MIRACLES IN
AOTEAROA
NEW ZEALAND

though
MIRACLES IN
AOTEAROA
NEW ZEALAND

TESTIMONIES FROM THE LIFE AND MINISTRY OF
R. WESTON CARRYER

Compiled by
Nick Klinkenberg and Josh Klinkenberg

© Copyright 2015—Nick Klinkenberg, Josh Klinkenberg
All rights reserved. This book is protected by the copyright laws of the United States of America. This book may not be copied or reprinted for commercial gain or profit. The use of short quotations or occasional page copying for personal or group study is permitted. Permission will be granted upon request. Unless otherwise identified, Scripture quotations are taken from the HOLY BIBLE, NEW KING JAMES VERSION®. Copyright © 1982 by Thomas Nelson, Inc. Used by permission. All rights reserved. Scripture quotations marked "NIV" are taken from the HOLY BIBLE, NEW INTERNATIONAL VERSION®. Copyright © 1973, 1978, 1984 International Bible Society. Used by permission of Zondervan. All rights reserved. Scripture quotations marked "NLT" are taken from the Holy Bible, New Living Translation, copyright © 1996, 2004, 2007 by Tyndale House Foundation. Used by permission of Tyndale House Publishers, Inc., Carol Stream, Illinois 60188. All rights reserved. Scripture quotations marked "RSV" are from the Revised Standard Version of the Bible, copyright © 1946, 1952, and 1971 National Council of the Churches of Christ in the United States of America. Used by permission. All rights reserved. Scripture quotations marked "ESV" are taken from the The Holy Bible, English Standard Version® (ESV®). Copyright © 2001 by Crossway, a publishing ministry of Good News Publishers. All rights reserved. Scripture quotations marked "NASB" are taken from the New American Standard Bible®, Copyright © 1960, 1962, 1963, 1968, 1971, 1972, 1973,1975, 1977, 1995 by The Lockman Foundation. Used by permission." (www.Lockman.org). Please note that it is the author's choice to not capitalise the name of satan.

Published by:
InFlame Publishing House
Tauranga, New Zealand
In partnership with:
Vision Churches International and Zoe Ministry Trust

Cover design: Paul Wayland Lee, LeewayCreative.com
Edit, layout and interior design: Carol Cantrell, Ron Cantrell

Dedication

This book is dedicated to all those who came to Jesus and received His healing touch through the hands of R. Weston Carryer.

Contents

Foreword	Christine Wratt, "Dad"	9
Foreword	Pastor Craig Clements	17
Preface	Nick & Josh Klinkenberg	21
The Story of R. Weston Carryer		25

Miracles in Aotearoa New Zealand Testimonials

Chapter 1	Hips, legs, Knees & Feet	37
Chapter 2	Head, Face, ENT & Neck	113
Chapter 3	Backs & Spine	173
Chapter 4	Cancer	255
Chapter 5	Shoulders, Arms, Elbows & Hands	273
Chapter 6	Abdominal & Internal Organs	311
Chapter 7	Heart, Chest & Respiratory	359
Chapter 8	Diseases, Disorders & Syndromes	393
Chapter 9	Overhauls & Unusual Conditions	445
Chapter 10	Skin	513
Chapter 11	Deliverance, Inner Healing & Other	523
Chapter 12	Infertility & Children Healed	551

"Keeping Your Healing" by Weston Carryer	609
Index	617
About the Authors	655
Resources	657

The following is taken
from the eulogy/tribute from
Christine Wratt,
the daughter of Weston Carryer,
on 24 July 2014, the day of the
celebration
of his life.

Dad

The Celebration of His Life

As he travelled the world and this nation, Weston Carryer was an evangelist, a pastor, a teacher, a pray-er for healings and miracles, and a trusted friend.

To me, he was my Dad, and my rock—one that was hard and solid, yet so warm and loving.

I am Christine, Dad's eldest child, and I would like to share about his life. I'm sure many who read this would have heard parts of what I am going to share because he was always excited to share his testimony and give God the glory.

I will always remember Dad for being so focused; it was all or nothing. His focus, and love for his family; his focus and hard work for many years on the farm, and then his focus after accepting Jesus and his faith which led many, many to Jesus for salvation and healing.

So in a nutshell, I'd like to share about Dad's family, his farm and his faith.

Dad was born on 14 October 1931 in Stratford to Ronald and Phyllis, known to me as Nana and Pop. Then a couple of years later, Kelvyn, his brother was born. Dad said, "Our family life was good."

MIRACLES IN AOTEAROA NEW ZEALAND

Dad always had an interest in animals and the outdoors. As a boy he was loaned a pony, and then a horse. Eventually he owned his first horse which he named, "Tommy." His first dog was called, "Turk."

Dad wrote his story for me a few years ago (see "The Story of R. Weston Carryer") and I created a book with photos for him, which he received on his 80th birthday. I'm going to share parts of what he wrote for that book.

"Our family life was good. Mum and Dad were both very interested in people, and as a result, there seemed to be visitors a lot of the time. I went to Stratford Primary School and then had 4 years at Stratford Technical High School where I passed what was then called, 'School Certificate.' After this I went to Massey College, followed by 6 months on a dairy farm in the Waikato. I graduated with a Diploma in Dairy Farming in 1950. I was then offered a job on a mixed dairy, sheep and cropping farm, in Southland. Following this, I was contacted by the Board of the Stratford Demonstration Farm and they offered me an assistant's position which I duly accepted and spent the next 2 years working there.

"I always had an interest in sport and played tennis in the summer and rugby in the winter. I played senior rugby in Southland at 19, and then back in Taranaki, I was included in the 25-man Taranaki playing squad and played for Taranaki B.

"During this year when I was 21," he went on to say, he was enjoying life—which included farming and rugby—but remembers becoming unsettled.

"I discussed this with my Dad. He told me that he had experienced the same feelings when he was my age and as a result worked his way on a boat from New Zealand to England where he had been born."

Then my Dad also decided to go to England and set sail in September 1953. Upon arrival he got a job working in Harrods, a large department store in London, and was a bread porter. On only the second day at work, Dad says he noticed this very attractive young lady who worked in the accounts section of the bread department. This was the beginning of a lifelong romance, and on 3 July 1954, Weston and Ruth—my Dad

The Celebration of Life

and Mum—were married in Brompton Holy Trinity Church in London. They honeymooned in Paris and hitchhiked through France, Italy, Austria, and Switzerland and then sailed for Canada, where they both worked for twelve months. In July 1955, they came to New Zealand and settled in Stratford.

Dad's father bought him a farm in Stratford where he share-milked for him for 2 years. During this time I was born—on 14th October—which always was and will continue to be special to share my birthday with my Dad.

Then 18 months later, my brother Colin was born. In 1957, Dad bought his first farm in Douglas—a very run down property. Dad obtained a town milk license and supplied milk to Stratford 365 days of the year. He said it was hard work, but it paid off as the returns from the farm trebled in the next seven years. While in Douglas, Lorraine and Paul were born.

In 1964, he sold up and bought a farm on the Plymouth Road in Oakura, twelve kilometres west of New Plymouth. Again, Dad worked hard and saw good returns. In 1968, he put a sharemilker on the farm, and as a family, we shifted to Tauranga where Dad bought a motel. After two years, we all returned to Taranaki where he bought a house in New Plymouth and bought more land to rear young stock. Eventually the farm was sold to my brother Colin.

Dad was a hard worker, and very committed.

He was also an amazing man who loved his family. I always saw his admiration and respect for his own Dad and Mum. Dad was a dearly loved husband of Ruth for 60 years, and there was always a special love for his four children. Although we have all caused him concern at difficult times in our lives, we knew he continued to love us. I will always remember my Dad being there for me—at the finishing line as I ran my races. He always took an interest in everything I did, like listening to me play the piano. And many years later, I married Lindsay, and we had our own three children. Dad loved to come and spend time with his grandchildren, Andrew, Christopher and Olivia.

My brother, Paul, married Reiko, and they had 2 sons, Iori and Youji, and he equally loved spending time with them. In May 2009, Dad became a great-grandfather and he shortened

Miracles in Aotearoa New Zealand

this to GG—GG to Annabelle, and then two years later, to Peyton.

Finally, I'll share about Dad's faith. When we become a Christian, we all receive a measure of faith. But Dad had the extra gift of faith and this enabled him to believe for the healing of miracles which he got so excited about, as many of you know.

He himself had experienced a healing of chronic backache which he had lived with for 17 years. One day he was on his farm in real agony laying on the concrete race! At exactly 12:00 noon this day, suddenly the pain went! Why did he experience such an amazing healing? There was a group of women—including his wife—who were praying, and at exactly 12:00 noon they prayed asking God to heal Weston's back, and God did. In his own words, Dad says, "God got my attention."

In April 1977, Dad gave his life to Jesus. In February 1985, he stepped into full-time evangelistic ministry, and talking about Jesus to anyone, anywhere became as natural to Dad as breathing. Most of all, he loved leading people in the nations, and people here in this nation, to Jesus. He had a special place in his heart for the Philippines and took 17 mission trips there. He even adopted a beautiful girl from the Philippines called, Caroline, as his daughter. Dad had a big heart and it just kept growing and growing. He also loved Israel, but that's another huge subject.

I feel so incredibly blessed to have been with Dad many times when he has shared his testimony and taught the Word of God. Other times, after visiting a church, he would phone me, and share about how many people accepted Jesus as their Saviour. Dad was a Kingdom man.

Dad ran this race until the end. The last three weeks of his life he spent in the Tauranga Hospital. Did this mean Dad just sat in bed all day in his PJs complaining? No, not at all! He still rose early in the morning, he prayed, and he read His Bible. Everyday he read a chapter in Proverbs, and this was one of his favourite books of the Bible.

Today it's the 24th July. Dad would have, at about 4:00 AM this morning, read Proverbs 24, so I've chosen verse 14 to share today.

The Celebration of Life

> *Know also that wisdom is like honey for you; if you find it, there is a future hope for you, and your hope will not be cut off!* (NIV)

Dad knew that hope.

I feel blessed because Dad and I discussed many Scriptures together. We loved getting out the concordances as we both have a heart to learn and teach. We also both loved reading true stories of men and women in the faith.

Again I feel blessed, because I spent the last week with Dad while he was in the Tauranga Hospital. I visited Dad every morning; he was up and dressed, visiting patients, helping the staff when he could, looking like he was in charge, feeling rested and refreshed, he made a special new friend called, Phil.

And the best story... One morning, a very sick man came into his room at 4:00 AM and he couldn't breathe. Dad felt so sorry for him. You guessed what he did next! He offered to pray for him, and the man accepted Dad's offer. Dad later found out that for the past five years, this man had been in and out of hospital and was waiting for two lung transplants. Dad would get so excited sharing stories of people who God had miraculously healed. Well, this one would have been in his next book. This very sick man went to have some more tests done after Dad prayed for him, and he was completely healed, and discharged from hospital!

Dad, you didn't get to publish this one, but I've shared it for you here and I know this would make your heart glad.

And Dad, I know you had many favourite verses, but one we often talked about was in John 14:12. Jesus speaking said,

> *Very truly I tell you, whoever believes in Me will do the works I have been doing, and they will do even greater things than these, because I am going to the Father* (NIV).

With your PhD—Preach, Heal, and Deliver—you had faith, and you did do even "greater", as Jesus said.

Pastor Bruce Monk said, "When you honour God, He will honour you." You always honoured God, and God honoured you.

Miracles in Aotearoa New Zealand

Dad, had you been able to read your Proverbs last Friday morning on 18 July, you would have read Proverbs 18:12, "Humility comes before honour." And Dad, you were a very humble man, and I was very proud of you.

I always remember you saying not to cry at your funeral because you wanted it to be a celebration of your life. I'm trying, Dad, mainly because I know you're in heaven perfectly healed and will be receiving your great reward. But I was fully expecting you to live into your 90s like your Grandad, and like Nana and Pop.

These tears are because you went so suddenly—and too early . . . I treasure the memory I will always have, and the photo of the last time we talked, prayed, and hugged in the Tauranga Hospital Chapel. I look forward to seeing you again, and in the meantime, I'm sure you'll still be praying for us all.

Love you, Dad.

xx

The Celebration of Life

Weston and his wife Ruth.

Foreword

Weston Carryer's life and ministry gave many people a glimpse into how much God cares for His people, and the heart God has for those who are yet to come into a relationship with Him.

The memory of Weston will long remain with hundreds of people up and down New Zealand. His influence stretches to Australia, the Philippines, Africa, and beyond.

This Taranaki dairy farmer never allowed the amazing miracles, which the Lord Jesus frequently did through him, to cause him to become proud, or to affect his concern and love for people.

Weston loved God, and he loved people.

It was not uncommon for him, upon meeting up with someone again a year or so later, to ask, "How is your ____ condition? I remember praying for you at such and such a meeting last year." People were amazed by this, and felt assured that the Lord Jesus Christ did really care for them and the challenges they faced.

Over the last 26 years or so, Weston's ministry has seen

Miracles in Aotearoa New Zealand

between 200 and 400 people each year put their faith and trust in the Lord. Along with this, many, many people have received healing, relief, and restoration in their relationship with the Lord.

There are many children who have been born to parents who, previous to being prayed for by Weston, were medically unable to have children. Weston jokingly mentioned one time about a couple who came back to him a few years later saying they now had four children, and could Weston now pray for them to have no more.

The gifts of the Holy Spirit were clearly evident in Weston's life and ministry—they included faith, working of miracles, healing, words of knowledge, prophecy and evangelism. Weston remained humble, totally dependent on the Lord Jesus to guide, to lead, and to empower him with the Holy Spirit's presence and power.

The healings demonstrated at meetings convinced and convicted many people of God's presence and the need for them to get into a right relationship with Him.

Throughout his ministry, Weston was hardworking, rising before most people to walk for up to an hour, just talking and meditating with the Lord. Phone calls, study, writing, prayer, travel, and meetings filled his days and weeks.

There is no doubt that Weston was a disciplined follower of Jesus. His ministry inspired hope and resulted in many people believing for the Lord to heal them and to work in miraculous ways in their circumstances.

Those who knew Weston were privileged to have known a wonderful man of God.

—Pastor Craig Clements
on behalf of the Trustees of Zoe Evangelistic Ministry

Preface

It is our pleasure to be able to present this book as a historical record of the Kingdom at work in Aotearoa, New Zealand. Our desire with this book is two-fold: to honour a man who lived unwaveringly for the glory of God, and to preserve a written record of the testimonies of God's power in our land for our children's children.

Honouring anointed men and woman who have gone before us is an essential part of receiving the spiritual inheritance we have in their lives. Weston Carryer was a gentle, humble, and inspiring dairy farmer who became a powerful healing evangelist. He saw hundreds come to faith in Christ every year as he ministered throughout New Zealand and further afield. He traveled tirelessly for nearly three decades ministering God's saving grace and healing power to people. Weston broke the mould in New Zealand and was able to do what not many before him had done: minister as an itinerant healing evangelist without the wage from a church.

There are few healing evangelists who have managed to compile and record so many firsthand testimonies. We felt it necessary to see these stories brought together in an exhaustive work that retained the integrity and honesty Weston displayed

Miracles in Aotearoa New Zealand

when first recording these testimonies.

The stories in this book are a powerful record of God's goodness and grace towards His people. We are excited to have a written record that we are able to pass on to future generations. In the same way that Israel was commanded to place twelve memorial stones on the banks of the Jordan River as a reminder for their children's children of the works of God in their land, so too is this book a memorial to the work of God in our land. We pray that this generation, and the generations to come, would be stirred with fresh faith as they read of God's goodness and His willingness to heal!

—*Nick Klinkenberg and Josh Klinkenberg*
Tauranga, July 2015

The Story of
R. Weston Carryer

This is the Lord's doing;
it is marvelous
in our eyes.
—*Psalm 118:23, NASB*

The Story of
R. Weston Carryer

Right from when I was a small boy, I can vividly remember having an interest in animals and the outdoors, and had a desire to become a farmer. My parents lived in Stratford, New Zealand, and Dad had a men's outfitters shop. However, there were a number of vacant sections around where we lived and the owners allowed me to use them for various horses that I managed to borrow.

The first pony that was lent to me for about five years was a Shetland which I used to ride usually at full speed without a bridle or saddle. The direction that he had to go was made clear to him by me hitting him on the opposite side of his head with a stick. He had a habit of stopping from gallop to dead stop and so many times, I flew off him onto the ground. My next horse also loaned was 17-hands high. By this time I had a bridle and a saddle and made sure that I did not fall off.

Dad then leased a farm at Te Popo as well as having his business. Our family—that's Mum, Dad, my younger brother Kelvyn, and I—would go to this farm for weekends. Dad gave me a horse of my own, Tommy was his name, and I spent a lot of time riding him—both helping with stock and pleasure riding. Another source of enjoyment for me was the first dog

Miracles in Aotearoa New Zealand

I was given by my uncle. He was a Scotch terrier-cross called Turk. With my grandfather's help I built a shed and bred quite a number of pigeons.

Our family life at home was good. Mum and Dad were both very interested in all sorts of activities and especially interested in people, and as a result, there seemed to be visitors a lot of the time. I went to Stratford Primary School and then spent four years at Stratford Technical High School where I passed what was then called, "School Certificate." After this I went to Massey College, as it was known in those days, for six months. This was followed by six months on a dairy farm in the Waikato as part of the course, and then a final six months back at Massey. I graduated with a Diploma in Dairy Farming in 1950. I was then offered a job on a mixed dairy, sheep and cropping farm in Southland which I accepted, and experienced an eventful time.

Following this, I was contacted by the Board of the Stratford Demonstration Farm and they offered me an assistant's position which I duly accepted, and spent the next two years working there.

I always had an interest in sport, and despite the fact that farm life was very busy, I managed to play a reasonable amount of tennis in the summer and rugby in the winter. I played senior rugby in Southland at nineteen and then back in Taranaki in my second season, I was included in the 25-man Taranaki playing squad. Although I never made it onto the field for Taranaki, I did play three games for Taranaki B.

Although I was really enjoying farming, rugby and life generally at age twenty-one, I became quite unsettled. I had never experienced anything like this before and didn't know what to do about it. One night I discussed this with Dad. He told me that he had experienced exactly the same feelings when he was about my age. As a result, Dad had worked his way on a boat from New Zealand to England, where he had been born, and lived for some of his early years.

I had always had a desire to see where both of my parents had come from. Consequently, I also decided I would like to see England, and so set sail on the old M.V. Tamaroa, in late September that 1953. This was the second to last trip it made.

The Story of R. Weston Carryer

It broke down twice on the way but finally after five weeks, we landed in London. I intended when I set out just to have a quick look at England, visit my many relations, and get back to New Zealand to continue with my career. However, being very energetic, and after being cooped up on the boat for five weeks, I wanted to get work upon arrival in England. The very next day I managed to get a temporary job at Harrods. They took on an extra 2,000 staff before Christmas and my position was a bread porter. On the second day at work, I noticed this very attractive young lady who worked in the accounts section of the bread department, and after a few more days, I asked her if she would come out with me. To my delight, she agreed to this.

Thus began a whirlwind romance. Checking out the rest of England—including the relatives—slipped from number one priority as I became much more interested in Ruth. In July the following year, 1954, we were married in Brompton Holy Trinity Church. We honeymooned in Paris for a week, followed by a hitchhiking trip through France, northern Italy, Austria and Switzerland. After this we sailed for Canada and both of us worked in Eaton's department store in Toronto for twelve months. In July 1955, we came to New Zealand and settled in Stratford where I had been raised and my parents were still living. Ruth was then six months pregnant with Christine.

With my best interest at heart Dad had bought a small dairy farm on the outskirts of Stratford. The idea was for me to work for him and then eventually buy it off him. I did sharemilk for Dad for two years and then decided that there was not enough future for me and my own family, and so I found a farm at Douglas. It was a very run down property—basically a ragwort-infested swamp. The owner was going bankrupt, desperately wanted to sell, and was prepared to finance me 100%. I accepted and shifted my family who now consisted of Christine and Colin as well as Ruth and myself. In hindsight it was not a good decision. To help generate income, I obtained a town milk licence, which meant I had to supply milk to Stratford 365 days of the year. The hard work paid off, and the returns from the farm trebled in the next seven years.

During this time we were blessed with the arrival of Lorraine and Paul. The oldest three children attended Douglas Primary

Miracles in Aotearoa New Zealand

School and did well, and I became very involved on the school committee. After seven years, the farm had become a viable unit, and after encouragement from Ruth, I sold the farm. This was a wise decision and we bought a much easier farm to run on the Plymouth Road which is twelve kilometres from New Plymouth. This farm already had a town milk supply licence and so I was able to milk my cows in the morning, shift them and milk them again at night on the new property, and then carry on. By this time, increasing farm production had become a focus in my life. I set about with a real will to increase the returns as I had in the previous seven years, and this time we were able to treble the returns in three years.

The three elder children settled easily into their new school at Oakura (Paul was only one) and became involved in nearly all sporting activities. I reluctantly became chairman of the school committee and held that position for the next four years. I also coached the rugby team, and one year, our team was runner-up for Taranaki for schools our size.

For some time Ruth's health had been troubling her and we decided that it might be beneficial to get off the farm. So in 1968, I put a sharemilker on the farm, and we bought a small motel in Tauranga and shifted there. We ran this for the next two years but I did not handle the shift into motel life very well. So after two years, we sold the motel and bought a house in New Plymouth. I also bought the farm adjoining my existing farm and leased two other smaller properties. We were then able to milk a lot more cows as well as rear young stock for both replacement dairy animals and the bulls for beef. Not long after this, I purchased another 100-acre block behind the main farm on Hurford Road. Things were going well, production continued to increase, and both our sons seemed interested in the farm. Colin had been working on the farm for some time.

I had always had some involvement in church and believed that I was a Christian, but really did not know what a true relationship with Jesus Christ was. Ruth had always been a church attender also, more so than me, and while we often all went to church as a family, she was the one who took our children to church when I did not make it.

In the early 1970s, Ruth started to get involved much more

The Story of R. Weston Carryer

and committed her life completely to Jesus Christ and became "born again." She shared all this with me but at that stage, I did not think I needed to make a commitment like this. However things started to happen in my life and I realized that although things externally looked good, there was a need in me that was not being fulfilled and I did not understand it.

For seventeen years I had lived with a chronic backache. Although it was always there, sometimes it was not too bad, but at other times, it was very severe and would prevent me from standing up properly and I would be buckled over. One day in real agony I was laying concrete on our farm race. All morning the pain had been horrendous when suddenly at exactly 12:00 o'clock, the pain just disappeared, and for the first time in weeks, I stood up straight. It was unbelievable. Nothing like this had ever happened to me before. I could not understand it. When I got home I shared what had happened with Ruth and she told me that she had been at a prayer meeting, and at exactly 12:00 o'clock, they had prayed for the Lord to heal my back. There was no doubt that I had been touched supernaturally by God.

God got my attention and I started really seeking after Him. I began to pray, read a Bible and go to Christian meetings. I was then invited to take part in a "Life in the Spirit" seminar. The idea of these seminars was for people to be baptized in the Holy Spirit. I did not know much about this, but took part. The seminar went over seven consecutive Sunday nights. During the first five weeks, those participating studied material on the Holy Spirit and on the fifth night, people were prayed for to be baptized in the Holy Spirit. During this seminar two things became very clear to me: one was that I was a sinner (like everyone) and I needed to repent and ask for God's forgiveness, and the second, that there was very definitely a hell, as well as heaven, and that unless I made a commitment to Jesus Christ, I would go to hell.

On the fifth night of the seminar in Brooklands Church New Plymouth, after a time of worship, the two men who were running the seminar asked for the first person who would like to be prayed for to come forward. I had no intention of being the first one but as soon as they asked, I was ejected from my seat and ran to the front. As they led me in a prayer of commitment to Jesus, I had an incredible experience of God's love (this has to be experienced to understand). I knew my sins were totally forgiven and I realised God's awesome power. My life was transformed at that moment. I knew I was a new person in Christ. This was 34 years ago in April 1977.

At this stage I did not know if God had anything in store for me. Two nights later Ruth and I were at a prayer meeting and a lady who did not normally come arrived. She said she was in a lot of pain and was terminally ill. She had dragged herself to this meeting for someone to pray for her and God to heal her. David Pearce was leading the meeting. He looked at me and told me to come and pray for her. I told him that he had the wrong one, but he insisted. I had never prayed for anyone before and felt very uncomfortable. However I did lay my hands on her and started to pray. I only said a few words and a miracle happened—the sickness and pain went, the lady stood up straight and shouted out, "I am healed!" Nobody was more surprised than me, but something happened in my heart at that moment. A passion to see people healed was birthed in me and I started to pray for sick people everywhere.

God gave me a real hunger for Himself and the Bible. I became very involved in Christian activities, especially sharing the gospel to see people saved and brought into God's kingdom.

About 1980, God started speaking to me about becoming a full-time evangelist. I had serious misgivings about this as I was not a natural speaker. But God, in various ways, made it plain to me that this was the call He had placed on my life. So in February 1985, in obedience to God and in agreement with Ruth, I stepped into full-time evangelistic ministry.

The last twenty-six years of my life has been amazingly eventful as I have travelled overseas and throughout New Zealand on many occasions to minister—God has opened doors for this to take place. I have seen many people come to faith in Jesus Christ as well as seeing the Lord heal countless numbers.

In summary, I just want to thank God for the wonderful life

He has given me, and especially for my family. Also, that He counted me faithful to call me into ministry, and for the joy of serving Him.

—*Weston Carryer*

MIRACLES IN
AOTEAROA

Heal the sick,
raise the dead,
cleanse those who have leprosy,
drive out demons.
Freely you have received,
freely give.

—*Matthew 10:8, NIV*

One

Hips, Legs, Knees, & Feet

Testimonies of healed conditions of hips (pelvis), legs, knees, and feet.

Hip (Pelvis), Hip/Leg

At a mission in Taumarunui where Weston Carryer was the speaker, I was chosen for healing. Weston mentioned there was someone present who was afflicted with osteoporosis (porosity and brittleness of the bones) and having suffered a hip fracture due to an accident. I went for prayer and was touched by the Lord but chose not to test my healing because I wanted verification from the orthopaedic specialist I was under. His inspection affirmed that the hip fracture had been completely repaired, that the osteoporosis is healed in the joint, and that I can start walking without the crutches I have been on for nearly six months. I am convinced that I was touched by the

Lord and that He will make sure my recovery is complete.

—*Audrey Banks*

At a Weston Carryer healing crusade, I went forward for prayer for healing of my right leg and hip. After that night, things started to happen in my leg. Knitting inside the leg went on for some time and God gave me back the two and a half centimeters which I had lost in that leg. I have had no pain either in my leg or hip since.

—*Gaelyn Lock*

I want to acknowledge the healing power which is in the name of Jesus Christ. I went forward for healing when Weston Carryer visited our church at Otaki. I had struggled with the problem that for over two years, both my hips were getting worn out, and it was such an effort to arise in the mornings. I was putting off the day when I would have to visit my GP to discuss a hip replacement (plastic fantastic) as it did not appeal to me in the least. Since Weston's visit I have had no more problems and I want to thank the Lord for His wonderful mercy. To God be the glory; great things He has done.

—*Alan Prior*

On 1 May 1994, Weston Carryer prayed for healing of my right femur (thighbone) hip joint which I broke on 29 November 1993. I was healed on the spot, and I have not used the aluminum crutches since. Weston also prayed for healing from insomnia. From that day I gave up the last of strong medications seven doctors given me to allay this affliction. This step was not easy but the Lord who has promised, "I am the Lord that heals you," is faithful and worthy of infinite praise.

—*Verna White*

Hips, Legs, Knees & Feet

I was born with misaligned hips and a short leg. As a result of this I experienced back pain which then led to very bad sciatica, which resulted in twenty years of continual medical and chiropractic treatment, none of which really helped. I was going through a time of intense sciatic pain which the doctor said would take months to heal when Weston Carryer came to minister in our church. During the meeting God revealed to Weston, through a word of knowledge, my exact condition and he asked me to go forward so he could pray for the Lord to heal me. As Weston prayed, God lengthened my leg; I saw and felt it grow. My hips and body were readjusted and went into place for the first time in my life, and the pain left completely. Since that night I have had no more pain and have experienced complete freedom in my body. Thank You, Jesus.

—*Janis Boyes*

I'd had trouble with my hip for the last three or four years. The pain would come and go, but the week before Weston Carryer came, the pain became constant. I went to the meeting believing God would heal me. On the last night the pain worsened, and I decided to go up for prayer. When Weston prayed for me I went down under the power. After I got up I realised that there was no pain. I have no pain since.

—*Phillip Bennetts*

I had a lot of pain in my left hip for about three years and it was getting more painful as time went on. Weston Carryer prayed for me and the pain left. Next day the pain came back as bad as ever, but I kept on praying and resisting the trouble and believing the Lord would heal me. He did! About three days later the pain had gone. Praise the Lord! My hip is in great condition. The Lord is wonderful, isn't He? I'm so thankful for your ministries.

—*Shirley Loeffen*

Miracles in Aotearoa New Zealand

In my early teens, a problem developed in my left hip, and this considerably affected me for the next twenty years. Whenever I would run it was always very painful. After I got married and became pregnant, I had to wear a special brace to prevent the hip from clicking out of joint. The doctor had to actually show me how to put it back in again. When out of place, it was extremely painful, and even when in place it was very uncomfortable. Five years ago I accepted Jesus as my Saviour, and discovered that He had also provided healing for my physical body.

One day, two years ago when experiencing terrible pain, I cried out and said, "God, I cannot keep going like this." He answered me and said that He would heal me at a Weston Carryer meeting. A few days later when Weston was ministering in our church, he spoke out my exact condition and also said that my left leg was shorter (which I did not know). He then prayed, and the Lord wonderfully lengthened my leg and healed my hip. I had two occasions when I had a slight twinge but ever since then I have had no pain or restriction and the hip has never clicked out of joint again. It is normal. Thank You, Jesus.

—*Joanne Kemp*

I was born thirty-two years ago with dislocated hips as well as scoliosis. The doctors were able to get one hip back into place when I was young but the other hip continued to trouble me and the doctors said that the scoliosis would prevent me from ever having a hip replacement. Over the years the pain continued to increase in my back and the doctors told me that I would end up in a wheelchair. I became more and more restricted in my movements and started to lose the feelings in my legs. Six years ago, I had to start having home help. I was on a lot of medication including anti-inflammatories (diazepam) and antidepressants. Also the doctor was looking at giving me a back fusion.

Because of the medication, my weight doubled. Three years

Hips, Legs, Knees & Feet

ago I attended a divine healing meeting in Ashburton where Weston Carryer was ministering and he prayed for the Lord to heal me. There was an immediate improvement in my back and over the next eighteen months, this improvement continued. Late last year I had a further x-ray and MRI scan done. The results were amazing—the doctor said I had received a miracle; my back is now the correct shape. I now do not have any pain or restriction or take any medication. I do not require any further medical treatment and my weight is now returned to normal. I am also weightlifting without pain. I now have a life! Jesus, I am so grateful.

—*Nicola Cameron*

I am so thankful for Weston Carryer coming to Dunedin. At approximately seventeen years of age I fell off my bike onto my right hip and seriously injured it. Then nine years ago I fell, landing on the same hip and tore my pubic symphysis, which are the ligaments that hold the pelvis together. This happened while I was pregnant with our second child, Hannah.

As a result of the second accident I was not able to walk at all for some time, nor could I sleep for long because of the pain. My doctor advised against further pregnancies. Twelve months after Hannah was born x-rays showed I still had seven millimeters of movement in my pelvis. This caused pain when walking, difficulty driving, many sleepless nights and depression.

When Weston came to Dunedin I desperately wanted to be healed but was not expecting a miracle from God to happen so fast. I was the first person Weston called out. He spoke out the exact details of the accident. I was stunned. Painfully, I very slowly shuffled my way up the aisle with assistance. As he prayed for me the power of God hit me and, in the snap of his fingers, I was healed. I leapt up and down and ran across the front of the church. I leapt up and touched the exit sign above the door and hopped, skipped, and jumped back to my seat, thanking God and Weston. Everyone was stunned, including me.

Miracles in Aotearoa New Zealand

For two years since I came to church, the worship team and the congregation had watched my painful determination to be in the choir and praise my God. After Weston's visit I went to an orthopaedic surgeon as I was still having travelling pain in my right hip and leg in spite of the healing in my pelvis. It was discovered that the L5 and SL bones were damaged and the disc between them had blown out completely. Also the sciatic nerve had been trapped as well.

Once again this year when Weston was ministering, first of all he called my exact condition and again I received a miracle and my back was instantly healed. Every day I had been taking twenty tablets in the morning, another eight during the day, plus another thirty at night. All the pain and restriction are totally gone; now I do not take any medication. I was also healed at the same time of asthma and allergies, and am now able to eat dairy products for the first time in nine years. God works and the devil is beaten. Lord, thank You so much.

—*Sarah Tregonning*

In 1993, when I was seven months pregnant, I jumped into a lake to save someone's child who was drowning, and this action broke my pelvis. I was bedridden until the birth of my baby; after the birth there was an improvement. Later I became pregnant again; this birth and pregnancy was okay. I became pregnant again and two months into this pregnancy my pelvis broke again. During the entire pregnancy I was confined to bed. I could not walk at all or even roll over in bed. After this baby was born, there was an improvement once again and I was able to do things in a limited way. Four years later the pelvis, for no apparent reason, broke again completely. For the next two years I was in terrible pain all the time; I could never get any relief at all.

In 2003, a major operation was done—a piece of bone in the form of a wedge was taken out of my left hip and hammered into the pelvis, the pelvis bone was completely fused, and plates and screws were put in. However, this operation was not successful. One long screw was penetrating my leg muscle and any movement caused excruciating pain. A scan done a

Hips, Legs, Knees & Feet

year later showed that the pelvis was still in two pieces and the doctors wanted to open me up again to attempt another fusion. This, even if it had been successful, would have resulted in a very long recovery period, when I would have needed to lie on my side all the time. I was really dreading going through this operation again.

While waiting for this operation, in late September 2004, my husband brought me to a divine healing meeting in Lower Hutt where Weston Carryer was ministering. At that stage I could struggle on crutches for a few metres, but I could not put any weight on my legs at all. My shoulders could not support me very long and any movement caused such pain and agony so that I did not even want to move at all. The only time that I did not experience terrible pain in both my hip and pelvis was when I lay in a swimming pool. As soon as Weston had prayed and asked the Lord to do a creative miracle and join the two parts of my pelvis together, he asked me if I would like to walk. But I was too frightened to because of what I thought the consequences could be, and so I did not try. One month later I went for my scheduled operation. The surgeon opened me up, removed the plates and screws, and discovered that the bone had re-grown; my pelvis was as it should be, and so he just sewed me back up. Within two weeks all pain and restrictions had completely ceased.

Prior to my accident, ten years previously, I had been a very active person; now I am very active again. The other day, as I was racing alongside my young son as he was riding his bike, I was marvelling at what the Lord had done. The only activities I cannot do are star jumps. Lord, I praise You and thank You for Your wonderful works.

—*Johanne Greally*

On a Friday, in November or early December of 2002, I decided that I had had enough of putting up with the pain and diminished mobility caused by degeneration in my right hip. So I made an appointment with my GP to begin the process of consultations for a hip joint replacement operation and to get stronger pain relief medication. The doctor carried out the necessary assessment, wrote a referral to an orthopedic surgeon, and prescribed stronger pain relief drugs. Previously, in January of 1998, I had had my left hip joint replaced and was told then that the other hip would need to be done in about two years time (2000).

Two days after my appointment, on the Sunday morning, Weston Carryer was visiting the church my wife and I attend in Pukekohe. He was preaching the gospel and conducting a service ministering healing through the power of God's Holy Spirit. We witnessed miracles and healings that Sunday morning, as we had done on previous visits by Weston. I had begun using the stronger medication. When he prayed for me, I felt my mobility improve. Within days I was able to play tennis and undertake physical activities I had been unable to do for some time.

When an appointment was made to see the surgeon in April 2003, x-rays taken showed that the clearance between the pelvis and the femur had improved. This meant that new cartilage had grown. Praise God for His healing power. Midway through 2006, at the age of sixty-five, I am able to climb around in the framing of new houses installing central vacuum systems and I am completely free of pain or medication. For that alone I am extremely grateful as the medication used to do nasty things to my digestive system. Since Weston prayed for me, my wife and I have tramped the Heaphy Track, Queen Charlotte Walkway, and the Abel Tasman track carrying our packs. There was no way I could have done that before. God is good, all the time, and His mercy endures forever.

—*Stu Ritchie*

Between 2002 and 2006, I went down the road of hip deterioration—a very painful condition I had to endure taking heavy doses of painkillers to get around. In 2004, x-rays revealed that my hip condition was moderate to severe, and hip replacement was inevitable. I could not lie on either side at all. I could not even vacuum and all housework was very

Hips, Legs, Knees & Feet

difficult. It became impossible for me to climb our house stairs and we were forced to sell our two-story house and buy a one level home.

In July 2006, we heard that Weston was conducting a healing meeting in Tauranga. As Christians, we knew that God worked powerfully through Weston, and he prayed for my complete healing.

As he prayed for me the pain went and I have never had any pain of any sort again in my hips. I already had an appointment with the surgeon again in August 2006 to have another x-ray. Even though my hips were feeling quite good, I wanted to compare this x-ray with the 2004 x-ray. The surgeon studied the two x-rays and said, "From what I can see on this (2006) x-ray there is absolutely no evidence that your hips need replacing at this time at all." The surgeon actually did some more special tests to confirm the result as he was so amazed.

Praise the Lord He has healed me. Thank You, Jesus.

—*Val Broadmore*

For some months I had been experiencing pain in my left hip which sometimes resulted in being unable to put any weight on my leg. It wasn't there all the time but would occur "out of the blue." It was a very disabling type of pain.

In early 2006, Weston prayed for me to be healed and the pain improved significantly. Within a few days it was gone completely and hasn't recurred. What an awesome, caring God we have as our heavenly Father!

—*Veronica (Ronnie) Hunter*

On Weston Carryer's visit to Cromwell in 2006, I came to his meeting just to listen. I had only joined the Lakeside Christian Church nine months before and was just a baby in the life of Christianity and knowing the Lord.

On the night of his meeting, Weston called for someone amongst us to come forward with a hip problem. I thought, *Oh, my goodness . . . maybe that's me . . .* but I didn't move from my seat. Firstly, because I didn't want to get up in front of people I knew because I thought maybe people will think I am a little crazy. And secondly, I didn't really know if I truly believed in God and the power of the Holy Spirit. So I just sat there and another lady went forward. Whew! I was so pleased. I watched Weston that night, with the grace of the Lord, heal and give hope to others, in awe, but still with apprehension.

I had had a problem with my left leg for many years. I couldn't step on it first—I always had to use my right leg and when I stood up from sitting I would have to just stand as I was so sore and stiff it would take a minute or so for me to be able to walk. The night of Weston's meeting I had my two-year-old grandson staying with me. He woke in the night and I got out of bed to attend to him. Halfway down the hall I realized I had no pain . . . funny . . . ! But I dismissed it as my imagination and went back to bed. Then, when I got up in the morning I noticed it again, so I went out to my steps and thought I would test my left leg. Wow! I could step up on it and my pain was gone! That was when I realized that the Lord had blessed me and healed my hip and that He did love me.

That night I went to the meeting in Cromwell and gave my heart to the Lord. I also attended Weston's Wanaka meeting and went forward for healing for a bad shoulder and my arm, which I had not been able to lift any higher than my chest. I had been going for physiotherapy for years with not a lot of success. That night the Lord healed my shoulder and arm and I have had no pain since. Since then I have been to Cambodia and worked as a volunteer, and in March this year (2007), I was water baptised in Cromwell. My life has changed so much since I opened my arms and my heart to Jesus Christ. Thank You, Lord, thank You, Jesus. I'm thankful for Weston's ministry.

—*Clarissa Bochel*

In April 2007, I was trying to control a bull. I was holding a rope attached to the head of the bull when suddenly he took off. I was unable to turn quickly enough and my whole body was pulled around very quickly, my hip became twisted and I

Hips, Legs, Knees & Feet

pulled one of my main muscles. The pain was severe. I could hardly move for weeks and pain relief did not help at all. This continued for the next eighteen months. I am a builder and I did manage to keep working, but by the end of each day my hip was very sore. There was also a swollen area on the waistline of my body.

Eighteen months later, at a divine healing meeting in Rotorua in October 2008, Weston Carryer prayed for the Lord to heal me. I did not experience anything significant as he prayed, but over the next forty-eight hours, the pain diminished until it had totally gone and full strength was restored to my hip. Now, four months later, my hip is one hundred percent healed and no pain has ever returned. The swelling on my waist has also disappeared as well. Praise the Lord.

—*Kevin Millar*

It was discovered when I was born that both my hips were out of alignment, which made me so pigeon-toed, that when I started to walk, I would fall over. As a result I wore steel braces on my legs every night until I was three years old to straighten the legs. Because the hips were twisted this also resulted in the legs being twisted. Although the braces did help they did not solve the problem, and a lot of the time, I experienced pain as well as being pigeon-toed.

In my late thirties, x-rays showed that the ball joints in the hips were badly worn and the specialist told me that I would need hip replacements. Over the next 10 years I experienced a lot of pain. Apart from the pain, when I was in bed at night, the hips would click out of position, and until my husband manipulated them back into place I would hardly be able to move at all.

In April 2009, I attended a divine healing meeting in Christchurch and Weston Carryer prayed for the Lord to do a miracle in my hips. I did not feel anything happen at the time, but a few days later, I realized that the pain had decreased and over the next several months, it almost completely disappeared.

Now, twelve months later, I only have slight twinges

occasionally. I now have full mobility and the hips do not click out at all. It is wonderful and I am most grateful to the Lord for what He has done.

—*Jan Van Zongeren*

I attended a divine healing meeting in Feilding where Weston Carryer was ministering. He had a word of knowledge for someone who was having problems in their right hip. Six weeks prior to this my right hip had been replaced and I was still having serious problems with it. However my left hip was worse. For at least ten years it had been painful, and for the six-week period following the right hip operation, the pain in the left one was very severe, 24/7. Apart from the daytime pain it would keep me awake at night.

I responded at the meeting when Weston spoke. As he prayed for me, all the intense pain completely went from my left hip, and both the left hip and leg were able to function normally. I have had no further pain of any sort since that moment, now six months later.

The right hip started to improve, and with further prayer and faith in the Lord, this hip is now also healed. So six months later, both hips are now normal. Lord, I am so grateful.

—*Mary Hurley*

For over 3 years, I experienced major problems with my hips. Pain was always there and I had difficulty walking. I could hardly get up stairs, and getting out of a chair was a real problem.

At times the pain was very severe and it would be too painful to do anything other than lie down. Most of the time I could never get comfortable in bed. I had bought a house and I wanted to do a lot of work inside and outside the house, but for the final year of my hip problems, I was unable to do any work at all.

Approximately three years ago I attended a divine healing

Hips, Legs, Knees & Feet

meeting in Turangi where Weston Carryer was ministering. During the ministry time, amongst other words of knowledge, he said there was someone there with serious problems in both hips. I responded and he prayed for the Lord to do a miracle for me. As he prayed the pain just went and strength returned immediately to my hips. Ever since that moment I have never had the slightest bit of pain and I am not restricted in any way. I am so grateful to the Lord Jesus Christ.

—Kia Paranihi

On and off for at least 25 years, my hips and lower back had troubled me. Most of the time I experienced discomfort and, if I was not very careful, aching would set in and it would take months to recover. I could not sit on chairs that were not padded or carry any weights like heavy grocery shopping.

Just over 2 years ago, I attended a divine healing meeting in St. James, New Plymouth, and Weston Carryer prayed for the Lord to heal me.

This condition has improved considerably and has made a huge difference in my life. Praise God.

—Billie Francis

In February 2012, my sister's hip and down her leg became very painful. The pain would shift from her hip to her leg or knee. She had many visits to doctors, who had no idea what could be the problem. They gave her many pills, even tranquilizers. X-rays showed nothing. She got to the stage she was on crutches and had used up most of her sick leave and holiday leave. She was in a position where she needed to work for income. The doctor decided to get an ultrasound. However, an appointment would take up to nine months.

When Weston Carryer visited Te Aroha in August 2012, he called someone out with pain in their hip. I instantly thought of my sister and, as no one put their hand up, I mentioned her. I stood in the gap and Weston prayed. I rang her after the service and told her what had happened. She claimed her healing.

Miracles in Aotearoa New Zealand

On Monday all the pain had gone. I sent her the *Keeping Your Healing* brochure to read. The pain did come back, but she stood on the promises of God. The pain went, and thirteen months later has never returned. Praise the Lord!

—*Tui Fisher*

Leg, leg/knee

I attended a healing meeting at Central Christian Family Church at which Weston Carryer was the guest speaker. I went up for prayer but I had great difficulty climbing the stairs. After Weston prayed for me, he asked me to go back down the stairs and run up and down them. At the age of sixty I thought, *You must be joking,* but said, "Okay, Lord, here goes." I didn't feel any different in any way, but ran up those stairs in faith. When Weston asked me if I had done it, I could only reply, "Been there, done that"—no other words would come out. But, praise God, I've had that healing to this day and I can climb up stairs comfortably.

—*Bev Schell*

I went along with some other "golden oldies" to a healing meeting where Weston Carryer was the speaker. For myself, my mobility had been reduced to the point where I could hardly move—where I needed assistance across the street, and so on.

I went forward for prayer and received an instant and miraculous healing. I am still walking freely, although I get tired if I walk too far. I now take things one day at a time.

—*Mavis H.*

I interceded for my family when Weston Carryer was here. He prayed with me for the needs of my family which I had written

Hips, Legs, Knees & Feet

on a prayer list as my family could not be at the crusade. Well, glory to God—my brother has been healed. He was meant to have an operation on his left leg because it was badly ulcerated. He no longer has any pain and the doctor says that since the ulcers have dried up, he has no need of an operation. Also, through his renewed faith in God, he is now coming back to church after being away from God for many years. I believe God has healed his heart again. Other members of my family for whom Weston prayed have also had good things happen to them. Praise God, for He is restoring my family's lives. I thank the Lord for all these healings.

—D. McC.

About twenty-seven years ago I had a nylon artery graft inserted in my lower body and upper leg. I was told by the doctor that my leg would last no more than twenty years because of the nylon, and at the end of that period, it would have to be amputated. Twenty years on, which was seven years ago, I started to have real problems in my leg, and the medical authorities said that they needed to amputate immediately. The pain was excruciating. At this time I attended a divine healing meeting where Weston Carryer was ministering. He prayed for me and I received an incredible miracle. God, through Jesus by the power of the Holy Spirit, totally healed me. For the past seven years I have had no pain, can walk in a straight line (something I could not do before), and I walk up to two and a half hours every day praising God. My leg is completely normal. Thank You, Jesus.

—Mies Lelieveld

I was born with one foot one-inch shorter than the other, and one leg one-inch shorter than the other. When Weston Carryer came to Tokoroa Apostolic Church on Sunday, 19 October 1997 for the healing meeting, I went up to get my leg and foot healed by Weston Carryer and God between them. Both my foot and leg grew and I saw it with my own eyes. I have been waiting for this to happen all my life. So you can see—and

MIRACLES IN AOTEAROA NEW ZEALAND

I know—that God is looking after me. God is good.

—*Stanley Seller*

While attending a healing meeting held by Weston, last year, I experienced a miraculous healing. I had my leg lengthened by approximately one inch. Approximately twenty years previously I was involved in a car accident and broke my right femur; when this knitted back together, I was left with one leg shorter than the other. I walked out of the healing meeting, with my right foot touching the ground, as it used to before the car accident. I remember feeling so happy. I will always remember that day, and it has strengthened my faith in God. When my faith (in my head) is fading, I can always stand up and remember when God healed my leg! Thank You, Jesus.

—*Cara Draper, Birkenhead*

In 1985, my left leg was broken, leaving me with a two-and-a-half-centimetre shorter leg and an ankle with relatively no movement in it. I was present at a Weston Carryer meeting in Mosgiel during April 1993, and went forward for prayer. Weston sat me in a chair and as the gathering watched on, I was healed. My legs are now even and my ankle has full movement. My doctor has confirmed the truth of the complete restoration. Let God be glorified.

—*Clive McKane*

In 1984, I broke my left leg (tibia) in a motorcycle accident and as a result spent ten months in plaster. My leg did not mend and ended up 2.2 centimeters shorter than the right one. I wore built-up footwear. To go barefooted was impossible. My leg had a callus on the side where the break was and it had a bend in it. All this caused me to have a sore back.

When Weston Carryer came to Mangakino in August 1993, I went along believing that, if I was called, God would perform a miracle on my leg. Weston said there were four persons present

Hips, Legs, Knees & Feet

with sore backs and one also had a short leg. He identified me as that one. Everyone gathered around. My leg went numb, and before their eyes, it grew to its rightful length. I walked out of the meeting in bare feet. The Mangakino doctor has confirmed that both legs are equally 48.5-centimeters between the knee and ankle. (Certificates of before and after are held on file.) There has been an ongoing healing since. Not only has the callus gone but there is no longer a bend in the leg. God is real and He still heals today.

—*Stephen Geange*

In July 2001, while playing for the New Zealand Silver Fern's netball team against Australia in Melbourne, I crashed into a wooden bench which was close to the court. This did not bother me a great deal at the time, but in November, when taking part in specialised training my leg became very sore, and I could not bear to put any weight on it at all. A medical diagnosis revealed that I had a classic stress fracture of the main front tibia in the left leg, being only the fourth person in NZ to have suffered this fracture over the last ten years. Three subsequent x-rays then showed that the break had been aggravated by training, and that it was not healing naturally, and I would have to go to Australia to have a specialized bone graft operation done. I really prayed that the Lord would somehow supernaturally heal my leg so that I would not need to have this operation. For the next three months I was on crutches and there was no improvement. In late February 2002 I attended a divine healing meeting in Christchurch where Weston Carryer was ministering and praying for the Lord to heal people. Late in the meeting I went forward, and as Weston prayed for me, I experienced the power of the Lord go into my left leg and heal the tibia. I dropped my crutches and started walking around normally with no restrictions or pain. An x-ray taken since has confirmed that the break was perfectly healed; I am now back on the netball court again. Wow! Thank You, Jesus.

—*Wilimina Davu*

Miracles in Aotearoa New Zealand

I'm thankful for Weston Carryer coming to Waitara some years ago to allow the Lord to work a miracle in my life. At a combined church service, as I was sitting in the congregation at the Waitara War Memorial Hall, Weston described the symptoms of agony in my back so accurately, that I knew the Lord wanted to do a miracle for me, and He did.

Ever since I had a sporting injury, roughly three years earlier, when my leg was broken, my right leg has been ten millimetres shorter than my left leg. Weston prayed for me and the Lord made it grow the full ten millimetres. My wife is a podiatrist and measures people feet in her profession. She measured my leg length and knows it is fully restored. I was severely disadvantaged before, especially in my ability to walk long distances. Now I am able to move freely, continue teaching at a boy's secondary school, to coach wrestling, and be an active husband and father. Thank You, Lord, and I praise You.

—*Wayne Kibby*

On Monday, 15 September, 2003 I went to a Weston Carryer healing meeting in Lower Hutt. I went up for my short right leg to be lengthened. As Weston prayed for it, the Lord did lengthen it to the same length as the left one. I found I could then, for the first time, in my life walk straight. I also went up for healing of sciatica in my right leg and hip, which had been seriously affecting me for six months. For five weeks I still had problems, but believed for my healing. Suddenly I realized after the sixth week on 27 October 2003 that I hadn't had any pain for five days. I used to go to the shops and had to sit down every five to ten minutes because of the terrible pain. One time I had to leave my trolley of groceries in much pain. I felt dizzy and sick and felt I would black out. Another time I felt I would black out with pain and walked out of the shop and sat on someone's fence. I wasn't fun to go out with. But it's been five weeks now and no pain! I can walk twenty minutes to the local mall, do the shopping, and walk twenty minutes home with no trouble! Praise the Lord. I'm healed.

—*Valerie, Wellington*

Hips, Legs, Knees & Feet

Being of a shy countenance when it comes to crowds I said to the Lord, "I'm only going to the front if he [Weston] says something really specific!" Sure enough he did and I didn't even see it coming. I knew it when he said, "Is there someone here who has had a lot of trouble with their left side, stemming from their hips?" This was blatantly obvious to me.

Three days before I had said these words to a friend of mine, not to mention the fact that I had, once again, fallen from my horse seven days earlier and was still on crutches because of my left leg, my hips, and so forth. So I raced up the front . . . well, as fast as two crutches and one useless leg would carry me. I got up there and Weston started praying for me. I felt this warmth, like a tranquilizer numbing effect, right across my back.

When Weston asked me if I can walk without my crutches I said, "Yes." I had attempted it but I could just get by. We walked across the church (in front of everyone, I might add). I had no pain.

Then he asked if I can walk a bit faster. So I did—still with no pain. Then he said, "Can you run with me?"

I thought, *No! No, no, no, no!* But then I knew it would be okay, so we ran. And guess what? Amazingly, there was no pain, no fear, no tightening of my muscles like I had expected. By this time the whole church was on their feet cheering and clapping.

God had healed me that day continually and rapidly. Now months later I feel terrific. I used to be sceptical—not quite believing. But I'll tell you, after that day of receiving the healing power of God—not just physically but emotionally—I will never be sceptical again. I will not listen to doubt and unbelief; I know it is God's will for us to be healed from anything. Do not fear, for with God, we can overcome everything! God bless you.

—*Michelle Humphries*

Miracles in Aotearoa New Zealand

I commute daily to Upper Hutt from Featherston on the train and then walk to work. Four years ago I noticed that during this walking time my legs, especially the shins, would really ache. This pain would continue for some time afterwards. This happened every day for three years.

One year ago I attended a divine healing meeting in Martinborough where Weston Carryer was praying for the Lord to heal people. He spoke out and said there was someone present who had shin splints, and described what effect it was having. I knew this was me as it was exactly what was happening to me. He then prayed for me. That same afternoon I went for a long, brisk walk and did not have any pain. I have never had any pain since in all of my walking. Thank You, Jesus.

—*Ngaire Greger*

Forty years ago, I developed a condition called "restless legs syndrome." This caused my legs to move continually a lot of the time when I was trying to sleep. It would always wake me, and on the nights when I was experiencing it, I would not get any sleep at all. This condition continued to get worse as I got older and over the last ten years it was terrible. Many nights on end I would get no sleep at all, and I was getting desperate as there was no medical cure for it.

In June 2005, Weston Carryer ministered to us in Te Awamutu and prayed for my healing. I am healed, set free, excited, and praising the Lord. I have had the occasional night when it has tried to come back, but I have rebuked it and praised the Lord and it has gone; then I have slept the rest of the night like a baby. I am thankful for Weston's *Keeping Your Healing* pamphlet. This has given me such understanding in my spiritual authority. Praise God.

—*Chris Gadsby*

Hips, Legs, Knees & Feet

For two years I had been unable to walk, even around my home, without using my walker. Even then it was always with real difficulty. When I went out I had to be wheeled in my wheelchair. Mobility had become a major problem for me.

I attended a divine healing meeting on the North Shore, Auckland in June 2006, where Weston Carryer was praying for the Lord to heal the sick. During the ministry time he prayed for the Lord to heal me. As soon as he had finished praying for me I realized that the strength had returned to my legs and I was immediately able to walk unaided and with confidence. I have been able to walk naturally ever since. It is marvellous. Lord Jesus, I am so grateful.

—Joy Torbett

When Weston came to minister at our church at North City Apostolic, Hamilton in November 2004, I was the last person in line to be prayed for. I worked part-time in retail and my legs ached from the standing. This had been troubling me for three years. Some nights I tossed and turned in bed, trying to get comfortable as my hips hurt and the pain rippled along my legs. After Weston prayed for me, I noticed no pain through the night and I know that God healed me. I testified to this in one of our Sunday services. I'm not that young and I worked nearly double my usual amount of hours leading up to Christmas. Jesus really helped me through this busy time in a job I enjoy. Two years later I have never had aching legs or hips again. Thank You, Jesus.

—Joy Leighton

For four years I experienced agony down the right side of my leg. This made walking very difficult—it affected my balance and I could only limp everywhere I went. I went to the doctor several times and was given different types of medication, but nothing helped in any way at all.

Miracles in Aotearoa New Zealand

At a divine healing meeting in Tokoroa in 1994, Weston Carryer was ministering, and through a word of knowledge, he described my condition. He asked me to go forward for him to pray for the Lord to heal me. As Weston prayed all the pain disappeared and has never returned over the last thirteen years. It was amazing.

—Julia Hohia

The grace, love and healing power of our Lord Jesus shone gloriously on Sunday, 19 February 2012, at Christian Renewal Fellowship in Whangerei where Weston Carryer conducted a healing meeting.

Awe filled the church as Weston called out different conditions and people went up to be prayed for and then returned to their seats. It was at this meeting our Lord Jesus spoke my condition to Weston: "There is someone over there with sore legs—the right one is the worst." Weston was pointing towards the area where I was seated.

I sat waiting to see if someone would respond. Weston repeated the condition. Much to my delight, our Lord Jesus was calling me to be healed.

For fifteen years, I have suffered with sport injuries which turned arthritic. In the later years, I have had sciatica which gave me great discomfort. I work in a bakery and before the end of the day, because of being on my feet all day, my legs would be so sore that I could hardly move them and I often had to have a break to give them some rest. Full of excitement and faith I went forward to receive my healing.

Weston asked me if I loved Jesus, and was I ready to receive my healing.

"Yes," I replied. Weston then prayed for me, and the pain I had at the time ceased. Then Weston told me to run. Now this is something I haven't been able to do for years. I ran with ease, like I had in my sport days. Praise the Lord. I returned to my seat. About five to ten minutes later my legs felt as though an electric current was flowing through them. It started at my toes and worked its way up my legs to my lower back. Then my

Hips, Legs, Knees & Feet

lower back started to pain. I moved around in my seat trying to get comfortable, thinking I would have to ask Weston to pray for me again.

At the end of the meeting I stood up—the pain had gone.

That afternoon I weeded and dug a very overgrown vegetable garden. Oh, I thought, now I've done it. I will suffer with sore legs and lower back pain. The pain I expected that evening and the next day never happened.

Since my healing over seven months ago, I have had no pain in my legs or lower back. May all the glory be given to our Lord Jesus for the healing I have received. Hallelujah.

—Pauline Marinkovich

I was born with a short tendon in my left leg, and this forced me to walk on tiptoes on both feet which considerably restricted my movements. As soon as I could, I started wearing high heels to try to hide the problem.

At a Christian healing meeting in Vision Church Fielding in September 2013, Weston Carryer prayed for the Lord to lengthen the short tendon, and as he prayed, I experienced my miracle.

At that moment, the tendon became warm and lengthened. Weston then asked me to run, which I was reluctant to do. However, I did run with ease across the entire length of the front of the church.

This has made a huge difference in my life. Although the tendon is almost (but not quite) perfect (but I know it will be), I have been able to run and walk normally for the last six months.

Thank You, Lord, so much for my healing miracle.

—Naomi Wells

For three years, I suffered from painful swollen feet and legs. There was constant discomfort and it was hard to walk at all. My legs looked unsightly and there was noticeable discolouration in the skin—especially on the shin because the fluid retention was causing the skin to be so tight. It looked like a big, coloured band around my legs and chronic pressure was always there.

Over this entire three-year period, I felt miserable and hopeless. I gained weight and it affected my sleep. It had a devastating effect on my personality and I wanted to isolate myself.

On 21 April 2013, I attended a divine healing meeting at Grace Vineyard Church, Christchurch, where Weston Carryer was ministering. During the ministry time he looked right at me and said that there was someone with foot and leg problems. I went up to the front and he prayed for me. He then said, "You won't have that problem any more." I felt better straight away, really flexible and even the arthritis in my hands felt better. The fluid just disappeared immediately.

The next morning, I awoke to complete freedom from pain, inflammation, and fluid retention, and was able to start walking for fitness again.

Now, nearly six months later, I am feeling fantastic. I walk at least thirty minutes every day and have lost several kilos in weight. My joy has returned. This has made an incredible difference in my life. Praise the Lord!

—*Bernie Mitchell*

I was born with my left leg shorter than the right one. Although it did not seem to affect me very much in my early life, when I reached my late thirties, I started experiencing problems. I had to have my left shoe heel built up, but even then I could not stand at all without experiencing extreme discomfort. This then went on for approximately ten years.

About ten years ago, at a divine healing meeting in Cromwell, Weston Carryer prayed for the Lord to lengthen my leg. As he prayed, I saw—and felt—my leg grow out to the same length as the right one. This has made a big difference to my quality of life. I now do not have to have my heel built up and I can stand normally without any discomfort. Thank You, Jesus.

—Rayley Thornton

Knees

I dislocated my knee. It was extremely painful for some two weeks and the doctor said it would probably be at least six weeks before there would be any improvement. I had a splint and needed a crutch to walk with. I could not put any weight on that leg at all. I went forward at a Weston Carryer meeting. Prior to this time I had never asked Jesus to be my Lord. As Weston prayed for me I experienced an amazing sensation. It felt as though a sandbag was being lifted off my knee. All the pain went, I suddenly realised God's love for me and I immediately asked Jesus into my heart. My knee was totally and instantly healed, through Jesus, by God. Praise the Lord.

—Cara Preston

I have been a born again Christian for five years now. We had Weston Carryer over here in Wanganui doing a ministry on faith. During his altar call he said there was somebody with a problem in their left knee. I responded. Weston prayed for me and I had instant healing. I had had problems with that knee for twenty-six years following a bus accident. But, praise God, I'm healed and can do lots more with my knee than I have for all those years. God is good. I have had other healings.

—Jenny W.

I injured my knee about two years ago playing basketball with the young people. When it ached I would put a knee band on it, hoping the pain would go away. At the North City Apostolic Church Weston had a word of knowledge for someone with a problem in the left knee. I paused for a moment to see if it was for someone else, then realised that it was a word for me. I went to the front and Weston asked me if I had seen a doctor about it. I said, "No." He sensed that I loved the Lord, asked me to raise my arms and he began to pray for me. I felt an awesome surge go through my body and as it focused on my knee; it felt like a spiritual operation was being performed. I felt real gooey-like. From that moment on I knew in my heart that God was doing a massive work in my body, in my hips and sacral area as well—not just my knee.

I had been going to the physiotherapist, but since the healing meeting, I have been told I do not need any more therapy. Praise the Lord. I kept praising and thanking the Lord for my healing, and going through all the steps that he outlined through the power of God's Word.

—*Hani Rhind-Turner*

For a whole year I was in agony twenty-four hours a day in both knees after I fell on them. For five months of the year I was on crutches and the rest of the time I hobbled with great difficulty. All walking was extremely difficult and I could not negotiate stairs at all. Both knees were very swollen the entire time. I went to a divine healing meeting at Mosgiel in 1997 where Weston Carryer was ministering and praying for the sick. As he prayed for me I felt the power of God literally hit me and was slain in the Spirit. When I got to my feet the pain and swelling were all gone, and my knees were totally healed. I jumped around and then danced before the Lord. What incredible joy. Thank You, Lord Jesus. Over the last twelve months my knees have been one hundred percent.

—*Helen Ludwig*

A friend at work asked me to a meeting which Weston Carryer was speaking at. As a result of my profession as a carpet

Hips, Legs, Knees & Feet

layer, I had suffered some cartilage damage to my knee, and it was necessary to have a small operation to repair the damage I had sustained in this occupation. It was also necessary to have physio to remove the scar tissue had resulted from the operation.

Weston said there was someone who had a damaged left knee. As I had nothing to lose, I got up, went forward, and Weston prayed for me. At first I felt nothing. A couple of days later I went to my physio appointment only to have the therapist say, "What have you done to your knee? I can find nothing wrong with your knee. I will have to cancel your appointments as everything is fine now."

Whilst I am not a Christian, I cannot deny what happened to me. And as I told my non-Christian mates, I cannot say, "It didn't happen," because it did.

—*(no name)*

In 1994, I badly damaged my left knee when I tripped and fell under a sanding machine. I experienced a lot of pain, was unable to use my knee, and could only walk with extreme difficulty. It was operated on, but there was no improvement. After the second operation fluid on the knee developed accompanied by severe swelling and then followed by continual infection for the next three years. During this time I had a total of fifteen operations but there was no improvement. At one stage I had a plaster cast on for twelve weeks.

In December 1997, at a healing meeting at Papamoa, Weston Carryer, who was ministering, said the Lord had showed him through a word of knowledge that there was someone there who had injured their left knee leaving it seriously impaired, and for the person to come forward for the Lord to heal them. As I was prayed for the pain left, everything went back into place, the strength completely returned, and for the first time in three years I ran! My knee has been completely healed through the power of Jesus Christ. Praise God.

—*Simon Perry, Tauranga*

Miracles in Aotearoa New Zealand

As a result of a hospital bed being pushed into my right knee, for seven years I had serious problems. My knee would not bend, was too painful to even touch and used to make audible noises when moved. I attended a divine healing meeting at Whangamata in early 1998 where Weston Carryer was ministering. I went forward for prayer and when Weston prayed, the Lord's power was released. The healing was not instant but within one month the knee was completely healed. Oh the joy of having a knee that functions after seven years. Praise You, Jesus!

—Noeline Wallace

As a result of a car accident twenty years ago, I sustained an injury on the same place of my left knee twice. I was advised by my doctor then that I would have problems as I got older. I am now fifty years old and have been experiencing discomfort and pain whenever I get up after sitting for long periods.

In September 2001, a small group of us went up to Wellington to be ministered to by Weston Carryer, an evangelist. At the meeting, Mr. Carryer said that there was someone there with a left knee injury which happened about twenty years ago and maybe been injured twice on the same knee. He said could that person please step forward as God wants to heal you right now. Believing that person to be me, I went forward, was prayed for, got slain by the awesome mighty power of Jesus Christ and returned home to Christchurch pain-free and with no discomfort at all. I thank my Lord Jesus Christ every day for the miracle of healing. Thanking You, Jesus, and my heavenly Father.

—Joyce Reid

In October 2001, when walking one day, my knee suddenly collapsed under me, and for the next sixteen months I suffered constant knee pain. I was placed on the strongest doses of

Hips, Legs, Knees & Feet

medication that were allowed out of the hospital, but these did not help, and the doctors told me that nothing could be done for me. Also, I had, by this time, had my knee operated on twice before. For the last three months of this sixteen-month-period I also suffered from bad nausea.

On the 16 February 2003, I attended a divine healing meeting in Tauranga where Weston Carryer was ministering. As Weston prayed for me, the Lord did a miracle—the pain and nausea instantly left and I started to run for the first time in sixteen months. I immediately stopped all medication, and have had no further pain or restriction since. Bless You, Lord. I am so grateful.

—*Nardia Bigwood*

I attended Weston Carryer's healing meeting in Hornby, Christchurch. I am in my seventies and have had a lot of knee problems. I have had two left knee operations over the years. You said someone sitting in a certain area in the church had a problem with the left knee and to come forward. Weston prayed for my knee and I have had no more trouble with it. I have just had a trip away for three days, and I did a lot of climbing up mountain forests with no trouble at all. It is wonderful. Weston also prayed for arthritis—it is so good. I keep claiming my healing. Thank You, God, for it. I loved your ministry and teaching.

—*Phyl Smith*

I have had sore knees for about six months and was wondering if I'd have to give up my trade of painting, decorating, and building. I just thought I would go up for prayer. Nothing seemed to happen, but since the service, my knees have been as good as gold. Praise God! I just forgot to tell him about my sore back.

— *David Florance*

Miracles in Aotearoa New Zealand

When Weston Carryer was in Christchurch in April, God gave him a word of knowledge about an injury to my right knee. I did not know it was for me at first because I never went to a doctor for a diagnosis. I knew a doctor couldn't help. After he prayed for me, I felt about eighty-percent of the pain leave immediately. I kept trusting the Lord to complete my healing until the pain was one hundred percent gone, which it was by the weekend. The realization of what God did came while I was doing a lot of work, which required much knee bending. I used to have unbearable pain after only a few knee bends. On Saturday, I was up and down dozens of times with no pain at all. Hallelujah!

—*Rev. David Scott*

On 28 May 2005, I was involved in a serious rugby incident. It resulted in my knee being split open. As I was carried off the field to be assessed by medical staff, I realized it was much more serious than I imagined. The split measured eight-centimeters wide and was quite deep, almost to the bone. I was therefore taken to a Medic Centre for further treatment. After an hour in theatre and eight stitches later, I was released. I did not feel any pain until later that night. I could not sleep for long periods of time for the next two days because the pain was extreme. I went to see my local GP on the Monday because the swelling had gone down to my shin and around the back of my calf muscle. Because of the severity of the pain I was prescribed stronger antibiotics. The next thirty-two hours were spent in bed. Although the medication helped ease the pain, I was still a long way from recovery.

I couldn't wait to attend the Weston Carryer healing meeting the following Tuesday night, even though I was in agony. As I entered the church auditorium in my wheelchair, I made sure I got a place up the front so that Weston could see me. Every time he would call out a condition I was praying that it would be mine. Finally a knee condition was called out, but it was the opposite of mine. Sitting there I thought to myself, in a

Hips, Legs, Knees & Feet

humorous kind of way, to cross my legs so that my injured left knee would be on the right side, but I couldn't even lift my left leg because the pain was too strong to bear. I remember sitting in my wheelchair listening to Weston Carryer's message, and praying in tongues as well, that tonight was going to be the night for my healing. As I went up the front, I found myself praying in tongues more and more. As Weston approached me, I explained what had happened to me just four days before.

He said to me, "Alright! Are you ready for your miracle?"

I replied, "Yes, I am."

After I was prayed for I felt the pain immediately go. The swelling around my shin and calf muscle had gone. I stood up out of my wheelchair and had two men assist me in walking. Once I got my balance I was able to walk by myself. To my own amazement I walked my wheelchair out. I give all praise and honour to God for His healing power. I can't wait to get back onto the rugby field again.

—*Tony Rikona*

About fourteen years ago, I dislocated my left knee twice. The doctors had to stabilize it by surgery so it wouldn't dislocate again. Last March, the right knee dislocated and relocated itself, causing me to have two weak knees. On 1 May 2005, Weston Carryer was in town, so I went to the healing meeting. When he asked for anybody who wanted to be healed to come forward, I went. I told him about my knees and how weak they were. As he prayed for me I could feel myself getting warm and my knees getting stronger. Weston then got me to run up and down the platform step in my church. Normally I would have been too scared of falling over and dislocating my knee again, but not this night. I ran up and down that step and really believe that God has healed me. The other day I ran up three flights of stairs. Normally I would have to rest at the top, but this day I went and did an hour's worth of grocery shopping first.

Almost eight months after being prayed for I have not even had the slightest twinge of pain at all. My knees both now have normal strength. After fourteen years of knee problems it is wonderful to be able to take part in normal activities. Thank You, Jesus.

—Janice Johnston

Four years ago my left knee was badly injured in a tractor accident. It was discovered that, apart from severe damage to the cartilage, the knee was so badly affected with arthritis the doctors said it was amazing I had any movement at all. The knee was operated on but there was no improvement. For the next two years I had to use walking sticks all the time to try to get around. One hundred and eighty metres was the maximum distance that I could ever manage to walk. During this two-year period there was no improvement whatever.

At a divine healing meeting in Whangarei in November 2003, I went forward at a healing meeting for Weston Carryer to pray for some other condition which I had. He then said, "I will pray for the Lord to heal your knees." My right knee was also badly affected. The healing commenced immediately and from that moment on I noticed a wonderful difference. Within six months my healing was complete. I now do not have any pain or walking restrictions. Recently I walked twenty-eight kilometres through bush without any problems. Thank You, Lord, for what has been a wonderful miracle. I am truly grateful.

—Richard Noall

I went to Weston Carryer's healing meeting at the Dunedin City Apostolic Church in March 2005. Ten years ago I tore the ligaments in my knees and they had never healed. Because of this condition I would experience throbbing pain in my legs for up to two hours after any exercise, and unless I stretched my legs after sitting for no more than five minutes my knees would ache as well. After Weston prayed for me I noticed an immediate, significant improvement and then the throbbing ceased completely. For some time now I have had no pain at all. Now fifteen months later after exercise I can sit in a normal position for hours with no pain. What wonderful relief! Thank

Hips, Legs, Knees & Feet

You, Jesus, and I'm so thankful Weston prayed for me and for his ministry.

—*Louise Dakens*

In May 2004, I slipped and fell over in the bath, landing on my knees. This resulted in my knee splitting down the middle. I was able to move the two pieces independently of each other and it was mushy between them. Although I was able to walk reasonably well if I was careful, bending my knee or trying to kneel was extremely painful. I attended a divine healing meeting at Napier in November 2004, where Weston Carryer was ministering. He spoke out words of knowledge that the Lord was revealing to him. When he said that someone had injured their left kneecap I knew this was going to be my time for my healing. I responded, went to the front and Weston prayed for me. Within one month my kneecap was totally healed and all pain ceased. Praise and glory to our great God.

—*Des Brightwell*

In a healing meeting in New Plymouth in 2004, Weston Carryer said that there was someone with a damaged ligament in their knee. I had experienced a lot of pain in my left knee, and it affected my ability to go for a run. I was using a lot of anti-inflammatory tablets to control the swelling and pain. After Weston prayed for me I knew my knee was healed. However, occasionally the symptoms would come back—almost like taunting me and challenging my faith to believe for my total healing. Now well over one year later, I realize I haven't had this problem or any of the symptoms for at least ten months. I have not used anti-inflammatory medication for the condition either. My knee is definitely healed. Praise God.

—*Ross Kernot*

For ten years, I suffered with excruciating pain in both knees. The cartilage in my knees was worn out completely and

Miracles in Aotearoa New Zealand

bone was rubbing against bone. I had difficulty walking and could not kneel down at all. I attended a divine healing meeting in Whangarei in November 2005 where Weston Carryer was ministering. During the meeting Weston, through a word of knowledge, spoke out my exact condition. As he prayed for me I felt the Holy Spirit come upon me in an amazing way. The pain went instantly. I ran up and down the stairs. Then, to my amazement, I started walking around on my knees singing loudly in the Spirit. It was exhilarating. Since that moment, eight months ago I have not had even the slightest sign of any pain in my knees and I can walk or kneel without any restriction. Lord, I am so grateful.

—*Emma Coyne*

I went to the healing ministry seminar at Whangarei in November 2007 that Weston Carryer was conducting because at the age of eighty I wanted to learn more. I have had to use a walking stick following a knee joint replacement ten months ago as I had an ongoing balance problem. I was always leaning to this weak side and by the end of the day had a hunched, aching back.

During the ministry time Weston prayed for the Lord to heal me and then took my stick and encouraged me to step out beside him. I realized that I was walking with upright carriage. From that time on I have never felt the need to use the stick for my balance or knee support and it is now seven months since I was prayed for. I drove the 117 kilometres home after being healed without having to angle my knee position on the accelerator. To God be the glory.

—*Lillian Appleton*

In 2003, while playing basketball I tripped and fell, damaging my left knee, which became very painful. I was unable to walk properly and could only drag my left leg. After two weeks I went to the doctor who sent me to the hospital; the x-rays revealed that my kneecap was shattered completely. An operation was then carried out to try to hold everything

Hips, Legs, Knees & Feet

together but, unfortunately, this did not work. A piece of wire used to join the shattered pieces of bone together pierced the skin and protruded out through the side of my knee.

I was then operated on again but there was still no improvement. Two more operations were then carried out and each time more bone was removed and I finished up with no kneecap at all. However, my knee was still no better and the surgeon told me that they could not do any more for me. From 2004 until September 2007 I had continual pain in my knee. I could not kneel at all, my knee would regularly swell up, give way completely at times, walking anywhere was a problem, and I wore a brace all the time to hold it together.

In September 2007, I attended a divine healing meeting at Victory Christian Centre in Lower Hutt where Weston Carryer was ministering. As he was ministering he said there was someone present with major knee problems in the left knee and for that person to come forward for him to pray for the Lord to heal it.

I went forward and he prayed for me; intense heat went into my knee and it was immediately stabilised. I then reached down and felt my brand new kneecap. Amazing! The Lord had given me a wonderful creative miracle. At that time I was not a born-again believer, but this creative miracle convinced me beyond all doubt about the love and power of Jesus Christ. A while later, I made a total commitment to Him and have followed Him ever since. From that moment, over twelve months ago now, my knee has functioned normally and perfectly in every way. Thank You, Jesus.

—*Taylor Morris*

I am a very active eighty-one-year old. Recently I went to Auckland to spend a week with my granddaughter. Unfortunately I tripped on one of the very steep streets and I injured my knee. The A & E said I had strained some of the ligaments behind my knee. After returning home my knee swelled and I could hardly move at all; it was getting worse and was incredibly painful. My friend took me to Grace Church in Christchurch where Weston

Carryer was holding a service. I told him I had been an elder in the Christian's Healing Ministry for many years when I was younger, and that I had seen the miracles. I looked him straight in the eye and said, "I believe."

Weston just said, loudly, "Spirit of infirmity, be gone." It was just as though someone had shot me in the forehead and I crashed so fast to the floor that no one had time to catch me. When I came to I got up and walked without any pain. This was over six months ago and I have had absolutely no trouble at all since then. I just thank and praise God that Weston was being so obedient to allow God to use His healing power through him. Praise You, God, for Your love for us.

—Mrs. Clare O'Connell

Seven years ago, I broke my ankle and it never healed properly. Then three years ago I tore a ligament in my knee and for the following six months I could not do anything. During this time my knee was swollen to twice its normal size. For the last seven years I was very limited in my movements and even more so during the last three years. The skin on my leg around my ankle was continually ulcerated. These ulcers, which were up the size of a fifty-cent piece, continued to grow on my leg and any walking would cause them to burst. For the seven years I walked on an angle because of this. Although an operation did help slightly, the pain in both my foot and my knee was horrendous for this entire period. The problems were unable to be medically resolved. During this seven-year period I became very negative, angry and bitter.

In June 2008, Weston Carryer prayed for my knees and ankles, and then he asked me to run around the stage. To my delight and surprise I did just that—not very gracefully and not as quickly as I used to, but I could move. My God had healed me. It was wonderful and, although I had previously accepted Jesus as my Lord and Saviour, I had never before experienced such peace of heart as I did that morning. I felt such a delicious peace of heart, mind and soul that I am hungry for that again. My negativity and bitterness left immediately after this

Hips, Legs, Knees & Feet

wonderful healing and my whole attitude and life has changed so dramatically. Thank You, Jesus, for my healing.

—*Krystyna Fatkiel*

I recently caught up with Weston at another healing service in Paraparaumu; he called someone up with left knee problems. I got up and went to see him as I'd had trouble with my knee for the past twenty years. The cartilage was wrecked from a series of accidents. It would always dislodge itself—a painful experience—and getting it back in was never easy, hurting a great deal. Once again, as Weston prayed, the power of God came through Weston and healed my knee. I felt a tingling sensation in my knee once I returned to my seat.

I was walking up a sand dune the other day and fell awkwardly on my leg. Usually in this kind of situation my knee would have popped out for sure, but no, it did not. It stayed in place perfectly. In fact, it would have popped out about three or four times by now. I was advised by doctors that the only way to fix my knee was to have a knee replacement operation. In the back of my mind I realised my knee would always trouble me. The thought of that, after having so many operations already, was something I really could not be bothered with. I was about to start taking glucosamine to help fix it as I really did not want to be a helpless little old lady stuck at home with a knee I could not pop back in.

The great news is, to this day so far, I have had no further trouble with my knee. Praise God. God really has worked a series of miracles in my life. I am truly grateful for His abundant blessings every day.

—*Nicole Williams, Ohau*

Several years ago, I fell and badly injured both my knees and the doctor believed that I would need a double knee replacement. It was then discovered that the cruciate ligaments inside the knees which hold the knee together had been ruptured and would not hold the knee together. For the next 3½ months I was in excruciating pain all the time. I could hardly walk at all, and during this period there was no improvement. I had physiotherapy but it did not help at all.

I attended a divine healing meeting in Kapiti where Weston Carryer was ministering. During the meeting he said that there was someone there who had damaged both knees and for them to go to the front for him to pray for the Lord to heal them.

I hobbled forward. He then prayed, looked at me and said, "Run across the front of the church."

I looked at him in amazement and then realized, *I have no pain!* I started to run and ran across the front of the church and back again with not the slightest bit of pain.

Since that time, several years ago, I have had no trouble with my knees at all. Hallelujah. Thank You, Lord Jesus.

—*Pam Anderson*

Nine years ago, when taking part in a church concert, a girl fell on my right knee and the A.C.L. ligament was torn. This never healed and it resulted in major restriction in my life. I was unable to do much with my knee at all. I had to stop playing football, and as a result of barely being able to exercise, my weight went from 90 to 142 kilos. My knee was always very painful and I damaged it four or five times during this nine-year period. It did not look like a normal knee. It became misshapen, with a piece of kneecap sticking out to the side.

However, this changed dramatically on 23 January 2011, when I attended a divine healing meeting in Auckland where Weston Carryer was ministering. As he was ministering he said that there was someone sitting where I was who had done this damage to their right knee and for the person to come forward for him to pray for the Lord to heal him.

I could not get to the front fast enough. Weston then prayed for me and I went down on the floor. As I was lying down, I felt my knee being reconstructed by the Lord. The whole knee became the right shape and size. It was incredible. I then got to my feet and ran at full speed around the church. Since that moment I have had no problem of any kind whatever with my knee. Thank You, Lord Jesus.

—*Scott Houghton*

I am forever grateful for the healing prayer I received from our Lord through Weston Carryer. When he came to City Church a few years ago, he asked the person sitting on the left side who had a painful right knee to come up and receive a healing. I said to my husband, "This is for me." I knew I was the one.

At that time I was taking painkillers and capsules for inflammation, plus wearing a knee support. The doctor arranged for me to have an arthroscopy and the result was that I had osteoarthritis and wear and tear and, in the future, maybe a knee replacement.

Praise God. The best news is that I have had a healing of my knee. I slowly weaned myself off medication, which is marvellous. I am a 73-year-old woman and I belong to an entertainment group who tap dance and go to rest homes and do private functions. I am so grateful to God for giving me the chance in realising my childhood dream of being a dancer, which I now can do. Not only dancing . . . I love to do my garden and also leisure marching each week. I am a grandmother and a great-grandma of four beautiful children. It is such a blessing to be able to do all that I do. God is so good. Praise be to God.

—*Ruth Scott*

After retiring from ministry in February 2010, my wife and I desired to serve the Lord in family ministry at YWAM, Crystal Springs, Matamata, and the date of 18 July 2010 was set for us to move to Matamata. But in March I damaged my knee and it deteriorated so that I assisted my walking with Grandad's walking stick.

I had several visits to Dr. Tim Lynsky, an orthopaedic surgeon. He booked me in at the New Plymouth base hospital for a knee replacement. Meanwhile my dream to serve at the YWAM base seemed to fade.

Miracles in Aotearoa New Zealand

I attended a combined church meeting in New Plymouth three months later in June where Weston Carryer was ministering. He prayed for the Lord to do a miracle for me and I am rejoicing that the Lord completely healed my knee.

My wife and I took up our position in Matamata on the planned date, and over the last two years, I have had no problem, pain or restriction in my knee whatever.

"I am the Lord who healeth thee," is an often-quoted Scripture as I tell others my story.

—*Stuart Helms*

For over ten years, I suffered terrible pain from what was diagnosed as permanently damaged ligaments at the back of both knees. Apart from the constant pain my knees were very swollen. This made walking very difficult and climbing stairs nearly impossible. During this entire time, I took at least four Panadeine tablets every day to try and ease the pain. A surgeon in the Palmerston North Hospital told me that this condition was inoperable, and that an operation of any kind would not help at all.

In September 2012, I attended a Christian healing meeting at the Centre Church in Paraparaumu where Weston Carryer was ministering and he prayed for the Lord to heal my knee. An improvement started immediately and within a few weeks, all the pain and swelling had gone. Over the past 6 months, I have had no pain and can walk normally. This has made a huge difference to my life. Thank You so much, Lord Jesus.

—*Shirley Button*

For over two years, I suffered from a very painful right knee which completely restricted me in all areas, but especially as a dancer. I could not kneel at all, and any movement was painful. The medical diagnosis was that the cruciate ligament was damaged and my knee would require surgery for the functionality to be restored.

Hips, Legs, Knees & Feet

Our Vision Church in Feilding hosted Weston Carryer for a healing meeting on September 5, 2012. Although I am a regular attendee at the church, I did not want to go that night. I was very tired, grumpy and I did not believe that healing was for me. I actually had a strange fear of healing meetings. I told my husband I was prepared to go for a short while.

Weston started ministering and after sharing some healing testimonies he said that the Lord was revealing some conditions that the Lord wanted him to pray for immediately. The very first condition he spoke out was a damaged cruciate ligament in someone's right knee.

I knew this was for me. In a flash I was on my feet and went to the front in pain for Weston to pray for me. As he prayed, the Lord instantly and completely healed my knee. I was able to bend the knee with no pain and the full movement was restored and for the last seven months the knee has been 100%.

That moment was a real significant God moment for me and the Lord really dealt with sacred cows in my life at that time.

I am so grateful to the Lord Jesus Christ for reaching out to me in such a wonderful way.

—*Karen Warboys*

For approximately 12 months, both my knees were giving me pain whenever I had to bend them at all. Getting up and down from a sitting position always hurt.

As a herd tester I had to climb in and out of cowshed pits and this became awkward because of this pain. The condition was getting worse and I was wondering what to do about it.

On October 5, 2011 (or October 17, 2012), I attended a divine healing meeting at St. Andrews, Matamata where Weston Carryer was ministering. He said that there was someone there experiencing pain in both knees and the left one was the worst one. This was exactly the case with me.

I went forward and he prayed for the Lord to heal my knees. Since that moment I have never had any further pain. I did not go to the meeting intending to be prayed for, but the fact that

Miracles in Aotearoa New Zealand

Jesus cared for me so much to reach out to me as He did shows that He really is looking out for me.

—*Pam Jeffs*

I am 67 years of age, and for the last eighteen years, I have had trouble with both my knees. The trouble started in the right knee, and the doctor diagnosed cartilage problems which he said would need an operation.

However, I was in no position to have this operation and so I did not proceed. Not long after this, the left knee also started giving me trouble and I found I was unable to run at all, which I had previously been doing. Soon after this, walking became very painful and so for the next eighteen years I became very limited in my movement.

On 1 December 2013, Weston Carryer came to my church, St. David's in Edgecumbe to preach and to minister healing. He spoke out my condition and I went forward for the Lord to heal me. The effect was incredible. All the pain instantly disappeared and has never returned. For the last six months, I have been able to walk briskly and jog for 65 minutes, six times a week, without any pain at all. Thank You, Lord. I praise You so much.

—*Sonny Mansell*

In February 2013, I was out our CRF church in Whangarei where Weston was having a healing meeting. Both of my knees and ankles had been continually aching for months and any walking was extremely painful.

Right as the start of the meeting Weston pointed to the section where I was sitting and asked the person who had the painful knees and ankles to come forward for him to pray for the Lord to heal them.

I responded, and as he prayed, they immediately freed up and the pain was gone! Six months on and everything is A-1.

Hips, Legs, Knees & Feet

The healing power of the Lord is awesome! I am so thankful. Ask, and thou shalt receive!

—George Bond

On 3 April 2007, at a healing meeting at South City Christian Centre in Christchurch Weston prayed for my injured knee. As a result of an old injury my knee was swollen, locked and very painful. Walking was painful and running was impossible. My symptoms were really affecting my life. After Weston prayed for me Jesus immediately healed my knee by about seventy-percent. It felt more stable, more flexible, stronger, and most of the pain was gone. Every day I thanked Jesus for the measure of healing that I had already received and the work He continued to do.

Today I have a total healing—one hundred percent! I walk and run without pain. I work out at the gym every week for three or four sessions. I'm thankful that Weston made himself available, and thank You, Jesus, for Your healing power and love towards us.

—Jo Gaul

Approximately two and a half years ago when getting into a truck, I fell and damaged both my knees. The left knee healed quickly but my right knee refused to heal and I experienced a considerable amount of pain for the next two years. At times walking was very difficult and my knee would completely seize up and I could not move it at all.

One morning, in September 2008, the pain was extreme and at City Life Church in Tauranga Weston Carryer prayed for the Lord to heal my knee. What happened was amazing. Immediately the pain went and my knee was able to function normally. Over the last eight months, apart from one day when I had slight pain for a short time, I have had no further problems with my knee. Lord, I am truly grateful to You.

—Nathan Thompson

Miracles in Aotearoa New Zealand

Feet, Heel/Feet, Ankles, Toes

I was present at a healing meeting at Mosgiel in May 1992, when Weston Carryer opened with a word from the Lord that someone on his left had punctured his heel and been left with arthritis. God wanted to heal it. He called several times and even pinpointed the area where I sat. It never dawned on me I was the person. Later in the week, I awoke to the realization that while I had no arthritis, I *had* stepped on a nail years ago. As a result, I have had a painful plantar (sole) facilitis over the last six to nine months. The heel has been healed since the meeting. God issued a promise and, true to His word, kept it.

—*Peter Ashton*

For years I have suffered from what I believed was one foot larger than the other. Invariably, I had blisters on my left foot because of the tightness of the shoe while the other one was fine. I used to get bad pains in my legs if I had been standing for long periods due to favouring the left leg and imposing the weight on the right one. I attended Te Nikau Bible School in January 1993, where Weston Carryer conducted a healing meeting. He said there was somebody present suffering from a sore left foot because it had no arch. Although I could not line up the facts, I knew the call was for me. Through Jesus Christ, God removed my affliction by giving me a perfectly normal arch. The next morning I put my boot on with no problem, but said, "Far out. I don't believe this," then I rebuked the thought, and claimed the victory in Jesus' name. I am healed and things get better every day. All glory to God.

—*Gail Henderson*

In 1994, a short log fell on my big toe and totally crushed it in many places. A year later I visited the doctor because the pain in my toe was so sore and I couldn't yet move it. The

Hips, Legs, Knees & Feet

doctor said to give it one more year. I used to feel so frustrated. After another year it was still the same. Weston called out my condition and I was totally healed. My toe can now dance. Praise the Lord.

—*Puhi, Whakatane*

I was born with a left clubfoot which by the time I was fully grown, was two and a half centimeters shorter than the right foot. My left leg was also two and a half centimeters shorter than the right one. At age fifteen I was in an accident which resulted in my good right foot ending up at an incorrect angle to my leg, making it very difficult for me to run.

I attended a Weston Carryer evangelistic healing crusade meeting in April 1994. As Weston prayed for me God, through Jesus by the power of the Holy Spirit, instantly healed all these conditions. My left foot is now exactly the same length as the right foot—my legs are of identical length and all abnormalities have gone from both feet. I can now run without any trouble. Praise God.

—*Lincoln Johnson*

God's healing power—what a wonderful gift. Although I have been a Christian for many years, I had not given much thought to miracle healing until one night God blessed me with one of my own. My wife and I had gone to a house group meeting where evangelist Weston Carryer was preaching. A real presence of God was there, and God was healing people and bringing them forward by a word of knowledge. The word "feet" came out which did not really suggest too much to me, but then the word "arches" came through and that really hit home. I was a harrier who enjoyed my running. For many years I had worn arch supports in my shoes as I had a problem with high arches. These supports were specially hospital-made every few years after new casts had been taken. Without supports, all my weight would press down on my feet giving me corns and all sorts of foot problems necessitating chiropody.

Miracles in Aotearoa New Zealand

In faith, I went forward. Weston laid hands on me and I was aware of a real heat coming down, then a total lightness as my body seemed to be floating up into the clouds. I felt a real love reaching out to me and a very peaceful feeling I knew to be God's presence. God's healing is perfect, but He does seek to reassure us. That night I removed all my arch supports and prayed that my healing be complete. True to His Word, God proved His healing.

The Dorne Cup race came up on the harrier programme and, without the benefit of supports, I ran it in the fastest time ever—faster than I had ever run before. Then followed half-marathons at Wellington, Palmerston North, and our own in Wairarapa—every one of which I ran faster than I had ever run before and all without supports. God's healing is complete and I know He healed my arches perfectly and enabled me to run faster just to prove it. Praise God for His healing grace. Never hesitate to go forward, in faith, and receive His gift for you; for His love knows no bounds, and He is there just wanting to share your life and give you His peace.

—*Pelham Ellis*

A night to remember: Weston Carryer had come to a healing meeting and the Lord gave him a word of knowledge that someone was having trouble with the arches of their feet. No one responded. Then it dawned on me—*It's me!* I was born with one foot longer than the other. My mother detested shopping for my shoes because one shoe fitted perfectly while the other would almost fall off. When I needed shoes for high school we went to the adjacent city. We visited a shoe shop where they had this new x-ray machine. We tried several pairs. None fit, so onto the machine I went. There it was—one foot longer than the other. It was a case of averaging them out and putting up with the pain. I would get sharp pains in the arches, and such pain in the heels I could hardly walk. I had cortisone shots in the heels. Over the years I learned to live with it.

As Weston began to pray, the funniest thing happened. It felt as if someone was tickling my feet. I began to laugh and could hardly stop. All joined in. When we looked, the feet were the same size. One foot had grown about twelve millimeters. What a blessing to be able to try on a pair of shoes and find they fit perfectly and, best of all, no more pain. What a mighty God we serve. Sometimes we do not have to ask . . . He just wants to give us a blessing.

—*Bill Snowdon*

On 27 April 1986, I slipped and fractured my left ankle. This was x-rayed and found to be broken in three places. A young Christian prayed with me at the time and we received the verse from Proverbs 4:12.

When you walk, your steps will not be impeded; and if you run, you will not stumble (NASB).

I clung to this Scripture in the following months and subsequent years, for the ankle breaks did not heal properly. Finally, in 1989, I went again for medical advice as the pain was almost unendurable. My visit was to a medical centre where there was choice of medical personnel. An x-ray was taken which showed calcifying of the ankle joint and wasting of the muscles and tendons as well. A suggestion was made that I be readmitted to hospital for the purpose of re-breaking the joint and inserting pins and a plate. Horrors!! Asking for time and for further consideration on the part of both myself and the medical team, I went home to pray. I told no person of the diagnosis.

The following evening, I attended my church fellowship-combined home group and youth group meeting at which Weston Carryer was to minister. As I walked into the gathering, Weston was giving an exposition on divine healings.

Then he said, "There is someone here with a broken ankle which has not healed. There is calcifying and constant pain to the knees which is beginning to spread to the thigh. You are considering an operation but God wants to heal you tonight." Now that had to be the Lord, for only I and the doctors knew what had been discussed one day earlier. I went forward, was prayed for, and released from the spirit of infirmity.

Miracles in Aotearoa New Zealand

The next day I went back to the medical centre for another check and more x-rays. We viewed the x-rays side by side. On one is the broken and deformed ankle, and on the other a perfectly restored ankle. The doctor said, "Shirley, we are in the healing business, but God is in the miracle business. This is a miracle."

Twelve months later I am in a "Rise Up" team and doing much walking. At a meeting God reminded me of the Scripture given in 1987. I realised I still had a slight limp. Asking a leader to pray for me, I had the leg grow nineteen millimetres from the ankle, and the hip socket go into place. Weston had a word the following Sunday concerning someone with an injury from a broken arm. That was me. It, too, was totally healed.

—*S. K. Currie*

I had broken a bone in my foot back in 1972. In June 1990, I broke another bone which had me on my back for nine weeks. I asked the Lord, unashamedly, to send an evangelist if He wanted me on my feet again to do His work. Weston Carryer came in late August. Praise God, I am walking around today totally unimpeded. I was healed of a hernia too. I was due to go to hospital for bed rest before tests. There was no bed available so I thank God as I am believing the tests will prove clear. I was, further, released from a spirit of fear of man caused during home life and, later, being unevenly yoked in marriage. Now I am on a new path and continue in awe of Jesus as He opens up new avenues of service to me.

—*Colleen Hillock*

In December 1989, I broke the bones in my heel when I fell out of a first-story window while in the throes of an epileptic fit. I had medical treatment at the time, even spending a period in hospital, but was told that as they were difficult bones to treat I may always have pain and would just have to get used to living with it. Months went by. They never healed properly and were giving me considerable and almost continuous pain. When Weston Carryer was in Dunedin in mid-May 1991, I

Hips, Legs, Knees & Feet

asked him to pray for relief from the pain and for the healing of those bones. Six weeks later, as I was praying, I realised I had had no pain for some time. I thank God for sending His servant, Weston, and give to God the glory for my healing.

—R. Chandler

I went along to a healing crusade in Auckland in 1992 at which Weston Carryer was the speaker. Through a word of knowledge, he invited someone who had a damaged foot to come out for prayer. When there was no response, he assured me God had told him it was myself. Since I could not recollect any accident which fitted the description given, I still did not go up. Time went by, and the whole incident returned to me. I wrote to Weston and he sent me a copy of his pamphlet, *Keeping Your Healing,* over which he had prayed for healing of my affliction. I simply placed this over the area around and below my left ankle, then praised God and thanked Him for His healing touch. I started to get pain in the foot late that very day. I realised it was, just as your notes said, satan the thief who was immediately endeavouring to destroy the gift of God by undermining my faith that the healing had been received. I resisted the urge to use the anointed notes a second time but, prompted by the Holy Spirit, accepted the healing had occurred and told satan to quit posturing. He did not persist and, from that day, I have had freedom from discomfort and from the occasional crackling sound which came from my foot.

—Nigel Griffiths

I was born without arches to my feet. This caused problems all my life. My feet ached continually while standing for more than a few minutes, and it was a real effort because of the pain this caused. I also had a curvature of the spine. I attended a divine healing meeting at Dunedin where Weston Carryer was ministering. During the meeting he said there was a person who had flat feet that God wished to heal at that moment. This had been revealed through the Holy Spirit. He did not call me out but simply asked me to stand. As I did so, the power of

Miracles in Aotearoa New Zealand

God, through Jesus, touched me in an amazing, awesome and beautiful way. Immediately, I felt arches develop in my feet and my back straightened up. I can now walk properly, and stand for long periods without any problems or pain whatsoever. I praise God for my perfect arches and straight back.

—*Adrian Murray*

For the last two years I had had a severe Achilles' tendon strain. I had physio eighteen months ago but the improvement was negligible. My right foot eventually corrected but the left was not getting any better. In November 1991, I went to a house group in Christchurch where Weston Carryer took the meeting. During the healing time I kept thinking, *I would love to have the Lord heal my foot.* Being somewhat shy, I did not go forward. Later, when it was time to leave, I was limping as usual, and a friend said I should have had my foot prayed for, but I had learned to live with it. Besides, other people seemed to have worse problems than I did. Next morning I woke to a burning feeling along the top of my foot. It went on for the rest of the day, slowly losing heat as the day wore on. Next thing I realised was that I had no pain in the tendon. I believe the Lord healed me through the hope expressed in my thought while Weston was praying. Thank You, Jesus.

—*Glenda Hay*

I am still trying, at age sixty-one, to come to grips with what took place at a healing meeting in Tauranga conducted by Weston Carryer in 1994, and the unusual experience of coping with an arch in my right foot, to see it straight and to find the overall walk is not all to one side. All my life the heel of my right leg was never fully down. At forty-one years, this impediment was accentuated by polio in the lower section of the leg, and then compounded by an accident in 1979, when the right ankle joints were fractured and fractures were sustained in each foot. The one in the right foot was on the outer edge which became a pressure point. In spite of all this, I managed to maintain an active life but some three months before the meeting the right

Hips, Legs, Knees & Feet

ankle kept throwing outward, and the foot was canting over to the extent that two pairs of shoes had had a hole worn in the side of each upper. Weston prayed over me and God, through Jesus Christ, gloriously healed me. I am still overawed by the immensity of it all.

—*Peter McEvoy*

In 1975, my Achilles tendon snapped, and for the next eight years I suffered considerably. It never healed. I was almost always in pain, while the ankle was invariably swollen. I attended a healing meeting in Stratford where Weston Carryer was ministering; I had gone there believing God was going to heal me. Right at the start of the meeting Weston said there was someone present with the condition I had, and for that person to come forward for God to heal whoever it was. I went forward immediately and was prayed for.

Within three days, all swelling and pain was gone and I have had no further distress or problems. For the last nine months, my ankle has been completely normal. I thank God who, through Jesus Christ, has healed me.

—*Dawn Reith*

I have had flat feet all my life, that is, until the night I went to a Weston Carryer healing meeting. He invited anyone who wanted healing to please come forward. So I did. I explained what was wrong, and that I got backache and sore legs from flat feet. When he had finished praying I looked down at my feet and saw the Lord had given me arches. I reflected, "I will never have to wear inner soles again." Later that night I went up to Weston and asked, just as a matter of curiosity, whether he would look at the length of my legs, and he did. Everyone came and had a look too. One leg was 2.5 cm shorter than the other. Weston prayed. God extended the shorter one to the length of the longer one. Praise God! I am thankful for Weston praying for me. Thank You, Jesus, for healing me. It was a night to remember.

—*Monique Nouens*

Miracles in Aotearoa New Zealand

I was born with flat feet which resulted in me having foot problems through my life. My feet were always in pain and I was limited in many ways because of this. Also the middle toe on each foot had never developed and they were less than half a centimetre in length. Weston Carryer was ministering at a divine healing meeting in Taupo which I attended. During the meeting he said that God had revealed to him that there was someone there who had flat feet and was also experiencing a lot of pain in their feet, and if they would come forward the Lord would heal them. I responded and as Weston prayed for me the Lord released His power. Not only did He give my feet arches, but the middle toes on each foot grew out to be the right length. Since that time, almost a year ago, I have had no pain or any problems in my feet. Praise the Lord!

—*Francis Jago*

I was born with flat feet which caused problems all my life . . . until recently. I had to wear special shoes, but despite this, if I was standing at all, by the middle of the day my feet were always aching. At a divine healing meeting in Tauranga where Weston Carryer was ministering, Jesus reached out to me in a very special way. He revealed through a word of knowledge to Weston that there was someone there who had flat feet accompanied by foot problems. I went forward and as Weston prayed the Lord caused arches to develop in my feet. Incredible—they were there for everyone to see. Since then I have had no foot pain. My feet are healed and normal. Thank You, Jesus.

—*Monica Willis*

I am so thankful for Weston Carryer praying for me to receive God's healing of putting arches in my feet. About two years ago I fractured my right foot and have had trouble with it ever since. After I fractured it I was told by my doctor that I had flat feet and that's why my feet have been painful. When

Hips, Legs, Knees & Feet

Weston prayed for me to be healed, the pain went instantly. It was amazing and my feet are no longer giving me pain. I was at East Street Apostolic Church when Weston came to Hamilton. God is amazing when you let Him do things with you in your life. I have been a Christian for about three or four years. God has helped me in the past with problems I have had. God has really helped me—especially with putting arches in my feet as now I don't have to wear supports in my shoes. Once again, I am thankful to Weston! God is great!

—*Tina Shorten*

For forty years I had flat feet. My brother also had the same problem but he had an operation as a child to have this corrected. On 16 April 1996, I attended a divine healing meeting at Wanganui. When Weston Carryer, who was ministering, revealed through a word of knowledge that someone had flat feet, I immediately responded. Imagine my joy, when as I was prayed for, I felt the bones in my feet move and I realized that Jesus Christ had given me arches. Praise the Lord.

—*Ian Little, Wanganui*

Ten months ago I broke my foot in two places. These breaks had never healed properly; my foot was always in pain, I was restricted and had to be very careful at all times. I went forward during a healing meeting at The Centre, Paraparaumu, where Weston Carryer was ministering. As soon as I had been prayed for I realized my foot was completely healed, and I was able to run around the church with no pain. Praise the Lord. Thank You, Jesus.

—*Maria Burland, Paraparaumu*

Our granddaughter, Angela, had her big toe put badly out of joint due to a horse treading on her foot, and was in constant pain and was obliged to wear a bigger size shoe. After Weston laid hands on her foot and prayed, her toe was completely and immediately healed—back into normal position, all pain was gone, and she has had no further trouble. Praise the Lord.

—*Ailsa Simpson*

Over a number of years the arches in my feet had dropped completely, and this was causing pain and all sorts of problems in my feet. I needed to wear orthotic soles to support my arches. In November 1999, Weston Carryer came to minister in our church in Hastings. The night before his first meeting I prayed that the Lord would give him a word of knowledge for me. When Weston asked for the person who had my condition to come forward, I responded immediately. After he prayed, I was lying, resting in the Spirit on the floor with my shoes off and the people in the front row saw the Lord form my arches.

Since that time I have had no further problems in this area in my feet. I have two perfect arches and no supports needed. Thank You, Jesus!

—*Leslie Walker*

In 1984, I slipped and broke my ankle, and immediately it was put in plaster by a doctor. Movement was very difficult, so the next morning I contacted Weston Carryer and asked him if he would pray for me. As Weston prayed I experienced all the pain going, so I straightaway returned to the doctor and asked him to remove the plaster as I knew my ankle was healed. He was very surprised at my request and even more surprised when he took the plaster off to find that the ankle was fully healed. Within a week I was able to walk normally, without any pain, putting my full weight on the ankle. Over the past sixteen years I have had no further problems with the ankle. Praise the Lord.

—*Barbara Chilcott*

While competing in a game of netball in 1993, I broke my Achilles tendon and as a result my foot was useless, as I had

Hips, Legs, Knees & Feet

no strength in it at all. A cast up to my knee was put on and the doctor said it would take between one and two years to heal and that I would be on crutches for some time. Two days later I attended a divine healing meeting on my crutches where Weston Carryer was praying for the sick. He prayed for the Lord to heal me. The pain immediately left and I knew that I was healed. I took the plaster cast off and found my foot was functioning normally. Two weeks later I was back on the basketball court. Praise the Lord!

—Marion TeKawa (Rotorua)

For all my life I suffered from flat feet. This caused pain a lot of the time in my knees and they would suddenly collapse from under me at any time, and I would fall over.

At a church service in Pukekohe, in December 2000, Weston Carryer was ministering and spoke out my condition. He said the Lord had revealed this to him, and for me to go forward for the Lord to heal me and give me arches. I went forward, and as Weston prayed the Lord gave me two perfectly formed arches in my feet. Since then I have had no pain in my knees and they never buckled again. This is wonderful. Thank You, Jesus.

—Val Harris (Pukekohe)

I am currently eighteen years of age and when I was quite young (about three and a half years old), my parents discovered that my right foot was slightly out of alignment. They took me to the doctor to see what could be done, but the doctors could not fix it. They decided not to do anything about it as it did not appear to be effecting my walking but was just one of those annoying things.

One day I was invited to a Weston Carryer healing service on Tuesday, 6 March in Wanaka. During the service Weston Carryer was praying for individuals to be healed by the Father in the name of Jesus. A few individuals were very pleased with God healing them on the spot. I then remembered about my

Miracles in Aotearoa New Zealand

bad right foot so I decided to ask for prayer. As soon as the prayer had finished I collapsed just before Weston was about to perform the laying on of hands. I felt the Holy Spirit coming into me; it was like a gust of wind and warmth. As I was falling many people watching heard a loud noise of a bone in my right foot clicking into place. When I got up I discovered that God had healed my right foot. My left and right feet are now perfectly in alignment and I have recently discovered that my right foot had been effecting my walking. God does heal today!

—*Alex Mercer*

I am writing to tell you about the wonderful healing I received when Weston Carryer prayed for me last month at Kevin Dixon's Friday night meeting. Weston prayed for my feet that were turned in, saying that God told him my pelvis was tilted. I know that God healed me instantly, and the pain in my back that was caused by this (which I can't remember ever not having) has completely gone. This is a great blessing as I work with elderly and handicapped people which requires that I do a lot of lifting and am on my feet all day. I am thankful for Weston's obedience to God.

—*Christine Potroz*

For ten years, I suffered with extreme pain in both of my feet. It was too painful to walk anywhere at all. I attended a divine healing meeting where Weston Carryer was ministering, and he said the Lord had revealed to him that there was someone who had the problem with their feet I had. I responded, and as Weston prayed, the Lord immediately healed my feet. I rejoice to say that ever since that moment several years ago, I have had no further pain or problems in my feet. Thank You, Jesus.

—*Shona Vick*

For over thirty years I continually sprained my ankles, and as a result they became out of shape. They bulged so much,

Hips, Legs, Knees & Feet

especially the right one, which made it look like it was on an angle to my leg. Besides this weakness, I would experience pain when standing for long periods or going on a walk.

I attended a healing meeting at my local church in Tauranga in January 2003, where Weston Carryer was ministering, and through a word of knowledge, he described my condition. I responded immediately and he prayed for the Lord to heal me. The next morning I noticed my ankles had been restored to normal shape. Ever since then I have had no further sprains or problems with them. I can walk distances, and stand without pain. Thank You, Jesus.

—*Lynn Flanagan*

I hope my testimony is an encouragement to others. For three years I suffered from deep throbbing pains in my feet. I eventually went to a podiatrist who made splints for my shoes. I had to wear these at all times, and did so for two years. Unfortunately, they failed to help, and I resigned myself to being in almost constant pain.

I have been a Christian for many years but it never occurred to me to ask the Lord to heal me. When I heard that Weston Carryer was coming to town with a healing ministry, I realised that the Lord was the answer to my problem. I was absolutely convinced that I would be healed, and when Weston called out that someone had sore feet, I was up like a shot. He prayed for me, and I went home safe in the knowledge that I was healed.

I'm sure you can imagine how gutted I was when the pain in my feet became worse and appeared in new areas. I was, however, firm in my faith and I claimed that healing with all my heart. After a few days, I realised that my feet were being reconstructed, and I had to throw away my splints because they didn't fit any more. It took two painful weeks before my feet were completely healed. Not long after that we went on a seven-week trip to England, and I think I walked non-stop for most of that time. Praise the Lord—my feet were perfect and still are.

—*Pam Pullar*

Miracles in Aotearoa New Zealand

For several months I had a sore foot every morning when I got out of bed. It felt like a stone bruise, but instead of going away, it gradually got worse each day. It got to the point where I felt like I had a large bee sting on the bottom of my foot every morning. During the day, the pain would gradually improve but the next morning it would be back and getting gradually worse with each passing week. The doctor told me I had Morton's Neuroma, which is when a growth occurs on the nerve inside the foot. The only known cure is to have it surgically removed.

Weston prayed for me at an evening service at Tauranga Worship Centre. The next morning when I got up, the pain and swelling were noticeably improved (about fifty-percent) but were still there. I kept thanking the Lord for my complete healing, and gradually over the next two to three weeks, the early morning pain subsided. For about two months now my foot has been completely back to normal—no pain at all. Thank You, Lord, for a healthy body!

—*Jane Hay*

In November or December 2001, I fell down some narrow stairs and badly twisted my ankle. The ankle was badly swollen and I couldn't bear the bedclothes on my foot so didn't sleep at all that night. The next night when I went to bed I asked the Lord to heal my foot as I would be travelling for forty-seven hours in a few days time. I had a good night's sleep and the next day though tender, it wasn't painful and the swelling had gone down. I had no problems on the way home, but a few weeks later I noticed a swelling on top of the foot and it would suddenly become very painful and weak. This would happen every few days at first, and then it became more and more frequent. Just as I was thinking I should have it x-rayed, I went to Weston Carryer's meeting in Christchurch in February 2002, and he called out, "The Lord is healing someone's left foot." Three times he called it out, and someone else put up their hand. As it wasn't painful at that time I didn't think it would be me. But a few days later, during a quiet time, I realised I hadn't

Hips, Legs, Knees & Feet

had the pain in my foot, and the swelling had gone! I haven't had any pain since. Praise the Lord!

—Margaret Hutton

Weston came to our church to minister and during his meetings he called out my condition, which was flat feet. I've had flat feet as long as I can remember. It got to the stage where I had to see a podiatrist and get some orthotic inserts made for my shoes (very expensive ones). This was to help with my walking and running posture to prevent injury due to "excessive pronation" (downward rotation). These inserts are quite annoying, as I had to basically use them in every shoe—something I was not keen to do for the rest of my life.

God heard my request, and I praise Him, because that night Weston called out my condition and God healed my feet. Weston and Ruth are now the proud owners of some very large and expensive inserts that I no longer have any use for as. Like a good Christian, I blessed them with the orthotic inserts! Nothing is too big, or too small, for God. The visual part of my arches improved slightly and now I actually have a footprint in the sand and no longer a flat-plank print. Two years on and I have no problems with my body at all; I have been running and doing all sort of things. Praise the Lord, and I'm so thankful for Weston.

—Hayden Robinson

Just over a year ago (mid-2003), I broke my ankle, which was then set and put in plaster. The day the plaster was taken off I again damaged my foot, and this resulted in a hairline fracture where the ankle had been broken. For the next twelve months I experienced considerable pain and it felt like the bones were not connected. I also needed support for my ankle to be able to walk at all and I could not wear jandals.

In August 2004, when Weston Carryer was ministering in our church, he said that there was someone who had broken their ankle, that it had not healed and was causing a lot of problems, and would that person come forward for the Lord to heal their ankle. I was so surprised, and although I knew it was me, I didn't move immediately. Someone else went forward, although it was not for this exact condition. As Weston prayed for the other person, heat went into my ankle and it was completely healed.

I can now run without any pain or restriction. Lord, You are awesome. I am so thrilled. I know that You care so much about me.

—*Diane Bottcher*

On 1 May 2004, while attending the healing meeting held in Helensville by Weston Carryer, he called out the condition of flat feet. I took my shoes off, took my orthotic inserts out of my shoes, and walked up to Weston in my socks with my inserts in my hand.

At first I wasn't sure if I had flat feet as I'd understood them to be twisted, so I explained this to Weston.

He replied, "Do you want God to heal you?"

I immediately shouted, "You bet I do!"

Weston then prayed over me and I went down to the floor under the power of the Holy Spirit. A peace came over me, and after a short time I started hearing excited conversations around me.

Three people sitting closest to where I was lying had witnessed the arches in both my feet forming perfectly. They were now shouting and praising God with excitement as I lay there under the anointing. I felt only slight movement in my feet, but they witnessed my feet being totally reformed and restored. Hallelujah! Praise God! When I got up we all celebrated together.

It is now twelve months since my healing and I haven't worn my orthotic inserts since that evening. I received my miraculous healing that night and to God be all the glory! Amen. The morning after my healing I wrote on the back of my orthotic inserts in felt pen: "Healed! In Jesus' name, Praise God! 1/05/2004—Weston Carryer healing meeting, Helensville."

— *Janice Archer*

Hips, Legs, Knees & Feet

In the year 2000, I badly twisted my left ankle and damaged the ligaments. As a result my ankle had to be in plaster for six weeks. After the plaster was removed I realized that my ankle had not healed. Sometime later I badly twisted it again and had to have it in plaster for a further six weeks. Once again it had not healed and for the next four years I was never able to put any weight on it, and was consequently unable to walk properly during this entire time. I always had pain; at times it was considerable and my ankle would also swell.

Weston Carryer was ministering in Flaxmere at a teaching meeting that I was attending in November 2004, and he said that the Lord had revealed to him that there was someone present who had damaged their left ankle some time ago and that this ankle had never healed. He asked would that person come forward for him to pray for them.

I said, "Yippee . . . that's me!" and immediately went forward. Weston then prayed for me, and before he had even finished praying, my ankle was healed. I jumped up and down on it several times. Since then, seven months later, my ankle has been normal. It is so wonderful what the Lord has done and I continually praise and thank Him as I am so grateful.

—*Chrissy King*

As a result of an acutely inflamed Achilles tendon my ability to move was severely restricted for five years. A lot of this time I could only hobble around and people were always asking me what was wrong with my leg. My doctor told me it would probably never heal because of the build up of scar tissue. A nodule grew on the outside of the tendon. I always had to be so careful with all my movements as there was a possibility that the tendon would snap.

At a divine healing meeting in Christchurch, in February 2003, Weston Carryer prayed for the Lord to heal my tendon. The Lord really answered the prayer and my tendon was healed. It wasn't instant, but over a two-month period the nodule disappeared. All the pain went totally, the strength fully returned, the limp went, and I have never had any problems with it since. Praise You, Jesus.

—Robyn De Mandeville

For many years, I had severe problems with both my ankles, suffering severe pain and swelling. Several years ago an operation was performed on them but this was not successful. The ankles continued to deteriorate, were very painful, and the swelling became worse and worse until in mid-2004, I could hardly walk at all. By November, I had to lie down nearly all the time and my ankles were so swollen the skin looked and felt like it would burst at any time.

I attended a divine healing meeting at Tauranga on 9 January 2005 where Weston Carryer was ministering. That morning I went, believing for the Lord to heal me. When Weston, through a word of knowledge, said there was someone present with my exact condition, I was so delighted and hobbled to the front as well as I could. As he prayed the swelling and the pain went—just went! It was amazing. I ran back and forward and jumped up and down. Since that moment over eight months ago, I have had no pain or suffering whatever and I can walk with complete freedom. Lord Jesus, I am so grateful for what You have done for me.

—Waiata Spurr

I was born with a clubfoot and had to have years of corrective surgery. Furthermore, my right leg was shorter than my left one. This, plus other factors, caused a curvature of my spine as well as seriously hindered my ability to run. I experienced lower back pain nearly all my life and sometimes this was severe. Then, over the last several months, I started to get severe pain in my foot and ankle area which prevented me from walking any distance. However, thanks to the grace of God and His wonderful healing powers, this radically changed on 10 July

Hips, Legs, Knees & Feet

2005 when I attended a divine healing meeting at Auckland where Weston Carryer was ministering. As Weston prayed for me, the Lord straightened my back, lengthened my leg, and healed my foot. It was amazing. I am now not restricted in any normal movements. I can run, walk long distances, and I do not have any pain at all. I am forever Yours, Lord Jesus.

—*Daniel Glover*

For over fourteen years, I had experienced trouble of the Achilles tendon. It caused me great discomfort and my ability to run was very limited. Limping was another factor I had to deal with. When the cold got in to it, I would not be able to function normally. It felt like my foot would just seize up and it would take a little while before I could walk properly. When Weston Carryer prayed for God to heal this condition, God's healing was immediate. I have not experienced any of the above symptoms since that night—fourteen years of pain and discomfort gone, just like that! Thank You, Jesus, You are truly amazing. *Arohanui ki a koe Te Arikinui.*

—*Vivian Rikona*

At the end of 2005, I was diagnosed with an Achilles tendon problem in both feet. This severely hampered any walking for any distance. In early 2006, I attended a healing meeting in Rangiora led by Weston Carryer. At the end of the meeting I requested prayer for my Achilles tendon problem and I received an immediate full healing in both feet. The next month while on holiday in Australia I experienced some soreness while walking every morning in the heat but continued to claim my healing, believing that I was totally healed. Now, to this present day, I can walk free of pain over any distance. Praise God.

—*Ralphia Henderson*

For at least the last six years I suffered from intense burning soles in my feet if ever I walked any distance. During a round of golf, I would have to stop, remove my shoes, and wait until the burning subsided as it was so severe. The right foot was the worst.

I attended a divine healing meeting at Waiheke Island in May 2006 where Weston Carryer was ministering. He spoke out and said that there was someone present who was suffering in both feet and this condition was the result of an accident many years ago. An accident to my back had caused this problem in my feet. I went forward for Weston to pray for me and the Lord blessed me by improving this condition immensely. Since that night, seven months ago, there has been only a very slight sensation of any burning and I am now not restricted like I was. Thank You so much, Lord.

—Anita Gibb

For approximately three years, I had a spur under my right heel. This is a sharp-pointed, bony growth. It made me hobble a lot of the time when I was walking and was very sore to stand on also.

Two years ago at a divine healing meeting in Tauranga, Weston Carryer prayed for the Lord to remove the spur; it simply disappeared off my foot within a short space of time. Thank You, Jesus.

—Pat Straayer

I ruptured my Achilles tendon six years ago and went to the emergency department where my foot was put in plaster. I was told they only operated on torn Achilles tendons in sports people, which I accepted at the time. I had pain and restricted movement, and when I turned my foot I could feel it pinching in my ankle. I went back to see an orthopaedic specialist who told me that it was a bad rupture and should have been operated on when I did it. He wanted to know why it hadn't been and I explained what they had told me at the time. He said it was now too late to operate on and told me to be careful how I stepped down off things as it could rupture again.

Hips, Legs, Knees & Feet

At a healing meeting in Whangarei, Weston had a word of knowledge, and although I had no pain at the time, I went forward for prayer. After I was prayed for I could move my foot right around and I have had no pain since. Praise You, Lord Jesus.

—*Roxanne Ruawhare*

I would like to praise the Lord for healing my foot at one of Weston Carryer's meetings in Hastings in 2003. Approximately forty-five years ago, I was practising long jump for high school sports. Unfortunately, instead of jumping from the correct mark I jumped from the edge of the pit. As a result I landed with my right foot on the opposite end of the pit. Although the pain was excruciating there was no swelling or apparent bruising. After some days I forgot all about it and never had any further problem. About two months before Weston came to Hastings, I started to get pain in my foot and suddenly remembered the accident I had all those years ago. At the time it was never x-rayed, so I have no idea what damage had been done. I began rubbing deep heat into it to help alleviate the pain.

At the meeting the Lord gave Weston a word of knowledge about someone who had an old injury in the right foot. It took me by surprise because I was going to ask for healing for pain in my elbows and knees, not my foot. He said that if the Lord didn't heal my foot, arthritis would set in. Weston prayed for my foot, elbows and knees. The pain in the joints left immediately. It took at least three months for the pain to completely go in my foot. It was a real test of faith because I knew the Lord had revealed the problem, and this meant that He was going to heal it—and He did. I sincerely appreciated Weston's ministry and know that he was a caring and humble man of God.

—*Pam Rowlands*

In early March 2005, as a result of an accident, I badly ruptured my Achilles tendon. For the next ten weeks I could not use that leg at all. I had to use crutches or a walking stick all the time. There was no improvement during this time and the doctor said that I would need surgery. I attended a divine healing meeting in Tauranga on 29 May 2005 where Weston Carryer was ministering and praying for the sick. I went forward on my crutches for him to pray for me with the usual great difficulty. As he prayed for me the power of God went into my tendon; all the pain left, the strength returned to the tendon and it was completely healed. I was able to put my crutches down and walk normally back to my seat.

Two days later we shifted house and I was able to lift heavy furniture. I have had no further problems with the tendon over the last two years. Lord, I am really grateful.

—*Gary Bedell*

About a year ago, for a period of about eight months, I suffered from severe foot pain every morning when I got out of bed. I would crunch my toes under and hobble to the bathroom. A last minute decision to attend a night service where Weston Carryer was ministering saw my neighbour and myself in the second-to-back row. I was called up for healing of fallen arches. Weston insisted that I remove my footwear so he could confirm my condition. I refused because I had been wearing Ugg boots without socks all day. After some discussion back and forth I finally agreed to remove one boot with a warning he might be the one slain on the floor. Weston prayed. I sat down with no immediate awareness of change. The next morning I got out of bed and one foot was completely healed; the other was still in crippling pain. Guess which one was healed? I went to my neighbour and told her. After almost crying together with laughter, I said, "Well, what do I do now?"

She said, "Apologize to God for your pride and ask Him to complete the healing." The following morning I strode to the bathroom with two healed feet and have never had any feet problems since. My heavenly Father has an amazing sense of humour and unlimited love.

—*Carol Nicoll*

Hips, Legs, Knees & Feet

One day in March 2007, when I was at work, I realized that my right foot had become painful. By the time I got home that night the pain had become horrendous. For the next five months the pain was there every morning and would increase through the day. My movements were extremely limited as walking was so painful.

I believed that the Lord would heal me and I attended a divine healing meeting in August 2007 where Weston Carryer was ministering. At the end of the meeting I asked him to pray for the Lord to heal me. As he prayed the very severe pain just went and the full use was restored to my foot. Apart from very slight pain about two days later I have had no further problems in that foot of any kind. It was a wonderful relief. Lord, I bless You and praise You so much for Your love and kindness to me.

—*Robin Nepia*

In September 2007, I tripped and fell, breaking five bones in my foot. My foot was extremely painful and so swollen that the doctor was unable to put it in plaster. Two days later I was invited by a neighbour to an evangelistic healing meeting where Weston Carryer was ministering. I attended on crutches as I could not even rest my foot on the ground at all. After Weston had shared some testimonies of healings, he said that the Lord had revealed to him that there was someone present who had broken their foot and the Lord wanted him to pray for their healing.

I did not know Jesus at this time and found all this quite overwhelming. However, after some encouragement from my neighbour, I hobbled forward and Weston prayed for me. The pain disappeared immediately; my foot became really hot and stayed that way for three days. God had reached out to me in amazing love.

That night I realized that Jesus was so real and that He really loved me. In fact, it was the first time in my life that I had experienced unconditional love and through the meeting, I had such incredible joy. Later that night when Weston asked people to accept Jesus as their Lord, I had no hesitation in doing so.

When I went back to have my foot plastered a week later, x-rays showed that the five broken bones were perfectly healed. Not only that, I had been born with a metatarsal bone out of alignment and that had been restored to its rightful place. Lord Jesus, thank You so much for healing, loving and saving me.

—Learna McBride

Late in 2007, Weston came for a series of healing meetings up on the Hibiscus Coast at Living Faith Church in Red Beach. I had a long standing problem with my left foot and ankle. I had broken my foot twelve years before, and then broke the same foot two years later. Each time my ankle had turned over and the ridge of my foot was broken. This had torn the ligaments in my ankle as well. About a year after the second break when I was walking on a grassy slope my ankle gave way because it was weak from the torn and stretched ligaments. So three times I had really wrenched that foot.

I have had so much trouble with that foot, because if I walked or stood on it for more than fifteen minutes my ankle would really swell up and would take between two to three weeks, or up to three or four months to settle down again! I would regularly come home from shopping at the grocery store and have to elevate and ice pack it.

There has been much prayer, many times for my foot over the last twelve years. I have had many different doctors' appointments and physio, etcetera. I even went to the All Blacks very own physiotherapist to get help, only to be told I had a lot of old swollen scar tissue in the ankle joint. They basically said there wasn't much that could be done but to get orthotics for my shoe as they would help to keep the pressure off it by lifting my arch up.

On the morning of Weston's first meeting as I was sitting there, I said—"Lord, please, please, please! Get him to call out my foot problem!" After calling out half a dozen ailments Weston said, "There's someone here who has broken your left

Hips, Legs, Knees & Feet

foot twice; you have a collapsed arch and this foot has caused you no end of trouble!"

Well, I shot out of my seat, and said, "Lord, that can only be for me!!" As Weston prayed for my foot to be healed and strengthened, I felt strength come into my ankle and leg bone. He told me to run back and forth up the front of the church. It felt different and I was very thankful—but the real test would be when I stood in line at the airport, and travelling to the USA with my leg hanging down for such a long time, as this would really set it off.

In the New Year, I made four separate flights and not once did I have trouble with that foot! I sincerely and gratefully thank Jesus! And I also am thankful for Weston—for his obedience and faithfulness to the call and gifts on his life!

—*Carol Haythornthwaite, Hobsonville*

Approximately sixteen months ago when Weston was in Whangarei in November 2007, I came to see him about a problem in my right foot which caused me pain when walking. I had four spots of a wart-like growth (some quite big) in the sole of my right foot which, according to my doctor, had to be cut out. That would have been very painful and prone to infections and I would have to walk on crutches for some time.

So I went to the front of the Christian Fellowship Renewal building where Weston had asked people to come who wanted to be healed and I told him about my problem. I've heard from other people that sometimes heat can be felt in the affected areas and I can testify to that. The moment when Weston released the healing power of our Lord, I felt intense but painless heat in specific points of my left foot and I thought, Oh my! The Lord has got it wrong—the problem is in my right foot. So when I got home I thought, Why did I get that heat in the left foot? I've never had any pain there. I had never had a look at the sole of my left foot—which is an effort anyway if you're over sixty.

When I checked it in the mirror I couldn't believe my eyes—I had the same stuff growing there too—which I didn't even know about, but the Lord did! So, I firmly believed that our Lord would heal both feet even though I told Weston about my right foot only. It took some months before I could see the diameter of the warts shrink and since then the affected bad flesh has continuously been replaced with new good flesh, so that now after a period of about one year, both feet are practically healed.

When I made a decision on the morning of Monday, 13 October 2008 (approximately three weeks before Weston would come to the CRF in Whangarei again), to give testimony to this miracle, I looked in my Bible to go on reading the Psalms. The first thing I saw was Psalm 51:

> *And call upon me in the day of trouble; I will deliver you, and you shall glorify me* (v. 15, ESV).

And that's exactly what I want to do; I want to give all the praise, honour and glory to our gracious and loving God.

—*Roland Gillespie*

Ten years ago I started having problems with my feet, and any walking would cause them to ache. I tried orthotics but they did not help. A podiatrist said that nothing could be done for my feet.

At a divine healing meeting in Waikenae, in February 2011, Weston Carryer prayed for the Lord to heal my feet and this is exactly what happened. Over the past ten months I have had no pain in my feet at all and I can walk as much as I want to. What a difference this has made. Thank You, Jesus.

—*Marilyn Kilpatrick*

In 2005, I ruptured the Achilles tendon in my right foot, and for the next six years I experienced severe pain and restriction especially when trying to walk. I continuously had to walk on the ball of my foot. The doctor said that I needed to have it operated on, but with family commitments, I was unable to take the time off required.

On Sunday, 1 May 2011, I attended Harvest Church in Rotorua as usual. I had walked that morning, and limped all

Hips, Legs, Knees & Feet

the way, as the pain was intense.

Weston Carryer was having a healing meeting in our church and I went forward for him to pray for me. As he prayed for the Lord to do a healing miracle for me, this is what happened immediately . . . just like that! Instantly the pain went and the movement and strength returned to my foot and ankle. I have had no further problems with the foot over the last six months.

Thank You, Lord Jesus.

—Carmelita Jolly

Thirty-one years ago, I sprained my left Achilles tendon. Shortly after, I sprained it again, and it was medically diagnosed as a "serious" sprain. Over the next thirty-one years there was no improvement to the tendon at all. I had been a keen runner and walker but was unable to run at all and always walked with a limp. Standing for any length of time would cause it to throb, and every night I took painkillers to stop the throbbing so that I could sleep. I could not go for any walks.

I attended a divine healing meeting at The Centre Church Kapiti where Weston Carryer was ministering in September 2011. Prior to the service I had said to the Lord, "I have had enough of this condition."

Right at the start of the meeting Weston said that the Lord wanted him to pray for the person who had damaged their left Achilles tendon many years go and it had never healed. I was so excited and jumped up and went forward. Weston then said that God was going to give me a new Achilles tendon. The moment I was prayed for the pain went and I found I could walk unhindered, with no limp, and realized that I could stride out and could walk normally.

That was six months ago and I can now really enjoy my long walks with no pain or hindrance whatever. This is marvellous after suffering for thirty-one years. Thank You, Lord Jesus.

—Dawn King

MIRACLES IN AOTEAROA NEW ZEALAND

Early in June 2011, I ruptured my Achilles tendon in my left foot as a result of a work accident. On June 12, I attended a divine healing meeting in City Life Church Tauranga where Weston Carryer prayed for the Lord to heal my tendon.

The healing was not complete immediately, although there was an improvement. I had it checked by the doctor who said that I had had a complete rupture of the tendon and that there had been a 15-mm gap between tendon ends, but that the healing had commenced. This was as a result of the prayer.

I did have plaster on for one week to help at this stage and then it was removed. For the next six weeks, I kept confessing healing Scriptures every day. Then on 8 August, the doctor said the tendon ends had fused together perfectly and that the tendon was completely healed.

I praise God for this and thank Him for His goodness to me.

—*Malcolm Gracie*

I was born with three extra bones in each foot. This caused me to walk with my feet turned right out at an angle to my legs. I was always in great pain in my feet and when I would walk home from school, the pain was excruciating. Any form of running was simply out of the question.

When I was 14, my feet were operated on and the three extra bones were removed. While this enabled me then to be able to walk straight, it did not reduce the terrible continual pain.

I attended a divine healing meeting at Eastgate Christian Centre in October 2012 where Weston Carryer was ministering, and during the ministry time he prayed for my feet to be healed. As he prayed, the power of God went into my feet and the pain immediately disappeared.

Weston saw the look of astonishment on my face and asked me to test my feet. I did something that I had never been able to do before. I jumped up and down several times with absolutely

Hips, Legs, Knees & Feet

no pain. Since that moment, over three months ago, I have had no pain or limitation in my feet. I can now run and take part in sporting activities and my feet are normal. Lord Jesus, I thank You so much.

—*Jonathan Worsfold*

Approximately seven years ago, I fell down some stairs and crushed my ankle. As a result, I had six screws inserted and needed eighteen stitches. For the next seven years, I had ongoing trouble. I had limited movement in my ankle and was not able to exercise.

I attended a divine healing meeting at Church Unlimited in January 2013 where Weston Carryer prayed for the Lord to heal my ankle. The ankle was immediately healed and I have been able to walk long distances with no pain. The arthritis in it has gone as well. At the same time, I was also healed of a sore back which had been troubling me for some time, and over the past five months I have been free of pain.

This was a wonderful experience and I am so grateful to the Lord.

—*Lyn Andrews*

Before Weston Carryer came to Waihi Beach Christian Centre in 2013, our pastor told us to start praying in advance for healing. I did this as I had an extremely sore left foot. The doctor told me I had Morton's neuralgia on the top part of my foot which I had for at least two years and then I developed a spur on the bottom part of the foot above the heel. This is an extremely painful condition and quite common. So between the two conditions, my foot was in pain most of the time.

At the healing meeting, Weston called out someone with sore feet—one worse than the other. The next day after being prayed for, my foot was really sore and of course I believed I hadn't been healed.

The day after that I told the pastor's wife that my foot was still

MIRACLES IN AOTEAROA NEW ZEALAND

really sore. She explained to me that the enemy was probably tricking me into thinking I had not received healing but I was healed. So every day, and whenever my foot hurt, I thanked God for my healing. I told Him because I had been called out, I knew I was healed, and I kept thanking Him through gritted teeth.

Eventually (I think it was about three months later), I realised that my foot was no longer hurting. I now still thank God a year later for the healing, and those chronic pains have not come back. Thank You Lord, for answering my prayer.

—Robyn Ruddell

He forgives all my sins
and heals all my diseases.
—Psalm 103:3, NLT

Two

Head, Face, ENT & Neck

Testimonies of healed conditions of the head, face, ENT, and neck (i.e., headaches, migraines, sinuses, collarbones, ear, nose, throat, etc.).

Head, Face - Injuries

Eighteen months ago I hit the right side of my face during a car accident. The blow to my head caused me a deal of pain besides which, the right side of my face would develop a burning sensation. Every time the burning and pain came back it would cause the sight in my right eye to blur and I could not see properly.

I went to see Weston Carryer and he prayed for the pain in my head, the burning to my face, and the blurring of vision. All three symptoms were there when he prayed over me, although not as severely as at other times. When he finished praying my face went numb. The pain in my head was still there, but the blurriness went and I could see much better. As I went to sit down I could taste blood at the back of my throat and the pain in my head went. Now I am healed in Jesus' name. I thank God for His every Word is true. He wants me healed and whole. He loves me.

—R.P.

Eyes, Vision

In July 1991, at a Ministry Education Programme, Weston Carryer prayed for healing of my right eye. Since February of that year, I had been troubled with a burst blood vessel. Praise the Lord for His healing power for my eye is now perfectly clear. A week on, at a healing crusade, Weston prayed against a sinus condition which had been with me for as long as I can remember. I was healed again and give glory to God.

—*Rebekah*

I am a thirty-five-year-old woman, who, for the last thirty-three years was totally blind in my right eye. In November 1991, I went to a healing meeting at the Apostolic Church in Christchurch where Weston Carryer was ministering. I went forward for prayer explaining about my blindness. Weston laid his hands over my eye and I was totally healed by God through Jesus Christ, and now I have excellent vision in my right eye as well as my left one. I have received a wonderful miracle.

—*Margaret Johnson*

I attended a Weston Carryer healing crusade at Napier in April 1990. I had an eye complaint that was bothering me immensely. It persisted from the time I completed a computer

Head, Face, ENT & Neck

course in March of that year. When an invitation was issued to go forward for healing, I went. On the way home after the meeting, I had to remind myself not to wipe my left eye as I had been accustomed to do. Remarkably, the soreness and irritation had gone and I do not need to visit the doctor.

—*Coline Scott*

When I was eight years of age my right eye was damaged by a stone, and for the next five years, the vision from that eye was just a blur. In October of 1994, I attended a meeting at the Tokoroa Apostolic Church. When Weston Carryer prayed for me, Jesus completely healed my eye and restored my sight so that now both eyes function equally and normally.

—*Santos Koia*

On 1 January 1991, I was beaten up and punched in the right eye by a man, and the ring on his finger punctured the eye. The retina was destroyed and the centre of the eye was badly damaged. The specialists wanted to remove it and give me a glass eye. My mother and I, did not agree to this, however, and so I kept my eye. I was classed as having three percent vision but, in actual fact, I could not see anything apart from having a slight sensation of light. I had to wear dark glasses all the time.

On 31 July 1998, at a divine healing meeting at Opotiki, Weston Carryer was ministering and he prayed for the Lord to restore my sight. I felt an amazing sensation in my right eye, and over a period of a few minutes, my sight was totally restored. Also, as a result of the beating, I had a lump on my head which the doctor was concerned could develop into a brain tumour. That also disappeared as Weston prayed for me. I just want to praise You, Jesus!

—*Tewihi Nye*

Miracles in Aotearoa New Zealand

For about three months I had a problem with my eyes. When I blinked it felt like I had grit in my eyes, and they were always itchy and sore. I also had a lazy left eye.

Last year I went along to one of Weston Carryer's healing meetings at the Apostolic Church. Weston placed his hands over my eyes and started praying. At that moment I could feel the Lord's warmth flow through my eyes and I was completely healed. It was only because of God's love for me—through His Son Jesus Christ—that I was healed, and I thank Jesus for the wonderful miracle that I received.

—*Katrina Marsh*

My sight had been deteriorating. At twenty-seven years of age, I was told by an eye specialist that because of the eye condition retinitis pigmentosa, I would be totally blind in eighteen months. He gave me a white cane and told me to get used to using it. I had just accepted Jesus Christ as my Saviour and had become a Christian. Two months later I attended a divine healing meeting in Taupo where Weston Carryer prayed for the Lord to heal me. My sight immediately stabilized, and over the next four years it continued to improve. On my last visit to the specialist, he was able to confirm what I already knew, that my eyes were now good. I have passed all the eye exams and I now have a driver's licence, and I am studying to be a teacher. Praise the Lord.

—*Tom Macedru*

I had to wear glasses ever since I was a little kid because of being on oxygen when I was born. This resulted in my left eye being lazy. I came to one of Weston Carryer's healing meetings in Hawera and he called out the condition of a lazy left eye. When he prayed for me I went down under the power of the Holy Spirit. When I came to, I looked over at the far wall. We were in a hall where there was an honours board with a whole lot of names on it and I realized that I could read it. Before I was prayed for, I couldn't see anything clearly at a distance, so I knew I was healed. That was three years ago and I haven't worn glasses since then, praise God. I am healed.

—*Nadia Vossen*

I live in Inglewood and I came to the healing meeting. I had been to an optician some weeks before and discovered I was seeing shadows when looking through a new lens at the A's, B's, C's, and the lines. The optician took fright and got an appointment with a specialist for me. I might say I was quite shocked too, and worried about the outcome. I used to have red and burning eyes, and for years had to continually put drops in them to ease the pain.

Then a Weston Carryer healing meeting was announced, so I made sure I would be there. The healing for my eyes was instant with immediate relief. The specialist confirmed my eyes are in good health. What a relief. Did I have stress or did I have a headache when I went to the optician? *No.* It was freaky. Anyway, the specialist said I don't need new glasses and that if anything goes wrong, come back to him. I give God all the glory for the healing of my eyes.

—*Valerie Allen*

Early in June 2005, I had a cataract removed from my right eye and a multifocal lens put in. The following day I had perfect vision in that eye. At the beginning of July 2005, I had the cataract removed from my left eye and another multifocal lens inserted. Over the next few weeks my sight went from being fine to a marked deterioration. I left for overseas at the beginning of September not being able to read printed material or writing and only able to read large signs and headlines with glasses. I had an appointment with the specialist for the day after I returned home. It was decided that the lens in my left eye was to be replaced as soon as possible. This was done, but unfortunately, it was not able to be fitted in the correct place, and so once again, I could not see properly. I was told that the specialist had used the multifocal lens twenty-two times, had four failures, and two of them were mine. My right eye lens could not be removed and so it was given laser treatment. This began months of treatment to try to find glasses that might help, but to no avail. In February 2006, I started having treatment in the public hospital, and in May, I was told that I had something wrong with both corneas as well.

In early June, I attended a divine healing meeting in Auckland where Weston Carryer prayed for the Lord to heal me. As soon as he finished praying, I realized that I could see and read clearly. It was amazing. After the prayer I went to the hospital for further scans and they showed no problems with my eyes whatsoever. The Lord had totally healed every part of my eyes. Now six months later, my eyes are still completely clear. Praise the Lord.

—*Barbara Drinkall*

In March 2002, I suffered a stroke, which amongst other things, severely affected my eyes and left me with double vision. My left eye also lost all movement; although I could move my right eye normally, the left eye was fixed in one place. To see anything at all, I had to shut my left eye. I tried wearing a patch over it, but that did not work. In order to read anything at all I had to shut my left eye completely. I was not able to drive a car. This affected my quality of life so much.

In March 2006, I attended a divine healing meeting at Burwood, Christchurch. Weston Carryer prayed for the Lord to restore my sight and I immediately received my healing. My vision once again is normal; I can see clearly and move my left eye. The Sunday after receiving my miracle I was confident enough to drive the car all around the hills.

Last week I had my eyes tested and the optometrist said that although the movement in my left eye is not quite one hundred percent, my vision is clear with absolutely no double vision. He was totally amazed and I am extremely delighted. The prescription for my reading glasses has not needed to be

Head, Face, ENT & Neck

changed; it is the same as it was before my stroke. Lord Jesus, You are awesome.

—Yvonne Clutterbuck

On Weston's last visit to The Centre in Paraparaumu in January 2006, I went forward in the prayer line for healing. Though my vision was fine, the problem was eyestrain, which had been with me for at least forty years but had gotten worse to the point where it became quite distressing. The eyestrain caused a continual blinking, and at times, excess fluid in my eyes. I have since learned this has to do with glands in the eyelids. I am now free of this problem. After years of people saying to me, "Stop blinking!" and the discomfort that ultimately developed, I am so grateful. I thank God, and also Weston.

—Gwen Bateman

My name is Ngaire Hampstead, and I attend Invercargill Christian Centre. In early 2005, I had cataracts removed from both eyes, but unfortunately, this left a film on both eyes. This restricted my vision and I was booked to have laser treatment to remove the film. A few weeks after the cataracts were removed, I attended a divine healing meeting in Invercargill where Weston Carryer prayed for the Lord to remove this film. My vision was instantly, fully restored. It was marvellous. In January 2007, I kept my appointment at the hospital where the examination showed that there was no trace of film on my eyes, and as a result, I did not need any laser treatment. I was healed by God. We serve an awesome God!

—Ngaire Hampstead

In November 2002, a firecracker went into my left eye and left me with partial blindness in that eye. I only had limited frontal vision and no peripheral vision at all. The medical staff at the hospital told me that nothing could be done for my eye at all. I was not allowed to have a driver's license, could only read with my right eye, and I regularly crashed into things because I was unable to properly judge distances.

On 1 July 2007, I attended a divine healing meeting in West Auckland where Weston Carryer prayed for the Lord to restore my eye. As he prayed the power of God was released in my eye and my full vision was restored. I was immediately able to see around the church, which I could not do before. My quality of life has changed dramatically and I have had my driver's license restored. Praise You, Lord Jesus.

—*Rachel Tricker*

Eight months ago at a healing meeting in Cambridge, Weston Carryer prayed for the Lord to heal me of iritis, which I was suffering from at that time. Iritis is an eye condition causing inflammation of the iris; pressure then builds up in the eye, which in turn affects vision and can turn to blindness.

On a previous occasion when this condition had developed, I had to go onto steroid drops every hour for weeks. I have had my eyes checked twice since Weston prayed for me and the optometrist has confirmed that there are no iritis cells in my eyes. Lord Jesus, I want to thank You so much.

—*Kay Brennan*

Seventeen years ago I was born blind in my right eye. The vision in my left eye was normal, but my right eye turned outwards very noticeably and had no vision at all. At the age of seven, my family was told by an eye specialist that nothing could be done for my right eye and it would be blind for life as well as being out of alignment.

This changed radically on August 26, 2012 at a divine healing meeting at Harvest Church Rotorua, where Weston Carryer was ministering and praying for the sick. Near the end of the meeting I went forward for him to pray for the Lord to do a miracle for my right eye. Weston placed his hands firmly over both of my eyes and prayed. He then removed the hand from my right eye and told me to open it. I opened it and realized that the Lord had given me a wonderful miracle as I had received perfect vision in my right eye. With my left eye firmly closed, I could see everything clearly, even very small print.

I was so excited and still am. The eye, although it had straightened fairly well, was not exactly where it should have been. But over time, it continued to straighten. And now, it has come into almost perfect alignment. Lord Jesus, thank You so much.

—*Shannon Howe*

I'm so thankful for Weston Carryer visiting Ruawai Community Church. My eyes had been achy and blurred when reading. They now are clear and don't ache any more. Thanks to Weston for believing and having faith in Christ.

—*Bronwyn Holt*

In February 2005, I went into Waikato Hospital for tests to be carried out so as to discover what was causing enlargement to my heart. While this procedure was being done, something went horribly wrong and a clot went from my heart into the area of the brain that causes vision. I became totally blind in my right eye. For the next twelve months the only thing that I saw out of my right eye was a horrible flashing. On many occasions this also caused my left eye to lose its sight as well, and I would have to be led around by someone for up to several days. Even when my left eye was at its best I could not read at all, even with glasses.

In February 2006, I went to a divine healing meeting in Turangi where Weston Carryer was praying for the sick. During the ministry time I went forward for him to pray for me. As soon as he had prayed, I opened my right eye and realized that the Lord had given me a wonderful miracle. My frontal vision was completely clear and I could see plainly. I still do not have peripheral vision in my right eye, but once again, I can read easily with both eyes and my eye does not flash at all. To be able to see once again is just so wonderful. Thank You, Lord Jesus. I am so grateful.

—*Carol Apanui*

Nose – Sinus, Polyps

Approximately twenty years ago my nose was damaged, and since then it had become more and more blocked, being especially bad over the last eight years. I had been using nose sprays over the whole time and was having to use stronger sprays to try and get some relief. I could not sleep lying down at night and had to be propped up with pillows. At a divine healing meeting in Tauranga in August 1998, Weston Carryer was ministering and the Lord revealed to him my condition through a word of knowledge. He then asked the person who had this nose condition to come to the front for the Lord to do a miracle. I immediately responded and as Weston prayed for me, I experienced the Lord's power. It felt like a vacuum cleaner blowing my nose out. Since then my nose has been totally clear all the time, and I can lie down and sleep. Praise You, Jesus!

—*Piki O'Brien*

I thank God, that through Weston Carryer I was completely healed from my sinuses and the chronic hyperventilation syndrome I was diagnosed with a year ago. I was healed instantly. I praise God, and gratefully thank the Lord for Weston and the work and healing he did around the world. Praise God! I am grateful to him from the bottom of my heart.

—*Janice Mantell*

For two years I had suffered from a serious sinus infection with polyps completely blocking both nostrils, so that I was unable to breathe through my nose at all. I had a continual, severe and very unpleasant nasal discharge through my mouth, as well as a swollen face, constant irritation, head oppression, cold and dizziness. I was due to have an operation, but was not looking forward to it.

I attended a Weston Carryer healing meeting and during that meeting, through a word of knowledge from the Lord, Weston described my exact condition. I went forward; he prayed over me, and God, through Jesus, totally healed me. I experienced heat in my nose, and within thirty minutes of being prayed for, the polyps were gone, along with the other problems. A year has gone by and I have had no relapses and can enjoy normal breathing.

—*Glennys Scott*

On 13 June, at the Levin Apostolic Centre, Weston Carryer prayed for me for a polyp in my left nostril. I am happy to say that the growth loosened off and came out of my nose exactly two weeks later. No more severe nosebleeds and no more blocked nose. Thank You, Lord! I always got a polyp in my nose during pregnancy and it usually bled profusely and grew very large, leaving me anaemic. When carrying my last child, I ended up in hospital to have the polyp surgically removed because my blood count was abnormal. So I am praising God for this happy miracle!

—*Debbie Witt*

I received my amazing miracle in March 2004. I had been praying to the Lord Jesus to heal my clogged-up nose—an ongoing problem since I was small. When I went to church that night, I just knew that the Lord would answer my prayer and heal my nose through Weston Carryer. When Weston mentioned about someone suffering from post-nasal drip (the mucus from a stuffy nose drips down the back of the throat and affects the oesophagus), I thought he said "post-natal drip." Since I don't have any kids, I did not bother going up the front right away.

Miracles in Aotearoa New Zealand

Just to be sure that I heard right, I asked my friend if Weston had said "post-natal drip" or "post-nasal drip." When my friend said "post-nasal drip," I stood up right away and asked Weston for the healing. He did what the Lord instructed him to do to fix my nose.

After the prayer, my nose cleared up straight away. Praise the Lord. Jesus is indeed the Great Physician. That night, the Lord Jesus not only healed my stuffy nose, but also my right shoulder. It is so edifying to glorify and have faith in the healing power of the Lord Jesus. Thank You, Lord Jesus, for the healing. And thank You also for your wonderful servant, Weston, who helped a lot of people through Your miraculous power to heal.

Three months later, I have been able to breathe clearly every night while asleep. This has been marvellous after many years of being woken continuously with a blocked nose and sinus congestion. I now feel invigorated every morning instead of being washed out. Thank You, Lord.

—*Evelyn Carr*

I attended a healing meeting in New Plymouth in April 2007. I went not expecting any healing nor was I really aware that I was in need of miraculous healing. However, God had other ideas! Around twenty-five years previous I was involved in a motorbike accident and broke my nose. This was operated on and reset. However, over the years I was aware that it wasn't a particularly wonderful result as breathing on one side of my nose felt restricted. In recent years this became a major nuisance to my wife due to my loud snoring at night, which seemed to be getting worse.

During the service Weston called out that someone was having difficulties with their nose as a result of a motorcycle accident. He also spoke of several other symptoms which were as a result of this. I was not aware of these other symptoms, but I distinctly knew God was saying that this was me. I went forward, and as soon as Weston started to pray, I felt the left side of my nose instantly clear and my breathing felt much better and clearer than it had for years.

Head, Face, ENT & Neck

Over the fifteen months since I was prayed for, it's amazing how much clearer my nose feels and I have slept far easier than I have in the past. My wife will testify that I do not snore at all now, much to her delight! It has even become apparent that my nose got straighter, having been crooked for twenty-five years. The left nostril is now bigger than before! I give all honour to God for my healing, and thanks to Weston for his obedience to God's calling.

—*Mark Brown*

For approximately three years, I experienced a chronic, infected right sinus. I could not breathe through my right nostril at all and large amounts of mucus would constantly drain out. I was on different antibiotics during this entire three-year period, which did not help at all. In fact, the infected area got bigger and steadily worse. I was facing an operation, which I was not looking forward to at all.

In January 2012, I attended my church, Eastgate Christian Fellowship, where Weston Carryer was conducting a healing meeting. During the ministry time, he prayed for the Lord to heal me. What happened next was astounding. The nostril instantly cleared, the infection went, and over the last seven months, I have not had the slightest problem with it. Needless to say, I did not need the operation or any more antibiotics. What a blessing! I am truly grateful to our Lord Jesus Christ.

—*Raewyn Everett*

Ears, Hearing, Balance

This is a short testimony of a wonderful healing with which God has blessed me. I had just become a born again Christian and was feeling on top of the world. Words cannot express the way I felt. You really have to receive it to believe it. One Sunday, I decided to go up the front for healing. Since the Lord had done many marvellous things for me that week, I just knew He would heal me from a complaint I had had from childhood. As a child I had suffered with bad earaches, and was always tripping back and forth to the doctors. The more I went, the more I realised none of them knew the cause or the remedy. After taking the prescribed medicines each time, the earaches still came back to haunt and taunt me, finally leading me to lose all hope in doctors and specialists. I even had had an operation on my left ear, but to no avail. Previously, every time I sat by an open window in a car, my left ear would ache terribly, or whenever I sat by a fan or in a draught, my ear would ache. Going out on a windy day was out of the question unless I had a hat on or my ears were plugged. Thirty-eight years had passed, and you can imagine how fed-up I was with this.

I praise God for giving me the courage and faith to accept prayer through Weston Carryer for this ailment. By God's grace I have been totally healed. My healing was not instantaneous. I believed that I had received it and had to exercise patience. One wet, cold, and windy day I was out picking mushrooms when I suddenly realised I did not have my ears plugged up or my hat on. You can imagine the expression on my face as it dawned on me. I just could not believe I was standing outside on a cold day and not feeling a thing. "Praise God. Praise God," was all I could say. There was not any need for anything because I was totally healed. This all happened three years ago, and I hope that this personal blessing has become yours too.

—*Rosina McGregor*

In August 1987, I went to a healing crusade at which Weston Carryer was the speaker. Twenty years prior to this, I had a plastic eardrum inserted following a swimming incident. The operation was unsuccessful, so I had learned to live with silence in that ear for all that time. I went forward for healing and Weston prayed for my affliction. The silence was broken by the sound of a distant jet plane and the voice of Weston asking, "Can you hear me?"

"Yes," I replied.

Head, Face, ENT & Neck

He then requested I block the other ear and asked, "Can you hear me?"

"Yes." He then told me to praise God and joined in praise with me. The prayer of a right-standing man in God's sight avails much when he calls on God and He answers by showing him great and mighty things.

—A.B.

Concerning the report on Evangelist Weston Carryer on 24 May, it was stated that the woman who received healing in an ear at Winton was not answering her telephone so the healing could not be confirmed. I am the woman, and I was not answering the telephone because I wasn't home. I can assure you I can now hear with my left ear which had been totally deaf for three years. I'm sure no one was more amazed than I, when immediately after Weston Carryer prayed for me, my hearing was restored in that ear.

In 1987, it was diagnosed that I had an acoustic neuroma, a rare growth on the acoustic nerve which controls hearing and balance, and I was advised that if this was not removed, I would eventually be confined to a wheelchair as my balance would be affected and my face would also become badly twisted. In March 1988, the operation was performed and the growth removed. God gave me a verse of Scripture in the early hours before the operation:

> *Let us hold fast the confession of our hope without wavering, for he who promised is faithful* (Hebrews 10: 23, ESV).

Whenever I am in hospital I always ask Jesus to take away any pain, and He does. I have had two previous major operations and the staff are amazed that I do not require painkillers. I was told I would wake up with a sore head and neck but there was no soreness. I had a difficult time convincing the staff of this until I told them that Jesus always bears my pain for me. The removal of an acoustic neuroma leaves the affected ear without hearing at all and I was told by the surgeon I would never regain it in that ear. This did not concern me very much

Miracles in Aotearoa New Zealand

as I was just grateful that the growth was found and removed without more damage being done. Being deaf in one ear had its drawbacks, especially with a group of people, but I was quietly confident that if the Lord wanted me to regain my hearing, He would grant it to me.

Over the next three years I had my ear prayed for by others three times that I can recall, but nothing happened. On 24 May, at Winton, the Lord restored my hearing instantly through Weston Carryer. The hearing in my restored ear is not as loud as in my other ear, but I am confident that with use, and God's continued healing, it will improve. I am now more thoroughly convinced that nothing is too difficult for God.

—*Ellen Zwies*

When I was younger, I used to do a lot of swimming which, as I grew older, caused me a lot of problems with my ears. I could not shower without ear plugs, because if water got in them, they would get infected. In 1981, I got an infection which took the doctor three months to control. The cure was not complete and I had problems almost constantly for the next seven years. In 1985, I got another bad infection. This time the side of my face swelled up like a balloon. It just about drove me crazy. The doctor prescribed antibiotics and took a swab sample. The result was I had to go onto a course of injections every day for three weeks, morning and night. It was not nice. Eventually, after injections plus two visits to a specialist, it cleared up, but I still had problems off and on. I used to rip at my ears all the time and they would get so sore I could not touch them.

In February 1988, I became a born again Christian. A few months later, I went to a healing meeting at my church where Weston Carryer would be speaking. He prayed over me. Since then I have had very little trouble. I shower now without plugs. I get a slight discharge on the odd occasion but I consider this just normal compared to the problems I had over the previous twenty years. To me, God has given me a healing. Praise God.

—*J.A. (Sonny) W.*

Head, Face, ENT & Neck

In 1990, I started to have problems with my ears and my balance. It got so bad that in 1992, I had to quit my job in a pulp mill after nineteen years of service. Doctors and specialists both advised there was no cure, and they could do nothing for the ears or the gland behind the ear causing the problem. It worsened to the extent where I had trouble walking to my letter box without wanting to sit or lie down.

Weston Carryer visited our East Bay Church at Whakatane in early 1993. He prayed for me, and I believed I had received my healing (Mk. 11:24), although I did not receive it instantaneously. For the next few weeks I got worse rather than better but continually claimed my healing. I slowly started to improve and, with encouragement from my pastor and church family, now I can function in a normal way again. I have maintained a good confession, speaking health and such positive Scriptures (i.e., 1 Pet. 2:24 and Phil. 4:13).

—*John Sim*

I am seventy-six, and God is restoring me to wholeness, almost as if by degrees according to the faith produced within me. One later part of my healing was granted when Weston Carryer visited our church. At the time, I was dependent on a hearing aid, besides which I had several noises of different pitches always ringing in my head.

I went forward for prayer and was slain in the Spirit. When I got up I was asked whether I could attend the next three nights. I did, and the same thing happened each time. I woke up the morning after the last meeting, minus my hearing aid, and *heard* birds tweeting. I could not believe it because I had never heard the far louder noise of a car starting up on the street before that. Sure enough, it was true. I still have one nasty noise left in my head but the Lord will get that one too. He blesses those who believe.

—*Russell H.*

Miracles in Aotearoa New Zealand

Over ten years, I suffered three bad attacks of Meniere's disease. In February 2000, I had been suffering extremely for almost three months. My symptoms included bad balance (just like being on a pontoon on moving water all the time), repeated episodes of extreme dizziness, vertigo, and vomiting. I could not walk in a straight line and was unable to cross the road without support.

I attended a divine healing meeting at Mt. Maunganui Apostolic Church where Weston Carryer was ministering. During the ministry time he prayed for the Lord to heal me. On the way home I knew that I was healed as all my symptoms had gone. The next morning I got out of bed and did a range of exercises which confirmed that I was healed. Hallelujah. Praise the Lord!

—*Prue Wakelin, Rangiwhia*

When Weston Carryer visited our church, The Centre, I came expecting a miracle, and I got it. I had always been partly deaf. But twelve years ago, I had an accident where boiling hot water was thrown over my face, which meant my inner ear was completely burnt out. As a result I was profoundly deaf in my left ear. Thank you, sir. I came looking for a miracle and I got it. I can hear now. I have one hundred percent hearing in both my ears.

—*Erone Thomas*

Ten years ago my right ear became badly infected leaving me totally deaf in that ear and making it very difficult for me to hear anyone. I found it especially hard to hear what people were saying, both in church and at home. I attended a divine healing meeting in Kapiti in February 2004, where Weston Carryer was ministering. As he started to minister, Weston said that some people would be healed by the Lord in their seats. At that moment I experienced an amazing warmth in my ear and it simply popped open. Immediately I could hear everything so plainly, and now six months later, I can still hear perfectly. Lord, I am so grateful.

—*Diane Bottcher*

Approximately nine years ago, a cyst grew in my ear and was sitting on the eardrum. This caused terrible imbalance problems and very regular dizziness. I had this for a whole year. I attended a divine healing meeting in Christchurch where Weston Carryer was ministering. During the ministry time he looked right at me and said that the Lord had revealed to him this condition that I had. He invited me to go forward so he could pray for the Lord to heal me. As Weston prayed, a terrific heat went right through me. Within twenty-four hours the cyst had completely disappeared and I have had no recurrence or dizziness ever since. Thank You, Lord. I am so grateful.

—*Ian Hamilton*

I was born with a hole in one eardrum, and because of this, I always had problems with my hearing and understanding what people were saying. I always had to lip read and I felt like a handicapped person. In March 2007, Weston Carryer prayed for the Lord to heal my ears and I am rejoicing to write that I can now hear much, much better. What an amazing difference! It is so wonderful to hear what people are saying and understand them. Lord, I am so grateful.

—*Julia Hohia*

For thirty-seven years I suffered from migraines. These occurred at least monthly and often lasted up to at least three days. I have had prayer for them in the past, but they continued to plague me, often confining me to bed in a darkened room. In April 2006, I was feeling extremely discouraged about the lack of improvement in the health of a young man my daughter was caring for. I decided to attend the City Life Church in

Tauranga where I knew Weston Carryer was ministering that day, hoping that God would encourage me in some way to keep on persevering in prayer for this young man.

Weston had a word of knowledge about someone present with excruciating headaches. Up to that point, I had resigned myself to the fact that these migraines were mine for life. So initially, I looked around the room expecting someone else to go forward. Only when no one responded did I think that perhaps the person Weston was referring to was me! I went forward for prayer and received an instant healing of my migraines as Weston prayed. It is now sixteen months later and I have not once had a migraine, nor have I had to buy any more pain relief tablets. On two or three occasions I have been aware that a migraine was threatening to take hold. But each time this happened, I immediately prayed against it and asked others to join me, and the symptoms disappeared. I am so very grateful to God for my healing and hope that this testimony encourages you.

—*Janet Eaton*

Neck – Top of the Spine, Collarbone, Neck-Shoulder, Throat, Voice Box

I suffered a tumour on my neck which was operated on, removed, but it grew again. The regrowth caused terrible twitching and pain on my face, head, neck, and shoulder. As a consequence of this, I was too sick to work and had to leave my employment. The tumour was the size of an egg at the time I attended a Weston Carryer healing crusade. I went forward after he had accurately described my condition. The power of God healed me and the lump totally disappeared. There has been no recurrence whatsoever. God also healed me of a chronic back condition at the same time.

—*Joy MacDonnell*

Head, Face, ENT & Neck

In 1963, while playing rugby league, both my collarbones were dislocated. Despite medical help and attention, the bones kept slipping out of their own accord. I had pain all the time and could not lift my arms above my head. Weston Carryer prayed for me at a healing meeting in April 1979. Through Jesus Christ and the power of God, both collarbones went back into place while I was being prayed for, and they have stayed in place ever since. I have continued to enjoy normal use in my arms and have had no pain whatsoever. Weston also prayed for the arthritis in my hands. The lumps disappeared immediately and movement was totally restored to them. Praise the Lord.

—Ron Kaeo

For fifteen years I suffered with a large goitre. I was always aware of this obstruction in my throat. I attended a healing meeting in Foxton in June 1990 conducted by Weston Carryer. I came forward during the ministry time and Weston laid hands on my throat and prayed in the name of Jesus. The next morning the goitre was completely gone. Now, one year later, I have had no further problems and my doctor has confirmed that it was totally healed. Praise the Lord!

—Harriet Wilson

Jesus certainly heals today. Two years ago, I went to a Weston Carryer meeting and went forward for healing when he said, "There is someone here with pain in their neck." After prayer, I spent the rest of the meeting with a terrible headache, so went forward again. God took away the headache and completely healed the neck pain which has not returned.

—Valerie Horton

I attended a meeting at St. David's-in-the-Fields in August 1994, where Weston Carryer ministered to me. God touched me and healed me. Three years previously, I had an accident in my home and damaged the top of my spine and could only turn my head slightly to the left or right. Now I can turn it in both directions and also look over my shoulders. Thank You, Jesus.

—*Pat Goodsir*

It is with great joy I write to you about how God healed me at Westside Apostolic when Weston Carryer prayed for me for the polyps in my throat. It was only two days before I was to be operated on. I didn't see the surgeon before theatre and I needed it verified, so I went on with it. When I came out of the anaesthetic the specialist said, "He couldn't find anything." I didn't say anything then, but wrote to him later that week enclosing a flyer of Weston's visit to our church and explaining what happened to me at the meeting. Then, last week, I had a post-operative visit to the surgeon where I was able to expand more, telling him some of the miracles Weston read out of his book. The surgeon accepted it well. I have testified many times in church, Aglow, to family and friends—some of whom do not believe, but that was to be expected.

I trust God will continue to use you in the healing ministry, and thank you for your obedience to Him. Wishing you God's richest blessings.

—*Maureen Purcell, Christchurch*

In 1988, a disc in my neck started to dissolve, which affected the action of the spine and caused terrible pain twenty-four hours of the day. I was operated on and the dissolving disc was removed and replaced with a piece of bone from my hip. There were five of us who had the identical operation at the same time. There was an initial improvement. But then, after a few months, all five of us experienced bones collapsing resulting in the same symptoms as before. We were all advised that we would need bone fusions.

In 1990, I attended a divine healing meeting in Whangarei where Weston Carryer was ministering. As I was prayed for—for

Head, Face, ENT & Neck

the Lord to heal me—all the pain and restriction went. To this day—eight years later—I have no problems with my spine or neck at all. The other four people had bone fusions and they all have neck problems and virtually no movement in their neck. Praise the Lord.

—*Geraldine Condon, Whangarei*

I suffered severe migraine headaches for approximately eight years. My vision would go completely and I would have to go into a dark room for several hours until I vomited, and then I would get some relief. I used to get three or four of these migraines every week. In 1989 I attended a Weston Carryer divine healing meeting in Opotiki. At the start of the meeting, Weston said there was someone present who was experiencing migraine headaches and he went on to describe the symptoms that I was having. He asked for that person to come forward. I went forward, and Weston prayed for the Lord to heal me. I have much delight in testifying that apart from one slight headache, I have had no more migraines over the last eleven years. Lord, You are wonderful.

—*Penny Walker*

As a result of a head-on car crash on 20 August 1999, my neck and shoulder were injured. I woke up Sunday morning knowing I would be healed, but at the same time, worried and apprehensive. You see, I had never been to an actual faith healing meeting before, although I had witnessed prayer. I just knew I had to go. On the Friday previous, my physiotherapist and I had decided that on the following Monday we would attempt to find another method to try and heal my neck and shoulder (right down to my wrist) as I still only had about forty percent use.

Arriving at my physio appointment Monday morning, she asked how I was feeling.

"I am fine," I answered. "I have been healed. Look at me!"

Slightly bewildered, she said, "Impossible! On Friday you

had only forty-three to forty-five percent use of your shoulder and neck."

"Well, look for yourself," I replied.

She then asked, "If you were to assess yourself, what percentage would you say you are?"

I replied, "At least ninety-seven to one hundred percent." I was still feeling a little bit tender around those areas because after service on Sunday, I washed blankets and duvet covers—something I had been unable to do for a month. Since that morning of 3 October (about two months ago), I have felt one hundred percent recovered. Bless you all.

—*Nesta Alexander*

In mid-2002, my son, Scott, was admitted to hospital when he became ill with what was diagnosed as a combination of glandular fever, tonsillitis, and sinus infection. The hospital doctors told me that it was one of the worst cases of this kind they had seen. He had only a one-centimetre opening in his throat. He could not eat solid food and was only able to sip water. They gave him a liquid antibiotic. Despite being on morphine, he was in excruciating pain and desperate. A few days later he was discharged from hospital but with no improvement. By this time, he had become suicidal, and I was very worried.

I contacted Weston Carryer who was ministering elsewhere in New Zealand; Weston rang back and prayed for Scott over the telephone. As he was prayed for, the Lord did a miracle. My son felt this huge weight lift, the pain went, and his energy returned. With Weston's prayer, his healing immediately commenced and was complete in a few days. Scott was back at work in ten days and has had no recurrence. Lord, You are wonderful.

—*Lynette Wright*

At Balclutha, on Monday, 29 March 2004, Weston gave a word of knowledge for "someone with a reflux problem which was beginning to damage their oesophagus." I responded (after

Head, Face, ENT & Neck

a kick from my wife), saying I was not aware my oesophagus was being damaged. After praying for me I have noticed that I can sing again with ease. Hallelujah.

Weston also prayed for my shoulders and arms, which had given me much trouble and some pain from occupational overuse syndrome (OOS). In fact, at the time, my right shoulder felt as though the muscle in my biceps had locked up. After prayer, my arm was quite free and I was able to move it with ease and without any pain. Thank you.

—*John McKenzie*

I was in a car accident at the age of seventeen years. For fourteen years I had experienced pain in my neck because the cervical vertebrae had been damaged. The day of the healing meeting I had been in such pain (muscular pain and a migraine headache) that I went to bed for the afternoon. Still in pain, I went to the evening meeting with my husband. Weston received a word of knowledge that described my injury. I went forward and God completely healed my neck. The tension was immediately released; my neck did not hurt to turn or bend it. Thank You, Lord! I have since had the best, most restful nights' sleep. I have once again been blown away by God's care for me. He loves His people so much. What a good God we serve.

—*Ruth Ramsey*

About thirty years ago I suffered whiplash in a car accident. This badly affected my neck and shoulder and resulted in severe pain a lot of the time, especially through the night. I would be woken around 2:00 AM practically every morning with what felt like a knife twisting in my shoulder. Eight years ago, Weston Carryer came to Lower Hutt for a divine healing meeting. Prior to the meeting, I was lying on the sofa crying with the pain and I cried out to the Lord, pleading with Him to heal me at Weston's healing meeting.

When the meeting started, Weston began to speak out words of knowledge for people, and one of the first conditions he described was what I had. I went forward, in severe pain, and he prayed for the Lord to heal me. The pain simply went as I was being prayed for and has never ever returned over the last eight years. Jesus, I am so grateful to be free!

—*Marion Callec*

At Tauranga Aglow in October 2007 where Weston Carryer was the guest speaker, he called out a person with neck problems. I received several digs in the back as it was well known that I had had a severe fall several months previously resulting in neck and shoulder problems. A lump had come up in my shoulder which was checked by the doctor and I had been given a referral for a scan the following week. Weston prayed for me, and praise the Lord! When I had the scan and x-ray, the lump had gone. My neck felt so much better and my shoulder was completely healed. Now I can, "Lift up the hands that hang down," and give continuous praise to God. Thank You, Lord, for Weston's ministry.

—*Evelyn Mountfort*

For thirty years I had suffered with neck problems and had an unsuccessful fusion in 1982. During this time I experienced a lot of discomfort, had many headaches, and also had chiropractic treatment. My husband and I attended a healing meeting in Tauranga in October 2007, taking a person along who needed healing.

Weston obeyed a word from God, stood in front of the section where we were seated and said that God wanted to heal someone with vertebra problems in the neck area, mentioning three vertebrae. Not thinking it was me I did not go forward. But the call was repeated, and my husband nudged me and said, "God is calling you." As Weston prayed, I raised my arms, and as God touched me through Weston, I heard three loud cracks in my neck.

To this day—fifteen months later—I have complete healing in my neck. Praise God. By the stripes that Jesus suffered,

Head, Face, ENT & Neck

we can claim our healing. Only believe and obey. Thank You, Father, in the name of Jesus our Saviour. Thank you, Weston, for obeying God by using the gift of healing.

—*Ruth Yeatman*

For about a year, I had a husky voice and real limitations in my singing due to having damaged nodules on my voice box. As a worship leader in my church, this was so difficult and very frustrating. I could not lead worship properly at all and my voice showed no sign of improvement during this period. However, all this changed dramatically when Weston Carryer prayed for the Lord to heal me at my church in Flaxmere. As soon as he finished praying for me, he asked me to sing over the microphone. I was shocked as I found my singing voice instantly healed and fully restored. It was amazing. I have been able once again to lead worship and sing to God's glory. Hallelujah! Thank You, Jesus.

—*Quinton Harmer*

I experienced severe migraines for most of my life which started when I was a young girl. Then when I was eighteen, I was in a car accident, suffering whiplash which caused the migraines to be more severe and more frequent—usually twice every month. I would have to go into a dark room for up to three days as I could not stand the light. This prevented me from fully being the wife and mother I wanted to be. Also, as a result of the whiplash, I suffered a lot of neck, back, and shoulder pain over the next fifteen years. The pain was always there and it restricted my movements. But, I just learned to live with the pain.

In July 2007, I attended a divine healing meeting in West Auckland where Weston Carryer prayed for the Lord to heal me. All the pain went immediately and the full movement was restored to my neck, back, and shoulders. It was marvellous. Occasionally I have experienced a small amount of pain, but when this has occurred, I simply claimed my healing and the pain has instantly gone. I also rejoice to write that I have not had a migraine headache for nearly two years since I was prayed for. All this has made a huge difference in my quality of life.

—*Susan Ryland*

Approximately twenty years ago, I developed a very sore and stiff neck where most of the time, I could not turn my head from side-to-side. Amongst other things it made driving a car very difficult. Soon after this I woke up one morning with vertigo and a balance problem. Very often, when I would lie down, the room would spin round. On many occasions I lost my balance when walking. At times, when I put my head down to tie my shoe laces, my head would really spin. Although I had various forms of treatment over this twenty-year period, there was no improvement in any of these conditions.

In October 2010, I attended a divine healing meeting at my church in Taupo where Weston Carryer was ministering and he prayed for the Lord to heal me. I am so delighted to report that all these conditions went immediately, and over the last fourteen months, there has been no recurrence of any of them.

This has made an incredible difference in my life, and I am so grateful to the Lord Jesus Christ for what He has done for me.

—*Helen Marris*

Weston Carryer came to our church, The Centre, in 2011 and I was really excited. I had been in a full contact Tae Kwon Do tournament and got whiplash where I couldn't even bend down to tie my shoelaces. The pain had gone from the right side of my neck and travelled down and across to my left hip; it was excruciating.

To add to this, my eldest son, who is one of the lead guitarists in the church's praise and worship team, had started developing severe pain and numbness in his left hand. The doctor had said that he would have to give up playing for quite a while and prescribed an anti-inflammatory medication.

Head, Face, ENT & Neck

My son and I sat through the morning service in pain, but our conditions were not called out. We were not able to stay afterwards for prayer as we had another commitment. My son said, "Don't worry, Dad. We can go up in the afternoon service." We came back in the afternoon and again our conditions were not called, but we were still expectant and so we went up after the service.

As we were standing and waiting in the prayer line, we both started smiling. We felt the joy of the Lord come over us and we started to giggle! Weston then came to us and prayed for my son's hand. I saw my son's face light up; he looked at his hand and then just started to smile. His hand was instantly healed. In fact, he was up and playing in the youth and main band the next week like nothing had happened!

Weston then turned to me and prayed for my back and neck. Instantly I felt a physical movement go down my right side; I felt it go down the middle of my back, and then it was gone! After that I had no pain at all. I could bend down, twist my back, and move my neck without pain! Perfectly healed six months later.

I thank You, Jesus. In gratitude,

—*Barry Hawkins and family*

Over ten years ago, I experienced a fall and injured the left side of my head and neck. This made it impossible for me to find any comfortable position at all when trying to sleep.

I attended a Christian healing meeting at Christian Renewal Fellowship in Whanganui in February 2012, where Weston Carryer prayed for the Lord to heal me. Since that moment over seven months ago, I have not had the slightest bit of pain in these areas and I enjoy a restful sleep every night. What a blessing after ten years of not being able to even have a decent sleep. Thank You, Jesus.

—*Anne McCaslin*

Miracles in Aotearoa New Zealand

On 17 March 2002, one of our daughters phoned us in Dunedin to say that there was a man with God's power who had healed people in the New Life Church in Ashburton that morning. She had been in the service and seen the healings. She asked us to bring her brother to Ashburton for healing in the evening service. I was filled with excitement. When we arrived in the church, we heard amazing stories of God's healing in so many lives. I could have listened to them all night.

When it came time for the visiting preacher, Weston Carryer, to call out the people God wanted to heal, I was amazed at each one being healed on the spot. Then he said, "There is someone present who had a whiplash-type injury to their neck."

I thought, *That is me!* but I looked around to see if anyone was responding. Since no one moved, I went forward.

He asked if I was a Christian, and how long I had had the physical complaint, and then stretched out his hand to pray for me. I have no idea what happened, because the next thing I knew, I was lying flat on the floor. When I got up off the floor and started to move my neck, it made loud clicking noises as I went back to my seat. I said to my husband, "You will be able to hug me in bed tonight." Ever since the accident of falling off a high stool that I had been standing on to reach into a cupboard many years previous, I could not stand the pain of being hugged any more, like we had always done before going to sleep.

I was so excited at being healed. After the accident, I had been to three top specialists who decided the pain in my neck was degenerative—even though there had been nothing wrong with it before the accident. They also decided there was nothing that could be done about it and that I just needed to live with the pain. I had never given my neck a thought while driving all that distance to the healing meeting. I had learned to live with it . . . and the pain. When driving a car, I would turn my whole body to see to the right and to the left. I didn't lift my head up too far because I couldn't, and I braced myself for the pain when I got a hug.

Head, Face, ENT & Neck

Now, all that was gone and I was fully healed.

To this day, nine and a half years later, I still marvel at the amazing healing I received. I can hang the clothes on the line so easily. It is very difficult to do so when you can't look up.

Truly we serve a mighty God. Until that point in time, I had not seen God's power of healing in operation in so many people's lives all at once. It was at the service that night also, that our son we brought with us gave his heart to the Lord, which was another cause for rejoicing.

—*Jessie Paton*

For approximately twelve months I had a very painful egg-sized lump on the side of my neck. Apart from the continual pain, it made it difficult for me to turn my head. I was sent to the hospital where tests were done, but there was no diagnosis of what it was. I didn't know what to do next.

I attended a divine healing meeting in Tauranga on 26 January 2014 where Weston Carryer was ministering. As he prayed for me, the pain completely disappeared. I was astounded when I felt my neck and realised that the lump had gone, that there was no pain, and I could turn my head freely with no restriction.

That happened over four months ago, and neither the lump nor the pain have returned and I have full neck movement. I am still amazed and so grateful for this awesome healing the Lord Jesus has done for me.

—*Raywen Kiwara*

In 1985, I had two big operations in Auckland to remove rare bilateral tumours from my neck. Unfortunately, this left me with unstable blood pressure, damaged nerves in my neck, and only one vocal cord which left me physically unable to sing.

However, life goes on and I learned to cope with these issues. For some time I hadn't been particularly well, and twenty-five years down the track, just prior to what should have been a joyous Christmas, I was advised I had another tumour. I was informed that this surgery would be incredibly complicated and dangerous, potentially resulting in an inability to speak, as well as needing a tube for eating and drinking, that is, if I made it through the surgery. Without the surgical procedure, however, the tumour would eventually "take over."

While I was naturally feeling pretty scared, I also accepted "Whatever will be, will be," and I figured I just needed to get on with living in the present. I was thinking, *How wonderful it would be if only I could just reach out and touch the hem of His robe and be healed like that woman.* But then I realised, *I can . . . at any time!*

I have known Weston for many years, and I immediately checked his itinerary to see when he would be in our home area. He was scheduled to come again in July (it was around March or April at that time) and I was due to have another scan in August.

I attended the healing meeting feeling incredibly positive. I was no longer fearful and had no doubts that faith would get me through . . . and it did! I came out of that meeting never doubting that I had received a healing.

I had my scan in August as scheduled and when I was advised there was no further growth, I was very tempted to respond, "I know that."

I continue to have annual scans, but over two years on, there is still no further growth.

I praise God, and give thanks for His healing power, knowing that it is through the power of the Holy Spirit *all* things are possible.

—*Jude Hansen*

I had been having problems with my neck for about twenty years because of osteoarthritis and degeneration. I am a healthcare worker and care for many clients on a day-to-day basis. This neck condition made my job very difficult as I had to be extremely careful all the time as certain movements would

Head, Face, ENT & Neck

cause severe pain. I am on the road all the time visiting my clients, and just turning my neck to reverse the car caused excruciating pain. At times I could not lie down at all and I would have to sit in my recliner in the lounge to sleep.

I attended a divine healing meeting at Harvest Church Rotorua in May 2011, and Weston Carryer prayed for the Lord to heal my neck. A short while after this I realized that I had no neck pain, and for the last two years, I have not had any pain or restriction whatever.

I am healed, and I thank and praise the Lord that I do not have that pain any more.

—*Yvonne Sims*

I attended a divine healing meeting at Ruawai on 15 February 2013 where Weston Carryer was ministering. During the ministry time I went forward for him to pray for me.

For several years I had suffered from reflux problems. As well as the severe stomach pain, my throat felt as if I was swallowing barbed wire when I tried to drink anything, hot or cold. I had taken Omeprazole every day this for several-year period which only gave very slight relief.

When Weston prayed for me, I went down under the power of the Holy Spirit. While I was on the floor, the Lord gave me a vision of my throat being relined with new flesh. Since that moment, now six months ago, I have been able to drink hot and cold drinks with no effect on my throat at all. I can also eat with practically no ill effect and my throat never ever feels raw.

This healing has made an incredible difference in my life and I praise and thank God for His love and healing.

—*Colleen Judge*

I became addicted to cigarette smoking when I was fifteen and by the time I was twenty-nine, I was smoking up to fifty cigarettes a day. I desperately wanted to give up and tried many times. I also tried different kinds of things in an effort to give up but the addiction continued. After eleven years of this heavy smoking, my throat became infected; for three years, I was on antibiotics to try to get some relief. While the antibiotic helped temporarily and would ease the pain for a while, my throat would not heal.

In February 2006, I attended a divine healing meeting in New Plymouth where Weston Carryer was ministering and praying for the sick. Through a word of knowledge he spoke out my throat condition and asked me to go forward for him to pray for the Lord to heal me. I responded, and as Weston prayed my throat, I was immediately healed and it has never troubled me again. Weston also prayed for me to be set free of smoking. The terrible craving that I had for cigarettes started to disappear and I was able to reduce the number I smoked steadily. By the beginning of May, I no longer had any desire to smoke at all. For the last twelve months I have not smoked at all. What incredible relief to be free of nicotine addiction. Thank You, Jesus.

—*Teresa Patu*

I broke my collarbone one day while working. A doctor confirmed this fact later and my arm was placed in a sling. I was unable to use it at all over the next two weeks and I was in a great deal of constant pain. I went to a Sunday service at the Bay Apostolic Church where Weston Carryer prayed for me, and as he did so, I felt the power of God, through Jesus, touch my collarbone. Heat was released into it and I felt the bones fit back into place. There and then I took the sling off and resumed using my arm. On a visit to the doctor next day, he examined me, and after expressing amazement, confirmed the healing and asked, "What happened?" Praise the Lord.

—*Wallace Hiha*

Head, Face, ENT & Neck

Headaches, Migraines

In March 1989, while suffering from pains in the neck and migraine headaches, I attended a meeting conducted by Weston Carryer. I was prevailed upon to go forward for prayer for healing and was healed. Praise and glory to God! From that day on I have suffered no pain or discomfort from either my neck or migraine headaches. In November 1989, at another venue, the Lord again called me forward for healing. Problems I had been having with my oesophagus for some time were completely healed. The Lord has blessed me with His infinite compassion and grace and has shown by blessing me in this manner His all encompassing power which serves as a reaffirmation of my faith in God and in Christianity.

—Susan B.

For eight years I suffered from migraine headaches. Every day I spent the best part of the day sleeping, unable to do anything. My children would get pretty frustrated because I couldn't spend much time talking to or listening to them. The logo in our home became, "Mum's in bed again with a headache." I would get a migraine and for about five days, I would be in and out of bed with a constant aching in the back of my head. I was always walking around with either a severe headache or a slight nagging headache that would be brought on by the migraine attack.

Weston Carryer came to East Bay Church, Whakatane, and I remember sitting on the left hand side of the auditorium in the third row from the front. He said, "There's someone in this area that suffers from migraine headaches and you've got one now. Please come up. God wants to heal you." I responded. I wasn't healed instantaneously, but my healing came over a period of time. I am now free of migraines and I am completely healed.

Miracles in Aotearoa New Zealand

I thank God that I'm no longer bedridden for long periods of time with migraines. Now you can find me leading a very busy, God-focused life.

—*Judy Katipa*

For four and a half years I suffered from migraine headaches every week. These used to cause vomiting and affected my eyes to the extent that I had to go to bed in a dark room. I attended a divine healing meeting in Mosgiel in 1996, where Weston Carryer prayed for me. I can rejoice to say that since that time, twelve months ago, I have not had any sign of a migraine headache whatever. God, through Jesus, completely healed me.

—*Susan Stewart, Mosgiel*

Eleven years ago, at twenty-two years of age, I was involved in a horrific car accident. I was thrown heavily out of the car, landing on my head resulting in brain damage. Following this, for the next several months, I suffered excruciating headaches accompanied by vomiting.

I attended a divine healing meeting in Waikanae where Weston Carryer was ministering. That night the Lord touched me and totally healed me. Over the last ten years, I have had no further headaches or vomiting. Bless You, Lord.

—*Robyn Clark, Waikanae*

For nineteen years I suffered continual, bad headaches following a motor vehicle accident when I was concussed. The doctor said that I would have them for life. I attended a healing meeting conducted by Weston Carryer in 1995. Weston prayed for me and God, through Jesus Christ, instantly healed me and I have never had a headache since. Praise the Lord for His healing power.

—*Jocelyn Huddlestone*

Head, Face, ENT & Neck

For at least thirty-five years, I suffered from severe migraine headaches. These always lasted two to three days and occurred regularly. My mother and brother also experienced this condition. I tried many different forms of medication over this period but nothing I tried would give me any relief. In September 2000, I went to a healing meeting in Masterton where Weston Carryer was praying for the Lord to heal the sick. He then spoke out my exact condition and said for me to come forward for the Lord to heal me. My husband immediately said to go forward, which I did. Weston then prayed for me, and I rejoice to say that ever since that time, eighteen months ago, I have never had a sign of a migraine. Thank You, Jesus!

—Kate Howard

My first memories of migraine headaches go right back to when I was a child, and now, for over fifty years, I have suffered very badly with them. They occurred regularly every few weeks over this entire time and would last up to three days. When experiencing them I would usually have to go into a dark room where I did not want anybody to come near me. I also could not eat or drink as this would make me vomit. I had to consume vast amounts of panadol to try to get relief. As a young man I was a very keen bike rider but had to give this sport up because of the migraines.

All this changed dramatically one night at a Christian healing meeting at Marton in 1999. Weston Carryer was ministering and he looked right over where I was sitting and said that there was someone who was experiencing severe migraine headaches, and for them to come forward for the Lord to heal them. I was very reluctant to move as this was all new to me, but under pressure from friends who were with me, I finally went to the front.

That night I received a miracle. I have never even had the slightest sign of a migraine over the past three years. Since that night I have not had to take any panadol. And at the age of seventy, I was able to start bike racing again and have recently

Miracles in Aotearoa New Zealand

won three New Zealand Masters Championship medals. The healing I received has made an incredible difference in my life. That night I realized that Jesus Christ is for real and I accepted Him as my Lord and Saviour. Praise the Lord.

—Andrew Vosper

In May of 2001, Weston Carryer was ministering at CRF, Whangarei. My husband wanted to go but I didn't feel like going because I had a bad migraine. My husband said that was all the more reason to go. So I went, rather reluctantly, not being fully convinced that God healed through these ministries. For years I'd been having migraines regularly every month without fail and this day was no exception. During the meeting I witnessed others wanting prayer and receiving healing. When invited for prayer, I jumped out of my seat to get to the front as my head was getting really sore.

Weston asked me what I wanted prayer for, and I said, "Migraines."

He asked if I had one now and I answered, "Yes, very much so."

He placed his hand on my head and prayed for the pain to go in Jesus' name, and it was like a switch had been turned off; the pain was instantly gone. One moment I was in pain, and the next second, no pain whatsoever. Praise God! I went home rejoicing and totally amazed. But when I went to bed, my head started to ache once again quite bad, so I got up to get a panadol. I looked at it and decided, *No! I'm not going to take it because I know God healed me.* So, I went back to bed and the pain gradually went away. From then on, I've never had another migraine since, where once I was having migraines regularly every month. I've been pain-free for three years. I give all the glory to God, but am also thankful for His use of His servant, Weston.

—Anselma Beckmann

Head, Face, ENT & Neck

Thirty years ago, I was involved in an accident, resulting in brain damage and whiplash. Because of this I suffered very severe headaches for this entire thirty-year period. When the headaches came they would usually last a whole week. In February 2005, at a divine healing meeting in New Plymouth Life Advance Church, Weston Carryer prayed for the Lord to heal me. I wish to confirm that since that moment I have never had any sign of a headache again. It is brilliant. Thank You so much, Lord.

—*Pamela Byrne*

Approximately eleven years ago I was badly injured in a car accident and was in hospital for two weeks with my neck in traction. I immediately started getting very severe, painful migraine headaches that would make me vomit. These migraine headaches (which would come approximately every two weeks) would not go away until I went to the doctor to either have an injection or have very strong medication placed under my tongue.

My husband and I came to New Zealand from South Africa in August 2004. A flyer came in the mail advertising a healing meeting in Stratford where Weston Carryer was ministering, and so I went along. That night I accepted Jesus as my Lord and Saviour and have attended church regularly ever since. Weston prayed for the Lord to heal my migraines. For the following seven days I had a headache from 7:00 AM until 4:00 PM each day. The following day there was no sign of any headache and nor have I had even the slightest form of any headache whatever for nearly two years. To be healed and free after nine years of terrible migraine headaches is just so wonderful. Thank You, Jesus, for saving and healing me.

—*Annina Smith*

Eighteen years ago my nose was damaged. Since then I have

had a lot of pain around my nose and very severe headaches. On the 9th of July 2006, you prayed for the Lord to heal me. I have not had any pain around my nose or a headache since. This is wonderful after eighteen years. Thank You, Lord Jesus.

—*Haiying Bedggood*

I was born and raised in Switzerland. When I was three years of age, I was accidentally pushed out through the window of a third floor building. Although my baby sister's pram cushioned the fall, the force with which my head hit the concrete badly damaged my skull. This prevented my skull from properly developing. From that day in 1935 until 2003, I had severe headaches every day, all day. On many occasions they were so bad that I could not stand light, noise, or movement, and I had to be in a completely dark room. As a boy I missed many days at school.

I emigrated to Whangarei in New Zealand in 1980. In 2002, a neighbour of ours who was aware of my condition persuaded my wife and I to go to a divine healing meeting at her church where Weston Carryer was ministering. I had not been to church for exactly fifty years and so I went along very reluctantly. At one stage during the meeting Weston pointed his hand in my direction and said that there was someone in the area where I was sitting who, as a result of an accident as a child, has had very severe headaches all his life, and would he come forward for the Lord to heal him.

My neighbour and my wife pushed me out of my chair and I went forward very unwillingly and with no expectation. Weston said, "Do you know Jesus?"

"Sort of," I answered. Weston then asked if I had a headache and I replied that I did not, but that if I hadn't taken medication I would not have been able to have been there at all. After that, I have no recollection of what took place. But since that night, I have not had any medication at all, and apart from one headache nine weeks later, I have been pain-free with no headaches of any kind over the last five years. This is marvellous after experiencing chronic headaches for sixty-seven years.

Head, Face, ENT & Neck

That night, as a result of how Jesus really reached out to me, I realized how much He loved and cared for me and I had no hesitation in accepting Him as my Lord and Saviour. I have been so thankful to follow Him for the last five years. Thank You, Jesus. I praise You and bless You.

—*Lou Conteese*

Before going to Weston Carryer's healing meeting in Auckland in September 2006, I had been suffering from very violent headaches for two months. I had to go to hospital on two occasions for treatment to get some relief. I could not even make the Friday night meeting because the pain was so bad. I attended the meeting on the Saturday night and Weston prayed for the Lord to heal me. My healing was instantaneous and I have had no sign of a headache for the last nine months. I know I am healed. Thank You, Jesus.

—*Gaylene Booth*

Twenty-four years ago a brick fell on my head. As a result I experienced terrible head pain which I would wake up with every morning. It was just like I would imagine a hangover would be. Along with regularly having a bleeding nose, my sinuses were also affected and they were especially bad in the springtime. In September 2006, I attended a divine healing meeting on Waiheke Island where Weston Carryer was ministering and he prayed for the Lord to heal me. I am rejoicing to write and say that I have never had even any slight form of a headache, or sinus problems, or nosebleed since I was prayed for, now over twelve months ago. Thank You, Lord Jesus.

—*Belinda Linnett*

When I was eighteen years of age, I was at a swimming complex when I fell two and a half metres and landed on a speed-slide, knocking myself out and then sliding into the pool. Fortunately I was pulled out of the water. It was discovered that my skull was fractured. From that time on, and for the next twenty-two years, I suffered from severe migraine headaches on average every two weeks. I would have to go into a dark room or closet and I usually vomited before the headache would go. I also completely lost my sense of smell as the tube connecting my nose to my brain had snapped. The specialist told me there was dead matter at the top of my nose between my eyes.

I attended a divine healing meeting at City Life Church in Tauranga in October 2007, where Weston Carryer was ministering. He said the Lord had revealed to him that there was someone sitting in the area where I was who suffered severe migraine headaches. Knowing this was me, I responded and Weston prayed for the Lord to heal my headaches and my nose.

I realised immediately that I had received a miracle in my nose as my sense of smell had been restored. I was able to smell a lady's perfume on my way back to my seat. To be able to smell again is marvelous—especially to be able to smell my wife's fragrance, because in our entire married life, I had never been able to do this. Now, eight months later, I have never had even a sign of a migraine headache. Thank You, Jesus.

—*Mario Laas*

I suffered from extremely severe headaches for over twenty years. The headache would usually be there for around a week, would then disappear for one or two days, and then return. The pain especially affected the area above my eyes in the forehead, and on many occasions, would develop into a migraine. I tried different forms of pain relief but none of them helped in any way at all.

Approximately fifteen years ago I went to a divine healing meeting in Tauranga where Weston Carryer was ministering—just to have a look to see what happened. Although I was a committed Christian, I did not know anything about divine healing. During the early part of the meeting Weston described exactly the condition that I had and asked for that person to go forward for him to pray for the Lord to heal him. I thought

Head, Face, ENT & Neck

to myself, *Not likely,* and I did not move. Weston then pointed right in my direction, and so I finally responded, went forward, and he prayed for me.

The result was staggering! Over the last fifteen years I have never had another headache like I had for that twenty-year period. I have had maybe three or four slight headaches which I have rebuked and they have instantly disappeared. This has made an unbelievable difference in my life. That same night as Weston prayed for me, the Lord also healed my neck of arthritis which had prevented me from being able to turn my head. From then on, I really did believe in divine healing. Thank You so much, Lord Jesus.

—Harold Kenny

Near the start of my last pregnancy, I had a condition come back that had tormented me in one of my previous pregnancies—severe headaches. I never used to suffer from any sort of headaches and I could never get to the bottom of what was causing this problem. Almost every day or two, I would be gripped by this dreadful headache, and the smallest thing would set it off (i.e., a door banging or even a sudden cough) and it would last for many hours (frequently still present when I woke in the morning). At times I was concerned I would have a stroke as the pressure in my head felt so intense.

I attended one of your meetings in Christchurch in April 2010, and you indicated the area where I was sitting and called for the person who suffered from severe headaches to come up. I was very surprised as I was not expecting to be called up. But I felt sure immediately that it was me; no one else moved so I went up and was prayed for. Praise the Lord. I have not suffered from this problem in this way since, now over twelve months ago. It ended that night! I'm so thankful for his prayer.

—Gwenda Smithies

I attended a divine healing meeting in Christchurch in April 2008, where Weston Carryer was ministering. He spoke out my condition and asked me to go forward for him to pray for the Lord to heal me.

I had intermittent cranial headaches that ordinary painkillers couldn't touch as well as restriction of neck movement. I had scans and manipulations done. My head would be pulled and twisted. Sometimes I got relief but it would only be temporary. Then if I looked up to the sky, or down into low kitchen cupboards, the headaches would start again. After many years of trying not to cause a headache, I learned to live with them when they came. Many people laid hands on my neck and prayed for healing, but there was no change, so I accepted it as my lot.

I could not believe my ears, and immediately thought it was for someone else. *It couldn't be for me, could it?* Well, no one else stood up. *Yippee!* I thought. I went up to the front so quick. This was my time. Praise the Lord. I was so expectant of a miracle.

Weston said, "Lift your hands to the Lord." A tremendous heat came upon my neck at the back and he continued to pray. The Spirit of the Lord came upon me, my legs "went" and I enjoyed peace and healing on the floor of the hall.

When I got up and sat in my seat, the heat of God's healing power stayed on me. I knew I was healed. I can move my neck freely in both directions, and today I looked up high in a tree and saw a bell bird, and no more headaches. God is so faithful. Praise His holy name.

—*Chris Bailey*

For well over 40 years, I suffered from very severe migraine headaches. Nearly every time they came, I would have to go to bed for up to 3 days, be in a dark room, could not eat anything at all, and even then would often vomit. Sometimes medication would help but not very often. I would get these at least monthly and sometimes it would be weekly.

On 6 May 2012, I was at a divine healing meeting in Harvest Church Rotorua where Weston Carryer was ministering. He was speaking out words of knowledge for various people and

Head, Face, ENT & Neck

said there was someone there who was experiencing migraine headaches.

I went forward immediately and he prayed for the Lord to heal me. I am rejoicing because I have never had a migraine headache from that moment and that was now over a year ago.

This has made a huge difference in my life. I can now plan ahead with confidence and do not have to waste all that time that I used to be confined to bed.

Lord Jesus I am so grateful.

—*Wendy Belworthy*

Mouth – Tongue, Speech, Teeth, Jaw

Charles Owen was born with a speech impediment, and apart from a distressingly limited skill in speaking the odd word correctly or clearly, he had no ability to communicate at all. He went to a healing meeting at East Bay Apostolic Church in Whakatane where Weston Carryer ministered to him. Jesus immediately released his tongue. His speech is now distinct, and he can communicate freely. Like the bubbling of an underground spring, words flow out of him and continue to do so. We, of the family, are rejoicing in God's goodness.

—*Bob Owen*

For two years my only means of communication and conversations was by written notes. I was a cleaner at the Taumarunui High School and lost my voice through poisoning due to the use of chemical aids in my work. Since I had nothing to lose by doing so, I went to a healing crusade conducted by Weston Carryer, and was healed by Jesus instantly.

—*L. Johnson*

Miracles in Aotearoa New Zealand

I was born with a short tongue which, by the time I had matured to adulthood, was approximately four centimeters shorter than is normal. This had been a lifelong impediment, and was the cause of constant sniggers and ridicule during my school years. I went forward for prayer at a divine meeting conducted by Weston Carryer at Gisborne Apostolic Church, and a wonderful miracle happened. As Weston ministered over me, Jesus lengthened my tongue. It is now the correct length and my speech is both fluent and normal. Hallelujah! I rejoice that Jesus is really alive today.

—*Elizabeth Humphreys*

I suffered a long time with a jaw that clicked loudly. I had been to the doctors on a number of occasions and was told that it was a loose jaw joint. I went to a Weston Carryer healing meeting and he prayed for me in the name of Jesus. I was overcome by the presence of the Lord and instantly the click disappeared. To this day I have had no further problems. Jesus has also healed me through Weston of two other personal problems.

—*June Morris*

I attended your recent healing meeting in Levin. I had been suffering from a tooth infection. I was supposed to see an orthodontist to have my gum lanced and the infection removed, as antibiotics to clear it had worked once but the condition had reoccurred. It had progressed so that the left side of my face had become numb and it was affecting the alignment of my teeth, and my jaw was not opening my mouth properly. You prayed for me and the power of God came upon me and I could feel my teeth being rearranged in my mouth. The infection has gone. I can open my mouth and the pressures in my jaw and ear have been healed. Praise the Lord! Thank You, Jesus.

—*Raewyn Moar*

Head, Face, ENT & Neck

As a result of an accident when I was at school many years ago, I suffered a severe problem in my jaw. This resulted in my jaw being very painful a lot of the time with it continually clicking, and often, locking. I was told nothing could be done for it. At a healing meeting in Auckland, Weston Carryer prayed for my jaw, and Jesus instantly and totally healed it. My jaw has functioned normally ever since. Praise God.

—*Julie Upton*

On Sunday night, 19 February 2006, I asked Weston to "speak life into my tooth," following recent dentistry.

He seemed a little surprised and said something like, "We can ask the Father for anything . . . absolutely!" My dentist had said, "We may be looking at a dead tooth," but he would know for sure because it will be ultrasensitive to hot liquids and not cold ones. He went on to say that it was not a problem because he could do root canal work drilling through my new $1,200 gold cap.

I thought, *That'll be the day!* I had toothache all that weekend as a hot drink would set it off again. As Weston prayed, the tooth started tingling and had a buzzing feeling. As I sat down, I said to Maureen, "The ache has just gone. It's fixed!" Now every time I have a cuppa, I'm just so thankful because what was as "good as dead" is just fine now—alive and well. Praise God!

—*Gerald Dravitski*

As long as I can remember I had always had trouble with my jaw, and when I had teeth removed at nineteen, the dentist discovered the jaw was dislocated. For the following twenty years it gave me a lot of trouble. The doctor diagnosed that arthritis had developed, and it was always very uncomfortable, and at times, very painful and would always make a cracking noise.

Miracles in Aotearoa New Zealand

Approximately thirty years ago I attended a Christian healing meeting where Weston Carryer was ministering, and he prayed for the Lord to heal my jaw. As he prayed, the power of God went into the jaw and completely healed it.

Since that moment thirty years ago, I have had full movement, no cracking pain or discomfort, or any problems with my jaw at all. Thank You, Lord.

—*Lorraine Williams*

Brain – Conditions, Injuries, Stroke, Epilepsy, Seizures, Bell's Palsy

Will man ever plumb the depth of God's grace and love? Recently, I attended a seminar on spiritual and ministry gifts given by Weston Carryer at Tikitiki. Ever since I suffered a stroke four years ago, I have had problems with one eye through soreness, double vision and a tear duct which no longer wept. Sometimes, I have had to wear dark glasses inside. I was sitting with my back against a wall in the Marae, but the sunlight streaming in the window opposite was too bright for the eye. I moved places to be more comfortable, then listened while Weston prayed for someone else with defective sight. For no apparent reason at all, my glasses fell off. As I bent down to pick them up off the floor, tears started to pour from my damaged eye. I praised God, and turned to look out the window into the fairly bright light. I could see far away quite clearly without double vision. My eye has remained excellent. Where once I had to use a large-print Bible, I now use a normal one. I remain forever grateful to our Lord.

—*Hector Waimotu*

One never ceases to be amazed that, no matter what the disease or affliction was, God healed in days of yore, and we

Head, Face, ENT & Neck

still witness that power day in and day out, today. Since the birth of a child in 1988, I became an epileptic and was having two or three seizures every month. At Wairoa in November 1993, Weston Carryer prayed for God, through Jesus, to heal this condition. I am delighted to testify eighteen months on, I have been completely healed by the Lord. Notwithstanding one minor turn very shortly after I had been prayed for, and caused by my own foolishness, I have been free of all epilepsy since that time. All praises be to He who healed me.

—*Pagett Newlands*

Around two years ago I was diagnosed as having Bell's palsy. The left side of my face was paralysed. My father contacted Weston Carryer for prayer support for my ailment. Since he was passing through Feilding two days later, he called at the house and prayed for the Lord to grant complete abatement from it. When I awoke the next morning I realised the movement had been restored to my face. I looked in the mirror and there was the confirmation. I have had no further sign of the palsy from that day to this. Praise the Lord!

—*Scott Proctor*

The heart-stopping phone call which turned our lives upside down came around 9:00 PM on Monday, 29th of January 1996. Our twenty-year old daughter, Jolene, had been staying in Whangarei for the long weekend. A doctor from Middlemore Hospital's A & E rang to gently inform us that Jolene had been involved in a car accident and was deeply unconscious. They were about to send her for a CAT scan, then she would be in the Intensive Care Unit for assessment. Little did we know how serious her condition was, and how our lives wouldn't be the same for a long, long time, if ever.

I rang my sister in Auckland, and she, with my brother and his wife, raced to Jolene's side and prayed for her, while the rest of the family (except our youngest daughter) drove to Auckland—an extremely long two and a half hours! On arrival we found our precious daughter lying quietly on the bed, looking peaceful, but so tiny and vulnerable, attached to all the tubes and paraphernalia of life support. The scan showed a tiny haemorrhage deep in Jolene's brain. She was on sedation to reduce swelling.

The following day, the sedation was eased off and the ventilator turned down, to see if Jolene would breathe on her own and wake up. Expecting her to open her eyes, sit up and say, "Hi, Mum and Dad. Sorry to give you such a fright," it was a heartache to see her become very anxious and restless, not focusing her eyes or seem in any way coherent. The doctors decided to put her back on sedation and life support so as to be able to take a second scan. Praise the Lord. The haemorrhage had stopped!

Two days after the accident, all the family was called together and the resulting discussion was devastating. From their experience and observation, the doctors gave us a very-little-hope scenario for ever having our precious daughter back as normal. They suspected a diffused axonal injury. In basic terms, this means that the nerve cell endings (responsible for sending and retrieving information around the brain) had become disconnected or torn during a huge shake-up, as would have happened as Jolene's car spun around, and then was hit from behind. Her lack of response and other actions, such as holding her arms rigidly on her chest, reinforced their diagnosis. She had all the symptoms of an extremely serious head injury. Basically, we were told there is a scale of recovery from this type of head injury: some people don't recover much at all, others to the point of mobility, others to being able to work part time, and in rare cases, totally recover. One doctor gave his gut feeling: we should prepare ourselves to have Jolene remain at the lower end of the scale.

My husband and I took in the facts as presented sympathetically by the experts, and desperately clung to our faith in a loving, miracle-working heavenly Father. During these life-shattering days, we tried to balance the reality of what was before our eyes with faith in God. People the Lord sent to encourage and support us were just such a strength. We discovered how desperately we need the family of God, and

Head, Face, ENT & Neck

how He uses different people in many different ways through prayers, visits, cards, meals, to name a few. The Lord also sent us a new friend— a close friend of Jonathan (Jolene's boyfriend) who had spent time praying and fasting as soon as he heard of the nightmare his friend was suddenly experiencing. He joined us all in Auckland and was such an encouragement. Two days before the accident, he'd felt led to learn a new song: "Have faith in God . . . never give up," was sung softly with friends around Jolene's bed. This helped birth a peace and a faith in our hearts to oppose that which we saw in the natural.

Six days after the accident, Jolene breathed on her own. Praise God, we were a small step along the recovery road, but so much more healing to come! Earlier on, my sister-in-law had encouraged me to read Jolene's quiet time diary in case the Lord had prepared her for a trial. On January 17th she had written, "After a time of suffering, I will restore you, and make you strong, firm and steadfast" (1 Pet. 5:10), surely a promise from God to hold on to.

By this stage there were many folk from our home church, and all around Te Puke, and in fact, in many places in NZ, and even overseas, beseeching heaven for a miracle. Friends, relatives and complete strangers prayed for Jolene's healing and restoration.

A week after the accident, Jolene was moved to Tauranga Hospital's Intensive Care. There we were faced once more with coming to a place of releasing our daughter into the Lord's loving hands. Noting Jolene's erratic heart rate and soaring blood pressure, a doctor asked us our feelings on what they should do if she had a cardiac arrest. He felt it would be best not to resuscitate. One momentary glimpse of hope came when our son asked her to squeeze his hand. He felt a slight pressure; we were reluctant to accept this as progress in case it was just an isolated incident.

A few days later, Jolene was stabilised enough to move into a ward. A Christian brother from Rotorua phoned and told me about an evangelist, Weston Carryer, who has a healing ministry and would be willing to come and pray for Jolene. Weston came on Friday, 11 February, eleven days after the accident. A nurse had put Jolene in a lazy-boy chair, but she was still all curled up and unresponsive. Weston prayed gently in faith, feeling a burden of compassion, combining his prayers with the hundreds of others assailing our Lord daily. Who knows which vessel God chooses to use? We were so touched that Weston cared enough to come. That very evening marked a milestone in Jolene's recovery. Jonathan arrived to visit and was thrilled to note a greater clarity in her eyes. He asked her to reach out and take his hand; slowly she did. From then on, she began responding to questions, squeezing our hands (or nurses and doctors hands) to answers. For the first time, staff began to get a more positive look in their eyes.

Weston called in a few days later and prayed again, rejoicing in progress, but believing with us for more. Following his second visit, Jolene began to speak, whispering one word at a time. We praised God for His miraculous healing power and mercy. Our pastors called and shared a precious time of communion round the bedside, adding their prayers of faith to the many others. Jolene began to become extremely restless, especially towards evening, so the hospital staff allowed us to arrange a roster of caring folk to sit by her bed through the night. This was especially needed to prevent her pulling her nasal food tube out. She was so determined to remove this annoyance that she became quite cunning, turning over and pulling at it before her caregiver had time to race around the bed! Weston dropped in to pray again. Another momentous step was to come. Our daughter, now being called the "star patient" and, "miracle girl," began to take her first faltering steps. She needed support, but was so determined that a couple of times, we found her on the floor after trying to walk by herself!

Following this remarkable progress (much faster than the experts believed possible; they would just grin and shake their heads in wonder!) Jolene was moved to the adult rehab unit where therapy could be maintained at a more intense level whenever she was awake. At this stage, she was said to be suffering from "post trauma amnesia." She knew who she was, recognised the family and people from the past, but couldn't remember what day it was, whether she'd had lunch, who had visited, and so on. To this day she doesn't remember any of

Head, Face, ENT & Neck

Weston's visits, even though he came again and prayed for her at rehab. Soon after that, on the 15th of March, with great jubilation and rejoicing, Jolene came home for good. A mere six weeks, yet at times it felt like an eternity! So began the long journey of recovery, from suffering to the hoped-for, believed-for restoration. Around the end of March, Jolene's short-term memory kind of clicked back into place and she was able to remember things that happened the day before and so on. Still needing more healing, we went to a meeting in April where Weston ministered, and he encouraged us to keep believing for God to complete His work.

Later in May, after working with the head injury therapists from Burton Circle (who, incidentally, were amazed at the speed of Jolene's recovery), she was given the green light to try a gradual return to work—two hours, three days a week. She managed simple coding tasks at her old job, working for a chartered accountant. Since then, her hours have built up until by December 1996, she was coping with twenty-seven hours a week, once more, according to her boss, a productive member of the office team.

I am so thankful to the Lord for His healing touch! To see Jolene today—off to the office, driving again, and being a part of society—is just a miracle. After doctors prepared us to accept a far different future for our daughter—perhaps in a wheelchair, dependent on us for the rest of her life—it is such a blessing to have experienced God's mercy as He healed her. At the point of writing her testimony, I am still believing God for more. Restoration equals complete, to the previous state. Jolene still suffers extreme fatigue, and at times has short-term memory problems. She has learnt to use a diary, a tremendous help, and is about to begin a polytechnic paper to finish the Business Diploma the accident so dramatically interrupted, possibly using a Dictaphone to tape the lectures.

My husband and I believe God used many people as instruments in Jolene's healing as He called them to pray and intercede. There was, however, very noticeable changes after Weston prayed for her—especially the times at hospital and rehab. The Lord must have chosen to use him as a willing vessel at these times. Together with the cries and pleadings of many caring folk, his prayers are being answered in God's time. May all the glory go to our heavenly Father!

—*Jolene's Mom*

On Christmas Day, 1996, I experienced a stroke which left me paralysed down my left side. Prior to this I had been a very fit woman and had been playing squash regularly. Over the next fourteen months there was slight improvement but I could not raise my arm at all, my leg movements were totally restricted, walking was extremely difficult and I could not negotiate any uneven ground or steps.

On 9 February 1998, at a divine healing meeting at Alexandra, Weston Carryer prayed for the Lord to heal me. The result was staggering and unbelievable. I immediately put my arm up above my head, and as Weston encouraged me, I started to walk normally; then without any effort I ran and kept running in the hall and right on out into the car park. Apart from my left hand which has ninety-nine percent use, the rest of my body has been completely healed. Praise You, Jesus!

—*Joenella Biddle*

On 28 February 1999, I developed Bell's palsy. The side of my face was twisted, and as a result, my mouth was screwed up so that I could not talk properly. A few days later I attended a divine healing meeting in Ashburton where Weston Carryer was praying for the Lord to heal people. I was prayed for, and I have much delight in testifying that by the 8th of March, I was completely healed. Hallelujah. Praise You, Jesus.

—*Patricia McLaren, Ashburton*

I had lost my sense of taste and smell, either or both of which my doctor said may or may not return. Weston Carryer prayed for their restoration. The ability to smell returned immediately. The capacity to perceive smell and taste fluctuated for a while but I was confident they would return completely if

Head, Face, ENT & Neck

one continued to believe as Weston's pamphlet, *Keeping Your Healing*, advises. Weston also prayed for my hip and leg and they have improved immensely. I praise God for all He has done for me and affirm that faith in His healing powers works wonders.

—*Pamela Buddendyk*

As a result of being badly injured in a car accident at four years of age, I developed toxic clonic epilepsy. For the next twenty-two years I suffered two or three grand mal seizures every week. This was despite being on the heaviest form of medication that I could take. This type of epilepsy is the most severe form that is possible to have. I lived in constant dread of never knowing when I was going to have a seizure, and it was impossible for me to enjoy any sort of a normal life. I would regularly wake up on the street, or at other places, surrounded by medical or ambulance personnel after a seizure, and I was taken to the hospital on many occasions.

I attended a divine healing meeting at Invercargill in March 2004, where Weston Carryer was ministering. He prayed for the Lord to heal me and the Lord gave me my wonderful miracle. My seizures stopped immediately and I have never had one since that night twelve months ago. There was also a one hundred percent improvement in my general health, and I now have so much more life. Six months later I had medical tests done and my doctor confirmed that I was no longer epileptic. He said that it was advisable not to instantly stop the medication, so I am now on half dosage which will continue to be reduced until I am off completely. Jesus, I am so grateful for the quality of life I now have.

—*Victoria Cannon*

I have had epilepsy from my early teens when I started having one of two seizures a year. In my early twenties, after I was married, my condition worsened and continued to do so, going into ten to twelve dizzy spells, with occasional blackouts and grand mal seizures. Later these blackouts became controlled by heavy medication but this was at the expense of having more frequent grand mal seizures—approximately every four to six weeks, and at times, two or three in two days. The medication made it very hard for me to work because I was so sluggish, my memory was dulled, and I could not remember people or things. To do anything at all was a real effort.

Six years ago, in April 1999, Weston prayed for the Lord to heal my epilepsy, and I am delighted to write that there has been an incredible improvement, both in the epilepsy and my general health. I have had four seizures in this six-year period—an amazing improvement. I can now function as a normal person, which is so wonderful. My quality of life today does not compare with how I was for many years. Lord, I am so grateful.

—*Lois Griffiths*

I thought I would share my testimony, thanking God for the work He has done and will continue to do in my life.

When I was around eight years old, I was having moments when I would phase out briefly. We mentioned this to our GP who sent us off to a paediatrician and onto an EEG, and later an MRI. The EEG showed I was having seizures, and we came to understand they were absence-type seizures. I was diagnosed with epilepsy. The MRI showed everything else was normal, which was good news.

The absence seizures were infrequent and I would wake up each morning either perfectly fine or in a state of absence. I was a swimmer, and as time went on, training increased and I became a competitive swimmer. Early morning starts, plus school and church, meant my family had to check and be sure each day that I was 100% before I went about my day.

As time went on the seizures became more frequent, medication started and was increased, and I had an additional medication which would pull me out of the seizure state. Being diagnosed with epilepsy didn't seem to be a huge bother because I didn't think it would have such a huge effect on my life at the time due to the fact that it was only absences. But by the time I was thirteen or fourteen, it became worse, and I had my first full-on general seizure and was taken into hospital.

Later on that year, it did take a huge toll as I was starting to understand I would never be able to drive unless I could be seizure-free for a year, and every type of medication had different side effects (mood swings, liver damage, intellect issues, etc.), and we had to choose the best out of a bunch where none seemed particularly effective or safe. It suddenly became very real that my life wasn't going to be great and I wouldn't easily be able to do everyday normal things like others do.

During this time I had a number of people praying for me, over me, laying on hands, and going to healing sessions. It was really hard on all of us in later times as we couldn't just get up in the morning and go for a walk or out for breakfast without being really sure I was okay. And it was such a fine line between being in an absent state or not. So many times we went somewhere but had to turn around and go home. I had several general seizures in this time and they were really scary and exhausting.

My mum talked to me constantly about healing. I would visit my aunt, and her prayer group would pray for me and over me. When I was fifteen, I finally agreed to go to the healing rooms at Church Unlimited and that was a really powerful experience. They told me I would be a great sports person. Earlier that week I had just received six awards at my college for sports, coaching, and sport leadership. I asked the Dan Downey Ministries for prayer also.

Last September, I went to the Weston Carryer evening meeting at Church Unlimited and went up the front for God's healing. After these events and prayers the seizures decreased, then I had a general seizure not long after that evening which was really discouraging, but we kept on trusting in God.

I am now happy to say that since August 2013 I have not had a single absence or general seizure, I have not had the "rescue" medication that pulled me out of the absences, and I am now weaning off one of the medications with no bad effects.

Miracles in Aotearoa New Zealand

I will now be able to get my driver's licence and it is such a wonderful feeling getting up each morning knowing that I am 100% good to go for the day. I can get up early to exercise or do whatever I like. This healing has been such a blessing to everyone in my family as well as me.

I look back and know that God was with me all those years in the pool, crossing the road, playing netball, etc., when I was perhaps not 100%. In later years it was so hard for my family to decide whether I was okay or not. The relief now is overwhelming for everyone, and I am so grateful to all those who prayed for me and with me.

Praise the Lord! I have been healed. God is so faithful and I thank Him every day for this healing!

—*Alex Mortiboy*

He Himself took our infirmities
and carried away our diseases.
—Matthew 8:17, NASB

Three

Back & Spine

Testimonies of healed conditions of the back (shoulder/neck/back/legs, back/hip), tailbone, disc/vertebrae problems, spinal abscesses, scoliosis, back pain, osteoporosis, etc.

Back, Osteoporosis

I attended a healing meeting in November 1989, at Te Awamutu, at which time Weston Carryer prayed for my back. God has totally healed my back which now feels great.

—Joan D.

I was a keen shearer and was getting bad back pains, so I went to a physiotherapist. When he did not cure me, I then tried my doctor's drugs before going to a chiropractor. None of these medications or their remedies had much effect. My doctor told me to think about giving up shearing. By this time my back was so bad I could not shear anyway. I was desperate.

I saw an advertisement for a healing meeting in Gore with Weston Carryer speaking. I went along to see what he could do for my back. Well! Once there, I felt the awesome presence of God. It was just amazing. My eyes were opened to His glory and so I accepted Jesus Christ as my Saviour and was filled with the Holy Spirit. When Weston prayed over me, I got my back fixed and have been able to carry on shearing—free from pain ever since. Praise be to God.

—*David Wilson*

Last year Weston Carryer was in our town and I attended one of his healing meetings. He called me up for prayer for my back. I'd had back pains for six to eight months. As soon as he prayed over me the pain went. I had been a Christian for only one or two months. The pain used to come back every now and then but I would rebuke it, in Jesus' name, and it would leave.

A year has passed now and the pain is completely gone. I also had uneven leg length, my left leg being shorter than the right. The physiotherapist had diagnosed that as the cause of the pain.

I attended a healing meeting this year when Weston prayed for the lengthening of my left leg. Both are now the same. God has healed me totally and I am grateful. The only way I can pay Him back is to be obedient to His will, and I ask for strength and courage to do that.

U.P.

On Sunday, 14 November 1999, at the Hastings Apostolic Church through a word of knowledge from God, you had a witness to conditions that I suffered from and you called me forward for prayer. I had lower back pain and a short leg with pain also going down the leg. As you prayed I could sense Jesus' mighty power and a growing sensation and other strange sort of feelings. After returning back to my seat I could not cross my legs because the lower back heat reconstruction process that I could feel was amazing.

On Monday morning, I had a sense to ring my GP and make an appointment to see him. It was on Wednesday, and at 10:00 AM I started to bike from Flaxmere to Havelock North, a thirty-four kilometre return trip. I allowed on hour to get there but it took only thirty-five minutes. I have never biked that far before because of the pain to my back and leg. My doctor was at the local hospital delivery room so I wasn't called into the surgery until 11:15 AM. He examined me and entered it on the computer. I came out of the door but stood outside the surgery door scratching my head. He called to me from the waiting room door to inquire what was wrong. I replied that I really need it on paper for a reference. He said he couldn't do it that day but to leave it until the next time that he saw me.

I didn't see him again until 2 February 2000, and he wrote this testimony:

> *This gentleman is a patient of mine. He has had a growth of his left leg, i.e., it is longer in the last year.*

On this visit to the doctor it took me approximately just under thirty minutes to bike one way. I ended up biking about fifty kilometres in total that day. The doctors have been trying to get me to put my bike down for a few years now. My new pair of long legs are both the same length. Praise to the Lord.

—*Ian Lincoln*

I went up and received prayer from Weston Carryer for alleviation from sinus and back problems. With each passing day I have steadily improved, and am even riding my horse again now. The Lord really did a healing work on me.

—*Janey Sparr*

For a period of six years I endured a sore back in silence. Only one person knew of my constant suffering. On a recent

Miracles in Aotearoa New Zealand

Saturday, I was awake all night tossing and turning because my back was so sore. The next morning, I went to church where Weston Carryer was the guest speaker. He called someone out who was in pain because of a sore back. When I went forward, I was informed it was due to one leg being shorter than the other. Praise God, I was healed there and then through Jesus Christ our Saviour. My leg was lengthened to equal the other and my backache went entirely. I believe it was He who healed me.

—*Bronwyn Tata*

Last year, Weston Carryer was in my church at Tawa and I attended one of the healing meetings. He called me up to pray for my back. As soon as Mr. Carryer had prayed, my back pain was gone. I had only been a Christian for one or two months. I had had back pain for six to eight months. I also had uneven leg length (my left leg was shorter than my right leg) and the physiotherapist had advised me this was the cause of the pain. Through prayer from Mr. Carryer my left leg is now the same length as my right leg.

The pain used to come back every now and then but I would rebuke it in Jesus' name, and the pain would leave. It has now been a year and the pain has completely gone. God has healed me completely and I am very grateful. The only way I can thank God is to be obedient; so I pray for strength and courage to be obedient to Him.

—*Urmila Patel*

In January 1975, I had a very bad fall while running in the rain and hurt my back. Some six or seven weeks later I went to see my doctor who put me into hospital where I was in traction for seven weeks. I went home, but two days later was readmitted and put back into traction for a further five weeks. Then followed five weeks in a plaster cast from the neck to the top of my thighs. As no progress was made, I was sent to Waikato Hospital to see a specialist who again admitted me immediately. There followed major surgery and after three weeks, I went home to convalesce. For the next eleven years I enjoyed considerable good health but then things started to go wrong again. I had been told that further major surgery would be needed to insert plastic discs.

In April 1989, Weston Carryer was speaking in our church and God miraculously healed me through him. I had to see the specialist again who could find nothing wrong and thus, no further surgery is necessary. Thank you, Weston, for the ministry God has given you and, as you continue to do His work, may you know the blessing of the Lord on your life. Glory be to God.

—Judy S.

I praise God for His goodness to me. Two years ago I had back trouble. My right leg was immobile. It was difficult to walk or bend. The pain was distressful. Friends in our house group prayed for me. I read the Word and prayed constantly, seeking a healing from God. After prayer at one group meeting the pain began to subside.

At a healing meeting, Weston Carryer laid hands on and prayed over me. I was surprised to recover most of my movement and to be able to touch my toes. I had always found that difficult since a back operation seven years previously when my left leg gave the same trouble. The specialist said at that time there was not a lot he could do and gave me a programme of exercises, which I followed. He also advised me to quit farming and find light work. I still have some symptoms as a reminder but have continued farming and undertaken heavy work. I praise God for He is our healer.

—Bruce J. Newton

I had a back problem for fifteen years which caused me constant and continual pain over this entire period. My doctor told me that because of what was wrong with my back, I would suffer this pain for the rest of my life. I attended a men's breakfast at East Bay Apostolic Church at Whakatane on 11 March 1995. This was a new experience for me as I had had practically no contact with any church. Weston Carryer, who was the speaker, said that the Lord had showed him that there was someone there who had the specific back problem that I had and he described my exact symptoms. I responded to his invitation to be prayed for. I found myself on the floor and when I got up, the severe pain had totally gone. I knew that I had been miraculously touched and healed by Jesus and I had no hesitation in asking Him to be my Lord and Saviour. Over the last eight months I have had no pain or restriction in my back whatever and I am still rejoicing over my salvation. Praise the Lord!

—*Wiki Iha*

For many years I had suffered with a sore back. I found it particularly bad when shearing sheep. In the lower left in the small of my back, I would experience a locking-up feeling. I would have to stop shearing and lie on the floor or stand against the wall for it to release. I went to a Weston Carryer meeting where he placed his hand on my back and prayed in the name of Jesus. I have never had that locking-up feeling since. I know Jesus has healed my back.

—*Lance Bishop*

Weston Carryer visited the Thames Women's Aglow. I had been suffering from a horrible nerve condition through my legs and lower back. I could barely walk. Just walking to the letterbox was a real chore. I couldn't ride the horses or walk around with my friends. I honestly thought I would need a wheelchair. I was on the waiting list for an MRI scan and doctors' thought I'd need an operation on my back—if the problem was "accessible." Outwardly there was no evidence of a problem, but inside, my legs were screaming.

I came to Weston for prayer and he asked, "Are you ready for your miracle?" I was more than ready! After I got up off the floor, I felt worse—much weaker. But the next morning, I jumped out of bed and realized that there was no pain and

Back & Spine

no weakness. I can do all the normal things again. I can even run again! There is sometimes a small twinge of a problem but I know I'm healed. I'll still go ahead with the scan but I know that God's already done the operation. I'm grateful that Weston let God use him.

—J. Wilkie

For approximately twelve years I suffered severe back pain. For the last five years I have had to have regular physiotherapy treatment which only relieved the pain briefly, but it always returned. I also suffered shoulder pain for at least nine years for which I was having physiotherapy that only temporarily relieved the pain. I also suffered continual pins and needles in my right hand for the last twelve months.

I attended a divine healing meeting at Tuakau in November 1999, and during the ministry time, Weston Carryer prayed for the Lord to heal me. As he prayed, all the pain went and it has not returned. I have full restoration in my back, shoulder, and hand. I want to jump for joy. Praise the Lord.

—Doreen Kihi

In 1976, I fell into a pit with a concrete base landing on my back and badly damaged it which necessitated me having to go straight to Waikato Hospital. I was treated there and remained for three months. From the time I was discharged until 1990 (fourteen years), I experienced continual terrible pain. In 1991, I had surgery which did not help. I then slipped down my house steps and once again, landed on my back, causing further damage.

In 1996, I had further surgery when two steel rods were inserted into my spine. Once again this did not help. The surgeon said that so much damage had been done, further surgery was necessary, which they did in 1998. This time the operation was done through my abdomen and two cages were inserted to try to support the spine. After this, I still experienced continual horrendous pain.

Miracles in Aotearoa New Zealand

In July 2000, I went to a divine healing meeting at Tauranga where Weston Carryer was ministering.

During the early part of the meeting, Weston said that the Lord had revealed to him that there was someone sitting just where I was who was in severe pain and to come to the front for the Lord to heal them. I went forward immediately, and as Weston prayed for me, it was like a bolt of lightning hitting me and I was thrown to the floor. Within a few moments the pain was totally gone and no pain whatever has ever returned. My restrictions are gone and I walk at least forty minutes every day. I am rejoicing and praising God continually. After my husband saw what happened, he had no hesitation in accepting Jesus as His Lord. Thank You, Jesus.

—*Margaret Lind*

I was born with one leg shorter than the other and this resulted in me having a twisted hip. Four years ago the back and hip started to ache and the pain continued to worsen. I was always in pain of some sort.

At a divine healing meeting in Tauranga in 1999 where Weston Carryer was ministering, I went forward for prayer for the Lord to heal me. Through the power of God, I was slain in the Spirit. As I was lying on the floor, I experienced my leg lengthen to the correct length and my hip and bones in the buttock area completely readjust. In fact, everything came into alignment. Since then I have had no pain of any kind whatever. Thank You, Jesus.

—*Russell Turner, Tauranga*

I had been suffering from a number of severe physical problems for a long time. My right leg was six inches shorter than my left one. I had had two operations on my back. Bolts had been inserted, but, this had not helped ease the pain that I experienced all the time. My right leg was continually numb and I always had a painful neck.

I attended a divine healing meeting at Hamilton in March

Back & Spine

1999 where Weston Carryer was ministering. He prayed for the Lord to heal all my illnesses. Amazing things happened. I saw my leg grow the full six inches to the exact same length as the other one. This has been medically confirmed; although, of course I know because of the way I can now stand and walk. All other conditions were healed that night, and all the pain and restriction has gone. Hallelujah. Thank You, Jesus. You are awesome.

—*Lavinia Davis, Hamilton*

Over a thirty-year period, I experienced considerable damage to my back in my work as a painter and paperhanger. For two years, from 1993 to 1995, I had to take painkillers every day to be able to work at all. The back deteriorated further, and despite medical help and painkillers (which by this time had become ineffective), I was forced to stop work completely in 1995.

In December 1997, at a divine healing meeting at Papamoa where Weston Carryer was ministering, I received a miracle. During the ministry time, Weston prayed for me and Jesus Christ healed my back. The next day my back was ninety-five percent functional, and within days, it was one hundred percent. I now have no pain and no limitation of any kind. What a God we serve.

—*Campbell Barlow, Papamoa*

As a result of a car accident twenty years ago, I badly injured my back. For the next seventeen years, I experienced considerable pain, was very restricted in my movements, and could only walk with a limp. During this entire seventeen-year period I had treatment from doctors, chiropractors, and physiotherapists but without any real help. I had to take painkillers the entire time to try and get some pain relief.

Three years ago, Weston Carryer prayed for the Lord to do a miracle in my back and this is exactly what I got. At that moment my back was healed and I am rejoicing and praising

Miracles in Aotearoa New Zealand

Jesus Christ every day for a pain-free, trouble-free back. It is marvellous after seventeen years.

—*Betty Pratt, Mt. Maunganui*

Following the birth of a baby, I had chronic back pain for five years. Although it would subside at times, it always came back. Weston Carryer prayed for me at a healing meeting. Nothing seemed to happen then, but he gave me his pamphlet, *Keeping Your Healing*, to read and follow. He told me to believe God and to thank Him in faith for my healing. The pain did persist for three days but I kept claiming my healing. Suddenly, the pain went and has not returned. Twelve months have passed and I have had no further pain or back problems.

—*Belinda Kingi*

I had suffered chronic backache for many years as a result of transitional vertebrae. I also suffered over a long period from an extremely painful hip and it had reached the point where I was unable to stand on my leg because of the agony of it.

In September 1991, I went to a healing meeting where Weston Carryer prayed for me, and through Jesus Christ, God healed both these conditions. Since then, I have had absolutely no pain in my back and apart from one or two slight twinges, my hip has been pain-free and the use is fully restored to my leg.

—*Pixie Craig*

I got two exciting healings from God at separate meetings where Weston Carryer was ministering. I had frequent problems with a sore back and went up to have it prayed for. Weston asked what was wrong and I told him of my back.

He looked me straight in the face and said, "You have got one leg longer than the other." I did not know whether I did or not, so I sat down, put my feet together, and sure enough,

Back & Spine

my left leg was shorter. Weston prayed, and the short leg went longer than the other then retracted to match it. In the six months since I have had no trouble with my back.

When I was five years old, I leaned over the stove and my t-shirt caught fire. This caused third-degree burns on the right side of my torso and underarm. The graft on my torso straight after the accident was successful. Ten years later, another operation was done, to try and make the underarm scar normal. During the operation the skin graft slipped and had to be done again a week later. After a fourth operation a year on, the scar on the underarm had not gone and was quite painful. Weston prayed for relief from the pain and it went instantly. Two years have passed and I am trouble- and pain-free.

—*Christine Lutze*

For several weeks I had very severe pain in my back and legs and was unable to walk without the support of a walking stick. A year ago, I attended a healing meeting where Weston Carryer was ministering. As he prayed for me, the power of God through Jesus completely and instantly healed me. During the last twelve months I have had no further problems or pain at all.

—*Julie Alexopoulos*

As the result of injury received in a motorcycle accident, I suffered severe pain in my back for ten years, and on many occasions, I was unable to move at all.

I went to a healing meeting at Mosgiel where Weston Carryer prayed for me. The healing, through Jesus, commenced then. I believed that I was healed and kept praising God, although I still had some pain. After about three days, the pain went away entirely and I have had no further symptoms of any kind over this last year.

—*Dave Lewis*

Miracles in Aotearoa New Zealand

We do indeed serve a God of miracles, one who is faithful to do what He has promised, one who bore all our infirmities, carried all our sickness; one who gives life more than abundantly, wonderful Counsellor, Prince of peace, Almighty God.

My name is Anne Van der Mije. I am forty-two years old, married to Gerard, and we have three precious daughters and a son-in-law who all love Jesus. I've been a Christian for thirteen years and I've experienced the power of God in my life from the moment I first asked Jesus into my life as Lord and Saviour. I first went to one of Weston Carryer's meetings in Rotorua in 1991. He called out one who had lower back pain. I had been in pain for about a year and under constant physio and chiropractic works, yet with no healing. X-rays showed the beginnings of crumbling, and blood tests showed I was post-menopausal at forty years—that's no joke.

In 1992, Weston came to Taupo. In the meantime, God showed me I had a fear of cancer. As I looked back on the symptoms, I related to different dealings I had with folk. I went to his meeting, and before it even started, he called for someone with the fear of cancer. I knew instantly that was me. Then Weston told me to wait, but promised God's deliverance. When it happened, I was released from all pain associated with my back and nerves. I have walked straight ever since and I don't have any stiffness in my hips. It's like God has given me a new rod in my back. The symptoms did return for about two months, but each day, I claimed healing in Jesus' name.

Now (1994) I do not have back problems like I did. Praise God, thanks to Jesus—I'm totally healed.

—*Anne Van der Mije*

When Weston Carryer was in Hastings speaking and ministering at the Apostolic Church, he called out someone with lower back problems. I spent the rest of the meeting on the floor! My problems had begun many years ago so that I was less and less able to move around, until a touch from the Lord reversed things. Praise God! However, though flexible, x-rays proved there was severe deterioration and this resulted in quite a lot of pain. I should not have been able to function as I did, especially as I was a preschool teacher. Recently, I had begun to get severe sciatic pain too. The doctor could offer no help. From the moment Weston prayed over me, that has completely gone! What's more, the other pain is much, much less. I am still believing I will one day be free of this pain altogether. I am so thankful for Weston's faithfulness as God's servant, and I wish the Zoe Evangelistic Ministry all God's blessings. I thank and praise Jesus Christ, my Redeemer and my Healer. Yours in Christ.

—Jeannie Sale

When Weston Carryer visited Victory Christian Centre in Lower Hutt in September 2001, I responded to a general altar call and asked for healing in my right shoulder. For about eighteen months previous to that, I had been suffering considerable pain in my shoulder, arm, and elbow. I could not raise my arm for any length of time and was very limited in my movement. It was also very painful when I picked anything up, did the vacuuming, or any job, in fact, involving pressure on that arm. My doctor recommended physiotherapy and painkillers. I had physiotherapy once a week and was given some exercises to do. The young lady who was my physiotherapist gave up her practice to have a baby and encouraged me to keep up my treatment with someone else as the shoulder needed a lot of work on it.

Since that night Weston prayed for me, I have experienced gradual healing in my shoulder so that now (twelve months later) I have absolutely no pain in my shoulder, arm, or elbow.

About two weeks ago (August 2002), I attended one of Weston's healing crusades at a church in Wainuiomata where I live. He actually called out my symptoms of degenerated discs in the back with pain going down the right leg. I knew of the degeneration because I'd had my back x-rayed. I had been suffering back problems for almost thirty years. In fact, I first slipped my back out the night before my wedding when I was sewing my head dress onto my veil (not the best timing!). There were many times when I had to call for help as my back would seize up and all I could do was take painkillers and wait until the pain eased off. It was very painful to sit or stand for too long.

As Weston prayed for me, I felt the power of God slam into me, and that's the only way I can describe it. I really believe that He operated on my back that night. Since then I have been pain-free. As he says in his pamphlet, *Keeping Your Healing*, it is no use praying for faith. Prayer does not make faith work. Faith makes prayer work. Thank you.

—*Isobel Mollins*

For six years I suffered from very severe back and leg pain. This pain was so bad and so debilitating that I had to physically lift both legs with my hands when getting up or getting out of a car. I had medical and physiotherapy treatment, but neither of these helped at all.

At a divine healing meeting in August 2001 at Rotorua, Weston Carryer was ministering and described a back condition which I did not know I had but the symptoms fit the description he gave. I went forward and he prayed for the Lord to heal me. Although the pain did not go immediately I realized that something had happened. A day or two later the pain started easing, and one month later, all the pain and restriction were totally gone. My back and legs were once again normal. Over the last twelve months I have had no pain at all. After experiencing such intense pain for over six years, this is marvellous. Lord, I thank You and praise You.

—*Shelly Brown*

In May 2002, Weston Carryer held a healing meeting in Tauranga. The Lord had encouraged me to go. I thought I was going to offer prayer support only, but through a word of knowledge, the Lord healed my lower back which had given me heaps of trouble in the past.

Back & Spine

The chiropractor had told me some of the problem was from an old trampoline injury as a teenager (which I had remembered) plus heavy lifting in nursing. I had been having reasonable pain-free days but long journeys of sitting, and at other times, I would get very uncomfortable in my lower back. When Weston called out these facts, I knew God was talking to me. It didn't take me too long to hit the floor! My back has been wonderful ever since. Praise God!

—*Faye Falloon*

In 1994, I did something to my back when shifting a refrigerator. It didn't hurt much at the time, but, the next day I could not move and couldn't even roll out of bed. I was off work and on ACC for the next month. I had physiotherapy but this did not help at all. When I went back to work at my job in a tannery, I was unable to work certain machinery because of my back condition. I had been a half marathon runner but found I could not run at all.

I came to a healing meeting in severe pain in Christchurch where Weston Carryer was ministering in February 2002. I went to the meeting really believing for my healing after eight years of constant intense pain. During the meeting, Weston, under the leading of the Holy Spirit, described the exact condition of my back and the symptoms I was experiencing. He asked for the person to come forward. He then looked straight at me and said it was me, and then I immediately went forward. As Weston prayed for me, the pain instantly went and I felt heat come into my back. Since that moment I have been running again ever since. Thank You, Lord.

—*John Campbell*

About twelve years ago a degenerative disease developed in my back. This got steadily worse and got to the stage seven years ago where my back and legs were so painful, that despite continually taking painkillers, I could not walk at all without crutches. It was extremely difficult doing anything and I spent most of the day sitting in the lounge. I had all kinds of medical treatment but nothing happened at all. I came to a combined church healing meeting in Inglewood in June 2002, where Weston Carryer was ministering and he prayed for the Lord to heal me. As soon as he prayed for me, I experienced an amazing burning sensation in my back and legs which lasted for three or four days. The pain then started to go, and three weeks later, I was able to stop using my crutches. Since then, apart from the odd, very slight twinges in very cold weather, I have had no further pain or restriction. I can walk distances, do all normal activities, including mowing the lawns. I am healed by Jesus. Thank You, Lord.

—*Kathy Northcott*

At the beginning of 2001, I attended a Weston Carryer healing meeting at North City Apostolic Church. I had been receiving treatment for a lower back problem which I had been told that due to my age and profession, there was very little that could be done except exercise and lumbar supports. This advice was really going to restrict my lifestyle. I have been a Christian for a number of years and had seen healings take place.

At North City Apostolic I went forward for prayer. I felt the Holy Spirit come upon me; I was very relaxed and at peace. I still had pain when I left the church. Three days later, however, I suddenly realized that the pain had gone and I was more mobile. I had received my healing. Praise God. It has been two years now and no pain.

—*Russell Barriball*

In 1963, as a soldier in the NZ army, I was stationed at Burnham military camp. One day we were on a training exercise called "rapid dispersals," which meant we had to jump out of a moving truck in full battle gear. Unfortunately for me, this resulted in severe injury because of the way I landed, and I spent the next four and a half months in Burnham hospital. For thirty-nine years after being released from hospital, I had severe pain in my back and both legs and had to wear a back

Back & Spine

brace as well as braces on both knees at all times.

I attended a divine healing meeting at Inglewood in June 2002, where Weston Carryer prayed for the Lord to heal me. As he prayed, the Lord did a miracle. The pain went immediately and has never returned. I have not needed any of my braces over the last fifteen months. I am rejoicing in God's goodness after thirty-nine years of agony. Praise You, Lord.

—*Owen Northcott*

I was at a Weston Carryer healing meeting at The Well of Life Church and this is my healing testimony. About six years ago before I became a Christian, Weston was at a combined church meeting in Taumarunui. My wife, who is a Christian, and another Christian couple, suggested that we go along. When the power of the Lord went through the first person Weston called forward to pray over, she went down on her back. I thought, *What's going on here?*

The next two people were called up with the same result. I had come to get healing for my back and neck which were deteriorating steadily. I was always in pain in both areas and very limited in my movements. I could not move my neck without noticeable clicking and grating. I had decided to leave for a short time; so when Weston pointed to our part of the congregation and spoke out my condition, I wasn't there to go forward. When I returned and my wife told me, I didn't believe, at the time, that the call could be for me because I wasn't a Christian and would have felt a hypocrite to receive something I didn't believe in. Now six years later I am a Christian and Weston came to the Well of Life Church again. I spoke to the Lord saying, "This man and I have unfinished business."

That evening I was the first called, and my back and neck were both healed after ten years of pain. As Weston prayed, the pain seemed to just jump out of my neck. I felt the power of the Lord and the complete healing was instant. The back healing commenced, and now four months later, it is ninety-five percent healed, I know any day it will be one hundred percent. It is so wonderfully different to how it was for all those years. I can

Miracles in Aotearoa New Zealand

now shear sheep without any pain. Through receiving these healings, I have been really encouraged in my walk with the Lord. Praise the Lord.

—Richard Loft

My husband, George, had a severe back problem, as well as muscular aches and pains. At a healing meeting, Weston called for someone who needed healing for a back problem. George answered that call and went up, in faith, believing. One week later we were sitting around after dinner and he said to me, "I'm fixed." At the time I didn't know what he was talking about, so I asked him again, and he responded by saying, "I am fixed. I can't feel any pain any more in my back." It is wonderful to see George move around without wincing to get up or stopping to do things. I knew when you were praying and George fell down, that the Holy Spirit had come over him, as he had never fallen down under the power of the Holy Spirit before when he has gone up for prayer, even though he still receives His blessing. Praise the Lord.

—Heeni Bond

About sixteen years ago, when I was in my mid-forties, I started to experience a major health problem. My back would suddenly lock up on me, I would experience excruciating pain, and my back would go into spasms, cause me to collapse and I would pass out completely. I lost count of the number of times that this happened. I was taken to hospital on many occasions. After ten years of experiencing this back condition my heart developed problems which required medical and hospital treatment. On one occasion my heart stopped completely, but thankfully, the medical people in the hospital were able to restart it. This period was a dreadful time in my life and I continually felt so terrible, and went down hill so much, that I was convinced that I would not see that year out. I could see no hope whatever as nobody seemed to be able to help me at all.

However, all this changed dramatically in November 2002

when I attended a divine healing meeting in Napier where Weston Carryer was ministering. During the ministry time as he was speaking out words of knowledge, he described my heart condition and asked me to go forward for the Lord to heal me. When I went to the front, he said that the Lord was also revealing this back condition which was caused by two degenerate discs and that he was also to pray for this healing as well. I am rejoicing that my back was totally healed immediately. I have never had any spasms since. My heart condition also started to improve, and now three years later, I am living a normal life. The latest scans that I have had have shown that my heart is now functioning normally. Praise You, Lord Jesus.

—*John O'Donnell*

On 4 May 2005, I was hit by a tree while I was felling trees in an operation. While I was walking through the bush in the bottom of a gully the top of a tree, which had been broken in a prior storm, fell off and hit me. I felt that I had hundreds of puncture wounds in my back. I was only able to stand for 10-15 minutes at a time and I was unsure when I would be able to return to work. I was off work for three and a half weeks, was suffering badly during that time, and I was also having terrible nightmares.

I attended a healing meeting where Weston was ministering. Weston spoke out my condition and after I explained the accident he told me that I have had the pain for longer than described. I explained that I had been hit by a tree seventeen years earlier but I had learned to live with the pain. Weston prayed for me and immediately I was healed and the nightmares stopped. I returned to work the following week. I have not had any problems since. The Lord saved my life when the tree hit me and then healed me through Weston. Praise the Lord! I'm so thankful for Weston's ministry. Today I have no physical problems at all and I am recently married. Awesome! Jesus Christ saved me, healed me, and blesses me continually. Thank You, Jesus.

—*Dale More*

Miracles in Aotearoa New Zealand

I went to a Weston Carryer healing meeting in February 2006 at Pukekohe where Pastor Craig and Jean minister. I asked Weston for prayer for the Lord to heal my very bad lower back pain. The pain had been constant for two years. This also affected my posture and bowel. As I was prayed for, all the pain went totally, and now eight months later, has never returned. My posture has changed and is a lot better; my whole body also feels so different. I have no more pain. It is sometimes hard to believe that it is gone because I was so used to living with the pain. But, believe it I do, because the pain in my lower back is definitely gone. Thanks to Weston and thank You, Lord Jesus.

—*Leona Wijohn*

In 1982, I fell off a ladder and injured my left shoulder and my back. This caused me to have continual pain for the next twenty years and I was unable to lift my arm above my shoulder. At night, if I ever rolled over onto my left side the pain would wake me up and then I had to wake my husband up to get him to shift me off the shoulder as I would be unable to move at all. I took painkillers every day during this twenty-year period.

In 2002, I attended a divine healing meeting in Tauranga where Weston Carryer was ministering. During the ministry time I went forward for Weston to pray for me. As he prayed, God's healing power was manifested and the pain instantly left in both my back and my shoulder. Full movement was restored to my arm. I could lift it to full height and rotate my whole arm.

Apart from one or two very slight niggles, which I have rebuked in Jesus' name and they have gone immediately, I have had no limitation in my back, arm, or shoulder. Thank You, Jesus.

—*Charlotte Read*

Over twelve months ago, I attended both the morning and evening services at a Weston Carryer healing meeting at City

Back & Spine

Life Church, Tauranga. I came with a very painful back. It was so bad I didn't know whether to sit or stand—nothing felt good. I waited for the Lord to call me through Weston, but it did not come. Even though Weston made a call for those who needed healing, I stubbornly did not go forward, deciding rather that God must call me.

Again in the evening, I sat waiting to be called; nothing came. Again Weston made the call that he would pray for anyone needing healing. I waited. Thank God I got over my stubbornness and went forward. I was the last person he prayed for that night and I received a miraculous and instant healing. At the end of the meeting I carried the heavy boxes of books to Weston's car for him when he left! I have had no further problems with my back since that time. I thank God for Weston's willingness to answer God's call on his life and be the tool that God uses for bringing healing. May God bless his ministry.

—*Dave Ludlow*

Three months ago, I suddenly experienced crippling pain in my back and could not move for a week. It was discovered that a disc had protruded and was completely out of alignment and I could need surgery. The pain was so severe that I would have preferred childbirth pain.

I saw a notice in Rotorua advertising a Weston Carryer healing meeting. The Lord had earlier healed me on two occasions at Weston's meetings and so I decided to attend on the Sunday morning. On the Saturday night before the meeting as I went to bed in severe pain, I knew that the Lord was going to heal me the next day.

The next morning as I got out of bed, the pain started to diminish. I went to the meeting and Weston prayed for me. The pain continued to diminish, and within two weeks, it had gone completely. Apart from a mild cramping sensation occasionally in one leg, over the last eight months I have had no further pain. It is awesome. Praise You, Lord.

—*Carol Nicoll*

Miracles in Aotearoa New Zealand

Eighteen months ago, I attended a divine healing meeting at City Life Church in Tauranga where Weston Carryer was ministering. I had a very painful back which had shown no sign of improvement. I was sitting in my seat and while Weston was preaching, the pain simply went completely and had never ever returned.

I am so grateful to the Lord for the wonderful way that He reached out and touched me like this. Thank You, Jesus.

—*Rosy Butcher*

For approximately ten years I suffered discomfort in my back. This discomfort was always there and I used to regularly try to manipulate my back to get relief.

On 15 February 2013, I went forward at a divine healing meeting at Ruawai where Weston Carryer was ministering, and he prayed for the Lord to heal my back. As he prayed, the discomfort just went and has never returned. I am so glad because over the last twelve months, my back has been—and still is—perfect. Thank You, Lord Jesus, for healing my back.

—*Bronwyn Holt*

I was born and raised on Rotuma Island, which is north of Fiji. When I was ten years of age, my father asked me to climb a very tall fruit tree to get some of the fruit. Unfortunately, the branch that was supporting me snapped and I fell twenty metres.

I broke an ankle and badly hurt my back. I was unable to get off my back for three months. This accident left me with a permanently stiff and sore back.

When I was nineteen, I was working on the rigging on a ship in Port Vila, Vanuatu, when the man holding the pulley rope that kept me up in the rigging mistakenly let it go. This time I fell thirty metres and once again injured my back.

Back & Spine

Although I had this continual pain and stiffness all the time in my back, I was determined to stay active. As well as working, I did weight training to try and strengthen it. At the age of fifty, the pain became too intense for me to do any weight training and I had to give it up.

Four years later, I attended a divine healing meeting in Tauranga where Weston Carryer was ministering. He said there was someone present who had had these injuries to their back and was in severe pain at that moment. I responded, and as he prayed for me, the power of God touched me and I was instantly and completely healed. That same day I started weight training again—lifting very heavy weights.

Over the last ten years I have not had any pain or restriction in my back at all. Thank You so much, Lord Jesus.

—*Kafoa Penjueb*

I started to experience back pain in my late teens. This condition had affected a number of the male members of my family and for the next twenty-five years this affected me. While I carried on with most normal activities, I was always suffering. A lot of the time it was not too bad, but then there would be periods of up to several weeks when I could not straighten up and the pain would be excruciating. It would take many weeks before the pain would ease at all.

Fifteen years ago, I was going through a particularly bad period, and I had been doubled right over for some time. I attended a divine healing meeting in Cambridge where Weston Carryer was ministering. He pointed to where I was sitting and said that a person there had the severe back condition I had and that the Lord wanted him to pray for that person at that moment.

I immediately went forward and Weston prayed for me. I did not feel anything at the time, and when I left the meeting, the pain was much the same. However, that night I slept soundly, and the next morning I literally jumped out of bed with not the slightest bit of pain. Before my healing, getting out of bed had been a real mission.

Miracles in Aotearoa New Zealand

Now over fifteen years later, although I use my back a lot and do a lot of bending, I have never had anywhere near the back pain I used to get. This has made a huge difference in my life. I am so grateful to the Lord Jesus Christ for what He has done for me.

—Harry Street

When I was thirty years old (in the year 2000), I was pulling on a pulley rope, in the course of my work, and it snapped causing me to fall backwards onto a rock. This did serious damage to my back and caused many complications. Over the next nine years I had to have six back operations. At one stage the back seemed to be improving. But then a cow rolled on me and caused havoc with the screws that had been screwed in to the back. The screws had to be removed and a cage was inserted.

However, in 2009, the pain started getting worse and worse. By 2012, my back continued to deteriorate so that I could not even walk without the help of a walking stick despite being on 160 milligrams of morphine every day. The pain also went down both my legs.

On the night of 15 February 2013, I attended a divine healing meeting at Ruawai where Weston Carryer was ministering. I went with a terrific expectation that the Lord was going to do a miracle for me. I was in the overflow room at the meeting working the closed circuit TV, and after a while, Weston called out my condition.

I could not get to the front fast enough. As he prayed for me the intense pain that I was in just disappeared and I immediately felt normality return to my back and legs. It was incredible. That was over seven months ago now and I have had no further pain or restriction in my legs or lower back. I am now able to live a normal life and was able to come off all morphine and other painkillers.

I am so grateful to the Lord for what He has done for me.

—Craig Mitchell

Back & Spine

I was in a car accident in 2001. A car coming towards us hit us head on. There were five people in the other car: three died on impact, one on the way to hospital, and one later that night in hospital. My injuries were to my neck and my shoulder as I held my hands out instinctively during the accident. The shock through my arms damaged my shoulders and neck as well as the whiplash.

I suffered from that day on with constant pain in my shoulders, back, and neck, where even a sneeze could throw my neck out causing it to be stiff for days. I could also not sleep on my right shoulder or use my arm too long. Headaches from the neck pain were also constant.

Weston Carryer came to our church and he had a word of knowledge about my condition. As he prayed for me, I felt a warm feeling start from my shoulder and move all the way down my back. My shoulder and back were healed, but I continued getting headaches, and the base of my neck was still in pain. When Weston visited again, I went up and shared that my healing was complete in my shoulder but my neck still ached. He prayed and I am now totally healed. No more neck, back or shoulder pain. No more headaches, and it has now been over eight months. Praise the Lord, for His love endures forever.

—*Deborah King*

In January 2012, I was miraculously healed by the Lord at a divine healing meeting at Church Unlimited where Weston Carryer was ministering.

I was born with a back abnormality. My back was out of shape but it was not discovered until I was 32. The x-rays showed that the joints on the left side of the spine were not separate which resulted in my body pulling down on the left side, and any bending would cause bones in the spine to crunch together. An extra bone was also growing on the hipbone and there were other abnormalities. Medical people told me that the conditions were inoperable.

Miracles in Aotearoa New Zealand

As a child, and then as a young person, I was still able to do things and live a reasonably normal life, although I suffered a lot of pain much of the time. Over the years the pain became worse, and the five-year period before my healing, it had been practically 24-hours a day. Apart from the continual daytime pain, the pain would wake me and keep me awake at night. All the different medication I tried did not help the pain at all.

When walking up stairs I had to place one foot on the higher step and then drag the other one up to the same level. A lot of the time I had to use a walking stick to help me move. I could not stand long enough to do the dishes, or make a piece of toast, or do many other simple tasks.

When Weston stood up and started to minister, he shared some testimonies. I knew that he was going to speak out my condition, and indeed, my condition was the first word of knowledge that he spoke out. I responded, and moved to the front of the church with difficulty—in extreme pain and using my walking stick.

As he prayed for me the Lord gave me my miracle. The pain completely instantly disappeared and strength came into my back. Weston took my stick and I was able to move freely and rapidly across the front of the church.

That night, for the first time ever, I slept on my back. I went to sleep praising Jesus and when I woke in the morning, I was also praising Him. Since that night (now over 12 months ago), I have never awakened with any pain at all. Occasionally, over the last 12 months, I have had very slight back pain, but nothing like I had for all those years. This has made a huge difference in my life and I can now live a normal life.

I am so grateful to the Lord for what He has done for me.

—*Julie-Ann Lucken*

About twelve years ago, a degenerative disease developed in my back. This got steadily worse and got to the stage seven years ago where my back and legs were so painful that I could not walk at all without crutches despite continually taking painkillers. It was extremely difficult doing anything and I

Back & Spine

spent most of the day sitting in the lounge. I had all kinds of medical treatment but nothing happened at all.

I came to a combined church healing meeting in Inglewood in June 2002, where Weston Carryer was ministering and he prayed for the Lord to heal me. As soon as he prayed for me, I experienced an amazing burning sensation in my back and legs which lasted for three or four days. The pain then started to go, and then three weeks later, I was able to stop using my crutches. This happen fifteen months ago, and since then, I have had no further pain or restriction apart from the odd very slight twinges in very cold weather. I can walk distances, do all normal activities including mowing the lawns. I am healed by Jesus. Thank You, Lord.

—*Kathy Northcott*

My name is Graham Petterson, and I am in my late seventies. As a child I was diving off a high board at the swimming baths and I hit the edge of the concrete pool. This caused severe pain for sixty years. I had to give up farming because of this. However, this changed one night when I went to a healing meeting in Waikanae eleven years ago where Weston Carryer was ministering. During the ministry time I went forward, and as Weston prayed for me, Jesus Christ totally healed my back. After sixty years of pain, I am rejoicing to write that over the last eleven years, there has been no pain whatever. Hallelujah! Praise the Lord.

—*Graham Petterson*

For fifteen years I suffered severe pain in my back and right hip caused by osteoporosis. Eight x-rays taken over this period showed continuing deterioration. When we built a new house in Turangi, my husband was advised to build a ramp for a wheelchair which the specialist said I would be confined to very soon. The medication I had taken for relief had caused a stomach ulcer.

I attended a divine healing meeting at Turangi where

Miracles in Aotearoa New Zealand

Weston Carryer was ministering. God revealed my condition to him and he asked me to go forward to receive a miracle. As Weston prayed for me, my right leg—which was noticeably shorter—lengthened, and all the pain and restriction went from my back and hip.

Since that time I have had no further pain and limitations, and my back, hip and leg function normally. An x-ray taken one month ago (five years later) confirmed that my back has been fully restored. The stomach ulcer was also healed completely at the same time. Hallelujah. What a mighty God we serve. I praise Him continually.

—Ces Johansen

About 1996, I went to a Weston Carryer meeting in Tauranga, and he had a word of knowledge for someone with osteoporosis. Just a few weeks earlier I had x-rays taken and there were three places in my spine affected with this. I was prayed for and God healed me.

On Boxing Day 1996, Weston, his wife, and I were sharing on God's healing, and I shared what God had done and what I was believing him for. Weston asked me what I needed and then said, "Let's pray right now."

My right foot had always been longer than my left, and we believed for it to shorten, and it did. I can comfortably wear shoes now.

In May 1997, in Tauranga, another word of knowledge came for someone with respiratory problems and with a spot on their lungs. I went forward, was prayed for, and can now breathe correctly and easily for first time in my fifty-seven years.

—Diane Oliver

Twelve years ago, I was diagnosed as having osteoporosis of the lower spine. I found sitting uncomfortable, especially when travelling, as I didn't like pressure on my spine. My back would ache when doing things such as gardening or leaning over a table.

Back & Spine

One night, I went to a healing meeting at Well of Life Church, New Plymouth. Weston Carryer called up a lady with osteoporosis at the beginning of the meeting. I wasn't going to come up as I felt I wasn't the one he was talking to, but my daughter-in-law insisted that I go up too. There was some improvement.

About fourteen months ago I was getting a lot of pain in my right leg again and I thought it was osteoporosis again so I decided I would go and have a bone scan to see how bad it was. I was really thrilled to find that my bone density was now normal apart from the left wrist, which was just outside being normal. The pain in my leg was a pinched nerve. I can only praise God for that healing.

—*Dorrie Brown*

For many months I suffered with lower back pain which was there practically all the time. Five years ago, in 2002, this became a lot worse and became very severe continually. Many mornings I could not get out of bed because of the pain. I went to my doctor on a number of occasions but was told that nothing could be done for me. I was taking eight panadex tablets every day to try to get some relief.

In May 2006, I attended a Sunday morning service at my church where Weston Carryer was ministering. As soon as he started to speak he said that the Lord had revealed to him that there was someone present with a severe lower back condition. He asked if that person would come forward for the Lord to heal her. I responded, and as Weston prayed for me, the pain left. It was amazing. I was able to move my back and touch my toes with complete freedom. Since that moment over fourteen months ago, I have not had the slightest sign of any back pain whatever. It is marvellous! Praise the Lord.

—*Michelle Twiford*

In 2001, when I was walking along the street, a drunk driver drove his car into me. The impact forced me over the bonnet and I experienced a bruised femur. For the next five years I suffered from pains in the lumbar region of my spine. This stopped me from being able to sit straight when either sitting or driving. The pain was always there. In March 2006, at a healing meeting in Christchurch, Weston Carryer prayed for the Lord to heal my back. It was amazing to feel the pain lift off me. For the last nine months I have been pain-free. Thank You, Lord.

—*Emma Campbell*

All my life I have been a fit and healthy woman. On 14 May 2007, I was riding a horse which unfortunately bolted. Standing in the saddle and straining with all my strength on the reins, I finally managed to stop the horse which came to an abrupt halt. This caused me to come down hard on to the saddle and as this happened I experienced horrendous pain in my back. I lost all control, was unable to stay seated in the saddle, and I slid off the horse onto the ground where I found I could not move at all. I was taken by ambulance to hospital where it was discovered that my back was broken in two places. For the next three weeks I could not walk at all. Then I started moving very slowly around with great pain on crutches.

On 10 June 2007, I attended a divine healing meeting in Te Awamutu where Weston Carryer was ministering. During the ministry time he described my condition and asked me to go forward for him to pray for the Lord to heal me. I went forward with great difficulty and in extreme pain. What then happened was absolutely amazing. All the pain just went and the full movement was restored to my body. I could bend, move my body sideways, and walk properly without any pain. It was incredible! Now, three months later, the only pain I get is when I try and lift heavy objects. Apart from that, my back has been wonderfully healed. Thank You, Jesus.

—*Moina Carr*

From the age of seventeen and until I was thirty-two I

Back & Spine

experienced severe back and neck pain. A chiropractor told me that I had the neck bones of an eighty-year old woman. This severe pain was with me nearly all the time and I took painkillers most days. I would also experience severe headaches at least twice a week which would last up to ten days.

Weston Carryer was ministering at a divine healing meeting in Tauranga on 28 October 2007 which I attended. During the meeting he spoke out a word of knowledge regarding my condition and I immediately responded. He prayed for the Lord to heal me. The pain persisted for three days, but I knew that the Lord had healed me and I kept believing and thanking him for my healing.

Suddenly after the three days, the pain left and has never returned to my head, neck, or back. I have been completely pain-free over the last eighteen months. I am healed by the power of Jesus Christ. It is marvelous. Lord, I thank You so much.

—*Annette Yeatman*

Two and a half years ago I slipped and fell, jarring my back. For the next six months I lived with a constant ache. This whole time I was restricted in many ways and there was no improvement in my back at all, in any way. One Sunday morning, late in January 2007, my husband and I drove from Masterton to Paraparaumu where Weston Carryer was having a healing meeting. During the ministry time, Weston prayed for the Lord to heal me, and the Lord gave me my healing immediately. As I left Weston's hands, I was completely pain-free. Over the last two years I have not had any pain or restriction at all. It is wonderful. Lord Jesus, I am so grateful.

—*Ngaire Greger*

Miracles in Aotearoa New Zealand

Sciatica

For eight years, after being in a traffic accident when my sciatic was crushed, I walked with a limp. My foot felt as if a spike had been driven through it and my calf and shin areas felt as if they were tearing apart. Previously, I had enjoyed an active sporting life. Now I could not run. I had two epidurals, wore custom-made braces, yet suffered continual pain. I had no sexual feelings.

When Weston Carryer prayed for me, I was completely healed and restored to the condition I was in prior to the accident eight years ago. My whole life has been transformed through the healing power of Jesus Christ.

—*Reg Trowern*

Several months ago, I went to your healing services at the Christian Renewal Fellowship Church in Whangarei. We had recently arrived from Zimbabwe where we lost our farm to a power hungry dictator, and I was not feeling very "holy," if you know what I mean. My wife and children dragged me to church and, although reluctant at first, I soon started enjoying the fellowship.

In one service I was sitting off towards the side (right near the back of the church) when you turned, looked right at me, and asked if anyone in that area was suffering from sciatic problems. Normally reserved and shy, I stood up and went to the front as I had been in pain for a couple of weeks, especially in the mornings. I also had calcification of my lower spine and had been suffering for some time. You then asked the Holy Spirit to heal me; I was slain in the Spirit and felt healed. For the rest of the day I had no pain at all. Being a real "doubting Thomas" and looking for possible logical, natural reasons as to why I was instantly pain-free, was normal for me; hence the long delay before writing to you.

Back & Spine

However, several months later, I am still free of pain and very definitely much better off than I was. The one time that my sciatic did start to hurt me a bit, I prayed for healing and demanded satan to leave me. I reaffirmed my belief in the power of the Holy Spirit to heal me and keep me healed. Since then I have been almost pain-free. The only conclusion I have is that the Holy Spirit has real power right now, and I am blessed that the Lord touched me. May God bless you and the work you are doing in Jesus' name. Regards, and thanks.

—Garth Richter

I went to the Weston Carryer healing crusade in Whangarei and he prayed for me. I had sciatica problems in my right leg which affected my entire right side. I had been having physiotherapy for six months and was also on anti-inflammatory medication, but was still in pain. That Friday night I believed for my healing. It was a gradual process over a several week period, although I claimed and believed I was healed the instant Weston described my condition. I sprang out of that chair praising God before he even prayed over me. The enemy told me for some time that I was not healed, but I just said, "Thank You, God. My back is totally healed." Hallelujah. I am now totally healed, and for over four months, I have had no pain at all. Thank You, Lord.

—Nicolette Franks

In December 2005, I developed a very painful condition which seriously affected my back and one leg. My doctor diagnosed sciatica. Over the next three months there was no improvement.

In March 2006, I attended a divine healing meeting in the Burwood School Hall, Christchurch, where Weston Carryer was ministering. During the ministry time I went forward and Weston prayed for the Lord to heal me. As Weston prayed, the intense pain disappeared immediately and no pain has ever returned to my back or leg over the past seven months. What

Miracles in Aotearoa New Zealand

awesome relief. Hallelujah. Thank You, Jesus. I know I am healed.

—Myra Hockstra

Five years ago, because of degeneration in a lower vertebra in my back, I developed sciatica. For this entire five-year-period I had excruciating pain from my back right down my right leg and foot every night. The pain was also there every day but not quite as bad. It would keep me awake at night and I felt like hitting my leg with a hammer. I would have to keep getting up regularly through the night to take pain relief, which rarely helped. It was just like having a bad toothache but in the buttock. It was extremely debilitating and it restricted me so much in every thing I wanted to do.

I attended a divine healing meeting in Invercargill on March 18, 2007, and Weston Carryer prayed for the Lord to heal me. What happened as he prayed for me was incredible. Every bit of pain left as he prayed, and I have not had even the slightest sign of pain ever since. This was twelve months ago. I am now not restricted in my movements at all and I simply cannot praise the Lord enough for what He has done. My life is so different. Our God is an awesome healing God and I love Him with all my heart.

—Ngaire Hampstead

For approximately six months, I suffered from severe back pain and sciatica down my left leg. Sitting for any length of time was extremely difficult. One day during a car drive from Dunedin to Christchurch and back, the pain was awful. Medication would temporarily help but the pain always came back—in the back and leg.

In March 2008, at a divine healing meeting in Dunedin, Weston Carryer, who was ministering, spoke out my condition. He described exactly what I had been experiencing, although I did not have the pain at that moment. I went forward and he

Back & Spine

prayed for me. Over the last three years I have not had any more of this back or leg pain. Thank You, Lord Jesus.

—*Fran Dawson*

One day, when I was in my late twenties, I was tossing a bale of hay over a fence and something went in my back. This resulted in very severe sciatica, and for the next six weeks I could hardly move and I had to lie down for the entire time. After the six-week period I was able to start work again but for the next over fifty years I would have regular recurrence of this problem. It would often happen after lifting something, or at times for no apparent reason at all.

In May 2010, at a divine healing meeting in Papamoa, Tauranga, Weston Carryer prayed for the Lord to heal my back which was in pain at the time. As he prayed the pain disappeared completely and over the last seven months, there has been no sign of it whatever.

At eighty-two years of age I am very grateful to the Lord for this marvellous healing that I have received. To be without pain is truly remarkable. Thank You, Jesus.

—*Jack Hartfield*

In May 2005, when Weston Carryer was ministering at the Christian Renewal Fellowship in Whangarei, he called out someone with sciatica in their left leg. It was definitely me! This condition had developed four years previously. It caused varying amount of pain in my back and leg. Sometimes it was very severe and my doctor said nothing could be done for it. Sitting for more than half an hour was impossible. I had to buy a better chair, and when working on the computer, I had to either kneel or stand.

I responded to Weston's invitation, and he then prayed for me and asked me how I felt.

I replied, "I will let you know when the back is healed and the pain is gone." I said this because at that moment the pain was just as bad. The pain persisted for some time but I continued to trust God for my healing. Then one day, the pain went totally and has not come back. I know I am healed. I can sit and even drive to Auckland and back without any problems. It is marvellous. Thank You, Lord.

—*Wayne Garton*

Spine, Vertebrae, Discs, Cerebral Palsy, Scoliosis, Sherman's Disease

For some time I had suffered from both a growth on my spine, and high sugar levels in my blood. Recently my brother visited me and remarked on my back. I told him God was going to heal it, and I prayed in private that He would for I was going to church services the following day at which Weston Carryer was to be the speaker.

I was seated at the rear and questioned God how Weston would see me back there. When Weston asked people to go forward for healing, I started out, and then heard Weston say, "There is somebody present who has a growth on their spine which God wants to remove." Since I had not discussed my condition with anyone there, I knew the Holy Spirit had revealed my need and the call was for me. As Weston prayed, the pressure of the growth on my spine went. At the evening meeting God, through Jesus, also healed me of the blood disorder. I am now doing things I have not done for ten years, and visits to the dietitian are unnecessary. Thank You, Lord, from a grateful heart.

—*Elsie Nicolson*

I was born with cerebral palsy and was half-paralysed down my left side. This condition is called hemiplegia. I had a seizure when I was six, which was when the cerebral palsy was

Back & Spine

diagnosed, although it had been caused by me having a stroke before I was born.

At eight years of age I had a bone graft done. A piece of bone was taken from my hip and inserted in my left foot but this did not help in any way. I walked with a very noticeable limp and would continually trip over because my left leg was very weak and was three-inches shorter than the right one.

I was always in pain and walking for more than five minutes would cause the pain to become excruciating. The pain had continued to worsen, and for the previous 2½ years prior to my miracle, was severe at all times.

I attended a Christian healing meeting at the Flaxmere Christian Fellowship where Weston Carryer was ministering and I went forward for him to pray for the Lord to do a miracle for me. I had determined that I was going to receive from the Lord as I had had enough of the pain and ridicule that I had experienced over the years.

I was standing as Weston prayed for me and as he prayed the pain got worse. He then told me to sit in a seat and I stretched my legs out and everyone could see how short my left leg was. As he then prayed, God lengthened my left leg to the exact same length as the right one.

I stood up and realized that all the pain had gone and my whole body was in correct balance. Since that moment I have never had any further pain of any kind. I can now walk normally and for long distances and my whole body now functions normally. I have had an amazing miracle and I am so grateful to the Lord Jesus Christ for the miracle I have received.

—*Shiloh Eriha*

In 1990, I attended a healing meeting conducted by Weston Carryer. By the grace of God I was to be healed by His healing power through His servant, Weston. In 1975, I fell from a twenty-five foot balcony. The fall seriously damaged vertebrae in my spinal column leaving me in constant pain for the next fifteen years. At first, I lived on prescription painkillers, and then on anything I could lay my hands on—including dope in

MIRACLES IN AOTEAROA NEW ZEALAND

many forms. In 1989, I gave my heart to the Lord Jesus Christ, went off all the drugs, and believed that one day the Lord would heal me completely. Still the pain persisted, that is, until the Lord led me to the meeting where He would perform a miracle healing in my life. I went forward following a word of knowledge given by Weston.

He asked me, "Do you believe the Lord wants to heal your back?"

I said, "I do. . . . Amen." I then felt the healing power of God fall and descend on me, spreading through my body and settling in my lower back. Within minutes, I was completely healed. As the last remnants of pain went from my back, it was as though a mask was being pulled off my mind. Oh, the blessed relief.

At this writing three months later, there has not been the slightest bit of pain whatsoever. I do truly praise the Lord—not just for His healing power, but because He loved me first.

—*Tai Kote*

When I was eleven years old I was diagnosed with Scheuermann's (Sherman's) disease, which drastically affected my lower back. Over the next thirteen years the effect of this steadily got worse. I had a lot of pain, which used to come and go. At times I simply could not get out of bed because it was too painful. I would take very strong painkillers, which sometimes did not help at all. Various doctors told me that there was no cure for Scheuermann's disease and that I would have to learn to live with it.

I attended a divine healing meeting in Tauranga during September 2002, where Weston Carryer was ministering and he received a word of knowledge for me. He said there was someone sitting right in the area where I was who had a long standing problem with their lower back. I responded immediately, and Weston prayed for the Lord to heal me. I felt warmth go right through my body. Since that moment twelve months ago, I have not had any pain whatever and my movements have not been restricted. I am involved in children's ministry, and to be able to bend over is marvelous. I am so grateful to the Lord for what He has done.

—*Kelly Hawthorne*

When I was twelve years old I was diagnosed with Sherman's disease. This is a genetic condition which causes a lack of blood to the tailbone. As a result the muscles around the tailbone became inflamed. This would cause severe pain at times and could completely immobilize me.

Two years ago, at twenty-nine years of age, my friend took me to a divine healing meeting in a Tauranga church where Weston Carryer was ministering. I had not been in a church since I was a small girl and I was not a believer in Jesus Christ. I had been in pain for three or four days at the time. As Weston prayed for me the pain instantly went, and I found I had great difficulty standing. I was touched in an incredible way by the Lord at that moment, and I will never forget it. I knew instantly that God certainly did exist, and that He loved me. Since then, I have had no pain in the tailbone area. After having to be so careful for seventeen years, and even then being immobilized, it is marvellous. Jesus Christ is now my Lord and Saviour. Thank You, Jesus.

—*Angela Leamans*

When I was nine years old I started to have serious back problems. I was always in pain, and my sister used to massage my back to try to give me some relief. At the age of twenty-three I was diagnosed with Sherman's disease, and my doctor told me that by the time I was thirty, I would probably be in a wheelchair. My insurance company cancelled my medical insurance when the Sherman's was diagnosed. I could never ever have a good night's sleep because of the pain and would spend some entire nights on the floor. I would get my children to jump on my back every morning to give me some relief. Two of my uncles, who are both physiotherapists, continually worked on my back.

Miracles in Aotearoa New Zealand

In August 2002, when I was twenty-eight years old, I attended our church in Lower Hutt where Weston Carryer was holding a divine healing meeting. During the meeting Weston had a word of knowledge for me. He described my back condition, and asked the person to go forward for him to pray for the Lord to heal my back. However, I simply did not believe that the Lord would heal me.

My children said, "Mum, you must go forward," and so I did. They all knew that I would be healed and I believe that the Lord honoured their faith. I was totally healed that night.

For the last three years I have not even had a twinge in my back. I feel wonderful and my quality of life is now so different. Jesus, You are awesome. Thank You for really loving me so much.

—*Paula Kohika*

While in my early twenty's I had been diagnosed with Sherman's disease after confirmation by x-rays and tests. Then I was told my activities would be limited, so accordingly, I learned to live with constant pain. There were times during the past thirty years when I was confined to bed rest, had many physio appointments, and suffered continual lower back pain. As the disorder progressed it affected both lumber and also thoracic parts in my spine. The x-rays revealed significant portions of my vertebrae worn; pieces were worn away and the corners worn and rounded out. I was told I had the spine of an eighty year old, with the bone being quite chalky. At times the pain went down my legs as well. There is no medical cure for Sherman's disease. It can pass through generations via the male line. In my case my Dad had this, I had it, and my son at eleven years old also has it.

I did not expect that God would heal me as I had received prayer many other times but had experienced no change or healing. However, Sunday, 9 April 2006, was different—very different. I attended Weston Carryer's healing meeting in Christchurch. With Weston's first word of knowledge, he requested a person to respond if they specifically had the

Back & Spine

symptoms as described above. I knew immediately it was for me and I went straight forward for prayer. As Weston prayed I was very aware of God's closeness to me. All pain in my back diminished within seconds. Weston asked me to bend down and touch my toes. For the first time in many, many years I was able to do so with absolutely no pain!

The freedom of movement and ability to function normally is a significant quality of life improvement for me. Now eight months later, apart from when I bend for long periods or lift heavy loads and experience temporary stiffness, I do not have any pain or restriction at all. What an amazing difference after so many years of continual pain. Lord Jesus, thank You so much.

—*Mike Gilligan*

I had been having bad pain for several months and had trouble sleeping because of that, as well as the added need to climb in and out of our van. Driving was not feasible due to the fact that I could not sit in the same position for more than a minute or two. It was quite frightening to me that I intended to go on a three-month holiday around the South Island which would require a lot of sitting. The physiotherapist told me that bad posture, and a succession of pregnancies, had caused two vertebrae in my back to squash together destroying the disc between them. I had an actual and obvious dent in my back.

At a healing meeting conducted in Whakatane by Weston Carryer, I responded to a call made for someone with a disintegrated disc between the fourth and fifth vertebrae to go forward. The Lord showered me with His power even after I went back to my seat. He restored my back completely, much to the astonishment of my physiotherapist. She could not understand how her treatment could work so well for it was like looking at a completely different back. I told her of my divine healing. Praise the Lord for His almighty love towards us.

—*Carrol Hammond*

Miracles in Aotearoa New Zealand

In March 1992, I went to a meeting where Weston Carryer was ministering. I was born with curvature of the spine. I am now twenty-six years of age and have had to bear a great deal of pain. I decided to go forward for prayer, and was instantly healed. As I was slain in the Spirit, I felt a sensation as if my stomach was being pulled or sucked towards my back. I then stood up and was able to touch my toes for the first time. I praise God for His enabling and Jesus, for His healing.

—*Sue Berge*

I received my first healing at a Weston Carryer healing crusade. He prayed that my spine would be healed, and God healed my spine. I became a new person without the back pain. The doctor had told me I would have to live with it as it was an extra congenital bone causing the pain. Now thanks to a caring God, I have no pain and therefore no need for the strong pain relief I was given. Please, I would like more prayer for my sons, Stephen and Tony. Tony has a stress fracture, and Stephen vertebrae problems. These cause my dear boys a lot of pain. Secondly, at the same meeting, God once again healed me of a very nasty rash on my arms and legs. The skin specialist had told me it was lichen planus, and it would keep recurring. Praise the Lord, it has never returned!

—*Shirley Button*

As a result of being assaulted twenty-four years ago, the vertebrae in my spine were badly damaged in several places. This caused continual, horrific pain in my back, shoulder blades, as well as severe migraine headaches. After x-rays the specialist recommended a spinal fusion, but he said there was only a two-percent chance of it being successful and so I declined the operation. I tried many other forms of treatment but was not helped at all.

Two years ago, I attended a Women's Aglow healing meeting

at Mt. Maunganui where Weston Carryer was ministering. I went forward in intense pain to be prayed for. As I was prayed for the pain went for the first time in twenty-two years. Since that time I have had no pain or any migraine headaches at all. The mobility has fully returned and I am not restricted in any way. Praise the Lord! Thank You, Jesus.

—*Mary Tregelgas*

In 1994, I was lifting a large container filled with ceramic wall tiles which caused me to get a sharp pain in my back. I spent the next year in constant pain not able to sit in a chair for any length of time and lying on the floor with a pillow under my back so as to ease the pain. I was living on painkillers twenty-four hours a day. After all sorts of tests and treatments, I finally had a body scan by a machine and was told that I had a prolapsed disc that was pressing on a nerve in my spine and that only a risky operation would ease the pain.

I came to New Zealand in 1995, and in less than a year came to know the Lord Jesus Christ. One evening whilst attending church, I came forward with my back problem to receive healing prayer from Weston Carryer. During the healing prayer I could feel my back heating up, and within seconds the pain had completely gone and has not returned since. I know that through Weston, Jesus Christ has performed a miracle on my back.

—*Roger Vankuylenburg*

For over three years, I had suffered terrible pain continually and took painkillers all the time to try and get some relief. This was because I had two slipped discs and a cracked vertebra in my back. In February 1998, I attended a divine healing meeting in Gore where Weston Carryer was ministering and I went forward for Weston to pray for the Lord to heal me. As he prayed I experienced the power of God go into my back. All the pain went and my back was restored to normal. Since that time one year ago I have had no more pain and am living a normal life once again. Thank You, Jesus.

—*Joy Matheson*

For a long time I had two degenerate discs in the lower part of my back which caused extreme pain nearly all the time. Walking was very difficult and painful and the doctor had told me that I would need an operation to have the degenerate discs replaced.

At a healing meeting in Tauranga, Weston Carryer, who was ministering, was praying for Jesus to heal the sick. God revealed my condition to him and he spoke out and asked the person who had the condition to come forward to receive healing. I immediately went forward, and as I was prayed for, the power of the Lord went into my back. The relief was instant and full use was restored to my back. X-rays taken since have confirmed that the Lord has fully restored the discs. What a joy, after all these years to be able to do aerobics, line dancing, and run with no pain or restriction.

—*Piki O'Brien*

As a result of a car accident in 1979, two discs were put out of place in my back. They used to grind together which caused pain off and on for eighteen years. At times I could not stand after a day's work. For twenty years I had also suffered from bronchial asthma with some very bad attacks early in 1998. In November 1998, Weston Carryer was ministering in our church. After preaching he asked people to come forward for the Lord to heal them. Through the power of Jesus Christ that morning, I was completely healed of both conditions. I can now do hard physical work all day with no pain or restriction and I breathe normally at all times. Praise the Lord.

—*John Jones*

Twenty-three years ago I was born with a vertebra missing

Back & Spine

in my back and my left leg was one inch short. This condition caused me to experience severe pain most of the time and I would have to have approximately three months off school every year because of this back condition. At one stage I was unable to play any sport at all for a whole year. I went to a number of specialists but was unable to receive any help. However, my parents took me to a divine healing meeting where Weston Carryer was ministering. As Weston prayed for me, Jesus did a miracle in my body. I saw and felt my leg grow to the correct length and my back was instantly healed. Since that moment some years ago I have had no further back or leg problems. What a God we serve!

—*Sharon Collins*

For approximately five years I suffered extreme pain from a slipped permeated disc in my back. At times, throughout this period, I would go to the chiropractor everyday for two weeks at a time but never received any lasting help. I was also having regular cortisone injections to get some relief which also did not last.

I attended a divine healing meeting in Stratford in mid-1999 where Weston Carryer was ministering. During the meeting the Lord revealed my condition to Weston and he spoke and asked me to come forward for the Lord to do a miracle. That night I was totally healed. I am now rejoicing that since that night I have had no pain or restriction, or medical or chiropractor help of any kind. Thank You, Jesus.

—*Hillary Kieft, Stratford*

I am writing to share my testimony of how God healed my back in three stages. Several years ago I fell from a galloping racehorse and landed on my head. The result of this accident caused the discs in my back to "squeeze" and resulted in many problem areas, from the lumbar region up to my neck.

1) In May 1995 (Mother's Day), I attended a Weston Carryer meeting in Levin. By word of knowledge given to Weston by the

Miracles in Aotearoa New Zealand

Lord, I went up to receive healing in my lumbar back area. When I got up off the floor the pain had gone. On Monday morning, I skipped into the physio office and the startled physio exclaimed, "Well, you don't look like anyone with a bad back!"

"My back is healed", I shared, "I want a clearance to go back to work."

"Are you sure?" she replied. "On Friday, you could hardly walk."

"Oh yes, I know, the Lord has healed me," I replied excitedly. I continued to work but had problems in the thoracic area of my back (between my shoulder blades). This area caused pain in my left shoulder that radiated right down my arm and into my hands. I prayed and asked God to heal that area, as He had healed my lower back. I knew God was telling me that my healing was complete, so I held on to that, trusting Him.

2) On 16 June 1996, I again attended a Weston Carryer meeting in Levin, and by the grace of God, received healing in my upper back. The relief! Oh, the joy! The pain and discomfort went instantly.

3) On 23 June 1996, Weston came to my home church in Foxton, where my ever-faithful God completed His promise and my neck was healed. The first thing I noticed when I got up off the floor was that my neck felt so strong. I knew I was healed. A doctor looking at my neck x-rays (without knowledge of my accident) once said, "You look as though you have been dropped on your head."

I then told him, "That is indeed what happened." I suffered from headaches that would sometimes last for two days and would not respond to painkillers.

My God came through a fourth time for me on 25 June 1996 at my home church in Foxton, once again, at a Weston Carryer meeting. I received healing for a pinched nerve between my toes. I had had three painful cortisone injections and an orthopaedic surgeon said that surgery would be necessary. Well, Jesus, the Mighty Surgeon, had His way! The tingling sensation has gone today. I feel truly blessed and I know now my healing is complete. Praise God!

Back & Spine

This is to encourage people to never give in and never let go of the faith He has placed in your heart. His wisdom is divine and His grace is sufficient for you. Amen and amen!

—*Jenny Boyd, Foxton*

While playing basketball at the age of seventeen, I fractured my L3 lumbar spine and it never healed. I also dislocated both hips and both shoulders. Medical examinations also showed that my spine was crooked, and my right leg was one and a half inches shorter than the left one. For seven years I was in constant pain.

In November 1998, I attended a church service at Te Puke where Weston Carryer was ministering and praying for the Lord to heal the sick. I had difficulty believing the healings that I saw taking place and I had never seen people falling over under the power of God. To me it was very scary, and I did not know Jesus as my Lord. I finally went forward. Weston asked me to sit down and lifted my legs. Because of the pain I could not straighten my right leg and so it was bent. As Weston prayed, God's power hit my body. My leg straightened, the pain went, and then I saw, and felt it grow out to be exactly the same length as the other one. My back, shoulders and hips were also miraculously touched by the Lord and I was completely healed of all conditions. All the pain and restriction instantly went, and five months later I am healthy and whole. I had no hesitation in believing that Jesus Christ is alive and that He loved me, and I accepted Him as my Lord and Saviour. Thank You, Jesus.

—*Murray Mahauariki, Te Puke*

About 1988, osteoporosis developed in my spine which caused serious problems, and in 1993, I had major surgery for this condition. However, despite the surgery, there was no improvement and I continued to experience a lot of pain and was severely limited in my movements.

When Weston Carryer was ministering in our church in

Miracles in Aotearoa New Zealand

Hamilton in 1996, the Lord revealed to him, through a word of knowledge, my exact condition and the symptoms I had. I responded to his invitation to be prayed for and for the Lord to heal me. As I was prayed for, I believed in faith that I would be totally healed by Jesus, and that is exactly what happened. Since that time two years ago, I have had no pain whatsoever or restriction. A scan six months after the prayer showed that God had performed a miracle because the bone density had been restored to normal. Thank You, Jesus.

—Muriel Finlay, Hamilton

For six years, I suffered from spinal trouble after being knocked down twice from my bicycle. For three of the last six years, I lived on painkillers; for the other three, I was treated through acupuncture. I was finding by this time I could not cope much longer with this severe pain.

Two years ago I was invited to go to a meeting where the speaker was to be Weston Carryer. I went along not knowing what to expect. When he asked if anyone wanted healing, I guess I was one of the first to go forward. Weston prayed over me, and for a little while that day, the pain eased up. Getting up the next morning, I found that pain in my spine was completely gone and it has never returned. I praise the Lord every day for all the healings and blessings He has given me in my life.

—Barbara

I went to a meeting at Fielding conducted by Weston Carryer with the intention that if a word of knowledge was spoken concerning my husband's back pain, I would "stand in" for him. About seventeen years ago, Peter had a fall and crushed the lower five vertebrae in his spine. Since bone was moving constantly over bone, this had resulted in considerable pain. Added to this, arthritis had settled in both hip joints over the last seven years and progressed down each thigh.

In the course of the meeting, Weston said that a person seated in the area where I was had arthritis in the left leg. I did

Back & Spine

not recognise the word as applying to Peter as my mind was attuned to the lower back. After a short delay, during which no one answered, Weston approached me and said the word was for me. I stood in for my husband and, praise His name, Peter was healed at home simultaneously. Many months have passed and God's healing remains perfect.

—Colleen Marsden

During Weston Carryer's visit to Fielding in 1999, I was called out by a word of knowledge concerning my back. Around fifteen years before this, I had been a truck driver and my contracts include moving forty-four gallon drums of oils and agricultural chemicals. Handling these damaged my spine in the area of the small of my back. The discs used to stick together and this caused a lot of pain and discomfort. If I remained in one position too long that area of my back would lose its flexibility, and getting it moving again was a painful process. I have a relatively high pain threshold and I could put up with the pain and discomfort, but invariably ended up going to an osteopath to have my back manipulated to free the joints up. The problem used to return within two weeks and the cycle would continue. It did not stop me from doing anything; it just hurt most of the time.

Someone else responded to Weston's word of knowledge at the same time I did and I must confess I thought, *Oh dear, it's not for me.* However after talking to me, Weston said it was me, and he prayed for my back. The only way I can describe the results is to say that from that moment onwards, I have not felt back pain at all. No pain, no discomfort. Nothing. Hallelujah! God is good.

—Peter Mercer

I suffered chronic sciatica for fourteen years as a result of a car accident, plus I had two degenerate discs in my back. I was in pain constantly, both in my back and down my left leg, and was very restricted in my movements. I attended a divine

Miracles in Aotearoa New Zealand

healing meeting at Papamoa in December 1997, where Weston Carryer was ministering. Early in the meeting, he described my exact condition and said that the Lord was going to heal that person. Having never been to a Christian healing meeting before, I was astounded. I had no idea that God was reaching out to me in such a miraculous way and did not know what to do. I finally responded, went forward, and Weston prayed for me. I had an incredible experience. All the pain went and the full use was restored to my body. I am still so thrilled at what God has done, and some months later, I have no pain or restriction. Thank You, Jesus.

—*Titihuia Pirirua*

One day, in 1996, I was shoveling metal and I suddenly experienced a terrible pain in my back and right down both legs. I was unable to move at all and was put straight into hospital where I was treated with morphine for three weeks. It was then discovered that a prolapsed disc was causing my sciatic nerve to be crushed, and I was operated on.

I was told that it was doubtful if I would ever walk again. However, I did manage to walk with the aid of a crutch, and for the next five years, I used the crutch all the time as I could not move without it. I was in constant pain despite taking up to six painkillers every day and also needing sleeping tablets to be able to have some sleep at night.

All this changed miraculously in September 2001 when I attended a Christian healing meeting in Levin where Weston Carryer was ministering. As Weston prayed for me, all the pain disappeared and I felt amazing warmth from my head to my toes. I fell to the floor under the power of the Holy Spirit, and then immediately I realized that the strength had returned to my back and legs. I got up, threw my crutch away, and jogged around the church with no pain. Ever since that night, over a year ago now, I have been able to walk, sit down, and ride a bike with absolutely no restriction. Lord Jesus, You are a miracle worker and I bless and praise You.

—*Neil Shotter (2002)*

Back & Spine

I suffered from back problems most of my adult life as I got older. They became more frequent and would sometimes put me out of action for a week or more. When I accepted Jesus into my life and found out that He had procured our healing on the cross, I would stand on the Word for my healing. It has never failed me.

About seven years ago, I slipped down some stairs in the ice. I landed very heavily and knew I had damaged my back. I managed to crawl inside and then began the long process of me "standing" on the Word and receiving partial healing (enough to get around). But every morning as I tried to get out of bed, the pain was becoming worse until I couldn't work. I was sent to a chiropractor who then sent me for x-rays because of the seriousness of the injury. The x-rays showed I had a definite kink in my spine. The chiropractor thought he may be able to fix it but it would take a long time. I went home in more pain than ever. All the while I was crying out to God to heal me. I honestly couldn't understand why I wasn't being healed.

One Sunday Weston Carryer was speaking at a local church. I went along after some prompting by family members. I didn't think I would be able to sit long enough because I was in such pain, so I went along under protest. After Weston had finished speaking he said, "There is someone here with a kink in their spine."

I don't know how but I moved so fast calling out, "Yes, yes, that's mine."

Weston said, "God just told me He is going to heal you."

Well, I had no trouble believing that. That night I was healed and have had no problems since. Praise God!

—*Gail Lester*

I was born with a back problem that caused degeneration in my spine. Because of this two discs in the spine became badly worn, and by the time I reached the age of twenty-eight, my back was sore all the time. This condition was revealed when

Miracles in Aotearoa New Zealand

I lifted a board sheet at work and collapsed under the sudden pain. An x-ray showed that apart from the degeneration, the spine was approximately 5-mls out of alignment. One day, five years later, as I leaned forward to turn the radio off, I experienced horrendous pain. I was taken to hospital the next day, and the medical authorities decided that I should have a spinal fusion. As well as other problems, the ligaments had been stretched and the pain was causing malfunctions in other areas including my bladder. However, I never did have the operation, and following my discharge from hospital, I was on a sickness benefit for three years. I could not stand on my feet at all without severe pain. All through this entire eight-year period I tried to work, but discovered it was impossible. I could not hold a regular job during the entire time. I came to accept the fact that I would be in pain for the rest of my life.

However, all this changed dramatically in November 2001 when I attended a divine healing meeting in Mangaweka where Weston Carryer was ministering. The week before the meeting I went for a walk and asked the Lord to reveal to Weston, very specifically, what was wrong with my back. As Weston started ministering, he said that the Lord was revealing specific conditions that He, the Lord, wanted to heal. Then, Weston began, first of all, to speak out exactly what was wrong with me. I then realized that the Lord cared about my disability and me personally, and that Weston was really hearing from the Lord. This meant so much to me that God would really answer my prayers like this.

As Weston prayed, the Lord did a miracle. The pain went totally and has never returned. Over the past twelve months I have been able to work doing heavy work in regular employment. I am not restricted. I can play with my children and I live a normal life. I am so grateful to Jesus for what He has done.

—*Darren Playford*

In 1989 (approximately), Weston Carryer visited my local church, The Wave in Opunake, Taranaki. I suffered, at that time, from an injury I received whilst maintaining a front-end loader in 1972. I had suffered from what were crushed vertebrae in my lower back. I was told after numerous examinations and physical checkups that it was not operable and that I would suffer for the rest of my life with continuous back pain.

I was sitting in the back row of the church with my granddaughter on my knee. That particular morning I remember I had severe back pain and I remember the Holy Spirit prompting me to attend. I did not know that Weston Carryer was visiting. When he came out, I think he prayed first, and then he said, "There is someone here who has five damaged vertebrae, and that person has the pain down the right side at that moment. God is going to heal them!"

To begin with, I didn't think he meant me, and then almost immediately my right side sciatic nerve pinched and I wasted no more time getting to the front. As I approached him, Weston lifted his hand and took authority over the spirit of infirmity at which time I felt the Lord's presence come over me, and I partially collapsed. The pain was reduced to a dull ache immediately and stayed for a week or so before going completely. I knew that I had been totally healed. Praise God!

I have shifted from Taranaki to Katikati, and have worked here ever since. I have no back pain at all and I carry out all sorts of heavy work including chainsaw work, which has not been detrimental to my healing in any way. I praise and thank Jesus for my healing. I praise and thank God for ministries like Weston Carryer's. May God bless you and keep you in His eternal peace. Yours sincerely in Christ.

—Ray Sarsfield

In January 1995, I suddenly experienced considerable pain in my back and was unable to move at all, and was then flat on my back for two months. Up to this point I had been healthy all my life, and very active in my job as a beekeeper. It was discovered that I had two prolapses in one disc in the back. I was off work for a further eight months and then had an operation. But for the next seven years, I still had major problems as the swelling continued to squeeze the sciatic nerve and cause continual back and leg pain. I found I could not operate the tractor, as sitting on a moving tractor seat was just too painful.

In June 2002, I walked into our church one Sunday morning as Weston Carryer was starting to minister. I suddenly knew that he was going to call out my condition first but I did not want to respond in the mind state I was in. Weston described my exact condition. I hesitated. He then repeated it. God then spoke to me at that moment and said, "If you do not obey you will not receive a blessing." I then went to the front with pain in my back. Weston prayed and touched me very lightly. I felt intense pins and needles go through my entire body. I could not stand and dropped to the floor immediately. My heart raced incredibly and I felt like I was going to die. I had never felt anything like this before. After awhile, I experienced the wonderful peace of God and was really touched in an incredible way by the Lord.

I got off the floor after some time, drunk in the Spirit. I don't know how I managed to drive home and my son said he had never before seen me park like I did that day. From the moment I got off the floor, over a year ago now, my back has been marvelous. I can drive the tractor and do all my normal activities. As well as my physical healing, I had a real refreshing in the Spirit and for a long time I walked on cloud nine. Jesus, thank You so much.

—*Neil Mossop*

About twelve years ago, I was involved in an accident receiving a serious back injury that prevented me from working for several years. During this time I was on a sickness and invalid's benefit. Through this entire period I was in constant pain, continually taking panadol or nurofen. Two and a half years ago, while trying to lift an object, I damaged my back again. This time sciatica developed; the pain went right down my right leg. An MRI scan showed two degenerate discs. The specialist recommended an operation. However, because of a previous bad experience concerning anaesthetic I was too concerned to have this operation. I was then on ACC for a further two years. I had also suffered from a very sore tailbone

Back & Spine

since I was a teenager when I fell hard on my lower back on concrete while skating. I could never sit still for more than about ten minutes because of the pain and discomfort.

I went to a healing meeting in November 2003 where Weston Carryer was ministering. During the early part of the meeting he pointed in my direction, saying there was someone (where I was) who had damaged their tailbone. He described the symptoms that I was suffering. I knew it was me and went forward for the Lord to heal me. It was astounding. All the pain immediately went from my leg, tailbone, and back. Some of the pain returned but at a further meeting Weston prayed for me again. Since then I have had no further pain whatever. I am now not restricted and I live a normal life. Jesus, I want to thank You.

—*Shannon Payne*

In 1961, when I was living in the Philippines, I had a fall and slipped a disc in my back. This caused severe pain in my back nearly all the time for the next forty-three years. The sciatic nerve became pinched, causing the pain to go down my legs. Over the years I developed arthritis in my back as well. On 13 June 2004, I attended a divine healing meeting at West City Christian Centre, Auckland, where Weston Carryer was ministering. I was in pain, like I almost always was.

As Weston started to pray for me I was slain in the Spirit. I woke up a short while later and when I got up, I realized that I did not have any pain. I was so excited. Since then I have not had any pain and I can move freely. Jesus, I thank You so much.

—*Rafina Valdez*

Two weeks before Weston attended our church, I fractured my seventh thoracic vertebra in my back during a rugby game. I had been sleeping in the Lazy-Boy chair to enable me to sit up. I was on methadone and in a lot of pain. The church elders came and prayed for me. I then came off methadone but still needed codeine and panadol and was very locked up.

I attended the Weston Carryer healing meeting at our church, believing for a miracle. My condition was not called out when Weston had words of knowledge but at the end of the meeting, I went forward for prayer. I was not healed straightaway, but the next day, I woke up and felt great. Doctors had told me I would be ninety-five percent better after three months, but God had healed me after two weeks. Thank You, Lord!

—*Radley Hungerford*

In April 2004, while working as a nurse, I fell when trying to hold a patient and badly injured my back. I went to physiotherapy, but this one treatment made my back a lot worse. By Mother's Day in May, it had become so painful that I could not sit at all. I had to lie down in a truck and be driven everywhere. I went to my doctor who immediately referred me to a specialist. An MRI scan was taken which showed that two discs were ruptured and pushed right out of alignment. The sciatic nerve was also badly damaged and this was causing severe pain down my right leg to my foot. From the knee down, apart from the extreme pain, there was no feeling at all. To move around I had to use a walking stick as I simply could not hold my body up. The specialist said I would need to have surgery, but I did not want this. As a nurse I was aware of what the outcome could be.

For the next nine months there was no improvement whatever. In February 2005 a Christian friend drove me in a truck (as I still could not sit up) to a healing meeting in Rangiora where Weston Carryer was ministering. As he was ministering, he said there was a person there with a serious back problem. Weston looked at me and said it was me. As he prayed for me, the pain went completely, and now over one year later, has never returned. I had lived on painkillers for the previous nine months but have not had any medication since. The medication had upset my stomach; that was healed at the same time. This amazing personal healing encounter with the Lord changed my life and I really have found the Lord in a much greater way. After being a stale Christian for twenty-five years I now have

Back & Spine

a real passion for Jesus who is so incredibly real to me. Lord, thank You so much.

—Lin Mason

Over two years ago, I chipped the lower third and fourth discs in my spine which caused excruciating pain. I had an operation which relieved the pain considerably but left me with pins and needles and numbness. Any walking at all was almost impossible and I could not go up and down stairs without holding onto something for support. There was no improvement at all over this almost two-year period.

I attended a divine healing meeting at North Shore in June 2006 where Weston Carryer was ministering. Through a word of knowledge he spoke and said the Lord had revealed to him that there was someone present who had injured numbers three and four discs and for that person to come forward to be prayed for.

I responded immediately and as Weston prayed for me, the Lord's power hit me and I was instantly, miraculously, and totally healed. After experiencing this chronic restriction I can now walk and climb normally, run if necessary (which I certainly could not do before), and I can even wear high heels! Lord, I am so grateful.

—Gay Torbett

One day, in early 2004, I suddenly experienced excruciating pain in my back and found I could not stand upright at all. Any movement became agony and so I was confined to bed. My daughter did everything for me. She would bring my breakfast into me before school and cook my dinner at night. I had to crawl to go to the toilet. The doctors discovered that my spine was degenerating rapidly and turning to chalk. They told me that my whole spine would need to be replaced by putting pieces of tube in one at a time.

One morning, in October 2004, I was lying at home waiting for my first operation when I had this strong urge to go to my church in Tokoroa. I had no idea why or who would be there. With great difficulty I managed to get there and discovered that Weston Carryer was having a healing meeting there. Weston started ministering and through a word of knowledge said that there was someone there with major degeneration in their back and asked for that person to come forward for him to pray for the Lord to heal this condition. By this time I could not get out of my seat so Weston came down the aisle and prayed for me. The pain immediately increased and went into my legs as well. I came back again for the night meeting, had further prayer from Weston, and went home to bed in absolute agony.

The next morning I found I could move my toes which I had not been able to do before. Then, very slowly, I started to get out of bed and realized that I had absolutely no pain at all of any kind anywhere. It was unbelievable! From that time, two years ago, I have not had any pain and I am not restricted in any way. I stand upright and I can run freely. I have received an amazing miracle. Thank You so much, Lord Jesus. I am so blessed.

—*Ann Wawatai*

I thank God for the word of knowledge He gave you at the healing meeting in Masterton about my back condition. When you said that someone was suffering in the thoracic area as a result of an injury, I knew that it was me. Six years ago I fractured a vertebra in the thoracic area of my back and this had left me with permanent chronic stiffness in my back, preventing me from standing properly. When you prayed for me I received an instant complete healing. I felt the Lord gently touch the exact area and was released from all pain and stiffness; I stood up straight for the first time in six years. What an amazing difference this has made! Thank You, Jesus, and thank you, Weston, for your obedience and love.

—*Sanchia Hooker*

I'm so thankful for Weston Carryer's visit to Caloundra Baptist Church, Australia. I had been in shocking pain in my

Back & Spine

lower back for six weeks before his visit. We thank the Lord that he prayed for me and we give thanks to God that He touched my spine. I haven't experienced any more pain. Yours in our Lord,

—*Anne McNaughton*

As a result of serious degeneration in my back I had a fusion done: my L3, L4 and L5 discs were welded together. This took place in South Africa in 1971. My back then did not give much problem apart from one time when I had to have an infiltration done. This is when a local anaesthetic was given in my back followed by an injection right into my spine to ease the pain.

However, in June 2007, I had a very bad fall, landing on my back. As a result I suffered excruciating pain. On 2 July, I had another infiltration done, but this made my back worse. My wife and I had booked to fly to New Zealand on 9 July and we carried on with our plans. I left for the airport on crutches but found that I could not even walk with them because of the pain and so I had to be put in a wheelchair. We arrived in New Zealand on 10 July and for the next forty days I was unable to walk and continued to suffer excruciating pain with no improvement whatever.

I attended a divine healing meeting in Tauranga on 19 August where Weston Carryer was ministering. By supporting myself on the back of chairs I managed to very slowly get to the front for Weston to pray for me. What then happened was astounding. I felt warmth go right through my body and all the pain went. I immediately got up and walked with no restriction or pain. I have been able to walk normally ever since, and sleep on my back and both sides. Lord, I thank You so much.

—*Martinus Swart*

One day, in 1986, when working on a building site, I was carrying two bags of cement on my back and someone challenged me to carry a third one as well. I did this but fell on some uneven ground and injured my back. This caused pain on and off. Then, one day in 1989, I seriously injured it again while lifting weights. As a result I was unable to work and was

Miracles in Aotearoa New Zealand

on ACC for four years. The x-rays taken revealed that there was continuing degeneration and the bottom of my spine was tapering off. The doctor said I had the spine of a fifty year old, although I was only thirty. He also said that when I reached fifty my spine would be like that of an eighty year old. In 1993, I was able to go back to work again but was always in pain. Many times the pain was excruciating and I could only lie down. Even bending over slightly could cause my back to go out.

In 2003, I was taken by my brother to a Christian healing meeting at The Centre Church in Paraparaumu where Weston Carryer was ministering. I was not a Christian, although I believed that God probably did exist. I was sitting in the meeting in severe pain when Weston looked in my direction and said there was someone sitting in the area where I was with a long-standing back problem. He said for the person to go forward to be prayed for. I refused to budge and he then came over to where I was and said the person was right in front of where he was standing. After a firm nudge from my brother, I finally went forward and Weston prayed for me.

I experienced a warm tingling sensation and when I sat down all the pain was gone. At that moment I realized that God is so real. I went back weightlifting that afternoon. One year later, I accepted Jesus as my Lord and Saviour and have followed Him ever since. Over the last five years I have done a lot of heavy physical work and weightlifting with no problems. Wonderful! Thank You, Lord.

—*Matt Brown*

Over the years, I have had several accidents to my back including having a stack of timber fall on me. Then seventeen years ago I fell twenty feet from a tree, badly injuring my back. I had to be hospitalized for six weeks. It was discovered that I had a crushed vertebra and also osteoarthritis. I was told I could end up in a wheelchair. Following my discharge from hospital I was off work completely for eighteen months and then was on light work for a further six months. I then went back to normal work. But for the next seventeen years, I always had back pain. I was restricted in my movements and I could never

Back & Spine

lie flat on my back as this was just too painful. Also, because of the condition of my back my head could not touch the surface I would be trying to lie on. As well as the back pain, I had sciatic pain going right down both legs and my knees were also badly affected and always in pain. I had no power in my legs and could not change gears in a car. I received an electric shock at work which caused a heart attack, and as a consequence, I could have very little pain relief. I did not know what to do.

I attended a divine healing meeting at Papamoa in August 2007 where Weston Carryer was ministering. He spoke out my condition including a number of details which could only have applied to me. I responded and he prayed for the Lord to heal me. I immediately fell to the floor under the power of God and it felt like I was lying in a bowl of rice bubbles. For some time I could hear and feel a snap, crackle, and popping as my bones were being realigned in my body. It was amazing!

When I finally got off the floor, Weston asked me to run, and for the first time in seventeen years, I did run. Since that moment of being prayed for twelve months ago, I have had no pain or restriction in my back or legs. My strength is fully restored. To function without pain, after experiencing it for seventeen years, is marvellous. Thank You, Lord Jesus.

—*Steve Gilligan*

I'm so thankful for Weston Carryer's visit to Whangarei and for him praying for me.

On 9 September 2007, I turned over wrongly and popped a muscle out of the sacral vertebra. I thought I would be okay but suffered much pain for six weeks before going to the doctor. I was sent to the physiotherapist and he said a muscle popped out and manipulated it accordingly. After three more weeks, and the gnawing back pain not getting any better, I went back to my doctor. A general health check was ordered along with x-rays. Everything was normal, except for a thirty-year-old sacral back injury that was now an "advanced degeneration of the sacral vertebrae." The x-ray revealed that the bottom sacral vertebra was crushed to half the size. That was shown to me on the Friday.

Miracles in Aotearoa New Zealand

On Sunday evening at the healing meeting, Weston called out, by a word of knowledge, exactly those symptoms. I went forward for prayer and the Lord healed my back. I had no more pain and much improved movement. Over a year later I have no more pain or restriction of any kind. Thank You, Jesus. You are the best. All glory and honour to Your wonderful name indeed.

—*Margaret Berridge*

For as long as I can remember I always had back pain. This pain continued to get worse as I got older and was restricting me more and more. I loved to dance but the pain would always stop me after a while and I was never able to become involved in any sporting activities. Pain relief medication never helped at all, so I didn't use any.

At 15 years of age, my back was x-rayed and it was discovered that I had been born with a vertebra out of place and this had caused further misalignment in my back.

In May 2009, I attended a healing meeting in Wanganui where Weston Carryer was ministering. Right at the start of the meeting he said there was someone sitting where I was who had a vertebra out of place who the Lord wanted him to pray for immediately. I went forward, and as he prayed, the pain disappeared. It was incredible.

For the next 4 months I was completely pain-free. But then the pain returned. Weston prayed for me over the phone, and after a very short period, I was again pain-free and have stayed that way ever since. What a wonderful difference in my life.

—*Lucrezia Fodie*

Sunday, 11 September 2011, I was healed from lower back pain. In 1959, I was nursing and caught an elderly person from falling out of bed. I had bad back pain including many periods of intense pain, and a lot of the time being unable to sleep because of the severity of the pain. Even at the best of times, I was always aware of pain. About thirty years ago, I was sent to

Back & Spine

a surgeon who, after x-rays, said I needed the lower vertebrae fused. For me this was not a good idea. I was told I would one day come back in a wheelchair asking for this operation.

However, God has been faithful. The previous night to being healed was an especially bad night and I was awake quite a bit with pain. I felt the Lord was saying, "Every time the pain starts, praise Me," so I had a good night praising the Lord.

As I write this, it is the 23 September. Have had a busy week since healing: four rounds of golf, mowed the lawns, and extra good time doing household chores. Praise You, Lord Jesus, for my healing, and for Your obedient servant, Weston and his wife, willing to listen and serve.

I had no intention of seeking healing until Weston described my condition.

It is now eight months since my healing. I have not had the slightest bit of pain or discomfort and I am rejoicing that after over fifty years of suffering, I now have this completely pain-free back. Thank You so much, Lord.

—*Bunty Cotton*

In 1980, as a result of an accident, a disc prolapsed in my back. Then in the early 1990s, I had another accident which resulted in another prolapsed disc in a different place in my back.

This made it difficult for me to work as a landscape gardener as I was constantly in pain. On many occasions I could not work at all, and sometimes simply could not move. At one stage I was off work for ten months. Medical advice was that I should have operations but I was reluctant to proceed with them. So for thirty-one years I suffered immensely with this very painful condition.

All this changed dramatically on Sunday, 6 November 2011 when I was in my church, Victory Christian Centre in Lower Hutt. Weston Carryer was conducting one of a series of divine healing meetings and he said that the Lord would heal some people as they sat in their seats. At that moment I had

Miracles in Aotearoa New Zealand

a wonderful encounter with the Holy Spirit. I became engulfed with this amazing sensation of love and power and the intense pain that I was experiencing just completely disappeared.

It was a wonderful experience for me and made me realize the incredible love that the Lord has for us. Since that moment seven months ago, I have not had any back pain or discomfort despite my work as a landscape gardener.

Thank You, Lord Jesus.

—*Robin Maskell*

On 7 September 2007, when I was 70 years of age, I was taken to Christchurch public hospital by ambulance and operated on for a spinal abscess. I spent five weeks there before being transferred to the Burwood spinal unit and was eventually discharged on February 5, 2008. They thought I would never ever stand or walk again and would finish up bedridden or in a wheelchair. Owing to God's grace and mercy I learned to stand and walk again in a very restricted way.

In April 2008, Weston Carryer conducted some gospel and healing meetings at the local New Life Fellowship. I struggled along to one of his meetings where he prayed for me. At that stage, I was really struggling with areas in my body. Apart from the immense difficulty in walking, I was completely incontinent in both bladder and bowel and had to have a bladder catheter.

After I was prayed for, there was a major rapid improvement, and just over two months later, I was able to stop using the catheter. This was huge. What an amazing relief. Also my walking ability was restored, and for the last four years, I have been able to walk reasonably normally without aid, although I do have to be careful with one foot. I need very little medication of any kind.

I am so grateful to the Lord Jesus Christ for what He has done for me.

—*Norman Maindonald*

Back & Spine

Approximately eight years ago I was working at a rest home. I was transferring a 90-year-old lady from a chair onto a bed. The other carer decided to let go of her but I knew if I didn't hold onto her she would be injured. As I took all her weight I felt a crunch in my back on the left side. The doctor sent me for a scan and it revealed that the L3 and L4 discs had collapsed; there was no fluid between them and it was bone on bone. A specialist said he could not guarantee an operation would help.

For the next eight years, I lived with severe back pain and chronic sciatica right down my left leg. For six of those years I was on drugs to try and ease the pain. I had to stop work completely for two years. I could not walk without a limp the whole eight years. I became depressed with this continual pain.

In October 2012, I attended a meeting at Flaxmere Christian Fellowship where Weston Carryer was praying for the sick to be healed. As he laid his hands on me, the Lord did a miracle. All the pain instantly left. He also prayed for my right leg to be lengthened as it was one inch shorter than the left one, and it grew to the full length.

Since that moment, now seven months ago, I have had no pain at all. I am now able to bike 20 kilometres with no stopping and no pain, and walk five kilometres and I am no longer depressed. This exercise has caused me to lose fifteen kgs.

This miracle healing has made a huge difference to my life and I am praising Jesus for my healing.

—*Eliza Nathan*

I had been experiencing severe back pain for approximately twenty years, and it had been getting progressively worse. My back would suddenly lock up and I would hardly be able to move at all, and I had sciatic pain all the way down to the knee on my right leg.

The doctor diagnosed three lower vertebrae out of alignment but said that I would have to live with it as it could not be operated on. I tried chiropractic and heat treatment, but neither of these helped at all, and I was becoming concerned.

On Sunday, 26 August 2012, my husband and I were in Harvest Church, Rotorua, where Weston Carryer was conducting a divine healing meeting. We had only just started attending this church and we had not seen healing take place in the church we had previously attended.

Weston said that there was someone present with three lower vertebrae out of alignment and severe back pain, and the Lord wanted him to pray for this immediately. I was very surprised and not used to this and didn't move. Weston said the person needed to respond then if they wanted their miracle, and so I went forward and he prayed for me. As he prayed, all the pain disappeared and I was able to touch my toes for the first time in many years.

Although I still have some limitations, with reasonable care my back is pain-free, which is marvellous. For that twenty-year period I had to take painkillers first thing in the morning and up to three times though the day to be able to keep moving. But now practically every morning I can just get up and take part in a normal days' activities.

Praise the Lord!

—*Julie Hansen*

I have been in desperate pain for a few months now with my back, been to the doctor three times, had physio and now booked into a chiro. But tonight, at City Life Church, Weston Carryer was praying for people to be healed and called out my specific details to come up and get prayed for.

It's pretty exciting to not feel pain any more and to know that God cares enough about me to tell Weston my details. He explained things exactly that showed on my x-ray last week. He said I had three degenerative discs at the bottom of my spine with terrible pain going off to the left leg. He also said I had a tailbone accident which I did rollerskating which has put my spine completely out of line (which the x-ray also showed).

Back & Spine

Then God told him He wanted to also heal irritable bowel syndrome. I'm pretty excited right now that God told Weston all those things and that He healed me tonight. Now I'm going to have to cancel my chiropractic appointment. I'm just so amazed and happy that we have a real live God who cares about me that much. I'm just so amazed.

Thank You God, so much. I went to bed for the first time not nearly crying with pain. I had no pain when I rolled over in bed and I had no pain when I got up out of bed in the morning (usually excruciating). Also taking the first three steps—no pain; sitting down and getting up off the loo—no pain; leaning forward to wash hands at basin—no pain. Praise the Lord!

—*Dianne Fearns*

On the 12 August, I attended a divine healing meeting at Orewa where Weston Carryer was praying for the sick. For the previous eight months, I had pain in my lower back and an x-ray showed deterioration of my lower vertebrae. Weston prayed for me, and over the next few days, the pain went. Before the prayer, I was taking painkillers twice a day but since the prayer, I have not taken any painkillers.

I wrote to Weston one month later advising that the pain had gone and I felt fine. Later on he phoned back to thank me for sending him my testimony. However, I advised him that I did have slight pain in my back. Weston immediately prayed for me over the phone. The pain went as he prayed and has never returned over the last eleven months.

This has made a huge difference to my quality of life and I continue to praise God every day for His healing power.

—*Fred Doidge*

In 1998, I fell and landed very heavily on the lower part of my spine. X-rays revealed that the lower vertebrae on my spin was chipped. For the next thirteen years I experienced a lot of pain; the pain was always there and was often excruciating.

During this entire thirteen-year period I was on medication to try and get some relief, but the pain continued to get progressively worse. I could never sit still for more than five minutes without severe pain. We always carried a deck chair for me to sit on wherever we encountered hard seats because it was just too painful for me to sit on them.

Weston Carryer was ministering in our church in Cromwell in April 2011. He spoke out my condition and asked for the person who had this condition to come forward for him to pray for the Lord to heal her. As he was speaking these words, a warmth started in the painful area, and as Weston prayed for me, all the pain instantly and completely disappeared.

Since that moment, two and a half years ago, I have not had the slightest pain or discomfort in my lower back area. What a marvellous difference after thirteen years of agony. Thank You so much, Lord Jesus.

—Jo-Anne Van der Koeff

For ten years, many of the discs, from my neck to the base of my spine, were out of place and my pelvis was also twisted. This resulted in constant pain despite having much physiotherapy, chiropractic treatment, and other forms of back manipulation. These various treatments would only ease the pain for about a day but then it always returned. In November 2000, Weston Carryer came to our church to minister and I saw the power of God heal people as he prayed for them. I then went forward. After Weston prayed for me, I returned to my seat and then experienced terrific heat right through the entire area where all the pain had been. After half an hour, the heat went, and I realized that all the pain had totally gone; it has never returned. I am now not restricted, and I am praising God for my miracle and being pain-free after ten years of agony. Thank You, Jesus.

—Louise Epsom

Eighteen months ago I was told by a specialist that I had a chipped vertebra in my back, and that a very difficult to perform operation was necessary to remove the bone chips. For some

Back & Spine

years previously, my back had been causing serious problems and on many occasions it would suddenly feel like electric shocks going through it. I would then have to lie perfectly flat. When I was on my way to Australia this happened and I had to be taken off the aeroplane in a wheelchair. Almost two years ago I attended a divine healing meeting in Tauranga where Weston Carryer was ministering. As Weston was speaking out words of knowledge, he described my condition exactly, and also that I had been advised to have an operation. I went forward for prayer and the Lord gave me a miracle; I have been completely healed. What amazing relief! Thank You, Jesus.

—*Peter Frame*

As a young man I was employed by a coal merchant and I carried a lot of coal bags weighing up to almost 200 pounds on my back. It was later discovered that this excess weight had crushed many of the vertebrae in my back. At about age thirty, I started to get backache, which got worse and worse. The pain spread into my hips and I had difficulty in moving. I was diagnosed as having osteoarthritis and Sherman's disease. When I was thirty-seven I was admitted to Queen Elizabeth Hospital Rotorua, and I was told that a double hip replacement was necessary. I decided that I would believe the Lord to heal me and declined the operation. For the next twenty years I lived on anti-inflammatory and painkilling pills. Despite the continual medication it felt like a dog biting on my spine all the time and I was very restricted in everything I did.

In May 2000, I heard that Weston Carryer was coming to Whangarei, and I knew that this was going to be the night that the Lord would heal me. I arrived an hour early, and after the worship, Weston started to minister with words of knowledge. The fourth condition he called out was my exact condition. I went forward as fast as I could. As he prayed the pain went from my back and right hip. He then asked how I was and I told him what had happened and he prayed again for my left hip. The pain then went totally and has never returned. Over the last twelve months I have had no pain whatever, no medication, and no restriction. I can sleep at night without being awakened all the time with pain and I feel better now than I did at twenty-five. Thank You, Jesus. To God be the glory!

—*Stan Dobney*

I wish to testify to a double healing I received in May 2000 from the Lord Jesus Christ. From 1983 until 1997, I suffered extreme pain from a bone growth which grew around and over my spine. The medical people who were involved in the decision-making involving my case said that it was too close to the spine to operate on. Apart from the severe pain, it prevented me from walking properly and I could only drag my right leg. I was admitted to Middlemore Hospital in 1983 where I was given injections through my tailbone, but these did not help ease the pain. For fourteen years I could not work or do practically anything else; other people did my housework for me.

I went to a divine healing meeting at Kaikohe in 1997 where Weston Carryer was praying for the Lord to heal the sick. As he prayed, I experienced the power of God go into my body in an amazing way and I was healed. Since then, over four years ago now, I have had no pain or loss of movement. I can do all my own work and am doing community work as well. My joints had also been affected as a result of rheumatic fever for which I had to take medication. I was also healed of this condition of rheumatism at the same time and no longer need to take medication. Thank You, Jesus!

—*Paro Stirling*

While employed as a freezing worker at Waitara in 1969, my back was broken through a work accident. I suffered severe bruising which I was told would never go away. Two discs became totally degenerate and there was no fluid in them. As a result of this I suffered from a pinched sciatic nerve for thirty-one years which caused extreme pain. I had to be extremely careful all the time as different movements would radically affect it. I tried all kinds of medication and finished up by taking fourteen to sixteen panadol tablets every day. Over this

Back & Spine

thirty-one year period I was only able to work approximately two years.

In mid-2002, Weston Carryer prayed for the Lord to heal my back, and as he prayed. I experienced a terrific click and it felt as if my back was being welded together. From that moment I have had no pain whatever and I believe my back is completely healed. I am now able to work full time with no restrictions. This is wonderful after thirty-one years of continual agony.

—Romanos Gregory

Tailbone, Spina Bifada

On a Sunday night in Whitby, Weston Carryer asked the person with back pain, especially in the tailbone area, to go forward for healing. The pain has gone. I believe the condition is healed. I also had a skin complaint which was like a rash. It was quite annoying and made me scratch for hours. Weston prayed for that, and the abnormal irritation was healed as well.

—Rene Stephenson

I was born with scoliosis of the spine and spina bifida. The second and third vertebrae in my neck were also malformed. In 1997, when I was fifty, I had a shunt put in my brain for hydrocephalus (or fluid on the brain). I have had several surgeries on my spine and have plates in place to cover the gaps where my spinal cord was exposed through the spina bifida. I had a deformity in the second, third, fourth and fifth vertebrae.

At the beginning of 2006, I had a fall which resulted in a lot of pain and I was put back in a brace. Although the pain was coming from my back the doctor thought the pain was coming from my hips as x-rays showed a piece of bone broken off into the hip socket. However, a specialist in Dunedin confirmed that I had a disc out and as it wouldn't go back in he was preparing to operate on my back. I was in a lot of pain; even with taking painkillers I couldn't stay on my feet for long. Short trips to the shopping mall meant that I find a seat at regular intervals to sit down. I could not even carry a Bible.

I attended a Weston Carryer healing meeting and was prayed for. Now, for the first time in my life, my back is straight and not twisted as it had been due to the scoliosis. For the first time I can bend, do my housework, garden, and I am pain-free. My neck is also stabilised. My specialist of eight years has confirmed my back as being in "pristine condition."

This has been such a testimony here in Invercargill that I have had opportunity to testify to the amazing healing power of our God, and have prayed for others and seen God healing them. Praise God!

—Lorraine Richard

When I was seven years of age, I fell on ice and damaged my coccyx (tailbone). For eighteen long years I was unable to sit for more than ten minutes without suffering severe pain.

I attended a healing meeting where Weston Carryer was ministering and through a word of knowledge, he asked me to go forward so that the Lord could heal me. As Weston prayed for me, the pain disappeared immediately. One of my legs which was shorter that the other grew to the same length as well. During the year which has since passed I have had only one minor twinge. I claimed my healing immediately. The slight pain I experienced disappeared and I have had no further discomfort of any kind. I praise God for His wonderful healing through Jesus by the power of the Holy Spirit.

—Christine Vaughan

In April 1996, I broke my tailbone (coccyx) through which I suffered terrible pain. Medical authorities told me that it would take at least twelve months before any healing at all would take place.

Back & Spine

At a healing meeting in July 1996, Weston Carryer, was ministering and received a word of knowledge that there was a person in the meeting who had broken their tailbone. He said if they would respond the Lord would heal them. I came forward, and as Weston prayed for me, I experienced the power of God go into my tailbone and instantly totally heal it. No more pain or restriction since that night. Praise the Lord.

—*Delwyn Pauro*

About four or five years ago, I went to one of Weston Carryer's healing meetings at Coastlands Church at Papamoa. We were visiting there and a friend asked me to go along. I had had a floating tailbone as a result of being kicked in the bottom. For about thirty years I'd had extreme pain—like an electric shock, often when I sat down. Weston named what was wrong with me and I went forward for my healing. Hallelujah! Weston prayed for me and since then I have never had any pain. I praise God for my healing. God bless his ministry.

—*Robin Stockman*

One day, approximately ten years ago, I fell down some concrete steps and landed very heavily on the base of my spine. I knew my tailbone was damaged. For the next ten years, I experienced considerable pain a lot of the time, especially when standing or sitting. I could not stand for much more than about fifteen minutes. I had to sit on a cushion when sitting to try to ease the pain.

I responded to a word of knowledge by Weston Carryer, at Tauranga one Sunday morning a year ago. He said the Lord was reaching out to heal someone who had damaged their tailbone. I knew it was me and went forward immediately. Weston prayed, and the Lord touched me and straightened my tailbone. Since then I have had no pain and I can stand or sit for long periods without any problems. Thank You, Jesus.

—*Mary Weatherall*

Miracles in Aotearoa New Zealand

On Sunday, 21 September 2003, at West City Christian Centre, Weston Carryer called out the symptoms of my lower back being crooked, and my tailbone going off to one side causing me to be lopsided. I caused this from sliding down a bank when I was young. The only thing that kept me from going up for prayer straightaway was because he said the person was in pain—which I wasn't at the time, but I had had a lot of pain in the past. All my life I had been depressed, and severely so over the last twelve months. I was on anti-depressants.

I was trembling—I had been reading the book, *Deliver From Evil*. I went up, and Weston prayed over me. I jumped and felt a spirit leave me. I felt my spine straighten like someone had reached in and bent it back into place. At first it was still a little bent but now it is straight. My trainer, Ben, at the gym checked it for me at the time. My muscles were sore for a while. My posture and walking has never been this straight before. Since that morning, I have had no more depression. In fact I am heaps better! Thank You, Lord Jesus, for this wonderful gift.

—*Rachael Hilton*

Six months ago I fell on a sharp rock at Waipa Cove, landing on my tailbone, damaging a small section that caused much pain and discomfort. My doctor said that medically he could not help me. I went forward at a Weston Carryer meeting and God graciously healed me. I now have no pain or discomfort in this area. Thank You, Jesus.

—*Muriel A.*

One day in 1967, when six months pregnant and while working in the garden on a Friday, I dislocated my tailbone. I was in severe pain all weekend and my husband had to pull me up as I simply could not even get out of a chair by myself. Because of the delay over the weekend in seeking medical help,

Back & Spine

permanent damage was done. This also caused problems later after the birth of my third child. For thirty-five years I suffered from quite horrendous pain at times. I had to regularly be pulled up from a sitting position. This was despite the fact that I was a very fit person. In March 2003, I attended a divine healing meeting in Christchurch where Weston Carryer was ministering. Through a word of knowledge from the Lord, Weston spoke out my condition and asked me to go forward to be prayed for. Since then I have not had any pain or discomfort of any kind in the tailbone area. I am totally healed. Lord Jesus, I am so grateful.

—*Kathy Huntley*

In February 2006, I attended healing meetings where Weston Carryer was ministering. On the Sunday morning Weston had a word of knowledge about someone who had fallen and damaged the base of their tailbone (the coccyx) and that as a result of that damage experienced difficulty and discomfort when sitting for only a short length of time. I stood up immediately and responded because for over forty years, I had experienced discomfort and pain in that very area due to falling off my bike at age ten. The doctor had diagnosed that was the area I had damaged.

As Weston began to pray, and even before he put his hand on me, I felt the power of God come on me and joy and laughter filled my being. I went gently down and sat enjoying this touch from God. I knew the test of my healing would be ahead because we had a car journey of five to six hours to cover. I am always uncomfortable on long journeys or sitting in one place for any length of time. To date, we have made three longer car trips and I know I am healed. To be able to step out of the car and experience no discomfort or stiffness is a miracle.

I am so grateful to God for His healing touch on that Sunday morning. What great joy to report, that eight months later, I have no pain or restriction in the tailbone or lower back area. Thank You so much, Lord Jesus.

—*Lareen Driscoll*

Miracles in Aotearoa New Zealand

In November 2006, I attended a healing meeting in Whangarei. Weston said that someone there had a tailbone problem. It was me. I had broken my tailbone eleven years previously and always had pain when sitting for long periods of time. When Weston prayed for me I felt my tailbone click. Over the last six months I have had no trouble sitting. Thank you, Weston, and thank You so much, Lord.

—*Sharyn Playford*

At six months pregnant I fell, landing on my tailbone. For the next several years this caused pain all the time when sitting; at times it would be excruciating especially when sitting all day. It was always a real struggle to sit, even on very soft surfaces. In February 2007, at a divine healing meeting, Weston Carryer prayed for the Lord to heal my tailbone and since that moment over two years ago, I have not experienced any pain when sitting. Lord, I am so grateful.

—*Belinda Linnett*

In 1973, while giving birth to my daughter, my tailbone was broken. I broke it again a few years later and I lived with the continual pain for thirty-four years. In the middle of 2007, I slipped on ice and landed on my lower back causing further damage. For the next seven months the pain was extreme and there was nothing the doctors could do for me.

I attended a Christian healing meeting in Taupo in February 2008 where Weston Carryer was ministering. He spoke out my condition; I responded and went forward for him to pray for me. When he prayed the Spirit of God came on me and I fell to the floor. Lying flat on a hard surface I realized that for the first time in years, I had no pain. By the power of Jesus Christ I was healed. When I got up Weston asked me to sit down hard on a wooden surface; again there was no pain. Now, ten months later, I have had no further problems. Praise God for His continuing healing power.

—*Sheron Northe*

On 9 April 2011, I was sitting in the congregation in Leith Valley, Dunedin, when Weston came over to the side of the church where I was sitting and stood right in front of me because I was in the front row. He said there was a person here with a crooked tailbone and God wanted to heal them. I was wondering who that could be.

No one came forward so he repeated it, saying, "Come out now, because God wants to heal you." Still no one came. Weston then stepped back and said, "If you have a crooked tailbone it is like this and this . . ." adding, ". . . you find it difficult to sit."

I said, "Oh, that is me. I even came to the meeting sitting on a cushion in the car."

As soon as Weston prayed for me, I was slain in the Spirit and while I lay on the floor, I could feel my tailbone wiggling round and round in a very quick motion. I stood to my feet and I was fully healed. The end of my spine felt like the rest of my spine. For as long as I can remember the base of my spine felt spongy and weird—not a bit like the rest of my spine and I often asked my husband how his felt because mine didn't really feel like bone.

When I lay in bed that night I was thrilled to feel bone there that felt like the rest of my spine and evenly positioned. I was so excited. I did not realize the full extent of my healing until I went to a conference in July. At the end of three and a half days I suddenly realized for the first time that I can remember, my bottom was not aching and I had sat still through it all. Usually I wiggled and squirmed wishing I had more padding on my bottom because it was so uncomfortable sitting.

Isn't God so good to tell his faithful servant Weston that I had a problem that I knew nothing about? I just thought that was how I was. I still marvel at the Lord's goodness. It brings me to tears when I realize the full extent of the healing God has given me.

Miracles in Aotearoa New Zealand

I'm so thankful to Weston and Ruth for coming so far from home to bring God's healing to His people, and more especially, to me!

—Jessie Paton

I want to give you my testimony of healing which took place four months ago at Grace Vineyard New Brighton Church.

In November 2012, I gave birth to my second son. He took some time to come out, and when he finally did come, I heard a loud crack. Unfortunately, this was my tailbone giving way.

From that moment I was unable to sit down at all. I thought it would heal and the pain would decrease over time, but it stayed so sore. It was impossible to feed my baby comfortably and driving was extremely painful. Just about everything caused it to hurt. Eventually my whole lower back suffered, and I could not even bend over to pick my baby up.

When you prayed for me I immediately felt a huge surge of energy and I fell to the ground. I lay for some time where I felt what I can only describe as a strong current going through my whole body—especially the pelvic and lower back area. I was unable to get up for some time.

When I finally did manage to get up, I knew I was healed. I immediately felt like going for a run. Since that moment I have not had the slightest bit of pain or discomfort. This is amazing to be delivered from such pain and I really want to thank and praise You, Lord Jesus.

Jesus certainly heals today.

—Julie Wightman

I come from a family with a genetic problem called spina bifida, which has resulted in severe back problems in family members, and I was one of those who were affected. My grandmother had to wear a brace for most of her life because of this condition. My mother and sister both have had ongoing

Back & Spine

treatment all their lives from chiropractors and other medical people.

I first experienced pain in my back when I was nineteen, and although I did not have it medically checked (I didn't want confirmation) I knew, and my mother also realized, that I had this same condition that was affecting the other family members. Over the next ten years I always had pain in some form. Some work would really aggravate it. The pain would be very severe at times and over this entire ten-year period, I continually took Cataflam to try to ease the pain. A hump also developed on my back and I became very worried and concerned that I would end up a cripple.

In March 2002, I attended a divine healing meeting in Timaru where Weston Carryer was ministering. That night I was in excruciating pain. Through a word of knowledge that Weston had about my condition I went forward for him to pray for the Lord to heal me. As he was praying, Jesus performed an amazing miracle. The pain just went and the hump disappeared instantly. Since that moment one year ago, I have had no pain or restriction of any kind. It is wonderful. Thank You, Jesus.

—*Kirsty Henderson*

I was born with spina bifida, nerve damage, and without the normal covering for protection over the tailbone area, which left the nerves totally exposed. Apart from back problems, this also caused a lot of trouble with my left foot. My doctor said that as I got older there was a possibility that I would not be able to walk.

I got married, and in 1994, gave birth to a baby. This caused the sciatic nerve to become squashed and resulted in further major problems in my left foot. Following this I developed hip problems, and by this stage, I could hardly lift my left foot off the ground at all. I was on continual medication for the pain with very little relief. Despite the fact that things in the natural looked hopeless, I did believe that the Lord would restore me.

Weston Carryer came to our church in Dunedin in March 2003, and I went to the Sunday morning service believing

MIRACLES IN AOTEAROA NEW ZEALAND

specifically for a miracle that morning. Two months prior to this weekend, I had had a scan and an x-ray that confirmed the damage was permanent and that nothing medically could be done for me. During the ministry time, Weston pointed to the area where I was sitting and said there was someone there who needed a miracle and had come that morning to receive one, and would they come forward to be prayed for. I responded and he prayed for my miracle, and I immediately received it. The transformation was amazing. I found I could lift my leg up high straight away.

Within three months all the symptoms disappeared. I am now not restricted in any way and I can even do star jumps. Now twelve months later I have no back problems, no pain, and I am on no medication. Lord, You are amazing. I am so grateful.

—Crystal Carran

All things are possible
to him who believes.
—*Mark 9:23*, NASB

Four

Cancer

Testimonies of healed diagnoses of cancer and/or suspected cancer conditions.

In 1988, our son was diagnosed as having leukemia. He was put on a two year course of radiotherapy and chemotherapy. At the beginning of 1990, my wife and I started going to church. Not long after, we had our son prayed over for healing by Weston Carryer at a crusade meeting, although I admit, neither of us was sure whether we believed in this or not. Within weeks, we gave our hearts to the Lord. About a week after my wife's conversion, she was praying one night and heard a voice telling her to take Nigel off his treatment as he was healed and did not need it any more. She kept this entirely to herself in case people would think she was dumb.

Days later, when we took our son for chemo treatment, the doctor wanted to talk to us about his blood count. Against all logic, it was normal. My wife remained silent, seemed to withdraw within herself, then quietly walked out of the room to be on her own. Nigel went through with his treatment. Back home she told me about the call from God. We did not know what to do or think, so I brought in our pastor, notwithstanding my wife's reservations in case he may think she was out of her mind. His wise counsel was that we should ask God for a further sign (e.g., Gideon's fleece, Judg. 6:36-40).

A week on, Nigel went for another blood test, and the count had jumped even more, despite the fact it should have gone down following his treatment of days before. Since then, the count has risen up and up each time. Because we were in a quandary over some difficult areas relating to the questions of accepting advice and of responsibilities, we decided to keep him on the treatment although we firmly believed he was healed. His two-year course ended last week. The doctor wanted an extension for six months because he could not—and still cannot—work out why the blood counts are staying so high. The specialist told him to call it quits as they had tried everything they could to get the blood count to where it should be. We really believe God has healed our son and thank Him, not just for His healing power, but also for guiding our family through the two most traumatic years of our lives.

—F. Wright

An examination in June 1993, diagnosed me as having cervical cancer stage three. It was recommended I go to day surgery for a clinical assessment, and I agreed. The name Weston Carryer came to me at the same time, and an appointment was made to meet him at the office of his church in New Plymouth. I was feeling very ill at this stage. When he prayed over me, I felt calm and believed without any doubt whatsoever I had been healed. Two weeks prior to the exploratory surgery in September, I felt two hands had turned my stomach completely around. I honestly felt it flip over, a feeling I had never experienced in my whole lifetime. Surgery was undertaken as arranged. On my return to the ward, I felt quite happy and alert, although three other ladies were really sick. The doctor visited them but bypassed me. It transpired that the operation found nothing,

Cancer

and I was completely clear. I thank the Lord for my healing.

—*Della Conroy-Croot*

I had not long before had a thyroid operation and been told that cancerous tissues had been found. I told the doctors I could not accept that because I knew there was a greater Physician who could do the impossible. I thank the Lord for my brother and his wife who noticed an advertisement for a Weston Carryer healing meeting at the Hillsborough Anglican Church in September 1993. My family flew over to be with me, and we all went. Weston, through a word of knowledge, said there was someone present who was in extreme pain. I was still overcoming the after effects of the operation. When he prayed, I was slain in the Spirit and experienced the healing power of God through Jesus Christ in a wonderful way. As I lay there, I felt something come out of my mouth. On my way back to my seat I noticed there was no more pain in my neck. I knew I was completely healed. Today, one month on, I had scans, and to the amazement of the doctors, all were clear, proving God, the Master Physician had indeed performed a miracle on me. I just want to praise Him and thank Him from the depth of my being for that. Along with the above, He has also healed me of a heart murmur, a skin allergy, and, I know, done a wonderful work on my body.

—*Georgina Rasmussen*

I had been suffering from cancer of the lungs for some time, was extremely ill, and undergoing morphine treatment to relieve the pain. I was unable to raise my arms at all. I went to a divine healing meeting at which Weston Carryer was ministering. In order to appreciate the precarious hold I had on life, it was known to some, but not me, that my life expectancy, according to my doctor, was no more than six weeks. Weston prayed for me and I was healed at that very moment. The use to my arms was fully restored while my lungs functioned as they should again. At my own instigation, I went off morphine two days later and have not had morphine, or any other form of

Miracles in Aotearoa New Zealand

medication or treatment, for this condition since. One year has elapsed, and I am still enjoying good health.

—*Ola Pocklington*

For many months I had been suffering unbearable pain in the lower regions of my body. My doctor advised me that they suspected cancer of the cervix and I was waiting for further tests to be carried out. I went to a Women's Aglow meeting in Gisborne in July 1993 where Weston Carryer was ministering, and he prayed for the Lord to heal me. The pain went immediately, and since that time, two and a half years ago, I have had no further pain or malfunction in this area of my body. Praise God!

—*Tuku Haerewa*

I thank God for my healing from the Lord. Five years ago I had been diagnosed as having cancer in the right kidney. Not only was I passing blood in my urine but was also vomiting blood, was in constant pain, could not eat, and was just skin and bone for I had lost almost seventy-six kilos (twelve stone). I went to a divine healing meeting where Weston Carryer prayed for me. In those few amazing moments of time, God swept all symptoms away instantly and made me totally whole. I have had no further vomiting or passing of blood, the pain has ceased, my ability to eat has returned, and my weight over time has recovered to normal. A recent scan showed that my kidney has been healed. I am continuing to thank God, through Jesus, for what He has done for me.

—*Roger Wimuta*

Having been diagnosed in November 1988 as having carcinoma of the left breast, I was duly admitted to hospital where a lumpectomy was performed. There followed six weeks of radiotherapy for twenty minutes each day, an experience in itself. Reporting to a visiting radiotherapist for a routine check, it was shattering to be told I had a large lump in my armpit,

Cancer

diagnosed as failed radiotherapy and further cancer. A date was set for readmittance to a private hospital.

My son asked my husband and I to go to a Weston Carryer healing crusade one night. We really enjoyed it. To me, the benefit and power became immediately obvious, and we thereon continued to go for the balance of the meetings. The many people there advised me to pray for and believe that the operation would be successful and the lump would not prove malignant. One can imagine the joy and relief for us all when, one week later, and after the mastectomy, the surgeon told me the lump was benign. We would thank Weston for his prayers and feel sure it was our total acceptance of God's great healing power which achieved this result.

—*Alison M.C.*

During the year 1989, I was prayed over by Weston Carryer and, by the grace of God, I was healed of cancer. Cancer had eaten away the second and third ribs in my back. After being prayed over, I was healed. A little later I had x-rays and it showed the ribs had started to knit together. With continuous prayer, and the reading of my Bible daily, I am now able to do the things I loved doing without pain. Praise God!

—*I.A. Anderson*

In November 1997, it appeared as if I was facing surgery because of several pea-size lumps in my left breast. My doctor believed that they were cancerous, and had scheduled a time for me to have one of the lumps removed for analysis. Immediately after this I attended a divine healing meeting in Papakura where Weston Carryer was ministering. During the service, Weston prayed for the Lord to remove all the lumps. I was believing for a total divine healing. At the examination the next week it was discovered that every lump had totally disappeared. The doctor laughed with relief and said there was absolutely nothing wrong. To the doctor, I gave praise to God for my healing. He then commented and said he wished other people had my faith. Thank You, Jesus.

—*Tracey Hunt*

In 1996, I was diagnosed as having cervical cancer. I went to a divine healing meeting where Weston Carryer was ministering and he prayed for the Lord to heal me. I am delighted to write that medical tests have shown that God, through Jesus, totally healed me.

—*Julie Upton*

In late 1999, lumps were discovered in my breast. Diagnosis then revealed that I did have cancer. At that stage, I did not know Jesus Christ as Lord of my life, but my son, who was a born again Christian, encouraged me to go to a divine healing meeting at the Pukekohe Apostolic Church where Weston Carryer was ministering God's healing power. I did attend, and during the meeting, I heard Weston say that Jesus had died for my sins and that all we need to do is repent and accept Jesus as our Lord; when we do this, our sins are forgiven and we are born again. I was very happy to accept Jesus as my Lord, after which, Weston prayed for the Lord to heal me. A few days later, I had further tests including a biopsy done, and when the results came, they showed that Jesus had totally healed me. No more cancer. Twelve months later I am living a healthy life and committed to Jesus Christ and my church. Thank You, Lord.

—*Val Marr, Whangaparaoa*

In 1990, I was terminally ill with cancer and was about to have a large malignant tumour removed. Weston Carryer was ministering in Foxton and he came to my house to pray for me. The surgeon duly operated and discovered the tumour was no longer malignant and there was no trace of cancer anywhere in my body. He expressed amazement at what had happened.

Cancer

Since that time six years ago, I have had no more treatment of any kind and am living a healthy life. Thank You, Jesus.

—*Percy Young, Foxton*

For over two years I had been having considerable trouble with my bowel. I was experiencing terrible pain and difficulty with bowel movements, and then I was unable to go to the toilet for two weeks. At this stage, I was told by my doctor after examination, that a cancer growth in the bowel was suspected and that I needed to have a barium x-ray as soon as possible. After hearing this I became a complete nervous wreck. I was then invited to go to a divine healing meeting where Weston Carryer was ministering in New Plymouth. That night I heard that I needed to accept Jesus as my Lord to have my sins forgiven if I wanted to come into God's kingdom. I accepted Jesus as my Lord, and then Weston prayed for my healing. That night, after accepting Jesus, I experienced the most amazing peace and joy that I had never known before. I knew that no matter what was going to happen to me, it did not even matter as I belonged to the Lord now. I knew He would look after me. Immediately after this, all the pain went and my bowel started to function normally. Five days later the barium x-ray showed that my bowel had been healed and there was nothing wrong. For the last four years I have had no pain or abnormal bowel function. Praise the Lord!

—*Bev Hamilton (Inglewood)*

Thirteen years ago I started to feel unwell and this condition was with me for all of this time. I also became more and more listless and doing anything at all finally became a major effort. Finally in October 2004, I was diagnosed with chronic lymphatic leukemia. I immediately rang Weston Carryer and an appointment was made to see him at his office. I am overjoyed to report that when he prayed for me, Jesus Christ blessed me with a wonderful healing. I immediately started feeling better, my strength returned, and I feel better now than at any other time in the last thirteen years. It is awesome to be well and energetic again. My last medical checkup has confirmed my blood count has come down. Lord, I am so grateful. Thank You so much.

—*Janet Finlayson*

In 1983, I was diagnosed as having cervical cancer and was operated on. However, even after the operation every smear test taken showed there were cancer cells still in my body.

In January 1997, I attended a divine healing meeting where Weston Carryer was ministering. I received prayer from him for this condition. The tests taken since that time have confirmed that God, through Jesus, has completely healed me. Praise the Lord.

—*T. M. K.*

For some time I knew that there was something wrong with my body. In early 2005, I was diagnosed with prostate cancer. My specialist strongly advised me to have the prostate removed, but I said, "No!" Three months later I attended a divine healing meeting in Whangarei where Weston Carryer was ministering, and he prayed for the Lord to heal me. I knew that the Lord had healed me. I was monitored for the next three months, and then in September the specialist informed me that I was completely healed and that he did not want to see me again. Lord, Your works are marvellous and I am so grateful to be healed of prostate cancer. Amen. No more cancer.

—*Pat Coyne*

For many years I had a mole on my back. Seven years ago, when it changed colour, I was examined by a doctor and then a specialist. A biopsy was taken and it was diagnosed as malignant melanoma, which is one of the worst kinds of cancer. An operation was performed but the surgeon said it had gone too far into my body and that nothing further could be done for me. Over the next six years I did all I could in the natural to

Cancer

help my body, which included drinking plenty of carrot juice. But I became thinner, more tired and very drawn.

Two years ago, in 2004, a friend invited me to a healing meeting in Flaxmere where Weston Carryer was praying for the sick. During the meeting he prayed for me. I noticed an immediate difference. I regained my weight, my energy returned and I felt just like I did ten years ago. I believe I am healed. I regularly read the pamphlet, *Keeping Your Healing,* Weston gave me. This has been a marvellous help. I was having medical check ups every three months but now they have been reduced to once a year. Thank You so much, Lord Jesus.

—*Elaine Hartigan*

In September 2005, I was diagnosed with cancer in my lymph nodes and was treated with medication. However, it was discovered that the cancer had gone into my breasts and I was told that I would need a full mastectomy. As a young wife and mother, I was devastated. My entire life was on hold.

In May 2006, I attended a divine healing meeting on Waiheke Island and Weston Carryer prayed for the Lord to do a miracle for me. One month later, in June, I had my next medical check and the tests showed that there was no sign of cancer. Praise the Lord.

Then in December after another series of tests, my oncologist confirmed that there was no sign of cancer anywhere in my body. I thank You so much, Lord Jesus, for healing me of cancer, and I simply cannot express the joy that I am experiencing as a result.

—*Belinda Linnett*

In 1973, I accepted Jesus as my Lord and Saviour and was water baptized in 1976. I married in 1979. But after five years of marriage, and when seven months pregnant with my second son, my husband left us and the marriage broke up. A pastor who prayed with me discerned and pointed out to me that I was full of anger, bitterness, and resentment. Right at that moment Jesus appeared to me in an open vision and told me very clearly that I had to totally forgive both my husband and my father. My father had left my mother after forty years of marriage. As soon as I forgave them, the Holy Spirit became my Teacher, Comforter, and Guide. From that moment, the Lord continually spoke to me through His Word, people, or songs.

I married Colin in 1991. Prior to my marriage I had been feeling ill, and one night, a month after our marriage, I became very ill and needed medical help. Tests and x-rays revealed that I had cancer. Then there followed thirty-nine trips to Wellington Hospital for multiple biopsies and tests and I was finally diagnosed with non-Hodgkin's lymphoma. The hospital doctors wanted to operate but I determined to believe God for my healing and refused the operation. God then clearly gave me this Scripture:

> *"For I will restore you to health and I will heal you of your wounds," declares the Lord* (Jeremiah 30:17, NASB).

My health continued to deteriorate but I continued to believe God. My immune system became very weak, I could hardly breathe, and I developed pneumonia. Then it was hospital again—chemotherapy and more antibiotics, but I was still believing God for my healing. God continued to greatly encouraged me and speak to me through His Word.

> *Therefore, do not throw away your confidence, which has great reward. For you have need of endurance, so that after you have done the will of God, you may receive what was promised* (Hebrews 10:35-36, NASB).

I was then further encouraged when Colin and I attended a divine healing meeting at Plimmerton where evangelist, Weston Carryer, was ministering. In the very first word of knowledge he spoke to the congregation, he described my exact symptoms. He then asked me to go forward for him to pray for me, which I did. Following his prayer, however, there was no obvious health improvement.

I was then given some tapes by the Singapore evangelist, Howard Willard, on the power of the tongue which further

Cancer

encouraged me. A short time later Howard Willard ministered in Levin, and Colin and I attended. He knew nothing about me, but during the meeting, he said that he had a distinct word from the Lord for me.

I shall not die, but live, and declare the works of the LORD (Psalm 118:17).

This was further encouragement for me. After this, I became even more ill though; even still, I kept on claiming and believing God's promises for my healing, particularly quoting all the specific Scriptures I had been given. During this entire time Colin was so loving and such an incredible support to me.

Weston Carryer then returned to the Wellington region to minister for several weeks. Because I was too ill and unable to get out of bed, he prayed for me at home on several occasions. Then, suddenly, God's healing power was manifested. On my next trip to Wellington Hospital for more scheduled radio therapy, I was examined by two different doctors who both said that they could not find any sign of cancer.

That was fifteen years ago. From that time, once I regained my strength, I have lived a healthy life. Our wonderful Lord Jesus healed my broken heart and my dying body. I cannot praise Him enough.

Jesus said unto him, "If you can believe, all things are possible to him that believes" (Mark 9:23).

—Raewyn Moar, Wellington

I had been a fit, healthy, active man all my life until five years ago when I noticed that all my energy had totally disappeared. I was a blood donor giving blood every three months; this is how it was discovered that I was seriously ill. I was then diagnosed with multiple myeloma bone cancer. Myeloma cancer is a malignant tumor of the bone marrow which causes the bones to dissolve. I was told I had no more than twelve months to live. I was sent to Waikato Hospital for five days of chemotherapy and radiation which nearly killed me. I developed septicaemia and was overdosed with morphine. I lost over twenty-five kilograms of weight in five days. After I was discharged there was no improvement in my condition. There was only one person who has been treated at Waikato Hospital that has not died with this illness.

I went to Weston Carryer's office and he prayed for the Lord to do a miracle for me. Many other people were praying for me as well. There was no immediate improvement in my condition, but it immediately stopped deteriorating. I carried on believing God for my healing, claiming the healing promises in the Bible. I did this for the next two years, and then finally, the blood tests showed my condition was improving. This improvement continued until I was completely healed. I did not have any further medical treatment. A doctor at Waikato Hospital told me that God was the only one who could have brought this healing about. I want to thank the Lord so much for this wonderful healing that I have had for this medically incurable condition. Thank You, Jesus.

—Phil Wright

Ten years ago, I had an operation for breast cancer, followed by six weeks of radiotherapy. The operation removed the cancerous growth and a number of lymph nodes. All was successful. But a while later, I developed intense pain in the bone under both breasts—particularly the right one—and I also developed an unbearable ache in the muscle area in my right upper back. The visiting doctor from Palmerston North told me that unfortunately, it was a side effect of the radiation treatment which I could have for the rest of my life.

At a healing meeting in New Plymouth in May 2008, Weston Carryer prayed for the Lord to heal this intense pain in my upper back. As he prayed I had a sensation of a very small tube of very sharp needles being poked into that area of my back. Since then, I have not had a return of that upper back pain or the pain under my breast.

This has been a wonderful relief in my life as I did not know what to do to get some relief. These healings took place over nine months ago. I want to thank Jesus so much.

—Sybil Gunson, Waitara

Cancer

I was medically diagnosed as having pre-cancerous cells in my breasts. These were small crystal-sized lumps. For the next three years, each annual examination showed they were still there. In February 2013, Weston Carryer prayed for healing of some other conditions I was suffering from. As he prayed, I felt this incredible heat in my breasts.

The next breast examination after I had been prayed for revealed that the cancer cells were no longer there. And along with that, all the terrible fear I had simply disappeared. I am so grateful to the Lord for what He has done for me.

—*Wanda Behre*

Last year, I went to Weston Carryer's healing meeting at the Presbyterian church in Matamata with some of our students and staff. I am the Director of YWAM Pursuits, Crystal Springs, Matamata. I had been diagnosed recently with breast cancer and had an operation to remove two small tumours and five lymph glands.

I went forward at the meeting and asked for healing and also asked for prayer for a clicky shoulder.

Weston prayed in Jesus' name for healing for the cancer and then for the shoulder. Immediately my shoulder stopped clicking and I could raise and lower it without pain. That increased my faith for the cancer healing. The doctors decided later that I didn't need chemotherapy and when I went for a checkup, the top oncologist at Auckland Hospital shook my hand and said I had made their day. He said they considered me a negative. Praise the Lord.

I returned to visit my GP eventually for a checkup and happened to mention that with all the drama with the cancer, I had forgotten to take the thyroxine I was meant to take each day for Hashimoto's disease (an autoimmune disease of the thyroid). I had had this incurable disease for 29 years. If I forgot to take the thyroxine for three days I would usually start feeling very tired and dizzy. I had been without it for weeks with no effect. The doctor (a Christian friend) smiled and sent me for a blood test and of course, that came back negative! So the Lord has healed me of three conditions in one go.

Thank You, Jesus. I'm so thankful for Weston's ministry.

—*Beryl Henwood*

In 1989, I was medically diagnosed as having cancer of the cervix. I had also had a stiff neck for twenty-five years, which prevented me from turning my head sideways. In addition, I had one leg shorter than the other which caused me much backache. I went to a meeting in Gisborne where I was prayed for by Weston Carryer to be healed by God through Jesus. Immediately, I was able to turn my head with no restriction or pain in the neck. My shorter leg was lengthened to the exact length of the other. And, my body was healed of cancer.

Three years later, I have had no further back or neck pain while medical tests have confirmed that my body is completely healed of cancer. In January 1993, I went to a healing meeting in Hick's Bay where Weston was again ministering and praying with people for God to heal them. He called for the person with flat feet to come forward. I had been born with this condition, and also had no small toe sockets. These impediments affected my feet markedly. As Weston prayed I felt things happen in my feet and, upon examining them, I discovered I had perfect arches where the feet had been flat previously, and that I had small toe sockets. For the first time in my life my feet were able to function as they should be able to. Praise the Lord.

—*Maria Dewes*

Four years ago (in 2002), I had an operation on one of my ears to remove a cancer growth, and approximately half of my ear was removed. Two years later, a further cancer growth returned in the portion of my ear that was still remaining. I attended a divine healing meeting in June 2006, and Weston Carryer prayed for the Lord to heal me.

Cancer

Within a few days, the growth completely disappeared and has not regrown—now well over two years later. I have had my ear medically checked twice and the doctor reported that everything was fine. Lord Jesus, I am very grateful for my miracle healing.

—*Trevor MacLean*

I had been a born again Christian for seven months and was having extensive tests for what my specialist thought was bowel cancer. I had already recovered from cervical cancer sixteen years previously. During the barium enema, I was told that part of the bowel looked inert and was not able to be inflated and bowel cancer was suspected at this stage. I was having a lot of severe pain and problems.

I attended Weston's healing meeting at our church and was prayed for by Weston. Two weeks later when I had the next lot of tests, I was told that there was nothing at all wrong with the bowel. All the pain and symptoms had, by this time, already disappeared and have never returned. At this same meeting I also received the gift of the Holy Spirit and the gift of tongues. Isn't God all powerful?

—*Val Smith, Tokoroa*

I had bladder cysts for more than ten years and this required regular surgery every four months at the Dunedin Hospital to remove them. These cysts used to cause bleeding from the bladder. After surgery, it took several days for the pain and swelling to go down. I was also very anxious each time I went to hospital as the doctor had told me this was a pre-cancerous condition. I also had a weak bladder.

I received prayer from Weston Carryer twice: once when he was in Dunedin two years ago, and last year in Cromwell where I live. After the last time he prayed for me, the cysts stopped growing immediately and completely. The last two medical examinations showed that everything was clear and there were

MIRACLES IN AOTEAROA NEW ZEALAND

no cysts at all. I find it amazing that I am clear after all these years. My weak bladder has also improved markedly. Thanks to the Father and Jesus for the marvellous healing miracle.

—*Graeme Brown*

The prayer offered in faith
will make the sick person well;
the Lord will raise them up.
If they have sinned,
they will be forgiven.
—*James 5:15, NIV*

Five

Shoulders, Arms, Elbows, & Hands

Testimonies of healed conditions of shoulders, arms, elbows, and hands.

Shoulders, Shoulders/Arms

For fifteen months I suffered from a collapsed muscle in my back. This problem caused my shoulder to drop down and cut off the circulation to the arm. During this entire time I had undergone physiotherapy. My arm had been strapped for a three-day period, unstrapped for one day, and then the process repeated again. The arm was purple in colour and had continual pins and needles. In 1995, I attended a divine healing meeting at Wairoa Apostolic Church. As Weston Carryer prayed for me God's power, through Jesus, went into the afflicted area and it was completely healed. Hallelujah.

—*Linda Strode*

Miracles in Aotearoa New Zealand

I became a Christian on 24 July 1989 with no great revelations of God. In August, I was working with my mother shifting bags of sand and pulled all the tendons in my shoulder muscle which then stopped me from moving my shoulder completely. I went to the doctor who prescribed painkillers, physiotherapy and cortisone injections. The physiotherapy stopped on 26 September having made little improvement to my shoulder. I had less than half the movement and was still in a lot of pain.

On Sunday, 1 October, I went to church to hear Weston Carryer speak not knowing what to expect. While he was preaching, I was feeling very sceptical about God healing people. In fact, I had more faith in my doctor than I did in God. The service finished and I went home without being prayed for. However, that afternoon I was encouraged to go and see Weston to be prayed for, which I did, but still felt very unsure of what might happen. When I arrived I was very nervous. Weston laid hands on me and prayed for my healing, after which he allowed me to lift my shoulder. I could lift it quite considerably more than I was able to do previously. He prayed for me to be baptised in the Holy Spirit and an incredible peace came over me and I spoke in tongues. One minute there was this peace, and then suddenly a burning sensation came on upon my shoulders. Owen and Weston both said I was burning, and they asked me how my shoulder was. To my amazement it was perfect.

I now know for sure God is real, and He loves me very much.

—*Julie Booker*

For two years, I suffered intense pain with a dislocated shoulder. I had received hospital treatment but this did not help in any way. I could not lift my arm above shoulder height. At a divine healing meeting at Hicks Bay conducted by Weston Carryer, he said there was a person present who had a dislocated shoulder. He prayed for me, and I was completely and instantly healed by the power of God.

Shoulders, Arms, Elbows & Hands

For the last twelve months, I have had no pain and my arm movement is not restricted at all. I realised that God was real and cared for me so I committed my life to Him. He has totally changed my life. Praise the Lord!

—Pine Poi

I am a thirty-year-old woman. At the age of seven I fell from a tree. My arm was fractured upon hitting the ground. Through the standard hospital care and plaster cast procedure, the arm mended. At the age of seventeen, while swimming at our local river spot, I was thrown into shallow water and landed on the rocky river bed. My right shoulder was damaged. From this time onward I experienced excruciating pain in my shoulder, neck, arm, and right hand. The pain appeared to subside as I became accustomed to it but I noticed that the movements in my right hand and fingers were becoming restricted.

Our God told Weston Carryer about such a hand at a home group meeting I was attending. I almost let the opportunity to receive healing slip by because I thought it a very insignificant matter if it applied to me. When Weston clarified the condition, I realised God wanted to heal me. I went forward for prayer. The pain is gone, my hand is strong again, and my posture has improved. The day after this healing I experienced a tingling sensation exactly in the place where my arm was fractured those years before. I do not understand why, but I know that the Lord had everything to do with it.

—Katarina Coake

Seven years ago I was involved in a motor accident, which caused severe injury to my right arm. After the subsequent operations the arm was three inches short through bone being removed, and my shoulder stayed in a permanently dislocated condition. In June 1997, I attended a divine healing meeting in Hamilton where Weston Carryer prayed for me. I was almost blown away when the power of the Holy Spirit, through Jesus,

Miracles in Aotearoa New Zealand

lengthened my arm so that it is now exactly the same length as the other one, and my shoulder is in its correct position. Praise God!

—*Trevor Martin*

Early in 1998, I suffered injury to my left shoulder due to over-exertion in aerobics. I was not able to do up my bra, tuck my clothes in without pain, fold my arms, or lift my left arm above shoulder height. Throwing clothes into the laundry cupboard sent shooting pain up my arm. Even driving a manual car and changing gears caused my arm to ache. I drove my husband's automatic car to avoid the pain. I nursed my arm at every opportunity.

In April, I finally went to my doctor who sent me to physio twice a week for treatment for a frozen shoulder. At home in between visits I carried out regular stretching exercises as directed by the physio. Many weeks of physio treatments passed by without any real improvement. I was referred to a second physiotherapist. A cortisone treatment was also suggested which my doctor administered. Following this, no improvement of any kind was noticed—only a whole lot of pain on the day of the injection. Physio treatments continued on a weekly basis. A specialist appointment was made for 21 October. I also went forward for healing prayer at church and home group on several occasions, but with no noticeable change.

In July, someone asked me what I thought God was telling me through all this. I shrugged and said I didn't know, but as I said this, I heard God tell me in a quiet, clear voice that He was going to heal me miraculously for His glory. What an awesome thought. I was elated but scared; excited but worried all at once. Needless to say, I prayed about this, and by the end of August sensed that God wanted me to go to Weston Carryer's next healing meeting. I found out that he was not coming until sometime in October, which seemed such a long time away. I believe God allowed this time delay so that more friends and family would know of my frozen shoulder. In that time also, two other people on separate occasions suggested I should go to Weston Carryer's healing meeting. This I took as confirmation.

Shoulders, Arms, Elbows & Hands

This bolstered my faith somewhat. I became even more sure that God was going to heal me at this meeting and even told a few Christians that this was going to happen. I still had times of real doubting though, feeling like I was being tossed in the surf like it says in James:

> But he must ask in faith without any doubting, for the one who doubts is like the surf of the sea, driven and tossed by the wind (1:6, NASB).

Nevertheless I made plans to go to Weston's next healing meeting on 13 October.

After a time of praise and worship, Weston Carryer gave several words of knowledge for various illnesses, including one for a person with a left frozen shoulder. I went forward and he prayed. Apart from my heart beating flat out, I felt no different when I was resting in the Spirit and I could still not get my arm above my waist at the back. So he prayed again and I could lift my arm about one inch higher up my back than before. Weston said that he was sure it would continue to improve and I went and sat down, armed with the pamphlet, *Keeping Your Healing*. By the time I got home, my arm was a little more comfortable to lift, but that was about all.

Over the next two days, I continued doing my exercises, as my arm felt like it needed stretching and strengthening badly. I also read and re-read the pamphlet given to me. After just two days I was able to undo the back button on my skirt, undo and do up my bras, fold my arms, hold them behind my back comfortably, and raise my arm to about forty-five percent. A week later, although there was noticeable improvement, I didn't feel confident enough to go back to the physio, so I rang to cancel my appointment. "As it happened" the receptionist was going to ring me because the physio was sick. By the time I saw her the following week, I could swing my arm around in large circles and get my arm well up my back without the pain I had felt before. The two physiotherapists who had worked so hard on my shoulder were amazed to say the least. This physio appointment also "happened" to be the last physio appointment I would get any ACC subsidy for. I never went back. As I felt I no longer needed a specialist consultation I also cancelled that appointment and saw my doctor instead who was thrilled to see that I was on the way to full recovery. I continued stretching my arm at every opportunity—so glad to be able to stretch it without any pain.

It is now 9 December 1998, and my arm is ninety-eight percent healed. I believe it will be one hundred percent healed thanks to the healing power of Jesus Christ through his humble servant, Weston. To God be all the glory. Amen!

—*Janet Eaton*

Ten years ago I was diagnosed as having a frozen shoulder. This continued to get increasingly worse until over the last five years, I experienced continual pain and my movements became more and more restricted until I could hardly move my arm at all. I had to give up playing tennis five years ago, and also had to give up my nursing job.

In October 1997, I went with two friends to support them at a divine healing meeting in Tauranga where Weston Carryer was ministering. During the evening Weston was speaking out conditions that people had, asking them to come forward to receive healing from the Lord. I was surprised when he said there was someone with a frozen shoulder. I went forward, and as he prayed the power of Jesus Christ went into my shoulder and it was instantly completely healed. Since then I have had no more pain or restriction and have been able to continue nursing. Hallelujah! Thank You, Lord.

—*Kaara Mete, Tauranga*

In February 1997, I fell against a concrete wall and damaged my left shoulder. From that moment on I could not raise my arm above my shoulder at all. The doctor diagnosed a frozen shoulder. Any movement with my arm resulted in real agony. Over the next three months it continued to get worse. In May 1997, I attended a divine healing meeting at the Christchurch City Apostolic Church where Weston Carryer was ministering. At the start of the meeting he had a word of knowledge for someone who had a frozen left shoulder. I went forward immediately, and as Weston prayed, the Lord instantly and completely healed my shoulder. All the pain went, the full movement was restored, and the next day the doctor confirmed that it was healed. Hallelujah. Praise the name of Jesus.

—Les Holland, Christchurch

Ten years ago I had an accident at work which caused severe damage to my right shoulder, and as a result of this, I was unable to use either my arm or shoulder. For the next nine years I was on A.C.C. as I was unable to work. During this time I had two operations and some bone was removed. However, there was no improvement at all, and I could not work for the entire nine-year period.

I went to a healing meeting in August 2000 in Nae Nae, Lower Hutt, where Weston Carryer was ministering the Lord's healing power. He spoke out my exact condition and said that the Lord had revealed this to him. He asked for the person who had this condition to come forward for the Lord to heal them. I went forward immediately, and as Weston prayed, the Lord healed my shoulder. All the pain went, the movement was fully restored, and the specialist later confirmed my healing. I was able to go straight back to work and I have worked for the last twelve months with no pain or restrictions. Praise You, Jesus!

—Elizabeth Young

Somehow, I unfortunately chipped a piece of bone in my left shoulder. This caused severe pain a lot of the time over a two-year period. It felt just like a giant crab pinching with its pincers digging into my shoulder. When Weston Carryer was ministering in our church, the Lord gave him a word of knowledge for someone who had damaged their left shoulder and was experiencing the symptoms that I had. I went forward. Weston prayed, and I want to praise God because He instantly

Miracles in Aotearoa New Zealand

healed my shoulder. I have had no more pain or restrictions ever since. Hallelujah. Glory to God.

—*John Walker*

Twenty years ago while playing rugby, my left shoulder was injured and was very painful. It stayed this way for several years. As well as continual pain in the shoulder, the pain went into my neck and down my left arm, and at times was so severe, it felt like I was having a heart attack. I finally went to a doctor, who told me I had a frozen shoulder that was so bad that nothing could really be done for it. I had a lot of physiotherapy, which did not help at all. Some ray treatment was tried, as well as pool exercises, but it got worse. By this time I could not lie on my shoulder, could not lift my arm at all, had lost seventy percent of the movement and seemed to be going in and out of hospital all the time.

All this changed completely when I attended a divine healing meeting in Tauranga where Weston Carryer was ministering. Weston said the Lord had revealed to him that there was someone present who had a major problem in their left shoulder. I responded immediately, as I had been really asking for my miracle. As Weston prayed, I felt the Lord's power go into my shoulder and I started moving my arm. By that night all the pain and restrictions were gone. This was incredible after twenty years. Since then my shoulder and arm have been one hundred percent and I am continually praising Jesus who is an awesome healer. Thank You, Lord.

—*Peter Whaanga*

I couldn't sleep on my left shoulder for thirteen years until Weston Carryer asked Jesus to heal me. Now I can sleep on it with only slight discomfort. My hip was also painful because I had fallen and damaged my tailbone. After a year of pain I am able to be totally free from unbearable discomfort.

—*Amanda Barber*

Shoulders, Arms, Elbows & Hands

I suffered soft tissue damage as the result of a motorcycle accident in January. My arm had become locked and I could not move it. After the accident we returned to church for the first time in ten years. A couple of weeks later, at a divine healing meeting in New Plymouth, Weston Carryer spoke out my exact condition. He asked me to come forward for the Lord to heal me. No one knew the pain I had in my right shoulder, not even my wife sitting next to me. I was healed one hundred percent. Today I can mow the lawns and carry my kids. I have never raised my hands to praise the Lord because I am shy and very young in Christ. But I now see that through God's power, the Holy Spirit and my faith, I can praise the Lord as He should be praised, and throw away my prescribed painkillers. All I really feel like writing is, "I love Jesus!"

—*James Rangi*

For several years I suffered with a frozen left shoulder. With the restricted movement in this shoulder I found it a nuisance at times. However, I became used to it and accepted it, especially when doctors said it was just part of the aging process. I know that this is not in accordance with God's will. When you mentioned about someone having a frozen shoulder, I had no option but to take a step of faith and come forward. After you prayed over me I was healed within an hour. I knew I was healed. My left shoulder is now as good as new; it is now better than my normal right shoulder. The next morning my wife, Janice, who because of prior commitments was unable to attend the Sunday meetings, was amazed at the improvement to my left shoulder. I was not only healed in a physical sense, I also received a wonderful sensation of feeling my heart strangely warmed. Praise God from whom all blessings flow.

—*Keith Brough*

While I was at work one day, over twenty years ago, I was hit very hard with a beam which came off a front end loader. This beam hit me on the shoulder and head, and the very impact knocked me to the ground. When I got up I discovered that apart from the terrible pain, I could not lift my arm at all. I was taken to the hospital and there it was discovered that the top of the shoulder had been knocked right out its socket. I then had a seven-hour reconstruction operation done and a number of steel pins were permanently inserted. It took three years for me to re-learn how to use my shoulder. For the next twenty years I experienced pain in the arm and shoulder. This was very severe at times, and other times not so bad, but I was always very aware of it, and it restricted my arm movements.

All this changed dramatically when I went to a healing meeting conducted by Weston Carryer at Cromwell in March 2004. The Lord had spoken to me and said He was going to heal me that night. Very early in the meeting Weston spoke out my condition and said that the Lord wanted him to pray for my healing. I went forward and he prayed for me and the power of God hit me. It was awesome. The pain went! Then full movement immediately returned and I spun my arm round and round. I was so touched. Since then, now fifteen months ago, I have not even had a twinge of pain in my arm or shoulder, and as a mechanic, I lift heavy weights. I can even do one arm press ups! Thank You, Lord.

—*Neville Hamilton*

One day when walking my dog on a leash, the dog suddenly bolted. My arm was pulled severely and it was discovered that my shoulder was damaged. From that moment on I had severe pain in it. I was unable to move my arm behind my back or raise it above my shoulder. In fact, any movement was very painful and the arm would go into spasms. Physiotherapy did not help in any way at all. There was no improvement at all during the next six-month period.

I attended a divine healing meeting in Christchurch in March 2005 where Weston Carryer prayed for the Lord to heal me. As he prayed for me my healing took place; it was instant. The full movement was completely restored and all pain was gone. Over

Shoulders, Arms, Elbows & Hands

the next few weeks some very slight twinges occurred but I had read the pamphlet, *Keeping Your Healing*, that I had been given and so I claimed by healing. There have been no more twinges now over the last ten months. Thank You, Jesus.

—Ralphina Henderson

In June 2001, following my divine healing in March when Weston Carryer prayed for me, my husband and I decided to take a trip to Australia so that I could catch up with family. I got up early one morning to go to the bathroom and found the hallway very dark. I fell down thirteen stairs into a basement and smashed my right shoulder in four places. I ended up in two different hospitals before finally receiving surgery. When I finally saw a specialist in New Zealand he said I would be lucky to ever be able to lift my arm higher than my shoulder. By December 2003, the severe limitations of movement in my shoulder were starting to get me down.

Then I heard that Weston Carryer was coming to minister in our church and I did not need any encouragement to go along. That morning, praise the Lord, my shoulder was healed. I came home on such a high and I showed my non-Christian neighbour how I could do things with my arm and shoulder that I had not been able to do for years. Without any pain I can reach higher, touch my left shoulder, and eat without my "wing" out. I have been truly blessed. Bless you lots, Weston. All praise be to God.

—Lyn Wells

I did not intend to ask for healing for my shoulder at this meeting we went to with Weston Carryer. I had been told you didn't keep going up for prayer for the same thing! I had been having trouble with my left shoulder for over a year and had been to a surgeon who twice had given me cortisone injections. The next step would have been an operation, which may or may not have worked. I would pray and go up for healing prayer whenever I could. As I couldn't get my arm behind my back or straight up or reach around to my right shoulder it was on the way to being frozen. When Weston called out the problem and said God was ready to heal it, I thought it must be for someone else! However, it was me! The Holy Spirit, through Weston, has healed me completely! Praise God.

—*Fern Blackler-Oliver*

I had a frozen shoulder, and I had been to the doctor, had x-rays done, an ultrasound, a cortisone injection, and months and months of physiotherapy. I couldn't lift my arm above my shoulder or hang the washing out. I had spent hundreds and hundreds of dollars trying to get relief.

I went to Weston's healing meeting and he called out my exact condition except that he said it was in the left shoulder and mine was in my right shoulder. So I walked up backwards so that it would be on my left side! He told me I had amazing faith! I was healed instantly. I was slain in the Spirit and when I got up I was healed. Weston got me to wave my arm around and around in circles and it became freer and freer. The following week when I went for physiotherapy (I had been going three times a week), the physiotherapist was amazed at the result and asked me what had happened. She had given up hope of it getting much better. It was not one hundred percent straightaway but within a month it was. The doctor had said it would be six months to two years before it came right and that I wasn't to expect a quick recovery. All up I had it for about four months. I have had no relapses.

—*Sue Jensen*

For over six months I suffered from an extremely painful shoulder condition caused by a calcium build-up in the tendon in the shoulder. The pain was very severe all the time, even though I was continually taking painkillers and anti-inflammatory medication. All shoulder movement was very limited and I was told I would need surgery for my shoulder to be healed.

Shoulders, Arms, Elbows & Hands

I attended a divine healing meeting in Ashburton in March 2006 where Weston Carryer was ministering, and during the ministry time he prayed for the Lord to heal me. Improvement started immediately and was complete within three months. For the last ten months my shoulder has been completely normal. Praise the Lord.

—*Maree Janden*

One day, in 2006, when I was lifting a box of books off the top of a wardrobe, I dislocated my left shoulder which came right out of the socket. I had surgery to put the shoulder back into place. The main muscle was cut and shortened and a steel pin was inserted to try and keep my shoulder in place but unfortunately this did not work.

For the next eleven months I experienced continual severe pain. I could not lift my left arm above ninety degrees. If I lifted it to the side, it would pull out of the socket. I would always feel the steel pin digging in. Depression set in, and at times I had to have medication for this. Physiotherapy was tried, but they gave up as this did not help.

On the morning of 1 July 2007, I attended a divine healing meeting in Auckland where Weston Carryer was ministering. Early on in the meeting, through a word of knowledge, he described my condition and asked me to go forward for the Lord to heal me. As he prayed, a real heat went into my shoulder and stayed there until the afternoon. As the heat wore off I realized my shoulder was completely healed. There was no pain and the full movement was restored to my shoulder and arm. I do not know whether or not the steel pin has been supernaturally removed, but ever since, I have never felt it penetrating into my shoulder at all. Although I am right-handed, five months later my left shoulder is stronger than the right one. My depression went at the same time and has never returned. Lord Jesus, I am so grateful to You for this miracle healing.

—*Muriel Rainer*

Miracles in Aotearoa New Zealand

For several months I had a serious on-going problem with the rotator cuff in my shoulder which totally affected both my arm and my shoulder. It was very painful and I was unable to lift my arm at all. Every day my children had to help me put my clothes on and I was very limited in everything I did. Over that period of several months there was no improvement at all. I went to stay with a friend for a break, and one afternoon, Weston Carryer and his wife called in to see my friend. He immediately offered to pray for the Lord to heal my shoulder. As he prayed, I received my healing. All pain and restriction immediately went and the full movement was completely restored. This was over eighteen months ago and I have never had any problems with my arm or shoulder since. Lord Jesus, I am so grateful.

—*Lu Taylor*

At the age of nine I suffered a fracture to my left clavicle bone. Throughout thirty-six years of my life, this shoulder has been a weak area, and I regularly felt numbness, pain and tingling. I would often wake in the morning with pins and needles in my arm.

I attended a Weston Carryer healing meeting in Te Awamutu and he called out someone with a frozen shoulder. Immediately the warmth of the Holy Spirit came into that area and I knew this was my time to receive a healing. I walked forward and received my healing. After Weston prayed, I was able to move my shoulder in all directions and not feel any pain. Over the last twelve months I have had no pain, numbness, or tingling, and my shoulder has been restored to full strength. Thank You, God, for choosing to heal me. Praise God.

—*Pauline Lea*

In May 2008, I attended a divine healing meeting at St. Andrews Presbyterian Church in Matamata which is my home church. Weston Carryer was ministering there. For

Shoulders, Arms, Elbows & Hands

the six months prior to attending this meeting I had been experiencing an extremely painful left arm and shoulder. I had been to the doctor and had also had many treatments with the physiotherapist, but this had not helped at all and the condition just continued to get worse. I could not lift my left arm at all without experiencing excruciating pain. Even putting sheets on the clothesline with one arm was extremely difficult. I refused to have the operation the doctor said I needed and decided to believe that the Lord would heal me at Weston's meeting when he came.

I went to the meeting with an incredible expectation that when Weston prayed, the Lord would heal me, and that is exactly what happened. After Weston prayed he told me to lift my arm. It just shot straight up without any pain or restriction. It was wonderful! Over the last twelve months, I have not had the slightest pain in my arm or shoulders. Thank You so much, Lord Jesus, for healing me. I'm so thankful for Weston praying for me.

—*Lorraine Robb*

In April 2008, I had a wonderful experience when Weston Carryer visited our church and held a healing meeting. I have been a Christian for many years. I believed God did heal people, but not me . . . Yvonne. I now realize, what a serious lack of faith that was on my part. That evening I was sitting there with what was probably called a frozen shoulder. I was prompted to go forward for prayer when Weston had a word of knowledge for a frozen shoulder and called for that person to go forward. Weston prayed for me and told me my healing could take time and that I had to keep believing for it. For "Yvonne," I did. I ceased going to a masseur, and in a very short time, I was able to do up my clothing behind my back and I had no more excruciating pain. Praise the Lord.

—*Yvonne Thompson*

In May 2006, I had hurt my left shoulder while working out

at the gym. I did not do much about the injury until November 2008 when the pain intensified.

I was sent to have an x-ray and an ultrasound. Both examinations showed problems and a tear in the tendon of my upper arm. It got very painful and I had to have two cortisone injections as well as physio for a long time. The pain was still there and it was beginning to get me down.

In 2010, we had a lovely visit from Weston Carryer and he prayed over my shoulder for the pain to go and also for the surrounding area to come back to its proper place. As he prayed I just believed for healing and trusted God to come through for me! His Word says, if you believe, He will do the rest. I am rejoicing for the wonderful healing miracle of God's power. The moment Weston prayed, all the pain and restriction went and complete mobility was restored to my shoulder. That was now two years ago and I have not had any problems with my left shoulder since.

I am so thankful for how God used Weston Carryer to touch someone like me and so many others. May our sweet Lord Jesus be given glory all the time.

Thank You, Father, in Jesus' mighty name.

—*Joyce Reid*

In 2008, I had a major traffic accident and my right arm was ripped right out of its socket and had to be reset. After this I developed a condition called "compartment syndrome." I had to have a fasciotomy to release the blood vessels to allow the blood to flow through them again. Unfortunately gangrene set in, and I lost tissue in my lower arm.

For the next three years I was in constant severe pain from my right shoulder, neck, head, and especially behind my right ear. Because of this, my spine was rigid and could not relax at all which resulted in back pain as well. During this whole time, I was on seven different kinds of medication, but still suffered chronic pain.

In March 2011, I attended a divine healing meeting in Twizel

Shoulders, Arms, Elbows & Hands

where Weston Carryer was ministering. During the ministry time he said that there was someone there with head, neck, and shoulder pain, a result of an accident that the Lord wanted him to pray for immediately.

I went forward, he prayed, and what happened next was amazing. All the pain instantly disappeared! That was twelve months ago. I have had no further pain and I am off all medication.

Thank You so much, Lord Jesus.

—*Dawn Ghoorah*

On 15 February 2012, I went to a healing meeting in the Paihia Baptist Church where Weston Carryer was ministering. Weston said during the meeting, amongst words of knowledge that he had for people, that there was someone there with a painful left shoulder. I had had this condition for over ten years and as well as it being extremely painful, I was unable to use my left arm. I could not lift my arm at all and had to have it tucked into my side like a useless wing.

I went forward and the pain went as he prayed for me. As I sat during the healing of others, it felt like my shoulder was on fire and the pain started to return. Then it stopped. Period . . . and it has never returned. That was now six months ago.

I have now learned all over again to use my arm. After so many years of not being able to use it, I astonish myself when I lift my arm high above my head. No excruciating pain . . . no pain at all.

My arm is normal and I praise God all day long. I'm so thankful for Weston.

—*Neville Turner*

In November 2010, a major problem developed in my right shoulder and I was unable to lift my arm above 30-degrees. I had no strength in the arm at all, which meant that I was unable to continue working. I had been working for an agricultural contractor and it was impossible to drive tractors or work machinery.

Miracles in Aotearoa New Zealand

A surgeon diagnosed the problem as a frozen shoulder and bursitis combined and said that it would take 18 months to get better. The pain, at this point, was so severe that it was very difficult to get any sleep at night, as I had to get up at least eight times to pack it with ice as well as taking painkillers.

In April 2011, I attended a divine healing meeting in Tapanui where Weston Carryer was ministering and he prayed for my healing. The healing commenced immediately and was complete within five weeks. I was then able to get a job milking cows on a 700-cow dairy farm. This required me to use both arms which I had no problem doing.

Since that time, now 15-months ago, I have had no further problems with my arm or shoulder.

Lord Jesus, I am so grateful.

—*Alistair Macdonald*

My name is Tania. I'm 27 and have been dancing since I was eleven years old. In the past few years I had developed an inflamed muscle in my shoulder and my collarbone (nerves) was in constant pain. It felt as if I was also being jabbed in the centre of my chest near my heart.

I came to a Weston Carryer meeting near the end of 2011 and went up for prayer to get healing for my upper back problems. I praise God for loving me and being such a merciful God, so much that He would heal me.

I was healed now twelve months ago and am so thankful that Weston was His vessel that He worked through. I can dance with ease now—just like David did in the Bible.

—*Tania Ulph*

On the 15 February 2013, I attended Weston Carryer's meeting at Ruawai. He had a word of knowledge for someone who had a frozen right shoulder. My right shoulder had been really painful for several years and was severely restricting many of my shoulder movements.

Shoulders, Arms, Elbows & Hands

After Weston prayed for me, there was an immediate improvement and the shoulder continued to heal until four months later when the healing was complete. I now have no pain or restriction and I am praising the Lord for His goodness to me. Thank You, Jesus.

—Colleen Judge

For approximately three years I experienced severe pain in my left shoulder and neck, especially when trying to sleep at night as it would wake me up almost every night. Apart from the pain, there would be pins and needles and many times I would not be able to move my arm at all as it would lock in a very painful position. It also restricted me when driving a car as I could not hold the wheel for long periods.

I attended a divine healing meeting in Helensville in September 2012 where Weston Carryer was ministering. He spoke out exactly what was happening to my arm and shoulder and asked for the person to go forward for him to pray for the Lord to heal him.

I responded immediately, and as he prayed, it felt as if the Lord was readjusting my body. It was amazing. Over the last six months, I have not had any pain or restriction in my neck or shoulder. Thank You, Jesus.

—Pam Foster

Approximately thirty years ago, when working in the Porirua Psychiatric Hospital, I was attacked by a patient. This caused a lesion between the 7th and 8th cervical disc and I also received a tear in the muscle in the right shoulder. This resulted in me being in hospital for the next two weeks.

For the next thirty years I lived in agony and nothing medically helped me in any way. For two years I wore a neck brace to try and get some relief. I was on various kinds of medication during this entire time to ease the pain and help me to sleep. During the entire thirty-year period, lifting my right arm was almost impossible.

Miracles in Aotearoa New Zealand

In February 2011, I attended a divine healing meeting in Porirua where Weston Carryer was ministering. During the meeting, he said that there was someone there who had a frozen right shoulder. I went forward and he prayed for the Lord to do a miracle for me. What happened next was incredible. As he prayed, all the pain left my back and shoulder, and I waved my arm round and round with no pain or hindrance.

That was now twelve months ago, and since that moment I have not had any pain or restriction in either my back or shoulder.

I am so grateful for what the Lord has done for me. Praise You, Jesus.

—*Ngaere Dolman*

I suffered from a frozen shoulder for nine months and arm movement was totally restricted. The pain was intense at all times and I could not get any relief until I went to a healing meeting at Gore where Weston Carryer was ministering. Through a word of knowledge from the Lord, Weston spoke out my condition and asked me to go forward for the Lord to heal me. As he prayed for me, all the pain went and the use was restored to my arm. Amazing! Thank You, Jesus.

—*Ron Aitchison, Gore*

Arms, Elbows

I would like to testify to the Word's healing power in my body after Weston Carryer's word of knowledge concerning my precise condition! I've been a hairdresser for some thirty years, and as a direct result I developed R.S.I. (repetitive strain injury) in both my arms. I have suffered with severe shoulder and back pain leading down into both my arms hindering me in a lot of ordinary mundane jobs, including my work as a hairdresser.

Shoulders, Arms, Elbows & Hands

But, no more! Since the power of God healed me in that healing service, I have been pain-free. When I was under the power of God, I felt the Holy Spirit adjust my back and I no longer have to have any spinal manipulation or treatment for my R.S.I. I am healed by the power of Almighty God to whom I give all the glory and praise. Hallelujah! I am so thankful for Weston's availability and pray the Lord richly bless and continue his ministry. In His love and service.

—*Miss Tonia Butler*
P.S. *I do have X-rays to prove the previous state of my spine.*

To say my husband is doing okay is a real understatement. I can't hold him back. He is almost 75 and has just built a 7½-metre veranda on his own, all by hand, and dug and cemented all the poles in. He climbed up over the roof with heavy beams to be gale-proof and roofed it in less than a week, praising God all day long. Now he is building a 6-foot high fence, lifting it all by himself. He is actually young again, and looks it.

My husband is a walking miracle—from an arm that he had tucked to his side and could only lift up with his other hand with excruciating pain for ten years, to powerfully swinging a hammer and getting stronger and stronger.

—*Matileena Turner*

On 25 October 1993, Karin fell off a horse at a friend's place in Wanganui. She broke her left upper and lower forearm. It was plastered in Wanganui, and we were advised to seek a specialist in Hamilton as the break was severe in the elbow area. The arm was replastered again in Hamilton, less than a week after the accident, but this time they put it into a half cast (the arm sits in a cast and is bandaged for support). Because of this Karin had a fair bit of movement so the arm set at the wrong angle. She couldn't straighten it totally and could not touch her left hand to her left shoulder. It would not reach.

Weston Carryer came to our church and Karin was prayed for on 29 Sunday April. God healed Karin's elbow. Praise God!

Miracles in Aotearoa New Zealand

This was mentioned to her doctor who said that sometimes bones can "click" back into place. I asked whether this would occur after twenty months and he replied, "No, probably in the first three to four months." I told him it had been about twenty months since the accident. So, he had to agree that something other than man would have had to have done this.

Then my younger son informed the doctor he had seen a lady's leg grow. The doctor is now probably not as sceptical as he had first been, but he was pleased with the result, as the only other way they could have "repaired" Karin's arm was to re-break it in the same place and reset it, with only a fifty-fifty chance of being better. God gave Karin one hundred percent in about five minutes. I'm so thankful for Weston being an open vessel for God. May God bless his ministry.

—*Heather, Keith & Karin Donaldson*

I am sixty-three years old. When I was nine years old I fell headfirst out of a tree from a height of about five metres. I put out my left arm to break the fall and my arm was severely broken. My neck was badly damaged and restricted in movement with considerable pain and discomfort. About fifteen months ago, I was ministered to by Evangelist Weston Carryer when he visited Pukete Apostolic Fellowship where I attend church. After over fifty years of discomfort and pain, I received healing and am no longer troubled by it. Bless You, Lord Jesus.

—*Barry Molloy*

My name is Dot Davidson, I am forty-five years old, and I live at Wanaka. I came to see Weston Carryer for prayer during his visit to the Apostolic Church here. I had been diagnosed with chronic R.S.I. in both arms, as well as, R.S.D. (reflex synopethat distrovy) in my left arm. I had been in plaster, and had braces for both arms. I had been to the clinic in Dunedin several times, had cortisone injections three times, and Guaethidine block done three times. (This is when they squeeze all the blood from your arm, then put on a tourniquet, and slowly inject the

Shoulders, Arms, Elbows & Hands

Guaethidine; this takes about forty minutes all up.) Following this procedure, my arm would have black blotches all over it and it felt dead, but it never stopped the pain. In the end, there was really nothing more they could do. I was told I would never work the same job, that the only job I would be capable of was a one-handed one, that I wouldn't be able to drive a car or even look after kids as I couldn't rely on my hands to work. I had partial feeling in the fingers of my left hand with no strength in either hand. I lived like this for at least two years. I couldn't even do my own housework. ACC sent someone to do that once a week. I was taking up to fifteen panadene tablets a day for constant pain. Just making a cup of tea was awful.

Weston prayed for me that night. It was the first time I had ever gone up for prayer as I was a new Christian. I cried, and I was so scared, but knew God was talking to me. When I got home that night my arms got really hot and they stayed that way for three days; it felt like they were burning inside. When the burning stopped, the pain was also gone, and it has not returned. I thank God every day for that healing. I am now housekeeping for other people who need it. I am even looking after children, which I love doing, and sewing baby clothes—most of which I give away or sell. There is now nothing I cannot do. The strength in my arms is returning and there is no pain. I am so thankful that Weston shared his healing gift with people like me.

—*Dot Davidson, Wanaka*

For over a year my arm and shoulder were in such pain that I could not move either of them. I could not hold anything in my hand and was continually awakened at night with the constant pain. In April 1995, I attended a divine healing meeting. I went forward and Weston Carryer prayed for me. I received a total instant healing, and my arm and shoulder now function as they should, for which I continually praise God.

—*Nell Davidson*

Miracles in Aotearoa New Zealand

In 1998, I was the driver of a truck that was involved in a head-on collision with another truck, and as a result, both trucks were written off. There was no safety belt in my truck and my right arm suffered severe tissue damage. This affected me for eighteen months and prevented me from lifting my arm above chin height. I was in intense pain all the time, just like a muscle ripping every time I moved.

I attended a divine healing meeting in Christchurch in March 2000 where Weston Carryer was ministering. Weston spoke out my condition and said for me to go forward for the Lord to heal me. I went forward, and as Weston prayed for me, it felt just like an electric blanket being wrapped around my arm. I suddenly realized that all the pain had gone and my arm was totally healed. I was blown away. I just marvelled at God. It was amazing. From that moment, over twelve months ago, my arm has been one hundred percent. Thank You, Lord.

—*Neil Leathart, Christchurch*

I used to play a lot of sport, and during a table tennis tournament in Gisborne, I smashed the ball so hard that I created a fracture in my elbow which resulted in six pieces of broken bone becoming lodged in my elbow socket. After my doctor had confirmed all of this to me, I had to re-plan my career. At that time I was playing cricket for Poverty Bay and had travelled to England several times to play semi-professional cricket. I decided to sit an art course which led me into completing a diploma in Maori art. Shortly into this art course, my elbow got much worse, to the stage that I couldn't perform or do the things I normally could due to severe pain. I eventually got to see a specialist who reviewed my injury and said that I was to be placed on the Rotorua Hospital public waiting list to await an operation to have the lodged bone segments removed that were still firmly embedded in my elbow. When the specialist informed me that I would need surgery to remove the bone pieces, he said the Rotorua Hospital waiting list could take a while. During my waiting, the pain in my elbow

Shoulders, Arms, Elbows & Hands

got to the stage where I couldn't hold a knife, toothbrush, or comb, or bend my elbow for fear of an excruciating pain which felt like broken glass being scraped across my elbow. I had seen the doctor about this pain and he couldn't do anything about it. My mother-in-law had applied kawakawa leaves, a Maori *rongoa* (medicine), to help alleviate and cure this pain, but to no avail.

Eventually, we heard about a healing meeting taking place in Mangakino. This was in 1993. My wife and I were very determined to go along and check it out. I was very wary and sceptical of this healing meeting which was being held in the St. John's ambulance rooms. But I knew the situation I was in was serious.

During this meeting Weston asked the crowd to bow their heads while he prayed and during this prayer he asked if anyone had been acknowledging or worshipping any other gods or idols other than our Father in heaven. I thought for some time, then raised my arm in the air. I knew I had been worshipping a carving, asking for wisdom, strength, and power to be provided to me by my dead. And also to Tane-mahuta, Tu matauenga, and other various atua (Maori gods), I had been praying to enhance my work, which in my mind, heart, and soul, I was committed to. I had been worshipping a Maori wood carving. During this prayer I was asked to come up to the front and be led through a salvation prayer of which I knew nothing about. As I stood up at the front (where it seemed to be before hundreds of people) I was asked to repeat a prayer after Weston. He began by praying, "Lord, I am a sinner . . ." but I couldn't say it. The whole place went silent and I froze. For about two minutes I stood there and wouldn't pull myself together by saying that I was a sinner. During these two minutes (which seemed like an eternity), Weston said to me on several occasions, "Just repeat after me . . ."

Finally he said quietly, "We have all sinned." After hearing this, my heart softened to a stage where my spirit of pride allowed me to say a prayer of repentance and salvation in front of everyone at the meeting. I must stress, though, that my heart still wasn't right with God and I hadn't truly accepted Jesus Christ into my life. I also said this prayer so I could get back to my seat and not be the centre of attention. Next thing I knew I was being led out of the church and into a side room to be given material on becoming a new Christian. It wasn't a natural feeling as I felt like I was being railroaded into whatever was happening. Also, as I mentioned before, my heart wasn't right with God. Eventually I got back to my seat feeling really shell-shocked. I witnessed many people going forward for healing.

Eventually, right at the end of the meeting, there was a final call for anyone who had not received prayer for healing to come forward and be prayed for. *Yes!* This was the ticket I'd been waiting for and I wasn't going to miss out on the possibility of getting healed. After I was prayed for, I still felt the same and left the meeting feeling bewildered and very doubtful about any healing taking place and what had happened to me earlier on in the meeting. It was some months later that I felt my elbow was improving, and I was eventually able to use my arm again in most normal ways. The severe pain had gone, but there still remained a slight twitch in my elbow.

In 1995, I was asked to visit my specialist in Rotorua for a final checkup before going in for surgery. I visited this specialist who invited me into his office after having x-rays taken just before. He said, "Take a seat, Mr. Matenga. I have some very good news for you. After receiving your x-rays, we discovered that the six fragments of bone which had been floating around in your elbow have disappeared—except one minute piece which I'm pleased to say, is not worth taking out as I am sure that I would do more damage opening up and getting into your elbow than what the one speck or piece of bone remaining in your elbow would do."

Wow! I cruised home rejoicing that I didn't need the operation, and, it also clicked that maybe this was a miracle from God. Remembering that I still hadn't accepted Christ truly into my life, I wondered, *Could God have really done this? Maybe so.*

In 1996, I committed my heart and life truly to the Lord Jesus Christ and was baptised later that year as a result of the Holy Spirit telling me to do so. Since then, God has done a mighty work in my life and also in my family's lives. God has appointed my wife and I as leaders in a home group and

Shoulders, Arms, Elbows & Hands

through our pastors, we have been appointed as elders to lead a local church on our marae here in Mangakino.

Glory be to our Father in heaven and my Lord Jesus Christ. I also praise God for Weston, and for the gift of healing He anointed him with.

My elbow is excellent at this present time after being told that I would have arthritis for the rest of my life. I still carve, and have recently completed a sixteen-foot log monument, commissioned by our local Iwi, as a monument acknowledging the hundred years of the signing over of Lake Wairarapa to the government of that day. The central theme of this carving was reconciliation: man to God, and man to man, with the cross being placed in the centre. I praise God that a new light shines through me, and for the gifts He has given me for His glory.

—*Lionel Matenga*

Last year Weston Carryer prayed for a cyst (the size of a ping-pong ball) on my elbow. As he prayed the power of God fell on me and I fell to the floor. I had it imprinted on my heart that I was healed. Over the next six months the cyst slowly got smaller. Now it is gone! Praise God.

—*Pat Heaslip*

Several years ago, I developed tennis elbow in one elbow. This was extremely painful, and my doctor explained that there was a piece of broken bone in the elbow that was rubbing on the other bone, and this was causing all the pain. He booked me in for an operation, and for a year while waiting for the operation, I was given a series of injections to ease the pain.

Weston Carryer came to our church in Lower Hutt, and during the ministry time, I went forward to be prayed for by him for the Lord to heal me. As he prayed, the healing commenced, and a week later I realized that all my mobility had returned. Now for the past six years my elbow has been wonderful, and I have had no problems with it. I never needed to have the operation. Thank You, Jesus.

MIRACLES IN AOTEAROA NEW ZEALAND

I have also suffered regularly from severe migraine headaches for as long as I can remember. When these hit, they would totally flatten me for about two days, despite a lot of medication. At a divine healing meeting several years ago, also in Lower Hutt, Weston Carryer prayed for the Lord to heal me, and I am rejoicing and praising God because I have never ever had the slightest migraine since that moment. Praise You, Lord.

—*Dawn Whaanga*

As a result of cutting my right hand, I developed a severe blood infection in my right arm and had to spend several days in the Christchurch hospital receiving intravenous treatment. After I was released from the hospital I discovered that I had very limited movement in my right thumb and suffered severe pain in my right arm, especially in cold weather. This was affecting my ability as a plumber, and often driving home at night, the pain would cause tears to flow down my face. After experiencing this for fifteen months, I attended a divine healing meeting in Christchurch in 2003 where Weston Carryer was ministering. During the ministry time Weston prayed for the Lord to heal me. Within twenty-four hours full movement was restored to my thumb, and since then, I have not had any pain in my arm at all. I praise You, Lord.

—*Paul Johnston*

For three years I was crippled by a work injury. Both my elbows were badly damaged and I was diagnosed with lateral epicondylitis, which is inflammation of the elbow. The epicondyle is the rounded end of the long bone in the upper part of the arm. This condition, apart from the continuous dull ache I suffered, prevented me from being able to hold on to anything and I kept dropping everything I attempted to hold. All the doctors, specialists and physiotherapy experts were not only useless, but some damaged me even more. I suffered at the hands of ACC for those three years.

My brother, David, encouraged me to go to a Weston Carryer

Shoulders, Arms, Elbows & Hands

divine healing meeting. I decided to do this and drove from Nelson to Christchurch to attend one of his meetings. Before the meeting, I sat in my car outside City Church in Christchurch on 27 April 2008 after the drive feeling tired, depressed and in pain. I opened my Bible and read Psalm 6, that is titled, "A Prayer of Faith in Time of Distress."

> *Have mercy on me, O Lord, for I am weak; O Lord, heal me, for my bones are troubled. I am weary with my groaning . . . The Lord has heard my supplication; the Lord will receive my prayer.*

For days before my trip I was in no doubt that God could—and would—heal me. What blew me away was that as Weston prayed for me, it was instant, intense and . . . wow! By Christ's power I was—and am—healed! No more doctors! Thank You, Jesus. After three years on ACC, and not being able to work, I now have a great job at Bunnings and love it. God bless you, Weston, and your work. Praise God.

—*Gordon Moore*

One day when I was working as a fisherman I felt my forearm tendon tear which resulted in severe pain. I also had damaged my elbow tendons and shoulder tendons. My physiotherapist told me that I should give up my job as a fisherman as treatment was not helping me at all.

I told my pastor about this and he told me to ring Weston Carryer. I did, and he prayed for me over the phone. The shoulder-tear healed instantly as he prayed and the healing commenced in the elbows. They were totally healed over a twelve-week period.

Shortly after this I attended one of Weston's meetings at Christian Renewal Fellowship in Whanganui. Weston prayed again for my shoulder tendons and also for the severe lower back pain that I had experienced for many years. I was instantly healed of both of these conditions.

Over the past twelve months, I have been able to catch fish without these very painful restrictions to my body.

Miracles in Aotearoa New Zealand

Lord Jesus, I love You so much. You have changed my life so much and I will always be so grateful to You for not only healing me, but saving me as well.

—*Colin Lowe*

Hands, Hands/Arms, Wrist, Fingers

One night I was sitting at home, sitting in the lounge of Balgownie House during a Christian meeting. This was where my new life all began for it was at this meeting I was asked by Weston Carryer if I needed prayer for anything. It happened that through repeating a once-too-often act of mischief my right hand was broken beyond repair. I went forward, closed my eyes, and he prayed for my hand. When he finished, he asked me how it was. It was on the tip of my tongue to say, "still the same," but instead I instinctively closed my hand. I had not done that for ever so long. I opened and closed my hand several times, smiled, and believed. It really blew me away. Praise the Lord.

—*Mason E. Randell*

In 1945, I almost severed one of my fingers. It was hanging on to my hand only by the skin. It was sown back on medically but for forty years I had no movement in it at all. It was completely stiff and was a much darker colour than the rest of the skin. In 1985, Weston Carryer prayed for me and God, through Jesus, healed my finger. The use was immediately and fully restored and the colour returned to normal. God, You are wonderful.

—*Barney Dewes*

For approximately three years I suffered from carpal tunnel

Shoulders, Arms, Elbows & Hands

syndrome. As a woodcarver, I found this very frustrating for my wrists were badly affected. My hands would not function correctly and for no apparent reason, I would often drop tools. My wrists would frequently become numb through the night. This would waken me and I would have to raise my hands above my head before feeling was restored. I had been told I needed an operation but this would have prevented me from working for some time.

I attended a divine healing meeting at the Rotorua Apostolic Church conducted by Weston Carryer. In his exact words, he said, "God has revealed that someone has carpal tunnel syndrome and if that person will come forward, he can be healed." I responded. Weston prayed for me, and God, through Jesus Christ, healed me forthwith. For the last year I have had no pain, numbness or restrictions in my wrists whatsoever. Praise the Lord.

—Lou Phillips

On the evening of Friday, 31 March 1989, I attended a healing service at Upper Hutt where Weston Carryer was the speaker. I went not seeking or expecting healing as I was scheduled for surgery four days later. This surgery was to be on both my hands as I was getting the most terrible pain in both during the night. As I relaxed in sleep this pain would come on and be excruciating. The only way I could get relief was to wear splints. This stopped my hands from relaxing thus avoiding pain.

On that night, God gave Weston a word of knowledge that someone had something wrong with their hands and he even indicated where I was sitting. I remember him saying that our Lord wanted to heal me, and he questioned, *Do you know Jesus as Lord?* and *Do you believe He can heal you?*

I replied, "Jesus is my Lord," but that was as far as I went as all I could think about was I was scheduled for surgery on the Thursday. I thought it too late to stop that. However, Weston prayed for me and I went home. That night I did not put splints on my hands and had a pain-free night. I did have a few pins and needles, which was all. As Saturday progressed, I became more and more sure our Lord had healed me. Sunday morning I went to see my pastor and told him I was canceling the surgery as I knew that God had healed me. He was delighted. Monday morning I phoned and cancelled the surgery, telling the folk concerned I did not need it as God had healed me. It is now two months since my healing and I have no pain whatsoever. Praise God.

—Beryl Russell

I have just visited the medical unit at Southland Hospital for an EMG examination to test for nerve damage in my hand, the outcome of a broken forearm six months ago. Since Weston Carryer's crusade, the pain in my left hand has ceased entirely. I have been able to iron and to peel potatoes without bringing on the pain. The EMG showed no nerve damage over the back of my hand where it was formerly most painful, confirming God's work of healing. Wear and tear means that I have carpal tunnel syndrome in both wrists which caused cramps, but that can be rectified easily. Now I know for what I am specifically seeking healing. I am so thankful for Weston and his healing message. Thank You, God, for Your power to heal and for the presence of the Holy Spirit who completed the work.

—Judith Stevens

In 1990, through an accident, approximately one inch was taken off my index finger. At a divine healing meeting in Mangakino in October 1997 where Weston Carryer was ministering, I went forward to be prayed for, and the Lord, through the power of the Holy Spirit, lengthened my finger so that it has now returned to its former, correct length. Thank You, Jesus.

—Clare Jessep

I had been on a waiting list for three years for an operation

Shoulders, Arms, Elbows & Hands

for carpal tunnel syndrome. Apart from the pain that I was experiencing, I was very restricted in both my job as a butcher and also as a guitar player. I attended a divine healing meeting in Foxton in June 1996 where Weston Carryer was ministering. The Lord revealed through a word of knowledge to Weston that there was someone there with carpal tunnel syndrome and for the person to come forward to receive a miracle. I responded immediately, and as Weston prayed, God instantly healed me. Since that time, fifteen months ago, I have had no pain or restriction of any kind. Thank You, Jesus.

—*Dan Tahu, Foxton*

For several years I suffered with carpal tunnel syndrome in my right wrist. During this entire time the wrist was either very painful or numb. I attended a divine healing meeting at the Wanganui Central Baptist Church in 1995 conducted by Weston Carryer. As he prayed for me, I experienced what felt like a surge of electricity go through my wrist and it was instantly totally healed. Since then I have had no further trouble in my wrist. I praise God for His healing.

—*Kaye Pikari, Wanganui*

On the 6 February 2001, I suffered electrocution by holding onto a farm fence at a parachute festival near Hamilton. (I found out after that the fence had been damaged by a truck, meaning that the current that was passing through this particular part was increased.) I immediately felt dazed and unsure of my steps. I grabbed hold of my right hand, which had turned partly black and purple from the electricity. In extreme pain, I went to the doctor who was there. I was in shock, shaking; my right hand was so hot and felt like it was burning. I could feel electricity through my whole body as I lay receiving treatment. The doctor dressed both of my hands with crepe bandages as both of my hands had burn marks. I could not move my discoloured hands all weekend. After the weekend my left hand returned back to normal slowly, as I did not grab the wire with this hand. My right hand became discoloured in response to cold. My right upper limb, in its entirety, ached and tingled, and the limb stiffened up. I went to a specialist and the doctors. The specialist wrote: "My impression is that there has been damage to the nerves to the right upper limb and this has affected their sensory motor and vasomotor functions. My expectation is that the nerves will slowly and steadily recover. However, whether recovery is complete or incomplete remains to be seen." He advised me that there was no treatment available to repair my nerves and suggested approximately two years recovery. I went to physiotherapy to maintain strength and suppleness to the limb.

On 20 March, Weston Carryer prayed for me. God had mercy and touched both of my hands in such an awesome way. I fell under the Spirit as God's anointing filled my body. I woke up with no pain. I walked outside of the church in the cold without my hands going purple. I could clap my hands, click my fingers and could shake hands which I was unable to do during the last two months. I can use both my hands fully with no pain.

—*Annabel Greenslade*

For several years I'd had pain in my left wrist off and on. Although I don't know the initial cause, it was always aggravated when I played the guitar. When Weston Carryer prayed for it, I didn't feel a thing, but I believed God had healed me. A recent x-ray had confirmed avascular necrosis of the lunate bone, which means that one of the carpals wasn't getting any blood supply and so the bone was dying. Once Weston had prayed for me, I knew the best way to test it was to play the guitar. No pain! I kept playing, and still no pain!

Since my doctor had assessed my wrist previously, I decided to ask him to check it out. He said the scaphoid has fused to the lunate, and two carpals have joined together! So the scaphoid is now supporting the lunate—hence no pain. I've had several occasions since when it felt sore, but when I've moved my wrist to see how sore it was, there's been no pain—so just a thought put in by satan. I have been thanking God constantly for healing me and have told lots of people—Christians and

Shoulders, Arms, Elbows & Hands

non-Christians. Now twelve months later I wish to state that the wrist is completely healed and I have had no problems over this entire period.

—*Emily*

Weston Carryer came to the Invercargill Prison early in 2001 to minister to the inmates. Praise God for the salvations and healings that took place among the many men that day. I am one of the Invercargill Christian Church Prison outreach teams that go into the prison each Saturday afternoon and Sunday morning.

During the service Weston called out someone who had had their left hand crushed years ago. That was me. I used to help groom and ride a friend's horse years ago when I was seven. The horse accidentally stood on my hand. Since Weston prayed and laid hands on me, the Lord has healed my hand. May God bless you and your family. Your sister in Christ.

—*Lorraine Simmons*

I am a member of City Life Church in Tauranga. At Weston's last visit in June 2007, which was a seminar on evangelism, I came for healing for a painful tendon shaft on my thumb. This was going to require an operation to fix it. He mentioned at the time that healings may occur over a period of time. Glory to God! Within a month it was totally healed. I am so thankful for Weston obeying his calling by God in His work.

—*Harold Rollo*

In 2004, I developed tendonitis. This condition caused my right hand to become very swollen and very painful. As an orchard worker it became very frustrating because I kept dropping my secateurs as I could not tell if they were in my hand or not. There was no change over the next two years and the severe pain and swelling were there all the time. In November

Miracles in Aotearoa New Zealand

2006, I attended a divine healing meeting in Flaxmere where Weston Carryer prayed for the Lord to heal my hand. As he was praying the swelling and the pain disappeared completely and my hand functioned normally. For the last twelve months I have had no trouble with my right hand at all. Thank You, Jesus.

—*Verda Curtis*

I thank God for the repetitive strain injury healing in my right wrist. For over three years this was very annoying and frustrating, and made it very difficult for me trying to work as a dental therapist assistant endeavouring to do forehanded dentistry. My right hand felt just like a dead fish.

—*Lorraine Robb*

Weston Carryer was ministering at a divine healing meeting in Rangi Ora in April 2008, and I was in attendance. During the meeting he spoke out my exact condition. I went forward and he prayed for the Lord to heal me. From that moment, now over twelve months ago, I have not had any problems with my right wrist. It was wonderfully healed instantly. I just want to thank the Lord so much.

—*Claire Harris*

In January 2007, when I was thirteen, I damaged my wrist which became very painful with no movement in it at all. Over the next five weeks there was no improvement in it. Then it was discovered that it was broken and was immediately put in plaster. For the next three weeks the pain persisted with still no movement in my wrist at all.

Two months after the injury, I attended a divine healing meeting in Winton where Weston Carryer prayed for Jesus to heal the break in my wrist. As he prayed all the pain went and the full movement was restored to my wrist. The plaster was immediately removed and I have never had any problem with

Shoulders, Arms, Elbows & Hands

my wrist since. Lord Jesus, You are awesome, and I am so grateful.

—*Santana Kirk*

Approximately seven years ago I developed carpal tunnel syndrome in my right hand and wrist. For two years this chronic pain and restriction was in my hand and wrist and completely prevented me from doing anything with my right hand. I could not even lift a plate. I was facing surgery but was putting it off.

At a divine healing meeting in Whangerei five years ago, Weston Carryer was ministering. Through a word of knowledge he said that there was a person there with carpal tunnel syndrome in their right wrist and hand. I responded, and he prayed for the Lord to heal me. As he prayed the pain instantly went and the full movement was restored. Over the last five years there has not been the slightest sign of it.

Hallelujah. Praise the Lord.

—*Dianne Langridge*

"He himself bore our sins"
in his body on the cross,
so that we might die to sins
and live for righteousness;
"by his wounds
you have been healed."

—*1 Peter 2:24*, NIV

Six

Abdominal & Internal Organs

Testimonies of healed conditions of the digestive/eliminative system, internal organs, blood, and gynecological problems.

Stomach, Abdominal, Digestive/Eliminative System, Oesophagus

I went forward at a Weston Carryer meeting, trembling like a leaf. I had bowel problems in the form of a foreign growth. God, through Jesus, performed a miracle and my prayers of faith were answered. I went into the hospital later for more exploratory tests only to be told by the surgeon the growth had disappeared.

—*Molly Ireland*

For nearly seven years, my friend Clara had been unable

Miracles in Aotearoa New Zealand

to eat a solid meal because her throat used to gag (balk) at swallowing food. I always felt terrible enjoying a beautiful meal of meat and vegetables while she ate nothing.

Weston prayed for her. Last week, she kept insisting she had received her healing. She actually bought a pie and we all praised God as she consumed every bit. It was truly a blessing as I watched her eat a full dinner.

—Mavis H.

Unfortunately, diverticulitis was part of my life for forty years. This extremely painful condition is caused by food becoming cemented in the bowel which then causes severe cramps to occur at any time. In my case, this was often at night. I was told there was no medical cure for my condition and I would have it for life.

In May 2001, I attended a divine healing meeting in Whangarei where Weston Carryer was ministering. At one stage he asked the person with diverticulitis to come forward for the Lord to heal them. I went forward immediately and Weston prayed for me. I am delighted to testify that since that night twelve months ago, I have not had any pain or discomfort of any kind. I know my bowel is completely healed by the wonderful power of the Lord. Thank You, Jesus.

—Eva Wright

I had always had a bowel problem; as a child I was told I had a '"lazy" bowel. I am now sixty-one years old and in the past few years, this has become a major problem in my life. I went to the doctor who sent me for x-rays, and then on to a specialist. All they could determine was that I had a case of diverticulitis and that this went all the way to the colon region. The lower bowel had lost its sensitivity and they said I would have to be on medication for the rest of my life. I did not believe that this need be so, because the Bible tells me that God wants us to be whole physically as well as spiritually. God led me to His laws of creation, cause and effect, and showed me that

Abdominal & Internal Organs

although all things are permissible, not all things are beneficial. I took all this to mean that we all eat the wrong things and take everything for granted. I was not satisfied.

Praise God. I was healed completely by Him at a healing meeting in July 1990 when Weston Carryer prayed for release from my birth infirmity. Now I am completely whole with my bowel functioning as normal. I praise God constantly for His loving kindness. I am thankful for Weston obeying God's calling on his life.

—*Myrtle Clark*

My name is Liz Rongonui—a child of God from Masterton. I'd like to share a wonderful healing I had some two years ago now. Ever since January of 1980 until about the end of 1986-87, I had recurring bowel trouble. I had nearly always been constipated and had to have some form of medication to relieve the pain. The doctor said he couldn't do anything for my complaint but that he could prescribe medication (Granacol) to make it more bearable. After meeting our precious Saviour (who was a bit more helpful) in April of 1985, I noticed that my complaint had worsened, and by the end of 1986 I couldn't stand it. I remember going to the toilet this particular morning and with all my heart and mind crying out, "Oh Lord . . . Oh Lord . . . help me. Please help me." I was so very desperate and in need.

Well, that very night, Weston Carryer arrived at our church. I remember sitting at the back watching—with much awe—people being healed of many various illnesses—both big and small.

Then I heard Weston say, "There's a woman here with a bowel problem."

Man, you should've seen me fly! He was still speaking when I skidded to a halt at the front. You would've thought there were buses running. I can't remember too much else of what he said, but, I know that when I tried to get up I felt like a concrete slab. So I thought, *Well, I can lie here a bit longer, I s'pose.*

Praise our ever-loving heavenly Father. That was about two

Miracles in Aotearoa New Zealand

years ago now and the whole event was instant and miraculous. I came to know Jesus for who He is . . . the same yesterday, today and forever.

—*Liz Rongonui*

Since I fellowship at the same church as Weston Carryer I have been able to call on his spiritual support on several occasions with wonderful results. Initially, I had difficulty due to my bowels not functioning properly, and an examination by way of a barium enema revealed I had a touch of diverticulitis. Then, at a later stage, I had an operation due to gallstones when the gallbladder was removed. Strangely, every time I had appointments with a doctor or at a hospital, Weston was at church the Sunday before and he strengthened me for what was to come.

On a recent Sunday morning when Weston was ministering, I was desperately in need of God's healing touch. As he prayed over me I was slain in the Spirit. When I went to rise up, I felt so sick I was forced to lie down a little longer. I knew God was doing something in my body—to my bowels. It was fantastic for I felt I was really under an anaesthetic. Even when I arrived home I had to lie down because I was convinced the operation God was performing on me was not finished. Truly, in the end, I was completely healed by God, through Jesus by the power of Holy Spirit. There has been no recurrence. I praise Him, for He is a worker of miracles and does give wholeness to those in need.

—*June Colbourne*

For four years I endured stomach cramps which used to buckle me right over with pain. I attended a healing meeting at Hicks Bay and went forward for prayer from Weston Carryer. The pain was very acute at the time. During the prayer the pain ceased immediately. God, through Jesus Christ, healed me and for the last twelve months, I have had no problems at all.

—*Agnes Poi*

Abdominal & Internal Organs

I was called out by Weston Carryer for healing of diverticulitis when I attended one of his meetings in New Plymouth in late 1994. I had had a lot of problems with this affliction over some years, even to having a piece taken out of the bowel which had fallen down.

When Weston prayed for me, God's power, through Jesus Christ, healed me gloriously. Praise be to our heavenly Father and Jesus Christ our Saviour.

—*Thelma Watson*

Praise be to Jehovah Rapha, our healer. I had been diagnosed as having a hernia for which I was due to have an operation, and I also had a stomach ulcer. I had considerable pain as well as much discomfort.

At a divine healing meeting at Tokoroa, Weston Carryer prayed for me. Since that time I have had no further physical problems relating to either condition. Furthermore, the doctor has confirmed that there is now no sign of the ulcer, nor is there any need for the hernia operation. Thank You, Jesus, for healing me.

—*Joan Johnson*

I went forward for divine healing at Glen Eden on Sunday, 24 September 2006. Weston Carryer was ministering and he asked me what my problems were. For years I had severe pain in my spine through arthritis. Every morning it was difficult to get out of bed because of the pain, and although it was worse in the morning, it never went away. I had also been diagnosed with diverticulitis. This caused a lot of bowel pain and difficulty going to the toilet. What happened as I was prayed for was amazing. All pain instantly left and I have not had any further pain or problems with these areas in my body over the last twelve months. I have felt so much peace with no more pain in my back or bowel. I thank the Lord every day for giving me strength and supplying all my needs and healing me.

—*Bernice Wonglyn*

For eleven years I suffered from ulcerative colitis, and for several months of every year during this eleven-year period, I had to take steroids and salazopyrin. This condition was accompanied by a spastic bowel.

I attended a divine healing meeting in November 1998 where Weston Carryer was ministering. The Lord revealed my condition to Weston; he spoke it out and asked me to come forward to receive my healing from the Lord. I responded immediately and that night I was totally healed of both conditions. Ever since that night, over a year ago now, I have had no sign of either condition and there is no longer a need to take steroids or medication. Thank You, Jesus.

—*Sue Dwen*

For several years I had been suffering from a severe stomach problem. This resulted in chronic spasm abdominal pain. The digestive system could not function correctly which also caused continual constipation. I attended a divine healing meeting at Queenstown in 1998, where Weston Carryer was ministering and he prayed for Jesus to heal me. I wish to testify that I had a wonderful instant total healing through my entire body. Thank You, Lord!

—*Lyn Kramer*

For approximately ten years I had a serious bowel problem. It felt as if I had a plastic bag inside me and was accompanied by daily dysentery and regular morning vomiting. In August 1996, I attended a divine healing meeting in Tauranga conducted by Weston Carryer who prayed for me during the meeting. That night, God, through the power of the Holy Spirit, totally healed me. No more dysentery or vomiting since that night. Thank You, Jesus.

—Ione Mooney

Early in 1993 I became very ill. I had severe stomach pains and was unable to eat or drink very much at all. This complaint continued and got worse, until I was passing out with the pain. I went from doctor to doctor trying to get answers and find some relief, but no one had any answers for me. I had many trips to our local hospital, and even went to Hamilton for tests. These tests were very extensive. One test had me drinking fluid and then being stood on my head on a machine while they x-rayed the progress of the liquid. This was all taking its toll on me and my family. Most of the time I was in bed unable to participate in anything.

After several months of this, we were told of a healing meeting that was to be held in our town. My husband and I went—both of us very excited, and full of expectation, that the Lord would deal with my illness. I went forward, and Weston laid his hands on me and prayed. I never felt a thing at the time of his prayer. But throughout the evening, the pain subsided, and after a few hours, we left. As you leave the hall, there is a twenty-four hour takeaway directly across the street. Lance wanted to buy fish and chips, but I was afraid. I hadn't eaten anything like that in months; it made me so ill. My darling husband looked me in the eye, and said, "Where is your faith?" So we bought the food, took it home, and it was lovely. The best part being . . . no pain.

However, just before going to bed I started to get my pain medication ready for the night just in case. Once again Lance asked what I was doing. He was right; I put the pills away, went to bed, and was blessed with the first good night's sleep in months.

A week later, I had another appointment at the hospital and the doctor was so proud that at last he had some answers for me. It seems that I had three huge ulcers. My stomach was a mess. He found it very difficult to believe that I didn't need any painkillers or medication of any sort. It took some convincing him, but in the end, another test was done that meant me standing on my head again. When these tests came back there were no ulcers and no sign there ever were any. There was no scaring at all. Needless to say the poor man was very confused and thought that I was insane when I gave all the glory to God and told him of my healing.

My life is full. I am happy and healthy and know that Weston coming to our town at that time was no accident. God sent him here and gave me the choice of believing and getting well or turning my back and suffering. I chose God. He is the cornerstone of my life.

—*Angela Te Ahuru*

For approximately four years I suffered with haemorrhoids. This condition was always extremely painful and was very embarrassing as the continual bleeding would soak my clothes. I was told by my doctor that the chances of a successful operation were not good.

However, at a church service at Invercargill in February 2000, Weston Carryer prayed for divine healing for me. I am delighted to write that by the next morning, the haemorrhoids had all disappeared and have never returned. Jesus completely healed me. Thank You, Lord.

—*Bruce Hagen, Invercargill*

For over forty years I was medically diagnosed as having a dysfunctional stomach. This resulted in me being allergic to many different foods, particularly anything fatty, and even some vegetables. Any time I ate any of these foods I would have violent diarrhoea and often pass out completely. As a result of these fainting spells, I suffered further injuries and was hospitalised twice.

I attended a divine healing seminar at Paraparaumu in August 1998, where Weston Carryer was ministering. Weston

Abdominal & Internal Organs

received a word of knowledge about my condition, and when he spoke it out, I responded immediately and went forward for prayer. That night the Lord completely healed me. Eighteen months later I am delighted to say that I now have no dietary problems of any kind after forty years of suffering. Hallelujah. Thank You, Jesus.

—*Peter Brock, Paraparaumu*

I am so thankful that Weston Carryer prayed over me asking the Lord to heal me. When he opened his healing prayers on the Tuesday night in Gisborne, I was the lady who shook like a leaf. I told him that I had bowel problems.

Well, a miracle has happened to me as my prayers have been answered by the Lord. Praise Him. I went into the hospital on 10 August for more tests and then was taken down to theatre for an exploratory. But the surgeon discovered the growth I had was gone, so my prayers were answered. I thank the Lord for that. I always believed He had healed me as my faith in the Lord is very strong.

—*Molly Ireland, Gisborne*

For five years I suffered from diverticulitis and was on constant medication which I was told I would be on permanently. Also, I needed to be on a very restricted diet.

I attended a divine healing meeting at the Te Awamutu Apostolic Church in 1995. During the meeting Weston Carryer prayed for me and the Lord healed me. Since that time the diverticulitis has totally gone, I have had no further medication and my diet is not limited at all. Praise God.

—*Lorraine Mills, Te Awamutu*

I praise and thank God for healing me of serious haemorrhoids after suffering from this problem for about two years. I could not sit, stand, or walk for long lest my haemorrhoids bled.

MIRACLES IN AOTEAROA NEW ZEALAND

When I got pregnant, my haemorrhoids got worse. I had to be bed-bound. Once during my pregnancy I was bleeding for four days successively. My gynaecologist advised me to be admitted into the hospital immediately as he was concerned that it might endanger the baby in the womb. After I gave birth to my baby, Olivia, I thought I would be better, but ironically, I was worse than before. This time my haemorrhoids were really bad and were like a cluster of grapes filled with blood. Again, I had to be bed-bound, not to mention that I even had to have my meals in bed. It was awful and I felt very depressed. My doctor advised that I should have an operation, and he said he would confirm it when I visited him for my six-week post-natal checkup.

Meanwhile, my pastor's wife visited me one day and I told her about my condition. That very day she called Weston Carryer to come to my house to pray for me. Thank God for using Weston. When I went for my six-week postnatal checkup, my doctor told me that no surgery on my haemorrhoids was required as they had already subsided. Praise and glory be unto God, for truly the Lord heals in His own time. I remember my church friends, my family and I were praying for my piles problem for two years, and during this time, it seemed that God was far away and was just not answering our prayers. But I believe He is in control of all things and was using that period of waiting to strengthen my faith in Him. God is good and has always been good. Like Paul says, "His grace is sufficient for us." Praise the Lord!

—*Patricia Lien*

I wish to testify to two healings that I received from the Lord when Weston Carryer visited our church in March 2000. Firstly, I had been suffering from haemorrhoids for at least five years and they were getting worse. I also had a condition affecting my left arm which resulted in a very sharp pain grabbing the arm and causing me to lose total contact of the arm. During the meeting Weston had a word of knowledge for someone who was experiencing this particular problem with their arm, so I went forward and he prayed for the Lord to heal the arm. I made no mention of the haemorrhoids, but imagine my delight a few

Abdominal & Internal Organs

days later when I realized that both the haemorrhoid condition and the arm were healed. For the last twelve months I have had no problems. Praise the Lord.

—*John Caird, Timaru*

For twenty five years I suffered from irritable bowel syndrome. It was extremely painful and the intensity of the pain continued to get worse. I passed blood practically daily, and if I ever went anywhere, I always wanted to be sure that I was not too far away from a toilet as I had many embarrassing moments of bleeding through my trousers.

I attended a divine healing meeting at Dunedin in February 2000, where Weston Carryer was ministering and he prayed for the Lord to heal me. I noticed an immediate improvement. Over a few months the healing became complete.

Over the last several months there has been no sign of this condition. My quality of life now simply does not compare with how it was for twenty-five years. To be pain-free, and to be able to go anywhere without embarrassment can only be appreciated when you have experienced this for twenty-five years. I am so thankful to Jesus.

—*Graham Hunter, Dunedin*

For the last four years I have been suffering from an increasingly deteriorating bowel problem. When Weston Carryer was ministering in Tokoroa on Sunday, 25 July, the Lord gave him a word that someone in the congregation had a bowel problem. I went forward for prayer to receive a miracle.

Twelve days later I went ahead with a prearranged colonoscopy. The whole large intestine was inspected and multiple samples taken for later biopsies. The surgeon's report confirmed, "No inflammation, no cancers, and every sample taken was normal, healthy flesh." Thank You, Lord, for the miracle. What a powerful, loving God we serve. Your sister in Christ.

—*Fran Ivin, Putaruru*

Miracles in Aotearoa New Zealand

For over forty years I suffered from severe colitis. The pain at times was very severe. I have had eight children and the colitis pain was worse than any labour pains that I ever had. After every single meal I had to rush off to the toilet and also go through the night.

In March 2001, I attended a meeting in our church where Weston Carryer was ministering. Weston spoke out my exact condition as the Lord revealed it to him, and he asked me to come forward for the Lord to heal me. I went forward immediately. As Weston prayed, the Lord instantly completely healed me, and I have had no further pain or abnormal bowel movement ever since.

I am so grateful to the Lord and truly rejoice in being normal after forty years. Thank You, Jesus!

—*Mary Dunick*

I am writing to you to give my testimony of my healing after Weston Carryer prayed for me at the St. Andrews Presbyterian Church in Matamata. The condition healed was colitis which God revealed to him that someone was suffering from at the service.

The colitis came on rather suddenly about nine years ago. About four different doctors couldn't figure out the problem and I had learned to live with the condition. It was a nervous type of condition with symptoms of colicky pain and frequent visits to the toilet (but not diarrhoea), e.g., every morning at the start of milking (I am a sharemilker) I would have to go back to the toilet, and often several times in the day. If I was doing something that might make me a bit nervous (like operating the sound system at church), I would go to the toilet at home before I left for church and once again before the service started.

After the healing on the Sunday, I did not go to the toilet for two days! I have never had to go during morning milking again and never had to go twice before doing the sound at church again. I have settled into a regular daily pattern! The colicky pain eased up, not going instantly, but has slowly decreased to the point now, where I might feel a fraction of that feeling about once every ten days. The intervals are getting further apart and the pain so little now that you have to ask, is that colitis pain or not? I totally believe it will disappear altogether forever.

The amazing thing is, I came to church that day with no intention of getting healed and I would not have even asked Weston to pray for the condition as I felt embarrassed that other people would hear about it. Crazy, I know. I had prayed for myself to the Lord over the years and I did believe it would be healed in the Lord's time.

I gave my life to the Lord when I was fourteen and I'm now thirty-nine. Since my wife did an Alpha course this year, and shared personally with others, we have both grown a lot closer to the Lord, and we believe our vessels are filled with the Holy Spirit. I am continually praising the Lord for my healing.

Thanks to the Lord for my healing and I'm so thankful for Weston praying for me.

—*Evan Lock*

I am writing this testimony to encourage you that at one of Weston Carryer's healing meetings, I was healed of a bowel complaint that I have suffered from for thirty-nine years. I had a kink in the lower part of my bowel since I was born and that part had no movement. The surgeon told me that it was a lazy bowel that wouldn't work unless they operated and took out that part. This kink has caused me to have much severe pain for a lot of my life and has not been nice to live with. I have had many tests, seen many doctors, and had dozens of treatments to try, but nothing has worked.

I attended Weston Carryer's healing meeting in Te Awamutu and Weston called out a complaint of someone who was at the meeting with a physical condition that needed healing. I went forward to receive healing and I felt the Holy Spirit instantly take away the pain and correct the kink in my body. I can now live my life without the cramps and now do not take any medication because that part of me is alive again.

I also am writing to give testimony for another healing I received at Weston's meeting. For eight months I have had pain in my left side and left breast. I had an operation to remove a growth which left a huge scar and much pain. The nerve endings were damaged and scar tissue was building up, pulling, and giving a lot of discomfort. At the meeting Weston called out someone sitting in pain, and I went forward and received instant healing; the pain left my body. I can now slap that side of my body and have no pain whatsoever. I am grateful for Weston's healing meetings. Praise to God.

—*Pauline Lea*

I have suffered from gastric reflux (hiatus hernia) for many years. I had vomiting episodes every two to three months because of this. When I ate, the food seemed to stick in my chest and gave me a sick feeling. Over the last few months I have had to take nausea tablets nearly every day. On 7 November 2004, I attended a healing service where Weston Carryer was ministering. He prayed for me for this and other conditions. Now, two months later, I have had no further nausea or required nausea medication, no problem with food sticking in my chest, no repeats, and no gastric reflux. It's been wonderful to be free of that nausea-sick feeling. I give God all the glory for this wonderful miracle.

—*Molly Kirk*

For almost as long as I can remember I have had digestive problems. Then just over two years ago I suddenly experienced excruciating pain in the lower abdomen and I almost passed out. I was rushed to hospital and diverticulitis was diagnosed. The same thing happened six months later and the hospital doctors said that if this continued to happen I would need to have an operation to remove part of my bowel, and I would need to have a bag for at least six weeks. However, they said they were very reluctant to do this because of other problems that could occur. I continued to experience pain a lot of the time as well as discomfort all the rest of the time.

Abdominal & Internal Organs

Then I attended a divine healing meeting at West City Christian Centre on 13 June 2004 where Weston Carryer was ministering. After praying for some conditions that the Lord had revealed to him, he then said there was someone in the congregation with diverticulitis in the section where I was sitting. I responded. While he was praying for me, I knew I had been touched in the area of my need and felt heat in the exact place. However, I went through a rollercoaster ride of doubts over the next two weeks. But then as I awoke on the morning of the 30 June, I felt so different. I knew I was healed and I felt such a peace. I knew then that my trust and faith in God over the previous two weeks had allowed Him to complete my healing.

Now, five months later, I have had no real pain and everything is functioning normally. I have had only a couple of small niggles, but have claimed my healing and they immediately left. I give all the glory to the Lord and I thank Him, because it surely is a wonderful miracle.

—*Heather Partridge*

For the past thirty-five years I had extreme indigestion. Some nights I would go to sleep and wake up three hours later vomiting up bile. All this time I was taking Losec liquid antacids and for the past six years.

I knew Weston Carryer was coming to Whangarei for some healing meetings and I prayed and really sought God. I went to the healing meetings expecting God to heal me.

During one meeting Weston spoke out my exact condition and asked for me to go forward for the Lord to heal me. I did go to the front and he prayed for me. Sometime after this I realized that I was healed and that I did not need any more medication, and I have not had any ever since. I no longer have that dreadful indigestion or digestive problems. It was a wonderful, notable healing. It has made an incredible difference in my life. Thank You, Jesus. I am so grateful.

—*Maureen Ward*

Miracles in Aotearoa New Zealand

I attended a divine healing meeting at the Equippers Church, Wanganui on the 24 April 2005. Weston Carryer named a condition I had which was reflux. He called me forth for God to heal me. After prayer I sat back down. The presence of the Holy Spirit was really strong on me that night. It is now eight months since Weston prayed for me and I have not had even one of the pills I had been on every night for roughly two and a half years. It was a prescription medicine (Somac) that I had tried to go without on several occasions. However, I could not stop taking it for more than thirty hours without being sick. Praise God for His loving kindness and care and for Weston's obedience to Him.

—*Hayden Stead*

All my life I suffered from bowel trouble with almost constant diarrhoea, and much of the time, I was nauseous. This had slowly, but steadily, got worse over the years, and over the past few years, had become more painful. I found that I was becoming more and more restricted in my diet.

On 20 March 2005, I attended a divine healing meeting in Invercargill where Weston Carryer was ministering and he prayed for the Lord to heal me. The week prior to this I had been doubled over in pain, moaning and groaning, and thinking I was dying. I was afraid to go to the toilet because of the pain. As Weston prayed for me I felt heat go right into the problem area and the Lord did a miracle for me. The next day I was totally healed. All bowel trouble and constant diarrhoea is now history. I have not had a sign of either problem since that night over a year ago now. I am rejoicing and praising God that I am free of these conditions after experiencing them for my entire life. Thank You, Lord.

—*Glenis Currie*

When I was twenty-two years old I developed a severe digestive

Abdominal & Internal Organs

and bowel condition. Every afternoon I would experience very painful stomachaches, and when I finished work, I used to go straight home to bed to get some relief. This carried on for ten years and was accompanied by diarrhoea and almost continual bloating. Medical tests never revealed anything.

I was encouraged to go to a divine healing meeting in 2001 by my mother-in-law who was a Christian. I was quite sceptical but did go forward for another condition to be prayed for by Weston Carryer who was ministering. As soon as he started praying for me, the power of God hit me and I could not stand and I fell to the floor. I had never experienced anything like this before and I realized that Jesus was for real. A few weeks after this I accepted Jesus as my Lord.

In 2004, Weston was again ministering in our district and so I went along to the meeting. I went forward to be prayed for by him for my stomach and bowel. I am rejoicing to write that I was immediately healed and have never had any of those problems again. What a huge relief. Thank You, Lord, for saving and healing me.

—Kathleen Brebner

I would like to tell you about healing I received at one of Weston Carryer's healing meetings at New Plymouth City Life Church last year. I used to have uncontrollable dysentery which kept me house-bound for much of the day. This had been going on for approximately ten years. It was really terrifying and totally restricted where I could go as toilet access was imperative. Although my condition now is not perfect, I am able to lead a normal life. I no longer get the chronic dysentery I used to get. Once again, I thank God for my healing, and am grateful that Weston brought God's healing to people.

—Peter Hoskin

When Weston Carryer was in Invercargill in March 2005 at Hawthorndale Community Church, he called for a person with a bowel problem and I went forward for prayer. For approximately

Miracles in Aotearoa New Zealand

six years I had suffered from a blocked bowel, despite taking laxatives continually. This problem necessitated me having to have enemas at least once a month, and at times, twice a week. This condition caused a lot of pain and was sometimes very severe and extremely debilitating.

I must say that God touched me on that day. I have been healed and I know that for the last twelve months I have not had a blocked bowel and have not needed any laxatives or enemas. I feel so free and God has done a great miracle. Thank You so much, Lord Jesus.

—*Vanessa Scobie*

For almost five years, I had irritable bowel syndrome. This resulted in me spending lots of time at the toilet in the mornings with weird pressure in my bowel that caused pain and nausea. I was healed of this condition when God used Weston Carryer at Grace Vineyard Church in Christchurch in March 2005. I was not instantly healed, but there was an immediate improvement. As I claimed my healing, the attacks became less. I have now been one hundred percent for several months. Thank You, Lord Jesus.

—*Samuel Skinner*

For some time I had experienced considerable pain in my stomach. It was not there all the time, but when it was, it was very severe. Early in 2006, I was medically diagnosed with a stomach ulcer.

At a divine healing meeting in Patea in May 2006, Weston Carryer prayed for the Lord to heal me. The pain ceased immediately and never returned. A subsequent stomach examination after this revealed that the ulcer had disappeared. Thank You, Jesus.

—*Marilyn Broughton*

Abdominal & Internal Organs

Following a major operation in early 2005, I continued to suffer pain regularly in my lower abdomen area. This persisted for twelve months and did not improve at all during this entire time. I attended a divine healing meeting in Invercargill in March 2006 where Weston Carryer prayed for the Lord to heal this condition. Since the prayer I have not had the slightest degree of pain. Lord, I thank You so much.

—*Sue Jones*

I wish to testify to a miraculous healing when you had a word of knowledge while ministering in my church in Christchurch in April 2007 regarding an irritable bowel problem. I responded as I had had this condition for more than twenty years. I had learned to live with and manage this condition. Apart from the severe pain, it caused so much restriction and simply controlled my life. As you prayed for me, the Lord instantly healed me. It was marvellous. My whole system seems to have changed and I now live what I term a "normal" life. Praise God for His wonderful mercy toward me.

—*Shirley Fraser*

In 2005, I was diagnosed with having a hiatus hernia and also gastro-oesophageal reflux. The reflux caused me pain most of the day and got worse after meals. This meant that I had to go to sleep at night sitting up. I had a permanent sore throat from the refluxing stomach acid and it had begun to wear away the enamel on my back teeth. My GP had me on the maximum amount of medication that she could. I was awaiting a gastroscopy and possible keyhole surgery for my hernia. I was on the waiting list through the public hospital system but was unlikely to get seen as my problems were not considered severe enough!

Weston Carryer came to our church at the beginning of 2006. I came forward for healing. After he prayed for me, there was a slight decrease in my symptoms. I knew that God had touched me through Weston's prayer so I held on in faith to the belief that God would complete the healing. From that night, I slept lying down, which I had not done for many months. I kept on with my medication and slowly over time, the symptoms decreased even more so that I slowly weaned myself off the medication totally. Over a period of three months, I was totally healed of all pain and discomfort—no more sore throats or heartburn, and no more pressure from my hernia.

My healing was not instant, but a process over time. So I would want to encourage people to hold on and believe for their healing! I'm so thankful for Weston, for his ministry, and above all, thank You, Lord Jesus.

—*Christine Graham*

Irritable bowel syndrome troubled me considerably for at least five years. It caused me to either have constipation or diarrhoea approximately every two weeks during this entire five-year period. It would often be accompanied by pain. There was no improvement at all during the entire time.

At a divine healing meeting in August 2007, Weston Carryer prayed for the Lord to heal me. Apart from a small attack a few days later, I have had no further problem with irritable bowel syndrome over the last five months and I know I am completely healed. This has been a really significant healing for me, and I just want to thank the Lord so much.

—*Claire Smith*

From 2004 until 2007, I had a debilitating condition affecting my stomach and bowel. Terrible pain would regularly come in my stomach and then within a short time, my bowel would bleed. This would then carry on for some time. I was prescribed medication from the doctor to try to control the bleeding but it did not help. I was booked in to have an ultra-scan in April 2007.

In March 2007, I attended a divine healing meeting in Gore

Abdominal & Internal Organs

where Weston Carryer prayed for the Lord to heal me. Since that moment over two years ago, I have never had any stomach pain or bowel bleeding at all. The ultra-scan that I had showed everything was normal. Both my doctor and the hospital staff were amazed. Thank You so much, Lord Jesus.

—*Barbara Gibson*

For approximately ten years I suffered from irritable bowel syndrome. This condition caused so many restrictions in my life as most of the time I had little, and at other times, no control over my bowel. Often when shopping I would have to frantically rush to the toilet, and this was terribly embarrassing.

At a divine healing meeting at Papamoa in June 2008, Weston Carryer prayed for the Lord to heal me. The result was amazing. I was completely healed and over the last twelve months, I have had no further bowel problems at all. I can now go for walks without any worry. This healing has made a colossal difference in my quality of life. Thank You so much, Lord.

—*Shirley Redfern*

For five years, I suffered terribly from ulcerative colitis. This chronic condition completely controlled my life as I had no control over my bowels during this entire five-year period. Wherever I went, I always had to make sure there was a toilet very close. But on many occasions, I did not get to the toilet in time, which resulted in me having to change my clothes and sometimes needing to have a shower.

In October 2010, I attended a divine healing meeting in Flaxmere where Weston Carryer was ministering. During the ministry time, he described my condition and asked for me to go forward for him to pray to the Lord to heal me, and I responded.

An improvement started immediately; within three months, the healing was complete, and I have had no further problems at all. In December 2010, I had a colonoscopy and the specialist said he did not need to see me for three years.

What a relief. Praise God.

—Peter

For at least twenty years I suffered from reflux problems. At the best of times I would have this burning sensation in my stomach, but it was always worse at night and I often had to get up because of the pain and the feeling of nausea. I regularly felt sick after my evening meal, no matter how careful I tried to be with my diet. I tried many different kinds of medication including Losec, but nothing helped in any way.

I attended a divine healing meeting in Matamata in May 2011, where Weston Carryer was ministering. During the ministry time he prayed for the Lord to heal me, and I am rejoicing to say that I was instantly healed.

Since that moment, now six months ago, I have had no further problems with reflux. No digestive pain, discomfort or burning, and I now sleep like a baby through the entire night. This has made a huge impact on my quality of life. Thank you, Jesus.

—John Stewart

I went forward at a healing meeting conducted by Weston Carryer at St. Andrews Church Matamata on the 5 October 2011, when he said that there was someone present with a reflux problem. I had experienced this reflux problem for at least 20 years. It would cause quite severe pain in my digestive system for several hours each time and this was happening on a regular basis.

I received immediate healing, and have been completely free of this severe pain ever since, now over twelve months ago. I am very blessed.

—Grace Benge

Abdominal & Internal Organs

On 24 December 2013, I ate some fried sushi. This totally upset my digestive system. That night I took some natural medicine and I felt a slight improvement. On Christmas Day I was afraid to eat anything, so I just ate heaps of salad.

On the 26th we went to Hastings to visit a friend. I had fish and chips, which totally upset my digestive system. I continued to have excessive acid reflux and just felt horrible. This problem, combined with the pollen in Hastings, triggered my asthma. I had to be admitted to the hospital for observation. The doctor prescribed some Losec to help relieve my acid reflux, but the problem continued for the next two weeks.

One morning, when I was having my quiet time, the Lord reminded me He has taken everything on the cross. On the morning of Sunday, 19 January 2014, the Lord said He would heal me. As I was walking into church, I heard the song, "I Am the Lord That Healeth Thee." I knew He was going to heal me. When Weston Carryer called out my condition, I was so excited because I knew my healing was on the way. Before Weston could pray, I fell under the power of God.

From that moment, now over four months ago, I have had no problems with my digestive system. Thank You, Jesus, for healing me.

—*Sylvia Edwin*

In mid-2004, I was diagnosed with oesophagus reflux and ulcers in the oesophagus. For the next three years this caused pain and burning a lot of the time. I always had to be extremely careful with my diet. I refused to take medication and there was no improvement at all over the next three years.

In August 2007, I attended a divine healing meeting where Weston Carryer prayed for the Lord to heal me. I am rejoicing to let you know that the Lord instantly healed me, and over the last several months, I have had no further pain or burning at all. It is marvellous. Thank You, Lord.

—*Maria Thom*

Miracles in Aotearoa New Zealand

For approximately two years, I suffered from irritable bowel syndrome, which was very inconvenient to say the least. I would suddenly have to rush to the toilet at least five times a day and never knew when this would occur. In 2002, my husband and I were going to the Australian outback, and I was very concerned as I did not know how I would cope with this bowel condition.

The night before we left I attended a divine healing meeting in Matamata where Weston Carryer was ministering. He spoke out my condition and asked me to go forward for him to pray for me for the Lord to heal me. I responded immediately and Weston prayed for me. I am delighted to report that by the next morning I was healed and have never had any recurrence over the last three years. I was able to relax and enjoy my trip to Australia. How different life is now. Thank You, Jesus. I am so grateful.

—Margaret McBurney

About six years ago, I lost my voice to such an extent that I could barely whisper. This did not help me at all in my job as a teacher! Doctors had some trouble diagnosing this problem but finally showed that it was acute reflux—a condition where, as I lay down to sleep at night, the acid in the stomach freely runs up the oesophagus to the vocal cords burning them badly. I was put on Somac, and this relieved the symptoms. In fact, if I was ever without this medication, I found it very difficult to sleep at night.

Unfortunately, as this condition deteriorated, the medication levels had to be increased to a point where I was reaching the maximum allowed dosage. The doctor was concerned and sent me to a surgeon for examination.

"Surgery is seldom successful," he said. "So hopefully the maximum Somac dosage will work for you." *This . . . I thought . . . for the rest of my life?*

Some months after this examination and diagnosis, I attended a divine healing meeting where Weston Carryer prayed

Abdominal & Internal Organs

for the sick. Weston prayed for me, in the name of Jesus, at the end of the meeting. As he prayed, I claimed my healing and trusted God. I continued to do this—claiming my healing and confessing my trust in God many times a day—especially during the first week after the meeting.

It has now been over four years since God healed me, and during this entire four-year period, I have been on zero medication and I sleep soundly. My voice is normal and strong, and I can even sing again! Thank You, God. I'm so thankful for Weston's faithful work.

—*Paul Reid*

Two years ago I had chronic stomach pains. I hadn't been able to eat much for a few weeks. At the time of the healing service, I had been off work and was due to have tests on the Monday to show what was wrong. On the Saturday, I had been unable to eat at all, and by Sunday morning, I was so ill, I couldn't bring myself to get up.

My parent's-in-law had discovered the service was a healing meeting and came to bring me. I came up for prayer with Weston Carryer. God touched me, and then I was hungry.

The tests on Monday were all clear. Since then I have had no more pain. Praise the Lord!

—*Shane Russell, Fielding*

Internal Organs

A scan revealed that the severe pain I had been enduring was due to a bout of gallstones. At that time Weston Carryer visited our church. I went up for prayer and was wonderfully healed by God. Later I had to visit my surgeon on an unrelated problem and he just said, "No stones." How marvellous God really is.

—D.S.

Weston Carryer was speaking at a normal service in his home church. I attend there regularly and went that day, even though I was feeling miserable with nagging pains in the stomach region. Weston commenced by calling on those whom God told him needed healing. He said there was somebody present who had cirrhosis of the liver and God wanted to heal that person. No response.

He asked God to show him who it was and then he called me out. He laid hands on me and prayed over me. Along with other problems I was facing at the time, you can imagine the added stress and emotional strain when told of an illness I did not know I had. The reaction from family and friends was mixed indeed, yet I had to believe I had had such an illness and God has sovereignly healed me.

Weston reassured me of this later. I went for several months without any pain whatsoever and then the pain started to come back. I now recognise that this was a lying symptom from the devil who was endeavouring to cause me to disbelieve my healing.

Because of the pain at this time I had an ultra-scan. When interpreting the pictures the doctor said, "There must have been something wrong with your liver at some stage for there is a scar showing on it. No worry. Whatever it was has healed over."

Since that time I have had absolutely no pain. I thank God for the affirmation of His healing power.

—Linda Hancock

About a year ago God healed me of a kidney problem. One

Abdominal & Internal Organs

kidney was infected and the other one was not functioning at all. I went forward at a meeting conducted by Weston Carryer and God healed me and set me completely free from this sickness. Now I praise the Lord and give Him back the glory and honour due to His name.

—*Vaine D.*

I want to testify to the wonderful healing power of God. I was plagued with sickness for over seven years in several areas of my body: bowel, kidneys, liver and bladder. Medical practitioners did not—or could not—give me relief. For the years 1989 and 1990, I was at the doctor's every two or three weeks. Medical bills took a sizeable slice out of the low family income. I was awaiting another appointment for surgery.

Through Jesus Christ, I received total healing from God in May 1991, when Weston Carryer held a meeting in Balclutha. As I was completely free of pain, I stopped going to the doctor. Meantime, my appointment for surgery drifted on and took nine months to confirm.

I saw my doctor and told him, "I received my healing."

Then, to my surprise, he posed, "But would you not want confirmation of this?" He thought I had left town because I had not been to him for months past. I had small exploratory operation and was totally relaxed about it because I was convinced God was in this and it would reflect to His glory.

To the doctor's amazement they found only scar tissue! Hallelujah! A wonderful pain-free year has come and gone. I feel I have had the shackles removed entirely from me.

—*Rhonda Booth*

Ten years ago, when pregnant with my second child, I developed a cyst which severely affected me and resulted in both the cyst and a kidney being removed. Ten years later, when five months pregnant with my third child, another cyst was discovered which the doctor wanted to remove. I would not agree as there was a fifty-percent chance of my child dying. But knew I had to have the operation after my child was born. After my child was born the cyst had grown to the size of a large grapefruit.

While waiting for my operation I attended a healing meeting conducted by Weston Carryer, at which he prayed for Jesus to remove the cyst and heal me. I did not really believe that this was possible or would happen.

Imagine my incredible joy when I went for my next scan and the doctor told me, "I do not know what has happened, but the cyst has completely disappeared." Now twelve months later I am enjoying wonderful health. Thank You, Lord.

—*Charmaine Haenga*

Every day I thank my spiritual Dad in heaven with my whole being in that He used Weston Carryer, His very faithful servant, to pray a healing prayer over my body in time of great need. My bladder became infected and bled rather badly. I visited my local doctor who then sent me to Timaru Hospital. I stayed there six days under a specialist surgeon, Mr Wilton, who, when he was sending me home, asked me whether I would try some antibiotics. I would finish the course of tablets, and after some time, my bladder would bleed again. So I would go back again to my doctor for more tablets. This was the routine for more than two years.

Then I decided to attend one of Weston's healing meetings in Temuka with two members of the Full Gospel Chapel. Weston put out a call for people needing prayer, and I took myself to the front of the meeting and explained my health problem to him. He prayed over me, and then I came back to my home in Timaru. When people get a healing from our loving Father God, we know it. For myself, I can confirm that this healing is absolute in my body (and this is the whole truth) after I attended Weston's healing meeting in Temuka more than eighteen months ago. In the love and grace of Jesus Christ.

—*Bill Robinson, Timaru*

Abdominal & Internal Organs

Since the age of nine, I suffered from continual, almost weekly, bladder infections which plagued my life. This was accompanied later on by very bad menstrual periods and regular vomiting requiring me to be admitted to hospital on several occasions. Following my marriage, I found I was unable to conceive.

I had been married for three years when I attended a healing crusade conducted by Weston Carryer. He prayed for me in the name of Jesus and I was healed of the infection. Within days, I became pregnant and now have a beautiful baby daughter. Glory to God.

—*Melanie Smith*

Back at the beginning of August this year, I rang and asked if Weston would pray for healing for the hiatus hernia which used to give me severe pain, especially after eating meals I was unused to. He did pray for me and I am grateful for his prayers, and very grateful that God answered them. For the last four months I have stayed with five different people, plus eating out at different restaurants, and not once have I experienced any hiatus hernia pain. To me that is a real miracle. To God be all the glory!

—*Dorothy Angus*

In 1996, I was diagnosed as having a ruptured artery in my stomach and was told by the surgeon that unless I had a major operation I would have only two, or at the most, three years to live. A few weeks later I attended a Christian healing meeting in Ratahi where Weston Carryer was praying for the Lord Jesus Christ to heal the sick, and I went forward. Weston laid his hands on me and prayed, during which time I experienced the Lord doing something wonderful in my stomach, and I knew I was healed.

Miracles in Aotearoa New Zealand

At my next medical check the same surgeon told me that there was nothing wrong and I did not need any further treatment or an operation. Thank You, Lord.

—Tom Hawira

I was, to be honest, a little sceptical about faith-healing meetings, even though I had received tremendous healings for emotional wounds. The whole idea of seeing people healed physically, while others were not, was a little bit of a stumbling block. I desired to see God move like this regardless, but I just wanted to try to get my head around it. Well, that was before I went to a church meeting where Pastor Weston Carryer was ministering.

I was called out of the crowd before the message was preached. I had suffered from severe abdominal cramps for approximately three to four years. My condition had become so severe and embarrassing that I found working alone in our store incredibly difficult. My cramps were so bad by this time that I had to be very careful what I ate and at what time. The pastor prayed about my condition; I felt the Holy Spirit upon me, but still felt quite unwell. I can't say it was an instant healing (although compared to conventional medicine, it was).

Within a week, God had totally healed me and set me free to do the work I had at hand. I was just recently speaking to a staff member about how things used to be, and how that now I could quite easily be at work by myself for a long period of time, where only a year ago I couldn't even imagine. God has truly set me free, and I know He can do it for anyone.

To the congregation I would say, don't spend another day robbed from the things God would have you do, but come forward and be healed and made whole by the power of the Holy Spirit. Isn't it great that we serve a mighty, all-powerful, awesome, living God where all things are possible?

—Anita Verneer

In 1993, my gallbladder became diseased. An ultrasound

Abdominal & Internal Organs

showed that it was rotten and needed to be removed. It could have burst, and if this had happened I would have been dead within minutes. The convalescence period after the operation would have been six months. The surgeon told me that if I did not have the operation, and if the gallbladder didn't burst, it would more than likely develop into cancer. Through this condition I was also experiencing tremendous fevers and extreme pain. It felt just like a fist under my rib cage all the time. Because of my circumstances, I was in no position to have this operation, and so I did not proceed. In 1997, pain started to develop in my hip, and over the next two years it got steadily worse until I was in severe pain all the time when walking. It just felt like broken glass in the hip.

I attended a divine healing meeting in Tauranga on 28 November 2000, where Weston Carryer was ministering. I also had arthritis in my left foot and I ached all over. As Weston prayed for me I felt an intense heat source like a very strong torch light just away from my face. When I sat down I felt the most extreme hot flush that I had ever experienced.

The next morning the gallbladder pain and the foot pain had gone, and have never returned. The pain in the hip decreased, and over the next three weeks almost went. I kept on believing. Then three months later, it was totally gone. Now two and a half years later, I have no pain or physical infirmities. I am fit and healthy and able to do hard physical work. Jesus, thank You so much.

—*Ruth Carter-Chalmers*

In May 2002, my Dad had a liver transplant. Everything was going well until late in 2003 when his body started to reject the liver. It deteriorated so fast and due to the fact that he had hepatitis C, he was unable to have another transplant. Dad became so sick that the doctors told him that he had less than one year to live and they were very doubtful of him living until Christmas the following year. We made plans to move back to New Zealand so that he could be with his family, but he became too weak to move at all. He would hardly ever leave the house and he slept eighteen to twenty-two hours every day. His skin and even his eyes went yellow, he bruised very easily, and he became a completely different person. His weight dropped by twenty kilograms to fifty-eight kilograms.

Weston Carryer came to our church at Caloundra on the Sunshine Coast in Queensland in August 2004. He prayed for my Dad for the Lord to do a miracle for him. Dad believed that he was healed, but I had my doubts. After church, people came round for lunch and Dad stayed awake all day. This was amazing as he normally went straight back to bed. The next day Dad got up and mowed the lawns and when my Mum saw this she stood at the window in awe with tears in her eyes. We were all so amazed. We couldn't believe it. We knew the following day he would be completely stuffed, but we were all very wrong. He got up and changed the brake pads on my sister's car.

My Dad wasn't completely healed straightaway, and he still had to go back to New Zealand for further treatment. That day I saw God move in my Dad and it didn't just affect him; it affected a whole family and I knew it was the start of something great. When Dad was tested for hepatitis C this year, the results came back negative. He doesn't have hepatitis any more, and his liver is healed. He is healed! He is back working as a glazier full-time and sometimes works sixty-hours a week.

—*Lucy Watson, daughter*

I had a shopping list of things when I came forward for prayer. I had suffered regularly with bladder pain. It was excruciating and would bring tears to my eyes. I have been completely free of pain in my bladder now. I haven't had any pain—not even a hint of pain since Weston prayed for me. So, praise the Lord, and I'm so thankful for Weston and his faithfulness as a servant of God.

—*David Hollingsworth*

For the last seven years, I have experienced recurring episodes of extreme discomfort in the urinary bladder. These episodes became more frequent and longer in duration. With nausea and bloatedness I would pass water over twenty times in twenty-four hours. It completely governed my mind and limited what I could do and where I could go. Leaving the house was not possible. Medical blood tests and urinary tests revealed nothing abnormal and no infection. I was given an anti-spasmodic drug which had the side effects of giving me a rapid, irregular heartbeat, trouble breathing, dry mouth, and nausea. The cure was worse than the cause! I discontinued using the medication. The next step was an ultrasound scan of the pelvic area, scheduled with a four-week wait.

At this time I saw a signboard in Tauranga advertising a healing meeting with Weston Carryer. I sensed that Jesus was my only hope of healing. The medical profession could not rectify this condition without drastic and undesirable measures. I took this door of opportunity in God and received the prayer of faith with Weston.

In the following three weeks, I gradually improved and returned to normal functions by the time the scan was done ten months ago. Wonderfully, the results of the scan were absolutely normal! I bless the Lord for His kindness!

—Andrea Jacobs, Tauranga

On a Friday night in August 2012, I started to feel very unwell. I then developed severe stomach pains and quite suddenly had great difficulty breathing. My daughter took me to hospital. It was discovered that I had a urine infection and fluid on the lungs and was very sick. I was put into ICU and put on oxygen and a drip. But despite the hospital treatment, I remained in a critical condition for 48-hours.

On the Sunday night my daughter rang Weston Carryer and asked him to pray for me. He prayed over the phone and then came into my room in ICU the next morning. He laid his hands on me, and as he prayed, the Lord did a miracle for me. The intense pain just went immediately, and two hours later, I was able to go to the ward.

A few days later I was discharged from hospital and have

had no further lung or bladder problems over the last 4 months. Praise the Lord.

—*Pushpa Dounder*

As a result of severe pain I went to my doctor in May 2003. I had a scan done and this showed a cyst 10 centimeters long. I received prayer and a month later a further scan showed the cyst had shrunk in size to 4.5 centimeters, but, I still had the pain.

On September 14, 2003, I attended a divine healing meeting in Lower Hutt where Weston Carryer was ministering and he prayed for the Lord to heal me totally. I had a further scan done the next day, which showed that the cyst had completely gone. I have had no further pain. Thank You, Lord.

—*Martha Chongo*

Gynecological

In 1991, my husband and I attended Te Nikau Bible Training Centre. Shortly after we started the course, I had a recurrence of menstrual pain which became quite severe. Six months earlier, an x-ray had not revealed the reason for the pain. I was now at the point where I was in constant stress two out of four weeks in the month. I went to a doctor who put me immediately on the waiting list at the Porirua Women's Hospital. After seeing a specialist in March, I was admitted to Wellington Hospital in August for an exploratory operation, eighteen months after the first signs something was wrong. We were told I had endometriosis, which cause a lot of internal problems, and possibly, infertility. This condition is common among women, but is quite serious, for it is not really known how it begins. It is progressive with little hope of a complete cure. Drug treatments are offered which have the potential of side effects worse than the disease and with no promise of a result. My husband and I had one month to understand the condition before revisiting the specialist to decide on what to do. I went through all the reasons why I might be sick: curses, unbelief, past sins, current sins—you name it—and I rebuked, cast it out, repented of, and stood against, all. I kept hearing God say, "Trust and pray." And, this is what we did.

In September, Weston Carryer came to take some lectures, during one of which, I went forward for healing. I felt nothing but believed in the power and love of God, and in the Scriptures which told me Jesus healed and still heals today. Weston gave me his pamphlet, *Healing in the Atonement,* and encouraged me to read the Scriptures and claim my healing. Then he added that he felt God was saying to just "trust and pray."

My husband and I returned to the specialist in early October. The results from the operation showed the condition was extensive and drug treatments were recommended. We decided to wait three months to, "give God a go," knowing the condition would worsen with each passing month.

In late October, I went to my local doctor as I was feeling very unwell and overdue for my period. Much to our joy, and medical profession amazement, we found that I was pregnant.

—*Petrina da Costa*

At the age of twenty-three, I had a hormonal imbalance caused through having cysts on my ovaries. For four solid years, thereafter, I did not have any menstruation. This gave me concern for the future as there was a possibility not only of being unable to conceive unless I had medication, a remedy which could not be guaranteed, but there was also a risk of developing cancer of the cervix.

Weston prayed for me to be released from this condition in September 1992. Exactly one month after that prayer a natural period returned for the first time in four years. It is now one year on, and although I have missed on one occasion, this normal function has featured regularly since. I had another scan taken after I had been prayed for and there is no evidence whatsoever of cysts on the ovaries. Thank You, Lord, for Your wonderful healing power.

—J.H.

For four years I suffered severe pain through having cysts on my ovaries. In April 1997, I attended a divine healing meeting where Weston Carryer was ministering. I went forward for prayer, and as Weston prayed for me, all the pain went immediately. I have had no further pain since. Thank You, Jesus.

—*Janine Rietweld*

I had given birth to two boys in 1990 and in 1993. In December 1994, I was diagnosed as having a retroverted uterus. In October 1995, God promised us a baby girl who we were to call, "Jemimah." In February 1996, I still hadn't conceived, and upon going to the doctor for a scheduled checkup, he considered at that time that there may be a problem and wanted to refer me to a fertility specialist. I wasn't particularly worried as I had been promised by God. I knew it was all in His time. So I said to the doctor that I'd leave it a couple of months, and went home.

Two weeks later Weston Carryer was in town and he prayed for my uterus to be corrected. Six weeks later I was pregnant and the doctor confirmed my uterus was in the right place. God had healed me through Jesus Christ.

In January 1997, I gave birth to a beautiful baby girl and we named her, Jemimah. Praise God.

—*Kristin Stace*

Weston Carryer was faithful to the call the Lord had for his life. In so doing, I am one of the many who have been blessed and healed through his ministry to the Lord, to the body of Christ, and to the unbeliever.

Abdominal & Internal Organs

I praise God! It is amazing to wake each morning and not have to fumble for the pain relief before getting out of bed. To be without constant pain brings such freedom in my life. I am no longer hampered or hindered in daily living. Having contended with endometriosis for approximately thirty-five years, eight abdominal surgeries, attended pain management clinic, and visited many specialists, I had been told they could do no more for me. Any further surgery posed grave risks they did not want to take. The last surgery had gone horribly wrong. The reproductive area had been totally removed many years ago, but I continued to grow cysts in the abdominal area as the endometrium which had escaped into the abdominal cavity had seeded cells that continually grew and caused extreme pain. Because of the many surgeries, there were extensive adhesions to my bowel, bladder and intestinal tracts. I was taking anything up to 1,000 mgs of Panadene six times a day, 100 mgs Diclax anti-inflammatory analgesic, twelve hourly, and even still, at times needing an injection of Pethidene or Morphine to manage the pain.

On the Tuesday, previous to Weston Carryer's 1999 visit to Helensville, I had met with two others to fast and pray through the day in preparation for his meetings. I was in considerable pain during the morning and ended up being driven to the doctors for an injection. He wanted to call an ambulance and send me to hospital. After much discussion, he relented and agreed to give me an injection on the condition I promised that if, after your visit on the weekend I was still in pain, I would go into hospital. Normally the injection works within twenty minutes and allows me to sleep at least four hours and dramatically reduces the pain. But it seemed to have no effect. Even though my prayer partners stayed and prayed throughout the day, there was no relief and I continued to vomit with the pain.

I came to the Friday night meeting in considerable pain, heavily drugged, but determined, *This time, Lord.*

Praise God. Weston was God's vessel and a channel through which He poured forth healing into my body. It is approximately

Miracles in Aotearoa New Zealand

twelve months now, and I have not taken any medication for that complaint. Hallelujah!

—*A. Brown, Parakai*

For approximately eight years, I experienced a retroverted womb. During this time I did have an operation. But through lifting, the womb went back out of position again. Although I did not experience a great deal of pain, it caused me considerable embarrassment. I was limited in my movements, and I could not walk downhill.

Early in 1997, I attended a healing meeting in Tauranga where Weston Carryer was ministering. During the meeting he said that God had revealed to him that there was a woman there with my condition. He went on to say, "If you will come forward, God will heal you." I responded and went forward. Weston prayed for me, and the Lord totally and immediately healed me. Since then, I have no pain, embarrassment, or limitations. Praise God.

—*Rita Jensen, Tauranga*

For approximately five years I suffered severe pain from endometriosis for which I had an operation, but this helped very little. At times the pain was so severe that I could not stand and had to crawl around the floor of my flat. I also experienced excessive bleeding and regular blackouts when I would pass out completely. I did not know how I was going to cope.

I attended a divine healing meeting at Eastgate Christian Centre in May 2000 where Weston Carryer was ministering. During the early part of the meeting Weston said that the Lord had revealed to him that there was someone present who had endometriosis, and for that person to go forward for the Lord to heal them. I was too embarrassed to go forward at the time. However, at the next meeting I did go forward and I am rejoicing to say that as Weston prayed for me, the Lord immediately healed me. Since that time twelve months ago, I have lived a normal life, and apart from one occasion when I did have a very

Abdominal & Internal Organs

small amount of pain, I have had none of the symptoms that plagued me for five years. Thank You, Jesus!

—*Tolu Magalelei*

There was no time in the 10:45 AM service at West City Church on Sunday, 7 April 2002, that I didn't feel there was going to be a strong message for me. Little did I know that Weston Carryer would be used to glorify God's wonderful love and grace to me. His perfect timing, like always, has taken my breath away.

This is my testimony: I walked in with endometriosis and I walked out cured! I had suffered symptoms that were affecting my health, marital bliss, and self-esteem. I suffered constant bloating that would make my stomach enlarge to appear about six months pregnant, along with nausea, dizziness, irritable bowel, depression, horrible furious cramps, and backache.

Instantly, the pain ceased, my stomach went down, and I am improving every day. Thank You, God.

—*Melissa Findon*

I am writing to testify to God's amazing love and healing power. Our son's girlfriend has suffered from endometriosis quite severely for some years and had an appointment for surgery that had already been cancelled once. I had been relaying the testimonies Weston Carryer had already received from others whom he had prayed for with this same condition, and also telling her how God had healed me of non-sclerosis Hodgkin's lymphoma.

Although both my son and his girlfriend were reluctant to come to Weston's meeting, the need outweighed their reluctance, and they came! I went forward with Nicky and Weston prayed for her. She was nervous, and a little sceptical, but afterward, she sat in the front row and watched as Weston ministered to others. She saw for herself the Holy Spirit moving on others as he prayed. After she had been sitting there for a few minutes

Miracles in Aotearoa New Zealand

she said, "Ooh, I feel strange . . . I feel all hot." I could tell that the Holy Spirit was ministering to her.

Nicky had a new appointment for surgery, and since it was difficult to get appointments, thought she had better keep it and go for the surgery. The doctors opened her up and looked, but could not find any endometriosis at all. God had healed her and confirmed it to her. Praise the Lord!

I'm so thankful for Weston's faithfulness to visit small towns and cities throughout New Zealand, spreading the good news of God's love and His willingness to heal and save everyone.

—*Raewyn and Colin, 12 December 2002*

For two years I really suffered from fibroids in my uterus. These caused me to have very heavy periods every three weeks. These difficult periods were always accompanied by nausea, vomiting for three days, migraine headaches and severe stomach pain. This condition also used to cause pain in my back, hips, and in my legs down to my knees. I tried medical help, but the pain relief I was given was not effective because of the vomiting.

I attended a divine healing meeting at Tauranga in September 2003 where Weston Carryer was ministering and praying for the sick. As he was ministering, he had a word of knowledge for someone who had my condition. He asked for that person to come forward for him to pray for the Lord to heal her. I thought, *Could this really be for me?* I then realized that the Lord really wanted to heal me, and so I went forward.

Weston then prayed for me, and the Lord performed a wonderful miracle. From that moment, eighteen months ago, I have not had any of those conditions that I experienced for two years. No more vomiting, nausea, migraines, or pain. I am now having normal periods every four weeks without heavy bleeding, instead of every three weeks as previously. I also used to suffer from premenstrual tension and that has completely disappeared. What an incredible difference in my life. My doctor has confirmed that the fibroids have gone. Jesus, I am so grateful.

—*Michelle Barton*

Abdominal & Internal Organs

I came to one of Weston Carryer's healing meetings in Whangarei at Christian Renewal Fellowship in November 2005 because of a cyst on my left ovary. This was a real test of my faith. I went forward for prayer and kept believing for my healing—that the cyst would go away, and it did. Later I was tested for CA125 twice and it came out negative. I went for another scan and the cyst wasn't there any more. Glory to God.

I received a letter from the chief specialist stating that there is now no abnormality within the pelvis at all which he said is excellent news. This means that I have been healed of endometriosis as well. The report which my own specialist read to me states that "the former mass [i.e., the cyst] is unaccounted for. . . . " The specialist said, "It is a miracle."

I told him, "It is God's miracle."

—*Anselma Beckmann*

I write to give the Lord Jesus Christ all glory and thanks for a healing in my uterus in 2006. I am so thankful for Weston Carryer's availability and obedience to the Lord in the ministry that He entrusted to him.

In early 2006, the results of a scan done privately, and then confirmed by a hospital radiologist, showed a solid mass measuring approximately three by four centimetres in the right adnexa. Adjacent to this mass was a complicated cyst with nodules attached and some pelvic fluid. As a result of these findings, the gynaecologist booked me in for a laparoscopy and possible laparotomy. Prior to this investigation I sought the Lord, asking Him to reveal to me any areas of sin in my life, of which I immediately repented. I also took hold of His Word as outlined in Weston booklet, *Keeping Your Healing*, given to me at one of his meetings on another occasion.

I cried out to the Lord for a word of encouragement. Amongst other things, He spoke to me, "My Word is near you, even in your mouth. Shall it not come forth to heal, save and deliver?" I rang Weston and he prayed for me over the phone.

Miracles in Aotearoa New Zealand

The laparoscopy was performed and no sign was found of the mass or the adhesions seen in the x-rays. Praise God for His mercy and His healing power to all that believe.

—*Barbara Peters*

As a result of tests being done in 2003, it was discovered that I had polycystic ovarian syndrome. In January 2007, I rang Weston Carryer and asked him to pray for me over the telephone. He prayed for the Lord to heal me. In December 2007, I had further tests carried out and these confirmed that the Lord had healed me. I now do not have polycystic ovarian syndrome. Thank You, Lord Jesus.

—*Nicola Gubb*

I suffered debilitating abdominal pain from endometriosis, a medical term for a condition where the lining of the womb sheds itself and attaches itself to other areas of the body. The pain that is felt with endometriosis is from the lining attaching itself to other internal organs and then bleeding as part of the menstrual cycle. I had numerous operations to laser off these lesions, which gave me temporary relief. The more operations I had, the more scar tissue was created, which in the end, just added to the abdominal pain.

Finally at thirty-three I made a decision to have a hysterectomy, as I had suffered this condition from my first period at age fourteen. The pain was so debilitating I could not walk at times. I had given birth to two beautiful boys and could not deal with the pain I was experiencing a day longer. The operation gave me temporary relief and stopped the situation from getting worse. However, the lining that had attached itself to other organs in my body was still there; over time the pain came back—not as bad, but it was still there. I suffered abdominal pain from endometriosis for twenty-three years. I also suffered from digestion problems.

I came to see Weston at the beginning of September 2008 at a church meeting in Paraparaumu. During the service, he

Abdominal & Internal Organs

walked over to the area where I was sitting. He then called out for someone with severe stomach pain and digestive problems to come up for prayer. My husband pushed me up saying, "That's you!" I got up and went forward.

Weston prayed for me, asking me to place my hands on my stomach. He then put his hand on mine. I was in pain as he was praying. When he placed his hand on my mine I could feel incredible warmth coming through him from God. As soon as he touched me I knew God would be able to help me. The power of God is truly amazing. It came rushing through Weston and healed me from my pain. This left such an impact on me that I became born again that very day. Not only was I saved as a result of this experience, but my husband and two children were also.

My abdominal pain has never returned. Not only did I receive a physical healing, but I received an instant cleansing of my soul. I felt ignited for God and felt a deep yearning to live my life the best I could for Christ. I could not deny His power and glory. My mouth was cleansed from swearing, my mind was healed from depression, my relationship with my husband was restored, and I felt free for the first time in my life. I felt completely uplifted.

I thank God for my encounter with Weston. I thank God for the blessing of healing. Since that day my life has made a complete turnaround for the best and I have not looked back. Each day I grow stronger for God.

Trust in Him; have faith in His works. He truly is an amazing God. God has worked a miracle in my life. I am truly grateful for His abundant blessings everyday.

—*Nicole Williams, Ohau*

When I reached puberty, I would haemorrhage each month during menstruation and lose large clots of blood. This was very debilitating and I would always have to take a complete day off from school or work. This condition did not abate even when I was in my late forties.

Weston Carryer was ministering at a divine healing meeting

Miracles in Aotearoa New Zealand

in Foxton approximately fifteen years ago and he said that there was a woman there who had this haemorrhaging problem. I responded and he prayed for the Lord to heal me.

I am rejoicing to say that the haemorrhaging stopped immediately and since then, there has been no sign of it whatever. What a wonderful difference this has made. Thank You, Jesus.

—*Mary O'Hare*

Weston Carryer prayed for me at a meeting at Eastgate Christian Centre. The 18 months previous, I had been getting very heavy periods. The problem had been getting worse over time so that by the time I went to Weston's meeting, I needed to be on medication for 3-days a month to stop the extremely heavy bleeding. I was booked in for an operation to fix the problem. After Weston prayed for me, my periods went completely back to normal! I have not needed or had any medication since, and it is now six months since he prayed for me. This healing has made a wonderful difference in my life.

Praise God for His healing! It has made for some interesting conversations at the hospital as I have explained what has happened at follow-up appointments! May God continue to bless Weston's ministry.

—*Christine Taylor-Agnew*

For approximately 5 years, I experienced severe bleeding problems. I would bleed every two weeks and this would last for 10 days. My doctor said that I would need a hysterectomy. I became anaemic, had to take iron tablets, and was also prescribed provero to prevent the onset of cancer.

In early 2011, I was prayed for at my local church and there was an immediate improvement. My periods changed to once a month, would only last for about 7 days, but the bleeding was still so severe for at least 72 hours that I had to stay home and could barely move around.

At a divine healing meeting in June 2012, Weston Carryer

Abdominal & Internal Organs

prayed for my complete healing and this is exactly what happened. My periods are now normal and I do not need any mediation of any sort. This wonderful healing has had a huge impact on many other areas in my life. I am rejoicing and praising the Lord so much for what He has done for me.

Thank You, Jesus.

—A. C. F.

All my life I had been a very healthy, fit, active woman. I was a scuba diving instructor, married with three children, and had been a committed Christian for many years. Suddenly in 1996, I developed chronic endometriosis and became very ill. I was menstruating every two weeks and bleeding very heavily. I became very anaemic, with pain and cramping in my womb, experienced fainting spells, and one day, I collapsed in the shower. Medical attention did not help at all and I was told that my womb needed to be removed. I was prayed for at many healing meetings and on other occasions, but nothing changed. After some time I became quite despondent.

A friend then told me that Weston Carryer was having a healing meeting in Papakura, and I very reluctantly allowed her to take me. I sat at the back of the meeting and was not at all optimistic about receiving healing. Weston spoke out words of knowledge and prayed for some people, and then said there was a woman present with a womb problem. I thought to myself, *That is not specific enough.* When no one responded, Weston—thank God!—persisted, and my friend then dragged me to the front. As I was walking forward I started to weep as I had reached out so many times before with negative results.

Weston then spoke and gently told me not to be embarrassed, that he knew that I had endometriosis, and that God was going to heal me. He then prayed for me twice. The second time he prayed, I went down very fast under the power of the Holy Spirit. While on the floor, my chin vibrated at speed for about twenty seconds, and I received deliverance. When I got up I was completely healed. Since that moment eight years ago, I have never had any further sign of endometriosis.

Miracles in Aotearoa New Zealand

Jesus, You wonderfully, instantly, healed me, and I thank You so much.

—Marie Francis

For well over ten years I suffered from endometriosis which caused me to always be in severe pain. My periods were very irregular, heavy, and often every two weeks. Ten years ago the pain became so excruciating that I was sent to Green Lane Hospital for treatment to get some relief. Four years later, I once again experienced the same excruciating pain. I was sent to the North Shore Hospital where I had three ovarian cysts, the size of tennis balls, removed. The pain after this still did not ease, and eight months later it was discovered that the cysts had grown back again. This time I was put on depo provero injections to shrink the cysts and help with the bleeding and pain. These injections did help.

Several months ago I attended a divine healing meeting in Auckland at West City Christian Centre where Weston Carryer was ministering. Weston said that there was someone sitting where I was who had endometriosis and for that person to come forward to be prayed for. I was surprised as I had brought a friend along for healing, but realized that I was the person that he was referring to. I responded, and Weston prayed for the Lord to heal me. I am rejoicing that as a result of what the Lord did, I am now off the depo provero injections, no longer need medication, no more pain, and I have regular periods.

What an incredible difference in my life. I am now well enough to go overseas on a short-term mission trip. Lord, thank You.

—Natalie Gillam

She thought, "If I just touch
his clothes,
I will be healed."
Immediately her bleeding stopped
and she felt in her body
that she was freed
from her suffering.

Mark 5:28-29, NIV

Seven

Heart, Chest & Respiratory

Testimonies of healed conditions of the chest, heart, ribs, sternum, and lungs.

Chest

In 1998, lumps had developed in my left breast which was also very tender and sore. I attended a divine healing meeting at Rotorua where Weston Carryer prayed for the Lord to heal me. The soreness went immediately, and a mammogram taken a few days later, showed that the lumps had totally disappeared. Thank You, Jesus.

—*Gaelene Jones*

I went to a meeting in Christchurch in November 1991, where Weston Carryer was the speaker. For over three years

Miracles in Aotearoa New Zealand

I had suffered from RSI (repetitive stress injury) in the upper chest and was in constant pain. The doctor diagnosed damaged nerve ends as the cause. I went forward for prayer and God healed me completely. I have had no pain in that area since. And, praise be to God, I can now meet the demands of my work and do the garden at home without any pain whatsoever. I have been a Christian for only twenty months, and in that time have found that God has become all in all to me.

—*Veronica Brosnahan*

There was a small lump under my left breast for nigh on ten years. Following a word of knowledge given to Weston Carryer I went forward for prayer. Not all healings are instantaneous. I was conscious for a month or so that the lump was still there but persisted in faith to believe it would disappear. You can guess my joy when, two or three months later, I discovered God had removed it and I was healed.

—*T.M.*

When Weston Carryer was ministering at West City Christian Centre, Glendene in May 2002, I was prayed for on the Saturday evening. I had a lump in my right breast, and only God knows what it was. I was waiting to go to North Shore Hospital for an examination.

I subsequently received my appointment and kept it. The result was a clear mammogram and ultrasound. "Perfect," the doctor said. The lump had gone completely. I don't need any further appointments. Praise God! Hallelujah!

—*Joan Breeze*

In March 2005, I fell off a chair, landed on a door jam, and cracked my ribs. Over the next several weeks, any time I sneezed, coughed, blew my nose, or even breathed deeply, I experienced pain. During this period of several weeks there was no improvement at all.

Heart, Chest & Respiratory

On May 15th, at a healing meeting in Whangarei, Weston Carryer prayed for the Lord to heal my ribs. I claimed my healing straight away. An improvement started immediately and within one week, I was totally healed. Thank You, Jesus.

—*Gillian Haworth*

I could hardly believe that the Lord would appear beside me on a bus on the road to Jerusalem! I had slipped in a bath at Galilee and cracked some of my ribs which were very painful. *How could I continue on a five-week tour of Israel and Jordan when I was in such pain?* I thought I would have to return to New Zealand. But the Lord had other ideas. He came to me in the person of Evangelist Weston Carryer. He prayed for me right then and there on the bus! He prayed again in Jerusalem. There was such a healing anointing on both occasions that I knew I was healed. Yes, I went to Masada, and on to Petra, and walked on the wall around the Old City of Jerusalem. I visited the Red Sea, the Dead Sea, and the Mediterranean Sea, and strolled in the soft sand around a Bedouin settlement. Thank You, dear Jesus, for arranging for me to have this divine appointment with your dedicated servant.

—*Helen Richardson*

As a result of the wonderful healing that the Lord gave me when Weston Carryer prayed for me in Cromwell in March 2006, I took my daughter, Janine, to his meeting in Wanaka two nights later. Janine had cracked her sternum. She was having terrible pain, was living on morphine, and had been unable to work for four months. She did not believe in the Lord and was reluctant to come. However, she did come and Weston laid hands on her and prayed for her. Her sternum was instantly healed. She has had no further pain and never needed any more morphine. As a result she has started coming to church with me.

So you see, through Weston, the Lord has blessed not only myself, but my daughter. God is always there for us. It is us

Miracles in Aotearoa New Zealand

that think we do not need Him. His door is always open to us. We have to learn to have faith in Him. I'm so thankful for Weston showing us that God is a living, loving God for all of us. All we have to do is open our hearts to Him.

—*Clarrisa Bochel*

For ten years I suffered from muscular spasms in my chest. This very severe pain would come at least three times every year, and every time I had to be hospitalized for treatment. Apart from the pain I experienced, my breathing was badly affected and I could not breathe without an inhaler.

Weston Carryer came to our church to minister over a weekend in November 2006. At the meeting on the Saturday night, I suddenly experienced the crippling pain and started to have the spasms. Weston immediately prayed for me and the spasms instantly stopped. Since that night, twelve months ago, I have never had any chest pain, spasms, or breathing difficulties. I am very grateful as I was not looking forward to another ten years of pain or more hospital stays. Thank You so much, Lord Jesus.

—*Ngaire Fraser*

In the late 1980s, I developed lumps in one of my breasts and medical advice was that they needed to be surgically removed. I was admitted to the Gisborne Hospital where the operation took place and the lumps were removed.

A short time later, lumps once again developed in my breast, and following further medical advice, I was again operated on and they were removed. Not long after this, lumps started to once again develop in my breast and I was advised that they needed to be removed, and so, a further booking was made for me for the operation.

Before the operation took place, however, I attended a divine healing meeting in Ruatoria where Weston Carryer was ministering. After Weston had preached, he started speaking out words of knowledge for various conditions that people

Heart, Chest & Respiratory

had. Then he extended his hand towards me and said that the person right where I was sitting was booked in for surgery but did not need to go ahead as the Lord was healing her at that moment.

This is exactly what happened. The lumps just disappeared shortly afterwards and so I did not have any further operation. Over the last 25 years, they have never grown again.

Lord Jesus, thank You.

—*Roberta Bradley*

Heart

When Weston Carryer came to Christchurch in March 2008, I went to his meeting at Travis Junction and he called out the condition of irregular heartbeat. I had been experiencing this. The doctor had given me a simple test on the heartbeat-measuring machine and had referred me to a specialist for a more in-depth checkup that was to cost $280. The doctor had added that it was not a major concern to her. So I thought, *Jesus can heal me.* My heart would not beat irregularly all the time, but when it did, I would speak healing to it in Jesus' name.

I was not thinking about this at all during the meeting, but when the condition was called out, I immediately went forward. Weston prayed for the healing power of Jesus to bring this irregularity into order. He then asked me how it was, but all I said was, "I will let you know," which seemed a very poor reply to him at the time. But now, fifteen months on, I have not had any irregular heartbeats. I thank Jesus for healing me and his faithful servant, Weston, for being the channel through which God could work.

—*Christine Bailey*

Miracles in Aotearoa New Zealand

For thirty-one years I had been in and out of the Taumarunui and Waikato hospitals with a severe heart condition caused by a collapsed heart cage and a collapsed heart valve. I was in constant acute pain, experienced great difficulty in breathing, and had to try and sleep sitting up, supported by eight pillows. I was due to have a bypass operation.

This particular night, my husband drove me to Ohakune to a healing meeting. When Weston Carryer prayed for me, the power of God, through Jesus Christ, touched me in an amazing way and I was completely healed. I have had no pain since that time and medical examinations have proved that my heart is now quite normal.

—*Olive Toataua*

In April 1989, I was led into going to one of Weston Carryer's healing meetings in Waikanae. I felt nervous and shy about going to a healing crusade as it was a completely new experience for me, even though I had accepted Jesus as my Saviour some time previously. I had been ill with chronic coronary heart disease for eighteen months. And in spite of a very caring and helpful Christian doctor, I was very weak, tired easily, often in pain, and using medication frequently, sometimes constantly.

Weston prayed for me when I went forward, and within a few minutes, I was no longer breathless or tight-chested. That night I had my first good night's sleep in a long time. The next day I felt much stronger and free from pain. After one or two days I realised I was completely healed. Soon after I went to my understanding doctor for a checkup and he confirmed I was really well again but said to take things gradually for a while. That is over a year ago. Now I am in better health than I have been for many years. During my illness by blood pressure had been worryingly low. Each three-monthly check now shows it to be perfect. I just praise the Lord every day for His loving kindness.

Thank You, Jesus. I have witnessed to friends and people I

Heart, Chest & Respiratory

do not really know very well, for I feel I must tell them of God's love for us all.

—B. Sharp

Eleven years ago I was diagnosed as having angina. This heart condition had affected a number of my family members—my mother, uncle, auntie and grandfather had all died through this condition. A year ago, Weston Carryer was ministering in our church in Fielding, and the Lord revealed to him through a word of knowledge that there was someone where I was sitting who had angina, and if the person would come forward, the Lord would heal him. I responded immediately and Weston prayed for Jesus to heal me. I knew I was healed. All the symptoms immediately left, and two weeks later at my next medical check, the doctor confirmed that there was nothing wrong with my heart and took me off all medication. For the last year I have had no further heart problems. Hallelujah! Praise the Lord!

—Brian Marshall

Eighteen months ago I was diagnosed as having Wolff-Parkinson-White syndrome. For six months I experienced the heart attacks associated with this condition. It would literally strike me and I would fall to the ground and be unable to move any part of my body at all for approximately thirty minutes. It was also very painful. At a divine healing meeting at Windsor in Christchurch in April 1997, Weston Carryer prayed for the Lord to heal me. Since that moment I have never had this condition again. I am healed! Praise God.

—Andrew Crozier

In 1995, I had an aneurysm of the heart, and was facing bypass surgery as well in Green Lane Hospital. My uncontrolled blood pressure was 200/190. I was in Whangarei Hospital when the aneurysm burst. Weston Carryer and Pastor Owen Shepherd came into my room to pray for Jesus to heal me, but the doctor said that I had only two hours to live. The result of what the Lord did was truly amazing. I suddenly realized I had received a miracle and wanted to go home. Two days later, I was taken to Green Lane where tests confirmed that not only was the heart healed, there was no sign of any aneurysm, nor did I need bypass surgery. For the last three years I have enjoyed wonderful health with no medication. Hallelujah! Praise the Lord.

—Mei Tariora

Most of my life I suffered from palpitations to the heart and this had a terrible effect on me. The heart beats would be up to one hundred and fifty per minute. As I progressed through life, the attacks became more severe and would last up to eight hours. I was on the strongest medication available but it did not help. I was waiting for tests at Green Lane with the possibility of an operation when I attended a Women's Aglow regional conference at Rotorua in October 1998 where Weston Carryer was teaching on divine healing. During the ministry time, Weston prayed for the Lord to heal me, and I was instantly completely healed. Since that time I have had no medication of any kind and no further palpitations. Praise the Lord.

—Heather Whitmore, Rotorua

Practically all my life I suffered from a heart murmur. At a divine healing meeting at Fielding in 1997 where Weston Carryer was ministering, I went forward for him to pray for the Lord to heal me. I was instantly healed through Jesus by the power of the Holy Spirit.

—D.H.

I was invited by a friend to attend a healing meeting at Rangiora led by Weston Carryer on 19 March 2002. I had been unwell with pain in my right arm and around the chest area for approximately eight months. I was sent for an ECG by my doctor

Heart, Chest & Respiratory

and he had recalled me a few days later with an appointment to see him. He said the ECG showed signs of angina and that with my family history of heart disease, he wanted to refer me to a cardiac specialist. The specialist suggested an ECG with a scan at the end of exercise, which was done three weeks later on 8 April. The result of these tests given to me by the specialist was that I had a normal healthy heart which was working very well.

During the healing meeting, Weston Carryer had a word of knowledge for someone with heart problems, and as I went forward, he said it was angina. After prayer, the pain was gone. While getting prayed for, and afterwards, I had a lovely warmth that stayed in the area of the heart. By faith, I have had to hold onto the healing I received at the meeting, thanking and praising the Lord, and rebuking the pain when it tried to come back.

I am feeling really well, and able to live without pain.

—*Elizabeth Boss*

In mid-2002, I was diagnosed with a heart murmur. As a result of this diagnosis, an appointment was made for me with a heart specialist. However, before I went to the specialist, I attended a divine healing meeting at Whangarei where Weston Carryer was ministering and praying for the sick.

During the ministry time, he prayed for the Lord to heal me. I kept the scheduled appointment and had further tests done. Each test showed that I no longer had a heart murmur. Jesus had completely healed my heart. Thank You, Lord.

—*Carol Wosthuizen*

For a long time I had been suffering from three heart conditions which were severely restricting my quality of life. I was classed as having a moderate leak from the mitral valve, angina, and a very serious irregular heartbeat.

In March 2001, I was at a divine healing meeting in Christchurch where Weston Carryer was ministering. As he started to minister, he said that the Lord had revealed to him that there was someone present who had angina and an irregular heartbeat. I was surprised at the Lord caring so much about me that He would reveal this. So I went forward for Weston to pray for the Lord to heal me. For about three months after this, I continued to feel terrible, but then I started to improve. From then on, there was continual, steady improvement until finally, the last ECG revealed that the angina was healed, the heartbeat is normal, and the leak from the mitral valve is now classed as trivial.

I am thrilled to testify that I now enjoy good health, and good quality of life, with no need of medication. I have indeed received a wonderful miracle from the Lord. Thank You, Jesus.

—Barney Guerin

At twenty-six years of age I went to the Waitakere Hospital to give birth to my third child. I became seriously ill and was sent to North Shore Hospital where I nearly died. A baby boy was delivered through caesarian section. The doctors then discovered that fluid was being retained around my heart, I had a leak in the mitral valve, and a heart murmur (which I was very aware of). For some time previous to this, I had been breathless all the time. I was discharged after eight days and told I would have to continue to take heart medication. When I returned home I still experienced the heart murmur and continual breathlessness.

In November 2002, I was invited to a divine healing meeting at Flaxmere where Weston Carryer was ministering and praying for the sick. I was curious so I went along. Early in the meeting he walked over to the area where I was sitting and said there was someone who had heart problems. I found my feet moving forward and made my way to the front. Weston started praying for me and I felt something like a hot flash of electricity go right through my body. I could not stand and fell over backwards— slain in the Spirit. I felt a real heaviness jump right out of my body. I got off the floor a different person.

After the meeting, I ran one kilometre home without

Heart, Chest & Respiratory

stopping and I was not breathless. I have had three checks since and my doctor has told me that my heart is now normal, although he advised me to continue taking my medication. I do not have the heart murmur and I can breathe normally. Today I am totally changed. I can now more than cope with my life and my three children. The Sunday after my healing blessing I went to church and recommitted my life to the Lord, and six weeks later, my husband did the same. Jesus changes lives and I am so grateful to Him.

—*Turei Pine*

For a lot of years I found that I got very quickly out of breath if I did hard physical activity. I put this down to my age. Then in August 1999, at aged sixty-nine years, I had blood poisoning and was admitted to hospital. The doctors managed to save my life, but were worried that the bacteria may have attached themselves to the heart. So they carried out an ultra-scan and this showed that although there were no bacteria on the heart, calcium had accumulated on one of the heart valves and was preventing it from operating properly. The doctor who carried out the examination said that I would require a heart valve replacement within two years.

Ten days later, my wife Anne and myself attended one of Weston Carryer's healing services at Oasis. I had been discharged from hospital but was having an antibiotic drip four times a day. My next drip was due at 9 PM, so that meant I had to leave well before that and would not be able to stay until the end of the service. The service opened with praise and worship, and when it had finished, Weston immediately announced that there was someone in the congregation with a heart valve problem. I went up to the front and he prayed for me.

It was several weeks later as I was involved in hard physical activity when I discovered that I no longer got out of breath quickly. It was clear to me then that I had been healed, but I really wanted confirmation of that. I was due to be checked two years later, but because I no longer had a problem, they could not use their resources to check me. Now, four and a half years later and aged seventy-four, I still do not get out of breath

Miracles in Aotearoa New Zealand

quickly and now have the confirmation.

This afternoon I had another ultrasound. The doctor found that there was still some calcium on the valve but it was not of any importance and the valve was operating normally. Thank You, Lord! We were so grateful that Weston used his God-given gifts in his ministry.

—*Patrick and Anne Clinch*

I have had an irregular heartbeat for at least forty years, and over the years, it became much more pronounced. My heart would thump so much at night that I could not sleep. I was always tired and felt sick most of the time. One day, early in 2003, I experienced pain in my chest and this pain also went down my body. It was all I could do to get my breath. I went to my doctor who sent me straight to hospital in the ambulance. There I was admitted to ICU where the doctors had to stop my heart and then mechanically restart it again. I was released some days later. Although I was on medication, my heart would still beat wildly at night. I was very listless in the daytime and continued to feel sick.

In February 2003, I went to a Christian healing meeting at Papamoa where Weston Carryer was ministering. He said there was someone there with an irregular heartbeat to which I immediately responded. As he prayed for me, I received a miracle from the Lord. My heart was immediately healed. It no longer thumps at night and I seep soundly right through the night. I had not been able to do this for many years. Three months after I was prayed for, I had my medical check and the doctor confirmed that my heart is now normal.

At the present moment, I am working on Kiwifruit starting at 6:00 AM, working twelve hours a day and feeling absolutely wonderful. Thank You, Lord.

—*Ruth Wilson*

On the 13 October 2001, I had a cardiac arrest and died. God, in His grace and mercy raised me up again. I was placed

Heart, Chest & Respiratory

on a tablet to slow my heartbeat to forty-eight beats per minute to prevent it from going into fibrillation again. Weston Carryer prayed for my heart a year later. Three months later I went to the doctor for a checkup and he found my heartbeat had gone up to fifty-four beats per minute. He couldn't understand why, even though I told him I had received prayer for healing.

Three months following that, I went again for a checkup and my heartbeat was up to sixty beats per minute. The doctor said, "You have the heartbeat of a thirty-year-old woman." It has been strong and steady ever since. Praise the Lord!

—*Norma Cockburn*

In February 2001, I was rushed to Taupo Hospital at 5:00 AM with very bad pains in my chest and I could hardly breathe. I spent two weeks in hospital undergoing extensive tests for angina. When I started to feel a bit better I was allowed home. I was home for only two weeks and the chest pains started up again, and once again, it was hard to breathe. I spent another ten days in hospital. This kept on going until May. After ten days in hospital in May, I was taken to Waikato Hospital for an angiogram. I spent one week in Waikato Hospital. Tests showed that it wasn't my heart after all, although I had had all the symptoms of an angina attack. I was sent back to Taupo, and was due to go back in to Taupo Hospital.

When I got home I was told that Weston Carryer was going to be at the Apostolic Church. I told my husband I wasn't going back into hospital, but I was going instead to the Apostolic Church the next night for healing. I knew I would be healed that evening. I wasn't feeling the best when I arrived.

Praise the Lord! I was healed instantly. I knew I had been healed, as next morning I was able to eat breakfast. Before that I was living on milk puddings as that was all I could keep down. Thank You, Lord. I have been so blessed to be saved. Now three years later, I have had no further heart problems.

—*Violet McEwen*

Around six years ago, I was diagnosed as having an enlarged

heart and fluid around my heart. These conditions caused many distressing symptoms as well as a lot of concern.

Four years ago, my thirteen-year old daughter attended a divine healing meeting at Whangarei where Weston Carryer was ministering. Near the end of the meeting Weston had a word of knowledge for someone with a serious heart condition who was not actually present at the meeting, but whom someone else had come to stand in the gap for. My daughter was already down the front as she had said to her Gran who had brought her to the meeting, "I am going down to the front for Mum's heart." She stood in the gap for me and I received healing.

My symptoms disappeared and I threw away my heart medication. Two years on, I have had no further heart problems. Thank You, Jesus.

—*Diane Friar*

In 2003, I realized that I could not walk up a hill without gasping for breath. My doctor sent me to a heart specialist who carried out tests. These tests confirmed that I needed to take heart medication. The medication helped until mid-2006 when my blood pressure dropped dramatically every time I stood up. Shortly after this I became so sick, and felt so terrible, that I was admitted to hospital overnight.

Early in 2007, it was decided that I needed to have a pacemaker inserted. I was given a heart monitor to record how my heart was working. I was told to work the monitor every time my heart malfunctioned and caused the chronic feeling. The monitor recorded that during the first week I had to use it eight times and ten times during the second week.

On 4 February, I attended a divine healing meeting in Auckland when Weston Carryer prayed for the Lord to heal me. I immediately noticed an amazing difference: I was not breathless and I didn't have to use the monitor again. On 16 February, I kept my appointment with the specialist and he confirmed my heart and blood pressure were completely normal. I have been taken off all medication and my heart is not giving any problems at all. Praise the Lord.

—*Barbara Drinkall*

For several years I suffered from an irregular heartbeat. On average, every second day I would experience shortage of breath and thumping in my chest.

At a healing meeting at Papamoa in August 2007, Weston Carryer prayed for the Lord to heal this condition. Since that moment, now over twelve months ago, apart from experiencing this slightly when I was very tired one day, I have not had these symptoms, and I feel so wonderful. Thank You, Lord Jesus.

—*Angela Leigh*

For at least ten years I had needed to be on medication for an irregular heartbeat, which the specialist told me I would need to be on for life.

I attended a divine healing meeting in New Plymouth in May 2010 where Weston Carryer was ministering. During the ministry time he said that the Lord had revealed to him that there was someone there who had an irregular heartbeat and would the person come forward to be prayed for. I responded, and was Weston prayed for me. I did not feel any different immediately after that. However, a while later, I went away for a holiday and forgot to take my medication with me. I suffered no harmful effects, and since that time over the last several months, I have had no medication. My doctor had said to let him know if I have any problems. Thank You, Jesus.

—*David Thomson*

Over the last forty years, I had been suffering from a heart murmur, and this had been steadily worsening. I was having regular dizzy spells and some of these were very serious. On two occasions I passed out completely and had to be driven

Miracles in Aotearoa New Zealand

home. All kinds of medication were tried on me, but it did not help at all, and some made me worse. For the last several years I had to spend most of my time lying down.

On 15 February 2004, I attended a divine healing meeting in Tauranga where Weston Carryer was ministering. He had a word of knowledge for someone who had a heart murmur. I responded, and he prayed for me, and for the first time in my life, I was slain in the Spirit.

I have received a wonderful miracle from the Lord. He has healed my heart murmur of forty years. What a difference in my life this made. With no more dizzy spells, and at age eighty-two, I am active again nearly all day, apart from a doze after lunch. I feel better than I have in years. I am really blessed. Lord Jesus, I thank You so much.

—*Ivy B. Pratt*

When I was five-years-old, I contracted rheumatic fever and spent some time in hospital recovering. Over the next thirty-one years I experienced aching joints, especially in the wintertime. Due to the rheumatics, I ended up with a heart murmur which prevented me from participating in a great deal of sports.

While I was at a Weston Carryer healing meeting (1992), I distinctly heard the Lord saying to me, "Heart murmur . . . heart murmur." I jumped out of my seat, told Weston, who then prayed for me, and God healed me. There were no more chest flutterings nor any tightness. They ceased. In December 1992, my husband and I decided to go to Bible college and we had to provide checkups. While I was having mine, the doctor asked whether I had ever had anything wrong with my heart, and I replied that I *used* to have a heart murmur. He checked and assured me I was all clear. I praise God for the healing He has given me.

—*R.M. Johnstone*

We are so thankful for Weston and Ruth's faithfulness to

Heart, Chest & Respiratory

God's calling. In November 2003, when Weston was in Orewa, he prayed for my mother, Margaret, who was going to have a knee replacement operation. Weeks before this time she had been taken to hospital with an angina attack. During her stay in hospital it was discovered that the heart had been damaged, and the doctors, at that stage, were not prepared to go ahead with the knee operation because they believed the heart would probably not handle the stress of the operation. However, after she was prayed for by Weston, her next heart check showed that the heart had been fully restored and was now normal. So at eighty-four years of age, she had her knee operation with no complications, and she is now mobile again. A further heart check after the operation showed no damage and no angina. The doctor said that she had a heart strong enough to take her through another eighty years. I know that this was a miracle that God had performed for her the night Weston prayed for her. Although she had to go through the knee operation, her heart was the real concern; but God healed her through Weston's ministry. Praise God, and I'm so thankful that Weston made himself available.

—*Michelle Coxhead*

Respiratory

After my childhood asthma returned in my mid-forties, I became reconciled to the fact that possibly this time it was here to stay. Early in 1990, I accepted Jesus Christ into my life, and some months later, attended a healing meeting where Weston Carryer was ministering. When he made a call for an asthma sufferer to come out, I went forward for prayer. The asthma didn't improve immediately but I continued to claim the healing as outlined in Weston's pamphlet, *Keeping Your Healing*. Being a new Christian, I believe God used my healing to strengthen my faith and trust in Him. As my condition improved, I lessened my medication to the point where, six months on, I am asthma-free

Miracles in Aotearoa New Zealand

and medication-free. God does not desert us; we stop believing in His healing power.

—*G. Shakespeare*

My memories of childhood are of always being sick through bronchial disorders, and this has continued all of my life. I had had prayer for asthma, but the bronchitis persisted, making sleeping difficult. Strenuous activity was also a problem because of the possibility of a bronchial spasm. I went to Weston Carryer's healing meeting with the hope that something might happen to release me from this affliction. Weston preached, and then started calling people out. I was one of them. After he prayed for me, I took a deep breath and found that my nose, which normally was blocked, was now clear, and so were my lungs. Since then, I have had a chance to see how my body performs in situations which would have normally produced a breathing problem, and I have come through them with no respiratory distress whatsoever.

—*Roger McBride*

I was healed of asthma at a Sunday evening service when Weston Carryer prayed for and laid hands on me. At first I was somewhat sceptical about being prayed over for healing, but immediately afterwards, I felt a release in my chest. During the following week, I decided not to take my preventive medication and I did not have any signs of asthma at all. This was quite amazing because I am outside in the cold every morning travelling to polytech. I walk from the Wellington railway station to the institute at 7.30 AM when it is often only 5° celsius. Normally, I needed my inhaler by the time I got to the polytechnic; but since I was prayed over by Weston, I have not used it once. And this was the middle of winter! I have also been riding my motorbike in the cold. No asthma. I have been healed.

—*Glen Davies*

Heart, Chest & Respiratory

I suffered from bronchial asthma for twenty-four years from the age of six months onwards. At a meeting in our church, Weston Carryer said through a word of knowledge that there was someone in the row where I was sitting who had a respiratory problem. It did not cross my mind that this applied to me, even though I had had an attack that morning. He walked up and said to me, "The Lord wants to heal you." I went to the front and he prayed over me.

From that day on, I have been free, and I thank God for healing me.

—*Ross Skilton*

"Where once he had difficulty breathing, and hurrying caused him distress, Weston Carryer prayed for Russell Thomson at Te Awamutu, and God released him from its grasp." This testimony was written on a letterhead offering "Solutions for business." God provided a solution for sickness.

—*For Russell Thomson*

All my life I have suffered from very bad asthma attacks which required me to go into hospital at least four times a year. At a divine healing meeting in Auckland I was prayed for by Weston Carryer. Since then I have had no asthma attacks and consequently have not been back to hospital. Jesus Christ heals.

—*Shantelle Kaukau*

In October of 1989, I was unexpectedly afflicted with asthma. The attack was severe. The Asthma Society gave me all sorts of medicine without any visible signs of improvement. Six months later, our daughter was called back to the Lord. During the tangi, one of my lungs collapsed. I was whipped away by

Miracles in Aotearoa New Zealand

ambulance to the Medical Centre and placed on the nebulizer. The doctors declared it was a touch-and-go affair.

My condition remained indifferent from then until September 1990 when I went to a Weston Carryer crusade. Through a word of knowledge he said, "God wishes to heal someone who has recently developed asthma." I knew that could only be me. I went up for prayer and was healed there and then. It has not come back. Praise God for the servants He raises to demonstrate the truths of His Word.

—Liza

From birth I suffered badly from asthma, and up until three years ago, was on prednisone and continually used a nebulizer. But even still, I was regularly hospitalized. My daughter, Genesis, experienced exactly the same illness also from birth and we were both on identical treatment. She also had numerous trips to hospital for the first ten years of her life.

In 1995, we attended a divine healing meeting in Taihape where Weston Carryer was ministering. He prayed for the Lord to heal us. Imagine our joy when we were both instantly completely healed! Since that time neither of us have had any sign of asthma and we have been able to donate the equipment we needed at home for asthma treatments to the hospital. Thank You, Jesus.

—Dawn Boswell

I suffered from asthma all my life and continually used a nebulizer until I went to a divine healing meeting at Gore in February 1988, where Weston Carryer was ministering and praying for Jesus to heal people. During the ministry time I went forward, was prayed for, and the Lord completely healed me. What a real blessing being able to breathe normally after gasping for breath all my life. Praise the Lord!

—Margaret Tamihana

Heart, Chest & Respiratory

I suffered very badly with asthma for twenty-five years and during this time was taking heavy doses of Prednisone. I also needed regular medical attention. In November 1998, I attended a divine healing meeting in Te Puke where Weston Carryer was ministering and he prayed for the Lord to heal me. I was amazed at what then happened. Immediately, for the first time in twenty-five years, I was able to breathe normally. The next day I felt like pinching myself to make sure that I had been healed—but I was! Since that time I have had no breathing restrictions and no medication. Hallelujah! What a wonderful Jesus we serve!

—*Frank Keno*

For seven years I suffered chronically with asthma. I constantly used a nebulizer and a hand pump for relief and had been hospitalized three times. Twelve months ago I went to a healing meeting where Weston Carryer was ministering. He prayed for me and I was totally healed that night. Since that night, over twelve months ago, I have had no further medication and can breath normally at all times. Thank You, Jesus.

—*Sue Kona*

For ten years I was a chronic asthmatic. During this time I had continual chest infections, pleurisy, bronchitis, and had double pneumonia five times. In one year alone I was hospitalized four times and almost died on two occasions. During this entire ten-year period, I was on a lot of medication as well as continually using inhalers. I was unable to stay in a job because of my continual illness. Two and a half years ago I went to Bible college at Hamilton but could not finish the course due to my poor health. I did not even have enough breath to be able to sing.

Two years ago, I attended a divine healing meeting in Hamilton where Weston Carryer was ministering. During

Miracles in Aotearoa New Zealand

the ministry time he prayed for the Lord to heal me. I am thrilled to testify that I was immediately healed. No more asthma, pneumonia, pleurisy, bronchitis, and certainly no more medication. I can sing and praise the Lord, and am not restricted in any way. What an incredible blessing life has been over the last two years. Thank You, Jesus.

—*Karyn Mitchell, Hamilton*

I was plagued with asthma and bronchitis all my life, until nine years ago when I attended an evangelistic meeting at Waikanae where Weston Carryer was ministering. During the ministry time Weston prayed for the Lord to heal me, and I am delighted to say that at that meeting, I was totally healed of both of these conditions. To be free after a life time is wonderful. Thank You, Jesus.

—*Joy Petterson*

I suffered from asthma all my life until I attended a healing meeting at Taumarunui in 1994 where Weston Carryer was ministering. During the ministry time Weston prayed for me, and the Lord, by the power of the Holy Spirit, completely healed me. Since that time I have never used an inhaler or had any sign of asthma. Praise the Lord.

—*Athol Tepu*

All my life I suffered from diseased lungs. I also had chronic bronchial asthma, and at some stage in my early life, I had developed a spot on the lung. I always had difficulty breathing which restricted all my activities and I was unable to exercise or walk any distance. Four years ago I was going to start a new job as a caregiver knowing that it would be very difficult for me because of my lungs, but I was trusting in the Lord in this situation.

In November 1997, on a Saturday morning, I attended a divine healing meeting in Hastings where Weston Carryer

Heart, Chest & Respiratory

was ministering. As I was leaving, I walked past Weston and he said to me, "The Lord has revealed that you have diseased lungs and He wants to heal you." He then simply prayed, and the Lord simply healed. I was stunned and felt very humble and of course absolutely delighted. I then started to feel my lungs fill completely with air. I had to get used to this because I had never experienced anything like this before. To be able to breathe normally was wonderful after forty-nine years of not being able to do so.

I started my job on the following Monday. Over the last four years, my breathing has remained normal with no bronchitis or asthma. What a wonderful Lord we serve.

—Kathleen Gibson

It was 1997, and a friend told me about an upcoming Weston Carryer meeting at Pukehina Beach in the Bay of Plenty. I was then living in Te Puke. I was sixteen years old at the time and for about two or three years, I had been suffering from extreme shortness of breath during any kind of physical exertion. I loved to run, tramp, walk, cycle and swim, but struggled with all of these, even for short periods of time. I love the outdoors and was frustrated and depressed because I began to put on weight that I could not lose (being unable to exercise).

Weston Carryer called for people that had lung or breathing problems to come forward. Without hesitation I went forward and was prayed for. Immediately I felt like I had a new set of lungs. The next day I went for a jog. Although it was a struggle at first, I prayed and believed with all my faith that I was healed. Today, I can participate in any physical activity, with no problems. Amen, and praise the Lord!

—Nicole Bellamy

I am so thankful that Weston Carryer prayed for me on Saturday night, 15 August, at Raumati Beach School. He prayed for a cyst on my back and then later for my asthma. The cyst has gone down a little, but my asthma has completely disappeared. In fact, I can breathe properly for the first time in about twenty-six years. Thanks be to God! I can't get over how deeply I can breathe; even my stomach has gone down and feels more comfortable. I believe asthma is a demonic force. I've had a few dreadful attacks the past few years and nearly died a couple of times—only thanks to getting prednisone and asthma medication in time made the difference. I also knew that God was with me and I've really been blessed to receive some wonderful healings of all kinds over the past couple of years.

—*Kaye Molony*

For eight years I had suffered from asthma and bronchitis. When exerting myself in any way, I needed to use a nebulizer to be able to breathe. At a divine healing meeting, Weston Carryer was ministering and received a word of knowledge about my specific condition. I responded and went forward for prayer and knew that I was healed by Jesus. The next morning, when out for my walk, the symptoms really endeavoured to come back. But I stood on God's Word—both written Word and His word of knowledge—and after about an hour, they left and have never returned. I am now completely asthma- and bronchitis-free. Praise the Lord.

—*Diana Woods*

On 25 February 2001, I attended my first healing meeting led by Weston Carryer here in Christchurch. For me, I had gone only to observe even though I have been a Christian for many years. On many occasions I had watched Benny Hinn on television and the healings that have taken place through him. However, I did not accept or understand what was happening.

On this particular evening, I was sitting to the right of Weston Carryer at our church. He came over, looked directly at those seated in our pews and stated, "There is someone in these rows that suffers from a left lung problem that has affected them for many years." I was rather stunned as I had had this

Heart, Chest & Respiratory

condition since I was four days old when I got consolidation of the lung. It had always caused me problems and at the age of four years, my parents were told by doctors to move up to the hills as it was believed I would experience better health. Over the years I was predisposed to chest infections and my lung capacity was lessened. I was always aware of not being able to take in air easily. I could hear my lung "clicking" in bed at night if I lay on my left side. My husband often could hear the sound, as it was that audible. As I also have a serious allergic reaction to antibiotics, the complications from chest infections were always a concern for me.

I did not want to accept that what Weston was saying referred to me. I looked behind me and to either side of me to see whom it could be that he was referring to. It all seemed unbelievable. When there was no response Weston moved away, but soon came back and insisted that this person was sitting in our pews with this condition. Much to the surprise of my husband (and myself too, I might add), I found myself walking over to him, so unsure of the whole experience. Weston laid his hands on me and asked if I had faith in the Lord. He said, "The Lord has the power to heal you."

I answered, "Yes, I believe," and down on the floor I went.

What I experienced was so profound! There was this extremely icy, cold feeling going down into my lung, as though I was in arctic conditions—it was so cold. I shook a lot, my eyes were closed but I could hear Weston talking as he began to pray over others. When I got to my feet, I was hungry to breathe in deeply and kept taking in deep, deep breaths. It was a wonderful, freeing experience.

In October 2002, I came down with a really bad chest infection that took me three weeks to recover. I continued to pray for complete protection of my left lung that I had totally accepted had been healed. I am pleased to report that as of March 2003, I am free of any damage to my lungs from that last infection.

I do not understand why He allowed that me to be healed when I was so very aware of others whose needs seemed so much greater than mine. And yet, some who attended that night were not healed. I can now say, without doubt, that God, in His grace, healed me that night in February 2002.

—*Anne Bately*

Weston came to our church on 13 June 2004, and while ministering, he said, "There is someone here who has a serious lung disease which is affecting both lungs, but that the left one is the worst." My left lung had collapsed some years previously because of this lung disease. The doctors in Greenlane Hospital had told me that within the next ten years, the right one would continue to deteriorate, so I would need to return to hospital for major surgery. My children were horrified and scared. For eight years I had been experiencing a lot of pain, was using two different asthma pumps a day, and was also on methadone, yet I was still gasping for breath most of the time. For eighteen years I had smoked marijuana, and although I tried desperately, I could not kick the habit.

I came to the front of the church, and as soon as Weston touched me, I fell to the floor. I experienced an awesome heat, and what felt like a golden finger touched me. The heat was amazing—something I had never felt before. This miracle I received was the most incredible experience I have ever had. It just felt like my lungs being put back together. Ever since that moment, I have had no pain at all. I can breathe normally at all times and I use no inhalers and have no medication. The desire to smoke dope was immediately taken away and I have not smoked anything since.

I found Jesus that night—I really found Him! Do I believe in Jesus? Yes, I do! All the grace and glory goes to our Jesus. He never left me—maybe I just forgot about Him. Not any more. He is my true love. Thank You, Jesus, and thanks to Weston. God's works are great. Amen.

—*Maria Warren*

In 2000, I developed emphysema, and as a result I had to be on oxygen bottles every day. I could not last more than a day or night without oxygen. If I tried to, I would pass right out, and so consequently I had to take the oxygen bottles everywhere I went, including shopping, which was very awkward. In total, I had to be on oxygen at least sixteen hours every day.

One day, in November 2002, I went to church, and very suddenly and desperately, I needed oxygen. I could not even climb up one stair and a lady took me into the main auditorium where Weston Carryer was conducting a divine healing service. He immediately prayed for me and I was slain in the Spirit and received a wonderful healing from the Lord. I immediately felt like a totally different person. I was able to breathe. It was wonderful.

I was given a pamphlet written by Weston, *Keeping Your Healing*, which I read every day for a long time. I reduced the time on my oxygen, and now two years later, I can breathe for hours without it. I can walk distances without gasping and my life has changed. I still do connect up to my oxygen bottle sometimes at night, but I don't really even need to do this as I can breathe well all the time. My quality of life been so changed, and I thank Jesus so much for what He has done for me.

—*Victoria Ataria*

In 1999, I developed asthma, and for the next five years, I needed to take medication which I was told I would be on for life. At a divine healing meeting in Hastings in November 2004, Weston Carryer prayed for the Lord to heal my asthma, and I am rejoicing to report that I was completely healed. Soon after being prayed for, I came off my medication and I have not had any sign of asthma ever since. Praise the Lord.

—*Judith Lambert*

I suffered from asthma for the first thirteen years of my life. I would have regular bad attacks, especially at night. Many nights my mother sat with me right through the night because of the difficulty I would have trying to get my breath. It was always accompanied by chest pain. When I was thirteen I went

Miracles in Aotearoa New Zealand

to a divine healing meeting in Flaxmere. Weston Carryer was ministering, and at one stage, he said, "There are three people right here (in area where I was sitting) who all have asthma, and the Lord wants me to pray for you." I was sitting next to two girls about my age, and unknown to each other, we all had asthma. So, we went forward, and as Weston prayed for me, I was slain in the Spirit. From the moment I got off the floor, I have not had any sign of asthma at all. That is over eight years ago. What an impact the Lord made on my life. Lord Jesus, I thank You so much.

—*Sharn Parkes*

My name is Irina Carson, and I want to thank the Lord for His great healing powers. For over twenty years I suffered very badly with asthma, and as a result of this, I could hardly breathe at all, despite using three different puffers morning and night. I also had a nebulizer at home which I had to be regularly hooked onto when the puffers were unable to help me get breath. I attended a divine healing meeting at West City Christian Centre, Auckland in November 2006 where Weston Carryer was ministering. I went, determined that I was going to be healed that night. And, God in His grace, reached out to me.

During the ministry time, Weston said that there was someone sitting just where I was who was suffering from chronic asthma and whom the Lord wanted him to pray for immediately. I went to the front. Weston prayed for me and the Lord immediately healed me. My gasping stopped within seconds and I have never had any difficulty breathing since. I have not used the nebulizer or puffers since that night ten months ago. Thank You, Jesus.

—*Irina Carson*

For at least twenty years I suffered badly from asthma. During this entire time, in order to be able to breathe, I had to use two "puffers" morning and night each day as well as being on steroids. Even then I was always wheezy.

Heart, Chest & Respiratory

Fourteen years ago, I was taken by two friends to a divine healing meeting in Amberley where Weston Carryer was ministering. During the ministry time he described my condition and asked me to go forward for him to pray for the Lord to heal me. I felt very uneasy about doing this but my friends literally pushed me forward. Weston prayed for me.

I was reluctant to stop using my puffers as I had been using them for so long. However, I began using them less, and then after a few days I realized that I could breathe normally without the puffers or steroids. Over the past fourteen years, I have had no breathing problems and I am so thankful to the Lord for healing my asthma. Thank You, Jesus.

—Maureen Haigh

On 20 April 2008, Weston was ministering at our church, Gateway Life Centre, in Rangiora. At the end of the meeting he called for anyone who had come for a miracle to come up to the front. About five years previously I was diagnosed with COPD (Chronic Obstructive Pulmonary Disease), that is, damaged upper airways for which there no medical cure. I was having to use an inhaler morning and night, plus during the day, depending on what physical work I was doing. A few weeks before Weston came down, I was starting to feel like I would have to start taking my inhaler during the night also.

I was the first one up the front for prayer and Weston asked what I needed healing for. I said, "I have COPD."

He asked, "What is that?"

"Chronic Obstructive Pulmonary Disease," I replied. Weston then laid hands on me and prayed for healing for my disease and I felt a burning feeling go right up through my chest. I collapsed onto the floor and I seemed to go into a deep sleep for a period of time.

After I woke up, I lay there for a while and then sat up. Weston asked, "How do you feel?"

I said, "Great." He then asked me to take deep breaths in to see if there was any difference.

Miracles in Aotearoa New Zealand

I answered, "Yes, there was." I was feeling like I could get more air into my lungs.

I do not use my inhaler now at all, even when I do physical activity or physical work. I am completely healed from COPD.

I am so thankful to Weston for being available to hear God's word. I thank God for my miracle, and I feel so humble that I received a miracle healing.

—*Stu Henderson*

For twenty years I suffered badly from asthma, and despite being on continual medication over this entire twenty-year period, I would still have asthma attacks at least twice a week. I attended a divine healing meeting in Masterton in August 1998 where Weston Carryer was ministering. Through a word of knowledge he described my condition. Weston asked me to go forward for him to pray for the Lord to heal me, which I did. As he prayed, I felt a very gentle anointing, and marvellously, I received an instant complete healing from the Lord. Over the last ten years, I have had no medication and absolutely no sign of any asthma. Lord, I am so grateful to You.

—*Pauline Watkins*

I came to Weston Carryer in faith asking for healing in my chest. Previously I had a scan up at the Whangerei hospital which resulted in a spot on my lung. (This happened to be on a Thursday.) I was advised to go back and have another scan four days later.

In the meantime Weston had a healing service at Christian Renewal in Whangerei. It was like I was blessed that God sent him to intervene. Praise the Lord. I went back to the hospital and the specialist looked at me and said, "I could have saved you travelling time. Whatever it was . . . it's gone."

I sincerely thank the Lord for miracles untold, blessings that unfold. God is wonderful. Amen.

—*Heeni Bond*

Heart, Chest & Respiratory

When I was five years of age, I was diagnosed with bronchial asthma, and from the age of thirteen I had to use two inhalers to enable me to be able to breathe. I could never run more than a short distance before I would be completely breathless and would experience severe pain in my chest in the right lung area.

Breathing was difficult when I woke up in the morning and it was a real challenge getting out of bed, although I wanted to get up. This condition was debilitating for me and caused many limitations.

In September 2013, I attended a divine healing meeting at my home church, Vision Church, in Fielding, where Weston Carryer was ministering. During the ministry time Weston said there was a person present who was suffering from severe asthma and was also experiencing a painful right lung. I immediately responded and went forward for him to pray for me. After he prayed, he asked me to hold my breath for thirty seconds, and I was able to comfortably hold my breath for a complete minute.

Since that moment, now six months ago, I have never used my inhaler, I have not had any breathing restrictions, or any chest pain, and I can now run without breathing difficulties. The asthma is now a thing of the past. Life is now so much better and I am so grateful to the Lord Jesus Christ for healing me. Thank You, Lord.

—*Naomi Wells*

At two years of age, I was diagnosed with severe asthma which affected me for the next fifty years. All sorts of treatment was tried on me. I had to use various forms of atomisers each day, as well as having medication. I had numerous injections and was hospitalised many times. My lung capacity was only 35% and I always had to have oxygen at home as I never knew when I would need it urgently. I was on prednisone for twenty years.

I was a lawn-mowing contractor with 140 customers. But as

MIRACLES IN AOTEAROA NEW ZEALAND

I got older, the asthma continued to get worse and I had to sell the business in my forties. Twelve years ago, I was experiencing particularly severe symptoms and I went to the doctor to see if he could give me something for relief. He told me that if I went home that night I would die, so instead he sent me immediately to the hospital where they kept me for the next few weeks.

When I was finally discharged, I heard that Weston Carryer was having a healing meeting in Fielding where I live, and I firmly believed that if I went, the Lord would heal me. As Weston prayed for me, the Lord delivered me completely. All those demonic forces came out of me and everyone in church heard the screaming.

Since that moment, now twelve years ago, I have never had the slightest sign of any asthma or any breathing difficulty. Although I am now retired, I am very active and do a lot of voluntary work. This has made an amazing difference in my life and I am so grateful to the Lord for what He has done for me.

—*Terry Horn*

A man with leprosy came to him and
begged him on his knees,
"If you are willing,
you can make me clean."
Jesus was indignant.
He reached out his hand
and touched the man.
"I am willing," he said, "Be clean!"
Immediately the leprosy left him
and he was cleansed.

–Mark 1:40-42, NIV

Eight

Diseases, Disorders, & Syndromes

Testimonies of healed conditions diagnosed as diseases, disorders, or syndromes.

Multiple Sclerosis

Although I have always believed in Christ as my Lord and Saviour, what God did through Him for me is far above my wildest dreams. You see, I suffered from multiple sclerosis and had to use crutches and two sticks for over five years. The doctor advised there was no known cure, and told me some time ago, I was doomed to a wheelchair existence. A friend took me to a church service in Inglewood in February 1993 at which Weston Carryer was ministering. I was invited forward by him for healing prayer and managed to get to the front only with support. While I was being prayed over, there was a blinding flash and a terrible explosion in my head as I was slain in the

Miracles in Aotearoa New Zealand

Spirit. When I got back on my feet, I felt I was floating. This was all so beyond human understanding and I admit to being frightened.

At 4:00 AM the next morning, I jumped out of bed and walked without sticks. I even asked, "What's doing?" then realised God had performed a miracle for I did not think I would ever be free again from sticks or a wheelchair. I have not had to use any support since and am free from all pain.

There is a follow-up. I attended another meeting two months on to witness to the healing power of God. I had prayer for a severe bout of painful and distressing shingles. When I rose the next morning, the pain was gone, and all that was left was the marks on the skin where the eruptions had been. I thank God for freeing me of all my troubles and pain.

I feel I must add this because I have wondered why God healed me. I am well known in the town and everyone was aware of my crippled state. They call me the "miracle man," but what they have witnessed is the awesome power and grace of a miracle-working God. What has come out of my healing is a unity in the town I have not seen before and a harmony in the churches which has surfaced because of it. This, in itself, is the miracle God has performed.

—*Fred Thompson*

For seven years I had been suffering from multiple sclerosis. Over this time I had become more restricted in my movements and had got to the stage where from my feet to my rib cage I had no feeling at all. Even when I broke a toe I didn't feel anything. Following advice from the specialist who I was under, we sold our farm because it appeared that I would not be able to work it much longer.

I was encouraged to go to a divine healing meeting in Christchurch where Weston Carryer was ministering. During the meeting I was prayed for by Weston and immediately felt one hundred percent again. It was amazing. God touched me in an incredible way. After he had examined me at my next meeting, the specialist confirmed that I was completely healed and since that time, which was three years ago, I have lived a normal life. Praise the Lord.

—*Rex Horrall*

For over seventeen years I have had multiple sclerosis, and had to resort to using a walking stick. This affliction affected my bladder as well as causing me to pass water almost hourly every night.

A friend asked if she could take me to a Weston Carryer healing meeting in Invercargill. Weston laid hands on me and prayed for God's help. He put my walking stick down and got me to walk without it. I have not used it since, and thanks be to God, I do not need it any more, though I am fairly slow.

From that night on I have not needed to go to the toilet more than once (early morning) and, as a result, am having such lovely, long sleeps. I still have bladder problems during the day, but, with such good nights, I can cope with these periods of weakness. The pain on the left side of my stomach leaves me very sore. I know that God is helping me quietly, and in His time I will come right. People are astounded I am looking so good and not using a stick. I feel like shouting and telling everyone how the Lord has helped me. I feel great and with each passing day, I will keep on getting stronger. He and I working together.

—*Linda Payne*

Up until the age of twenty-five (which was ten years ago), I had been a fit, healthy, active person. However, ten years ago, I started developing strange symptoms, including unusual feelings in my feet and legs. These could not be explained. Then over the next several years my body deteriorated significantly in many other ways. This affected me mentally and there was a serious decline in my energy level. I then started having problems with my left leg and numbness in parts of my body. These symptoms would fluctuate considerably. The vision in my left eye deteriorated to about twenty percent and I was diagnosed with optic neuritis. I would become very dizzy, and at times, trying to focus my right eye or even doing simple tasks became impossible. After further physical and mental deterioration, at age thirty-three (two years ago), a neurologist diagnosed my condition as multiple sclerosis. This was devastating to me as I was told nothing could be done for me. I found this very depressing.

One year ago, in March 2007, I was invited by my friend to some Christian healing meetings where Weston Carryer was ministering. Although at that time I had no Christian belief, I thought, *I can't lose anything.* So my husband and I attended the Friday night meeting. During the meeting, as Weston prayed for people, we saw the Lord perform obvious healings and I was really encouraged. Late in the meeting, I went forward and Weston prayed for me. I didn't feel too much happen at the time, but we went back on the Sunday night and he prayed for me again.

The next morning I realized that my vision was completely normal, my energy had been fully restored, and my whole body was functioning exactly as it should. The mental problems I had been experiencing, as well as the fears, were all totally gone. I had been completely healed by Jesus Christ. I could not doubt this in any way. A few days later my husband and I climbed mountains, which I could never have done before. Over the last twelve months I have lived a healthy life and Jesus is now the Lord of my life. It is marvellous to have been healed supernaturally of a very serious, medically incurable disease. Thank You so much, Lord.

—*Janine Morgan*

Eating Disorder

For practically all my life I suffered with anorexia and depression. Even when I was in kindergarten, I can clearly remember having this terror of being overweight and having

Diseases, Disorders & Syndromes

depression. From the age of 15, I was on antidepressants. These conditions completely controlled my life, and at this age of 15, I firmly decided that if I got over a certain weight, I would take my life. I had a mixture of 300 pills that I used to carry with me at all times and I was ready to take them at a moment's notice to end it all. After practically every meal I would throw up, but did not let anybody know about this.

At the age of 18, I went from my hometown of Feilding to Whanganui to live for a while. I had never ever been a church attendee at all. One Sunday morning, I was walking past Equippers Church in Whanganui, and a lady spoke to me and gave me a hug, which had a profound effect on me. She invited me into the church for the service. I went in, enjoyed the service, and started to attend the church.

I then shifted back to Feilding and started attending Vision Church, and there I accepted Jesus as my Lord. However, I still had the anorexia and depression.

In September 2012, when I was 19, I attended a divine healing service where Weston Carryer was ministering. During the ministry time I went forward for him to pray for me for deliverance from both the suicide compulsion and the anorexia.

As he prayed the power of God hit me in an amazing way. I went onto the floor, and for the next hour I was unable to stand on my feet. At the end of the meeting I had to be carried out, taken home, and put to bed. I was shaky for the next 48 hours.

During that time I was totally healed of both the anorexia and depression, and I immediately stopped taking all medication. I became so aware of the love that God has for me. My life was truly transformed immediately. Over the last seven months, I have been able to eat what I like. I have no depression and I just want to live my life for Jesus.

Thank You, Lord.

—*Rachel Gorniot*

At age thirteen I developed anorexia and bulimia. My parents realized that I wasn't eating, and they got medical advice, but I was unable to be helped in any way medically. That was when I realized that I had to eat. Although I realized that I had to eat, my stomach could not handle it and I would have to go to the bathroom and vomit it all back up again. At the age of twenty, after having this for seven years, I vividly remember thinking and wondering how my health could possibly last, and if I was ever going to be free of this terrible condition. I had sore kidneys, constant stomach pains, headaches, mood swings, acne around my mouth, sores on my hands, and chronic tooth grinding. Because of the bulimia, the acid from my stomach affected my teeth and they started to rot. I had to have some teeth removed. I tried to stop myself from getting sick but the feeling of having a full stomach was more than I could handle. I needed more than will-power.

Then, when I was aged twenty-two, Weston Carryer came to our church. I remember praying that God would not reveal to him my symptoms because I knew that the media makes jokes of eating disorders. I was scared of being judged if anyone found out. I had tried so hard to disguise my condition from everyone. Then Weston called out internal problems. Well, that was good enough for me. I was up like a flash and as soon as he started praying I was on the floor. I felt heat go down my throat, lungs, stomach and into my back. I was miraculously healed instantly: physically, mentally, emotionally, and of the horror of the memory of continually vomiting. The Lord also took away the terrible shame that I always experienced. It was amazing. I never thought once more about being sick or not being able to eat normally. Eating just comes naturally now. I am living a healthy and normal life. Lord Jesus, I want to thank You so much.

—*Kera-Leigh Johnson*

Fibromyalgia, Chronic Fatigue Syndrome

On 2 August 2000, I went to Weston Carryer's place for

Diseases, Disorders & Syndromes

healing of fibromyalgia which I had been suffering from for at least four years. This condition used to cause me considerable pain and extreme fatigue. Weston laid hands on me and God healed me then and there. I only had a small amount of faith for healing. I did not think that God would heal me because I wasn't worthy enough. But God saw my small faith and unworthy feelings and He healed me. Yes, me!

I just thank God again and again for healing me, and I have told others—some non-Christians—who think I am strange. I am so thankful for Weston being God's servant and the one instrumental in my healing.

—*Judi Rogers, Mt. Maunganui*

I just want to praise the Lord for healing me of fibromyalgia. For some years I have suffered pain all over my body, especially in my joints. Just to carry a bag, kneeling, and bending was very painful, and with that, I always seemed to be very tired. In August, 2002, a specialist diagnosed fibromyalgia and prescribed steroids and a relaxation programme.

In November 2002, I heard that Weston Carryer was coming to Hastings and I decided to attend one of his meetings. On Sunday morning after he had shared testimonies of other healings, Weston said that he was going to pray for people. Up until the time of my diagnosis, I had never heard of fibromyalgia and was absolutely amazed when the first condition that the Lord revealed to Weston was mine.

I came forward and he prayed for me and the Lord healed me immediately. This is over a year ago now and I am completely healed. I am grateful to the Lord for His amazing healing and for Weston's ministry.

—*Glynn Burtenshaw*

From early 2003 until April 2004, I suffered a lot of pain all over my body. My left shoulder was so painful I couldn't lift my arm. The doctor thought that I probably had fibromyalgia which has no cure. As a mother of three young children, I felt absolute desperation.

In April 2004, I heard that Weston Carryer was coming to a friend's church in Helensville. So, I went there, feeling a bit unsure but hoping for healing.

At the beginning of his ministry, Weston spoke out my exact condition. I got up immediately and went forward for prayer. The pain left me instantly and I could lift my arm. I had seen miracle healings happen to other people but that night, I received my own miracle. I couldn't stop crying. Now I can lift up my hands to praise the Lord, and two years later, I have never had any sign of pain anywhere in my body.

—*Haiying Bedggood*

Until fifteen years ago, I was a very fit, healthy, extremely active woman with fantastic energy. I picked up a virus suddenly and then developed chronic fatigue syndrome. Everything in my life then changed. I had no energy; my immune system could not resist numerous conditions. I became anaemic, continually developed infections, was subject to many severe headaches, and became suicidal. I lived on antibiotics, but found doctors could not help me at all. Any reasonable activity during the day (i.e., children's school functions) would leave me totally stressed out the following day.

I attended a divine healing meeting at Tauranga in November 2003 where Weston Carryer was ministering. During the ministry time, he prayed for the Lord to heal me. As I was being prayed for, I received an amazing miracle. The fatigue left immediately. I have gone off all medication, I am no longer anemic, my energy has returned, and I have totally changed. I am a normal person again.

At the same meeting I was also healed of a dermatitis rash that I'd had on my temple for years, which meant that I had to apply ointment to it every day to keep it away. Since being prayed for, it has totally gone—no further ointment is needed. Praise You, Jesus.

—*Helen Collins*

Diseases, Disorders & Syndromes

Prior to four years ago I was a healthy young woman, but in 2003, my health deteriorated very markedly. I didn't know what was wrong. I was experiencing chronic pain over most of my body and became very depressed. I was finally diagnosed with fibromyalgia and chronic fatigue syndrome. For the next three years I needed to take antidepressants most of the time and I also had eating disorders.

I attended a divine healing meeting in Auckland in September 2006, where Weston Carryer was ministering. I was in a very bad condition physically, mentally, and emotionally. Weston prayed for my healing and broke the power of the spirit of death over me in Jesus' name. I immediately experienced a release in my spirit and an amazing peace came over me. The tears just flowed as I had a deep cleansing. That night I was healed physically, mentally and emotionally. I was a totally new person.

Nine months later, apart from slight pain down my left side when I get overtired, I do not have any of the conditions that I had experienced for three years. There was a period in November 2006 when some of the symptoms did try and come back, but I stood in faith and they have not returned. No more antidepressants, and once again, I am living a normal life. Lord, I am so grateful.

—*Andrea Wonglyn*

For at least two years, I suffered severe pain in most joints in my body through having fibromyalgia. The pain was always there and I could not get any relief from it. I attended a divine healing meeting in Tauranga in October 2006, and Weston Carryer prayed for the Lord to heal me. As Weston prayed for me, the Lord really touched me in a wonderful way and I experienced, amongst other things, a tingling right through my body. By the time I got home, all the pain had gone. I had a wonderful release in my body. I also had an unexplained energy that made me feel twenty years younger. I was able to touch my toes for the first time in years. Now seven months later I have had no pain whatever and feel really great. To be free of fibromyalgia is wonderful. All praise and glory to Jesus my healer.

—*Barbara Sawyer*

I had been a fit healthy woman all my life until seventeen years ago when I developed glandular fever. This affected me for six months. Following my recovery I was okay for a further six months until I experience a bad dose of flu which quickly developed into chronic fatigue syndrome and totally debilitated me for the next two years. During this entire two-year period, I had to sleep or rest for sixteen hours a day. I was unable to get out of bed until mid-day and would have to be back in bed around 8:00 PM. I lost all my power of concentration and couldn't understand what people were telling me. There was no improvement at all over this two-year period.

I attended a divine healing meeting in Winton where Weston Carryer was ministering. I told him I was sick, and tired of being sick and tired, and he prayed for the Lord to heal me. Nothing changed that night or the following day. But the next day I woke up completely healed and have never had the slightest sign of chronic fatigue ever since. It was incredible. For the last seven years I have been running a large sheep, beef and deer farm singlehandedly and enjoying great health. Thank You, Lord. I am truly grateful.

—*Marilyn Allan*

Jesus is working in my life in a wonderful way. My husband, Ted, and I were visiting our son Greg's church, The Centre in Paraparaumu in February 2007 where this healing ministry was happening. We had never witnessed healing like this before and were really excited. At the start of the meeting we watched two women and two men healed in front of our eyes. Then Weston Carryer who was ministering, made a call for a medical condition, fibromyalgia. I had not heard of this complaint. When no one answered, he explained the symptoms, and I thought,

Diseases, Disorders & Syndromes

Gosh . . . that is just what I have!

For over five years, my body had been aching severely just about everywhere. This was debilitating and causing considerable restriction in my movements. I thought that it was an age affliction, but now I know different. I knew immediately Weston's call was for me. I went up to the front, full of confidence and faith in Jesus, to receive the healing through him. All pain and aches went immediately.

Now, four months later, I have not had any pain of any kind in my body. It is marvellous. I thank and praise Jesus every day for I know it is by His stripes that I have been healed. I am so thankful for Weston's ministry.

—Coral Ann Favell

Weston Carryer prayed for me over the years and I will share my good news. I went to an evening meeting at Life Advance Church where I was healed of pain associated with chronic fatigue syndrome. I had that pain continually for more than ten years and it was very severe at times.

I would like to mention one thing I believe the good Lord used to help me, as this may help someone else: release from guilt and condemnation. I know we are free of guilt and condemnation when we are born again (as Jesus took this from us), but some of us struggle with it and I know that held me back from receiving complete healing. Not any more, though! All glory and praise to Jesus, and I am so grateful for Weston's faithfulness in prayer.

—Gaylene Haub

One day eight years ago, I experienced severe pain suddenly in my chest, arms and back; I thought I was having a heart attack. I was taken to hospital where tests were carried out. The pain was so bad in my back that every time my back was touched, I would scream. The tests revealed that my heart was not the problem, but what was diagnosed was fibromyalgia. I was treated in hospital for a week. The doctor prescribed anti-

Miracles in Aotearoa New Zealand

inflammatory medication and antidepressants which he said I would be on for life. For the next seven years I experienced terrible pain in various parts of my body—especially in my back—which was never free from this chronic pain. Every single winter during this seven-year period I had to go back to hospital for extreme pain and be treated with morphine.

Twelve months ago (November 2004), I attended a divine healing meeting in Flaxmere where Weston Carryer was ministering. During the meeting he said that the Lord had revealed to him that there was someone suffering from fibromyalgia, and asked for that person to come and be prayed for. I was really stunned but went forward and he prayed for me. Within forty-eight hours every bit of pain went from my body and I have never had any pain whatever since then. It is incredible! To be able to live a normal life again after seven years of terrible, continual pain is just so marvellous. Jesus, I am so grateful.

—*Glennis Little*

Allergies – Food, Seasonal, Environment

Weston Carryer prayed for my release from hay fever when I stayed with him during a tour of the Covenant Players. I have not had any hay fever since I left New Plymouth. Praise be to God our healer. I was so thankful for his encouraging faith.

—*Sue Christensen*

When I was in my early twenties I developed chronic hay fever, which I had continually for twenty years. I always had a runny nose, running eyes and cold sores all around my mouth. I had to get up regularly through the night with the symptoms and it left me with no energy. The tablets the doctor prescribed did not help at all.

Diseases, Disorders & Syndromes

At a divine healing meeting in Invercargill fourteen years ago, Weston Carryer prayed for the Lord to heal me. There was an immediate improvement. Over the next two months, the healing was complete and I have not had any hay fever since. Praise the Lord.

—Glennis Currie

For sixteen years I suffered from severe food allergy problems. I was unable to eat any dairy products, or food containing yeast at all during this entire time. My daughter, Rachael, suffered from the same allergies and eczema as well. We were both prayed for by Weston Carryer and, through Jesus Christ, we were both completely healed by God. We can each eat any normal food now without any ill effects, while Rachael's eczema has totally gone. Praise the Lord.

—Helen Moller

One year ago, Weston Carryer prayed for the Lord to heal me, and now I am healed of a dairy food allergy I had for three years. I couldn't eat anything with even a trace of milk protein in it without coming out in welts and being terribly itchy. As soon as I was prayed for, I went and bought a chocolate bar on my way home. It tasted so good! Having the allergy was an annoying inconvenience and I am so thankful to not have to be a burden to my husband or to people we eat with! Praise God.

—Rebekah Wilson

Weston Carryer came to my church in April 2006. I had been unable to eat any wheat products or products containing gluten for about six months. I had not been diagnosed with this intolerance problem, but when someone told me that my symptoms of diarrhoea, constipation, severe headaches, stomach cramps, fainting, and discomfort after eating could be food intolerance, I decided to change my diet. I stopped eating products containing wheat or gluten that I either knew about or found out about, and I also cut back on eating dairy products. My symptoms ceased and only seemed to return if I couldn't resist eating something that I really used to enjoy, even knowing that it contained these ingredients.

I soon became very religiously restrictive in what I ate. I checked the labels of everything that I ate, not just for gluten, but also for fat and sugar levels. This food intolerance had become an obsession. At one stage, I recorded everything I ate and would think myself into feeling sick if I ate anything that I saw as bad. Even if it didn't contain gluten, I would be disappointed that I had eaten something I saw as bad. I began to think that I wasn't losing any weight by just eating healthily and exercising. I thought I was too fat, so I tried throwing up.

I had only done it a few times before Weston came to town. By that time, I was beginning to see how much of a grip on my life this food obsession thing had become. I just wanted to be free of it all and I believed that God could do that. I felt so guilty about it that I couldn't talk to anyone about even thinking of throwing up.

I went to one of Weston's healing meetings and the testimony he read of a girl that God had healed of bulimia through his ministry blew me away. I was nearly crying, and desperately wanted to be free myself, but did not feel that I was deserving or good enough. Weston spoke out, by the leading of the Holy Spirit, that there were three people in the meeting with the fear of cancer. This was also something that I had been struggling with. I was absolutely terrified of being diagnosed with cancer, and every time I felt a little bit sick, I dreaded what could be causing it.

After the meeting I went forward and received prayer for both the food intolerance and resulting obsession, and for the fear of cancer. Praise God, I have been eating bread ever since! Headaches and stomach cramps came in fits, to begin with, after about a week. I prayed against them and claimed the healing that God had given me. Now, six months, later I can eat any normal food without experiencing diarrhoea, constipation, headaches, stomach cramps, fainting or discomfort. Thank You, Jesus.

Diseases, Disorders & Syndromes

—Tania Mounsey

I attended a divine healing meeting in New Brighton, Christchurch on Friday, March 23, 2012. In the last word of knowledge Weston Carryer had for the evening, he said that there was someone with an allergy that affects the digestive system. I did not respond immediately as I had gone to the meeting hoping for healing for a sore arm and neck which I had injured in the earthquake in 2011.

I had always heard the allergy I was born with described as "anaphylaxis" and is life-threatening at the severe end of the scale. For instance, if I had a tiny bite of a cake which had an egg, my mouth would burn, itch, and swell, along with my lips. If I happened to swallow that bit of cake, it would burn my throat and I would have severe stomach cramps, or vomit and my throat would swell. I had to have antihistamine tablets to keep my breathing going and my pulse would be rapid and blood pressure drop and I would feel dizzy. Once, my Mum, who is registered nurse, rushed me to hospital where I had to be given adrenaline to keep me alive. Egg white is hidden in many foods, wine, and even some medicines. So I got used to living my life around this particular ailment. I could not even touch many foods without this terrible reaction.

Firstly, you prayed to break a curse off my life, and then prayed for God's healing power to heal me. At that moment I was completely and instantly healed of this awful disease! I went home and told my children who were very happy—my 14-year-old son asked if he could break an egg over my head! Of course I said, "No!" and tested my healing slowly over a day or two—although I really knew the first moment I had some food with egg as usually the symptoms were so sudden and unbearable and now I had no symptoms at all.

The 27th March was my daughters' 16th birthday and she made a three-egg birthday cake. When I ate that cake with my children, they were also convinced that I am healed. Since then I've baked a lot with eggs and told all my family and friends who are amazed. Thank You, God, for healing me.

Miracles in Aotearoa New Zealand

When my daughter was about seven, she had a dream one night that God healed me of this allergy—and now that is a reality. Over the last seven months I have been able to eat any normal food with absolutely no adverse reaction at all. Another wonderful result of the healing has been a real strengthening in my immune system. I have gone through the Christchurch winter months with only a slight cold, whereas I would usually be very unwell the whole winter. I am so thankful for Weston's ministry.

—*Gabrielle Hall*

I am a dairy farmer who for many years had operated my farm and milked the cows. Approximately 16 years ago, I developed what was medically described as an allergic reaction to cowshed environment. This causes the skin on my hands to dry, then crack and peel off. It was extremely painful and a lot of the time I was in real agony. Doctors told me that I would have this condition for life. I had to pay someone else to milk for me, and it looked as if I would have to sell my farm, which was daunting for me as I had only ever dairy-farmed.

After having this condition for twelve months, I attended a divine healing meeting in Galatea fifteen years ago. Weston Carryer was ministering and he prayed for the Lord to heal me. There was an immediate gradual improvement, and within two months, the healing was complete. Over the last fifteen years, I have not been troubled with this condition and I am still milking cows. Thank You, Jesus.

—*Eric Smeith*

When I was in my early twenties I developed chronic hay fever which I had continually for twenty years. I always had a running nose, running eyes, and cold sores around my mouth. I had to get up regularly through the night and I had no energy. The tablets the doctor prescribed me did not help at all. At a divine healing meeting in Invercargill fourteen years ago Weston Carryer prayed for the Lord to heal me. There was an

Diseases, Disorders & Syndromes

immediate improvement in my condition, and over the next two months the healing was completed. I have never had any hay fever since. Praise the Lord.

—Glenis Currie

Other –Blood Pressure, Blood Disorder, Hepatitis, Thyroid

I experienced blood pressure for twenty years and was on medication the whole time.

Following prayer at a Weston Carryer healing meeting, my blood pressure was immediately restored to the correct level where, as medical tests have shown, it has stayed ever since. Praise God.

—J. Batley

Two years ago, when Weston Carryer conducted a healing meeting in Te Awamutu, my son was healed through Jesus of toxoplasmosis, a protozoal disease contracted from animals, which has a distressing effect on tissues throughout the body. He had been very sick indeed for some six months but was healed straightaway. My son and I were also healed at the same meeting of eczema, and it has not come back. My parents were so astonished with my son's transformation that they went to the final session and gave their hearts to the Lord.

In September 1994, Weston returned to Te Awamutu, and I went up for prayer. I had muscle trouble in my right arm which gave lots of pain. The doctor's painkillers did not work, but Jesus took it away immediately and for good.

—Margaret Bent

MIRACLES IN AOTEAROA NEW ZEALAND

Approximately five years ago in Opotiki, I was healed of hyperglycemia. After work, I left Whakatane and travelled to Opotiki for the meeting, thinking my daughter would enjoy hearing an evangelist. We were late and found seats at the back of a packed hall. About two sentences into the message, Weston Carryer stopped and said God wanted to heal someone of hyperglycemia. I went forward and was prayed for. Sometime later I went for a blood test and found my blood was normal. I have not had any symptoms since. Praise the Lord.

I am writing to tell the story of the healing that I received after Weston's prayer. I came forward for prayer when he came to Word of Life Church around July of 1998. I had been diagnosed as having M.E. (Tapanui flu) in March 1995, but had already had it for some time before that. Although I wasn't bedridden, I was constantly tired and would catch infections and bug after bug. I was also in Accident & Emergency at the hospital for serious allergic reactions from time to time. This condition seriously affected my marriage (December 1994) and isolated me from people because I wasn't able to go out very much.

After Weston prayed for me last year, I was very sick for two weeks. Then one day, I was in bed, feeling very sorry for myself, and the Lord said to study up on the verses in the Bible that talk of healing. So I did this, but not really believing them. I looked up four Scriptures a day, read them out, and said out loud that I believed it, even though I didn't feel it. Within a week I noticed a difference. After a month I was completely healed. It doesn't mean that the enemy doesn't still attack me through unbelief, but my faith in God's healing work is now so solid that I won't accept unbelief any more! For a long time now I have not had even the slightest hint of M.E. and life is so wonderfully different.

—*Rebecca Provan*

I wish to convey to you my testimony that I had a high S.E.R., which is a blood infection. I am pleased to say that I was healed by God at a Weston Carryer healing at the Apostolic Church service in Gisborne. Praise the Lord! May God bless the

Diseases, Disorders & Syndromes

Carryer family in a mighty way, in Jesus' name, amen.

—*Annie Horsfall, Gisborne*

As the result of a blood transfusion when I was approximately two years old, I developed hepatitis B. For the next twenty-one years, this drastically affected my life, and upon leaving school, I found I was limited in the type of work I could do. Medical tests had confirmed this condition. One of these tests done was on 8 January 2002 and the medical reading was:

HB2ag – reactive, anti-HB core—reactive, anti-HBs 0 IU/mL – negative.

These tests meant I had a hepatitis B infection.

I attended a divine healing meeting later that year in November 2002, where Weston Carryer was ministering. He prayed for the Lord to heal me. I knew I was immediately healed. I had never before felt like I now did.

I was able to get a much better job that I really enjoy. My whole life was transformed. Three months later on 17 March 2003, I had my next laboratory test done and the tests confirmed that the Lord had healed me. I do not have hepatitis B any more. Thank You, Lord.

—*Daniel Kyte*

Approximately ten years ago I realized that my body was not functioning as it should and my energy level became very low. Medical tests revealed that my thyroid was not working properly and that I had a condition called hypothyroid. The doctor told me that I would need to be on a medication for life. However, I was very reluctant to go on permanent medication and decided to believe the Lord for my healing; so I did not take any medication at all. For the next two years, I really struggled with my very low energy levels.

Eight years ago I attended a divine healing meeting in Lower Hutt where Weston Carryer was ministering. Although I was a committed Christian and believing for God to heal me, I had

MIRACLES IN AOTEAROA NEW ZEALAND

never been to a healing meeting before. To say the least, I was very sceptical about being healed at the meeting. Weston had words of knowledge for people and then he prayed for them. He then invited anyone else who had a need of healing to come forward. He stressed that he didn't need to have a word of knowledge for people for the Lord to heal them.

I went forward in a line with a lot of other people and determined that I was going to fix my eyes on Jesus, which I did. People were slain in the Spirit, and then Weston came to me. He then commanded a spirit of infirmity to leave me and I had an amazing experience. I felt something like a flickering fish tail as it comes out of the water come up from inside my knees, go right up inside my body and come out of my shoulders. I had never experienced anything like this before. Three weeks later I had blood tests taken which confirmed that I had been healed. My energy level had already returned and for the last eight years I have once again been a fit, healthy, active person. Thank You, Jesus.

—*Pam Andrew*

Our son James had a condition of very low platelet levels in his blood leading to spontaneous bruising and internal bleeding. This could have serious consequences. When Weston Carryer first prayed for him at All Nations Christian Fellowship in Tauranga a couple of years ago in 2004, his platelet levels went up to the normal level for the first time. This came in handy because he fell off the first floor balcony onto some concrete steps within a couple of weeks of the prayer. I believe God saved him because he only suffered a fracture in one bone of his foot; he was racing around in three days. After this event, his levels gradually decreased until the second time Weston visited our church about a year later. I reported the above and requested further prayer for him. Following Weston's prayer, his platelet levels increased to a normal level, and have remained so ever since. Thank God!

—*Robin Deal*

Diseases, Disorders & Syndromes

The Lord truly works in interesting ways, and here is why I can say that. Eleven years ago, in March 1996, I was diagnosed with a blood condition and was booked to have more tests done in Christchurch hospital. A good Christian friend, involved with the Full Gospel Business Men's Fellowship in Rangiora knew of my problem and told us of Weston Carryer's meeting in Amberley to be held the evening before I was to have the tests in Christchurch.

My husband and I went along to the meeting. Part way through Weston's speaking, he stopped and said, "There is someone here with a blood condition."

I waited to see if anyone else would respond; no one did, and Weston repeated what the Lord was telling him. Our friend from Rangiora looked at me and I knew what he was saying, even with no words spoken. My husband also made a gesture to me to respond. Before this time, I had experienced the Spirit of the Lord working in this way and healing me. So I was not ignorant of the fact that it truly was the Lord in His love and goodness answering my prayers, and the prayers of family and friends for me to receive healing in my body.

I went up and Weston prayed for me. The power of the Lord's Spirit came upon me and I collapsed backwards onto the floor. I lay there for sometime and I could feel the healing power of Jesus going through me. I knew I was being healed. No one told me I was healed; I just knew that I knew that I was healed.

My husband and I went to Christchurch Hospital the next day and it took hours of waiting to have the tests done; but I had no fear because I knew I was healed. And, sure enough, when the tests came back to my local Amberley doctor, everything was normal—not one thing was abnormal. I was totally and completely healed by Jesus. And to this day, I am still totally and completely healed. Hallelujah. Praise Jesus' holy name.

—*Donna Chambers*

On 26 June 2007, I attended a healing meeting where

Miracles in Aotearoa New Zealand

Weston Carryer was ministering. I was healed of a condition that I had been suffering with. I had felt tired and unwell most of my life—always needing lots of sleep and having to push myself to do anything as it was all an effort. Even though I had lots of sleep I still felt continually tired. I didn't know why. I was living on cans of energy drinks and coffee just to get through the day. I changed my shifts to afternoon shifts as I couldn't get up in the mornings.

After I had prayer at the healing meeting in July, I have lots of energy and I feel heaps better. I can't believe that I ever felt as bad as I did. I feel ten years younger and I haven't needed any more energy drinks since. This might not seem like much of a testimony to anybody else, but it is to me. Thank you!

—*Anne Blackler*

In December 2007, I suddenly developed very high blood pressure but I refused to take medication. Over the next two months this had a drastic effect on my body. I was gasping for breath all the time. Even after going to the letterbox and back I would feel faint and would have to sit down for half an hour before recovering. If I ever leaned over, I would almost blackout.

At a divine healing meeting in February 2008 in Taupo, Weston Carryer prayed for the Lord to heal my heart and heal the high blood pressure. The Lord instantly completely healed me. I immediately felt radically different. I was able to go to the gym for a solid thirty-minute workout with no problems of any kind.

Two months later, in April, I had a gamma-scan done which proved my heart is now one hundred percent with normal blood pressure. Thank You, Jesus.

—*Sheron Northe*

After the birth of my children I suffered from post-hyperactive thyroid for up to six months. However, after the birth of my third child, it didn't seem to be disappearing and I quickly lost a lot of weight and felt generally hyper. Although

Diseases, Disorders & Syndromes

I was completely exhausted, I would wake up about every two hours at night and I was unable to ever relax at all. The doctors at the hospital talked about radiation but I didn't really want to go down that path. I was on medication, and had been for more than a year; the monthly blood tests I was having continued to reveal what was wrong.

When I went to the Weston Carryer healing meeting in 2006, I felt sure that if God wanted to heal me, my condition would be called out. But as the night went on, that did not happen. At the end the meeting, it was opened for everyone to go forward for prayer, which I did. And then, I thought, *Maybe I'll experience the presence of God as I am being prayed for.* But this didn't really happen either. Weston's prayer was only a few words; but in faith I believed God had healed me. I stopped taking my pills that night. I guess part of me knew that my blood tests were in two weeks time and if nothing had changed I would be back on the medication again.

I kept reading Weston's pamphlet, *Keeping Your Healing*, that was given to me at the meeting over and over and I found this very helpful. It was a long two weeks of doubt, excitement and trusting God. When the doctor phoned to say my blood levels were fine and to come back in a month, I knew I had received God's healing.

This was eighteen months ago and I am now monitored every three months. I am continually amazed. The first few months were the hardest in trusting God for my healing. Having a sickness that affects your energy levels often gives you an excuse for not doing things, but that has been taken away. I praise God for His healing and this journey of trust.

—Louise Bocxe

In 2003, I was diagnosed with hepatitis B. This had a devastating effect on my life as there is no medical cure for this condition.

In May 2006, I attended a divine healing meeting in the Auckland area where Weston Carryer prayed for the Lord to heal me. In January 2007, I had my next medical check regarding this condition. The results came back negative. No more hepatitis. The Lord had completely healed me. One month later I had a liver test done and was absolutely delighted to be told that my liver has been fully and divinely restored. It is now in perfect condition. Lord, I am so grateful. I really praise You.

—B.L.

Arthritis

I have had arthritis in my neck, shoulders and lower back for many years. The condition has been verified by x-ray. People have prayed over me a number of times and I have believed for healing, but without result.

During Easter of 1990, Weston Carryer laid hands on me. Since then, I have been free from pain in my neck and shoulder. The symptoms did return to that area temporarily but I rebuked satan and the sickness, in the name of Jesus, and it went. Although my lower back still troubles me, I have absolute confidence God wants me totally healed and I am believing for that soon.

—J.S.

I had suffered from osteoarthritis in my spine and hips for some years and was greatly restricted in my movements. I was unable to stand up straight and had to be helped out of bed. I was having daily dosages of painkillers and sleeping tablets. The doctor stated that within months I would be crippled completely. As well, I had to use a large magnifying glass to read with.

My brother-in-law persuaded me to go to a healing meeting, and there after preaching, evangelist Weston Carryer, prayed for me. I experienced a warm and tingly sensation, and the power of God instantly healed all the osteoarthritis in my body

Diseases, Disorders & Syndromes

and restored my eyesight so that I can see and read unaided today. I have no further pain and am not restricted in my body in any way.

—Ray Lambert

Weston was in Taupo at the Apostolic Church on another healing crusade. I went, as I needed God to heal me of arthritis in both knees. I love walking and they had been hurting a lot. All praise and glory to God in heaven! I am healed.

—Shirley Button

How can I possibly forget that night in Mosgiel when God, through Jesus Christ, healed me at a Weston Carryer healing meeting? I went to the meeting with acute pain. The arthritis from which I suffered was such that I could not raise my right arm. What a wonderful healing. Even now—and without fail—upon waking in the morning, my husband says to me, "Raise your arm," and it goes right up in praise to my God. I still have pain in my hands, but am convinced it will go in time, for every day I give thanks for what He has done for me.

—May Reid

It was just another FGBMFI meeting at which Weston Carryer was giving his testimony. However, for my wife, it had special significance. Through prayer, and laying on of hands, God healed her of arthritis. She now has free movement in her neck. What a joy to see her loading up the trailer with rubbish without hurt or hindrance. We certainly have a God who can do great things.

—B.D.W.

I want to testify to the healing power of God. I was completely cured of arthritis during a Te Nikau summer school at which

Miracles in Aotearoa New Zealand

Weston Carryer was teaching. My doctor, indeed, *no* doctor has found a remedy for this affliction. I attended different churches searching . . . searching for something which escaped me. In August 1988, I received Jesus into my heart and was baptised in water and the Spirit.

In my Christian walk, God had, over the following two years, redeemed me from many of my sins. When I went forward for healing, Weston pointed out that holding on to grudges, and the like, was a complete block to receiving anything—especially healing—from the Lord. I had continued to hold grievances involving unforgiveness, bitterness, and hatred. This was the root of my complaint and the key to my searching because once I had confessed and named the people against whom I had resentment, God forgave me and I was healed me completely. I can now visit these people knowing that God has set me free through His Son Jesus Christ. This same healing power of God is available to you. Believe, and in faith, receive.

—*Elizabeth A. Davey*

I had suffered arthritis for several years. My arms and shoulders were especially affected and I was unable to raise my arms above shoulder height.

I attended a divine healing meeting where Weston Carryer was ministering. As he prayed for me in the name of Jesus, I experienced an amazing sensation. All the pain went in a second, and my arms shot up above my head with such force, I thought they were going to shoot out of their sockets. I was completely healed, and since that time (twelve months on), I have had no further arthritis problems.

—*Win Flutey*

I worked in a saw mill, and contracted arthritis due to chemical poisoning. The first symptoms developed in my wrists before spreading through my whole body. For three months, I was bedridden, and then was very restricted in any form of activity for close to eighteen months. I could not work, and

Diseases, Disorders & Syndromes

neither was I doing very well in my Christian walk.

I was invited to go forward at a Weston Carryer meeting in Inglewood for healing to my wrists which were especially bad. They were healed instantly. I awoke the following morning to the realization that my whole body was healed. I have not had the faintest ache since then, praise the Lord!

—*Bruce Saywell*

For at least ten years I suffered constant pain from arthritis in my back. This restricted me considerably in my movements.

I attended a divine healing meeting at Pukehina in late 1996 where Weston Carryer was ministering and he prayed for the Lord to heal my back. I didn't experience anything at the time, but the improvement started the next morning. Over the next two weeks, the pain disappeared. And now, two years later, the only time I ever get any very slight temporary pain, is when I exceed my natural limitations. Thank You, Jesus.

—*Elizabeth Bunting*

In 1996, Weston Carryer came to Wanganui and ministered in our church. He had a word of knowledge about arthritis, but he described where it had begun and where it had gotten to in the person's body. *That was me.* My whole upper body—from my hips to my shoulders, including my hands and lower back—were infected with this disease. I had been born with it. I was forty-nine years of age when Weston came, and I responded to God's Word.

I went down to the front where Weston prayed. I got up from the floor and went back to my seat. Then, all of a sudden, I was hot all over. Before this, I could never sit too long, lay down for too long, drive my car, or do any work around the house for too long. The pain was horrific. When I sneezed, I could not walk for two or three days. Now I have had three years of divine healing where I can do all the things I could never do before.

This may seem silly to some, but my disease became a

friend to me over the forty-odd years. Once the Lord opened my eyes to see that this was an enemy and not a friend, my healing came. It was a divine appointment for me that day. Thank You, Jesus. Praise the Lord!

—*Barry Smith*

For approximately a year, my whole body had experienced severe pain through arthritis. My son and daughter-in-law persuaded me to go to a divine healing meeting in Taupo where Weston Carryer was ministering. I did not believe for one moment that I would be healed and was very reluctant to even go forward for Weston to pray for me. I finally did go forward, was prayed for, but didn't feel any different at all.

The next day, however, I realized all the pain had gone and my body was not restricted in any way. I then knew Jesus was for real, that He had wonderfully healed me, and I was then delighted to accept Him as my Lord and Saviour. Since that time, over six years ago, I have not had any arthritic pain at all. What a joy living is now. How I love Jesus.

—*Tai Tito*

For several years I had arthritis in my jaw. Apart from the continual discomfort, it also affected my speech, and nothing I tried could help or relieve it in any way. I attended a divine healing meeting in Hamilton fourteen years ago where Weston Carryer was ministering and praying for the sick. During the ministry time he prayed for the Lord to heal me. Within three days, all the symptoms of arthritis had gone from my jaw and I have had no discomfort or restricted speech ever since. Thank You, Jesus!

—*Lorraine Williams*

At the age of sixteen, pain developed in my right hip which I later discovered was the onset of arthritis. Over the years this pain became more and more severe. Finally, it became very

Diseases, Disorders & Syndromes

difficult for me to walk, and in 2001, at the age of seventy two, I was told that I needed a hip replacement. In September 2001, I attended a healing meeting in Lower Hutt where Weston Carryer was ministering and praying for the Lord to heal people. As he prayed for me, the Lord did a wonderful miracle. All the pain just stopped and the full movement was instantly restored to my leg. After all these years this was incredible.

Soon after this I went for my next x-ray, and the doctor told me that my x-ray revealed that there was now nothing wrong with my hip. He said, "Here, look for your self." Over the last twelve months I have had no pain and can move freely at all times. Lord, You are wonderful.

—*Sarah Hotai*

I am delighted to share a wonderful healing that I received from the Lord earlier this year. For at least eight years I had arthritis in my back and most of my joints. I was always aware of it. A lot of the time it was extremely painful, and just getting out of bed in the morning was very difficult. I just had to roll out and try and not hit the floor too hard.

At a divine healing meeting in Auckland, I went forward for Weston Carryer who was ministering to pray for me. The pain just went immediately. The next morning, I just could not believe how I got out of bed normally and was able to kneel on the bed to open my curtains for the first time in eight years. Since that night I have had no pain and it is so wonderful being totally pain-free. Thank You, Jesus.

—*Margaret Hamilton*

I am forty-two years old and I had osteoarthritis for two years. For the last six months I had been in continuous pain, suffering sleepless nights because of the pain and I would cry sometimes because the pain was too much. I had to put up with the pain until it got unbearable when I would take some painkillers. I was under a specialist who I last saw in August 2003. It was then that he told me I was too young to have a hip replacement, but because my hip had deteriorated so much since January, he would see about putting me on a waiting list next year (2004) in March. But of course the waiting lists are anything from one to two years.

I belong to the Apostolic Church and knew that Weston Carryer was coming in about six-weeks time. On the 4 October 2003, I came along to one of the healing meetings at night. On the Saturday I was in a lot of pain, so much so that the pain was throbbing in both my hips. I said to myself, *Well, if I am going to get healed, today is a good day because I am in a lot of pain.* I had been sitting there all night watching Weston pray for other people to be healed. Pastor Dave got up to say that it was 9:00 PM and asked Weston if he wanted to finish because it was late. Well, of course, my heart saddened with disappointment, and I thought, *That's it . . . I am not going to be healed.*

Weston must have told the pastor that he had one more person to pray for because then he said, "There is someone in this area that has a problem in their left hip." Well, straightaway I put my hand up. Weston asked me questions, and then asked, "Are you in pain?"

"Yes!" I replied.

So he prayed for me, and instantly my pain was gone . . . just like that, the pain was gone. I began crying. I could hardly believe it because the pain was just terrible, and in a moment, it had gone. If anyone has a degenerative hip, they will know the pain I am talking about. I just couldn't believe that the pain had gone. I even had no sleep that night because I kept waking up to see if I was in pain (ha ha!). Since then I have had no further pain, and I do not walk with a limp any more. It is really amazing. Truly you have no idea what it is to be pain-free!

I have always been a physically active person and road cycled for twelve years doing competitive cycling. But with my hip the way it was I could not cycle much as it was too sore. Now I can ride my bike without pain, and I am able to put pressure down on my left side when I turn the pedals without experiencing any pain either. My husband can't believe it himself (although he does). He is just so amazed and has been telling different people as well. His words are, "Believe me, I know she's been healed."

Diseases, Disorders & Syndromes

I kept asking myself, "Why me? Why have I been healed?"

I even asked my husband, "Is it because I have done this or that?"

But he said, "I'm sure God heals everyone, Leeanne."

One thing that has come out of this is God's love for me and that His love is overwhelming. I truly believe that all things are possible through God and we just have to focus on Him. Through God working in us, we can see how great His love is. I praise God that people-miracles still happen. It happened to me . . . no more pain! I am pain-free.

—*Leeanne Wilson*

When I was twelve, I developed severe arthritis in my right knee. For the next few years this totally restricted me. My knee was continually swollen and very painful. The pain went down to my toes. A lot of the time I had to crawl to get around. Many nights, usually at around 3:00 AM, my parents used to carry me to the bathroom to put my knee under the cold tap to get some relief. I used to cry watching the other kids play sport.

Eight years ago (when I was sixteen), Weston Carryer came to minister in our church at Tokoroa. I knew that the Lord was going to heal me that morning. As soon as Weston started ministering, he said that there was someone present with a badly affected arthritic right knee. I was so excited, and hobbled up to the front as fast as I could. As he prayed the swelling disappeared. It was awesome. The pain went. I started to run up and down the front of the church. I cried and cried and cried.

After hardly being able to move for four years, I took up touch rugby and became a New Zealand All Star representing my country. I have never had any further problems or any pain with my right knee ever since then. Thank You Lord. I am so grateful.

—*Sharon Teheko*

Miracles in Aotearoa New Zealand

For the last three years I have had major problems walking and not knowing when my legs would give way. Throughout this entire time I had to use two sticks to be able to move at all and any walking was very painful. The doctors took x-rays and said it was arthritis in my hips; yet the pain was in one thigh. Recently I had a fall in the bath, which was of great concern.

On 30 May, 2004, when Weston Carryer was at Son City Apostolic Church, Gisborne, I went up for prayer. Weston laid hands on me, the pain went immediately, and I have been able to walk without sticks or any pain ever since. God is good. Praise His holy name.

—Charlotte Knight

I attended a Weston Carryer healing meeting in Paihia in November 2004 and witnessed many healings. Weston said there was someone present with arthritis in both knees that the Lord wanted to heal. I had been suffering with arthritis in both knees for years. All leg movement was very painful and difficult. The authorities at hospital had told me that I needed a double knee replacement but were not prepared to operate because of my age. I am eighty-seven years old.

Weston prayed for me and the Lord healed me. I was able to walk freely back and forth at the front of the church. Now, months later, I am walking distances and everything is still wonderfully operational. Jesus is Lord. I'm so thankful for Weston's ministry.

—William Witstyn

For at least three years I suffered with arthritis in both knees. This restricted my movements greatly. I had to use a walking stick to aid me and I couldn't get upstairs or lift my legs up at all. During this time my son got married overseas but it was impossible for me to go because of my very restricted physical ability. I was in pain all the time. Although I was a

Diseases, Disorders & Syndromes

committed Christian, I didn't think that God would heal me. About five years ago, Weston Carryer was holding a healing meeting in Alexandra and a friend insisted that I went with her. During the meeting Weston said there was someone present with arthritis in both knees. I responded, went forward, and he prayed for me. Weston then asked for me to lift my legs up and I found that I could. He then said for me to walk without my stick and I found that I could do that also. My knees were completely healed that night and I have never had any pain since or needed to use my walking stick. My doctor was amazed. This wonderful touch from the Lord turned my life around and gave me an even greater love for Jesus. Lord, I give You all the praise.

—Alice Cundall

For approximately ten years I suffered from very painful arthritis in both my knees whenever I tried to climb steps or stairs. I attended a divine healing meeting at Papamoa in June 2008 where Weston Carryer was ministering. He prayed for the Lord to heal me. The pain immediately started to diminish, and then over a period of time, it disappeared completely. Now, six months later, the pain has not returned, apart from a very slight twinge occasionally. This healing has made a great difference to my quality of life and I am very grateful to the Lord. Thank You, Jesus.

—Lynne Bold

In 1996, I developed severe arthritis in my right hip, and experienced severe pain for two years. Medical x-rays showed that I needed a hip replacement and I was booked in to have this done. In 1998, I attended a divine healing meeting at Queenstown where Weston Carryer was ministering, and I went forward for Weston to pray for the Lord to heal me. The healing commenced immediately, and then the hip continued to improve dramatically until it was complete a short time later. I have not needed a hip replacement, and over the last three years, have had no pain or restriction at all. I have actually fallen over twice, landing heavily on my right hip, and yet, no

Miracles in Aotearoa New Zealand

harm was done. As well as totally healing the hip, the Lord seems to have supernaturally strengthened it. Praise the Lord.

—*Maureen Jenkins, Queenstown*

Over twelve years ago, osteoarthritis developed in both my knees. This caused continual pain, which would wake me up at night and make it very difficult for me to get up from a sitting position, as bending my knees was extremely painful. I didn't know how I was going to put up with the continual pain I was experiencing, as at times it was so severe. The muscles in my legs were also sore, resulting in severe pain.

I attended a divine healing meeting at Eastgate Christian Centre in January 2012, where Weston Carryer was ministering. During the ministry time he prayed for the Lord to heal my knees and legs. As soon as he had prayed, he asked me to lift my legs, and I was astounded that I could lift each one easily. All the terrible pain and stiffness had gone.

That was now almost two years ago, and since that day, I have been able to sleep right through every night with no pain. I can now walk normally nearly all the time for up to a kilometre before my knees start getting a little sore.

Once in a while I do have some pain in my knees, but nothing like it was before Weston Carryer prayed for me.

Thank You, Jesus—my Lord and my healer.

—*Chiara Giglio*

For several years I experienced very severe back pain. The prescribed pain relief from the doctor did not help in any way. I tried deep heat and any treatment I could find to help ease the pain, but to no avail. Hospital x-rays showed arthritis in the spine.

In June 2006, at a divine healing meeting in Tokoroa, Weston Carryer was ministering and he prayed for the Lord to give me a miracle. As he prayed the severe pain went. It was

Diseases, Disorders & Syndromes

incredible. I was able to run up and down in the church and I was so excited.

This happened eighteen months ago and I have never had the slightest sign of any pain in my back since. Lord Jesus, I am so grateful.

—Julia Hohia

For approximately twenty years I suffered with lower back pain. X-rays showed I had lower back damage and arthritis. I was never without discomfort and at times the pain was very severe, limiting what I could do. Any physical activity would cause severe pain and I could never sit for long periods of time. I also had a stiff neck as a result of a work injury and could never turn my head properly.

One Sunday in January 2011, we went to our church not knowing it was a healing service led by Weston Carryer. During the ministry time Weston described my back condition and also said that the person had just had it x-rayed (which I had). He asked me to go forward for him to pray for the Lord to heal me.

I went forward in pain, in both my back and neck, and as Weston prayed for me, all pain in my back and neck went immediately. By His stripes I was healed. Since that moment over nine months ago, I have not had any pain again. I can now lift things and sit for long periods in complete comfort.

I give praise to the Lord.

—Kevin Turner

Almost twenty years ago, arthritis developed in my fingers and made it impossible for me to move them. With six children to look after I had to continue to try and use my hands, but it was very difficult. This was a genetic condition which my mother and sisters had as well.

Twenty years ago, Weston Carryer came to the Apostolic Church in Hastings for some divine healing meetings. I had just started attending this church. Although I had been a Christian a long time, the church I had previously attended did not practise divine healing, so this was new to me. During the ministry time Weston prayed for the Lord to heal me.

An improvement started immediately and within a short time my healing was complete, and for the last twenty years there has been no sign of arthritis in my fingers at all.

I have done—and still do—a lot of knitting for Missions Without Borders, and if it was not for my healing, I would not have been able to do this. This healing has made a huge difference in my life. Thank You, Lord Jesus.

—*Margaret Love*

Over the past few years I have had a great deal of pain in my shoulders and knees due to degenerative arthritis. Twenty-seven years ago I was in a car accident and suffered severe bruising to my knees which left my left knee, in particular, with permanent damage to the kneecap.

In October 2003, at a healing meeting at our church, Weston called out the condition of arthritis across both shoulders. I went up in real pain at the time and received immediate healing in my shoulders, and have never had even a twinge of pain there since. I was so excited that I forgot to ask him to pray for my knees. Since then my knees got progressively worse and I had to go up and down stairs holding onto something while bringing both feet onto one step at a time. Several times my left knee collapsed under me and I fell.

When Weston returned for his next healing meeting in July 2004, I went up really believing for a miracle. As Weston prayed for me, I felt my knees tighten and stretch and I knew even before I ran up the steps to the stage that my healing was immediate. I can go up and down stairs, get in and out of my car with no trouble, and have no restriction in bending my knees. I can even play soccer with my great-grandchildren. Thank You, Jesus!!

—*Val Smith*

Diseases, Disorders & Syndromes

My name is Hine Moeke and I live in Gisborne. I am seventy-eight years old and I've been a Christian for over thirty years. I am writing this testimony to speak of the mighty healing power of our Lord Jesus when He touched my life in a special way four years ago. I had arthritis is my hip and I had to have a hip replacement! After the operation I was told I would be walking within ten days. After ten days I came home; but two days later as I was driving my car, I hit a parked car. In trying to free the wheel, my hip that had been operated on came out of its socket! The pain was terrible, unbearable.

I went to the doctor and he said there was nothing wrong! I went for an x-ray; they said, "Nothing wrong." I was still in pain. I really thought I was going to die. I phoned Hastings Hospital and I told the office girl what had happened, and that I thought my hip had come out of its socket. After spending three days at Napier Hospital I was finally operated on in Hamilton, at Waikato Hospital, and given another hip replacement. I was in there nearly one month, and was in a lot of pain. When I left Waikato Hospital I was on crutches. Three weeks later, I went into Gisborne Hospital for yet another operation on my hip as I was unable to walk. I came out of Gisborne Hospital still on crutches and remained on crutches for the next six years.

Thankfully, I was not in pain even though my hip was not properly healed! Four years ago, I went to Perth, Australia for a holiday. By the second day my back was in pain and I ended up in Perth Hospital. I was told that I was taking the wrong pills and these were causing damage to my kidneys. As a result of this medication, I nearly died. I was in hospital for one month where I went through a lot of tests and my medication was changed. I came back to New Zealand on crutches with a prescription for the right medication and I began to feel much better.

I had a lot of prayer for healing. Then I heard Weston Carryer was coming to Gisborne! I couldn't drive, but someone from our church took me to the meeting. Weston Carryer called out, "Someone here has been having trouble with their right hip."

I looked around thinking it could be someone else. I stood up with my crutches. Weston Carryer asked, "Is it you?"

Miracles in Aotearoa New Zealand

"Yes," I replied.

So he prayed, and then he asked me, "Do you believe the Lord will heal you?"

"Yes," I answered. Weston then laid hands on me, and putting both of my legs together, he prayed for me from the top of my head right down. Then he said to me, "Keep believing."

I returned to my seat on crutches. While I was getting into my seat and putting my crutches down, I felt I should get up without my crutches and take a step out of my seat. As soon as I stepped out and I took the first step, I felt the strength that I could walk—so I called out loudly to everyone, "I can walk! I can walk!" Everyone was looking and praising the Lord. I got hold of my crutches and threw them across the church to the door and I said, "I will never go back on my crutches again!" I was jumping and praising the Lord. Since then (which is four years ago), I have never used my crutches. The doctor suggested that I use a walking stick sometimes, but I seldom do! I would rather walk without my stick! I don't take pills!

In finishing my testimony, I thank God that He has filled me with His Holy Spirit and gives me understanding of His Word. Although I'm seventy-eight years old, I feel younger than sixty years. I mow my lawns, I help people, and I drive and take my grandchildren to school. I get tired, have a rest and then I'm strong again. I thank God He has healed me, and without Him and His help, I wouldn't have lived this long.

—*Hine Moeke*

A few weeks ago Weston was in Taupo at the Apostolic Church on another healing crusade. I went, as I needed God to heal me of arthritis in both knees. I love walking and they had been hurting a lot. All praise and glory to God in heaven! I am healed again.

—*Shirley Button*

I attended a healing meeting conducted by Weston Carryer.

Diseases, Disorders & Syndromes

He said God had given him a word of knowledge that there was someone present with an arthritic shoulder problem. I believed it was me, so went forward for healing. When I returned to my seat, I felt as if I was on fire. Noises of bones being put into place commenced then and continued through to lunch time the following day. Praise God, I can now do many arm and neck movements that were impossible before. Thank You, Lord, for my gracious healing.

—*Joy Ellis*

Diabetes

My mother, who is in her seventies, has suffered from diabetes for several years. She controlled it with tablets and holding to a regulated diet. In October 1989, the sugar level rose dramatically. Her GP tried to stabilize the problem by administering different medications of varying strengths and imposing a stricter diet. This was all to no avail. A figure much over six on the scale is a cause for concern. For weeks her sugar level hovered between the 16- to 17.8-mark. Finally, the doctor said he could do no more to help and advised her to attend a hospital to learn how to self-administer insulin twice daily. An appointment was made.

My mother is not a believer. Almost coincidentally with the doctor's advice, God was ministering in our church through His servant, Weston Carryer, and I asked him to pray that mother would not need insulin injections and would be healed. I am young in the Lord and have a long way to go, but God, in His infinite mercy, gave me the faith to believe for her healing. I visited mother next day and told her that which I had done and what I believed. I was so convinced of her healing, I persuaded her to agree that when she went to the hospital, she would ask for further tests before she was provided with any unnecessary medication. She was a little sceptical, but promised to do so because of my insistence. She then showed me a small scold between the index finger and thumb of her right hand. That evening it blew up into a huge blister so she visited her GP the

Miracles in Aotearoa New Zealand

following day for treatment of the burn. That was two days after the prayer request. While there, he took the opportunity to do a routine blood test for sugar level. Praise God, it had dropped to ten. The doctor was very surprised but extremely pleased.

Some three weeks on, the hospital gave mother a thorough medical check. The level was in the range six to nine. The report from the hospital doctor stated her blood sugar level was perfectly normal for a person of her age and under no circumstance would he recommend insulin injections. He did suggest that her family doctor continue to monitor levels closely. The GP's nurse, who knew nothing of my prayer request, said, "Something miraculous appears to have happened."

—F.I.

At the time I went to a Weston Carryer healing crusade, I was receiving medical attention for diabetes. I was called forward for prayer. At its end, Weston suggested I go back to my doctor, and this I did when my three monthly check was due. He advised I was "as normal as any usual person." The next check is six months on. There are no restrictions on what I eat. I still do the finger (pricking and blood) testing occasionally only to find I remain continually within limits. I praise God for His perfect healing power.

—Margaret S.

The same week Weston Carryer visited St. John's Hastings I had been diagnosed as having diabetes. I went forward for prayer and Weston prayed for me. All this year I have been having tests checking my sugar levels, and each one of the tests have come back normal. Praise be to God who uses obedient servants.

—Gladys McKay

God is good. For over ten years I was a diabetic. In March

2001, doctors at the hospital told me that I must immediately go onto insulin because of what was happening to my body.

However, about two days later I attended a divine healing meeting in our church in New Plymouth where Weston Carryer was ministering. During the ministry time he prayed for the Lord to heal me. Later that night I checked my blood and found that it was reading six, which is completely normal. I was delighted, but then acted very unwisely by eating all kinds of food which I knew were not good for me. My reading then went back to fourteen—I was staggered! However, that night God spoke to me about my bad diet. I repented, and immediately changed to a normal, sensible diet and immediately the reading went back to six and has stayed there over the last sixteen months.

I now know that the Lord healed me that night in March 2001 of diabetes. I also now realize that my body is a temple of the Holy Spirit and that I need to look after it and eat sensibly—not in a restrictive way, but just eat sensible food. Thank You, Jesus.

—*Piri*

I was most blessed to be prayed for by Weston Carryer during a visit to the Well of Life in New Plymouth in March 2000. I had suffered from diabetes for five years and was on the verge of needing to take insulin. I also suffered from tennis elbow and needed to wear a supportive brace every time I played tennis. Thanks to our Almighty God, I was healed instantly. I chose not to continue with my diabetes medication immediately. Normally this would have resulted in tingling sensations in my fingers and toes and a general feeling of unwellness. However, I have not experienced any of these symptoms since. Praise God!

Although my doctor did not believe I was healed due to my sugar level remaining high, I stood firm in my faith, proclaiming that I was definitely healed. Right up until this day, I have not experienced the slightest sign of diabetes. Concerning the tennis elbow, it so happened that I had a competition game the day following Weston's visit. Yet again I chose to firmly believe that I was healed and did not wear my brace, thus resulting in never needing to wear a brace again. I continue to play tennis for both the "A" grade competition and mid-week ladies, and still to this day have not had any trouble.

So, in finishing, I would like to acknowledge the only and greatest healer, my heavenly Father. All praise, honour and glory belongs to Him.

—*Helen Grindlay*

In November 2001, my doctor diagnosed me as diabetic. I told my doctor that I wanted to have another child but he said that it was far too risky in the condition I was in. He referred me to a specialist whom I met with in March 2002. The specialist also confirmed that I was in no condition to have a baby. Not only would there have been major problems for me, but also the baby could have been badly affected.

I attended a divine healing meeting at West City Christian Centre, Auckland, in April 2002, where Weston Carryer prayed for the Lord to heal my diabetes. As he prayed I knew that the Lord had done a miracle. There was no doubt in my heart that I was healed. My next specialist check was in August 2002, and the specialist was astounded at what had happened. My blood was normal. I also found that I was having no more problems keeping my weight under control as I had in the past. I was taken off all medication. I was then able to immediately conceive, and on 30 June 2003 gave birth to a healthy baby boy. Jesus, I am so thankful. Bless You, Lord.

—*Rachael Pal*

I have a family history of diabetes. When pregnant with both of my sons, I experienced gestational diabetes, but this cleared up each time after each son was born. However, in March 2006, I was diagnosed with diabetes and had a reading of fifteen. For some time prior to this I had been feeling very tired and nauseous. I immediately changed some eating and lifestyle habits, and although my blood sugar level did reduce,

Diseases, Disorders & Syndromes

I was still extremely tired and nauseous.

At a divine healing meeting at City Life Church, Tauranga in July 2006, Weston Carryer prayed for the Lord to do a miracle for me. As soon as Weston had prayed for me I knew I was healed. The abnormal tiredness and nausea immediately left and I felt well again, like I had not felt for a long time. Three months later blood tests confirmed what I already knew—the Lord had healed me of diabetes. A later blood test in April 2007 once again confirmed my complete healing. Lord Jesus, I am so grateful.

—Lisa Becroft

Autoimmune Diseases: Crohn's, Coeliac, Lupus, Graves', Hashimoto's, MS, Polymyalgia, Rheumatoid Arthritis

Praise God, I am healed. Prior to God healing me I suffered from coeliac disease. My name is Jill and I am in my mid-thirties.

Let me tell you what my life was like when I was a coeliac. The disease is a genetic, incurable illness which affects the normal processes of the digestive system. It is controllable, through diet, by not eating any substance containing wheat, oats, barley and rye. This eliminates many foods such as bread, pastry, cakes and biscuits, to name but a few. Going out for dinner or away on holiday was quite a hassle. Any intake of forbidden food results in severe illness—chronic diarrhoea, weight loss, abdominal pains, and distention. When I heard Weston Carryer was coming to our town, I told God that I did not feel that I could go forward and ask for this incurable disease to be healed.

"Lord," I prayed, "if You want me to be healed of this, You will have to call me."

Well, on 22 May 1990, Weston spoke to our women's group.

Miracles in Aotearoa New Zealand

The meeting concluded with a healing ministry. Through a word of knowledge he said, "There is someone here with a bowel problem." That is exactly what coeliac disease is. A diagnosis is made by doing a small bowel biopsy test. I stood and Weston prayed for me. God sovereignly healed me. Ever since then I have been eating a normal diet including all the foods coeliac sufferers must not eat—food that before would have had me very, very ill. No longer do I have coeliac disease, praise our God.

—*Jill T.*

For at least eight years I suffered from a very debilitating condition called lupus, and over the last five years that I had this condition, I suffered terribly. There is no medical cure for lupus and it was terminal. It causes the immune system to turn on itself and destroys the good body cells. It seriously affected my kidneys, caused rashes over most of my body, and robbed me of all my energy. Over this five-year period, I was in bed most of the time.

I attended a divine healing meeting at Hastings in November 2000, and I was prayed for by Weston Carryer who was ministering. An improvement started immediately and continued steadily over the next four months until the healing was complete. During this time I kept claiming my healing and I believe that this is essential. I was then examined by two doctors who both stated that all the symptoms had gone and they could find no trace of lupus. Over the last eight months there have been no symptoms. I was also healed of M.E. at the same meeting by the Lord and all the symptoms went within three weeks. What an awesome Jesus we have!

—*Colleen*

I am finally writing regarding my healing. It happened on the night of the healing meeting in Timaru in 2006. I asked for prayer for a few things including the coeliac condition I had. I was familiar with the symptoms as my Mum had been diagnosed

Diseases, Disorders & Syndromes

with it a year or so prior after suffering for years. My locum GP advised me to reduce the gluten in my diet but didn't offer any tests. I ended up completely excluding all gluten products as even a teaspoon of beef stock in a casserole or flavouring in potato chips would trigger a reaction. The reaction was high stomach pain within two hours, acid reflux, and then speedy downwards exit of stomach contents leaving an unwell feeling for a couple of days. I coped well with a different diet at home, but potluck dinners, eating out and travelling were tricky with bread, pasta, pizza, pies, batter, and most baking excluded.

The next day after the healing meeting I had a piece of normal toast for lunch with no ill effects. I was at Waimate for a woman's weekend camp following this and took no special food with me. I enjoyed a normal diet for the weekend except I couldn't eat much as I felt so full—God's way, perhaps, of easing my body into it. It was great to have all the women rejoicing with me. I am so thankful for Weston's ministry. I believe that New Zealand will continue to see more of God at work in this way.

—Janice Bernard

I had been quite sick for about two years: I was very tired, anemic and losing weight. I was diagnosed as having coeliac disease. Many foods had to be excluded from my diet—wheat, rye, barley and oats, and any manufactured products which may contain them. I had to buy specialised food such as gluten-free bread, biscuits, cereal, pasta and baking ingredients. My body would no longer accept the "normal" food I was eating.

At an evening meeting in February 2000 at the Invercargill Christian Centre, Weston Carryer had a word of knowledge for someone who had stomach problems (from "food poisoning"). I didn't think that my condition had originated from food poisoning, but I went forward anyway. I was prayed for, and Weston told me to eat anything. So, I went home and had a piece of toast, which I wouldn't normally have been able to have. I was okay in the morning so I thought I would have porridge (that would be the real test). I was fine after that so I knew that I was healed.

Miracles in Aotearoa New Zealand

I prayed that I would be able to pray for people, and that they would also be healed of coeliac disease too. I rang two people (Paul and Cheryl) I knew that had it and told them I would pray for them. Months later, on 5 May, Cheryl rang me and asked me to pray for her; I did, and she also was healed. The next day I saw Paul and I asked him if I could pray for him. I did, and he was also healed from coeliac disease. Later, Paul brought his sister Ann to me for prayer, as she also had coeliac disease; she was also healed. They are both buzzing and are so pleased to be able to eat "normal" food again—no more reading labels of the food in shops! Praise God.

Being healed certainly lifts your faith level. Paul, and his sister Ann, both had coeliac disease for twenty years. To this day Paul, Ann and myself, have been healed totally.

—*Debbie Peninsula*

In 1998, I was diagnosed as having an overactive thyroid, which then developed into Graves' disease. From that time, until December 2005, I would take thyroid medication as directed until my thyroid function tests became normal, and then when the endocrinologist allowed me to, I would stop the medication. After a time my thyroid would return to being overactive and I would go through this cycle again. I was believing that I was healed and while I was waiting for my healing to come about I would confess the word of healing over my life. When Weston Carryer came to our church, I would go up for prayer.

In March 2004, I gave it one more go and was allowed to stop the medication. However, by December 2005 I had become quite ill and had come to the end of myself. I could no longer bear the ravages of Graves' disease in my body and soul. I agreed to have radioactive iodine therapy. The odds are slim of a patient becoming normal after this treatment; some remain hyperthyroid and are given a second radioactive iodine treatment, but most become hyperthyroid and medication must be taken for the rest of the patient's life. The last two outcomes were not an option for me; Jesus had promised me healing and that was what I wanted! With that in mind, in early January

Diseases, Disorders & Syndromes

2006, I had the radioactive iodine treatment; if anybody could do anything now, it could only be Jesus!

At the end of that month, in January 2006, Weston Carryer returned to our church for a healing meeting. During the praise and worship time in the last meeting, the power of God came upon me and remained with me until some weeks after that meeting. The swelling in my thyroid went; vibrancy, energy and health returned to my body. By August 2006, eight months after radioactive iodine therapy and nine years after the initial diagnosis of Graves' disease, my blood tests have remained normal with no treatment. I no longer require blood tests or any medication; my thyroid is normal. Jesus has done what no one else could do. Finally, I have it, the complete manifestation of my healing! What Jesus has done for me, He wants to do for you!

—*Karen Phillips, The Centre, Paraparaumu*

Five years ago my health collapsed drastically. An Auckland specialist diagnosed MCS (multiple chemical sensitivities), a disorder of the autoimmune system. I had become allergic to many everyday stimuli, including a severe intolerance to dairy products and gluten. Even the smallest amounts caused extreme fatigue, weakness and illness. I could only eat food I had prepared myself as there were so many ingredients that seemed to cause illness. It was unbelievable.

I went to a meeting in Wanganui where Weston Carryer ministered (in 2011). The Lord gave him a word of knowledge of reflux and resulting stomach pain. I surely had the stomach pain and went forward for prayer. Within a few weeks the pain and discomfort alleviated significantly.

In October, six months later, I went to Weston's meeting in Edgecumbe whilst staying at my daughter's home. He prayed for me again—for the chemical sensitivities generally. I did not feel anything differently at the time, but that very afternoon began being able to eat a normal diet: a small taste at first, with no reaction, so I tried something else. I tried foods I had literally not even been able to touch for the last five years or

Miracles in Aotearoa New Zealand

more: regular bread, butter, milk, yoghurt, cheese, marmite, avocado—with not the slightest adverse effect. They taste so good!

I thank the Lord so much. He knows exactly what our situation is, doesn't He? I'm so thankful for brother Weston and his faithfulness with the gifts God entrusted to Him.

—*Joan Harrow*

For a long period of time I slowly developed very sore muscles, and got weaker and weaker. As a builder it became very difficult for me to work. The muscle soreness continued to intensify and I developed twitching and experienced spasms which would keep me awake at night. The doctor diagnosed polymyalgia.

I eventually became so weak that even picking up a cup of coffee required two hands. By this stage I could not work at all. I also discovered that my brain function was diminishing, which was very alarming.

In March 2011, I attended a divine healing meeting at C3 Church Christchurch, where Western Carryer was ministering. During the ministry time, Weston said there was someone there with a medically incurable condition especially affecting the muscles, and the person had come believing that day for a miracle. That was me. Two of these conditions applied to me although I didn't know it was a medically incurable condition.

I responded and Weston then prayed for me. The next day I felt better. My wife and I stood on God's Word for my total healing, and 48 hours later, my strength started to return. I then realised how weak I had actually been.

I was still puzzled about what the medically incurable disease could be. My wife and I prayed, and the Lord revealed to my wife that it was motor neurone disease, which is a condition that we knew practically nothing about. I went back to the doctor and asked if the early symptoms of motor neurone disease were similar to polymyalgia and she said, "Yes."

Over the next five weeks I got a lot stronger and was able

Diseases, Disorders & Syndromes

to start an exercise regime. Then, three to four months later, my mind started to function at a reasonable standard and continued to improve until once again, I was able to be highly organised. Eighteen weeks after being prayed for, I was able to work again and even started playing squash.

Now, three years later (March 2014) at 49 years of age, I am working on-site as a builder with three apprentices, and working to the capacity I did in my early-30s. This is truly a miracle and I am so grateful to the Lord for my new lease on life.

We saw a documentary on a man in Australia who was battling motor neurone disease and his symptoms were mine to a "T," along with other things I didn't even realise were part of the disease. This, we believe, confirmed what the Lord had healed me from. Praise You, Jesus.

—*Grant Maitland*

I'm so thankful for Weston Carryer's prayer. I attended a healing meeting at Tauranga in a school hall when visiting New Zealand around 27 January 1998.

I had suffered from a chronic disease—an inflammatory bowel disease called Crohn's disease—for about two years. I am twenty-three years old. The specialist doctor told me I had an incurable disease. For a short time I took strong doses of steroids and also took other medication. This treatment was to be for the rest of my life. My symptoms included ulcers and inflammation in the large and small bowel, chronic fatigue, eye inflammation, joint inflammation, throat infections, chest infections, ear infections, bladder infections, low blood pressure, blackouts, high fevers, ulcers in mouth, ulcerated lips, sores around mouth, rash over my whole body, loss of memory, loss of voice, severe pains, bleeding from bowels, frequent dehydration, vomiting, collapsed veins. My eyes were always black all around and my skin went grey. I went down to only forty-nine kilograms—like a skeleton. I could not always tolerate food and so mostly lived on liquid food from the chemist. Toward the end of last year, I got a bad cold and became dehydrated; my veins collapsed and my temperature went to the end of the thermometer and I had a fit. As a result my heart was damaged. I could only go to work a few days a week and would need to sleep the rest of the week.

This is to let you know how sick I was, and that since Weston's prayer, I have taken no medication whatsoever and all my symptoms have disappeared. I now go to work five days a week, church one night, Bible study one night and polytechnic two nights.

—*Kathleen Llewellyn*
(Since then, Kathleen's specialist has confirmed that she has been completely healed.)

In August 1995, I was diagnosed as having Crohn's disease, a condition which severely affects the functioning of the body and especially the bowel. Over the next three years, with prayer, there was a slight improvement.

At Queenstown in 1998, I attended a divine healing meeting where I was prayed for by Weston Carryer for the Lord to heal me. All my symptoms immediately disappeared, and now one year later, I am enjoying excellent health. Praise the Lord!

—*Samantha Conner*

For many years I suffered with Crohn's disease which is a badly affected, very painful colon condition for which I was on steroids. I attended a divine healing meeting in Hamilton in 1996 where Weston Carryer was ministering. Following a word of knowledge, Weston called out my condition and said if I would respond, the Lord would give me a miracle healing. I went forward and Weston prayed for me. I rejoice to say that God totally healed this debilitating condition. I have had no further pain and am off all medication. Thank You, Jesus.

—*Cherie Sawyer*

Diseases, Disorders & Syndromes

In September 2002, I was working at a part-time job with special needs children and I suddenly felt sick. From this, my symptoms escalated to constant diarrhoea, nausea, vomiting, abdominal pain, fever, bleeding from the bowel and fatigue. I began to rapidly lose weight. My husband took me to the Thames Hospital outpatients department where all sorts of tests were done. The results showed the haemoglobin level in my blood was very low. My doctor made appointments for me to have an ultrasound scan and a colonoscopy. Biopsies on my bowel were also done. Over this period of five months my weight went from eighty-four and a half to sixty-seven kilos. I became very weak and had to have help.

In January 2003, I was diagnosed with Crohn's disease which is an inflammatory bowel condition for which my doctor said there was no cure. I knew I was dying. As well as this, it was discovered that I had a three-centimeter ovarian cyst which was causing lower abdominal pain as well as the excruciating continual pain from the crohn's. As a result of medication, my vision became blurred and I could no longer drive a car.

In May, I rang Weston Carryer and an appointment was made for me to see him in his office. He asked me if I had faith for the Lord to heal me and my reply was, "Yes." He placed his hands on me and the power of God touched my body like a lightening bolt and I dropped to the floor. Weston then said I was set free from a spirit of sickness.

At my next medical appointment my doctor was amazed at the transformation that had taken place. He couldn't believe that I was the same woman that he had been treating and asked me what had caused this miraculous turnaround. I told him my faith in Jesus had healed me.

I went off all my medication. Over the next eighteen months, the pain decreased steadily and totally ceased in September 2004. Since then I have had no pain whatever and my body functions normally. I thank the Lord so much because I am not going to die, but live! Praise You, Jesus.

—*Karen Reece*

And He came up and
touched the coffin;
and the bearers came to a halt.
And He said, "Young man,
I say to you, arise!"
The dead man sat up
and began to speak.
And Jesus gave him
back to his mother.

–Luke 7:124-15, NASB

Nine

Overhauls & Unusual Conditions

Testimonies of healed conditions classified as an "overhaul—anything with 3 or more healings, as well as unusual conditions.

The family has always considered me to be a little odd. You see, I have suffered for some time from a familial disease. I attended a healing meeting at Beachlands in September 1993 when Weston Carryer was the speaker. God, through Jesus, granted me a miracle and cured me. The tremors have ceased, the major depression has gone, my balance is normal, and my memory is improving. I can run and caper again . . . something denied me for five years. I laud Him each day for my miracle.

—Nancy Perry

Weston Carryer came to our church in Dannevirke and held healing meetings there in late 1989. Through a word of knowledge, Weston spoke of some things which I recognised

Miracles in Aotearoa New Zealand

were physically wrong with me. I responded, went up to the front, received prayer, and the Lord touched me. The Lord healed me of a broken bridge on my nose and it was reshaped back to what it had been. The soles of my feet were also uneven and as I was being prayed for, I could feel them being flattened out.

Weston also prayed for the upper part of my spine which had been damaged when I was younger. It was strengthened and healed. A few other minor things were wrong with me and the Lord healed them as well. Praise be to God!

—*Lynn Garrick*

I want to share what Jesus did for me at a meeting conducted by Weston Carryer in July 1991. Maybe somewhat misguidedly, I was reluctant to go or to ask God for more help because He had already given me so much comfort and guidance since I had asked Him into my life. I thought I was managing quite well, although I was suffering from damaged nerves, a partially paralysed hand, a frozen shoulder, shortened right leg and, most frightening of all, a very large growth pressing on my spine.

Weston called me up for prayer. The strong words, the light touch and God's compassion filled me to overflowing. I wept as I realised that, despite telling no one of the latter affliction, God knew my need and wanted to heal me. I accepted His love with enormous gratitude. As I came to myself, I discovered the very large lump was nearly gone, the effect on my spine had vanished, and my hand moved. My whole body has functioned perfectly since. I know God wants us to have faith in His miracle-working powers and to accept His promises for our wholeness.

—*Rhonda Svendsen*

I had been a Christian for only six weeks so you can understand my nervousness over going forward at a healing meeting held by Weston Carryer at Foxton in mid-1991. But I was so desperate because I had suffered for twenty-six years

Overhauls & Unusual Conditions

from back and neck pains as well as gallbladder problems. There was little I could eat which did not buckle me up in so much pain. I would have to go to Levin each night—week in and week out—for physiotherapy where they would put me in traction. I left feeling worthless and washed up. Latterly, I was at the stage where I could not sit, lie down or stand up for long periods. I had hit rock bottom. I cried out to the Lord, "If this is meant to be life, I would rather be dead." I had a doctor's appointment on the day of the meeting. I argued that I had nothing to lose by going to the healing meeting. So I cancelled the doctor's visit and then turned to the Lord and prayed as I have never prayed before.

Weston laid his hands on me. I felt no difference that night, yet, while the pain remained, I was totally convinced I had been healed. The next day I was reduced to tears with the pain which became so acute and, propped against the wall, I thanked God for my healing over and over and over. A sister questioned how I could thank Him when I was in more pain than before. My reply was, "I just know I am healed."

Praise God, on the third day, He lifted me from the pit of hell. When I got up that morning I knew I was free. I went outside and weeded the garden, carted and stacked firewood, and then did other chores I had been unable to do for so long—all accompanied with songs of praise to the Lord at the top of my voice.

What a joy to be able to eat what I like again. One year on, Weston prayed for my flat feet to be given arches. The Lord gave them to me. Praise God that He always answered my prayers.

—*Karen Hansen*

I went along to two healing meetings at which Weston Carryer was the speaker. At the first, I received from the Lord healing to my neck which was damaged in an accident some eight years previously, and to my left knee. The latter had hampered me since a mishap nineteen odd years ago. I also received prayer for a freeing up from fear—a fear of man which had hindered my walk with God. How can one fear God when

Miracles in Aotearoa New Zealand

one is bound by man? Since then many truths have flowed freely from the head to the heart.

At the second meeting I was more open to stating a personal problem of a prolapsed uterus. It has been corrected, as has my other (right) knee. Praise God for His goodness.

—*Yvonne P.*

I had a bad car accident in August 1986 and was taken to hospital with two broken ribs, a smashed left wrist, fractured skull and a left leg I could not move because of the pain in two parts of it. The doctors thought I might lose the leg and it was in plaster for a year. Once out of plaster, I went back to my work as a head store man but had to give it up because my injuries were giving way under the strain.

I attended a healing ministry conducted by Weston Carryer in April 1990. God spoke to him of a person who had been in a bad accident that He wanted to heal. That day, God performed a miracle by mending every single part of me and putting everything back into place. Four months later, I went for my final checkup knowing I would be cleared for heavy duty, and I was. Praise God we can live in peace and without the pain and hurting.

—*Peter (L.H.)*

In August 1990, Weston Carryer visited our church. At that time I had spinal and lower back problems along with persistent headaches. I was prayed for and was completely healed at that time. In the next twelve months dermatitis developed over my hands. I would wake up nights in extreme pain.

Weston again prayed for relief from this physical affliction and mental ills as well. I was cured. All praise to God who cares for us.

—*Mary Severinsen*

Overhauls & Unusual Conditions

The Lord healed me. I had had constant pain in my back and leg for five years. My right leg was shorter than my left. I also suffered from migraines. As Weston prayed for me, all the pain went completely. Both legs are now equal and migraines are a thing of the past. I believe Jesus is my Saviour, that He is the Holy One, and that He is real.

—*Colleen*

During a period of eighteen months, Weston Carryer has prayed for me for a number of ailments. Nearly all have been remedied. I have been cured of cigarette smoking and healed from haemorrhoids. Instant relief came from sinus headaches, backache, and a sore neck. I also asked for prayer for such things as parenting and release into ministry gifts, and God has answered those requests in His own inimitable way. I have been delivered from many fears, which I willingly parted with so that God may be effective in my life.

—*Rangi Barton*

I would like to share with others the miracles I received from God through Jesus, by the power of the Holy Spirit, at healing sessions in Pukekohe where Weston Carryer was conducting services. At a meeting in 1992, Weston prayed for my release from the spirit of alcohol to which I had become addicted over a span of eight years from age fifteen. From that night onwards, it has not been a stronghold, and still is not, and I enjoy the absolute freedom from it. That same night I received the Holy Spirit and was given a new language and speak in tongues wherever and whenever I can. Two years later I was prayed over by Weston against migraine headaches (something I had suffered from since I was fifteen), and a backache in the lower part of the spinal canal caused by an epidural anaesthetic to relieve pain during childbirth. Since then I have been totally relieved of each affliction. It is so wonderful to be able to stand

and walk around for longer periods without discomfort and also to be able to read and concentrate more without the intrusion of migraine headaches. Awesome! God does heal!

—*Char Apanui*

I was nothing until He found me. He has proved His love for me and made me a new person both spiritually and physically. I attended a summer soul school at Te Nikau Bible Training Centre where Weston Carryer was lecturing. As was his custom, he prayed for healing for the students and, during the next three days, God performed miracle upon miracle on my warped limbs and afflicted body. For about three years I had suffered progressively with increasing swelling in my feet and ankles. I watched in amazement as the swelling disappeared. I felt I had new feet. I had a troublesome back due to curvature of the spine. I could place my fist in the base of my back. When Weston prayed for me on day two, I could feel my spine straighten out. Where there are back problems, often one leg is shorter than the other. I returned for further prayer and watched my right leg lengthen to equal the left—a fact witnessed by many and verified by differing levels of suntan on my legs. Greater relief came on the third day. I was born with an abnormality in my hips which caused me limited movement and shortened my steps. This, to my constant embarrassment, made me appear to waddle as I walked. I received prayer for healing and felt a stirring sensation like a grabbing, shaking, tilting movement. I then began to walk and run freely.

Later, I went back again for prayer for my shoulders which were also restricted in action and truly painful to move. Once again, God healed me and relieved that pain by freeing up my shoulders. For many years I have had very limited sight in my left eye. The vision had worsened until I was almost blind in it. As Weston prayed, the focus became clearer and clearer until God restored the sight completely. There were other things for which I received prayer but these will take the test of time to be confirmed. His Word says He heals, and He does!

—*Donna Parrish*

Overhauls & Unusual Conditions

As a result of a serious motor accident, I suffered from whiplash, bad headaches, a leg problem, and other body ailments. I also had a cyst on an ovary.

I went to a healing meeting where Weston Carryer prayed for God to heal me. The power of the Holy Spirit really touched me, and in a flash, I was healed of every one of these conditions. A scan later proved that the cyst had been divinely removed. Praise His holy name!

—*Tanya Kendall*

For some time I had been suffering from a bad back, shoulder and knee, besides glaucoma in my eyes. I had been losing sight in my right eye quite rapidly, and was warned by the specialist that on my next visit I could expect to need laser treatment as a hospital outpatient.

In the latter part of 1993, I went to a meeting where Weston Carryer was speaking. He prayed for release from all of my afflictions, and God, through Jesus and the power of the Holy Spirit, healed me absolutely. The following morning I had blurry vision for around two hours. I realised it was satan trying to discredit my healing, so I rebuked him in the name of Jesus, told him I belonged to Jesus, and immediately my eyes returned to normal.

Since I was totally convinced God had heard Weston's prayers, on my next visit to the specialist I told her about this and that nothing would be wrong. Her examination confirmed I had been divinely healed. In June of 1994, I suffered a retinal ulcer in my left eye which was distressingly painful. A different specialist prescribed drops. I asked my own pastor for healing prayers. It cleared quite rapidly and the drops were discontinued after two days. Later I saw my own specialist for a checkup. I was able to read the bottom line of the eyesight chart with each eye, something unachievable for many years. Normally a retinal ulcer will leave a permanent scar but, she

Miracles in Aotearoa New Zealand

said, "You have no scar at all." I thank God continually for what He has done for me.

—*Margaret Rasmussen*

In 1978, I had a motorcycle accident in the Karori tunnel. Result: a subdural hematoma, shoulder injury, paralysed left arm, lost kidney, lost spleen through rupture, prescribed medication, developed depression and anxiety, had epileptic-type seizures when asleep, became alcoholic, on drugs, passed through three rehabilitation centres.

Saved 1985: healing process started; backslid; went to prison; marriage broke up.

Recommitted my life in 1988.

In 1990, Weston Carryer prayed for me. His pamphlet, *Keeping Your Healing*, kept me going. All the pain, depression, fits are now gone; my memory is restored; I'm stronger physically; arm paralysis gone totally. . . arm one hundred percent.

—*Peter Clark*

For two years I had trouble with my legs. I had great difficulty walking and was in extreme pain all the time. I had additional problems due to a prostate gland and a "tennis" elbow which prevented me from lifting my left arm.

My wife encouraged me to go to a Weston Carryer healing meeting and I went, somewhat reluctantly, mainly to please her. Much to my surprise Weston, during the meeting, called out my conditions and said God wanted to heal me. I went forward and experienced the healing power of God in a wonderful way. Later in the meeting I was born again and baptised in the Holy Spirit. Next morning I realised I had been healed in every part of my body, and now several months later, my entire body operates as it should without pain. My whole life has been transformed by God's saving and healing power.

—*Ted Batley*

Overhauls & Unusual Conditions

I attended a series of meetings in our town at which Weston Carryer was speaking. During the course of the outreach God virtually healed me by installments. At the second meeting I was prayed over for healing from genital herpes, an ailment which had been with me for nine years and recurred about five times in each year. Nothing seemed to happen that day but within two days the blisters had dried out and fallen off leaving a pink mark of healed skin. Following a word of knowledge at the third meeting I received prayer for bronchitis. For nine years it had come on every winter. I believe I will never have it again. The next day it was the turn of sinus and hay fever. I had had a continually blocked nose for four years, was always blowing it and was never without a handkerchief. The healing was complete. At the Sunday service I was having difficulty holding up my head as a pain in my spine was getting unbearable.

Weston prayed for me and I was slain in the Spirit. The neck, which had troubled me a few days before, was completely healed and the pain in the spine area went. Things became perfectly normal instantly. I praise God and thank Him for making me whole.

—*Ann N.*

As a child I fell from a swing and injured my lower back. When I was in my twenties I was told that my back was twisted at the base of my spine, but, it didn't give me any bother until about 1995 or 1996. Then for two years my back gave me chronic pain. I went to see Weston Carryer in Queenstown in 1997 with great expectations. I read my Bible before leaving and Weston read the same passage that I had. Then a word of knowledge brought me up the front—three things Weston said, actually—and my back was healed. I felt like I had been to a chiropractor. I was walking on air. I rang my daughter in Christchurch to say Weston was going to be there two weeks later. She was also called up through Weston's word of knowledge and had her back dramatically healed as well. She had been having problems with it for about eighteen months. Also she had been

Miracles in Aotearoa New Zealand

bothered with urinary infections for two years, very frequently and she was cured of that as well. She had a tingling in her lower abdomen when Weston prayed for her and she has never had one since. Praise God. I have witnessed to so many people. I feel so excited.

My son came to Weston in Waikanae the end of last year with a leg and back problem. He was powerfully touched. His back wasn't healed, but he was healed within. He has lost all his anger and is a different person. Everyone notices. God has been so good to us! Thank you.

—Alison Marshall

I had had ongoing back pain, neck and shoulder problems, sciatica, migraines, and general lowness, and have seen various specialists over a period of about twenty-three years. Then a car accident sixteen years ago left me with a damaged and locked-up spine, excruciating pain at times, and an inability to be able to play the piano for any length of time. Over the past couple of years, my condition had deteriorated to the point where I was constantly in pain and unable to sleep through the night. I also was suffering from cystic ovaries and a prolapsed bowel.

These were my conditions when I attended a divine healing meeting at Milton in early 1998 where Weston Carryer was ministering. After Weston prayed for me, although I still had pain, I knew that the Lord had done something and I felt taller. That night I slept soundly all night, woke free of pain, and over the past twelve months, have had no pain whatever. Jesus Christ has made me completely whole.

—Adele Pilato

It is with grateful thanks and much delight that I write to Zoe Evangelistic Ministry to inform you of my healing from God during one of Weston's healing crusades to Napier. It was a great blessing and privilege to speak to Weston in person and I have been further encouraged to share my miraculous healing.

My healing from God happened last year during Weston's

Overhauls & Unusual Conditions

healing crusade to Napier at All Saints Church in Taradale, on a Sunday evening service. Weston had a specific word of knowledge about my back injury and associated complications and called me up to the altar for a divine healing. I have included in my letter copies of two letters written by my orthopaedic surgeon, Mr. Gale Curtis, who had investigated my back injury in Hastings Public Hospital with a discogram just a month or so prior to my healing.

My back injury occurred on 20 December 1995, at my home. I was digging out a fence post, pulled on the post and fell back on a pile of dirt and onto another shovel on the ground. I fractured my L3 vertebrae and collapsed and tore L 4/5 and L5 /S1 levels of my back. This injury was initially diagnosed incorrectly and simply treated as a "strain" of the back. I was sent to physiotherapy. After unsuccessful months of treatment, and when my condition didn't improve, the physiotherapist referred me back to my GP as my mobility had deteriorated and my pain had increased unbearably. Finally, in June 1996, just prior to my fortieth birthday, extensive x-rays were carried out and the condition properly diagnosed. My fracture at L3 had healed with uneven union and the two other areas of injury L 4/5 and L5/S1 had collapsed and bulged. I had continued to work part-time as a teacher aid, and as a new single parent with two young daughters, I had continued to care for my home, property, and children.

I was a fairly new Christian fellowshipping at Taradale Baptist Church and belonged to Napier Women's Aglow Fellowship. The care and practical support during this time was such a help. The prayers and loving ministry were of great strength and comfort and always so unconditionally given.

On 24 July 1996, I was admitted to Napier Public Hospital for an epidural injection to promote healing and pain relief of my spine. The events which followed became a living nightmare. Some of the epidural anaesthetic travelled up into my brain causing the condition of "status epilepticus"—uncontrolled grand mal brain seizures. For twenty-one days I was in ICU and a medical ward, severely sick. Because of the extent of the violent seizures my back became more irritated. My young family, home, property, and job all became a great worry. I was

Miracles in Aotearoa New Zealand

informed, upon discharge from hospital, that because of the seizures and the medication I was put on to control them, I wouldn't be able to drive for one seizure-free year.

The rest of the year (1996) was a very tough time; I needed home help to assist with the children, to buy groceries, and help with some housework. I was fairly housebound, and from being so well, fit and active six months prior, it was a very limiting and hard place to be. I became very reluctant to want to go places and was always very aware of the grand-mal seizures and their associated problems (i.e., falling down, incontinence, and the strong medication effects which made me quite drowsy, depressed, and caused memory loss). My children were always so helpful and loving, and often missed out on many things because of the lack of transport and my limited mobility.

I stopped fellowshipping each Sunday and hadn't returned to work. My secular friends were very supportive but soon continued on with their own full, busy lives. My Christian friends, especially my very close ones, continued faithfully to support, care and pray for the girls and myself. My neighbour (a non-Christian) called them "angels with cell phones," as she always saw their visiting car and the many kind things they did for us.

After Christmas, early in 1997, I was finally seen by Dr. Gale Curtis, an orthopaedic surgeon. He was very quick to order further tests and help me. After a CT scan showed the three affected areas of my back, he admitted me to Hastings Memorial Hospital for a discogram to assist him with the spinal surgery, he assumed he would need to perform on me later in the year. The letters I have enclosed were written to my employer and A.C.C. to keep them up-to-date. I haven't enclosed the more extensive letters I have copies of because of their more personal nature. I returned to work, only two hours a day in February 1997, but still needed home help.

Just a few months after my final discogram diagnosis I was sitting at home in my lounge room on a Saturday night. My girls had gone to their dad's for the night and I was feeling pretty low, depressed, lonely and in pain. My faith had been fairly low and because I wasn't fellowshipping regularly I felt

Overhauls & Unusual Conditions

pretty removed and isolated. My Christian friends were my greatest source of bringing me "light." The Lord revealed to me that night, in my very desperate place, that I needed to seek great wisdom for healing and have hands laid on me, and that I needed to move forward and seek this healing, and also that I needed to be anointed with oil, and take communion. I felt a warm feeling on my right temple and smelt a very fragrant smell. It felt like warm oil. I prayed to the Lord for help that night . . . I really cried out.

The next morning a friend rang and said she was going to the Taradale AOG Church and asked would I like to come with her. I had never been there before but the pastor, Ken McLouglin, was an advisor at Napier Women's Aglow. After the service, Pastor Ken called for anyone who needed healing. I was standing at the back of the church as my back had become too painful to sit for long periods. I felt my legs take me forward. I received communion and was anointed with oil. I smelt the fragrance of the oil again and it felt warm on my temple, even though it was cold. Pastor Ken invited all the church to come to All Saints Anglican Church to hear Weston Carryer, the evangelist-healer, and encouraged us all to come with them. They were not having their usual 6.30 PM service, but going there instead.

That night, ten minutes before the meeting began, I decided to go on my own down to All Saints Church. The church had about eighty people in it, and after the most beautiful worship, Weston was introduced. After giving his testimony of his back healing he said he had two words of knowledge. The first one described every detail of my back and even acknowledged some associated medical problems. A man who was sitting next to me told me, "You had an appointment with God tonight," and urged me to step forward. I couldn't believe the Lord would choose me to receive a healing touch from Him.

Weston asked me, "Do you know the Lord loves you?"

I said a quiet, "Yes."

Then he asked, "Do you know the Lord can heal?"

I said a very sure, "Yes."

MIRACLES IN AOTEAROA NEW ZEALAND

Then he asked me, "But do you know the Lord can heal you?" I couldn't answer and began to cry. The reality was I knew in my heart the Lord could heal, but *heal me*?

I raised my hands and Weston said, "Receive your healing now."

I stood there for about five minutes and he asked me how I felt. I said, "I feel straight!" which I did. Tall and wonderful and straightened up! I returned to my seat and I felt a warm tingle all over my back and down into my hands. I sat there and smiled and cried some more. When I came out of All Saints that night, it was a warmish evening and the palm trees looked as tall as I felt.

When I came home about 9.30 PM, my girls were watching TV. I stood in front of the TV set and then did this "glorious" forward roll on the carpet in front of them. My eldest daughter said, "Mum, where have you been and what have you been doing?" They were so overjoyed to see me moving so painlessly and free. We did a few more forward rolls for fun and good measure. The next morning on my way to work I called into two special friends' houses to show them my healed back. At work my workmates couldn't get over what a change in my physical condition. I told them all it was a "divine healing" from the Lord. I was so excited on the Sunday night I could hardly sleep but felt so full of joy and energy. The next day was amazing. It was so apparent to Christians and non-Christians that something wonderful had happened.

Many things moved me deeply about my healing:

- The revelation on the Saturday night before about me stepping out and receiving healing, of being anointed with oil and receiving communion.

- The opportunity on the Sunday to attend AOG and go to All Saints for the healing meeting; to be called out.

- The expectancy and love of the congregation at All Saints Church to receive not only healings themselves, but the anointing to heal others.

- The desperate place I was in physically, spiritually, and emotionally; not fellowshipping and low in my faith.

- The constant faithful prayers of my Christian friends always believing in a healing for me.

- The gentle anointing for healing I felt in my back and hands that night at All Saints which now becomes such a powerful blessing when I pray for others who are sick; the feeling and the desire to gently lay my hands upon them with the Lord's healing anointing to flow into them.

- The way my personal testimony has blessed others and how even my Christian friends have been able to speak to their families, friends and workmates about my healing, to offer them hope for their own personal circumstances with a real "living" account.

- But, mostly, I have been touched by the Lord's amazing love, grace and mercy for me; that He can meet us in our greatest need.

- The desire of my heart is to see others healed, restored and set free.

I visited the orthopaedic surgeon for another consultation one month after my healing. He was very impressed at my improved condition. I asked him to discontinue any A.C.C. and home help assistance. He told me to come back and see him in twelve months time, and cancelled any further surgery plans. I take no medication at all. I have had no further seizures.

—*Susan McConnell*

Greetings from the Philippine Islands in the mighty name of our Lord Jesus Christ! I thanked God for His wonderful healing power and for using Weston Carryer to pray for my illness. I really praised God and thanked Him for my complete

Miracles in Aotearoa New Zealand

deliverance. Last May 1999, Weston was ministering in Pastor Ben Acebis' church. In that meeting one night, God revealed to Weston that there was somebody in the congregation who was suffering with pain in the neck going down to the back, and radiating to the right hand. That was me, and I stood up in front without delay and he prayed for me. Praise God, I received my complete healing at that moment.

I had been suffering for nine long years. It only started by pushing an operating table back in February 1990, when I was working as a nurse in Saudi Arabia at that time. The pain became worse and I was in a cervical neck collar for the first month. I was not able to work with my right hand; somebody had to do it for me—especially paperwork.

X-rays were done and diagnosed as tendonitis. The doctor told me that I would have to manage the pain with analgesics for life. The tendon in my right arm was overstretched, therefore, it would not return to the normal shape. Different analgesics and liniments were used but they only relieved temporarily. Steroid injections were administered, and I was having daily physiotherapy even, but still the pain was there. Of course, I also asked God to relieve me from this misery. Thanks to God for using Weston to cast all the pain away. I really got an instant healing. Praise God!

From that moment on, I had no more pain relievers, no more physiotherapy, no more liniments applied, nothing any more. I am completely healed by our Almighty God. I immediately informed my friends in Saudi Arabia who knew my condition very well. I testified the miraculous healing power of our Lord Jesus Christ. Hallelujah!

One more victory; God extended my father's life. October 4, 1999 he underwent two operations. We took him to the hospital as an emergency case. His abdomen was so distended that they decided to open him up. It was found out that the large intestines were twisted. There was no way to release it except to perform a colostomy.

We were about to discharge him after ten days when my dad's abdomen again became distended. Nothing came out through the naso-gastric tube and into the colostomy. They decided to re-open him. He was in crisis especially as he was already seventy-one years old. They found inside that there were adhesions in his small intestines pressing the large intestines and blocking the passage. But God is really great, for that crisis passed.

—Ludie Grace Sanchez

In 1985, at fifteen years old, I was involved in a car accident. My back was broken in three places, one disc was crushed, my spinal cord was damaged, my left kneecap was crushed, my left femur broken, my right ankle was broken in four places, my collarbone was broken, I had head injuries, and two broken ribs. My left leg, as a result of the injuries, had shortened and was crooked.

On 22 November 1998, at a Weston Carryer healing meeting, God lengthened my leg and straightened it. It was my last healing I needed to be completely restored in the different areas that had been affected.

1985 — Doctors said I would not walk again. God had a purpose and plan.

1986 — Doctors told me due to internal injuries, I would never conceive a child. I have since given birth to four children.

1995 — I was healed from arthritis.

—Michelle Bird

The last time Weston Carryer was in Dunedin at the Word of Life in July 1999, he said there was someone in the church who had had a lot of accidents. My fifteen-year-old son, Andrew, had had eight accidents for which the required medical treatment is fifteen months. Three accidents included breaking his ankle with a bat trying to hit a cricket ball, and breaking his pelvis jumping on a trampoline. However, the last two were the most serious. He had a stab wound to his arm, spending two nights in theatre and four days in hospital. Four weeks later when that finally healed, he was punched in the teeth by boys he didn't even know while out delivering circulars. Two weeks later Weston came to our church. Andrew went up for prayer. He has not had another "accident" since. I thank God for sending Weston that day. It was His perfect timing.

—Karen Robinson

At the age of four, I was placed in an orphanage by my parents where I remained until I was sixteen. After leaving the orphanage, I started drinking and smoking heavily and soon became an alcoholic. I injured my back and also developed a severe stomach condition. To ease the pain, I drank all I could and used drugs. I got married but that did not last. I attempted suicide, and spent some time in Porirua Psychiatric Hospital. Then, through my law-breaking activities, I was detained in prison for two-and-a-half years and later served one-and-a-half years in Mt. Crawford prison. For forty years my life was a nightmare. At sixty-eight years of age, after four unsuccessful stomach operations, numerous treatments and operations on my back, having to wear a brace for thirty-five years, and having also developed emphysema which made me continually gasp for breath, I had no hope.

However, my daughter had accepted Jesus Christ as Lord of her life and had become a Christian. She had been praying for me for sixteen years and started taking me to church. At a church service I heard that there was a healing evangelist called Weston Carryer who was coming and I became curious as I had never seen an evangelist before. I attended his meeting and saw many people being healed of their conditions by the Lord as Weston prayed for them. I then went forward, and what happened is absolutely mind-boggling. The Lord healed all my sicknesses and addictions.

It is now twelve months since I was healed. The Lord has done for me what the doctors said could not be done. I have not had any discomfort in my back. The brace that held me together for thirty-five years is not needed. I am completely healed in Jesus' name. I have not had any stomach problems and I am

Overhauls & Unusual Conditions

eating anything I fancy. I do not use my inhaler and I am on no medication at all. Driving and walking are not a problem. I can now go to my letterbox and climb up my back steps without gasping for breath. The desire for cigarettes and alcohol was taken away, and I have put on weight. No longer am I skin-and-bone. My nights are no longer full of bad dreams. I am free, and Jesus Christ is my Lord! I have not been to a doctor ever since that memorable night twelve months ago. Thank You, Jesus.

—*Alan Rod, Titahi Bay*

I was facing surgery for a prolapsed womb which had caused major physical conditions in my life. Also, I needed surgery to remove a large polyp in my nostril which had been there for a long time and was getting larger all the time. It was visible, like a large boil, and blocked the nostril causing breathing restrictions.

At a church service in Lower Hutt in September 1999, Weston Carryer prayed for the Lord to heal both of these conditions. Imagine my delight the next day when I discovered that the polyp had fallen out of the nostril. I also realized that I was having no womb problems, and the next medical check confirmed that my womb was indeed healed. Twelve months later, my womb and nostril are functioning correctly and I am rejoicing and praising God. Thank You, Jesus.

—*Zarida Standeven, Lower Hutt*

My name is Wiki Tepu and I want to testify to the wonderful healing power of Jesus Christ in my life. For thirty years I suffered from chronic migraine headaches which affected me for days at a time, often causing total blackouts.

I was also taking medication three times daily for arthritis which was causing a lot of pain and limiting my movements. I attended a divine healing meeting with my husband at Taumarunui in 1994, where Weston Carryer was preaching and ministering to the sick. Since Weston prayed for the Lord to heal me I have had no more migraine headaches, no arthritis or medication. Hallelujah! Thank You, Jesus.

—*Wiki Tepu, Taumarunui*

In 1987, I was knocked off my push-bike by a car and my body was badly injured in a number of ways. My left arm was badly broken and the doctors wanted to amputate it at the shoulder, but I refused to give permission to do this. I finished up with an arm that would not straighten properly, was also five inches short and was always very painful. My back, leg, and neck were also injured and I was hospitalized five more times for further treatment, especially for my back. My right leg finished up being two-and-a-half-inches shorter than my left leg and I had continual severe pain in my lumbar region.

I attended a divine healing meeting in Tokoroa, in November 1996, conducted by Weston Carryer. I went forward for prayer for God through Jesus to heal me. One after another, as each of my conditions were prayed for, all were healed: my left arm grew out and straightened; my leg lengthened; my back and neck came into alignment. For the first time in nine years, I was a whole person. I was overjoyed to say the least. Thank You, Jesus, for loving me and healing me in such a wonderful way.

—*Daphne Te Nahu, Tokoroa*

I was a greenhorn-Christian of only six weeks standing when I answered an invitation to go forward for healing at a Weston Carryer meeting at Foxton in June 1991. I was far from sure what might, or could, happen. I had three problems. I harboured a lot of hatred against my stepfather for all the ill-treatment dished out to me as a child. I knew I had to forgive if I wanted to walk the path Jesus trod. I also had rheumatoid arthritis in both hips, and an affliction in which the skin grows over the discs of the spinal cord and would have, in time, made my back as stiff as a board.

When Weston prayed over me I was slain in the Spirit. I felt the Holy Spirit wrestling, as if it were a demon, with a ball in my

Overhauls & Unusual Conditions

stomach, pushing it over to the left side, then with tremendous force, pulling it down the inside of my left leg and driving it out through my left foot. There was no pain. When I sat down I felt so warm inside and so full of love. Hate was gone. Apart from touches in my right hip, the arthritis has gone. Prayer will do the rest. Weston gave my wife a passage to read, and that night she did so aloud. My backbone began to wriggle up and down and I could feel the skin being pulled free from the joints. I said, "The Lord's working on me again." At its end, I jumped out of bed and touched my toes, something I had not done for a very long time. I thank God He has set me free both in body and soul.

—*Ron Hansen*

In the summer of 1990, I went to a summer school of evangelism at Te Nikau Bible College where Weston Carryer was our teacher. During the ten days, I had prayer for three things which had caused me much trouble over the years. I had had bronchitis for three months every winter for many years, and I have never had it since. That was eleven years ago now. I also had prayer for problems that I had in my womb, which was from freemasonry curse. I had carried five babies to between five and six months into pregnancy, and then they had died; and yet I had to go through the processes of induced labour and birth each time. My womb was cursed, and this was lifted through prayer, and has behaved in a healthy manner since. I also had prayer for my back which was injured when I was nineteen [I was forty at the time of Weston praying] and that part of my back has never given me any trouble since then. Today I went for prayer for a recent injury which damaged my back and arms. I am believing for total healing for these. I am so thankful for Weston being a deliverer of the healing touch of God so faithfully for so many years.

—*Mary Gemmill*

I was born blind in my right eye, and all my life was under an eye specialist because of the problems with the right eye. In

Miracles in Aotearoa New Zealand

November 2000, I attended a divine healing meeting in Hastings where Weston Carryer was ministering.

During the meeting God revealed to Weston through a word of knowledge my condition, and he then asked me to come forward for the Lord to heal me. He then laid his hands over both eyes and prayed. After that he removed his hand from my right eye and I discovered that I was able to see perfectly. The Lord had given me sight in that eye which I had never ever had. Twelve months later I can see clearly and I have not needed to go back to the eye specialist.

Thirty years ago, my knee was damaged in an accident. This knee continued to deteriorate until two years ago when it became so painful and restricted, I had to have a knee replacement operation. Unfortunately, it did not work and I was no better off.

In November 2000, at the healing meeting in Hastings, Weston prayed for the Lord to heal my knee. As he prayed, I experienced a wonderful warmth around the knee and down the leg, and full movement was immediately restored. Over the last twelve months my knee has functioned correctly. At times there has been a very slight amount of pain but nothing like it was for thirty years. To be able to move freely is absolutely wonderful. Thank You, Jesus. Praise the Lord!

—*Dawn John*

In November 1995, I fell off a ladder and received compression fractures in two vertebrae in my back. I was taken immediately to North Shore Hospital and then transferred to Middlemore Hospital. A CT scan revealed that as well as the two vertebrae fractures, the nerves from the back of the left leg were severed. The doctors said that I would never walk again without support. I was told that I would have to spend twenty-six weeks in hospital: eight weeks flat on my back, ten weeks in rehabilitation, and then a further eight weeks undergoing other treatment.

I was visited by my South Auckland F.G.B. president in hospital who prayed for me, and the feeling returned to my leg. I decided that I did not want to complete the treatment in hospital, and one month after the fall, I discharged myself. The hospital authorities said that they would not take any responsibility for what would happen to me. With the aid of a brace, I managed to hobble around for the next three months, but I was in continual intense pain all the time. It was all I could do to move at all. Also, as a result of a broken wrist, my carpel tunnel was damaged and I had been unable to close my hand for some time.

In early March 1996, I attended a F.G.B. meeting in West Auckland where Weston Carryer was ministering. During the ministry time, I went forward for him to pray for me. I was in terrible pain. I remember Weston starting to pray for me and the next thing I knew, it was sometime later when I woke up on the floor with a lot of other people also on the floor. I discovered that my hand was closed. My hand was working again and the wrist was healed. I then wondered how on earth I was going to get up as it was four months since I had been able to do this. To my absolute amazement, I simply got up and discovered that all the pain and restrictions I had were totally gone. I went to the bathroom, took my brace off, and then came back into the hall and did a series of back exercises. Jesus had totally healed my back. Over the last four years my back has been completely normal. Praise the Lord!

—Jim Foster

In June 2000, Weston Carryer came to Stratford for one of his healing meetings. I had only been a Christian for a week or so and was very excited and full-on for Jesus at this moment— being very anxious and excited at the same time at what Weston did at healing meetings. From what people had told me at church, it sounded awesome at what God did and I wanted to see God work powerfully and miraculously in people's lives. So I went along on the night to see miracles happen.

I have been an asthmatic all my life and always had to carry an inhaler with me wherever I went. It was an essential part of my life and was just like carrying your keys with you all the time. My asthma was particularly bad when the weather was cold. The cold air affected me so much, that, if I was outside on a cold morning, I would have asthma within minutes, which made it particularly hard to play winter sports.

Halfway through the healing meeting, Weston called for an asthmatic to come forward for prayer. I went to go forward but someone else stood up before me. I thought, "Oh no! I missed my chance." But I got another chance to go up. Praise the Lord! Weston started praying for my asthma to be healed, and the Holy Spirit hit me hard and fast, and I had carpet time for the first time. What an experience! What a night! From that night on, my asthma has been ninety-percent better and I can play sports and be out in cold air now. Hallelujah! I believe with all my heart that God is going to heal the remaining ten percent. God is powerful and mighty and can heal! Amen! I claim my healing each day in the name of Jesus Christ. I thank Jesus for my healing and love Him so much that I can't describe how I feel!

I had another opportunity to attend Weston's healing meeting in Hawera in June 2001. I went along mainly to support the Hawera church. I was not expecting to get prayer for anything. From a baby, I have had quarter vision in my left eye. It never bothered me; I got used to using my right eye for all my vision. I had glasses in my early primary school years to help correct my vision in my left eye. However, after years of wearing glasses, my vision never improved and the eye specialist told me that my vision in my left eye would never improve or could get worse. This did not bother me too much as I had become so dependent on my right eye.

However, Weston said, "Who is the person with the lazy left eye?" Well, that shocked me.

I thought, *That's me. I've got to go up!* So up I went for healing. The Holy Spirit hit me fast and hard again and I had carpet time for the second time. While I was down on the floor, my left eye felt very hot underneath and I knew God was healing me. Before, my only vision in my left eye was an outline of objects. If I looked at a person up close, all I could distinguish was an outline of the body, no features whatsoever. However, God healed me. Awesome! And now I can see eyes, mouth, nose,

Overhauls & Unusual Conditions

ears, and so forth, on a person. Praise the Lord! I can now see detailed signs and words where before I couldn't.

I love the Lord so much and thank Him every day for my healing and breath. Jesus can heal you as well. All you have to do is believe it in your heart. If you ask, you will receive. Jesus is mighty and powerful! Don't hold back for your healing. God is awesome! I give Him all the glory! Jesus Christ is Lord. Thank You, Lord. Amen!

—*Catherine Old*

I am excited to tell you that I have had three significant healings from the Lord after receiving prayer from Weston Carryer at two of his meetings. The first time was at Tauranga Intermediate School in about 1996 when I had been suffering intense emotional pain and grief for at least three years. I was particularly tormented by a sharp stabbing pain that went through my heart, accompanied by a feeling that there was a big gaping hole where my heart should be. This sensation was with me day and night. After the prayer, the pain began to fade and that empty feeling was replaced with a sense of joy and hope—something beautiful instead of something so ugly—and I was able to move on a journey to emotional health and stability.

I attended another healing meeting at Oasis Christian Centre Tauranga and asked Weston to pray as I was seeking healing in my body. For several years I'd experienced extreme pain in my body. I had pain on the right side of my face affecting my ear, jaw, and teeth. I'd had wisdom teeth removed, a root filling done and consumed copious amounts of pain medication, but nothing helped. Nerve pain was suggested as a diagnosis, but no relief found.

Also, over several years, I'd had seven operations: five of those surgeries were for endometriosis. However, I experienced ongoing pain and illness. During the last surgery for a hernia repair, an enlarged nerve was released from scar tissue and divided. Unfortunately in the years that followed, I experienced severe nerve pain associated with the operation site. There was no cure—medical or otherwise—except for my hope in the Lord. During the prayer, I never felt any pain relief, but in the days that followed, the pain in my face area receded until it was totally gone. For the first time in years I was free from it.

Also, I have noticed a significant improvement in the other affected areas. I praise God for this. I am continually amazed at His unfailing love towards me regardless of Him choosing to heal me or not. I truly serve an awesome God. I am thankful for Weston sharing God's truth and love with me and others.

—Leonie

When I came to Weston Carryer for prayer at the beginning of November 2001, my doctor had just told me that I had acute reflux indigestion problems which also triggered my oesophagus into a spasm. This had been a problem on and off for about two and a half years. My doctor also said I would have to have Gaviscon every night and may need to see a specialist. This condition was extremely painful and I never knew when my oesophagus would go into a spasm. I would just about faint with the pain and the attack often lasted for half an hour at a time. My main concern was that the attacks would become more frequent during my pregnancy because "normal" indigestion usually occurs during pregnancy anyway.

When I came up for prayer I had just had an attack the previous weekend. I had been fasting (a church breakthrough fast), and my personal breakthrough was healing in this area. The prayer Weston prayed was simple, and I found myself on the floor for what seemed like ages. He also prayed for anxiety to go in my life too. I know this condition is partly due to stress. During that Sunday after the prayer I didn't feel any different but believed that God had done something. It was the next day (Monday) that I felt a noticeable difference. It's hard to explain what or how, but my mind, body, and whole outlook seemed different. On Tuesday, I told my church leaders at the staff meeting, and I also had a chance to share my testimony of healing with some Jehovah Witnesses.

It's now been seven months since Weston prayed and I

Overhauls & Unusual Conditions

haven't even had the slightest niggle of anything that I had been having (i.e., tight and/or aching chest, palpitations, or full indigestion). With my pregnancy I have had a little bit of heartburn but I know it's just the normal sort, not the horrible kind I was getting. I knew God would heal me. I still give thanks and praise to Him for it today.

Also during my pregnancy, some ultrasound scans picked up on a low-lying placenta. At thirty-two weeks I had another scan which then revealed some large blood clots close to my cervix and the baby's head, as well as the low placenta. My midwife, therefore, wanted me to have an elect caesarian. The risk of these blood vessels bursting during labour was too high to have a normal birth. I was quite shocked and disappointed and said I would get my family and friends to pray. I then remembered Weston was visiting our church again, so I arranged to get a babysitter for our other two children. My midwife, at this stage, had booked me in to see the obstetrician at the hospital to make a date for the caesarian, and I had another scan appointment within the following week.

Again, when Weston prayed, it was a very simple prayer. Even though I felt nothing change right then, I just trusted that God would answer. I must admit that on my way to the scan appointment I was nervous and dubious. I wasn't too sure whether God would answer this prayer because I wasn't in dire straits, or in pain, and lots of women have caesarians. It was just my heart's desire to have a normal birth like my other two had been.

But as I was thinking on all this, I felt God challenge me, asking me, "Is it an important issue to you?"

I answered, "Yes."

Then I believe God said back to me, "If it's important to you, it's important to Me—no matter how big or small, because I love you." Well, I had a peace in my heart after that. And the scan revealed a complete change. It was hard to get a direct answer from the doctor, but basically, there were no threatening blood vessels to be seen near the cervix or the baby's head! My midwife was also very surprised! She cancelled the appointment to see

Miracles in Aotearoa New Zealand

the obstetrician and now I am looking forward to a natural labour and birth.

—*Jan-Marie Mills*

P.S. My baby was born naturally and healthy. Glory to God!!

I give all praise and glory to our Lord Jesus Christ for healing me after Weston Carryer so kindly prayed for me during his visit to Invercargill at the FGBMF meeting. For the past twelve years, I have had diverticulitis, where approximately sixty centimetres of the large bowel was severely affected. It was a painful and most unpleasant complaint, and most unpredictable.

Since he prayed for me I have not had the slightest twinge, and it was so wonderful to be well again. I keep thanking and praising Jesus.

That night, Weston gave a call for someone with damaged vertebra in the neck. I'm so thankful that he also prayed for this condition. Jesus healed me of that too. I had damaged my neck back in 1961 and had developed a hump; so I used to avoid wearing collarless garments as my hump looked like what Angus bulls have. Almost three years ago, I fell on steps and landed very hard on the back of my head on the concrete floor at the wool store when we had taken our wool in. That fall took many months to recover from. At some positions, I would get a strange vibration coming into my ears from my neck. It was a bit scary as I thought it would stay like that for life. I got a lot of neck aches and stiffness also. Well, praise the Lord! The hump has gone, my neck looks normal now, and the grating vibration has gone. I have a little stiffness but I keep claiming my healing in the name of Jesus.

I'm so thankful that Weston, came to Invercargill and for praying for me, for his obedience, dedication, love, and faithfulness to our Lord Jesus Christ. We loved his testimony. As a farmer, he had a compassion for his stock, and he was a wonderful shepherd for Jesus.

—*Ruth Stewart*

Overhauls & Unusual Conditions

I came to the healing service held at Tokoroa Apostolic Church on 5 October 2001. At the end of the service, when Weston Carryer called for anyone who hadn't received ministry to come up, I came for healing of fading eyes, a redundant bowel, and a prolapsed uterus. Now I don't have those problems. When I got home, the Holy Spirit prompted me to check the prolapse. So I did, and it wasn't there any more! I got this complaint back in February 1982, after the birth of my daughter. I lifted something far too heavy, and did the damage then.

I'm so thankful for Weston being faithful to the Lord.

—Jan Morton, Rotorua

I wish to report the blessings of healings I received from the Lord through Weston Carryer's prayer for healing ministry. The first time I attended one of his meetings was in New Plymouth soon after I moved here from Tauranga in 1994. I had much trouble over the years with an arthritic condition of my neck. It caused pain, lack of flexibility, and at times, pinched a nerve that severely affected the movement in my right arm. I used to regularly visit a chiropractor to have adjustments made. Weston had a word of knowledge, prayed for my condition, and I had a healing. Since that time, I have not needed a chiropractor's adjustment.

At another meeting Weston had a word of knowledge regarding an irregular heartbeat to which I responded. I have not had an irregular heartbeat since.

In early 1988, I felt very distressed with much pain. My back, shoulder, arms, and legs—my whole body—ached. A blood test showed up an inflammation. The doctors didn't diagnose my condition specifically and sent me home with painkillers that didn't even take the edge off my pain.

Weston held a meeting here and had a word of knowledge to which I responded. There was an immediate improvement and it continued over a period of six months. I would meditate on the Scriptures from the pamphlet, *Keeping Your Healing*, claim healing for myself, and thank God for it nearly every day.

One warm, sunny day, I woke up so refreshed and happy. I had no pain at all, hardly dared to believe it, and have never had this pain again. Thank You, Lord.

—Erika Bonnevie

My testimony involves much more than physical healing, marvelous as that was. Eight years ago I married a businessman. Unfortunately, his business ran into severe financial problems through a person not paying money owed to him. To help the situation, my husband, Steve, started to work incredibly long hours which caused major stress.

One night a customer, supposedly to help him with the stress, introduced him to the drug "speed," and very soon he progressed to "P." He immediately became hooked on "P," and very soon was heavily involved. His personality changed completely and he became violent. One night he pushed me across the room. I landed very awkwardly and either broke or badly damaged my left foot. Despite the terrible pain I was too embarrassed to get medical help. The foot finally did heal to a degree, but for the next three years, I was very restricted in what I could do. I was unable to put any weight on that foot at all.

During this time I prayed and cried like I never had before for Steve and for our marriage. Finally, the Lord broke through in Steve's life and he was able to totally stop taking drugs so that his normal nature returned. I was so pleased, but still felt like I had been run over by a bus. I was very low emotionally.

The two of us went to a divine healing meeting in 2003 where Weston Carryer was ministering. He had a word of knowledge for someone with a specific tailbone problem. I also had this condition and I knew it was for me, but I said, "Lord, please . . . more confirmation." Weston then had a word for someone who had badly damaged their left foot which had never healed. I shouted to myself, *Lord, You really do care about me.*

Weston prayed for my foot which was immediately healed.

Overhauls & Unusual Conditions

All the pain went and the full movement was restored. He then prayed for total restoration in the lives of both of us and this happened immediately. Our marriage is restored and we are both whole in spirit, soul, and body. Steve is now helping people who are suffering like he was. Jesus, You are so awesome.

—*Tracey Fawcett*

At the beginning of April 2002, I tore and pulled both the hamstring tendons in both of my legs playing basketball with my two grandsons by firstly not doing any warm-up stretches, and secondly by wearing unsuitable footwear. Over the ensuing weeks my legs became like heavy useless logs. I could scarcely walk up the slight incline to our house. Going shopping to the mall was an impossibility, getting out of a chair and standing up was an agonizing experience. It felt like I would never properly walk again. It also became increasingly so difficult to turn over in bed that I resorted to using my shoulders to push and take the weight off my body. As a result of this action I tore and damaged the left rotator and elevator cuff muscles attached to the AC shoulder joint and lost most of the use of that arm. I began months of physiotherapy and exercises.

Although I had previously been to the Philippines as part of a ministry team with Weston Carryer, witnessing many healings, and had also received healing for other conditions myself, I did not think to contact Weston for prayer or refresh myself on his teaching pamphlet, *Keeping Your Healing*. Towards the end of 2002 (in October or November), Weston came to our church in Tauranga. By this stage my legs had improved apart from some tightness of the ligaments still and an inability to run, but my arm remained very restricted and painful.

I went to the meeting wanting prayer and healing. Weston called out a painful left arm condition. Two other people responded quickly and I (foolishly) decided that the call was not for me and did not go forward, thinking and deciding that I would claim the healing where I was. My arm did improve a little.

In February 2003, Weston was again back in our church

Miracles in Aotearoa New Zealand

and I had just been appointed his secretary. The first condition he called out was a painful restricted left arm, so I immediately responded this time. I had not told him about this condition or my other foolish decision. I did not receive an immediate return to full use. But over the following weeks, there was a continual progression, until in April, I realized that I was doing things that had previously become impossible.

In November 2003, I had a long delayed flight to London, staying in unfamiliar beds, carrying a shoulder bag around the city. Then two weeks later I had an extremely bumpy flight to Cape Town to stay with my son. I was aware my neck and shoulders had become sore with stiffness. After about a week in Cape Town I woke up one morning and I could not lift my left arm (not even to turn on a tap). It ached from the shoulder to well below my elbow. It just felt like it was broken through the middle. Even though my husband prayed for me, I felt totally miserable, just wanting to go home; yet I was to be there another six weeks. After thirty-six hours I decided that the situation was ridiculous! There was no reason to suggest that it was, in fact, broken, and furthermore, I had been healed. I decided that I needed to take positive action with praise and worship playing CDs (at night as well) and reclaim that healing, to thank Jesus for it, and remind satan he could not steal it back from me. By the next day all the symptoms had disappeared and, praise God, I was able to carry on having a good time with my family.

—*Jill Clark*

The skin irritation I had which Weston Carryer prayed for about three years ago is completely gone, and I have had no recurrence. On his visit, he prayed for my back and arm. The arm pain diminished immediately, and though the back pain was still there, once I returned to sit down, I knew God had touched me. The arm pain also flared up again. However, it gave me great confidence that they were both only temporary. By Monday, I noticed further gradual improvement. Each week there was further gradual improvement to the point where now I am able to sit and type this testimony without pain. I also get a full night of sleep. I am very grateful for that as at one point

Overhauls & Unusual Conditions

I was only able to sleep for three hours. Sitting was also very painful. Thank You, Lord.

—Richard Baxter

I want to write about three healings that the Lord has given me through Weston's ministry. My father died some years ago of prostate cancer and this resulted in me having a real fear of dying of the same condition. Several years ago I started having prostate problems and this fear intensified. When Weston was ministering in Dunedin in March 2000, he spoke over me and said that I would never die of cancer and broke the fear of it over my life. Later, when I did have a prostate operation, both the operating surgeon and the anesthetist told me that the P.S.A. count was only just over two and it was extremely unlikely that I would ever develop prostate cancer.

One year later at a meeting in Dunedin when Weston was speaking out words of knowledge, he pointed in my direction and said, "There is someone who has a bad migraine headache now." For at least twenty years I had suffered from bad migraine headaches and I had a really severe one at that moment. I went forward, he prayed, and I was slain in the Spirit. The headache had gone before I got up, and I have never had one since.

In April 2004, once again in Dunedin, as Weston was ministering, he said that there was someone right in the front where I was sitting with carpal tunnel syndrome. I had been diagnosed as having this after having a bad infection in my wrist. Once again I was slain in the Spirit, and my wrist was immediately healed, and is now completely supple. I am so grateful, and I praise You, Lord Jesus.

—Terry Templeton

Somewhat reluctantly I attended an F.G.B.M.F.I. weekend camp at Punawea in Otago in August 1998 where Weston Carryer was our speaker. The reluctance was because of a bad attitude I had towards Weston at that time.

During the first meeting Weston started to speak out words

Miracles in Aotearoa New Zealand

of knowledge. First of all, he said there was a man there who, as a result of a motor bike accident, had injured numbers three and five vertebrae in his spine. He asked that man to come for prayer for his healing. Years before I did have a motor bike accident and the x-rays had shown that these vertebrae were damaged. This had badly affected my back and I was having medical treatment at the time.

I knew I needed to respond and I went forward and was slain in the Spirit. As I came round I heard Weston say that there was someone there who was suffering from a particular eye problem that I had. This caused constant irritation and I had the eye drops to relieve this in my pocket. Weston then prayed for this as well. That night the area of my back affected was completely healed and I have never had pain there again. The eye irritation also disappeared.

These healings plus one other physical healing that I received that night were truly wonderful. But, the greatest healing that I received that night was with my attitude. The Lord really dealt with me over this, and during supper that night, I got things right with Weston. Eight years later, I still marvel at how much the Lord cares about us and how He wants to deal with these issues in our lives because He wants us whole in spirit, body, and soul. Lord, I am so grateful for Your amazing love.

—*David Stewart*

We have been so blessed by Weston Carryer's ministry over the years. Just a brief update: Russell, whom Weston prayed for with a bad back, is still bouncing around free and fit as a fiddle, rejoicing in God's goodness. Shane, who had broken bones in his foot that had never healed properly, continues to talk about there being no pain—even when he jumps onto the concrete floor off the top bunk. He can now bend three of his toes which he hadn't previously been able to. God is good.

—*Jeff Low, Chaplain, Invercargill Prison Chaplains*

In the winter hockey season of 2001, I rolled my left ankle.

Overhauls & Unusual Conditions

I damaged the tendons, ligaments and the nerves, and as a result of this, I could not balance very well. The physiotherapist told me that it would have been better if I had broken it, as I would not have had any long-term damage. I continually rolled my ankle for the following five years and it was always very swollen and puffy, and I could never see the anklebone.

On 20 December 2003, I collapsed at home one morning. My mother thought I had taken drugs and that I was dead. However, I was not on drugs. From that day on, I experienced many faint and dizzy spells and would feel a sharp, piercing pain on the left hand side of my chest in the heart region. I was checked out many times by doctors, had ECGs and scans on my heart. These found nothing. I used to get the pain just every now and then; but then it began to stay there—dragging out and getting worse at times. It always felt tight and it could often put me in tears.

On 27 April 2006, I was working a shift at a hotel management school where I slipped on the kitchen floor and landed flat on my back. I was taken to hospital by ambulance because I couldn't move and my ankles wouldn't support me. X-rays were taken and they showed that nothing had been broken. However, I did sprain my whole back, from the top of the neck to the bottom of my spine, and I was told it would take a while to heal. I was put on anti-inflammatory medication and painkillers. My neck had become so stiff and sore that I could not move it from side to side more than a few centimetres without wanting to scream in pain. After spending the entire weekend completely bedridden without any improvement I rang the hospital. They informed me to follow up with a GP who then referred me on to physio treatment. I had been told I was not going to be able to work for a week; the doctor had wanted to give me longer. I was having physio every other day and I was not feeling any better than when the accident had happened.

My physiotherapist encouraged me to go to a Weston Carryer healing meeting. Weston was having a healing meeting that Sunday, 14 May 2006, at the Park City Church in New Plymouth, and the physio suggested that I should consider going. I was really tired but I finally talked myself into going.

I heard Weston describe a few things that had me thinking,

that could be me . . . but then something else was added to the condition and I thought to myself, *He didn't mean me.* At the end of the service I went up to get prayer for my injuries. I fell backwards under the power of the Holy Spirit. When I woke up from that, I could move, I felt looser than I had been. I actually thought I was dreaming, so I took my time in getting up. When I finally got up, I moved my head from side to side, and it moved further than it had before, and it didn't hurt. Then I twisted my back from the hips as if to stretch it and I found I could see behind me, so I bent down—all the way to the ground while keeping my legs entirely straight. Previously I had not been able to bend down more than maybe 10-cm, otherwise I had to bend with my knees and keep my back straight. I was in shock, I think, to discover I could do this!

When I got back home I was so happy! I skipped into my friends' room, and with great excitement I showed them all how I could bend down. It was the best feeling ever! My smile was huge. For the first time in three weeks I went and played three games of pool one after the other, until I couldn't bend over long enough to get a good shot. I was low in faith before my fall and wandering off my Christian walk. But now, I thank God for what He has done. I thank Him that He has blessed Weston with this gift of healing and that Weston obeyed this calling. God truly is wonderful and amazing. He should be shared with everyone! I fully believe in God's existence and the great power He holds.

Over the past five months, apart from a very brief period of pain for one day when I fell on my back again, I have had no pain at all, no dizzy spells, or pain in my heart region. My ankle is fine, the full strength has returned (all the swelling disappeared when it was prayed for), and I can now see my anklebone.

—Christine Coursey

Over the past fifteen years I have struggled with acute pain and decreasing movement from strokes. I also suffered with increasing arthritis and I needed continuous pain relief every day. On 26 April 2007, I attended a divine healing meeting in

Overhauls & Unusual Conditions

New Plymouth where Weston Carryer prayed for the Lord to heal me; I received a marvellous instant healing.

I am now pain-free and off all pain medication, enjoying remarkable movement every day. Housework and gardening are now a breeze to get through, and walking for an hour is bringing me great joy once again. I have been able to knit a shawl for my grandchild with no pain or restriction in my fingers. Prior to my healing this was impossible.

I am thankful for Weston's gift of healing. Praise be to God.

—*Judy Moratti*

For over thirty years, I suffered from irritable bowel syndrome, and over this time, it had got progressively worse. By early in 2007, all my food was going straight through me. In March 2007, my immune system suddenly broke down and this radically affected my whole body. I developed candida and chronic fatigue; my digestive system could not handle food at all. I could not work properly and lost my job. I felt terrible and was experiencing severe internal pain all the time. Despite medical attention there was no improvement at all over the next five months and I did not know what to do. I was really ill for this entire time.

In August 2007, I heard Weston Carryer was having a healing meeting in Papamoa. I desperately wanted to be healed so I attended. During the ministry time, Weston said that there was someone present with irritable bowel syndrome and would that person come forward for him to pray for the Lord to heal her. I immediately went forward and then Weston prayed for me. The internal pain went instantly, and I clearly remember that night marvelling at being without pain for the first time in five months. Over the next few weeks, my other healings came, and now today (2008), my digestive system is working as it should and my food is supplying the correct nourishment to my body. I am eating wisely. My energy has returned and I am now able to resume work. The effect on my life has been huge and I am so grateful to our wonderful Lord Jesus Christ for restoring my health.

—*Ann McArthur*

Miracles in Aotearoa New Zealand

I was involved in a motor accident on 6 August 2006, and sustained compression fractures of the L1 and L2 vertebrae, whiplash and brain trauma.

I attended Weston Carryer's healing meeting in Whangarei in the following November. For the entire three months since the accident, I had continually experienced severe back spasms that were extremely painful. I would call them grade ten.

Weston called me up for arthritis in my right foot which I also had. He laid hands on me and prayed for my overall healing. I was immediately slain in the Spirit and crashed to the ground causing considerable discomfort and pain. I eventually hobbled back to my seat, which was no more than six metres away. By the time I sat down, my back was feeling very different. I sat down normally for the first time since the accident. I think I was in shock, so I went out to the foyer and touched my toes and did twists, etc. Perfect!

Although my back was still a little stiff, and I had to exercise it to regain its full strength, the most important thing is that the excruciating pain has never returned over the last seven months. My foot is also much better. I'm so thankful for Weston's prayer, and our glorious Saviour Jesus Christ.

—*Wayne Jeffs*

As a result of a wonderful healing I had previously received from the Lord when I attended a Weston Carryer healing meeting in New Plymouth, I drove to Papamoa in the Bay of Plenty to attend another Weston Carryer healing meeting. Early in the meeting, Weston said that there was someone present with intense lumbar pain, arthritis in the left knee, and right hip. This was me and I went up again. Weston then prayed for me, and the Lord completely and instantly healed my right knee. When I sat down after the Lord had worked over my lower back, I had the sensation of a small bar sliding just slightly from left to right in my lower back and all the pain went.

Now, over six months later, all the pain has gone from my

Overhauls & Unusual Conditions

back and knee. My hip still gives a defiant hit now and again, but nowhere near as bad. I am believing for that to also be totally healed. Lord, I just want to once again thank You so much. I'm so thankful for Weston and Ruth.

—*Sybil Gunson, Waitara*

My name is Tania Williams. I am married to Andrew and have two wonderful sons aged 19 and 16, and two older stepchildren. I gave my heart to the Lord 12 years ago as a solo mum and divorcée. It's the best and most exciting thing ever. He helps me with life's challenges and brought meaning and hope into my life. No matter what comes my way, I know that ultimately I have Him right there loving me like no one ever could. He's real, and He still heals today.

I'm excited, honoured and privileged to tell you about the healing that Jesus has performed in me! Not only was I healed from multiple sclerosis, but later via telephone with Weston, I received Jesus' healing for migraines, coeliac disease (gluten intolerance), and food allergies.

I staggered off to a Weston Carryer healing service at Park City Church—with an emphasis on *staggered*! I remember I had such bad fatigue that day. In fact, I rarely made it to church because fatigue and weakness made it near impossible to sit erect for so long.

Weston prayed an assertive prayer over me and had me test my walking. Then he added a bit more prayer . . . and that was it. No pomp and ceremony, just a simple prayer. I was like a stunned mullet, twirling my walking stick as I swaggered out of church . . . emphasis again on the *swaggered*! This was such a strange feeling . . . to be able to feel my legs and have strength enough in my legs and torso to stand up really straight. Wow! I'd gone from someone who was looking to buy a wheelchair (which, by the way, I had to use while on our honeymoon 4 years previous) to someone who could now hop on one leg with no worries! And my vision!—perfect! In fact, the amazing thing was that my brain processed all things sensory just perfectly now, even if I was tired. Real, bone-numbing fatigue was a thing of the past. I could look around and process what I was seeing, move a limb, touch something, hear sounds, think of things to say and speak words—all as naturally as God had intended. The sensory processes flowed immediately without effort. It was like being born again . . . again!

It's been a year now since I was healed. I am very grateful to our Lord Jesus, but also for Weston Carryer and his team at Zoe Ministries who have continued to communicate with me and pray.

It hasn't, in all honesty, been an easy ride at times. For one thing, the closeness I still had to mates with MS weighed heavily on me . . . and two of them around my age are now in a rest home.

Adjusting to relationship changes was another. My relationship with the Lord changed. I was so reliant on Him before, but now I found myself self-sufficient and had to re-programme myself and begin a new routine. My relationship with my husband Andrew changed also. He married me with MS so there have been some adjustments there.

Being in amongst life and people was pretty "freaky" at first as I was used to being on my own pretty much as people just tired me out with sensory overload. Nowadays I can enjoy all the opportunities without feeling overwhelmed. Here are a few—

- I'm going to my first women's conference in June!
- Joined a women's group here at St. James.
- Go off to watch rugby.
- Flew to Wellington to see my sister.
- Take my dog up to Merrilands Domain regularly.
- Joined a bible study group.
- Have had people over for dinner.
- Started my jewellery website.

There are so many things I can do now thanks to God's healing! What an amazing difference there is in my life now since my healing!

Overhauls & Unusual Conditions

- No more pain. It is such a miracle and a relief.
- No incontinence—bowel and bladder healed!
- No cognitive problems—I can think straight.
- No slurring or hesitant speech—sometimes strangers thought I was drunk.
- Able to go out in the evening—even to Cliff Richard!
- No pain medication or other MS-related meds.
- No walking aid.
- No dropping and breaking things.
- Normal vision.
- I can hop on one leg—left or right—without falling over.
- Skip like a young girl.
- No wobbling about or legs giving way.
- My head doesn't wobble like a nodding dog you see in the rear window of a car.
- No numbness or leg twitch.
- No falling over—I used to go splat and have wrecked several pairs of trousers.

Something else I'm faced with is where I fit in the workforce. I was originally a PA, but times have changed after 10 or so years of being ill. Plus I'm a different person now. It's just been a year of discovering and adjusting to the new opportunities and choices I have.

It finally dawned on me that I still need some healing in the areas of fatigue, leg stamina and coordination which took me awhile to work out. I really didn't know what was the "norm" after ten years of being abnormal! By the way, I read of two others divinely healed of MS by the Lord at Weston Carryer's healing meetings and one was climbing a mountain the week

Miracles in Aotearoa New Zealand

after her healing and the other was dancing. So I thought to myself, *Well, this isn't just me not being fit, or a matter of retraining my legs to walk or run.* (I've been told I run like Forrest Gump!) Yeah! It was a relief to figure this out and I feel certain the good Lord has more healing coming my way in His timing.

I want to stress that I have had soooo much healing . . . not just one thing, but about four disabilities. I am excited when I think of the possibilities ahead. Praise the Lord.

—*Tania Williams*

My name is Louise and I'm writing this testimony of thanksgiving for several miraculous healings after Weston Carryer (and later, my senior pastor) laid hands on me and prayed for my neck, back, and shoulders during his ministry at our church in Riccarton at Easter 2009.

My neck, which had some stiffness (recurring after a whiplash injury in a nasty car accident July 2002), has been completely free since his prayer. My mid- then lower back areas also became totally pain-free within 10 days of prayer for the first time in over twelve months after being severely damaged in two work injuries (March 2008).

These back injuries, plus those in both rotator cuffs, all occurred during long shift hours working in my much-loved healthcare occupation in Otago. These combined painful and distressing injuries resulted (after my GP's strong recommendation) in the sad termination at 61 years of age, from that happy, fulfilling and, I believe, Holy Spirit-led employment, plus ending more than 7 years in my chosen field of career and Christian endeavours.

I required several courses of both voltaren tablets and physiotherapies for approximately 10 months as my mobility was severely impeded during my daily living skills (e.g., showering, dressing, shopping, and sleeping, etc.). Both shoulders were x-rayed, and later ultra-scanned, showing recent deep tissue damage in both rotator cuffs and I was referred to a "top" shoulder surgeon at Mercy Clinic in Dunedin.

I saw this specialist just before Weston's arrival here in

Overhauls & Unusual Conditions

Christchurch and he had, upon examination, decided to proceed with a 2-part surgery using a pin to mend the deep tear still visible in my right shoulder, and shave some bone in order to relieve pain and increase this right arm's mobility again—all scheduled for within 6 weeks of that March appointment.

After Weston's very timely visit, and with more prayers of agreement with Pat Robertson of 700 Club, and close personal friends also in those crucial weeks, I received a special rhema from our Lord Jesus, "I don't want you to go ahead with that surgery." I then received a miracle in this previously painful shoulder and was soon able to demonstrate normal movements (i.e., full-circle swings, etc.), to not only my GP and ACC case manager, but also testified in a letter requesting the cancellation of that upcoming surgery with my specialist. He eventually replied giving his consent for the time being. However, I am gloriously free of all pain and all restrictions in both shoulders and have been functioning fully now for these past 10 to 12 months. Hallelujah!

I am fully recovered, even with sufficient grace, strength and unction to dance before my holy and powerful Lord Jesus again! I have been off all A.C.C. supports since before Christmas.

All glory, honour and praise to our holy heavenly Creator and His glorious beloved Son, our Lord Jesus Christ, and Holy Spirit, for all their miraculous restorations in my life. With much love in Christ.

—*Louise Wallis*

I am eternally grateful for what Weston Carryer has done through our Lord and Saviour Jesus Christ. This testimony is for my youngest son, Rihare, who had asthma and eczema for most of his life, and it had got worse as he grew older. I took over being the sole parent of my children in May 2003 and had to deal with these afflictions on my own, which was extremely hard.

Rihare's asthma got so bad that he nearly died twice, and the eczema was heartbreaking as well. He had his eczema since he was about two, and it was so bad that three-quarters of his body was covered in it! He needed a special cream as every other cream made him scream in agony.

I used to cry, thinking that as a father, I am the protector of my children. Yet I couldn't do anything to take the pain away from my son. I would sit and hold him until he went to sleep so he wouldn't scratch himself and cause any more sores. His whole body hardly had a clear patch of unscarred skin as the eczema was rampant! I was a young Christian at the time and I heard that Weston was coming to our church again.

I knew that if I was expectant, my son would be healed. (I know now that I should have gone up for my pastors to pray over my son for healing. But I was new in the Word.)

Weston came to our church, The Centre in 2004. When he said that there was someone with a severe breathing disorder in my row, I grabbed my son and rushed to the front. Weston prayed over him, and instantly his breathing changed. I asked if he could pray for his eczema, and he did.

We went back to our seats and I could see a physical change on my son immediately. His face had softened. (His face was always a little dark and he always had a pained look about him.) It was so awesome!

I went up for prayer for my leg because I had snapped my cruciate ligament and it hadn't healed properly. I still got a lot of pain when I exercised, but the doctors, physios, and the surgeon that had operated had said there wasn't much more they could do. I knew that God is the God of miracles and was determined to get my leg healed. Weston prayed for me and my knee became instantly hot. He asked me to run and do some jumping, which I did, and there was no pain!

I went back to my seat and my son had a look of amazement on his face, so I asked him what was up. He smiled and said, "Look!" I looked as he was pointing at his arm which was totally clear of any scarring! I looked at his tummy and back and they were all clear of the hideous scarring! Halleujah! Praise God.

I have not had any problems with my knee and my son has never had any more asthma or eczema for six years. In fact, he is grading for his black belt in Taekwondo in a week and he is

Overhauls & Unusual Conditions

the school champion for cross country!

I thank You, Jesus. In gratitude,

—*Barry Hawkins and family*

Weston Carryer came to our church in Ashburton on 27 March 2011 and I was a one-year-old Christian. The day he came, I had it in my heart to be healed. I had a lot of symptoms and pain in different areas of my body, and so I came in great expectation.

Weston prayed for migraine headaches which I had also had for twenty years. These would flatten me for around 24-hours. Since then the first early signs of a migraine have shown themselves occasionally, but I have immediately claimed my healing and they have instantly disappeared. So for the last ten months, I have been free of them.

As well Weston prayed for the Lord to heal my insomnia, and this has improved by 80%.

At that meeting I was also healed of sciatica. I was sitting in my seat while Weston prayed for someone else with sciatica. I had had this sciatic pain down my leg, which was very severe at times, for at least ten years. It simply disappeared as he prayed and has never returned.

I am so grateful to the Lord for all the healings that He has done for me and it has really encouraged me in my Christian walk. Thank You, Lord Jesus. I believe in Your miracle working power.

—*Julie Wightman*

For over seven years I suffered with pain in both my shoulders, back, and right down both legs. A lot of the time the pain was excruciating and would prevent me from doing anything. The pain was always there, and even at the best of times I would only be able to garden for five minutes without having to come inside and sit or lie down.

Miracles in Aotearoa New Zealand

The tablets I was prescribed did not help in any way. In October 2011, I was having a particularly bad time with the pain in the shoulders, back and legs and I could barely move at all. A leaflet came in our letterbox advertising a Christian healing meeting where I live in Flaxmere. Weston Carryer was ministering and I decided that I must go to get healed.

During the early part of the meeting Weston spoke out my condition and I slowly struggled to the front. As he prayed all the pain disappeared and I was able to run across the front of the church. Since that moment, six months ago, I can work and garden for long periods with no pain. My whole life is now so different. Thank You so much, Lord.

—*Taei Tere*

All glory, honour and praise to our wonderful, loving, healing and merciful God. I woke up this morning with great excitement knowing that God was going to do something huge in my life today. I came to the morning service and was surprised by the things God healed me from. It was not what I expected.

I was completely healed from a bladder problem, a hernia, an irritable bowel problem and side effects that I was having from going off twelve years of mental health medication for my post-traumatic stress disorder. Wow . . . all that in one morning.

This afternoon I was sitting at my sister's house deciding what I was going to ask for healing from tonight. God had better plans for me. During the evening service, I felt uncomfortable and sat and fidgeted in my seat. God put on my heart to recommit my life to Jesus which I happily did, as my Christian walk had been less than desirable.

At the end of the service I went up for my healing. When Weston came up to me, my idea of what I wanted to be healed from went out the window. God wanted to heal me of my crippling fear I'd had since I was three and I'm now fifty. I was terrified of the dark, being alone, and of evil spirits which I sometimes saw that were going to get me. These fears have worsened since my husband died 4½ years ago.

It is 4.30 AM the next morning (1 Feb. 2010) and I've been

Overhauls & Unusual Conditions

asleep since 8:00 PM last night. I want to write this while it is still fresh in my mind. I am here alone but I'm not afraid. Last night was the best night's sleep I've had in years—free of fears and nightmares.

Thank you, to my wonderful Father, for Your love, healing and great mercy. I'm so thankful for Weston's obedience to God and for being a vessel for God to heal me through. I will be grateful for this healing for the rest of my days. At last I can say is, I am free!

Now, nine months later, I want to confirm that I am completely healed of all these conditions and symptoms that plagued my life for all those years. I am now able to live the abundant life that Jesus has made available for me according to John 10:10, and I am grateful to the Lord.

—Karen Van Veen

On a special night in 2005, at our Kauri Coast Christian Fellowship in Dargaville, visiting Evangelist Weston Carryer arrived. He asked anyone who wanted prayer and healing for any sickness to come forward. I needed prayer. I'm a guy who is 6 foot 2 inches tall, overweight, and I had many sicknesses. I had high blood pressure, an enlarged heart, and I had no cartilage in my knees. When Weston prayed for me I felt the warmth of God's hand on my heart and on my knees. The Bible teaches us that if you've got faith as small as a mustard seed and believe that you are healed, then you are healed (Matt. 17:20). Praise the Lord. God is good . . . all the time!

I stopped taking my pills and then I visited a doctor (who wasn't my own doctor). He asked me if I was still taking my pills at the right time. I replied, "No, because my God has healed me." His response was that God couldn't do that. I disagreed with him.

On 4 December 2006, I made an appointment to see my doctor for confirmation of my healing. He checked me over and could find nothing wrong with me: my heart was normal, my high blood pressure was normal, and there was no pain or restriction in my knees. There is nothing our Lord Jesus cannot do for you.

People, God delights to give us what we ask for when it is in His will. Never underestimate His desire to respond to our prayers. Be encouraged by the Lord's strong reminder that there are some things that only God can do—saving people is one of them. Praise and glory to our Lord Jesus Christ for the miracles He gave me.

—*Norman Booth*

As a result of a collision with a hospital trolley, for at least five years I suffered problems in my left knee. I could not walk straight, had a limp, and had to continually take Incidid tablets for relief. Owing to a childhood injury to my head, I also suffered from migraine headaches which occurred regularly, and apart from the pain, would cause me to vomit. As well as these conditions I experienced continual back pain.

Eleven months ago at our church in Hastings, you prayed for the Lord to heal all these conditions. I am delighted to write to let you know that all these conditions were healed instantly. I can now walk without a limp, no medication is required, I have no knee or back pain and have not had a sign of a headache since. Lord Jesus, I want to thank You.

—*Ben Revell*

One day in August 2003, I succumbed to a virus infection. This developed in to a bad chest infection and I would shake and shiver uncontrollably. This condition worsened rapidly and affected my whole body, and within a week I could not walk, drive my car, or do any housework at all. I experienced horrific muscle pain and my blood pressure went right down. I needed support to move. Many blood tests and other tests were done as well, but nothing definite was diagnosed. The medication I was given did not help, and so I did not stay on it.

In May 2004, I attended a divine healing meeting in Whangarei where Weston Carryer prayed for me for the Lord to

Overhauls & Unusual Conditions

heal me. At this stage I was not as ill as I had been, but was still far from well and was suffering with many symptoms. There was then a significant improvement and my body continued to improve until July 2004 when the last symptom went from the back of my heel. During this entire time I continually quoted healing Scriptures. I want to thank Weston and the other people in my church who prayed for me and supported me during this time. Above all I want to thank the Lord who has completely healed me of that chronic sickness. Praise You, Jesus.

—*Gillian Haworth*

While riding my motor scooter I was hit by a car, was seriously injured, and not expected to live through the night. However, I survived, but for the next twelve months I suffered continual chronic headaches. My knee and surrounding area was numb with no movement and I could not bend it at all. I was on continual medication.

I attended a divine healing service in Tauranga where Weston Carryer was ministering. As Weston prayed for me, the Lord did a miracle—the feeling came back into my knee, and I was immediately able to bend it like I could prior to the accident. My headaches have ceased and I take no more medication. Praise the Lord.

—*Tania Jackson*

I am in my early sixties. I had a nasty fall in which I hit my face between my nose and upper lip on the edge of a washtub. The force of the fall affected my whole body. The marks and bruises were obvious and extensive. As the days ticked by, I knew I had to seek help, and with the leading of the Lord, I went forward at an altar call for healing at a service where Weston Carryer was the speaker. I was slain in the Spirit, and immediately felt the healing power of God right through my body. The marks and bruises disappeared. It was a tremendous experience and so wonderful to feel completely healed. All praise and glory to our Lord and Saviour, Jesus Christ.

—*Joan D*

Miracles in Aotearoa New Zealand

Twenty-one years ago I was involved in a horrific car crash in which a person was killed. I did not have a seat belt on and received severe whiplash to my neck. After a while I started getting terrible headaches and neck pain which were so severe, that childbirth labour was mild in comparison. The medication I was on for pain relief, which hardly helped the pain, actually caused deterioration in my kidneys. I accepted Jesus Christ as my Lord in late 1999.

In March 2000, I attended a healing meeting at Christchurch Apostolic Church where Weston Carryer was praying for the Lord to heal the sick. As soon as he started to minister, he described in detail what had happened to me and asked the person whose condition he had just described to go forward for the Lord to heal her. I had never experienced anything like this before and was too scared to go forward in front of everybody, but did go up later and Weston prayed for me. I am overjoyed to say that God instantly healed me. Over the last twelve months, I have had no pain or restriction or any medication. Thank You, Jesus.

—*Deborah Ditmer, Christchurch*

I will share the wonderful healings I have experienced as Weston Carryer prayed for me and God's healing power was released into my body. About seven years ago, I was set free from migraine headaches that I had suffered from since the age of thirty years. They would last three days, and occurred every three to four weeks. I would not be able to work during this time. I would have to lie still in a darkened room, I would see stars, and vomit. I had injections given by the doctor, but nothing really helped. That is, till I was prayed for by Weston, and praise God, they have never returned. A miracle!

I suffered from bad sinus problems, which effected me every winter with one to two bouts. In April 2002, I was prayed for by Weston and praise God, no further attacks.

On 28 September 2002, I was again prayed for—this time

Overhauls & Unusual Conditions

for arches in my feet. I was slain in the Spirit and on the floor. Intense heat went through my body—the first time I have experienced this. The heat remained in my body for some time. I now have good arches in my feet. In fact, all through the last week I experienced tightening in my arches. I had just paid for artificial foot arches the day before on 27 September. I am believing to have that $200 returned supernaturally to me.

I thank and praise God for His wonderful healings, and for Weston's great obedience to the call God placed on his life. I pray and ask God to use me to pray for people's healings, for His glory to be manifested, and the captives set free.

—*Marian Esterbauer*

Approximately seventeen years ago I was in a car accident which caused numerous serious head injuries requiring months of medical treatment. This resulted in severe trauma in my life, including regular mini-seizures, severe continual headaches and caused me to have a fall. I became very depressed, and I experienced what I now know were demonic forces trying to destroy me; I became suicidal.

About five years after the first accident, I was knocked out again when a metal gate swung and hit my head in exactly the same area of my head where the impact from the first accident was.

I did not know what I was going to do to get help. Approximately six months after the second accident (which was now ten years ago) I was driving my car and I saw a sign advertising a Weston Carryer healing meeting. I knew I had to attend, and so I did.

That night I heard the gospel and accepted Jesus as my Lord and Saviour. Weston prayed for the Lord to heal me. What happened was amazing. That night I was completely healed of the headaches and mini-seizures, and delivered from all depression and suicidal tendencies. My whole life was transformed.

Over the last ten years I have had no mini-seizures or headaches. I have had to deal with some minor episodes of

Miracles in Aotearoa New Zealand

trauma symptoms, but they have been nothing like they were before the Lord healed me, and now I have no depression or suicidal tendencies. I am a transformed woman by the power of Jesus Christ. Thank You, Lord.

—*Wendy Pearce*

As a result of a car accident two and a half years ago, my pelvis was broken in six places. My right hip, right femur and right tibia were also broken. I was in hospital for five weeks and a metal rod was inserted from the right leg to the hip. As a result of the operations my right leg was twenty-five millimetres shorter than my left leg. After being discharged from hospital, I was unable to walk at all for seven months and I suffered excruciating pain. One year later a bone graft was done. This did not work and an infection developed in my hip; things generally got worse with continued severe pain. Six months after this it was discovered that cancerous cells had developed in my uterus, and I had developed polycystic ovarian syndrome as well.

I heard that Weston Carryer was coming to New Plymouth in February 2006 to minister and I really believed that the Lord would heal me at one of his meetings, so I attended. Initially, I was disappointed when Weston didn't call out any of my conditions, but later in the evening, I went forward and he prayed for my miracle.

For two days after the prayer the pain persisted and then it suddenly disappeared from everywhere in my body. It has never returned over the last five months and I know I am healed. My legs are the same length, I am not restricted in any way, and I can bend my leg normally. Tests done since have revealed that the cancer cells in my uterus have totally gone and the polycystic ovarian syndrome is also healed. Lord, Your works are marvellous and what You have done for me has convinced me of the amazing love that You have for me.

—*Dana D'Ath*

Overhauls & Unusual Conditions

In October 1989, I went to a healing crusade. After responding to a word of knowledge through Weston Carryer, I was healed of curvature of the spine (which was later confirmed by a nurse) along with various lumps and sores. This latter problem had been with me since I turned to Christ and away from drugs and alcohol abuse. In addition, my left leg grew to the same length as my right one—a miracle witnessed by those who stood about me. The next day, the Lord gave me a vision of the ten lepers who went to Jesus and were healed by Him. One only returned to thank the Lord. He was a Samaritan. I believe, and still do, that the Lord was asking me to be as that one. So, I returned to glorify God and thank Him publicly for the healings I had received. I told the assembly all, and as I sat down, the Lord granted me a further healing. As a young teenager I had been refused entry to public swimming baths, had been called a "leper," and was threatened with dismissal by an employer because of the lumps which had grown on the calf of my right leg. Surgical removal proved a failure because they always grew again. On the night I gave testimony of the healings I had received, the Lord chose to also heal me of those emotional hurts and memories.

—*Elizabeth C.*

When I was eleven years old I had an accident that was to lead to a lot of pain and suffering later in life. I was cycling to school when, men working on telephone lines dropped one just as I went underneath it. The wire caught me across the mouth and ripped a tooth out as I was flung to the ground. I got over the shake-up and was more upset about the tooth than the rest of me. Life went on fairly well—teenage years, marriage and family. Life was full and busy.

Looking back, however, I can see that my health and vitality was getting worse. I had a lot of headaches, and neck and back pain. I never seemed to be able to get enough air into my lungs and would find myself taking a really big breath quite often. My body felt like it had a big suit of lead on it and my legs just didn't want to move. The headaches got worse and no doctor could find out why. I could feel my strength going and in 1987, my body gave up and I could not do anything. During the months before this happened, I was confused, depressed, and suicidal. I stopped breathing one day because my brain couldn't get the message to the lungs. I was a mess physically and emotionally, and continually racked with pain. During all this, my precious Jesus was my comfort and I never let Him go. There were times when I wanted to jump off the upstairs deck and finish it all to be free from pain. However, my precious Saviour was so much part of me, I knew I could not do it.

One day I was standing at my sink so confused and in despair I cried out, "O Lord, I am going crazy," and, immediately, I heard in my spirit, "I have not given you a spirit of fear but a sound mind." He knows us so well. I was sent to a specialist who, of course, couldn't find anything wrong, as usual, and he referred me to a psychiatrist. I was screaming inside and knew that no man can get inside me; only Jesus knows me that well. I felt like a little girl with no control over what was going to happen to me. Due to a lot of circumstances, and God's intervention, I never did keep that appointment. The specialist told me I had personality problems and to go home and get on with life the best way I could. I was devastated; and if I had not been a Christian, would have walked out in front of a car right then.

My husband was desperate to find the answer for my health. He was working for a chiropractor and told him my story. I went to this doctor, and through x-rays, he found problems with the top two vertebrae affecting the stem of the brain. He said that this had been caused by a very bad sideways fall. I was able to trace it back to the cycle accident thirty-six years before when the bones would have been soft and still growing. He was totally amazed that I was still upright and walking. The pain was still terrible, and the treatment was extremely painful. I was told it would take at least two years to be anything like normal. During this time I had lots of prayer and love and support from friends and family especially from my wonderful husband. Life became much better; still lots of pain, but more bearable. I began to live life again, was able to drive the car

Overhauls & Unusual Conditions

and run my home and do the garden. I even took on the job of being a nanny for a doctor to a little baby—then two and then three little ones. I was coping, or I thought I was, fairly well. The headaches were often still there and the breathing still the same.

In February 1998, while in the South Island, I had very bad back and chest pain. I was a bit concerned but would not go to a doctor because I was not going to let anything spoil that special holiday. When we came back to the North Island the pain got worse, with all the symptoms of heart attacks, and all the drama that goes with it. I was put on the treadmill, and all was well, but, the pain still didn't go away. Again people prayed, and I fasted, and was anointed with oil. I tried all sorts of natural herbs and some seemed to help with the pain. Again things seemed to get quite a lot better but I would still get the terrible pain in the lungs and crushing in my chest, and found it hard to breathe. In October 2000, I took really sick; again looked like heart problems. I had little sleep and lots of pain, more prayer and crying out to God. On November 20, 2000, I was seen by two chiropractors at the same appointment and was told that my skull was out of alignment and the part of the brain that controls the emotions was squashed. So a lot of questions were answered as to why I had not coped and had been so irrational at times. Also, they found that the chest muscles were adhered to my ribcage, so the lungs could not expand to get enough air. Answers at last! I was to start the long painful treatment for all this on 4 December 2000.

On 22 November, I was told about a Weston Carryer meeting on 28 November and was encouraged to attend. A couple of days later someone else said the same thing. I had been to so many healing meetings, and had so much prayer, I didn't want to hear anybody else tell me that I hadn't been healed because I didn't have enough faith. I really felt too sick to be bothered going to another healing meeting. I said to the Lord, "If one more person asks me to go, then I will." It was Monday afternoon now, so I felt sure that it wouldn't happen. At 9:15 PM I received a call from someone who doesn't usually phone me saying she really felt I should go to the meeting the next night.

Miracles in Aotearoa New Zealand

I went to the meeting, still feeling so sick, and I said to the Lord, "Okay, if this is really You, I want a word of knowledge." I really didn't go to be healed. My faith was about floor level right then. I sat there watching others being prayed for, and then Weston called for a neck injury. I thought, *That's me*, but my husband said, "No, it's not." I stood up and by that time someone else was at the front having prayer. I started to walk up, and he called for something else. I thought, *Okay, that's not me*. Then Weston noticed me, and called me forward. I told him a little of my story . . . about my problem.

He said, "Are your ready to receive your healing?"

I said, "I sure am," and my arms shot in the air. I was struck like lightning and was thrown to the floor. Immediately I started breathing normally. Wonderful . . . lungs full of air and the pain went. Electricity was going down my arms and through my hands, and I could not get them off the floor. I did not hear what Weston prayed over me, and he certainly didn't touch me—only the power of Jesus. I was down there for one hour, but it seemed like five minutes. The next day I could not believe the vitality and joy that I had. I was able to do things that I could not have coped with before. I kept saying, "Lord, I can't believe this." But it was real. On the 3 December, I had my sixtieth birthday, and what a wonderful present God had given me. People kept saying, "You look so different." Yes, I have the joy and spring in my step. Some of my friends find the new bouncy me a little hard to cope with at times, but I know that God has healed and restored the person He created me to be. I don't know why He chose to heal me that night or why it took so long. I know that it's not how much faith we have or what we do or don't do that decides if God will heal us. I am so grateful that I reluctantly went to that meeting and walked to the front. Thank You, Lord, for Your love and faithfulness to me.

—*Jeanette Ellis*

In 1984, at the age of seventeen, I fell down twenty concrete steps and as a result I suffered very bad neck and back damage. This caused extremely severe, continual pain in both my neck and back for the next twenty-four years. Many times

Overhauls & Unusual Conditions

over this period I could not walk at all. At other times I would just suddenly collapse. I never had a day without pain over this entire twenty-four year period.

In 2001, I had my tailbone removed to try and help but this caused me to lose all bladder control, and I became incontinent. A stimulator was then inserted in my lower back to stimulate the nerves to cause my bladder to work.

I attended a divine healing meeting in Papakura on 2 February 2008 where Weston Carryer was ministering and he spoke out my condition, asking me to go forward for him to pray for the Lord to heal me. As he prayed, all the pain and restriction disappeared. It was incredible.

For the last eight months I have had no restriction in my neck or back. I have had some very slight pain in the lower back area but I believe that this is the stimulator which needs adjustment from time to time. My quality of life is now wonderfully different and I am so grateful to the Lord. Thank You, Jesus.

—*Denise Levy*

In 1964, as a result of an accident, my back was severely injured and I had to give up all sports including playing tennis for the rep team. In 1972, when I could no longer bear the pain and could only walk a few yards on crutches, a disc was removed from my back. However, this was not satisfactory, and in 1981, two further discs were removed from my back. Bone was taken from my hip to strengthen my lower back.

Over a forty-four year period I experienced a lot of pain, and at times, it was excruciating. Recently, after more x-rays, it was discovered that I had several fractures and narrowing of discs in my neck and shoulder area which caused a lot of pain and restriction in my neck. My right leg was also one inch shorter than my left one.

On Sunday, 13 April 2008, I went to a healing meeting in Dunedin where Weston Carryer was ministering. As he prayed for me I felt the power of God go into my body, and amongst other things happening, I felt, and saw my right leg grow.

Miracles in Aotearoa New Zealand

On 16 May, I had my medical checkup; my doctor measured my legs and confirmed they were now the same length. On 9 June, I visited my specialist for my neck and shoulders and he said I have great movement in my neck. My back, neck, and shoulders are now completely free of all pain and I have freedom of movement. I give praise to the Lord and thank Him every day for the marvellous healings that have wonderfully blessed me. Thank You, Lord Jesus.

—Joan Hammer

All my life I have lived with pain. I attended Weston Carryer's meeting in Victory Christian Centre in Lower Hutt in November 2012, and his first word of knowledge was for the back condition that I had. Whatever the Lord had for me, I wanted it, and I immediately went forward for Weston to pray for the Lord to minister to me.

Prior to this meeting I had suffered a lot of back pain from this condition. As a child I would often have to lie on the floor for long periods to get some relief from the pain. I also had very sore knees and ankles. My hip would hurt badly and it would continually wake me up in the night. My leg pain at times would also wake me, but the hip pain was different and very cruel. I would also get stabbing pain in my left arm and shoulder, and x-rays had shown that the shoulder was damaged.

If I received even a little knock to my knees, it would cause my legs to collapse from under me and could take up to an hour before I could stand again. As a result, I had many falls. During one fall, I damaged my tailbone, which was very painful and made sitting for long periods difficult.

As Weston prayed for me, the back and hip pain just went. I was so relieved to be without pain, tears flowed gently down my face. The healing was not instant like with some of the other conditions, but Weston prayed for me twice more over the phone.

Although I do have a slight niggle in the back occasionally, now, just over a year later, the difference is huge. It is wonderful to be without that constant and severe pain.

Overhauls & Unusual Conditions

I now have no pain at all in my hip, shoulder, tailbone, or legs; my knees are a lot stronger, and I can sleep soundly through the night. These healings have made a colossal difference to my quality of life and I am so grateful to the Lord for what He has done for me. Thank You, Jesus.

—*Suzanne Green*

I come from a family, of whom many suffered heart problems. This, combined with years of physical abuse, caused me to develop serious heart conditions, which according to my doctor could have caused my death at any time. I had been a professional wrestler, and as a result of this, the bones in my feet had been damaged and I could hardly walk. As well, through wrestling, several discs in my spine were injured, which caused considerable pain.

I attended a healing meeting in Porirua in August 1999, where Weston Carryer was preaching and praying for the Lord to heal the sick. During the meeting the Lord revealed to Weston that there was someone there who had my exact condition stating that if he would respond, the Lord would heal him. I went forward, was prayed for, and the immediate result was that all three conditions were healed.

One year later I can now walk properly. I have had no back pain at all after years of agony, and the doctor has confirmed that my heart is healed. What a God we serve!

—*Ray Holland*

For ten years I suffered terribly from a terminal autoimmune disease. This caused heart failure, liver problems, an enlarged spleen, and I was in dreadful pain all the time despite having at least 800-milligrams of morphine daily. I was treated every six weeks, during which, cell counts of spinal fluid would be taken from my back, just to keep me walking. This procedure always had devastating effects on my body.

In May 1997, I attended a divine healing meeting at

Miracles in Aotearoa New Zealand

Ashburton where Weston Carryer was ministering. He came down to the back of the church because I could not get up. As Weston prayed for me, I experienced a miracle in my body. All the pain and restriction went!

The next morning I got out of bed on my own for the first time in years. The next week my blood count had risen considerably, and it is now almost to the point where the specialists are going to stop the checks. I can ride a bike again and do all the things I have not been able to do for the last ten years. Life is wonderful again. I thank God who, through Jesus Christ by the power of the Holy Spirit, has healed me.

—*G. Mc*

For all of my life I had been sick and had been on antibiotics continually ever since I was a small child. In 1995, I attended a divine healing meeting, although I was not a Christian at that time. For the five years prior to attending the meeting, I had suffered chronically with M.E. I had a kidney infection which was causing me to urinate blood, and I had just had my appendix removed. I felt dreadful and did not care if I lived or died. I went forward for prayer and Weston Carryer prayed for me.

The next day every symptom and affliction had totally gone. For the last twelve months I have enjoyed wonderful health with no medical treatment or antibiotics of any kind. I realized that our heavenly Father, through Jesus, had totally healed me because of His amazing love. He is so real. Soon after this, I accepted Jesus Christ as my personal Saviour and I am living an amazing happy and healthy life.

—*Kim Taylor*

Unusual Conditions

I just want to thank Jesus for giving me an overall healing in my whole body at a Weston Carryer healing crusade, especially

Overhauls & Unusual Conditions

the relief from the shortness of breath which had afflicted me for some sixty-one years. There are two things of which I have no doubts whatsoever: Jesus has given power to His servants to heal just as His Word said He would, and Jesus is willing to heal no matter what your spiritual state is.

—*Maria Apanui*

When my daughter was thirteen months old I was smitten with a stomach infection. Other than prescribing antibiotics, the only advice my doctor gave me was to stay away from fried or fatty foods and eat nothing but boiled meals and salads. The infection itself healed during the course of treatment only to leave behind the peculiar difficulty after every meal of not being able to swallow normally. The saliva would either not go down and sit halfway in my throat, or it would not stay down and come back up again leaving me no option but to spit it out. As time went by, this condition grew worse, requiring me to spit all the time. I also had to get out of bed every night to clear my throat because the saliva would either coagulate or regurgitate, which made swallowing and sleeping impossible.

I was seriously considering another visit to the doctor around the time Weston Carryer came to minister in our church at Rotorua. I went forward for prayer for something else, and more or less as an afterthought, asked him to pray for this condition also. Following the service, I went home and ate a fried meal. Half-an-hour later I realised I continued to swallow normally. That night I slept right through and woke with a clear throat next morning. My daughter is now over twenty so I praise the Lord for healing this affliction which plagued me for nineteen years.

—*Glenis Sayers*

Three weeks before my baby was due to be born it was discovered that the baby was in breech position. As I had a history of difficult births with my other four children, it would have been necessary for me to go to Waikato Hospital for the birth. I had also suffered from haemorrhoids through the entire pregnancy.

I attended a divine healing meeting in Thames in late 1996, where Weston Carryer prayed for these conditions. The baby turned around in my womb immediately to normal delivery position, and the delivery time was under two hours. I had never experienced a birth like this before. The haemorrhoids were totally gone within three days of being prayed for. Thank You, Lord.

—*Karen Reece, Thames*

I was diagnosed as having a hormone imbalance in my body, and for three years, this caused severe pain in my vagina especially when walking. During this time I was treated with estrogen but had no relief. In April 1997, at a Christian healing meeting I was prayed for by Weston Carryer for the Lord to heal me and I was totally healed. I have had no more medication and no more pain. Thank You, Jesus.

—*Heather Harrison-Lee*

I would like to testify to God's goodness regarding prayer I received from Weston Carryer in 2001 when he visited The Centre. As a congregational member of the church, I had gone that morning with an expectant attitude to receive my specific miracle. Weston started speaking out words of knowledge and had mentioned that someone had come specifically that morning for a miracle. He said that person was sitting on his left hand side. That person was me, and I came up for prayer.

I was thirty-six weeks pregnant with my third child and the baby I was carrying was facing the wrong way. Weston prayed that the baby would turn around and that I would have an excellent birth with no complications. Well, later on in the early hours of that morning, I awoke with the most amazing pains and I could feel the baby turning in my stomach, positioning himself correctly. Then, a few days later, I was told by my midwife that the baby had turned around and was ready and

Overhauls & Unusual Conditions

waiting in the perfect position for birth—which I already knew due to your prayer. There was no need for a caesarian section any more! The birth was quick, fast, and the best I have ever had. Praise God!

—*Karen Ngatai*

While I was at work just over five years ago, I suddenly experienced a terrible sensation. I had severe chest pains and felt just like I was floating. I was rushed to the doctor but nothing specific was diagnosed, then or later. For the next five years I suffered a lot of pain. I had to give up work. I progressively became more and more restricted in my movements, and then for four months I could barely walk at all. I was taking a lot of medication.

It was in this condition that I attended a divine healing meeting at Invercargill in March 2004, where Weston Carryer was ministering. I was not a Christian but I was desperate and prepared to try anything. During the ministry time, with the help of other people, I managed to get to the front to be prayed for. As Weston prayed for me I felt the Lord's power go into my body and the pain started to go. I knew then that Jesus Christ was alive and I asked Him to be my Lord. Within a few days all the pain and restriction was gone. I went off all medication for this condition. Over the last year I have had no sign of this condition. I am now totally committed to Jesus. Thank You, Lord, so much.

—*Gary Wilson*

Four years ago, as a result of experiencing flu-like symptoms for some time, I went to a doctor and he prescribed penicillin for me. I took the first tablet immediately, and within minutes, I went scarlet all over my body and had this horrendous itch. I managed to get back to the medical centre and then collapsed and went into cardiac arrest. When I woke up I was being given an injection. I was then taken to hospital in an ambulance. I was discharged the following day, but for the next three and a half years, I felt terrible the whole time and could not get any help from doctors or specialists. I had to force myself to go to the supermarket and only going out when absolutely necessary. It was always difficult to breathe and I passed out completely on two occasions. I did not know what to do next.

In February 2007, I was invited to a divine healing meeting in Tauranga where Weston Carryer was ministering and praying for the sick. I had never been to a healing meeting before. As Weston prayed for me, the power of God knocked me backwards onto the floor. Within two weeks of being prayed for, my health was completely restored and I have not had any further symptoms for the last nine months. I am still amazed at what the Lord did for me.

—*Judith Watson*

For a number of years, I had a condition which affected me in different ways. I would become breathless, and walking even short distances was impossible. My hands were always freezing and my feet went almost black. I became so limited in what I could do.

Five months ago, I rang Weston Carryer and he prayed for me over the phone. As he prayed for me, the Lord completely healed me. The normal colour returned to my feet, and the iciness just went from my hands. I was no longer breathless and I was immediately able to walk around the entire golf course with no restriction or stopping.

I just want to praise the Lord for my healing. What a difference in my life.

—*Harriet Tregoweth*

I was born with a rapid heartbeat, which at times was up to 300-beats per minute. In my early years, different medications were tried, but they only helped temporarily and the heartbeat would revert to how it was.

I was never able to run at all. Whenever I did try, I would have to stop immediately as my breathing was impaired and

Overhauls & Unusual Conditions

I would have a sharp pain around my heart area. Sometimes it would be weeks before the pain went and normal breathing resumed.

An operation was tried when I was thirteen, but this was not successful. When I became pregnant with my first child, the heart action changed and the beat became very irregular.

In September 2013, I attended a divine healing meeting in Helensville where Weston Carryer was ministering. He pointed to a side section of people where I was sitting and said there was someone there with an irregular heartbeat that the Lord wanted him to pray for. I went forward, and as Weston prayed for me, a miracle took place. My heart immediately started to beat regularly and at the right rate. I experienced an incredible surge of energy and my whole body felt marvellous, so different to how it had always been. That night I had difficulty sleeping because of this new energy, and I realised this must be how normal people feel.

Since that moment, now over seven months ago, I have had an entirely new lease of life. I exercise regularly now, which I couldn't do before, and am training to run a charity marathon. I don't take any medication. My life is now so different to what it was for all those years. Thank You so much, Lord Jesus.

—*Suzanne MacCracken*

I have had problems with my legs all my life. Whenever I scratched them, I would end up with sores for periods of eight months and more. Sores also developed from nowhere. Doctors called it cellulitis, that is, inflammation of tissues of the body which is evidenced by pain, swelling, or redness of the affected area. Once I had an operation on a leg when one and a half pints of pus was removed. When children were near me, I was always wary because even the slightest touch by them meant agony.

Praise God, Weston prayed against the condition and it has been removed. I am 22 stone (139kg), can walk as far and as

Miracles in Aotearoa New Zealand

fast as anyone else, and run where I am not slowing anyone down.

—*M. A. Boyce*

I had leptospirosis, caught while farming, and had suffered violent headaches ever since. Weston Carryer prayed for me on Queen's birthday weekend in 1995 at the City Life Church, Tauranga. I have not had a headache since. Praise God.

—*Royce Wynyard*

I'm so thankful for Weston Carryer praying for me at the Hornby Presbyterian Community Church (February 2003). The doctors were concerned that the blood salts in my system were very low and not improving, as expected. My daughter and son-in-law brought me forward at the altar call and we explained this condition, and Weston specifically prayed for healing. The power of God caused me to fall from the wheelchair.

I am happy to be able to tell you that the results of the blood tests last week show a remarkable improvement, so much so I don't have to have the medication, which has given me very harsh side effects in the past. I am so thankful to Weston and thank God for the way He uses the gift of healing that He gave him.

—*Audrey Scott*

For seven years I suffered badly from M.E. Prior to this condition afflicting me I was capable of being a full time school teacher, but chose to be part time in order to look after my children. However, after getting this illness I was only capable of teaching part time as a relieving teacher. I felt as if I had the flu all the time, but worse still, about every six weeks I would have very bad episodes when I literally could not do anything at all. I dreaded these times. Nothing medically was any help to me at all.

Overhauls & Unusual Conditions

Two years ago I attended a divine healing meeting in Christchurch where Weston Carryer was ministering and he prayed for the Lord to heal me. My healing commenced immediately, and over a period of a few months, my health steadily improved to the point where I had my life back. I no longer have these bad episodes and the worst I feel these days is occasionally feeling slightly off colour.

I am now well and ready to teach full time again once the position I am looking for becomes available. Lord, I am so grateful for what You have done.

—*Robyn De Mandeville*

As He entered the village,
ten leprous men
who stood at a distance met Him;
and they raised their voices, saying,
"Jesus, Master, have mercy on us!"
When He saw them, He said to them,
"Go and show yourselves
to the priests."
And as they were going,
they were cleansed.

–Luke 17:12-14, NASB

Ten

Skin

Testimonies of healed conditions of the skin, i.e., eczema, dermatitis, psoriasis, warts, scars, etc.

Eczema

At a meeting at Paraparaumu Family Church on 27 May 1990, Josh was healed completely from food allergies—widespread swelling from eggs, severe widespread eczema from birth due to dairy products. He was unable to eat eggs, dairy products, and at times chicken or beef due to these allergies. Two days before he was prayed for, he had reacted to some milk he had taken before we could stop him. From the time he was prayed for and healed, he has had no dietary restrictions and no side-effects. Previously his reaction to egg had been so immediate that if he had put his hands in the water of a soaking bowl containing traces of egg white, his hands would immediately swell. Afterwards, nothing . . . he reacts in no way at all.

—*Jill Knox, Paraparaumu*

Dermatitis was part of my life for nineteen years. In August 1987, Weston Carryer conducted a crusade in Ruatoria. A number of us from Gisborne attended. I had not gone in expectation of a healing for myself. During one meeting I was called out for my particular complaint. Weston took hold of my hands and advised me not to pray because he would. I remember the words, "In Jesus' name, be healed." My first reaction was to think, *Well, that was not much of a prayer.* Despite the thought, I did believe for healing.

It is now April 1990, and to this day I have not had the itching or the bleeding hands which I often woke up to after a night of scratching while asleep. I have not purposely tested my healing but have had to use many strong detergents and cleaning agents on occasions without a rash or a pimple appearing. From a very simple prayer, and much faith, God has healed me!

—*Sal Nikora*

I suffered from a very itchy skin irritation on my arms and legs which I had for about six months. I attended a healing meeting where Weston Carryer prayed for the Lord to heal me. The itch and skin inflammation went after about three months and I have not had any problem for over nine months now. Thank You, Lord.

—*Richard Baxter*

In November 1999, at a Full Gospel Business meeting I asked Weston Carryer to pray for a weepy sore which was about two-and-a-half-inches long that I'd had for two years or more. I had been to my GP but his first reaction on seeing it was,

Skin

"Ooh, yuk! What a mess." This remark didn't make me feel too great, I can tell you. The doctor prescribed cream that I was to apply three times a day, and then I was to go back to him after a week. My husband told my doctor that he thought it looked like some type of skin cancer but the doctor's reply was, "We will see what happens in the next week." I never found out what this thing on my neck was as I was too embarrassed by the doctor's reaction. I never went back. My husband would try and tell me to go back but I just let it fall on deaf ears. If people spotted this thing on my neck their reaction was the same as the doctor's. I knew, at this stage, what a leper must have felt like. I started to keep it covered at all times.

The night I asked Weston to pray for me, my first words to him were, "Please don't say, 'Ooh, yuk!' to what I am about to show you on my neck."

Weston's reply to me was that he would never do that and he then proceeded to pray. Nothing much happened that night, but a few days later, while having a shower, I asked the Lord if He would please heal this thing supernaturally. At the end of that week, Weston was to hold a seminar on the Saturday and take both services at the Hastings City Elim Church, which I attended. It was at the Sunday evening service that I went and asked Weston to pray for this thing again. As I had been selling Weston's books for him, I was the last person to be prayed for. Nothing happened that night but a few days later, the thing on my neck was disappearing.

Now, praise the Lord, all that I have on my neck is a white scar which looks just as if I had had an operation. Quite often I am asked if I have had an operation on my neck. I explain, "No, I didn't have an operation. But Jesus healed me of a thing that I'd had there. He was the Surgeon." It has been great to let people see what the power of God can do.

—*Kathy Grooby*

I suffered from psoriasis for several years and decided to go forward at a healing service at my church where Weston Carryer was speaking. I praise God because His healing power came upon me. I have had no return of this itching skin disease over the last two years. I claim the victory in the name of Jesus Christ, my Lord and Saviour.

—*Meryl Sears*

I recently watched a programme on television about faith healing, featuring Weston Carryer and Bill Subritzky. During the broadcast of the programme, I was reminded of my own healing after being prayed for at a Weston Carryer meeting. I have been carrying his pamphlet around, *Keeping Your Healing*, ever since it was given to me at the Apostolic Church in November 2000.

At the service, Weston called for someone with psoriasis to come forward. I was not sure it was me as I only had small amounts of psoriasis. Weston was insistent, so I said I have a little bit of psoriasis. I went up still unsure why psoriasis and not something major, like a stroke. Father God ministered to me so swiftly and I was out on the floor for a long time being ministered to—crying and laughing and shaking. I remember trying to stand but could not get above about two feet. The Holy Spirit wasn't done with me until He was done with me!

Well, the first thing that happened was the itching went. Psoriasis—no matter how much it itches and you scratch—weeps and flakes, and you scratch more just to be free of the itch. Now the psoriasis site on my knee has lovely new skin and no sign of where it was. The psoriasis that was on my scalp and up the back of my head has also gone. My hairdresser can't believe it. Here I am some ten months later and I am psoriasis-free.

—*June Lott*

I heard from a friend that Weston Carryer had a healing ministry. I went to one of his meetings in September 1990, with the expectation of being totally healed of both a rare eczema condition, which had been with me since the age of fourteen, and unbearable abdominal pains. The latter were triggered off

Skin

by certain things such as jobs, food, and stress and so on. I answered the call to go forward for healing. Weston prayed against a curse and healing from my infirmities in Jesus' name. I am now absolutely free. I know, because I do not have to use creams and lotions any more, besides which I can do certain jobs and eat certain foods now without distress. I thank God for Weston's ministry and for His healing me.

—*Cheryl Eade*

For fifteen years, I suffered from severe psoriasis. I had continual itching and my skin used to peel and fall off everywhere I went. I was so embarrassed that I always wore clothes which covered me completely in order that people could not see this hideous scaling on my arms and legs. At one stage I was hospitalised for a month with this condition but nothing could be done medically for me.

Two years ago I attended a Christian healing meeting and when Weston Carryer prayed over me, I was healed totally by God through Jesus. The itching stopped straightaway, and within a few days, all the skin was restored to normal. Praise the Lord.

—*Noreen Thomas*

Almost a year ago I had been suffering from psoriasis of the scalp as well as the body. To be honest it was more of a nuisance than anything else—but it was a nuisance that I was sick of (no pun intended). At a divine healing meeting at Kapiti Coast, Weston Carryer called out this condition. He prayed for me and I went down on the floor. Though I didn't feel anything at the time, as soon as I got back to my seat, my wife commented that all the scaliness and so forth, seemed to be going. By that afternoon there was a marked improvement. Within a week—no flaky bits, no brushing stuff off my clothes, no itchiness! Totally healed! Praise God! And it hasn't come back since!

I thank God for my miracle! I pray that it may be an encouragement to others.

—*Barri Dullabh*

Miracles in Aotearoa New Zealand

When I heard that Weston Carryer, a healing evangelist, was coming to our church, Good Life Community Church, Queensland, I wanted to be there to receive healing. I have been suffering from dermatitis for ten years in a mild manner, but severely the last three years. It is a skin condition that reddens and ruptures the central part of my face. Only recently married, I wanted my former clear skin back. So I decided to go the evening service by myself without my husband and our one-and-a-half-year-old son.

After the main part of the service, everyone could go up for prayer for healing. Weston Carryer prayed for me briefly, specifically praying against the curse that causes sickness. I went down in the Holy Spirit and felt this light flurry of activity around my back. When I got up, I decided to go to the ladies to see if my face had improved. I didn't notice any change. So I decided to go home. As I was walking to the car and driving home I noticed that I was walking and sitting very erect, unlike ever before. I thought to myself, *I just feel good because I've had an evening out by myself*—something rare for me. But when I got up the next day, I knew I had been absolutely, totally healed of my long-term arthritic back—something I didn't ask for because I hadn't any idea how bad it was until I was healed.

For more than eight years I have been going monthly to chiropractors to have my back adjusted to avert pain. In one brief encounter with the Living God, my back was totally restored with new discs. I grew 3.5-cm as proof and it was easy to carry myself lightly and erectly. I kept my usual appointment with the chiropractor two weeks later to verify my healing. I didn't say much at first, just that I felt good. He didn't have much to do because my back would put itself right if I misaligned it. He said it is much better and since then instead of monthly, I go six weekly just for maintenance, and they have very little to adjust. Now, nine months later, I have absolutely no pain or restriction of any kind. My face has improved dramatically; however, some of the rash still lingers. I praise God for His mercy and love.

—*Julia Corradetti*

Skin

When I was about eight years old I had two chronic skin conditions on my feet for a year. No amount of treatment would make them disappear. I could not sleep at night and I would be in terrible pain. These conditions made it very difficult for me to participate in sports, especially gymnastics which I loved. If I did participate, my feet would immediately blister.

My Dad took me to a divine healing meeting in Invercargill where Weston Carryer prayed for the Lord to heal me. I was healed almost immediately. The skin cleared and I was able to have relief from these two chronic conditions. For the last seventeen years I have had no further skin trouble. This healing convinced me of the love the Lord had for me and I have followed Him ever since. Praise be to God.

—*Emma Campbell*

For over six years I had psoriasis over my entire body all the time. This caused chronic continual itching for which I could never get any relief. I tried many different crèmes, but nothing helped in any way.

I attended a divine healing meeting in Winton in March 2007, where Weston Carryer was ministering. During the ministry time, he prayed for the Lord to heal me. Within four days all the psoriasis had cleared up and the itching had completely stopped. Over the last twelve months there has been no sign of it at all. What a wonderful joy it is to be healed. Thank You so much, Lord Jesus.

—*Mark Officer*

On 13 November 2011, I took my daughter Zara to Harvest Church where Weston Carryer was having a divine healing meeting. Zara had eczema and I had taken dairy and citrus out of her diet and was using no soap or detergent products on her skin or clothes. It was particularly bad on her upper body and any exposed skin—especially the back of her neck—and it would be scratched till it bled leaving her neck raw. She had

suffered this condition for approximately four months.

During the service Zara's condition was not called but I took her forward at the service's end and she was prayed for. It took a couple of days to clear and I continued to pray over her. Within a fortnight it had gone completely—no more bleeding necks or upper arms. Over the last five months there has been no more sign of it whatever. Praise God. She now loves a bubble bath. Hallelujah.

—*Bridget Gifford*

I am seventy-years old and for thirty-five years, I had psoriasis on the soles of my feet. They first had the form of pustulous lumps, which then went into a brown scale and then peeled off. I had been treated by dermatologists and skin specialists for all of the thirty-five years. Every night I had to rub ointment on my feet, wrap them in glad wrap and then put socks on for the entire night to get some relief from this chronic continual irritation.

However, when Weston Carryer was at the Invercargill Christian Centre in March 2006, I received prayer from him for this condition. While he held my hands I received a jolt—similar to an electric shock. About seven days later, I had no lumps or scales left on my feet. Six months later they still look clear. I praise the Lord and give Him all honour and glory.

—*Shirley Morehu*

As a result of having had shingles eleven months previously, my left arm was covered in swollen scars which would not go away.

At a church service in Wanganui in July 2001, Weston Carryer prayed for the Lord to heal and remove all the scars. Two days later, all the scars, except for one which had considerably reduced in size and was almost gone, had totally disappeared and my arm was normal. I am rejoicing and praising the Lord. Thank You, Jesus!

—*Lynne Ruscoe (Wanganui)*

When evening came,
many who were demon-possessed
were brought to him,
and he drove out the spirits
with a word and
healed all the sick.

–*Matthew 8:16, NIV*

Eleven

Deliverance, Inner Healing & Other Conditions

Testimonies of healed conditions through deliverance, as well as other conditions not defined in a general category (i.e., inner healing, insomnia, depression, abuse, anxiety, fear, bedwetting, emotional trauma, addictions, etc.).

For approximately twenty years, after being expelled from high school for attacking my form teacher, my life was a disaster. From an early age, the big time for me was drinking, womanizing, and at a later stage, indulging in drugs. Even though I would settle for a period, the cycle would recur time and again. I spent time in Borstal and in prison. My lifestyle cost me my first marriage, and my second marriage was breaking up for the same reasons. Ultimately, I asked to be taken back, but was refused.

One night, I heard my wife and her friends talking of going to a healing crusade conducted by Weston Carryer. I was curious so offered to take them. The people were nice and I did not feel left out. I had predetermined that in no way was I going to become a Christian. How wrong I was! When the call for salvation came, my hand went up, even though I did not put it up. Somebody did it for me. Man, was I scared! Since all heads were bowed, would anyone have seen my hand raised? Weston asked for all who put their hands up to go forward and accept the Lord into their hearts in front of everyone. Man, that was freaky. With my wife alongside me, I went and had prayer for all my addictions, and also asked the Lord into my heart. I fell backwards and had the sensation that a mighty hand had gripped my stomach and wrenched something out. I felt it physically. I had decided I was not going to fall back when Weston prayed over me. Wrong, again. By this stage I was past worrying because something had happened to me and my whole body felt really strange, just as if I was floating on a cloud. Since that day my life has been great. Once I would have been afraid of what people thought. But the day after my conversion, I was up first thing in the morning and off to tell as many friends as I could before going to work, of the mighty things which had taken place. What I had been searching for all my life, I have found in becoming a Christian.

I must thank my wife for the years she has stood besides me and helped me. If I was asked to summarize my spiritual and physical healing in a single, graphic phrase, it would read simply this: From hell to Jesus Christ.

—W.H.

I went to a meeting conducted by Weston Carryer, during which he spoke on "being anxious." I thought, *Yes, I know all about that.* I am aware it is a sin, and even had underlined all the appropriate verses in the Bible to remind me. Anxiety indicates you do not trust God to care and provide for you. I had thought I was overcoming that. Weston continued on about "guarding your heart." I was conscious of the need for this in the physical. The night before the meeting I had a terrible pain which I thought was my heart, although I was unsure. I wanted to avoid that happening again but wondered how. When I went forward for prayer, I did so rather sheepishly, for God's Word informs us to be anxious about nothing. Despite conviction to the contrary, I was actually producing the fruits of it. Weston prayed for release from this affliction. A few days later it was confirmed the sharp pain was probably my heart under tension. Since I had been freed through prayer I had to believe I would be guarded and protected from stress. Strangely, disciplining myself against being anxious had the reverse effect, so I prayed, "Lord, I cannot do this by myself. Please help me and show me how." That night I had the most awful nightmares and awoke with strong palpitations. I realised I needed God to penetrate the subconscious and remove the obstruction from there, as well as restore the heart areas affected by stress. I am thankful for Weston's prayer for healing of the emotional, and of stress pains across the neck, shoulders and arms that has contributed to a greater sense of well-being and ability to cope again. God is performing a wonderful healing. Now, when I become anxious, I stop and thank the Lord for showing me His better way.

—*Marie Campbell*

For twenty-one years I have been a bedwetter—a problem which is not only irksome from a health point of view, but is distressing mentally too. It is a very socially restricting disorder. In late 1990, I attended a Weston Carryer Crusade and was prayed over for this affliction. I have been cured physically and the lurking fears and doubts are also gone. I thank God each day for my healing and claim continued freedom from ills.

—*D.W.*

When Weston Carryer was in Feilding recently, I asked for a release from the power of fear over my life. I had become afraid of driving on the open road as a consequence of a car accident. This weekend I drove to Waipukurau with so much confidence I knew the Lord had given me a release from this fear. Praise His name.

—*L.W.*

Miracles in Aotearoa New Zealand

I'm so thankful for the time and prayer Weston Carryer gave me in making the healing power of Jesus available through the gifting God gave you. And I'm thankful too, that he was so faithful to the calling on his life. I'm aware it's not always been easy, and has actually been an offering or personal sacrifice to Him —and a sweet aroma before the throne of God our Father.

In 1994, at Weston's farewell service at New Plymouth Apostolic Church, I went forward for prayer, and asked him to pray for complete healing of my nervous system (which had been very sensitive and obviously not functioning as it should . . . from birth I think). Something happened that night which restored a measure of coordination. Before that I had not been able to carry certain things like trays, or cups of tea in each hand at once. That evening after I went home, I found myself carrying a tea in each hand, as if I had always done it. That ability has remained. Weston Carryer was God's faithful ambassador.

—Lorna Messenger

For at least fifteen years, I suffered from manic depression and on numerous occasions, had been confined to psychiatric institutions. I was also an alcoholic. Doctors stated I would have to be on medication for the rest of my life. I went to a healing meeting where Weston Carryer was ministering. He prayed for me for deliverance from depression and alcoholism. Several days later, I realised I had forgotten to take my medication and became aware that I no longer had need of it. Now, four years later, I have had no medication nor depression. I have no desire for alcohol either and lead a normal life. I had another wonderful healing from the Lord at a later date.

For three years I suffered terribly from constipation and other bowel problems resulting from a twisted bowel. I attended a further meeting at which Weston was ministering where, through a word of knowledge, he asked me to go forward because God wanted to heal my bowel. He prayed for me and, by the power of the Holy Spirit, through Jesus, God completely and instantly healed me. I praise Him for His love and my transformed life.

—C. J.

In my early twenties, I suffered anxiety neurosis (a mental disorder, which was a very frightening thing to live with). I was prescribed a drug called Ativan to relieve the distress, and became really addicted to it. I was taking six other drugs at the same time. Five years ago I gave my heart to Jesus and committed my life to Him. Some time after, I was tuned to Radio Rhema and heard Weston Carryer speaking. I rang to talk with him, missed out, but left my number. He rang the next day and when told of my anxiety neurosis, prayed for me and recommended I read Philippians 4:4-8 every day for a year.

> *Whatever is true, whatever is noble, whatever is right, whatever is pure, whatever is lovely, whatever is admirable—if anything is excellent or praiseworthy—think about such things* (NIV).

I carried this out faithfully. I thank God each day that within the year, I went off all the drugs and have been completely free from any distress or disorder for four years.

—Mary Dunick (Invercargill)

Thanks be to my Lord and my God for His love, power, goodness and faithfulness to His Word. Through the ministry of Weston Carryer, the Holy Spirit revealed that I was suffering from a spirit of rejection, and I received prayer against it. Two days later I was put to the test. I visited my husband's parents to find she was having a nap after receiving news of an impending operation while he was distressed for his wife. As he waited for her to awaken, I asked if he minded me praying for her. He became angry, attacked my faith, told me I was being brainwashed, and felt quite threatened. Between silences, I continued to quote Scripture to support my belief, telling him he must be born again of the Spirit to enter the Kingdom of

Miracles in Aotearoa New Zealand

God. Amazingly, no matter how much abuse he threw at me I felt only love and compassion for him. I did finally pray with her and asked God to heal her in Jesus' name. I am truly grateful to God for this opportunity to witness. It is now over to Him to draw them to Himself through Jesus Christ and the Holy Spirit.

—*S.H.*

I began smoking as a teenager and had been smoking about fifteen cigarettes a day for ten years. Even though I knew it was bad for me, I did it anyway. I went to a healing meeting at the Lion's Den where Weston Carryer was praying for the sick. I had no intention of giving up smoking and had left my smokes in the car so nobody would see them.

A man went up for prayer and Weston said, "This man wants to give up smoking." So he asked if anyone else wanted to give up as well. To my surprise I responded and received prayer. On the way home I grabbed my cigarettes and threw them out the window. Thank God I have been free for eight years.

—*Charmaine Robinson*

About September 1991, I travelled from Invercargill to Dunedin to attend a Weston Carryer healing meeting. I had a craving for bananas, eating five to eight kilograms a week. To keep my weight down I had to exercise—running, cycling, swimming, weights, and so forth—to keep this craving under control. Weston suddenly said that there was someone present who had an addiction to bananas. I was out of my seat like a shot. He prayed for me and instantly my craving left me. I will now eat and enjoy only three or four bananas a week. Praise God.

—*Don Munro*

For fourteen years, I suffered very badly from anxiety disorders and had been on medication for this for four years as well as being on antidepressants for two years. I always had terrible irrational fears, especially a major fear about death, and had psychosis towards medication.

I attended a divine healing meeting at New Plymouth in August 1997, where Weston Carryer was praying for the Lord to heal people. I was a new Christian at the time and I still marvel at what Jesus did that night. As Weston prayed for me, the power of God came upon me and forced the demons (which been controlling my life) out of me and I had an instant total deliverance. It was amazing. Since that night I have had no more fear, no more antidepressants or any other medication. I am rejoicing in being completely fear-free. I am now a normal person. Hallelujah! What a God we serve!

—Debbie Croton, New Plymouth

Weston Carryer visited Taumarunui Apostolic Church on Sunday, 3 May. This is my testimony. I used to smoke twenty-five to thirty cigarettes a day. I had tried to stop, but the craving beat me each time. I even tried patches; they didn't work either. I have been a smoker for over thirty years. That evening I asked Mr. Carryer for God's healing touch. He said, "If God takes away the desire to smoke, do you promise never to put another cigarette in your mouth?"

I said, "Yes, I promise." I had my last cigarette just before going to church that evening. I have not smoked since. No desire! No craving! No withdrawal symptoms! Praise the Lord; He is so good! My family are delighted; they used to say that there was always a smoke haze around me.

Thank You, Jesus. Thank You! I'm thankful that Weston Carryer was God's healing instrument here in New Zealand. Praise be to God Almighty for His wondrous love.

—E. Ryan

I have been a smoker for over forty years, trying just about everything there was on the market (i.e., Nicobrevin, chewing gum, patches, going cold turkey even) to try and break free from the habit. But, to no avail. I became a Christian in September

Miracles in Aotearoa New Zealand

of 1995 at the age of fifty-seven, and on Sunday, 16 October 1995, I attended a healing meeting led by Weston Carryer. He invited anyone who needed healing to come to the front to get prayed over. I thought, if Jesus can't help me, no one can. I found myself up the front asking Jesus to help me break free from my addiction to smoking. I was slain in the Spirit, and immediately, the desire for nicotine left me. I came through without any withdrawal symptoms, and to this day, 1 March 1997, I can honestly say that I have never touched a cigarette and have no desire to do so in the future. Isn't God good? I wondered why I left it so late in my life to find Him. I know He loves me and I love Him. Praise the Lord.

—*Dorrie Espener, Taupo*

My life had been empty with no inner peace, no contentment, no joy, everything destructive, all of which had led to ill-health, suffering, and much physical sickness and pain. Over many years, and applying orthodox medical diagnoses, no practitioner could detect a real physical cause for my condition. Finally, God cleansed and forgave me, and when I focused on Him, a miracle happened. The Lord Jesus touched me and made me whole. He used Weston Carryer as His instrument to heal me completely from osteoarthritis, a bone-crippling disease. All honour, praise and glory be to Almighty God for the compassion, love and fulfillment of all He promises and freely gives to all.

—*"A Child of God"*

God healed me. I was deep in the depths of despair wondering how I could face the future. My life was a mess: I had emotional and sexual problems; I could not relax, and my mind was a whirl of tormenting thoughts. As a mother, I was unfit and cried constantly. I did not know where to put myself or how to cope with any situation. During a Weston Carryer healing crusade, I was totally healed by God. My life is tolerable now and each new day is a challenge.

—*L.S.*

Deliverance, Inner Healing & Other

I went to a meeting conducted by Weston Carryer, albeit rather reluctantly, distressed, confused, grieving, and in pain from all the anguish of some twenty-one years accumulation. To begin with, our beautiful twenty-six-year-old unmarried Christian daughter came to us with the shattering news she was pregnant. My husband, as yet non-Christian, was devastated. It was a very difficult time but God brought me through fairly quickly. The wee chap was born late 1986. He was born handicapped—yes, a Down's boy. I shed many tears but God taught me some very precious truths. Today, he is my pride and joy and latterly, that also of my husband. In mid-1987, my younger sister who suffered from a bad heart, died. It was a shock and one I was not prepared for. Eight months later, my father, with whom I was very close, also died. In June of 1988, our dear and very much loved son of thirty who had been redeemed and restored by God about five years previously, was killed in a horrific car accident caused by an eighteen-year-old drunken driver. With his death came a deep, gaping hole and a constant tearing, unbearable pain.

Shortly after this I received prayers for deliverance at a meeting, but these had a reverse effect. I confess I had hit rock bottom and was ready to opt out. I reasoned, in the natural, that if this was all that God could do, I had nothing to lose by changing sides. It was at this point a close friend invited me to spend a few days with her and go to hear Weston as she believed God wanted to minister to me. I can assure you I wanted no more of God's ministering for I had had more than enough. Fortunately, her persistence prevailed. I went forward for healing and was absolutely enveloped in, and overwhelmed by, His compassion. I was completely healed, restored and renewed. He has taken my pain and replaced it with peace, my confusion with assurance, my grief with joy, and my doubts with certainty. Truly, He is "able to do exceedingly more than I am able to think or ask" and He is bringing life out of death.

—B.N.B.

Miracles in Aotearoa New Zealand

Weston Carryer prayed for us both at his home. I came because of insomnia problems. I had felt the Lord ask me to come to Weston. After his prayer, my sleep patterns began to improve. By the end of February, I was fully healed. All told, I had had the problem for six months, sometimes going several nights without sleep, and developing a growing dependency on sleeping tablets which were giving me much concern. I really do praise the Lord for His great healing. In fact, every morning I thank Him for His goodness.

—*Peter Brock*

I had been suffering from post-trauma syndrome for sometime. It had been so bad that it had affected my relationship with those around me. It had so affected my self worth and confidence that I had to be put off work with little chance of returning. It all started in India while I was travelling with some other Christians to a nearby village. A motorcyclist was travelling the other way, and when we started to get closer, he swerved into our path. The van veered off the bank into a tree. The people in the van were cut and bruised. As I made it to the road to see if the man on the motorbike was alright, I witnessed that the insides of his head were laying all over the road. But after the prayer I received from God, I have been able to return to work, rebuild good friendships, prove myself competent in the workshop, sleep better, and I have just completed a series of unit standards to prove to my employers that I am a competent worker. I thank the Lord Jesus Christ for the healing, and for Weston taking the time to pray for me.

—*Andrew Hoogland*

About 1984, I developed a very painful condition that affected my entire body from my neck to my feet. Apart from severe pain, my movements were becoming more and more limited. Two and a half years later when I became unable to shift the gear lever in the car I went to the doctor. There was swelling in many parts of my body and my fingers just looked like sausages with the skin being so taunt, and parts of my body were blue with inflammation. I was referred to Queen Elizabeth Hospital in Rotorua and became a patient there for three and a half weeks. The specialist diagnosed zero-negative polyarthritis. I was put on very strong medication and told that I would need to take it for life.

In 1988, I went to a divine healing meeting in Tokoroa where Weston Carryer was ministering. In his message he explained that God forgives us when we accept Jesus as our Lord and that we must also forgive everyone, no matter what they have done or said to us. This really spoke to me and I realized how much unforgiveness I had in me. Weston also said that if we harbour unforgiveness it will cause physical sickness in our bodies. I immediately totally forgave everybody for anything they had done to me. Weston then prayed for the Lord to heal me. I stopped all medication that night, and over a short space of time, all pain and swelling went and has never returned. Now fifteen years later, I am living a healthy life. Thank You, Jesus.

—*Atawhai Marriner*

Last year in February, I attended a healing meeting conducted by Weston Carryer at the Hornby Presbyterian Church. Even though I had previously experienced God's healing touch, I went with a totally open mind. Many went forward when their specific ailments were called, and almost all received immediate help. Towards the end of the meeting the call came for any who felt they may still have need of healing. My friend who had invited me said, "Well, if you want to, then go." So I went forward, and while standing waiting, and without prior thought, bowed my head and said, "Lord, let it be me—let it be my turn." At my request Weston prayed for my depression which had been a long-term problem, and also for my diabetes, a more recent problem. Before I even reached the floor, I knew my depression and diabetes had both gone completely!

It was so good lying comfortably on the floor, thanking and praising God that I was in no hurry to get up. Now a year later,

Miracles in Aotearoa New Zealand

I'm still very thankful for feeling so great, and I give thanks and praise to God for His compassion and for this miracle. Also I'm thankful that Weston was a willing agent of God's healing.

—*Liz Boyd*

God used Weston to heal me, around May 2001 at Alive Church, Kelston Girls School. Weston prayed for my internal organs that God would heal my kidneys and liver that had been very badly damaged over a period of thirty-seven years of drinking alcohol and taking all manner of drugs. At the time that Weston prayed for me, my kidneys were healed and I have continued to be healed by God physically, mentally, morally, emotionally, and spiritually. I have been set free from addictions, and never enjoyed better health than I do today. Mighty is the healing power of Christ Jesus. Bless His Holy name.

—*Warwick Anderson*

For quite a few years now I have suffered from depression and neck pain. I had refused antidepressants from my doctor after hearing how bad they can be, so I was praying to God for a healing. I have been a Christian for just over a year and have also been battling to understand the Bible and what God was trying to teach me. I came to Weston's healing meeting and prayed so hard for God to help me. Weston called out to someone who had been for recent blood tests, and even though I felt deep down it was me and my heart was beating fast, I didn't go up. After the meeting, God spoke to me and told me to go up. Weston prayed for me and I felt an awesome presence of God as my head and neck felt warm and tingly. I had never felt such peace and assurance in my life. I can confidently say that God healed me that day and I have been a different person. I have so much energy and no pain in my neck. I am taking in every word in the Bible and no more depression. Thank You, Jesus.

—*Tracey MacLeod*

Deliverance, Inner Healing & Other

I pray that my testimony may be a source of encouragement to anyone who has shared any of the sufferings I have endured. I suffered with Post Traumatic Stress Disorder and depression most of my life until I came to one of Weston Carryer's healing meetings. I believe I was healed the instant he prayed for me. I want you to know that we have an enemy who seeks to destroy us. He tried his best to destroy me and I almost allowed him to because of the choices I made. But praise God, I am a living testimony of the healing power of our Lord and Saviour Jesus Christ. It is hard to describe my life on a few pages so I will be as brief as I can.

Between the time I was born, until I reached the age of four and a half, I had stayed with a number of different families, mostly aunts and uncles, due to my real parents fighting all the time; I was separated from my two brothers in those times. I was adopted when I was four and a-half years old by my uncle, his wife, and their four sons, one of whom is mentally impaired and violent when he is upset. Six family members have sexually abused me; three abused me when I was around the age of two. I found this out when I met my real father thirty-two years later; he told me that he was one of them. My stepfather started to sexually abuse me when I was ten or eleven years of age and the abuse was almost daily. This went on for years. Two of my stepbrothers were also sexually abusing me and I told no one about the abuse. I was attending Sunday school around the time it all started.

I isolated myself from the family as much as I could because I felt that I didn't belong and spent all my spare time in my bedroom after all my chores had been done; even then I wasn't safe for very long. My stepmother worked full time and she had no idea of what was happening. I ran away from home around the age of fourteen only to be raped in the two weeks I was gone. I rang home and my stepfather picked me up. We stopped at the pub, and I told him what had happened to me. He told me not to tell anyone about the incident, and he continued to sexually abuse me. I told a friend and it was strongly suggested that I see a doctor. He came with me to tell my stepmother, but her response to me was, "Don't tell lies . . . and if it happened, you probably enjoyed it."

At age fifteen, I tried to commit suicide and I became a patient in the psychiatric hospital for a few months. I got a job at the hospital through a rehabilitation scheme and moved into the nurse's home while I worked there. I started going to the pubs and nightclubs, searching for some kind of sanity, because I thought drinking hard liquor would be the answer to my problems. I had a relationship with a guy who physically and emotionally abused me, and I got into trouble with the law. It was around that time that the sexual abuse by my stepfather was revealed to my stepmother. He denied it and she didn't believe me, and so I was branded a liar. I was baptised while I was in this relationship. We had a son who I later adopted out because I could not cope with the beatings and living in fear; I didn't want my son to grow up in that environment. My son's father stalked me for a long time after I left him, and at times tried to kill me when he found me. I started hitting the pubs full time around the age of eighteen to try to cope with the guilt and pain, only to be set up, and again I was raped.

I met my real mother when I was twenty-one only to find out that she was involved with the occult—palm readers, tarot cards, crystal balls etc. Out of curiosity—and by choice—I got involved as well. Just prior to meeting her, I had become a born again Christian. I got pregnant again just after meeting my real mother and was married at twenty-two to my daughter's father. I started having flashbacks of the trauma I had endured, and some time after, I abandoned my husband and daughter. I fell away from the Lord big time. I sold the house, bought a van (that I lived in), and got involved with all the wrong people—smoking and dealing drugs, drinking alcohol, and partying for almost twelve years. I started to isolate myself and didn't even like to be seen in public, so all the people I knew came to see me. I had between thirty to forty people visit me every day and night. I had been on the invalids benefit due to a back injury during those years. It was then that I had been diagnosed with post traumatic stress disorder.

After years of being in that rut I met my second husband and moved out of the city I was living in to start a fresh life. I still smoked marijuana and drank three to four casks of wine a week just so I could sleep at night. I went to church, only to go home and get stoned and drunk, reading horoscopes, living in sin, and I believed that it was okay for me to do that. After realizing the mess I had made of my life through the wrong choices I had made, I decided to be obedient and do things God's way and let him take control. After making this firm decision that my only hope was in the Lord, I attended the healing meeting where Jesus gave me my amazing, transforming deliverance as Weston prayed for me.

I no longer have any more flashbacks. I have now stopped smoking drugs and drinking alcohol. I now have nothing whatsoever to do with witchcraft or the occult. I have been re-baptized and now feel comfortable to be seen in public again. I am studying at the polytechnic in an effort to get qualifications for a job and I am really well, praise God. I have a wonderful relationship with my daughter and my relationship with my stepmother is being restored. I have a wonderful supportive husband, and we give our lives to Jesus every day. I put my armor on every day and live one day at a time. I have got wonderful friends now, most of whom are Christians. I am happy and at peace. Praise God. I thank and praise the Lord for anointing people like Weston Carryer, and the pastors of the church, to give healing to those who choose to believe in the healing power of Jesus Christ. All glory to our heavenly Father. Thank You, Lord.

—*God's Child*

I was diagnosed with clinical depression and obsessive compulsive disorder by my doctor and was advised to start taking antidepressants. Weston Carryer came to Faith Bible College where I am studying. He shared his testimony and said that the Holy Spirit was naming conditions to him that He wanted people to be free of. I prayed that if this was the day that I was to be free of this illness, that Weston would name my condition. Weston asked who was really battling with depression. I immediately came up and he prayed for me. I saw my doctor on Sunday at church (he is a Christian) and told him

Miracles in Aotearoa New Zealand

what had happened. He looked at me and said that he could see that the depression had gone. As I was only diagnosed a few days before Weston came, I felt I didn't need the medication any more as it hadn't even started working. It is now three months later, and I feel wonderful. I'm thankful for Weston ministry, and thank You, Lord.

—*Graham Aitchison*

When I was twenty-six years old I was diagnosed with bipolar disorder. As far as mental illnesses go, I was very ill. I was committed under the mental health act and treated in the acute wing of a psychiatric hospital with major tranquilizers. After compulsory treatment I was advised that I would be best to take a mood stabilizer medication. I followed the psychiatrist's advice and took lithium. I frequently struggled with depression. I felt I had to work so hard just to get through each day and stay "normal" (whatever "normal" is).

At age thirty-three, I had an unplanned pregnancy. I really could not face a future of bringing up a child on my own with a mental illness and the medication I had been on could be damaging to the unborn child. I was desperate. I went to one of Weston Carryer's healing meetings at the Ashburton New Life Church. At the end of the meeting he asked anyone who wanted healing to go to the front of the church. A lot of people responded that night. I was standing in the middle of the people, shamed out at both the stigma of my illness and the shame of my unplanned pregnancy. When Weston asked what I wanted healing for, I quietly explained that I was pregnant and also bipolar, which was what I wanted healing for because I had stopped taking my medication to protect my unborn child. Weston prayed for me and I remember the prayer being quite brief and I almost felt a little short-changed; it all seemed insignificant. I unceremoniously walked back to my seat and somebody handed me a pamphlet about how to keep your healing.

Now over three years later, I remember that night as very significant. From that day on, I have not needed to take any medication. I had a choice of going under a specialist during

Deliverance, Inner Healing & Other

my pregnancy to have my medication monitored. I didn't go on medication but agreed that I would go under a specialist if there were any signs of mental illness. I remained well throughout my pregnancy—in fact I felt better, because without medication, I seemed to be able to think clearer, and my short-term memory came back along with a greater ability to concentrate.

I had a healthy and content 9lb 1oz baby boy ten days before my thirty-fourth birthday. I have remained well ever since. Because of my illness, I had visits from the social worker from the community mental health team, and occasionally went and saw a psychiatrist. One day I went to the mailbox and opened a letter from the mental health team. It simply stated that I no longer required their services and that if I do have any future problems to contact a GP. It also said they had sent a letter to my GP saying that they felt I no longer required their services.

I believe I have been totally healed! I am now able to dream dreams for my future, which I was not able to do with my mental illness. In the not-too-distant future, when my son, Joseph goes to school, I want to do my Bachelor of Nursing. This was something I could only dream of when I was sick, but now it may become a reality. Also, my desire to travel and visit other cultures, which has been strong since I was young is now a possibility too. I thank the Lord so much for my healing, and I really want my life to be pleasing to him. Words cannot express my gratitude to the Lord and also to Weston's ministry!

—*Lynne Whiting*

Although I had been a Christian for some time, when my husband and I shifted to Tokoroa I had not become connected to a church. As a result of this, plus the fact that I had been grieving over the death of a son for a long time, I had become depressed and felt completely brokenhearted. I had been taking medication for the depression and I did not know what to do any more. I saw a notice advertising a healing meeting at the Tokoroa Apostolic Church where Weston Carryer was ministering and I went along. As Weston started ministering, he said, "There is someone present who is suffering from a broken heart and depression whom the Lord wants me to pray

Miracles in Aotearoa New Zealand

for immediately." I went forward, and as Weston prayed for me, the Lord ministered to me in an amazing way. The power of the Holy Spirit hit me and I was rapidly thrown backwards. My mouth opened and I cried out very loudly and experienced all these dark spiritual forces just pouring out of me. All my internal pain and depression went instantly and completely. I had a wonderful deliverance.

I immediately started going to church and have been very involved there for three years. The following year when Weston was back in Tokoroa in our church, he once again had a word of knowledge for me. He said there was someone there with high blood pressure and an irregular heartbeat. I had both these conditions, and so I responded, and he prayed for me. Once again the Lord ministered to me and I was totally healed. I am now off all medication. I was also healed of degeneration in my spine which caused crippling pain a lot of the time. Now I have no back pain at all. As a result of these experiences with the Lord, my life has been transformed, and I have such a love for the Lord. During worship I find I am continually weeping for joy. What an awesome Jesus we have.

—*Ann Lovelock*

I suffered post-traumatic stress syndrome after an incident on our farm when the armed offender's squad came onto our property because tenants in a second house were harbouring a man who was being sought by the armed offender's squad. Our house was also surrounded and we were interrogated as they thought that we were also involved. As a result I was unable to sleep at night properly for over a year. Weston prayed for me, and the Lord totally and instantly healed my insomnia. Thank You so much, Lord Jesus. It is marvellous to sleep soundly every night.

—*Joan Christianson*

When I was six years old, my Mother was taken to the Porirua mental institution and for the next six years, my younger sister and I lived in an orphanage as our Father was unable to look after us. During this time I was made responsible for my sister. Later on, at the age of twenty, my sister developed schizophrenia and I looked after her for some years. Possibly because of my background and events in my life, I slowly became depressed and fought this depression for over thirty years without fully understanding my feelings.

Several years ago, I attended a divine healing meeting in Masterton where Weston Carryer was ministering. During the meeting Weston looked right at me and said that there was someone in the area where I was sitting who had battled depression for years, and would that person come forward for him to pray for the Lord to heal them. I responded immediately and Weston prayed for me. After this I realized that I did not have the sick feeling in the pit of my stomach any more, and I had a joy and peace in my heart that I had never ever previously known. This is wonderful for me and I am so grateful to have been healed by Jesus Christ through His servant.

—*Gaye Gosling*

For sixteen years, I suffered terribly from depression. This started when I was aged seventeen and the desire to commit suicide was never far from my mind. On several occasions, I did try to take my life, but fortunately, never succeeded.

I became a Christian early in 2007, and in May, I attended a divine healing meeting in Auckland where Weston Carryer was ministering. I went forward for him to pray for me for a physical condition.

He looked at me and asked, "Do you ever had thoughts of suicide?"

I replied, "Yes! Many times."

Weston said, "We really need to deal with this," and he prayed for me accordingly. The result has been amazing. I have never been depressed for one moment since then (over twelve months ago) and I have certainly had no thoughts of suicide. Instead, I have a joy I never thought was possible. I do not need to have any medication and my life has been transformed. Lord

Miracles in Aotearoa New Zealand

Jesus, I am so grateful for what You have done for me.

—*Susan Ryland*

At a healing meeting at Te Awamutu in June 2008, Weston Carryer preached and showed us how Jesus Christ paid the penalty for our rejection so that we could be set free in all areas of our life. He then asked people to stand if they had felt rejected in their life. Immediately the Holy Spirit came into my heart and I knew He was talking to me.

I had suffered depression a lot of my life but didn't know the root cause and at times in my life I had been so desperate for God to take this depression away. I felt rejected by my own family: brothers, sister, and mum and dad who do not follow God. There were times in my life when I wanted to commit suicide. I had given my life to Jesus in 1989 but was still feeling unable to belong to a family. Two weeks before Weston came to Te Awamutu in 2008, I was battling depression and having thoughts of suicide. I was desperate, in pain, and needed God to fill my void. I had hidden this for a long time because I was a Christian and Christians are not meant to feel or think like that. Well, guess what I did? I stood for prayer!

Thanks to God, I am now free of feeling desperate, helpless, unwanted, and wondering where I belong. I have not felt attached anywhere throughout my life; now all I want to do is worship God and belong. Let God have the glory for setting me free. The change in my life over the last twelve months has been truly amazing.

—*Pauline Lea*

I was born on the 19th of April 1973, but my life only really began on the 27th of April 2008 after a healing I received at a Weston Carryer healing meeting held at City Church in Christchurch. Satan had stolen the first 35-years of my life, but through God's grace, I am now able to live the life God sacrificed His only Son for. My black hole was finally filled with God's everlasting light that Sunday service.

Deliverance, Inner Healing & Other

I had lived a life that could only be described as a living nightmare. Four weeks before the healing meeting, I started praying for an accident to happen in my life. Thankfully Christchurch buses never seem to arrive on time and I held on till the healing meeting, but only by a thread. I wanted to live, but I just didn't want to go through the pain any longer. After 35-years of barely surviving, I had finally come to a point of surrender. I couldn't fight it any longer. I would love to say I prayed through the night or read the Bible while standing on my head, but I was in no state except to lie in bed. I had nothing left in me. Things were getting to a ridiculous stage and I knew I only had a couple of days of surviving left in me.

I rang an emergency health service desperate for help. A health worker came to visit me and so I told them about the healing meeting that was to be held the very next day. I awoke the morning of the meeting, but was very unwell. And although I felt this was my last chance for a miracle, I could not even manage to get out of bed to go to the service until God provided His first miracle for me that day. The person from the emergency service rang me that morning before church to make sure I went to the healing meeting. They weren't even saved, and during my 12-years of being a Christian, nobody had ever rung me up to get me out of bed for church, although at times I wish that someone would have done that. I still struggled to get out of bed, but I finally managed and arrived at the service half an hour late and sat down at the back of the church.

My life was on a knife's edge, but nobody would have ever known. I knew that at the start of a meeting Weston usually had words of knowledge for various conditions that people had. He called for someone in my section who had come especially for a medical miracle. I went up to the front where he laid hands on me and I was slain in the Spirit. The Holy Spirit ran up and down my body like vibrations for around ten minutes as I lay there. I could hardly stand afterwards as it felt like I had just run a marathon. Instead I sat in the front row as Weston told me that I should believe things would be better for me from now on.

I didn't feel any different at the time until a couple of days later when I awoke one morning and realised I felt different,

Miracles in Aotearoa New Zealand

like happy. I can't describe it any other way. I just felt happy. I thought I had experienced happiness before, but this was a different feeling altogether. The best way that I can describe it is that feeling you have when you've been really sick and then suddenly recover, and that feeling is better than if you had never been sick in the first place. I now live that happy feeling every day. I never actually realised that life could be this good. It's way beyond anything I could have ever imagined. Nothing in my life has changed. It's just that I've changed. I realise that people won't see a big difference in me, but I do. To me I'm like a totally different person, but at the same time, I'm still the same old Matt.

I have no idea why God chose me to receive a healing. I didn't deserve it, but I do know His timing was perfect to the day. What a gracious God we serve. When Paul wrote in the New Testament that he was the biggest sinner that ever walked the face of the earth, I think it was only because he had never met me. Only by God's grace, and nothing else, was I brought out of my sufferings.

Bipolar Disorder can only be described as a living hell. I have great empathy for those still struggling with this illness. My only regret is that others continue to suffer as I enjoy my life, having done nothing to deserve it. I have asked God why He chose me for a healing and I felt that He replied by reminding me that although we all sin and deserve hell, He still sacrificed His only Son so that we all could have the opportunity to enjoy heaven. There is no other answer. It's only through God's love and grace that I can now live, what to me feels like heaven on earth, and not the hell on earth I deserve.

> *Then should not this woman, a daughter of Abraham, whom Satan has kept bound for eighteen long years, be set free on the Sabbath day from what bound her?* (Luke 13:16, NIV)

It is now two years since my miracle. My life is simply wonderful. No longer do I have any suicidal thoughts. I love living, I have almost finished my business management course at Vision College, and I am looking forward to being able to help other people.

Deliverance, Inner Healing & Other

My medication has been reduced steadily and I am only on a third of the amount of what I was taking. Fairly soon I will be off all medication. The only reason I still need any is to make sure I sleep well.

And yes, I do believe I am a walking living miracle. God is so good.

—*Matt Doolan*

For 53 years I had smoked cigarettes and I had been unable to stop no matter how hard I tried. I attended a Christian healing meeting in 2008 in Pahia where Weston Carryer was ministering, and he prayed for the Lord to set me free from this addiction.

The next morning I got up, did my usual four hours of farm work, then came in and had my breakfast. While having my cup of tea after breakfast I started to crave a cigarette. I always used to roll a few smokes, put them in a tin and carry them in my pocket for when I wanted them. This morning I rolled three, put two in the tin and lit one. I tried to smoke it but I found I couldn't, so I threw it away. Later on in the day I tried the second one, but had to throw that away as well. Now, four years later, the third one is still in the tin. I have not smoked at all and have no desire to do so.

Lord, You are amazing, and I just praise and thank You for my complete deliverance.

—*Kara Davis*

This miracle has had a huge impact on Shiloh's quality of life. For years she was ridiculed and put down because of her condition and this had a demoralizing effect on her. Her whole personality has changed and her self-esteem has grown immensely. She is now a confident happy seventeen-year-old who loves the Lord.

Her father and I, along with Shiloh, are rejoicing and continually praising God for what He has done for our daughter.

—*Paula Eriha*

Miracles in Aotearoa New Zealand

In 2005, I began having remorse over a decision I made. I became preoccupied with not having our farm any longer and began to wake up a lot a night, worried and fretting. I became depressed. We were living in Christchurch, and I found living in a suburb, squashed in with other buildings and people, added to my mental state.

Living continual regret without any respite took me down into deeper and deeper depression. Even though my wife and friends prayed, it did not make any difference. It got to the stage where I did not sleep at all—all night. One night I saw fire and thought it was hell. I heard voices. They were telling me that if I ended my life, then this terrible suffering would end.

I was committed to Hillmorton psychiatric hospital and given some strong drugs. One was called risperidone—it was a brain tranquilliser and it prevented my mind from racing. I had friends visit. One day some old farming friends from Southland arrived. When I saw my farming friends, the wife begin to sob and weep at the sight of me, and I knew I was severely mentally disturbed and in a very bad way.

At night in the hospital I could sleep for about five hours each night, but I did not let on in fear of the authorities keeping me in longer or giving me an electric shock. Gentle Christian music was given to me to play in the night. Then at night I would awake and feel huge demonic pressure on me. It was an enormous fear and torment, and I thought my mind was going to blow up and I would be insane for the rest of my life. In hindsight, I know this attack could have made me much worse.

So I began to call out to Jesus in a whisper (so the nurses would not hear). I proclaimed his name repeatedly, "Jesus . . . Jesus . . . Jesus . . ." over and over. It was such a fight for my mind—for my life. I was determined not to let this thing make me go mad. After about fifteen minutes of this fight it went away. It happened four or five more times, but each time the attack got weakened as I said, "Jesus . . . Jesus . . ."

A pastor gave me communion, and after that, these horror attacks went away. I was released after 3 weeks. At a checkup consultation I asked the head psychiatrist if I would be like this for the rest of my life. She said, "It is likely you will be on those pills for the rest of your life."

My wife took me to a Weston Carryer meeting. The atmosphere was one of true compassion and not emotional massaging and manipulating-hype. Before the meeting I cried out to God to give Mr. Carryer a word of knowledge for me.

Then the moment came. He said, "There is someone here with a serious mental illness and you have been in a psychiatric hospital. The Lord desires to take you off all pills. I leapt to my feet—didn't care what others thought. He prayed; and I felt love run all over me like oil running over me.

I went home with hope in my mind. I continued having counselling and slowly began to get better. It was important I told God everything on my mind and confessed and proclaimed.

We went to Southland and lived in a rented country cottage and the soothing streams and countryside. The work of our Father's hands got me better and better.

Then in 2009, four years later, I asked the doctor to consider taking me off all pills. He agreed. Since then my mental health has got better and better. I am a new man. I have been healed by the supernatural and unfathomable power from on high.

There is so much more our Lord has for my wife and I and I feel like I am a beginner. Praise to the one true God and His son, Jesus.

—*Alastair Macdonald*

As a teenager I was moody and suffered from bouts of depression, excessive sorrow and sadness, and always carrying a heaviness which really weighed on me.

This had started when my pet corgi died suddenly when I was eleven. I was very fond of him and used to play for hours with him. He became ill in the morning. I went to school that day, and when I returned home, he had died and my father had buried him. This devastated me.

Miracles in Aotearoa New Zealand

Approximately nine years later, I attended a divine healing meeting where Weston Carryer was ministering and he had a specific word of knowledge for someone whose pet had died while he was a young pre-teen, and that a spirit of grief had attached itself to that person resulting in depression and sadness.

I was shocked! God cared about me! I responded to the word of knowledge, and Weston prayed for me and a weight lifted off me. Since then, over twenty years, I have known lightness of spirit and joy and have not suffered from the heaviness, sadness, and depression that plagued me through my teenage years. God is good and He cares about us! Praise God!

—Stephen Collecutt (Pastor)

He went in and said to them,
"Why all this commotion and wailing?
The child is not dead but asleep." But
they laughed at him.
After he put them all out,
he took the child's father and mother
and the disciples who were with him,
and went in where the child was.
He took her by the hand and said to
her, *"Talitha koum!"* (which means
"Little girl, I say to you, get up!").
Immediately the girl stood up and
began to walk around
(she was twelve years old).
At this they were
completely astonished.

—Mark 5:39-42, NIV

Twelve

Infertility & Children Healed

Testimonies of healed conditions of infertility and also testimonies of children that were healed.

For three years, the abiding wish of my husband and I was to have a child. During that time I had been treated by a gynaecologist, but had still been unable to conceive. The two of us went forward at a divine healing meeting where Weston Carryer prayed for us to have a child. One month later, I discovered I was pregnant and am now the mother of twin boys. We truly received a double portion.

—*Donna Goldsworthy*

I am thankful to Weston Carryer for re-introducing me to the Lord God, and through Him and Weston's prayer, for making my dreams come true. On his visit to Dunedin, I came to witness the miracles that the Lord performs through Weston.

For the past ten years I have suffered with anorexia, being

Miracles in Aotearoa New Zealand

hospitalized twice. My husband and I have been trying to conceive a child for the last four years but without success. I have been undergoing fertility treatment and feeling very despondent, and at times suicidal.

On the night that Weston called me up from the congregation, he placed his hands on my head and prayed that the Lord would do away with my fear of food and that God would heal my reproductive system. Well, this has happened. Within six weeks of Weston's prayer, I became pregnant and I am now six weeks pregnant. Being reunited with God, I feel immensely grateful for each day that I am alive. I believe that He is an amazing God, able to make dreams come true and for happiness to be within anyone's reach who is willing to let the Lord into their heart.

—*Emma Gallagher*
Note: *Seven and a half months later, Emma gave birth to a healthy baby.*

For eighteen months, my wife and I had been trying to have a child but without success. The doctor had told us that the chances of us ever having a child were very slim indeed. This was as a result of tests that we had undergone. At a healing meeting in Christchurch conducted by Weston Carryer three years ago, he prayed for us that God would heal this condition. We praise God that He did heal us and we now rejoice in being parents. Thank You, Jesus.

—*Jeff & Jo Cotton*

For years I suffered discomfort in my womb, and after a year of marriage, my husband and I tried to have a child. However, I was unable to conceive. After a year of being unable to conceive, I went to a Christian healing meeting where Weston Carryer prayed for the Lord to heal me. Imagine my joy when one month later I found myself pregnant and all discomfort totally gone. Thank You, Jesus.

—*Joanne Conde*

Infertility & Children Healed

As a result of not being able to conceive and have a child after being married for twelve months, I had a medical checkup. The tests showed that I was not ovulating and the doctor thought I probably never had. Weston Carryer was ministering in Kaikohe early in 1997 and I asked him to pray for my condition. My husband and I both believed that through the prayer, God would heal me, and both of us stood firm on His Word. I received no medical treatment.

I am now six months pregnant and looking forward to the birth of my baby. God is faithful.

—*Bobby Loader*

I had never had a normal menstrual cycle at any stage of my life. After we married, my husband and I wanted to have children, but I was unable to conceive. I attended a divine healing meeting in Queenstown in April 1996, where Weston Carryer was ministering and he prayed for the Lord to bless us with children. Within days I was pregnant, and now four years later ,I have two lovely children, and am pregnant with my third. We have a God of abundant blessing! Thank You, Jesus.

—*Julie Jenkins, Queenstown*

For a year my husband and I had been trying to have a baby but I had not been able to conceive, even though I had previously had a child. I had been taking Clomasine for some months, but this had not helped.

In August 1998, Weston Carryer prayed for the Lord to give me a baby. My Christian midwife worked out that I became pregnant within forty-eight hours of being prayed for when it was not my fertile time. This had to be a miracle from the Lord. I am now the mother of a three-month-old baby girl. Thank You, Jesus.

—*Justine Watkins, Fielding*

Miracles in Aotearoa New Zealand

For several years I had suffered from having miscarriages (ectopic pregnancies), and during this period, I had been unable to have children. I was prayed for by Weston Carryer at a healing mission, and God, through Jesus Christ, totally healed me. Since then I have had no more miscarriages, have had two children, and have also been healed of other female problems relating to this condition.

—H. H.

After having two daughters I found that I was unable to conceive again, and my husband and I really wanted to have a son as well. I was examined by a doctor who said that I had become sterile; he also told me that I would never be able to bear any more children. Nine years then passed without our son.

On 6 May 2000, Weston Carryer was ministering in our church at Kaikohe and I suddenly knew that God was going to give us our miracle son. I went forward for ministry, and as Weston prayed for me, I experienced an amazing sensation in my womb so that I knew I was healed. I did not become pregnant immediately but continued to believe.

On August 2, 2002, I gave birth to our beautiful baby son. Jesus, we are so grateful.

—Sarah Pakai

I was diagnosed with polycystic ovarian syndrome at the age of twenty-one in 1997. All my life I have lived with irregular menstrual cycles that could often last five to six weeks at a time then cease for at least six months. Polycystic ovarian syndrome can also mean pregnancy is more difficult to achieve. My husband and I found this out after trying to start a family. My gynecologist sent me to a fertility specialist who worked with regulating my menstrual cycle. After twelve months, I finally

Infertility & Children Healed

started to have a monthly cycle; however, my hormone levels were still too low and abnormal.

Weston and Ruth came to our church in March 1999. Weston did not call out my condition, but I wasn't bothered. I knew he would pray for anyone wanting God's healing. That night I was prayed for and left feeling excited in my spirit by what God can do. If you have ever suffered from infertility, you will know the deep pain it causes and how becoming too hopeful or excited can deal another devastating blow with another negative result. Even so, I was excited.

In June 1999, after my hormones began to function normally for the first time in my life, we conceived a beautiful gift from God. She has just turned three. I'm grateful for Weston and Ruth. Thank You, our wonderful Lord, Jesus Christ.

—*Lisa Anderson*

My husband and I were married in 1999, and in December of that year, we decided to try to have a child. I found I could not conceive and was diagnosed with polycystic ovarian syndrome and was told that there was only a six-percent chance of me ever having a baby.

In May 2000, my husband and I visited my mother in Hamilton. On the Sunday morning we went with her to church where Weston Carryer was ministering. During the ministry time, he prayed for the Lord to heal me so that I could conceive. Three months later, the doctor discovered that I was eight-weeks pregnant, and that meant I had conceived during the first month after being prayed for.

Six months later I gave birth to beautiful, healthy baby boy. We give all the praise to the Lord to whom we are so grateful.

—*Sherrill Eden*

My husband and I have known each other for fourteen years. Eleven years ago, we started living together and tried to have children, but I was unable to conceive. We both accepted

Miracles in Aotearoa New Zealand

Jesus Christ as Lord of our lives and then realized that to be in right relationship with the Lord, we needed to get married. We did marry. But through this period of ten years of being together, we were unable to have children. We never used any form of contraception during this entire time.

In April 2002, I attended a divine healing meeting in Taupo and Weston Carryer prayed for the Lord to heal me so that I could conceive. I am rejoicing to testify that two months later, it was confirmed that I was pregnant.

In February 2003, I gave birth to a wonderful little girl who we have named, Olivia Rose. Thank You, Jesus.

—*Jackie Ramsay*

My husband and I had been trying to conceive a child for twelve months without any success. My doctor had told me that there was less than a fifty percent chance of this happening as a result of me having had endometriosis for twelve and one-half years. I did, however, manage to conceive, but then miscarried on 18 March 2002. I was devastated. However, two weeks later I attended a divine healing meeting at Auckland, and Weston Carryer prayed for the Lord to heal me and give us a baby.

I became pregnant immediately, and on 8 January 2003, gave birth to a baby girl. Truly she is a gift from God. Thank You, Jesus.

—*Kerry Ward*

In 1996, I was diagnosed with chlamydia. There was evidence of an ectopic pregnancy that I miscarried. Because the hair follicles in the fallopian tubes had been destroyed, the egg from the ovum could not be transported to the womb. The doctor's diagnosis was barrenness. Weston did a home visit in 1997, where he prayed for me that I would be blessed in childbearing.

It is now 2003, and we are expecting our third child. Only God could have made these blessings possible.

—*Rose-Lee Trego*

Infertility & Children Healed

Weston Carryer visited our church in Ashburton at the end of March 2003, and my husband, two young children, and I heard him speak in a Sunday morning service. At that stage we had been praying to God for about six months for another baby. God had been speaking to me through His Word and I believed His promises, but I had been feeling depressed since the start of the year because I couldn't understand why our prayers had not been answered. I also knew that I was coming under attack from satan who was causing me to doubt God's Word and His goodness to me. But I seemed to overcome the problem myself.

At the end of the meeting, Weston invited anyone who had a need to go forward for prayer. I felt shy about going forward in front of everyone, but I knew that it was something God wanted me to do. Our whole family went forward, and firstly, Weston prayed for the spirit of depression to be lifted from me. Immediately I could feel that a great burden had been lifted from my shoulders. Weston then prayed against any problems of infertility and that God would bless our family. I came away from that meeting feeling a great relief knowing that God would bless us with another baby in His perfect timing. Although I went home trusting God and being happy to wait for any period of time for His blessing, I became pregnant the month following the meeting!

We had a baby boy, Samuel Ross Holland, born on 29 December 2003. He is a healthy little boy and we are enjoying him. I truly thank God for Weston Carryer's ministry and the power of intercessory prayer.

—*Linda Holland*

When I became a teenager I started to have female problems. I experienced a lot of pain and excessive bleeding. I had all the symptoms associated with hormonal imbalance, but it was not diagnosed at this time. I got married in 1996. My physical problems continued until 1999 when it was discovered that I

Miracles in Aotearoa New Zealand

had polycystic ovarian syndrome and a hormonal imbalance as well.

Two weeks after this medical diagnosis, Weston Carryer came to Dunedin where he ministered in our church. He had a word of knowledge for a woman with a hormonal imbalance problem. I responded and he prayed for the Lord to do a miracle for me. My husband and I were both overjoyed when it was discovered that two weeks after being prayed for I became pregnant, and now five years later we have three children. I am also thrilled to write that medical tests have confirmed that I do not have polycystic ovarian syndrome, my hormone levels are normal and I do not have the pain I used to get. All these physical problems were healed by the Lord when I was prayed for. Jesus, I am so grateful.

—*Tania Bron*

In September 2003, after thinking we had had a miscarriage, I got bad stomach pains. The doctors found that I had an ectopic pregnancy and I would need to be operated on. My husband and I prayed that they would be able to save the tubes, and praise God, they did. Five months later, after trying to get pregnant without success, Weston came to our church in New Plymouth. He called out that there was someone there with womb problems. I hadn't had that, as such, so I sat there. Next, he elaborated saying this woman had a type of endometriosis and may not realize it. I thought, *Is that me?* Knowing endometriosis caused irregular bleeding, I said to my husband, "Is that me?"

He replied, "I don't know . . . just go up." I did, and Weston prayed for me. The Holy Spirit filled me, and I was healed. I knew it; I had a vision of a positive pregnancy test. The next week I took a pregnancy test, and, praise God, the vision was correct and I was pregnant.

Now, I am delighted to write that on 12 October 2004, I gave birth to a lovely baby girl. Thank You, Lord.

—*Philippa Annand*

Infertility & Children Healed

My husband and I had desired to have a second child for almost four years. After much prayer we did not feel God was directing our paths towards medical intervention. However, preliminary tests had revealed no reason for the secondary infertility. This was an incredibly challenging journey for me as to be a mother was something I not only enjoyed, but had waited a long time for. My dream of a large family had come to a sudden halt after our son was born. Over the last four years I sought God to help me overcome the shame and guilt I felt and also the overwhelming feelings of failure that had accompanied the infertility. I knew what God said about barrenness and about receiving miracles. I held on to these praying that God would fulfill His promises to me. I finally came to the point where I replaced this "idol" of fertility with our loving Saviour. Once again my life could be lived for God, and not for another child.

On 16 May 2004, Weston came to a Sunday meeting at the Tauranga Worship Centre. At other meetings that I had been to that he had held, I prayed fervently that I would be called to receive healing, but had left disappointed and despondent that it wasn't the right timing. On the night of 16 May, I felt God impressing upon me to go along to see testimonies of His hand at work in others lives. So, I was shocked when he called us out and was so specific—even to the area we were sitting in. I sat for a moment in fear of admitting my struggle to our church, but with encouragement from my pastor's wife that this was for me, I took a step of faith.

By 10 June, we were pregnant—four years exactly to the day my son had been due. I'm currently in my ninth week of pregnancy and feel fantastic. I couldn't wait to share the "great things the Lord has done" for us. We pray that our testimony will serve others and give them hope where there is none. We are thankful for Weston's faithful work, and I can say with Hannah:

> *I prayed for this child, and the LORD has granted me what I asked of him* (1 Sam. 1:27).

MIRACLES IN AOTEAROA NEW ZEALAND

My pregnancy was not easy and led to a c-section, but God's hand never left us and His intervention was evident throughout. On 1 March 2005, we came to the end of our journey: a healthy 9lb 13oz baby boy—Flynn Caleb Tanner.

—*Adelle and Jeff Tanner*

I gave birth to a baby boy several years ago. However, since then, it had not only been very difficult for me to conceive, but I had not been able to carry a baby to full term, and during this period I had two miscarriages. The main reason for this was because I had polycystic ovaries. This was very discouraging for me because I desperately wanted to have another child. On Sunday, 18 April 2004, I went up for prayer at my church where Weston Carryer was ministering. He prayed for the Lord to heal me so that I could have another baby. Two days later on Tuesday, 20 April, I went to Tauranga Hospital for a pelvic scan and it was discovered that there was nothing wrong with my ovaries. Praise Jesus! I used to have polycystic ovaries, and now I don't. Amen! Two weeks later, in May, I became pregnant.

On February 5, 2005 I gave birth to Isaac James. I'm thankful for Weston, and thank You so much, Lord.

—*Trish Weggery*

Firstly, let me say thanks to God for hearing and then giving me the desires of my heart. As a teenager I was diagnosed with polycystic ovary syndrome. Back then, this didn't impact my life greatly except for the specific symptoms related to the syndrome. It wasn't until I was married and my husband and I started trying for a family that the full implications of polycystic ovary syndrome became clear. Eventually, after several years and successful fertility treatment, we had our first daughter. Needless to say, I still look at her and give thanks to God for giving her to us.

When our first child was about three years old we decided we would love another child to complete our family, so we headed down the same track with fertility treatment, and so

Infertility & Children Healed

forth. After two years I fell pregnant and we looked forward to once again holding another precious baby. At thirteen weeks, however, I lost this baby, and following this miscarriage found that for some unknown reason, the fertility treatment had lost its effectiveness. The specialist told me to "take a break," and we decided to trust that God would enable us to conceive on our own.

Nearly a year later, still no pregnancy and I was beginning to look at other women with their babies and feel such a deep sense of grief and despair. Looking back, I believe that the passage in the Bible that says is completely true.

Hope deferred makes the heart sick, but a longing fulfilled is a tree of life (Prov. 13:12, NIV).

Then in October 2003, I heard through family that Weston was going to be holding a healing meeting at a local church. My husband and I went along and listened to all the wonderful testimonies of God healing people's sicknesses and afflictions through Weston's ministry. At the end of the service I went forward for healing prayer and can vividly remember Weston speaking over me that I would be pregnant within three months. I didn't feel anything special happen to my physical body, but I did go out feeling a new spark of hope.

November came and I had this really excited feeling that I was pregnant. I contacted my specialist and asked her to arrange some blood tests to confirm what I secretly knew in my heart had happened. I can remember being told the tests confirmed I was in the very early stages of pregnancy, and just sitting there grinning like a Cheshire cat and shaking with joy.

Nine months later I was still grinning like a Cheshire cat as I held our new little baby girl, Olivia.

God is so good! I find myself praising God for our two girls in the strangest moments during the day . . . when I'm washing a grubby top for the third time that day, when I'm extracting half-chewed food from between the sofa cushions, and especially in the evenings as I tuck them both into their beds. I'm thankful for Weston's prayer, and praise be to God for the miracle of our two children. He has indeed fulfilled the longing in my heart.

—*Tonia Dowman*

Miracles in Aotearoa New Zealand

Six years ago we were told we had medically one percent chance of having children. On 26 April 2006, we were invited to go to Weston Carryer's healing meeting in Invercargill by a family friend who had been attending his seminars. We had received prayer before, and to be honest, went with limited expectation except knowing that God was able.

We really appreciated Weston's sensitivity to our circumstance and his genuine, simple prayer. To our utter amazement and joy, we discovered the next month we were one hundred percent pregnant. Praise God!

One week ago, our beautiful son, Emmanuel John Highsted, was born (January 2007). We are thankful for Weston's faithfulness and thank God for showing us His great mercy.

—*Julian & Sarah Highsted*

In March 2001, I came to a Weston Carryer meeting at Main Street Church in Stratford. I had just got engaged and children were in our long-term plan as a married couple. There was one small problem, though. Five years earlier I had been told that the chances of my being able to conceive children naturally were very slim. I had been diagnosed with polycystic ovarian syndrome. An ultrasound confirmed that I had cysts growing around each of my ovaries, which were preventing an egg being released each month resulting in my having only two or three periods a year.

I decided to come to Weston's meeting and receive prayer. I had faith in God and trusted that I would be healed. One of the desires of my heart was to be a Mum and I knew on that night in March 2001, my healing process was going to begin. As Weston prayed for me, I could feel the power of God at work in my body. I can't describe exactly how it felt other than it was wonderful. As each month rolled by the Lord was healing me—I was a "normal" woman and it felt great after nine years of not being "normal" and wondering what was wrong with me.

Nathan and I married four months later in August 2001,

and six-weeks later, I fell pregnant. We couldn't believe it—pregnant! We were over the moon. Thomas was born on 17 June 2002, followed by his sister, Rebekah on 31 May 2004. Around May 2005, Weston came to Main Street Church again. As I sat listening to testimonies and witnessing miracles and healings, I felt the prompting of the Holy Spirit to go forward for healing once more! I had another wonderful experience, soaking up the work of the Holy Spirit. The Lord still had some work to do in me!!

On 1 August 2005, Nathan and I found out I was expecting another baby and we were speechless. Another miracle, another blessing! But the Lord had another surprise in store for us. On 17 November 2005, we found out we were having identical twins. Poor old Nathan didn't know what to do—stand up, sit down, take his hat off or put his hat on. "Four kids . . ." he exclaimed, "and two of those twins! How are we going to cope?" But the Lord is good; we have survived their first year. They are now fourteen months old and just lovely, lovely boys.

We must say a huge thank you to our heavenly Father, and we're so thankful for Weston's ministry. If he hadn't come to Main Street Church, I probably wouldn't have had the opportunity to go forward for prayer and receive healing, and I wouldn't have had four wonderful children in the space of three and a half years. Isn't God awesome?

—*Natalia Hodge*

For four years, I was unable to conceive a baby. As recorded in the first testimony I wrote that three weeks after Weston prayed for me, the Lord gave us a wonderful miracle, and I discovered that I was pregnant. On 1 March 2005, Flynn Caleb Tanner was born.

There is now a wonderful follow-up to this. On 17 December 2006, Liam Joshua Tanner was born weighing 11 lb 7 oz. It wasn't an easy pregnancy or birth, but it is an awesome testimony of God's grace and mercy on my life, and especially Liam's. I'm thankful for Weston's support, prayers, and encouragement for us.

—*Adelle Tanner*

Miracles in Aotearoa New Zealand

My husband and I were married in 1982. We then went overseas for seven years and when we returned back to New Zealand, we tried to have our family. Unfortunately over the next three years I had four miscarriages. This was devastating to both of us.

In 1992, I attended a divine healing meeting in Queenstown where Weston Carryer was ministering. He prayed for me. He specifically prayed that I would conceive again, have healthy pregnancies, that things would go well, and that I would have healthy children. Eight weeks later I conceived and after a good pregnancy, gave birth to Jarrod. Then twenty-three months later Rueben was born, and then marvel of marvels, two years and four months later Lucy and Emily arrived.

Looking back, I now believe that going through what I did taught me to really believe God's Word, to continue to trust Him, and never to give up hope. Lord Jesus, I am so grateful to You for giving me the desire of my heart as my four children are such a wonderful blessing.

—*Tracey Campbell*

My husband and I decided when we got married that we would like to have a few children. We were blessed with our first three, but tragically, we lost our fourth baby through a miscarriage. For the next three years, we tried to have another baby but I was unable to conceive. Early in 2007, I was prayed for by our pastors, Carey and Janine Clow. Then in May, at a divine healing meeting at our church in New Plymouth, Weston Carryer prayed for me. Within a month I was pregnant, and in February 2008, I gave birth to our beautiful baby daughter. Lord, we want to thank and praise You for Your indescribable gift.

—*Kathy McInnes*

When my husband and I got married one of our real heart

Infertility & Children Healed

desires was to have a family and so we immediately tried to do this. However, I was unable to conceive. I was then checked medically, but there was nothing discovered that would have stopped me from becoming pregnant. For three years we tried but still no pregnancy.

Weston Carryer came to our church in Invercargill to minister in March 2006. When he started to minister he shared some recently received testimonies of healings and miracles that he had seen the Lord do, including one about a woman who had never been able to have children. She had then come to one of his meetings and so he had prayed for her. The Lord had healed her and she now had children. My husband and I were ministering to the church children and were not in the main auditorium at the time. Our pastor then came through and told us what Weston had said. Later my husband and I went forward to receive prayer.

I strongly felt at that moment that, as blind Bartimaeus had spoken out his desire publicly to Jesus to be healed, I needed to do the same. So I proclaimed my fervent desire publicly. Weston then prayed, and I felt things happen inside of me; it just felt as if the Lord was putting something in to place.

Two weeks later, I was pregnant, and in December of that year, I gave birth to our beautiful daughter, Tennille. Lord, we are so grateful to You.

—*Angela Waddell*

God is not a one-hit wonder. I know true well that His miracles are abundant. I know because He gifted His miracles to me. I had endometriosis for thirteen years, and during the first six years, I had countless admissions to hospital for emergency surgeries or pain management. I was told that the damage to my body was so significant, that there was little or no chance of me being able to conceive. I was even offered IVF—and I wasn't even married! Although it was a struggle, I decided to put my trust in the One who has never failed me—Jesus Christ. He knew His perfect timing for me, even if His opinion differed somewhat from the "experts."

Miracles in Aotearoa New Zealand

After I got married, we decided to try for a family straightaway. Unfortunately, our first pregnancy resulted in a miscarriage. I was devastated, but vowed to hang on to God and the truth of His Word. Within twenty months we experienced two miracles. God blessed us with Isaak, and shortly after, with Eli. People told us we should be happy with what we had and move on. But I knew deep in my heart that there was one more baby for us.

My endometriosis symptoms were severe and it looked hopeless. Year after year went by and there was no pregnancy. During this time Pastor Weston Carryer came to our church to preach and pray for miracles for those who needed them. It felt like my heart was in my throat as I heard Weston call out different conditions, illnesses and diseases that God had revealed to him and that God wanted to bring healing to.

Then, there it was: "There is someone in this room who has endometriosis. . . ." I was prayed for, that I would receive healing and to be able to conceive. A few months later, I was booked in for surgery for the endometriosis. But I can testify that I had to phone and cancel the surgery as I was indeed pregnant.

It was a delight to see Weston a year later and to be able to show off my big belly! God is great! I now have a gorgeous baby girl, Amaliah (which means, "work of the Lord"). God is generous and abundant in pouring out His blessings and miracles. He is not stingy and He does not ration out the miracles. To be free from endometriosis after all those years is marvellous.

—*Tanya Pohio*

My husband and I had four children in four years, the last two being twins. Because of a haemorrhage after the birth of the twins, and an electrical heart complaint, we opted for my husband to have a vasectomy. After this I felt convicted by God that we should let Him decide whether to give us children, and prayed and repented. Finally, my husband was to have an operation and we arranged for him to also have a vasectomy reversal at the same time. This was after twelve years.

Infertility & Children Healed

No pregnancy happened for five months. Weston Carryer was at our church in September 2007. I went forward for prayer, believing for a child. I did not reveal what the need for the prayer was; Weston prayed and said God would do something special. Four months later I was five weeks pregnant! We now have a beautiful son, who at eleven days early, was born on his father's birthday, with a speedy labour and no haemorrhage. God sent a Christian midwife who prayed with us against blood curses and I had minimal blood loss. Praise God! He does "exceedingly, abundantly above all that we ask or think" (Eph. 3:20)!

—*Melody Woodward*

My wife and I were married just over 3 years ago. After one year we tried to have a child but my wife Clare was unable to conceive. Another year later, when she had still not conceived, we attended a healing meeting at our Park City Church in New Plymouth, on 27 November 2011, where Weston Carryer was ministering. He prayed for us to be able to have a child. We were delighted when eight weeks later, she became pregnant. In October 2012, Clare gave birth to our son Jonathan. We are praising the Lord for what He has done for us.

—*Brian Barnfather*

I came to the meeting in Feilding in about September 2010. At the time, I had been trying for a second child for four years. All blood tests and scans came back within the acceptable parameters. We had no idea what was wrong or how to deal with it.

I heard about the healing meeting and came along. The first testimony that Weston read out was about a lady who had tried for some time to have a baby. That got my attention! The letter went on to say that after going up for prayer she conceived quite quickly. Wow! That was like God spoke directly to me, declaring, "I did it for her, I will do it for you."

After the message, when we were called forward for

MIRACLES IN AOTEAROA NEW ZEALAND

prayer, I went up and shared my issue. As Weston prayed, I felt a warmth move through me and truly believed God could answer my prayer. I conceived in November 2010 and was, understandably, ecstatic. God had fulfilled a great desire and answered my long-prayed prayer. I could hardly contain my excitement.

January 29, 2011, my dream was shattered as I miscarried at 13 weeks. I was devastated. How could God allow me to get pregnant and then take it away? The next few months were difficult as I had many doubts and was very confused (Prov. 20:24).

As time went on I realised I felt God had betrayed me, and I also realised I had a choice to make: either say my whole life was a lie and give up, or sort it out. I had made a decision when I was 17 that, no matter what anyone said or did, or no matter what happened, I was in this thing for life and would stay committed to following God.

So I got into the Bible and found time and time again others who had similar experiences (Ps. 9:10)—a promise, vision, or direction from God, only to seem to have it thwarted.

- Abraham and Sarah were promised a child and waited 25 years for that to be fulfilled.

- Joseph was given a vision that he would be in a position of power over his brothers and family, only to be found in a foreign jail.

- David was anointed king and spent many years on the run for his life and lived in caves.

Job really got to me. The Bible introduces him as an upright, blameless man who feared God and shunned evil, and yet, look what happened to him. Everything was taken away—wealth, flocks, herds and his children—but his response was an immense challenge to me personally. To go through such tragedy and say, "The Lord gives, and the Lord takes away, blessed be the name of the Lord." Wow!

Through these lives and many others, I got a conviction in my being that God is in control; He sees the big picture and allows tough things to happen. I resolved that as long as I hold tight to Him and seek His way (Prov. 3:5-6), He will bring me to victory—no matter how long it takes or what I must go through.

We are here for a reason, and I think if we just lift up our heads and commit to living God's way we can impact the people around us for Him (2 Cor. 1:3-4). I certainly wouldn't choose to go through it, but the lessons learned are invaluable. I finished the year with a greater understanding of God, and my faith had been strengthened.

On 26 October 2012, I gave birth naturally to God's precious gift, my second child, Nicholas.

I'm so thankful for Weston and all the team (Rom. 15:13), but mainly, thank You, God.

—Michelle Flynn

Weston Carryer prayed for us at Grace Vineyard in March 2012, that we would conceive a child. Praise God, we did conceive almost immediately!

Although we hadn't been married very long, medical opinion was that there was a cloud over our chances of having children—issues which Weston also prayed for (such as, endometriosis and fibromyalgia). Praise God, those issues have also not given any trouble during the last year and I have had no further pain, which I used to have from the endometriosis.

Although it was a protracted and very difficult birth, we are thankful and very blessed to have a beautiful baby boy, Judah Emmanuel, now almost three months old.

I'm thankful for Weston's ministry. It has blessed us so much!

—Rob & Emmy Carson

I started living with the man who was to be my husband thirteen years ago, and over the next three years, I was able to have two children. We tried to have a third child, but I had five miscarriages.

Miracles in Aotearoa New Zealand

Medical examination and tests done at that time revealed I had major internal problems with numerous body parts out of place. I was told the chances of me conceiving were very slight, and even if I did conceive and manage to carry the baby to full-term, the baby would almost certainly have major physical or mental disabilities.

By this time I had accepted Jesus Christ as my Lord and Saviour, had married and I believed the Lord would want me to have another healthy child. I attended a divine healing meeting at Cromwell in April 2012 and Weston Carryer prayed for a miracle for me: that I would conceive, carry the baby full-term, and that the baby would be normal.

I conceived straightaway, and in January 2013, I gave birth to Parker James. All tests and scans to date have shown us he is a healthy boy. Now, in November 2013, ten months later, Parker is fantastic and we are rejoicing and marvelling at how well he is doing. I am so thankful to the Lord for what He has done for us.

—*Emma Campbell*

On the morning of 9 November 2012, I phoned Weston Carryer in desperation to ask him to pray for me. I was ten weeks pregnant and had started bleeding.

This pregnancy was an IVF pregnancy. My husband and I had a beautiful eight-year-old daughter, Megan. We really didn't want her to be an only child and so we had been trying for the last almost seven years for another child. After four miscarriages and two cycles of IVF, I was finally pregnant again, but then the bleeding began.

I must just say that many Christians may be sceptical of IVF and don't believe it is God's way. However, God was so gracious to me through the entire time. A few days before our baby was implanted in me by the doctors, God gave me the verse in Isaiah 43:13:

> *No one can deliver out of my hands, when I act who can reverse it?* (NIV)

Infertility & Children Healed

Another verse is:

> *No one can snatch anyone out of my hand, no one can undo what I have done* (NLT).

This verse was confirmed again through a friend, a few days later. You would think I would have trusted God, believing this child was in his hands, but instead, I fretted and stressed through the entire pregnancy, always wondering when I would lose this baby!

You prayed that the spirit of miscarriage would depart, and the bleeding stopped. A few hours later I had a scan done. I was told the baby looked perfect!

Despite a difficult pregnancy I am so happy to say we welcomed our perfect baby girl, Eden Elizabeth, on 26 May 2013. She is now almost one. She is the sweetest little thing, and I thank God daily for her. He has filled a big hole in my heart. I thank God daily for her. He has also strengthened my faith through all of this.

I'm so thankful that Weston prayed for me on the phone. His prayer was a lifeline at that time.

—*Raquel Naude*

My wife and I had been married for ten years and had been trying to have children for the last five years. We had been praying that the Lord would bless us with a child. We didn't receive any medical treatment as my wife, Jasmine, had the conviction that she didn't have any physical infirmity preventing her from becoming pregnant.

On 30 June 2013, we attended a divine healing meeting at Church Unlimited Auckland, where Weston Carryer was ministering. He shared a testimony, so much like our situation, of a couple who were married for ten years and unable to have children. He had prayed for them, and then God had given them their child. We knew from that point that the Lord had something for us that night.

When Weston prayed for Jasmine, she felt a leap in her spirit and experienced this sensation for an hour afterwards.

Miracles in Aotearoa New Zealand

We went home praising God, firmly believing that she would have a baby.

Two days later, on 2 July, we took a step of faith and went to a shop and bought two sets of baby clothes—one boy and one girl set. The shop assistant became very confused when we told her that Jasmine had been prayed for two days previously and consequently we believed she was pregnant.

Tests a week later confirmed that Jasmine was pregnant, and in March 2014, our son, John, was born. Thank You so much, Lord Jesus.

—*Ajay Makal*

In 2012, we called Weston Carryer from the U.S.A., and he prayed for my husband and me for a child. I had previously had three miscarriages.

We are excited to say that on 13 May 2013, I gave birth to our son, whom we named, Zachariah James Bray Weidnecht.

Zachariah means, "God remembers," and James means, "God protects." We praise God for this precious child. We are so thankful for Weston's part in this.

—*Erick, Katrina & Zach Weidknecht.*

My husband and I have been married for eleven years. After five-and-a-half years our first child was born. During the next four years, I had a miscarriage, and subsequently, was unable to conceive or had further miscarriages. I was then diagnosed with a condition called "anti-phospholipid syndrome." This condition causes the placenta to make blood clots which clots the placenta off and the baby then dies. Nothing medically could be done for me during this four-year period. It is a type of autoimmune disease. Two years ago I attended a divine healing meeting in Whangarei where Weston Carryer prayed for the Lord to do a miracle for me. Five weeks later, it was discovered that I was pregnant, and I am delighted to write that I am the

Infertility & Children Healed

very happy mother of a ten-month-old baby. Lord, we are so grateful.

—Joy-Lynn Abplanalp

Children Healed

My grandson, Samuel, was born with one clubfoot. His leg was put in plaster when he was three days old. The plasters were changed until his foot was operated on at six months. Because of this condition, one leg was considerably shorter than the other, as was his foot, and he had no arch in his foot. This meant he had to wear special insoles in one shoe, and my daughter had to buy two different pairs of shoes to get one pair Samuel could wear. It affected his balance, and he walked with one shoulder much lower than the other. He was to have an operation at about sixteen where they would break his thigh bone, and put screws in it to let the bone mend gradually, building up a longer leg. Because of the pain involved in this operation, my daughter felt that this was a decision that Sam could make for himself when he reached sixteen.

Although my daughter is a Christian, she didn't really believe in God's miracle healing power for today. When I told her of the healing meetings last year, I didn't know whether she would come or not. However, God spoke to her, and she did come.

On the Friday night when Weston prayed, God grew Sam's leg so it matched the length of the other one. On the Saturday night, God grew his foot, and put an arch in it. Praise God!

It has been a year now, and Samuel is almost thirteen years old. He can skateboard, do roller hockey, and many things he couldn't do before. I'm thankful for Weston's faithfulness, and praise God for His miracle working power. And praise You, Jesus, that You loved us enough to die for us and send Your blessed Holy Spirit to minister in power through your servants.

—Kath Harris

Miracles in Aotearoa New Zealand

My baby daughter, Kaela, was born on 26 January 2005. As a result of her having very little mobility, tests were carried out which showed she had a very small ball joint in her left hip socket and this hip socket was also very shallow. This meant that the ball joint was unable to fit into the socket. In January 2006, our church leaders prayed for her, and she was then able to crawl very slowly.

In March 2006, I took her to a divine healing meeting in Timaru where Weston Carryer was ministering. He prayed for the Lord to do a creative miracle. The change in Kaela was huge immediately so that her mobility increased significantly. From that moment the ball joint grew steadily and went back into the hip socket, which also changed shape to become the right shape to hold the ball joint in place.

The x-rays taken in April 2007 showed that everything is one hundred percent and her actions certainly prove this. She has no restriction in any of her movements and can run freely. We have received a wonderful creative miracle, and Lord Jesus, I am so grateful.

—*Larni McCartney*

During my married life I adopted and raised twelve children and also raised one of my daughter's children, Maringiwai. One day, when Maringiwai was six-years-old, she fell off the jungle gym at school, and because of the resulting injury to her body, her legs were completely paralysed. She was unable to walk or stand at all. She was immediately taken to Tauranga hospital and was there for the next six weeks. During this time there was no improvement in her condition.

After six weeks in hospital, she became very despondent and on a Friday morning as I was visiting her, she cried and cried and cried and pleaded with me to take her home. With the doctors' permission, and after finding out everything I had to do for her, I took her home for the weekend.

When taking her back to hospital on the Sunday afternoon,

Infertility & Children Healed

I passed what I saw was a sign advertising a Weston Carryer divine healing meeting the following Tuesday night in Otumoetai, Tauranga. I stopped the car to have a closer look, but discovered that there was no sign. This had to be an amazing supernatural "sign" from the Lord just for me. I checked and found out that this meeting was indeed being held and I was convinced that if I took Maringiwai to the meeting, the Lord would do something wonderful for her.

I asked my neighbour, Liz Forrest, if she would help me. The following Tuesday, we picked Maringiwai up from Tauranga Hospital, carried her to the car, drove to the meeting and we both carried her in. During the early part of the meeting Maringiwai was very still but when Weston started ministering, her body started jerking. Then Weston said that there was someone there who was unable to walk and the Lord wanted him to pray for that person immediately. Liz and I then carried her forward and Weston prayed for her. We then put her on the floor, and she was able to stand unaided, although she still could not walk.

Over the next forty-eight hours she steadily regained more body movement and two days later she was able to walk and run with complete freedom. This was fourteen years ago and Maringiwai is now an air hostess in Australia and has always been so appreciative for what the Lord Jesus Christ has done for her. I still also praise and thank Him.

—*Piki O'Brien*

In September 1994, our six-year-old son, Gideon, was in a motor vehicle accident in which he received a broken back. We were told by staff at the hospital it was a miracle he had not received any neurological damage due to the dislodging of two vertebrae. Things were serious, for with any unstable fracture, one wrong movement could cause paralysis. Initial diagnosis was that Gideon would have to spend eight weeks on his stomach on a spinal bed to allow the vertebrae to return to their normal position. X-rays showed later that the vertebrae had moved and were stuck to each other giving a more serious condition than before.

Miracles in Aotearoa New Zealand

The chaplain called in Weston Carryer for prayer for healing, after which we were flown to Starship Hospital in Auckland where Gideon was operated on the following day. There were some astonishing results. The operation, in which his spine was fused by bone graft taken from his hip, was scheduled for six hours, but took only three. He was given no antibiotics, and was the only spinal case not to be put into intensive care. The surgeon advised that although he had a rare injury, he was the only one who could now walk. Three days on, he was fitted with a brace, and within two further days was walking unaided. Gideon was discharged one week after the operation, has had no side effects, and is even able to play contact sports. I know God was with us throughout the ordeal, and I thank Him for the power of prayer. We are forever grateful to Him.

—*Rebekah Christian*

Isaiah was born on 8 January 2000—nearly a millennium baby, but not quite. He was our second baby, with Jasmine having been born nearly four years earlier in 1996. When Isaiah was about six months old and trying to sit up we noticed his back seemed to have quite a bend in it when he leaned forward, something we couldn't remember with Jasmine. I asked our GP about it at our next visit. She agreed it didn't look quite right, and made an appointment at Dunedin Hospital with the orthopaedic specialist. An x-ray with Isaiah lying on his front, showed a 19-degree curve in his back. The specialist confirmed a tentative diagnosis of infantile scoliosis. He said, at the time, it occurred more often in boys and often corrected itself by the time the child was five years old. We had another two specialist appointments between then (mid-2000) and September 2001. Over this time the curve moved progressively to about 30-degrees. The specialist was becoming a bit more concerned at the progression and started to talk about the possibilities—an operation to fuse his spine being the worst case, with at least a brace until he was five if the curve didn't get any worse.

Isaiah was late walking, and at the appointment in September 2001, a good x-ray of him standing was taken. It showed a 42-degree curve. The specialist wasn't happy and said we had to prepare for an operation. To operate on Isaiah when he was this young and fuse his vertebrae, plus add rods, was not a good outcome. It would mean he would lose his height with his back unable to grow where it was fused, but also, many operations over the years as he grew.

The tests began—an MRI scan and various neurological tests—to make sure he was fit to have an operation and there were no other underlying causes. There weren't. In November, Isaiah had his first brace fitted. At our specialist visit in December, the doctor said we would be preparing for an operation in the New Year. He scheduled another pre-op x-ray. We waited over the Christmas period.

Since his diagnosis we had sought prayer from our friends and church family, and continued earnestly in prayer over this time as well. In January 2002, the x-ray showed a small decrease in the curve of 41-degrees. The specialist took this as good news, and held off on the operation. In March 2002, Ananton Pillai invited us to one of Weston's healing meetings—at the Shoreline New Life Centre. He prayed for Isaiah at the end of the meeting.

May was x-ray time again and the good news was a curve reduced to 33-degrees! In December, that year (2002) it was down to 27-degrees! Now we were down to annual visits—with December 2003 showing a further reduction to about 19-degrees. We could take the braces off! December 2004, showed more progress with the curve now 11-degrees—only slightly more than what's considered normal. We are now on annual visual examinations only from now on.

Although the specialist won't confess it as a "miracle," I've done a lot of research on the internet, and nowhere have I found evidence of a 42-degree curve correcting itself. In fact, many are operated on once they pass 30-degrees. Our doctor held off because of Isaiah's age. The specialist was very surprised at the dramatic decrease in curve between January and May 2002—this was the time we received the most concentrated prayer, and prayer from Weston.

Ken and I believe God has healed Isaiah miraculously. Isaiah is now a very healthy and active five-year-old. He has

Miracles in Aotearoa New Zealand

a loving heart for people and a very winsome personality. He knows Jesus has healed him and tells people so. We believe he is an evangelist.

—Nicola Holman

Note: Nicola sent x-rays of Isaiah's spine showing the 42°, 33°, and 27° curvature of his spine which are on file at Weston Carryer's ministry.

In January 1993, my three daughters—then aged six, ten and twelve—were all suffering from an untreatable pustular type of infection called "molluscum virus." This was causing an infectious weeping rash on their bodies, especially over the stomach area. They had been experiencing this for approximately six months and no medical treatment could help in any way.

Weston Carryer came to Hicks Bay to minister in January 1998, and I told him about my daughters' condition. He explained that God, through Jesus, could heal the three children and he simply prayed for the Lord to do this. The infections started to disappear the next day and continued until two or three weeks later they were totally gone on all three children. There has been no recurrence of this medically incurable condition. Thank You, Lord.

—Pauline Somersby

When our son, Ricky, was six months old he developed very severe asthma. He had to be attached to an auto-inhaler four times a day to try and prevent attacks. Despite this, he still had frequent attacks which would last up to four days. During this time, he had to have Ventolin every two hours.

At a Weston Carryer healing meeting, I went forward and stood in for prayer for Ricky. Weston prayed for him for God to heal him through Jesus, and then told me to lay hands on him when I went home. This I did. Apart from two very minor signs of asthma in the first three weeks after being prayed for, he has

Infertility & Children Healed

had no further asthma in the past twelve months and is now living a normal life. A grateful mother,

—*Tanya Kendall*

I have twin sons who are five years old. They were born more than six-weeks premature. Therefore I was given steroids to develop their lungs when it became apparent they would be born soon. One son had begun to cough a lot, especially at night even in the middle of summer. I would get up to see him several times a night to cover him up and see if he was cold and so on. This was taxing on me but, even more so, I was concerned at an apparent weakness, compared with his twin who slept peacefully each night. I realize that when someone has an infection they will be coughing, but Andrew just coughed when there was no sign in the day of any infection.

When Weston came to Helensville and prayed for Andrew the coughing just stopped. All winter he has slept peacefully like his twin. Praise You, Jesus. I am thankful for Weston and his wife, for giving of their time and themselves.

—*Jennie McKeown*

For six years, from the age of seven to thirteen, I had at least two hundred warts on my knees, hands and up my arms. There were far too many of them to be burned off without leaving permanent scarring. I was given an acid-based ointment which was supposed to remove them without scarring. But, if one disappeared it was immediately replaced with another one. They became quite painful as they would split in two on the finger joints and knees. My hands, arms and knees had to be taped when playing sports. Apart from the pain and discomfort, it was very embarrassing and I became very shy.

Six years ago, I went to a divine healing meeting in Wanaka where Weston Carryer was ministering and he prayed for the Lord to heal me. He specifically prayed for the warts to disappear within one month. By the end of the month they had all gone and I have never had one since. This healing really

Miracles in Aotearoa New Zealand

impacted my life and made me aware of how much the Lord was personally interested in me. There have been times in the last six years, as a teenager, when I have temporarily wandered from the Lord, but then, when I would look at my hands, I would remember and realize how much He loves me. Thank You, Jesus.

—*Nathan McLachlan*

I would like to testify to a wonderful healing that my son, William, received at a divine healing meeting at Living Faith Church, Orewa, in August 2011, where Weston Carryer was ministering. William had been toilet trained for over a year when suddenly, not long before his fifth birthday, he started losing all control over his bladder. His bladder would suddenly empty without any warning. Apart from the terrible embarrassment that it was for him, the fluid had a very strong smell.

This problem continued after he started school, and on a number of occasions we were contacted by the school who asked us to come and change his clothes. We took him to a doctor who determined it was either fungal or bacterial. The doctor gave him antibiotics, which did help with the smell, but did not help the bladder problem in any way.

We went to another doctor who was unable to offer any help at all. We were referred to a specialist who did a scan and then told us that he could not find any reason for what was happening, and he referred us back to the first doctor who told us that he thought it was psychological and he could not do anything for him.

A year after the problem started we attended the divine healing service and my wife was convinced that the Lord would heal William. During the meeting we took William forward. Weston prayed for him and I am delighted to testify that he was completely healed that day.

Since that moment twelve months ago, he has had full normal bladder control. What a wonderful relief this has been for our son, and we are so grateful to the Lord Jesus Christ.

—*Gary Mueggabury*

Infertility & Children Healed

Our twelve-year-old daughter suffered severe kidney pain for some fifteen months. The first inkling of a problem was when blood appeared in her urine about four years ago. IVP x-rays showed she had deformities in her ureter tubes. Despite many visits to specialists, both locally and out of town, the most they seemed to be able to do was to prescribe increased painkilling drugs without actually correcting the issue.

My nephew saw her in distress and called in Weston Carryer. He prayed over her in our home and, by the grace of God, she is healed. Several weeks have now passed without the need for either drugs or visits to doctors. Our daughter is pain-free. Praise God!

—J.M.

When Hannah was four-and-one-half, she was having difficulty hearing at home. The teachers at kindergarten had also shown concern and referred us to a child health doctor. She did tympanograms both in winter and summer. Each time they showed a flat eardrum, especially in one ear. She had "glue ear", a build up of fluid behind the eardrum. This could be remedied by having grommets inserted, so we booked her in with an ear specialist at the hospital.

We had Weston Carryer for dinner, and while Hannah was sleeping we asked him to pray for her. The next day, and particularly at night, we noticed a vast improvement. Her loud snoring had disappeared and was replaced by normal to louder breathing. We eventually got to see the specialist. He examined Hannah's ear, looked at me with surprise and said, "There is nothing wrong with her," and dismissed us. All I could think was, "Jesus, You healed her."

—Pauline Terry

When my daughter, Jessie, was four years old, she was hit in the right eye with a pellet from a gun. This caused the retina

MIRACLES IN AOTEAROA NEW ZEALAND

to be detached resulting in total blindness in the eye.

At a divine healing meeting in the Porirua Apostolic Church two years later, Weston Carryer prayed for her vision to be restored and Jesus healed her. The sight in her right eye is now absolutely normal. Praise the Lord.

—*Maxine Gardner*

Levi was born 17 May 2001 with bilateral cleft lip and palate. His plastic surgeon is Martin Reese from Kids First Middlemore Hospital, Auckland.

After Levi was born, we had doctor after doctor telling us that it would not be an easy road, but we believed all was going to be well. We were told Levi was going to need around eighteen operations over a period of time, and also from the age of nine and up, he would need to have orthodontist work done for the reshaping of his mouth and correction of the jaw. This meant he would have to have bone grafts as well as plates and braces. The hardest thing that I had to deal with as a mother was not being able to feed him. He had special feeders, and so forth.

Weston Carryer came to Stratford Main Street Church and also to The Vine Church at Hawera when Levi was six weeks old. We took Levi to those healing meetings and Weston prayed for him at both churches. We noticed that immediately after the prayer at Hawera, the shape of the outside of Levi's mouth had changed. It had grown and come down to the exact size and shape that it was supposed to be. As a result of what God did, Levi has only had to have two operations instead of the eighteen predicted.

Four months after he was prayed for, Levi went to Auckland for the first operation which took seventeen hours, and the next day a further two-hour operation was done. The surgeon had said it was extremely unlikely that Levi would ever develop teeth, because he had not had a top jaw to start with. He also said that if any bottom teeth came through, they would probably be rotten and he would need a massive amount of orthodontic work done. Levi returned to the hospital's plastic surgeon in August 2003, and he is very surprised with him.

Infertility & Children Healed

Levi has two perfect jaws, a full set of healthy teeth, and his mouth is completely normal. We are rejoicing that Levi does not need any more operations or treatments of any kind.

Levi is our fifth child, and we have seen God move in His healing power big time. It was very hard for the first few months but we had God in our lives, so we knew about His healing power for those who stand firm in His Word and believe.

We believe Levi was born that way for a reason so that he too, would have a powerful testimony he could share with people and touch their lives. He is a living, walking testimony to the healing power of the Word of God. We believe in immediate divine healing, but encourage others to know that sometimes, healing can also happen over a period of time—in God's own time, not ours.

—*Hillary and Peter Kieft*

In September, at Victory Christian Centre, Weston Carryer prayed for my granddaughter aged two years and two months. Abby was deaf due to nerve damage when she was born; she was only making animal-like noises. Weston prayed for God's complete healing for her ears, her hearing and speech. A miracle took place that day . . . God completely healed her.

From that day on she could hear; she came when we called her. She put her ear next to her cat and laughed when she heard him purr. She was surprised when she heard herself laugh. Words were soon being spoken; she started repeating the words we spoke to her. Now six months later she is speaking in sentences. Everyday we are given opportunity to praise God as more words are being added to her vocabulary. I love telling her how God healed her. She is now raising her hands to Jesus and singing, "Jesus loves me." Thank you.

—*Marie Marsh*

My daughter was born with a hematoma on her head—half the size of her head. After many doctors' visits and scans it was established that the hematoma would go away, but it would take four to six months.

At the 2001 Apostolic Leaders Conference, Weston prayed for my baby. She was three-weeks old. The lump didn't disappear immediately. That particular weekend was a long weekend and we were going away. When we arrived home four days later, the lump was gone and my baby's head was normal.

Another great thing that happened through this healing was that people asked, "What happened to the lump on her head?" We were able to share and testify that God is a miracle-working God. Amen! What man said would take four to six months to heal, God healed in four days.

—*Rita Gamlen*

We noticed from an early age our son Daniel was having difficulty focusing his eyes on specific objects, and that his left eye would drift out of alignment. At four years, he was diagnosed with a lazy left eye with very little vision, and very poor vision in his right eye. The optometrist said that because of the condition of his eyes, he would never be able to drive a car later in life. From the age of four, he had to wear very thick lens glasses, otherwise everything was completely blurry to him.

When Daniel was nine, on 15 February 2013, we took him to a Christian healing meeting at Ruawai where Weston Carryer was ministering, and Weston prayed for the Lord to do a miracle for Daniel's eyes.

This is exactly what happened. He immediately took his glasses off as the Lord had given him perfect sight and both eyes were completely normal. This has made a huge difference in Daniel's life. He is now looking forward to playing rugby and not missing his tackles as he can now see his opponents.

We are so grateful to the Lord Jesus and we are all continually praising Him for what He has done for Daniel.

—*Bronwyn and Shawn Holt*

Infertility & Children Healed

I brought my grandson to Weston Carryer for healing. Over a period of ten years he used to wet the bed every night. The only suggestion made by doctors was that he should bathe in a hot tub of water and wash under the foreskin of his penis. These instructions were followed consistently, but to no avail. Since Weston laid hands on and prayed over him, my grandson has been wonderfully healed by the mighty power of God. Bless His holy name.

—R.W.

I was a single parent of twins—a boy and a girl. When my baby boy was about fourteen-months-old, he began to sleep only two hours of the twenty-four. He would scream and cry continuously. He persisted in banging his head against the walls and furniture, and when I approached him he would bite and scratch me, while continuing to scream. He was under numerous doctors for diagnosis, and in an attempt to calm him he was on heavy doses of medication, equivalent to valium-type drugs. Matthew was also constantly being hospitalised, often for four of the seven days. Despite this heavy medical involvement, no doctor was able to tell me what his condition was. Subsequently, he was booked into the Wellington Hospital for a brain scan.

During this time, I was not coping with the pressure and was delving deeper into drugs and alcohol. Emotionally I was becoming detached from Matthew, and when he was twenty-months-old, I initiated proceedings to place him in foster care. It was at this point that I decided to take him to my parent's home so he could be farewelled.

During this visit, my sister went to a healing meeting with Weston Carryer. The Lord Jesus met her need for healing and her subsequent testimony caused me to have hope. The next day, I attended the Weston Carryer meeting myself.

Despite my good intentions, while in the meeting, I hated every moment and wanted to run out—very badly! However,

Miracles in Aotearoa New Zealand

I managed to stay, and toward the end of the service Weston pointed at me, and said, "Your son is sick and God wants to heal him. Will you come up so I can pray for him?" Although still very much wanting to run from the building, inside I felt the warmth of hope growing. I nodded at Weston, and went to the front.

Weston laid hands on my baby and began to pray. Matthew went berserk. He jumped from my arms and ran straight toward the walls. Once there, he attempted to scale them screaming and yelling the whole time. Weston followed him, laying hands on him where possible and continuing to pray. Suddenly Matthew stopped his frantic activity and became settled. Weston said that the Lord had told him it was epilepsy. Weston then prayed for me, and I invited Jesus into my life. I immediately felt the true force of hope despite never having felt it before. This was the first time my emotions had been able to believe in hope.

After the meeting we left and went to my parent's home. Many of my extended family were also at the house, and that night after Matthew had been put to bed at 7:00 PM, we all began to watch the clock. Remember, that for the previous six months, Matthew had woken at 9:00 PM each night and begun the screaming. The clock continued through the hours . . . 9:00 PM . . . 10:00 PM . . . 11:00 PM . . and Matthew continued to sleep. We went to bed.

On the Tuesday, we had a doctor's appointment. As I entered the surgery, without my saying a word, the doctor asked, "What has happened? Matthew looks as if he is better."

I replied that God has healed him, and added, "It is wonderful." The doctor examined Matthew and confirmed that he had indeed been healed. From that time, all the specialist appointments were cancelled, and despite the heavy drug dosage that Matthew had been subject to, he required no weaning from them. God is so good.

Matthew is now twelve years old and has continued to sleep well at night. He has shown no signs of the previous disorders. At the same meeting, although it was not specifically prayed for, I was completely delivered from my alcohol and drug addictions. During the next four to five weeks, God healed Matthew and my relationship. We continue to have a very good relationship.

For me, the biggest lesson of that time was learning that God alone is our hope. He continues to be that hope for us. Thank You, Jesus, and I'm so thankful for Weston's prayers.

—*Michelle Oliver, Taradale*

Wow! How empowering Weston's healing meeting was in Invercargill. Eugene, our five-and-a-half-year-old son had silent reflux, a condition which was finally picked up when he was five months old. He had developed a major anger problem, which could have been caused by the continual 24/7 discomfort from the reflux. If we overlooked his anger, he was funny, quick-witted and caring; but we could only rarely see this. Our day-to-day battle with trying to find peace within Eugene, was completely wearing our family down. Most days all activity regarding Eugene would cause him to scream. We did not know what to do and were at the end of our tether.

In March 2006, we were invited to take Eugene to a divine healing meeting in Invercargill where Weston Carryer was ministering. During the ministry time Weston prayed for the Lord to heal Eugene. What happened was amazing: he was a totally changed boy immediately.

Since that moment, eighteen months ago, Eugene has lived what we regard as a normal boy life. Our family atmosphere has totally changed. The terrible tensions that used to exist have gone. We knew our beautiful boy was there—somewhere. Thank You, Lord Jesus. We have found him.

—*Rebecca Gay*

Our son, Zacharias, was born with both feet turning inwards quite markedly, and we were told that he would need operations to rectify this problem.

One month later, we took him to a divine healing service where Weston Carryer prayed for him. As he was being prayed for, his left foot straightened completely, and over the next four weeks, the right foot also straightened. The medical authorities have said that there is now nothing wrong with his feet and that he needs no further medical treatment. Thank You, Jesus.

—*Helen Ropitini*

In September 1996, our twin boys, Joshua and Calem, were born. Joshua was the first born and was discovered to have talipes (clubfoot). He was a little feller. The surgeon advised us that his leg would need to be plastered in order to help correct the foot. But because he was so little, all that could be done for him was to tape his leg until he was strong enough to have it plastered. For two months we had to take Joshua (and Calem) to Starship Hospital every week to have the tape changed. Over time he gained the strength needed to have his leg plastered. For the next four months we were in and out of Starship once a week getting his plaster changed.

The surgeon wanted to operate on Josh at six months to correct his foot to the right angle, and we agreed. The surgeons did the operation which they said was a success. It was hoped that his leg would grow in the right direction. However, Josh still needed to be seen by the surgeon, so for the next three years, he was being seen at regular intervals.

When Joshua was three, the surgeon had some disappointing news: what they had hoped would happen had not happened. Josh's leg did not grow in the direction they had hoped it would. As a result his foot was in the right place but his leg bone had continued to grow to the left. They said he would need an operation to break the leg and twist it to the right position. As it was, the effect of his leg growing the wrong way had caused a discrepancy in height, with Josh's hip being in the wrong place and consequently one leg was shorter than the other. The ongoing appointments continued to happen, up until 2005.

When Weston came to our church last year, I told him about Josh's clubfoot. He understood everything about it and made mention about another young boy whom he had prayed for and was healed by Jesus. Weston prayed that Josh's leg would be

Infertility & Children Healed

straightened and that his hips would be healed in the process.

We had another trip to the surgeon in Wellington. It was unusual and amazing! The intern came in to examine Josh's leg and made Josh do some walking, etc. She went out, and then came back with the surgeon, and they did the same again. They went out, and then came back a while later with Josh's notes. They explained what had happened to Josh's leg and hips, showing us how straight his leg had become, and even showed us how the hips had become even and were in the correct position. The surgeon looked rather puzzled; however, I had a big smile when they said that they do not need to see Joshua again. Jesus, thank You so much.

—*Miha Emery*

Our son suffered from chronic asthma the first four years of his life. He had to have steroids all the time, use inhalers and a nebulizer, and was hospitalized twice. He also suffered from food allergies and had to live a dairy-free diet. We had to keep a heater on in his room all night, every night.

We took him to a divine healing meeting in Hastings on 18 February 1996, where Weston Carryer prayed for him. God, through Jesus Christ, completely healed him. He went off all medication that night and his asthma and food allergy problem went and have not returned. He now lives a normal life. We praise God because of what he has done for our son, Mitchell.

—*Jason & Julie Thomson*

My daughter, Waiora, experienced really bad asthma for the first two years of her life. She had to have medical treatment at least every month. I took her to a divine healing meeting at The Centre Paraparaumu in August 2000, where Weston Carryer prayed for the Lord to heal her. The Lord did instantly heal her and she has had no more breathing problems ever since. Thank You, Jesus!

—*Natasha Ochkas (Lower Hutt)*

Miracles in Aotearoa New Zealand

Twenty-three years ago, I attended a divine healing service in Plimmerton where Weston Carryer was ministering. I took my three-year-old daughter, Stacey along because she had been diagnosed with underdeveloped kidneys, which was a real concern. I was sceptical about divine healing as a result of my Brethren background but was willing to go for her sake.

During the meeting, Weston was speaking out words of knowledge for various conditions that the Lord was revealing to him. He said that there was a woman present who had a lump in her left breast and she was very fearful of it being cancer, and would she please come forward for him to pray for the Lord to heal her. I had had this lump in my left breast for about three years and not only was I too scared to have it checked, but I was terrified of it being cancer.

However, I did not budge from my seat. Weston waited and then when no one responded he looked right at me and said, "If it helps you to come forward, I am eyeballing you right now." I just stared back.

Later in the meeting when I took Stacey forward for him to pray for her, Weston asked me why I had not come forward for my own healing and why was I so afraid of cancer. I told him everyone was afraid of dying of cancer. Weston then said that he was not afraid of dying of cancer, and the Lord wanted to set me free of this fear.

Weston then prayed for both of us. Tests following showed that Stacey's kidneys were healed and fully developed to normal size. The lump in my breast totally disappeared within 48 hours and I had the most wonderful deliverance from the fear of cancer. The fear simply went as Weston prayed and I have not had the slightest concern ever since.

My husband and I have been pastoring now for many years. I have been able to pray for many people and have seen them set free from this terrible fear of cancer. In a number of cases, the cancer in their body has gone into remission and some have been completely healed.

Lord Jesus, I am so grateful to You for the way you healed

Infertility & Children Healed

Stacey and myself and set me so wonderfully free from that fear of cancer. My life was truly transformed at that moment.

—Cathy Harrison

My son developed asthma when he was four and he had to use inhalers. Yet despite the inhalers, he would suffer from very severe attacks.

One day when he was seven he had a very severe attack. As a nurse, medically I knew that I should have taken him to the hospital. However, we were having a healing meeting at our church that night where Weston Carryer was ministering, and I knew if I took him along, the Lord would heal him. He also was convinced that he would be healed.

Weston prayed for him and he was slain in the Spirit. His asthma went immediately and has never returned over many years.

—Wendy Belworthy

In January or February 1995, we wrote to Weston Carryer telling him of our son, Stephen's, bedwetting problem and asked if he would pray for his healing. This he did and then wrote to us advising of this, and also, how he had broken a family curse which he believed had been over our son's life. The results were as Weston suggested—not completely immediate, but over a period of time. The initial results, although not complete, were still a thrill. Stephen went from five to seven wet nights a week to just one. We did not experience seven dry nights for many months.

Even prior to Weston's prayers did we never believed God could heal him, nor following. We continued to trust in God. However, the breakthrough did come; but would you believe it? He went from one wet night a week to one wet night a month. This must have continued for twelve months or so.

We now rejoice: Stephen has not had a wet night for the last two months or so. We are so thankful for Weston's prayerful concern, and want to acknowledge God's graciousness and faithfulness.

—John & Joy Hunt, Red Beach

Our daughter was nine years old when she was diagnosed with a medical condition called polynephritis. This caused multiple kidney infections during which Hannah experienced a lot of pain in her kidneys and back. She regularly had urinary tract infections; this also caused high fever, nausea, and generally she would be very unwell. Once she was hospitalised for ten days. Because Hannah had this condition for a long time before it was diagnosed, we were told by the doctors that there was permanent damage to her kidneys. As a result of this damage she was, therefore, having scans to monitor any further deterioration.

In 2001, we attended a divine healing meeting in New Plymouth where Weston Carryer was ministering. He prayed for Hannah's healing. After she was prayed for, the next scan showed an improvement in her kidneys which the doctors said could not happen medically or naturally. The next scan showed further improvement, and then a short time after that, her healing was complete. Over the last eight years Hannah has had no kidney problems, infections, back, or kidney pain or any of the symptoms she had experienced prior to her divine healing. Lord Jesus, we are so grateful to You.

—Pastors Beth and Chris Lee

When she was five months old, our daughter, Aileen, sustained a head injury in an accident. X-rays were taken which revealed a fracture to her skull. For years she had recurring headaches. She also had a problem coordinating her balance which was partly due to late development. Upon examination, the doctor found that she had one leg slightly shorter than the other.

We attended a Weston Carryer healing crusade with Aileen where, by a word of knowledge, he described the symptoms

Infertility & Children Healed

of the accident so accurately. We took her forward for prayer and God healed her. She has had no headaches since. We also requested prayer for her shorter leg. It grew. Aileen was excited about seeing and feeling her leg grow and she has testified to many about it since. Weston also prayed for relief from asthma and eczema. She is now sleeping at night free from constant coughing and her eczema is much reduced. God is so good.

—*Evan & Janet Pallesen*

Ever since birth, our daughter, Joy Ann, had suffered from very bad asthma, eczema over most of her body, major food allergy problems, and conjunctivitis as well.

Our family attended a divine healing seminar at Motueka where Weston Carryer was ministering. The Lord revealed someone was suffering from the conditions Joy Ann had. She went forward, Weston prayed for her, and the Lord healed every condition. Apart from one very minor bout of asthma, none of these illnesses which had plagued her for the first seven years of her life have recurred in over twelve months. We all marvel at God's wonderful power and love.

—*Wayne Klenner*

My name is Catherine, and I'm eleven years old. My Nan and I have been going to the Hastings Apostolic for about two years now and we love it there. It feels like family. When Weston and Mrs. Carryer were there, I came up and Weston prayed that my mum and dad, who are separated, would be reunited and saved so we can belong to Jesus as a family. I also came up because a lady we know did a horoscope for my mum and me. It said that I was accident-prone and I would have lots of infections. I had an irritating, running eye, sore hips, itching body, sore legs and sprained feet. Weston prayed for all these things, and except for itchiness, and my mum and dad, they're nearly better.

I especially wanted to tell about my school's sports day. Usually during any games or sports days, I sprain or twist an ankle, foot, finger or all of them! And I usually don't have a very good attitude to it all, and hate them. Well, not this time, thanks to Weston's prayers and God. I had a great day! First I made up my mind to have a good attitude towards it; I ran like the wind, jumped high on the high jump, crawled low on the under-over obstacle course, and got my name recorded twice for good participation!

Through all these things that have happened, and what my Bible says, I really know that He is truly the one great God and I love Him and want to do whatever He wants me to do, just like Weston. Love from,

—*Catherine Watson-Paul*

In 1992, I took my grandson, Vincent Hastie, to a divine healing meeting where Weston Carryer was ministering. He was several months old and had been completely covered over all of his body with eczema. Despite medical treatment, it had not improved at all, and his doctor had said that he would have it for life. Following prayer that night there was an immediate improvement, and it started to disappear. After a period the eczema went completely and has never returned at all. I praise God for His wonderful healing.

—*Helen Master*

After my granddaughter Madison was born, we discovered she had a serious eczema problem. Her body was covered with it most of the time and the skin would also erupt which was most unpleasant for her. In November 2001, when she was two-and-a-half years old, I took her to the divine healing meeting in Hastings where Weston Carryer was ministering and he prayed for the Lord to heal her. Madison later told her mother, "That the man put his hand on my head and asked Jesus to heal my eczema."

Within forty-eight hours all eczema had gone from her body, and in the last twelve months, has never returned. Thank You, Jesus.

—*Margaret Grove*

Infertility & Children Healed

My name is Samantha Kern and I am fifteen years old. When I was about twelve, I was jumping on my friend's trampoline having a great time. Then all of a sudden I tripped as I jumped and I landed on my tailbone on the metal frame of the trampoline. It really hurt and I was sure that something was wrong with my tailbone, but I never got it looked at or x-rayed or anything. The years went by and it was still hurting and I still didn't know what was wrong with it. I couldn't sit down in the same position for longer than a few minutes.

Then about three or four weeks ago, I heard that Weston Carryer were coming to Jireh Fellowship in Lyall Bay, Wellington, so I went to hear him speak, not knowing at all what he was going to be speaking about. I was privileged to be called up the front by Weston to get prayed for, and through him, God sent a heat over me while he were praying for me. When I got up, God had healed me. This experience has greatly improved my faith in God, and I can now sit down any way I like and for however long I like.

—*Samantha Kern*

I took my little three-year-old girl to church at Whakatane Apostolic. While she was asleep, I asked Weston to pray for her because for months before that night, she had been bleeding from her bowels every time she went to the toilet. The doctors had checked her out, but they were baffled to know what it was. She went into hospital where a dye was inserted into her body to find the problems. Nothing worked. The next stay was a major operation to cut her open to find the problem; still with no result.

That night when Weston prayed in 1991, we went home and thought nothing of it. The next day she had no bleeding. She was completely healed. Praise God. Since that time she has had a completely normal bowel.

—*Anela Carroll Mulae*

Miracles in Aotearoa New Zealand

Our daughter, Desiree, had a serious operation, and after having to go back to the surgeon was told that a hernia had developed. She was to see the surgeon again in a couple of days.

In the meantime she went forward on an altar call where Weston laid hands on her and prayed for her. On going back to the surgeon the next day, she was informed there was no hernia, as it "seemed to have gone." On another occasion Weston, by word of knowledge, called for someone who had trouble with their oesophagus, and again, our daughter went forward and was completely healed as Weston prayed and laid hands on her. That was two years ago and she remains healed.

—Ailsa Simpson

For six years my daughter (who was seven at the time) suffered from what was described as a lazy bowel. This caused serious problems, and throughout this entire time she was on strong medication.

We attended a divine healing meeting at Mosgiel in April 1995, at which Weston Carryer was ministering. She responded to a word of knowledge that the Lord gave to Weston for someone who was suffering from this condition. Weston prayed for her and the Lord completely healed her. Within one month she was off all medication and has had no problem with her bowel ever since. Praise God!

—Megan Conway

My grandniece, Debbie, was born with a hole in her heart, and for the first two years of her life this caused her considerable distress. She had great difficulty in breathing all the time.

When she was two, I took her to a divine healing meeting at Rotorua where Weston Carryer was ministering, and he prayed for the Lord to heal her. She was immediately healed and her

Infertility & Children Healed

breathing became normal. At the next medical check the doctor informed us that there was nothing wrong with her heart. Ever since then (which was six years ago) she has lived a normal life. Praise You, Jesus.

—*Awhina Parkinson*

Our grandson, Ryan, was born in May 2004, and at the age of two months old was diagnosed with bilateral kidney reflux which had him hospitalised a number of times.

In 2006, when Ryan was two years of age, Weston prayed for a complete healing and restoration to normal function of his kidneys and everything associated with them. We had to wait a year (until mid-2007) for the next ultrasound and testing.

To the absolute surprise of the technician, there was no reflux to be seen. She checked and double-checked but found none. There was still a small amount of scarring to one kidney—just to remind us of what had been present—but this has no effect on the working of his kidney. I knew in my heart that Ryan had been healed a year earlier so it was great to have that confirmed. Now, two years later, he is still healed of that condition. Praise the Lord.

—*Wilma Van der Hulst*

I was born with a leaky heart valve which was diagnosed when I was two years of age. I was then under a specialist for the next eight years with the possibility of having to have surgery. In 1996, when I was ten years old, I was taken by my mother to a Christian healing meeting in Rotorua where Weston Carryer was ministering. He prayed for the Lord to heal me and I was instantly, completely healed. At my next specialist appointment, after examining me and being able to confirm that there was now nothing wrong with my heart, the specialist words were, "We will give glory to Him who is greater." I also continually give God the glory and thank Him so much for my wonderful miracle.

—*Alena Witene*

Miracles in Aotearoa New Zealand

My son, Manaia, was born with a condition called tetralogy of the heart. This condition has four key features:
- A ventricular sepal defect.
- Many levels of obstruction from the right ventricle to the lungs.
- Aorta lies directly over the sepal defect.
- The right ventricle develops thickened muscle.

At seven months of age, he was rushed to Greenlane Hospital and went through major surgery. He was one of the first in the world to have his heart out of his body for over six hours and live. We were then told that he could need further surgery when he was six years old and that there would only be a fifty percent chance of him living. Around his sixth birthday, he started having breathing problems, he became very lethargic and turned blue. The doctors were monitoring him at this stage. It was a really sad time watching him having to sit there going blue and trying to breathe when other kids were having fun.

I heard through my church that Evangelist Weston Carryer was coming, and I decided to have faith that God would heal Manaia through him. Well, Weston prayed for my boy and God did the miracle. After the prayer, we took Manaia back to the doctor, and after extensive tests, he was given a clean bill of health. Truly amazing!

That happened just over one year ago now. My boy has twice the amount of energy as your normal child, and plays soccer and touch rugby. When I asked the Lord if He would give my boy the heart he needed, I promised Him I would give Him mine. Lord, thank You so much.

—*Leicester Ashwell*

I phoned Weston Carryer on Monday, 2 January 2012, and asked him to pray for my grandson, Taylor Bateup. For a few months now he had been having trouble with his windpipe

Infertility & Children Healed

clicking in and out of position and giving him pain and having difficulty swallowing. Recently on a trip to Australia, it clicked out and wouldn't click in again. Taylor was in a lot of pain and his uncle ended up taking him to hospital there. They were unable to do anything for him as they had not come across this before, although he was seen by several specialists. They suggested he see a specialist when he returned to NZ.

On return to NZ, his mother took him to the hospital and they were unable to find what was wrong. They prescribed pills for pain. He couldn't eat or drink and found swallowing difficult and had to spit out his saliva. He was becoming lethargic and everyone was very concerned. I asked my daughter if I could ring Weston and ask him to pray for Taylor. She and Taylor agreed. My daughter and I had both been praying and laid hands on him and were expected that God was going to heal him. However, we hadn't seen any change.

I phoned Weston and explained. I placed my hand on my grandson's photo as Weston prayed and I felt an anointing as he prayed and sensed, "It was done." Taylor was healed. Weston told the foul spirit that was afflicting my grandson to go in Jesus' name and not to return. Three days later he went to the doctor and was told he was completely fine—breathing normally, eating and drinking. And now three months later, he has had no further problems.

I thank God for His mercy and grace and His goodness and faithfulness in healing my grandson. Praise God. I'm so thankful for Weston and his kindness and faithfulness over the years in the ministry God gave him.

—*Mary O'Hare*

When our daughter Sarah was eight years old, she suffered terribly from pain in her bladder. When this pain came—which it did regularly, usually at some stage every day—although she desperately wanted to go to the toilet, she would be unable to do so and she would scream in agony.

This went on for almost six months and we took her to doctors and specialists, but they could not do anything for her.

Miracles in Aotearoa New Zealand

She was referred to a pain specialist. I did not know what to do.

We attended a divine healing meeting in Tauranga where Weston Carryer was ministering, and during the meeting, he said that there was someone there who was suffering with a painful bladder. I immediately took her forward and he prayed for her.

She was completely healed that night and has never had any further bladder pain again since that moment over fifteen years ago. Lord Jesus, we are so grateful.

—*Sarah Kite*

I would like to testify to God's healing power that we experienced at a healing meeting through Weston Carryer's ministry. In 1998, when our son, Jason, was four years old, he experienced an epileptic fit. It happened one night around 9:00 PM. Jason had been in bed for around two hours and everything was quiet as though he was asleep. Our older son just happened to go into his room and noticed that Jason had vomited. When we went up to check him out, he was not only choking on the vomit but he was already having an epileptic fit.

As my wife had grown up with a brother who experienced this condition, we knew we had to seek medical help. Jason was rushed to hospital where they induced him with drugs to bring him out of the seizure. He also had to have a CAT scan to see if there was any long-term condition.

About six months later, Jason again experienced another epileptic seizure in which it was only by God's grace again that we found him in time before it was too late. This time the doctors said that because it was his second seizure, it may be something that he had to live with for the rest of his life. The only treatment was a lifetime of drugs. We didn't want these as we had seen what it had done to my wife's brother. We went to a specialist and they also gave us the same outlook: controlled drugs was his only hope of managing this epileptic condition. As Jason's parents, we really struggled with this decision.

About a month later, in March 1999, Weston was ministering at the Shoreline Christian Centre in Dunedin. We didn't go

Infertility & Children Healed

there thinking that God would heal our son; but when Weston gave an altar call, I felt an urge to take Jason up to the front to be prayed for. Weston's prayer was simple, and his words to me were, "Just have faith . . . believe. . . ." Those words really spoke to me—that if I believed and had faith, then God would heal Jason.

That was nine years ago. Jason is now fourteen years old and he has never had another seizure. We praise God for His healing power, and we are so thankful for Weston's ministry.

—*Graeme Hastie (Jason's Dad)*

I want to let you know about the wonderful healing our son experienced from the Lord after Weston Carryer prayed for him three years ago. He was born with dyslexia and because of this, it was difficult for him to learn a lot at school. He was bullied a lot, and his father and I had instructed him not to fight back. He became extremely discouraged, and this continual bullying had a drastic effect on his life and personality. He developed anxiety disorder which developed into severe obsessive compulsive disorder. At this point, demonic forces drastically affected him. He could visibly see these demons taunting him. He would scrub his hands and feet daily until they were bleeding, sometimes two hundred times a day.

For the next two years I had to home school him as he wouldn't leave the house at all, and he had great difficulty sleeping. One morning I was suddenly alerted by the Holy Spirit and I rushed upstairs to discover that he had tied a rope around his neck, had tied the other end to the balcony and was just about to throw himself over and hang himself. I only just caught him in time.

A few days after this, I managed to get him to a Christian healing meeting where Weston Carryer was ministering and Weston prayed for his complete deliverance. He immediately started to improve. We were then able to send him to a Christian school where he was able to function normally as they really supported, encouraged and prayed for him.

He has now changed schools and has been able to cope

Miracles in Aotearoa New Zealand

with this. Although he is still classed as mild OCD, he is able to live a normal life with no suicidal tendencies, no compulsions, and he knows the Lord has healed him.

We are so grateful to the Lord for what he has done for our son.

—A.G. (name withheld)

Michelle Dodunski, a sensible, quiet girl of thirteen, was troubled with pain in her feet for about eighteen months. The symptoms had reached the point where she could no longer play running sports, and was also forced to cease gymnastics, a sport she enjoyed.

An examination by an orthopaedic surgeon revealed she had "bilateral tibialis posterior insufficiency in both feet." Moulded plastic orthotics (insoles) were provided, and while they gave some relief, her feet were painful when walking barefoot. It was expected things would settle as she matured. In November 1993, Michelle attended a Weston Carryer meeting in Fielding, was prayed for and advised her arches would be restored.

Her medical record (held on file) has this final note dated 23 December 1993:

> *Examination today reveals a normal gait . . . There is some flattening of the longitudinal arch on weight bearing. The arch is quite well restored on toe walking without discomfort. There is no tenderness over the tibialis posterior tendon. Clinically, her symptoms have resolved. No further specific treatment is necessary.*

Michelle herself agrees she has no further problems.

—Michelle Dodunski

Tanya is a pretty, vivacious nine-year-old. At the time she attended a healing ministry conducted by Weston Carryer. However, she was a hurting, self-conscious child whose urge was to shun everyone. Around her mouth she had a hideous,

Infertility & Children Healed

scaly rash which was an acute embarrassment, and which was making her withdraw into herself. She was also suffering from a swollen face, an ulcerated mouth, high fever and inflamed tonsils, besides which, she had a rash covering her face, arms and legs.

Late morning, Weston laid hands on Tanya and offered a simple prayer of faith for her healing. By 5:00 PM the fever had left her, the sores on her mouth had dried up, her tonsils were no longer painful and the skin rash was reduced to patches here and there only. To God be all glory because our eyes saw this happen. Tanya herself knew it was God who had healed her. She waited up until after her father got home from the late shift he was on so she could show and tell him of her healing. Tanya went back to the doctor next day. His report was:

Blood test:	Normal	Urine Test:	Normal
Fever:	Gone	Tonsillitis:	Cleared
Mouth Sores:	Cleared		

He said to her, "Tanya, you sure are a mystery. I have never seen anything like this before."

—D. McC.

My son suffered from continual ear infections for the first five years of his life. He was on medication practically all this time, and because of his hearing problems, he could not speak very well.

I took him to a divine healing meeting at Mataura in 1995, and Weston Carryer prayed for Jesus Christ to heal him. I praise God that he was healed that night and he has had no more infections at all. His hearing and his speaking are normal and he excels at his schoolwork. Thank You, Jesus.

—Karen Turipa

Twenty years ago, my daughter was born with phenylketonuria, which is a very rare disease and causes retardation to the brain. Twenty years ago this June, Weston

Miracles in Aotearoa New Zealand

Carryer was in Rotorua and through his healing prayers and the love of God, my daughter is still with us and very well.

—*Patsi Grace, Rotorua*

Carmen Northe was born mentally retarded and with the added disadvantage of severe scoliosis. At age fifteen, medical authorities decided she should be operated upon, not only because of the condition of her spine, but also due to the rapid deterioration which was taking place in her body.

Her mother took her to a divine healing meeting at Taupo where Weston Carryer was ministering. When he issued an invitation for people to go forward for prayer for healing, Carmen enthusiastically responded. This reaction was totally contrary to the response one generally received from her. Within two weeks of her being prayed for, her back was straight. Over a further period of time, everything in her back was corrected, perfected and made completely normal. Thank You, God, for Your wonderful healing.

—*Mother of Carmen Northe*

Keeping Your Healing

R. Weston Carryer

"Go your way;
and as you have believed,
so let it be done for you."
And his servant
was healed
the same hour.
–Matthew 8:13, NKJV

Keeping Your Healing

by Weston Carryer

Matthew 8:17 tells us that Jesus "took our sicknesses" and "bore our diseases," while 1 Peter 2:24 tells us that by His [Jesus'] stripes we "were healed."

You can see by these two Scriptures that God has provided physical healing for us, as well as salvation through Jesus.

Very often at healing meetings, or on any occasion when God's healing is ministered to people in any of the biblical ways, healing can be received; people will receive their healing and all their symptoms and pains will disappear.

However, in some cases, over a period of time the symptoms may come back and then people often think that they have lost their healing. This is not true. This counterattack is from the devil, and the Bible tells us in John 10:10 that satan has come to kill, to steal, and to destroy. We also see in Mark 4:15 that any time people receive any blessing at all from God, whether it be salvation, baptism in the Holy Spirit, or healing, that satan will immediately try and take it away. He does this immediately before the Word of Truth can be established and grow in the believer's life.

The following are steps you can take to help you maintain your healing.

Miracles in Aotearoa New Zealand

1. Believe you have received it.

Mark 11:24 tells us to believe we have received it and it will be ours. Accept by faith that you have received your healing. Thank God continually for healing you. Not all healings are instantaneous. In fact, a lot of them do take time and you will often have to be patient. Hebrews 10:35-36 says,

> Do not cast away your confidence which has great reward. For you have need of endurance, so that. . . you may receive the promise.

At times, further ongoing prayer may be necessary.

2. Use your authority as a believer.

If the symptoms *do* start coming back, then recognise the source they are coming from. They are not from God. They are from satan. Realise that through Jesus, who has defeated all the power of the devil (1 Jn. 3:8), you can stand against them and demand that they leave you. You are not demanding of God, but of satan. In Luke 10:19, Jesus said:

> I have given you the authority. . . . and over all the power of the enemy, and nothing shall . . . hurt you.

3. Make sure you are living in right relationship with God and each other.

In Mark 11, straight after Jesus told us to believe that we had received when we pray, He tells us in verse 25 that we must forgive. We can see clearly when looking at this account in the Bible that these two thoughts cannot be separated. If we are to receive and retain anything which God has given us, then we must forgive as God forgives us. In Isaiah 43:25, God tells us that He forgives and forgets for His sake. How much more do we need to do this for our own sake! In maintaining right relationships, we must live in peace; 2 Timothy 2:24 tells us we must not be quarrelsome.

4. You need to increase your faith and walk in love.

Romans 10:17 tells us that ". . . faith comes by hearing, and hearing by the Word of God," and so we see that we must read the Bible, which is the Word of God. This is the only way we can develop our capacity for faith. It is no use praying for faith. Prayer does not make faith work; faith makes prayer work. Galatians 5:6 also tells us that faith works by love, and so we must operate in Bible love. We are told in 1 John 2:5 what Bible love is:

> *Whoever keeps His Word* [is obedient to the teaching of the Bible], *truly the love of God is perfected in Him.*

5. Maintain a good confession.

Our spirit is designed to reproduce in itself that which it hears come out of our mouths. You should speak health, well-being, etc. Familiarise yourselves with Scriptures such

MIRACLES IN AOTEAROA NEW ZEALAND

as Matthew 8:17, 1 Peter 2:24, and Psalm 103:3. Do not talk about "*my* bad back . . ." and so on. Do not claim them. They are not yours any more.

6. Do not listen to any doubt or unbelief.

Just as faith comes by hearing (and hearing and hearing) God's Word, so doubt and unbelief come by hearing negative reports. Mark 4:24 states:

Be careful what you are hearing. The measure [of thought . . .] *you give* [to the truth you hear] *will be the measure* [of virtue . . . (God's power)] *that comes back to you—and more* [besides] *will be given to you who hear* (AMP).

Luke 8:18 in the same parable states:

Take heed how you hear.

Many people will probably want to tell us that maybe we will not get healed, or that healing is not for everyone; immediately reject this unbelief. Do not let Jesus marvel at our unbelief (Mk. 6:6) but rather let Him marvel at our belief in Him (Matt. 8:10).

7. Do not let fear come upon us.

Fear of any kind is not from God and the Bible states 365 times that we are not to fear. If the Bible tells us to do it, then we can. Fear will always distort the truth and make us believe things which we should not believe. In 2 Timothy 1:7 it states:

Keep Your Healing

God has not given us a spirit of fear, but of power and of love and of a sound mind.

Hebrews 21:4-15 tells us that Jesus has delivered us from the bondage of the fear of death.

8. Have no anxiety.

1 Peter 5:7 tells us to cast all our cares on God because He cares for us. Philippians 4:6 says,

Have no anxiety about anything (RSV).

9. Confess your sins.

Confess any unconfessed sins to God once, then receive complete forgiveness and then forget all about it. Obviously, stop all deliberate sin (Jn. 5:14). 1 John 1:9 states:

If we confess our sins, He is faithful and just to forgive us our sins and to cleanse us from all unrighteousness.

10. Know that it is God's will for you to be well.

Erroneous teaching has said that sickness is a "cross" to bear. This is completely false. We take up our cross voluntarily. If we believe sickness is a punishment from God, then we have no right to ask for healing from God, a doctor, or anyone else.

Miracles in Aotearoa New Zealand

We should certainly not ask a doctor to pit his skill against the power of God.

God wants us well in our bodies. He still loves us just the same, whatever physical state we are in of course, but He provides the means for us to have health. Let us enjoy it.

11. Keep our bodies fit.

Corinthians 6:19 declares that these bodies we inhabit are not our own, but they belong to God, and therefore, we have the responsibility to do all we can to look after them.

Make sure to get enough exercise. Fast walking for at least half an hour gives our bodies three times as much oxygen—an essential ingredient in combating cancer, as well as benefiting our heart.

Become wise in eating habits by eating the right food and not overeating. Eat plenty of fresh fruits and vegetables (1 Cor. 9:27, Phil. 3:19).

12. God heals so that we can reveal His glory.

Psalm 118:17 declares that we are preserved to "declare the works of the Lord," which means we need to testify about our healing as well as sharing the gospel.

In Mark 5:19, the Bible records that after Jesus had healed a very sick, troubled man, He told him to go, return home, and tell what great things the Lord had done for him.

I am the Lord, who heals you.
—*Exodus 15:26, NIV*

Index

A

abdominal
   cramps   340
   cyst   344, 347
   pain   329, 516
   swelling/bloating   349

Abplanalp, Joy-Lynn   573

accident
   bicycle   220, 464
   car   64, 151, 161, 167, 181, 197, 204, 216, 221, 296, 428, 448, 451, 454, 461, 482, 486, 494, 495, 496, 531, 575
   horse/horseriding   202, 217, 307
   motorcycle/motor scooter   52, 183, 281, 452, 493
   sport injury   54, 66, 227
   work injury   224, 228, 466, 492

A. C. F.   355

Achilles tendon   86
   inflamed   97
   limited movement   99, 100, 106
   pain   99
   snapped/broke/ruptured/sprained   87, 90, 100, 101, 106, 107, 108
   walking aid   101

addiction/abuse   534
   alcohol   449, 452, 462, 497, 526, 536, 586
   cigarette smoking   145, 449, 462, 528, 529, 545
   drugs   586
   food   528

A.G. (name withheld)   602

Aitchison, Graham   538

Aitchison, Ron   292

Alexander, Nesta   136

Alexandra   166, 425

Alexopoulos, Julie   183

Alive Church   534

Allan, Marilyn   402

Allen, Valerie   117

allergy/allergies   405
   antibiotics   383
   cowshed environment   408
   dairy   42, 405, 513, 589
   life-threatening   407
   many foods   318, 483, 513, 593
   skin   257
   wheat products   405
   yeast   405

All Nations Christian Fellowship

412
All Saints Anglican Church 457
All Saints Church 455, 457
Amberley 387, 413
A., Muriel 246
anaemia 123, 354, 355
anaemic 400
Anderson, I.A. 259
Anderson, Lisa 555
Anderson, Pam 74
Anderson, Warwick 534
Andrew, Pam 412
Andrews, Lyn 109
aneurysm
   burst 365
angina 365, 367, 371, 375
Angus, Dorothy 339
ankle(s)
   broken/fractured/ankles 72, 83, 86, 90, 95, 109, 194, 461, 478
   calcification 83
   damaged ligaments 97
   pain/swelling 78, 83, 98, 502
   restricted movement 90, 97
   sprained/twisted/swollen 92, 94, 450
   torn ligaments 104
   ulcerated 72
Annana, Philippa 558
anonymous 63, 530, 537

anorexia 396, 397, 551
anti-phospholipid syndrome 572
anxiety/neurosis 452, 470, 524, 527, 528, 530, 601
Apanui, Carol 122
Apanui, Char 450
Apanui, Maria 505
Apostolic Church 114, 116, 184, 294, 371, 410, 417, 422, 427, 430, 494, 516
Apostolic Leaders Conference 584
appendix removed 504
Appleton, Lillian 70
Archer, Janice 96
arm(s)
   fractured, broken 275, 294, 464
   injury/damage 275, 288, 452, 465
   muscular problem/pain 409
   needed amputation 464
   numbness/pain/tingling/pins and needles 286, 291
   pain/limited mobility 137, 185, 281, 291, 293, 295, 296, 320, 407, 473, 476, 502
   paralysed 452
   shorter 275, 464
   tendon, tear 288
   tissue damage 296
arthritis 417, 461, 463, 480

Index

back/lower back 227, 416, 419, 421, 427, 518

foot/feet 341, 482

hand(s) 133, 417

hip(s) 220, 419, 420, 424, 425, 429, 482

injury/sport injury 58

jaw 159, 420

joints 421

juvenile 419

knee(s) 65, 68, 423, 424, 425, 428, 430, 482

leg 220

neck 155, 416, 417, 473

shoulders/arms 416, 417, 418, 428, 431

spine 315, 426

upper body 419

whole body 418, 420

wrists 418

Ashburton 142, 166, 285, 489, 504, 557

Ashburton New Life Church 538

Ashton, Peter 80

Ashwell, Leicester 598

asthma 42, 216, 333, 375, 376, 377, 378, 379, 380, 381, 382, 384, 385, 386, 388, 389, 467, 487, 578, 589, 591, 593

Ataria, Victoria 385

Auckland 57, 74, 85, 118, 153, 159, 285, 356, 372, 377, 386, 401, 415, 421, 434, 541, 556

Australia 230

autoimmune condition 503

B

back 201

abnormality/misaligned/hump 197, 214, 251

broken 202, 242, 461

degenerative disease 198, 231

disc(s)-damaged/degenerated/misaligned/prolapsed/slipped/permeated/ruptured/chipped 42, 185, 191, 193, 215, 216, 217, 221, 222, 223, 226, 227, 228, 229, 235, 237, 238, 461, 501, 518

fusion 231

hip/back pain 180, 199

injury/work injury 100, 176, 178, 179, 181, 182, 187, 188, 191, 194, 196, 203, 207, 223, 226, 231, 232, 237, 242, 453, 455, 464, 465, 501, 536

leg/back pain 183, 185, 186, 187, 188, 198, 207, 225, 227, 233

limited mobility/restriction/chronic stiffness 177, 178, 181, 189, 200, 210, 216, 221, 225, 230, 232, 235, 242, 250, 462, 464

lower back/legs/nerve-neurological damage-condition 178, 184, 186, 188, 192, 202, 206, 231, 448, 464, 482, 575

619

MIRACLES IN AOTEAROA NEW ZEALAND

neck/back pain 189, 203, 268, 447, 460

pain/locking up/deterioration/problems/sprained 39, 52, 54, 92, 132, 173, 174, 175, 176, 177, 178, 179, 181, 182, 183, 185, 187, 189, 190, 193, 194, 195, 196, 199, 225, 237, 449, 451, 454, 476, 478, 479, 486, 489, 492, 497, 500, 502

posture affected 192

shoulder/arm/back pain 292

spasms 190, 482

surgical operation(s) 176, 179, 180, 196, 501

traction/plaster cast 176

vertebra degeneration/crushed/cracked/missing/fractured/misaligned/chipped 206, 213, 214, 215, 216, 220, 224, 227, 230, 232, 233, 234, 237, 239, 240, 241, 455, 466, 478, 482

walking aid 183, 196, 198, 202, 222, 228, 231

Bailey, Chris 156

Bailey, Christine 363

balance, abnormal 445, 592

Balclutha 136, 337

Balgownie House 302

Barbara 220

Barber, Amanda 280

Barlow, Campbell 181

Barnfather, Brian 567

Barriball, Russell 188

Barton, Michelle 350

Barton, Rangi 449

Bately, Anne 384

Bateman, Gwen 119

Batley, J. 409

Batley, Ted 452

Baxter, Richard 477, 514

Bay Apostolic Church 146

Bay of Plenty 381, 482

B.D.W. 417

Beckmann, Anselma 150, 351

Becroft, Lisa 435

Bedell, Gary 102

Bedggood, Haiying 152, 400

bedridden 418

bedwetting 525, 585, 591

Behre, Wanda 267

Bellamy, Nicole 381

Bell's palsy 161, 166

Belworthy, Wendy 157, 591

Ben Acebis' church 460

Benge, Grace 332

Bennetts, Phillip 39

Berge, Sue 214

Bernard, Janice 437

Berridge, Margaret 234

Biddle, Joenella 166

Bigwood, Nardia 65

bilateral kidney reflux 597

bilateral tibialis posterior

620

Index

insufficiency 602
bipolar disorder (see also "manic depression") 538, 544
Birkenhead 52
Bishop, Lance 178
B.L. 416
Blackler, Anne 414
Blackler-Oliver, Fern 284
bladder
    bleeding 338
    cysts 269
    infections 338, 339
    pain 342, 599
    pre-cancerous 269
    problems 224, 337, 342, 490
bloating 327, 343
blood condition 413
    low salts 510
blood infection
    arm 300
    high S.E.R. 410
Blood platelet levels
    low 412
blood poisoning 369
blood pressure 409
    high 365, 414, 491, 540
    low 364
    unstable/uncontrollable 143, 365, 372
blood sugar
    high 208
B.N.B. 531
Bochel, Clarissa 46, 362
Bocxe, Louise 415
Bold, Lynne 425
Bond, George 79
Bond, Heeni 190, 388
Bonnevie, Erika 474
Booker, Julie 274
Booth, Gaylene 153
Booth, Norman 492
Booth, Rhonda 337
Boss, Elizabeth 367
Boswell, Dawn 378
Bottcher, Diane 96, 131
bowel trouble/pain 313, 315, 316, 321, 326, 327, 330, 337
    bleeding 330, 595
    blocked 328
    dysentery 331
    growth 311, 319
    "lazy" 312, 323, 596
    redundant 473
    twisted 526
Boyce, M. A. 510
Boyd, Liz 534
Boyes, Janis 39
Bradley, Roberta 363
brain
    diminishing function 440
    epilepticus 455
    haemorrhage 162

MIRACLES IN AOTEAROA NEW ZEALAND

injury/damaged 148, 151
trauma 482
breast/breast cancer
    cancer 258, 266
    lumpectomy 258, 267
    lump(s) 259, 260, 359, 360, 362, 590
    lymph glands removed 267
    mastectomy/needed 259, 263
    pre-cancerous condition 267
    radiotherapy 258
breathing 596
    difficulty 343, 377, 380, 498, 508
    shortness 505
breathless 368, 414, 508
Brebner, Kathleen 327
Breeze, Joan 360
Brennan, Kay 120
Brightwell, Des 69
Broadmore, Val 45
Brock, Peter 319, 532
bronchitis 376, 379, 380, 382, 465
Bron, Tania 558
Brosnahan, Veronica 360
Brough, Keith 281
Broughton, Marilyn 328
Brown, A. 348
Brown, Dorrie 201
Brown, Graeme 270
Brown, Mark 125
Brown, Matt 232
Brown, Shelly 186
B., Susan 147
Buddendyk, Pamela 167
bulimia 397, 406
Bunting, Elizabeth 419
Burland, Maria 89
burns
    third-degree 183
Burtenshaw, Glynn 399
Burwood 118
Burwood School Hall 205
Butcher, Rosy 194
Butler, Miss Tonia 293
Button, Shirley 76, 214, 417, 430
Byrne, Pamela 151

C

C3 Church Christchurch 440
Caird, John 321
Callec, Marion 138
Caloundra 342
Caloundra Baptist Church, Australia 230
Cambridge 120, 195
Cameron, Nicola 41
Campbell, Emma 202, 519, 570
Campbell, John 187

Index

Campbell, Marie 525
Campbell, Tracey 564
cancer
    armpit 258
    bone/multiple myeloma 265
    bowel 261, 269
    breast 258, 260, 263, 266, 267
    cervical 256, 258, 260, 262, 268, 269
    ear(s) 268
    kidney(s) 258
    lungs 257
    lymph nodes 263
    malignant melanoma 262
    malignant tumour 260
    pain 257, 258
    prostate 262
    ribs 259
    thyroid 257
candida 481
Cannon, Victoria 167
carpal tunnel syndrome 302, 304, 305, 309, 477
Carran, Crystal 252
Carr, Evelyn 124
Carr, Moina 202
Carson, Irina 386
Carson, Rob & Emmy 569
Carter-Chalmers, Ruth 341
C., Elizabeth 497
cellulitis 509

Central Christian Family Church 50
Centre Church 76, 107, 119, 130, 140, 232, 402, 439, 488, 506, 589
cerebral palsy 208
Chambers, Donna 413
Chandler, R. 85
chest
    infection/virus infection 379, 492
    muscular spasms 362
    pains/severe 507
    tight/aching 471
Chilcott, Barbara 90
chlamydia 556
Chongo, Martha 344
Christchurch 47, 53, 60, 65, 66, 71, 79, 86, 94, 97, 114, 118, 131, 155, 187, 202, 205, 212, 247, 282, 296, 300, 301, 328, 329, 359, 363, 365, 367, 382, 394, 407, 440, 494, 511, 542, 552
Christchurch City Apostolic Church 278
Christian Fellowship Renewal 105
Christian, Rebekah 576
Christian Renewal Fellowship 58, 141, 204, 207, 301, 351, 388
Christianson, Joan 540
chronic fatigue syndrome 400, 401, 402, 403, 481
chronic hyperventilation syndrome 122

Miracles in Aotearoa New Zealand

Church Unlimited 109, 169, 197
Church Unlimited Auckland 571
cirrhosis of the liver 336
City Church 75, 542
City Life Church 79, 108, 131, 154, 192, 194, 238, 307, 435, 510
C.J. 527
Clark, Jill 476
Clark, Myrtle 313
Clark, Peter 452
Clark, Robyn 148
cleft lip and palate
    bilateral 582
Clinch, Patrick & Anne 370
clubfoot 573, 588
    leg shorter 81, 98
    restricted movement 99
Clutterbuck, Yvonne 119
Coake, Katarina 275
Coastlands Church 245
Cockburn, Norma 371
coeliac disease 435, 436, 437, 483
Colbourne, June 314
colitis 322
    ulcerative 316, 331
collarbone(s)/clavicle
    broken/fracture 146, 286, 461
    dislocated 133
    nerve pain 290

Collecutt, Pastor Stephen 548
Colleen 436, 449
Collins, Helen 400
Collins, Sharon 217
compartment syndrome 288
Conde, Joanne 552
Condon, Geraldine 135
conjunctivitis 593
Conroy-Croot, Della 257
constipation 313, 316, 330, 526
Conteese, Lou 153
Conway, Megan 596
COPD 387
Corradetti, Julia 518
Cotton, Bunty 235
Cotton, Jeff & Jo 552
Coursey, Christine 480
Coxhead, Michelle 375
Coyne, Emma 70
Coyne, Pat 262
Craig, Pixie 182
CRF church 78, 106, 150
Crohn's disease 441, 442, 443
Cromwell 45, 60, 240, 269, 282, 361, 570
Croton, Debbie 529
Crozier, Andrew 365
Cundall, Alice 425
Currie, Glenis 326, 409
Currie, Glennis 405

Index

Currie, S. K. 84
Curtis, Verda 308

D

da Costa, Petrina 345
Dakens, Louise 69
Dannevirke 445
Dargaville 491
D'Ath, Dana 496
Davey, Elizabeth A. 418
Davidson, Dot 295
Davidson, Nell 295
Davies, Glen 376
Davis, Kara 545
Davis, Lavinia 181
Davu, Wilimina 53
Dawson, Fran 207
Deal, Robin 412
deliverance 83, 355, 397, 406, 412, 460, 517, 524, 525, 526, 527, 528, 529, 530, 531, 532, 533, 534, 537, 540, 541, 542, 545, 547, 548, 571, 585, 587, 601
  curses 465
De Mandeville, Robyn 98
demonic oppression 495, 529, 540, 546, 601
depression 41, 285, 349, 396, 397, 401, 445, 452, 456, 495, 498, 526, 533, 534, 535, 537, 539, 541, 542, 546, 547, 557
dermatitis 400, 448, 514, 518
despondent 552, 574
Dewes, Barney 302
Dewes, Maria 268
D. H. 366
diabetes 431, 432, 433, 434, 533
diarrhoea 318, 326, 327, 330, 405
diffused axonal injury 162
digestive problems 324, 326, 332, 407, 481
Ditmer, Deborah 494
diverticulitis 312, 314, 315, 319, 324, 472
dizzy spells 373, 479
D., Joan 173, 493
Dobney, Stan 242
Dodunski, Michelle 602
Doidge, Fred 239
Dolman, Ngaere 292
Donaldson, Heather, Keith & Karin 294
Doolan, Matt 545
Dounder, Pushpa 344
Dowman, Tonia 561
Draper, Cara 52
Dravitski, Gerald 159
Drinkall, Barbara 118, 373
Driscoll, Lareen 247
drug rehabilitation (passed through) 452
drug user 209, 384, 452, 462, 497, 523, 536
D. S. 336

Dullabh, Barri 517
Dunedin 41, 84, 85, 206, 249, 251, 269, 321, 461, 477, 501, 558, 600
Dunedin City Apostolic Church 68
Dunick, Mary 322, 527
D., Vaine 337
D. W. 525
Dwen, Sue 316
dysentery 316, 327
dyslexia 601

E

Eade, Cheryl 517
ear(s)
    acoustic neuroma 127
    balance/problems 129, 130, 131
    cyst 131
    deaf, partially deaf 126, 128, 130, 131, 581, 583
    dizziness/vertigo/vomiting 130, 131
    earache 126
    eardrum 126, 131
    glue ear 581
    infection(s) 128, 130, 603
    Meniere's disease 130
    required hearing aid 129
    ringing 129
East Bay Apostolic Church 157, 177
East Bay Church 129, 147
Eastgate Christian Centre 108, 348, 354, 426
Eastgate Christian Fellowship 125
East Street Apostolic Church 89
eating disorders 401
Eaton, Janet 132, 278
ectopic pregnancy 554, 556, 558
eczema 405, 409, 487, 516, 519, 593, 594
Eden, Sherrill 555
Edgecumbe 78, 439
Edwin, Sylvia 333
elbow(s)
    broken/fracture 293, 296, 299
    cyst 299
    injury/work injury 300, 301
    lateral epiconylitis-inflammation of the 300
    pain 101, 185
    tendons 301
    tennis 433, 452
Ellis, Jeanette 500
Ellis, Joy 431
Ellis, Pelham 82
Emery, Miha 589
Emily 307
emotional problems 525, 530, 531, 534, 541, 571
    low 474

Index

pain/grief/hurts/despair 469, 497, 539, 547, 561
emphysema 384, 462
endometriosis 344, 347, 348, 349, 351, 352, 355, 356, 469, 556, 558, 565, 569
epilepsy 84, 161, 167, 168, 586, 600
    toxic clonic 167
epilepticus 455
Epsom, Louise 240
Equippers Church 326
Eriha, Paula 545
Eriha, Shiloh 209
Espener, Dorrie 530
Esterbauer, Marian 495
Everett, Raewyn 125
eye(s)
    blind/partially blind 114, 115, 119, 120, 121, 465, 468, 582
    blinking, excessive 119
    burst blood vessels 114
    cataract(s)/surgery 117, 119
    double/blurred vision 113, 115, 118, 121, 160
    dry tear duct 160
    injury, damaged, fixed 115, 118
    iritis 120
    lazy 116, 468, 584
    misaligned 120
    optic neuritis 396
    retinal ulcer 451
    retinitis pigmentosa 116
    sore, irritation, itchy, red, burning, excess fluid 114, 116, 117, 119, 121, 478, 593
    vision deterioration/restriction 116, 117, 119, 160, 416, 450, 451, 473, 584

F

face
    burning sensation 113
    injury 493
    pain 469
    paralysed 161
fainting spells 318, 479
Faith Bible College 537
Falloon, Faye 187
Farrell, Peter 332
fasciotomy 288
fatigue 483
Fatkiel, Krystyna 73
Favell, Carol Ann 403
Fawcett, Tracey 475
fear 525
    of cancer 184, 406, 477, 590
    of death 529
    of man 84, 447
Fearns, Dianne 239
Feilding 48, 77, 161, 525, 567
femur
    broken 38, 461, 496

Miracles in Aotearoa New Zealand

FGBMF 472, 514
FGBMFI 417, 477
FGBMF West Auckland 467
F.I. 432
fibromyalgia 399, 401, 402, 403, 569
Fielding 59, 220, 221, 365, 366, 389, 390
Findon, Melissa 349
fingers
    genetic condition 427
    injury/pain 304, 427
    shorter 304
    stiff 302
Finlay, Muriel 220
Finlayson, Janet 262
Fisher, Tui 50
Flanagan, Lynn 93
Flaxmere 97, 139, 209, 263, 308, 331, 368, 386, 404, 490
Flaxmere Christian Fellowship 209, 237
Florance, David 65
flu-like symptoms 507
Flutey, Win 418
Flynn, Michelle 569
Fodie, Lucrezia 234
foot/feet
    arches, high 81
    arches, improper 82, 86, 446, 495
    broken/fractured 84, 88, 89, 103, 104, 474, 478
    damaged/deformed 85, 108, 209, 503, 587
    discoloured 508
    flat (no arches), fallen arches 80, 85, 87, 88, 89, 90, 91, 95, 96, 102, 268
    growths/blisters 105, 519
    injury/swelling 59, 101, 450, 593
    larger/longer 80, 200
    limited mobility 103, 251, 503
    misaligned 91, 92
    Morton's Neuroma/neuralgia 94, 109
    pain/burning soles 82, 85, 92, 93, 94, 99, 102, 103, 106, 108, 204, 602
    plantar facilitis 80
    walking aids 105
forearm
    broken 293, 304
    tendon tear 301
Foster, Jim 467
Foster, Pam 291
Foxton 133, 218, 260, 305, 354, 446, 464
Frame, Peter 241
Francis, Billie 49
Francis, Marie 356
Franks, Nicolette 205
Fraser, Ngaire 362
Fraser, Shirley 329

Index

Friar, Diane 372
Full Gospel Chapel 338

G

Gadsby, Chris 56
Galatea 408
Gallagher, Emma 552
gallbladder 447
    diseased 340
    gallstones 335
Gamlen, Rita 584
gangrene 288
Gardner, Maxine 582
Garrick, Lynn 446
Garton, Wayne 208
Gateway Life Centre 387
Gaul, Jo 79
Gay, Rebecca 587
Geange, Stephen 53
Gemmill, Mary 465
gestational diabetes 434
Ghoorah, Dawn 289
Gibb, Anita 100
Gibson, Barbara 331
Gibson, Kathleen 381
Gifford, Bridget 520
Giglio, Chiara 426
Gillam, Natalie 356
Gillespie, Roland 106
Gilligan, Mike 213
Gilligan, Steve 233

Gisborne 258, 268, 319, 410, 424, 429
Gisborne Apostolic Church 158
glandular fever 402
glaucoma 451
Glendene 360
Glen Eden 315
Glover, Daniel 99
goitre 133
Goldsworthy, Dorothy 551
Good Life Community Church 518
Goodsir, Pat 134
Gore 174, 215, 292, 330, 378
Gorniot, Rachel 397
Gosling, Gaye 541
Grace Church 71
Grace, Patsi 604
Grace Vineyard 569
Grace Vineyard Church 60, 328
Grace Vineyard New Brighton Church 250
Gracie, Malcolm 108
Graham, Christine 330
Graves' disease 438
Greally, Johanne 43
Greenslade, Annabel 306
Green, Suzanne 503
Greger, Ngaire 56, 203
Gregory, Romanos 243
grief, spirit of 548

Griffiths, Lois   168
Griffiths, Nigel   85
Grindlay, Helen   434
Grooby, Kathy   515
Grove, Margaret   594
Gubb, Nicola   352
Guerin, Barney   368
Gunson, Sybil   266, 483

H

haemorrhoids   318, 319, 320, 449
Haenga, Charmaine   338
Haerewa, Tuku   258
Hagen, Bruce   318
Haigh, Maureen   387
Hall, Gabrielle   408
Hamilton   57, 89, 180, 220, 275, 379, 420, 442, 555
Hamilton, Bev   261
Hamilton, Ian   131
Hamilton, Margaret   421
Hamilton, Neville   282
Hammer, Joan   502
Hammond, Carrol   213
Hampstead, Ngaire   119, 206
Hancock, Linda   336
hand(s)
  broken/fractured/crushed   302, 307
  cold/freezing   508
  damaged/injury   197, 304, 305
  fingers/hand restricted movement   275
  numbness/pins and needles   140, 179, 303
  pain   140, 303, 460
  paralysed   446
  tendonitis   307
Hansen, Jude   144
Hansen, Julie   238
Hansen, Karen   447
Hansen, Ron   465
Harmer, Quinton   139
Harris, Claire   308
Harris, Kath   573
Harrison, Cathy   591
Harrison-Lee, Heather   506
Harris, Val   91
Harrow, Joan   440
Hartfield, Jack   207
Hartigan, Elaine   263
Harvest Church   106, 145, 238, 519
Harvest Church Rotorua   120, 156
Hashimoto's disease   267
Hastie (Jason's dad), Graeme   601
Hastings   90, 101, 184, 380, 385, 399, 427, 436, 466, 492, 589, 594
Hastings Apostolic Church   174, 593
Hastings City Elim Church   515

Index

hatred   464

Haub, Gaylene   403

Hawera   116, 468, 582

Hawira, Tom   340

Hawkins, Barry   141

Hawkins, Barry & family   489

Haworth, Gillian   361, 493

Hawthorndale Community Church   327

Hawthorne, Kelly   211

hay fever   404, 408, 453

Hay, Glenda   86

Hay, Jane   94

Haythornthwaite, Carol   105

headaches   133, 218, 400, 405, 448, 451, 493, 494, 495, 497, 510, 592

   chronic/severe/excruciating/vomiting   148, 151, 152, 153, 154, 155, 197, 203

   cranial   156

   sinus   449

head/skull

   damaged/fractured/injury   152, 154, 448, 461, 495, 592

   pain   113, 141

heart   190, 372

   aneurysm   365

   breathless   368, 369, 372, 373

   calcium accumulation   369

   cardiac arrest   370, 507

   chest pain   370

   chronic coronary   364

   damaged/problems   375

   enlarged   371, 491

   failure   503

   fluid retained   368, 372

   hole in   596

   mitral valve leak   367, 368

   murmur   257, 366, 367, 373, 374

   needing bypass operation   364, 365

   pacemaker needed   372

   palpitations   366

   rapid heartbeat   508

   required heart valve replacement   369

   tetralogy   598

   valve collapsed   364

heartburn   471

heart murmur   368

heart valve

   leaky   597

Heaslip, Pat   299

heel

   arthritis   80

   broken bones   84

   injury   80

   pain   82

   spur   100, 109

Helensville   96, 291, 347,

400, 509, 579
Helms, Stuart 76
hematoma 583
hemiplegia 208
Henderson, Gail 80
Henderson, Kirsty 251
Henderson, Ralphia 99
Henderson, Ralphina 283
Henwood, Beryl 268
hepatitis B 411, 415
hepatitis C 342
hernia 84, 315, 469, 490, 596
herpes
   genital 453
H.H. 554
Hibiscus Coast 104
Hicks Bay 268, 274, 314, 578
Highsted, Julian & Sarah 562
Hiha, Wallace 146
Hillock, Colleen 84
Hillsborough Anglican Church 257
Hilton, Rachael 246
hip(s)
   clicking out of joint 40
   degeneration 43, 44
   diminished mobility 43
   dislocated 40, 219, 429
   fracture/broken 37, 243, 496
   injury 41

   joint replaced 429
   leg pain 38, 49
   lower back pain 49
   misaligned 39, 47
   muscles pulled 47
   pain 39, 40, 41, 45, 47, 48, 49, 55, 57, 167, 182, 280, 341, 502, 593
   replaced surgically 38, 44, 48
   replacement needed 44, 47, 241, 421, 425
   restricted mobility 41, 48, 184, 251, 450
   sacral 62
   socked abnormality 574
   twisted 46, 180
H., Mavis 312
Hockstra, Myra 206
Hodge, Natalia 563
Hohia, Julia 58, 131, 427
Holland, Les 279
Holland, Linda 557
Holland, Ray 503
Hollingsworth, David 342
Holman, Nicola 578
Holt, Bronwyn 121, 194
Holt, Bronwyn & Shawn 584
Hoogland, Andrew 532
Hooker, Sanchia 230
hopelessness 462
hormonal imbalance 345, 506, 555, 557

Index

Hornby 65
Hornby Presbyterian Community Church 510, 533
Horn, Terry 390
Horrall, Rex 395
Horsfall, Annie 411
Horton, Valerie 133
Hoskin, Peter 327
Hotai, Sarah 421
Howard, Kate 149
Howe, Shannon 121
H., Russell 129
Huddlestone, Joycelyn 148
Humphreys, Elizabeth 158
Humphries, Michelle 55
Hungerford, Radley 228
Hunter, Graham 321
Hunter, Veronica (Ronnie) 45
Hunt, John & Joy 592
Huntley, Kathy 247
Hunt, Tracey 260
Hurley, Mary 48
Hutton, Margaret 95
hydrocephalus 243
hyperglycemia 410
hypothyroid 411

I

Iha, Wiki 178
immune system dysfunction 481
incontinent 236, 501, 580
indigestion problems 325, 470
infantile scoliosis 576
infections 593
   prone to 400
infertile 339, 344, 345, 346, 461, 551, 552, 553, 554, 555, 556, 557, 558, 559, 560, 561, 562, 563, 564, 565, 567, 569, 570, 571
infirmity, spirit of 83, 412
inflammation 473, 533
Inglewood 117, 189, 199, 393, 419
insomnia 38, 41, 56, 454, 489, 532, 540
Invercargill 119, 167, 206, 244, 318, 326, 327, 329, 395, 405, 408, 472, 507, 519, 528, 562, 565, 587
Invercargill Christian Centre 119, 437, 520
Invercargill Prison 307
Ireland, Molly 311, 319
irregular heartbeat 363, 367, 370, 373, 473, 540
irritable bowel syndrome 239, 321, 328, 329, 330, 331, 334, 349, 481, 490
   passing blood 321
itching 507, 514, 593
Ivin, Fran 321

J

Jackson, Tania   493
Jacobs, Andrea   343
Jago, Francis   88
Janden, Maree   285
jaw
   clicking/locking/loose joint   158, 159
   dislocated   159
Jeffs, Pam   78
Jeffs, Wayne   482
Jenkins, Julie   553
Jenkins, Maureen   426
Jenny W.   61
Jensen, Rita   348
Jensen, Sue   284
Jerusalem   361
Jessep, Clare   304
J.H.   346
Jireh Fellowship   595
J.M.   581
Johansen, Ces   200
John, Dawn   466
Johnson, Joan   315
Johnson, Kera-Leigh   398
Johnson, L.   157
Johnson, Lincoln   81
Johnson, Margaret   114
Johnstone, R.M.   374
Johnston, Janice   68
Johnston, Paul   300
Jolene's Mom   166
Jolly, Carmelita   107
Jones, Gaelene   359
Jones, John   216
Jones, Sue   329
J.S.   416
Judge, Colleen   145, 291

K

Kaeo, Ron   133
Kaikohe   242, 553, 554
Kapiti   74, 107, 130, 517
Katipa, Judy   148
Kaukau, Shantelle   377
Kauri Coast Christian Fellowship   491
Kelston Girls School   534
Kemp, Joanne   40
Kendall, Tanya   451, 579
Kenny, Harold   155
Keno, Frank   379
Kernot, Ross   69
Kern, Samantha   595
Kevin Dixon's Friday night meeting   92
Kibby, Wayen   54
kidney problems   337, 581
   cancer   258
   cysts   337
   damage   429, 534
   deterioration   494
   dysfunctional   337
   infected   337, 504
   surgically removed   452

Index

underdeveloped 590
Kieft, Hillary & Peter 217, 583
Kihi, Doreen 179
Kilpatrick, Marilyn 106
King, Chrissy 97
King, Dawn 107
King, Deborah 197
Kingi, Belinda 182
Kirk, Molly 324
Kirk, Santana 309
Kite, Sarah 600
Kiwara, Raywen 143
Klenner, Wayne 593
knee(s)
   accident/injury/sport injury 61, 63, 64, 66, 68, 69, 70, 71, 73, 79, 466, 493
   cartilage damage 63, 68, 69, 73, 78
   collapse 64
   deteriorated 75
   dislocated 61, 67
   joint replacement 70
   kneecap/crushed/shattered 70, 461
   ligaments, damaged/torn 68, 69, 72, 73, 74, 76, 447
   limited mobility 62, 63, 65, 68, 70, 74, 76, 78, 492, 493
   locked/stiff 64, 79
   no cartilage 491
   pain 61, 62, 63, 64, 65, 66, 68, 69, 70, 73, 75, 76, 77, 78, 79, 101, 451, 488, 502
   past surgery 65
   problem(s) 61, 65
   recommended surgery/replacement 73, 75, 424, 466
   swelling/fluid 62, 63, 69, 72, 76, 79
   walking aids 68, 70
Knight, Charlotte 424
Knox, Jill 514
Kohika, Paula 212
Koia, Santos 115
Kona, Sue 379
Kote, Tai 210
Kramer, Lyn 316
Kyte, Daniel 411

L

Laas, Mario 154
Lakeside Christian Church 45
Lambert, Judith 385
Lambert, Ray 417
Langridge, Dianne 309
lateral epicondylitis 300
Leamans, Angela 211
Lea, Pauline 286, 324, 542
Leathart, Neil 296
Lee, Pastors Beth & Chris 592
leg(s)
   amputation needed/potential

51, 448
broken 52
calf/shin pain/damage 204
fluid retention/swelling 59, 67
fracture, stress fracture 53
limited mobility 46, 50, 54, 57, 58, 59, 448, 452, 461
numbness 180
pain 46, 53, 54, 57, 58, 59, 167, 449, 451, 452, 489, 593
paralysis 574
pinched nerve 201
post surgery problems 51
restless legs syndrome 56
shin splints 56
shorter/longer 39, 51, 52, 54, 59, 60, 87, 99, 174, 176, 180, 182, 200, 209, 217, 237, 268, 446, 449, 450, 461, 464, 496, 497, 501, 518, 592
stiff 46
surgery needed 51
tendon/ligament damage/pulled hamstrings 475, 488
tibia 52, 53
ulcerated/sores/lumps 51, 497
walking aids 53, 55, 57, 204
Leigh, Angela 373
Leighton, Joy 57
Leith Valley, Dunedin 249
Lelieveld, Mies 51
Leonie 470
leptospirosis 510
Lester, Gail 223
leukemia 255
   chronic lymphatic 261
Levin 158, 217, 222
Levin Apostolic Centre 123
Levy, Denise 501
Lewis, Dave 183
L.H., Peter 448
lichen plarus 214
Lien, Patricia 320
Life Advance Church 403
life/lifestyle transformed 523, 530, 537, 541, 545
Lincoln, Ian 175
Lind, Margaret 180
Linnett, Belinda 153, 248, 263
Little, Glennis 404
liver
   problems/damage 337, 503, 534
   transplant/post surgery 341
Living Faith Church 104, 580
Liza 378
Llewellyn, Kathleen 442
Loader, Bobby 553
Lock, Evan 323
Lock, Gaelyn 38

Index

Loeffen, Shirley 39
Loft, Richard 190
Lott, June 516
Lovelock, Ann 540
Love, Margaret 428
Low, Chaplain Jeff 478
Lowe, Colin 302
Lower Hutt 43, 54, 71, 137, 185, 212, 235, 279, 299, 300, 344, 411, 421, 463, 502
L.S. 530
Lucken, Julie-Ann 198
Ludlow, Dave 193
Ludwig, Helen 62
lungs 382
    cancer 257
    collapsed 377
    diseased 380, 384
    fluid on the 343
    morphine treatment 257
    spot on 200, 380, 388
lupus 436
Lutze, Christine 183
L.W. 525
Lyall Bay, Wellington 595

M

MacCracken, Suzanne 509
Macdonald, Alastair 290, 547
MacDonnell, Joy 132
Macedru, Tom 116
MacLean, Trevor 269
MacLeod, Tracey 534
Magalelei, Tolu 349
Mahauariki, Murray 219
Maindonald, Norman 236
Main Street Church 562, 563
Maitland, Grant 441
Makal, Ajay 572
Mangakino 52, 297, 304
Mangaweka 224
manic depression (see also "bipolar disorder") 526
Mansell, Sonny 78
Mantell, Janice 122
Marinkovich, Pauline 59
Marriner, Atawhai 533
Marris, Helen 140
Marr, Val 260
Marsden, Colleen 221
Marshall, Alison 454
Marshall, Brian 365
Marsh, Katrina 116
Marsh, Marie 583
Martinborough 56
Martin, Trevor 276
Marton 149
Maskell, Robin 236
Mason, Lin 229
Master, Helen 594
Masterton 149, 230, 388, 541
Matamata 77, 267, 286,

322, 332, 334
Mataura 603
Matenga, Lionel 299
Matheson, Joy 216
Mavis H. 50
M.C., Alison 259
McArthur, Ann 481
McBride, Learna 104
McBride, Roger 376
McBurney, Margaret 334
McCartney, Larni 574
McCaslin, Anne 141
McC., D. 51, 603
McConnell, Susan 459
McEvoy, Peter 87
McEwen, Violet 371
Mc., G. 504
McGregor, Rosina 126
McInnes, Kathy 564
McKane, Clive 52
McKay, Gladys 432
McKenzie, John 137
McKeown, Jennie 579
McLachlan, Nathan 580
McLaren, Patricia 166
McNaughton, Anne 231
MCS (multiple chemical sensitivities) 439
melanoma
   malignant 262
memory problems 445
menstrual

back/hip/leg pain 350
cramps 349
difficult 339
dysfunctional (infrequent/no menstrual period) 345, 553, 554
heavy bleeding 350, 353, 354, 557
nausea/vomiting 350
pain 344
vomiting 339
mentally disturbed 546
mentally retarded 604
mental torment 530
Mercer, Alex 92
Mercer, Peter 221
Messenger, Lorna 526
M.E. (Tapanui flu) 410, 436, 504, 510
Mete, Kaara 278
migraines 131, 135, 147, 148, 149, 150, 151, 154, 156, 214, 300, 350, 449, 454, 463, 477, 483, 489, 492, 494
Millar, Kevin 47
Mills, Jan-Marie 472
Milton 454
miscarriage(s) 465, 554, 561, 564, 568, 572
Mitchell, Bernie 60
Mitchell, Craig 196
Mitchell, Karyn 380
Moar, Raewyn 158, 265
Moeke, Hine 430

Index

Moller, Helen 405
Mollins, Isobel 186
Molloy, Barry 294
molluscum virus 578
Molony, Kaye 382
Mooney, Ione 317
Moore, Gordon 301
Moratti, Judy 481
More, Dale 191
Morehu, Shirley 520
Morgan, Janine 396
Morris, June 158
Morris, Taylor 71
Mortiboy, Alex 170
Morton, Jan 473
Mosgiel 52, 62, 80, 148, 183, 417, 596
Mossop, Neil 226
Mother of Carmen 604
Motueka 593
Mounsey, Tania 407
Mountfort, Evelyn 138
mouth
    ulcerated 603
Mt. Maunganui 215, 399
Mt. Maunganui Apostolic Church 130
Mueggabury, Gary 580
Mulae, Anela Carroll 595
multiple sclerosis 393, 394, 395, 396, 483
Munro, Don 528
Murray, Adrian 86
muscular aches and pains 190

N

Nae Nae, Lower Hutt 279
N., Ann 453
Napier 69, 114, 191, 454
Nathan, Eliza 237
Naude, Raquel 571
nausea 65, 326, 343
neck
    chiropractic treatment 138
    clicking 189
    damage 294, 407, 447
    disc/dissolving/degenerative 134, 142, 144, 501
    fusion 138
    headache/migraine 137, 138, 139
    injury/traction/surgery/damage 135, 137, 138, 143, 151, 291
    pain 132, 133, 135, 137, 140, 145, 147, 180, 449, 454, 497, 500, 534
    restricted movement/stiff 134, 135, 139, 140, 156, 268, 294, 427, 479
    shoulder/neck/back pain 135, 137, 138, 139
    tumour/lump 132, 143
    vertebrae damage/malformed/hump 137, 138, 243, 472

whiplash 137, 139, 140, 142, 151, 197, 451, 482, 486, 494

Nepia, Robin 103

nerves, damaged/pain 184, 446, 469

nervous system 526

New Brighton 407

Newlands, Pagett 161

New Life Church 142

New Life Fellowship 236

New Plymouth 69, 76, 124, 146, 201, 256, 261, 266, 281, 315, 373, 433, 473, 479, 481, 482, 496, 529, 558, 564, 567, 592

New Plymouth Apostolic Church 526

New Plymouth City Life Church 327

New Plymouth Life Advance Church 151

Newton, Bruce 177

Ngatai, Karen 507

Nicoll, Carol 102, 193

Nicolson, Elsie 208

Nikora, Sal 514

Noall, Richard 68

non-Hodgkin's lymphoma 264

North City Apostolic Church 57, 62, 188

Northcott, Kathy 188, 199

Northcott, Owen 189

Northe, Sheron 249, 414

North Shore 57, 229

nose

  bleeding 153

  blocked/clogged/seasonal allergies 122, 123, 153

  breathing restricted 124

  broken/damaged 124, 151, 446

  crooked 125

  polyps/nosebleeds 122, 123, 463

  post-nasal drip 123

  sinus infection/problem 122, 125

  sinus problem 175

Nouens, Monique 87

Nye, Tewihi 115

O

Oasis Christian Centre Tauranga 469

Oasis, The 369

O'Brien, Piki 122, 216, 575

obsessive compulsive disorder 537, 601

occult practice 536

occupational overuse syndrome (OOS) 137

Ochkas, Natasha 589

O'Connell, Mrs. Clare 72

O'Donnell, John 191

oesophagus

  damage 136

  spasms 470

Index

Officer, Mark 519
Ohakune 364
O'Hare, Mary 354, 599
Old, Catherine 469
Oliver, Diane 200
Oliver, Micelle 587
Opotiki 115, 135, 410
Opunake, Taranaki 224
Orewa 239, 375, 580
osteoarthritis 421, 530
   back 232, 241
   hip(s) 416
   knee(s) 75, 426
   neck 144
   spine 416
osteoporosis 37, 199, 200, 219
Otago 477
Otaki 38
Otumoetai 575
ovaries
   cysts 345, 346, 351, 356, 443, 451
overall healing 504
Owen, Bob 157

P

Paihia 424, 545
Paihia Baptist Church 289
pain 288, 401
pain, chronic 448, 452, 469, 473, 502, 503, 532

Pakai, Sarah 554
Pallesen, Evan & Janet 593
palpitations 471
Pal, Rachael 434
Papakura 259, 355, 501
Papamoa 63, 181, 222, 233, 245, 331, 370, 373, 425, 481, 482
Papamoa, Tauranga 207
Paraparaumu 73, 89, 119, 203, 232, 318, 352, 402
Paraparaumu Family Church 513
Park City Church 479, 483, 567
Parkes, Sharn 386
Parkinson, Awhina 597
Parrish, Donna 450
Partridge, Heather 325
passed out 373, 508
Patel, Urmila 176
Paton, Jessie 143, 250
Patu, Teresa 146
Pauro, Delwyn 245
Payne, Linda 395
Payne, Shannon 227
Pearce, Wendy 496
pelvis
   bedridden 42
   bone fused 42
   broken 42, 461, 496
   limited movement 42
   tilted 92
   twisted 240

Peninsula, Debbie 438
Penjueb, Kafoa 195
Perry, Nancy 445
Perry, Simon 63
Peters, Barbara 352
Petterson, Graham 199
Petterson, Joy 380
phenylketonuria 603
Phillips, Karen 439
Phillips, Lou 303
Phillips, Piri 433
physical abuse victim 503, 536
Pikari, Kaye 305
Pilato, Adele 454
pinched nerve 473
Pine, Turei 369
Pirirua, Titihuia 222
Playford, Darren 224
Playford, Sharyn 248
pleurisy 379
Plimmerton 264, 590
pneumonia
    double 379
Pocklington, Ola 258
Pohio, Tanya 566
Poi, Agnes 314
Poi, Pine 275
polio 86
polyarthritis, zero-negative 533
polycystic ovarian syndrome 352, 496, 554, 555, 558, 560, 562
polymyalgia 440
polynephritis 592
Porirua 292, 503
Porirua Apostolic Church 582
post traumatic stress disorder 490, 532, 535, 536, 540
Potroz, Christine 92
Pratt, Betty 182
Pratt, Ivy 374
pregnancy/birth problems 320
    baby in breech position 505, 506
    bleeding 570
    bleeding haemorrhoids 320, 506
    cervix/blood clots 471
    haemorrhage at birth 566
    low-lying placenta 471
    planned caesarian 471
    risky birth 471
premature birth(s) 579
Presbyterian church 267
Preston, Cara 61
Prior, Alan 38
Proctor, Scott 161
prostate problems 452, 477
Provan, Rebecca 410
psoriasis 515, 516, 517, 519, 520

Index

psychosis 529
pubic symphysis
   torn 41
Puhi 81
Pukehina 419
Pukehina Beach 381
Pukekohe 44, 91, 192, 449
Pukekohe Apostolic Church 260
Pukete Apostolic Fellowship 294
Pullar, Pam 93
Punawea 477
Purcell, Maureen 134
P., Yvonne 448

Q

Queensland 342, 518
Queenstown 425, 442, 453, 553, 564

R

Radio Rhema 527
Raewyn and Colin 350
Rainer, Muriel 285
Ramsay, Jackie 556
Ramsey, Ruth 137
Randell, Mason E. 302
Rangi, James 281
Rangiora 99, 228, 366, 387

Rangi Ora 308
rape victim 535
rash 214, 243, 603
   infectious weeping 578
Rasmussen, Georgina 257
Rasmussen, Margaret 452
Ratahi 339
Raumati Beach School 381
Read, Charlotte 192
Rebekah 114
Red Beach 104
Redfern, Shirley 331
Reece, Karen 443, 506
reflex synopethat distrovy (R.S.D.) 294
reflux 333, 334, 439, 587
   gastric reflux (hiatus hernia) 136, 145, 324, 326, 329, 332, 333, 339
   gastro-oesophageal reflux 329
   oesophagus 333, 334
Reid, Joyce 64, 288
Reid, May 417
Reid, Paul 335
Reith, Dawn 87
rejection, spirit of 527, 542
repetitive strain injury (R.S.I.) 292
   arms 292, 294
   upper chest 360
   wrist(s) 308
respiratory

infections 383
restricted mobility/movements 348, 403, 507, 510
Revell, Ben 492
rheumatism 242
rheumatoid arthritis
   hips 464
Rhind-Turner, Hani 62
rib(s)
   broken 461
   cage collapsed 364
   cracked 360, 361
Riccarton 486
Richard, Lorraine 244
Richardson, Helen 361
Richter, Garth 205
Rietweld, Janine 346
Rikona, Tony 67
Rikona, Vivian 99
Ritchie, Stu 44
Robb, Lorraine 287, 308
Robinson, Bill 338
Robinson, Charmaine 528
Robinson, Hayden 95
Robinson, Karen 462
Rod, Alan 463
Rogers, Judi 399
Rollo, Harold 307
Rongonui, Liz 314
Ropitini, Helen 588
Rotorua 47, 106, 120, 145, 156, 184, 186, 193, 238, 359, 366, 505, 596, 597, 604

Rotorua Apostolic Church 303
Rowlands, Pam 101
R.P. 114
Ruatoria 362, 514
Ruawai 145, 196, 290, 584
Ruawai Community Church 121
Ruawhare, Roxanne 101
Ruddell, Robyn 110
Ruscoe, Lynne 520
Russell, Beryl 304
Russell, Shane 335
R.W. 585
Ryan, E. 529
Ryland, Susan 140, 542

S

Sale, Jeannie 185
salvation 178
Sanchez, Ludie Grace 461
Sarsfield, Ray 225
Sawyer, Barbara 402
Sawyer, Cherie 442
Sayers, Glenis 505
Saywell, Bruce 419
Schell, Bev 50
sciatic(a) (pain, damaged, nerve pinched) 39, 42, 54, 58, 185, 204, 205, 206, 207, 221, 222, 225, 226, 227, 228, 233, 237, 242, 251, 454, 489
Scobie, Vanessa 328

Index

scoliosis   40, 243, 604
   restricted movement   40
Scott, Audrey   510
Scott, Coline   115
Scott, Glennys   123
Scott, Rev. David   66
Scott, Ruth   75
Sears, Meryl   516
seizure(s)   495
   childhood   208
   epileptic-type   452
septicaemia   265
Severinsen, Mary   448
sexual abuse victim   535
sexual problems   530
S.H.   528
Shakespeare, G.   376
Sharp, B.   365
Sherman's (Scheuermann's) disease   210, 211, 212, 241
shingles   394, 520
Shoreline Christian Centre   600
Shoreline New Life Centre   577
Shorten, Tina   89
shortness of breath   381
Shotter, Neil   222
shoulder(s)
   calcification   284
   clicky   267
   collapsed/inflamed/torn muscle   273, 290, 291
   damage   276, 279, 280, 282, 283
   dislocated   219, 274, 275, 282, 285
   frozen   276, 278, 280, 281, 284, 287, 290, 292, 446
   injury/work/sport-related injury   192, 197, 275, 279, 280, 283, 452, 487
   neck/arm pain   275, 288, 291
   pain   46, 124, 137, 179, 185, 280, 285, 289, 295, 451, 454, 489
   pain arm/shoulder   287, 291
   restricted mobility   46, 274, 279, 284, 287, 289, 450, 502
   rotator cuff problem/pain   286, 475, 486
   tendons, pulled/torn   274, 301
sickly, lifelong   504
Sim, John   129
Simmons, Lorraine   307
Simpson, Ailsa   90, 596
Sims, Yvonne   145
sinus problems   453, 494
S., Judy   177
Skilton, Ross   377
skin
   chronic condition   519
   cyst(s)   381
   irritation   476, 514
   scars   520

MIRACLES IN AOTEAROA NEW ZEALAND

sores on the 514
Skinner, Samuel 328
S., Margaret 432
Smeith, Eric 408
smell, lost sense of 154, 166
Smith, Annina 151
Smith, Barry 420
Smith, Claire 330
Smithies, Gwenda 155
Smith, Melanie 339
Smith, Phyl 65
Smith, Val 269, 428
Snowdon, Bill 83
Somersby, Pauline 578
Son City Apostolic Church 424
South City Christian Centre 79
Sparr, Janey 175
speech impediment 157, 158
spina bifida 243, 250, 251
spinal cord damaged 461
spine/spinal column
 back to leg nerves severed 466
 base-twisted 453
 calcification of 204
 curvature of the/crooked/ misaligned 85, 98, 214, 219, 238, 240, 246, 450, 497
 damaged/fractured/crushed vertebrae 209, 219, 221, 503
 damaged/top of 134, 220, 223, 446, 448
 degeneration 223, 229, 232, 540
 growth on/abscess 208, 236, 242, 446
 pain/locked up 453, 454
 surgery 219
spleen
 enlarged 503
 ruptured (surgically removed) 452
Spurr, Waiata 98
stab wound 461
Stace, Kristin 346
Standeven, Zarida 463
St. Andrews 77
St. Andrews Church Matamata 332
St. Andrews Presbyterian Church 286, 322
St. David's 78
St. David's-in-the-Fields 133
Stead, Hayden 326
Stephenson, Rene 243
sternum
 cracked 361
Stevens, Judith 304
Stewart, David 478
Stewart, John 332
Stewart, Ruth 472
Stewart, Susan 148
Stirling, Paro 242

Index

St. James New Plymouth 49

St John's Hastings 432

Stockman, Robin 245

stomach

   aches/pain/spasms 145, 316, 317, 327, 330, 335, 343

   cramps 314

   dietary restrictions 505

   dysfunctional/problems 318, 462

   infection 505

   ruptured artery 339

   ulcer 200, 315, 328

   unable to eat or drink much 317

Straayer, Pat 100

Stratford 87, 151, 217, 562

Stratford Main Street Church 582

Street, Harry 196

stress-related physical conditions 517, 525

Strode, Linda 273

stroke 118, 160

   pain 480

   paralysed 166

   restricted movement 166, 480

subdural hematoma 452

suicidal 397, 400, 495, 498, 536, 541, 542, 544, 552, 601

Sunshine Coast 342

Svendsen, Rhonda 446

swallowing abnormality 505

Swart, Martinus 231

T

Tahu, Dan 305

Taihape 378

tailbone (coccyx), broken/damaged/floating/dislocated 226, 243, 244, 245, 246, 247, 248, 249, 250, 280, 474, 502, 595

Tamihana, Margaret 378

Tanner, Adelle 563

Tanner, Adelle & Jeff 560

Tapanui 290

Taradale 455, 587

Tariora, Mei 366

taste, lost sense of 166

Tata, Bronwyn 176

Taumarunui 37, 189, 380, 463

Taumarunui Apostolic Church 529

Taupo 88, 116, 140, 184, 248, 414, 417, 420, 430, 556, 604

Tauranga 45, 65, 79, 86, 88, 93, 94, 98, 100, 102, 108, 122, 132, 138, 143, 154, 180, 186, 192, 193, 194, 195, 200, 203, 210, 211, 216, 231, 241, 245, 278, 280, 307, 316, 341, 343, 348, 350, 374, 400, 401, 412, 435, 441, 469, 475, 493, 508, 510, 575, 600

Tauranga Intermediate School

469
Tauranga Women's Aglow 138
Tauranga Worship Centre 94, 559
Tawa 176
Taylor-Agnew, Christine 354
Taylor, Kim 504
Taylor, Lu 286
Te Ahuru, Angela 318
Te Aroha 49
Te Awamutu 56, 173, 202, 286, 319, 323, 409, 542
Te Awamutu Apostolic Church 319
teeth/tooth
    damaged 462
    dead 159
    infection 158
    ripped out 497
    toothache 159
Teheko, Sharon 423
TeKawa, Marion 91
Templeton, Terry 477
Temuka 338
Te Nahu, Daphne 464
tendonitis 460
Te Nikau Bible College 465
Te Nikau Bible School 80
Te Nikau Bible Training Centre 344, 450
Te Nikau summer school 417

tennis elbow 299
Tepu, Athol 380
Te Puke 219, 379
Tepu, Wiki 464
Tere, Taei 490
Terry, Pauline 581
Thames 506
Thames Women's Aglow 178
The Centre 89
The Wave 224
Thomas, Erone 130
Thomas, Noreen 517
Thom, Maria 333
Thompson, Fred 394
Thompson, Nathan 79
Thompson, Yvonne 287
Thomson, David 373
Thomson, Jason & Julie 589
Thomson, Russell 377
Thornton, Rayley 61
throat
    closure/gagging 136, 312
    infection/chronic 146
    pain/severe 145
    polyps 134
thumb
    limited movement 300
    tendon damage/pain 307
thyroid
    post-hyperactive 414

Index

tibia
  broken   496
Tikitiki 160
Timaru 251, 436, 574
tired continually   414
Titahi Bay 463
Tito, Tai 420
T., Jill 436
T.M. 360
T. M. K. 262
Toataua, Olive 364
toe(s)
  dislocated 89
  immobile 230
  injured 80
  pain 80
  pigeon-toed 47
  underdeveloped 88
Tokoroa 58, 230, 315, 321, 423, 426, 464, 533
Tokoroa Apostolic Church 115, 473, 539
tongue
  short 158
tonsils, inflamed 603
Torbett, Gay 229
Torbett, Joy 57
toxoplasmosis 409
Travis Junction 363
Tregelgas, Mary 215
Tregonning, Sarah 42
Trego, Rose-Lee 556
Tregoweth, Harriet 508

tremors 445
Tricker, Rachel 120
Trowern, Reg 204
Tuakau 179
tumour
  malignant 260
Turangi 49, 121, 199
Turipa, Karen 603
Turner, Kevin 427
Turner, Matileena 293
Turner, Neville 289
Turner, Russell 180
Twiford, Michelle 201
Twizel 288

U

ulcer 200
Ulph, Tania 290
unforgiveness 418, 533
U.P. 174
Upper Hutt 303
Upton, Julie 159, 260
ureter tubes abnormality 581
urinary tract infection 343, 454
uterus/womb
  cancerous cells 496
  fibroids 350
  prolapsed 448, 463, 473
  retroverted 346, 348
  tumour/growth/mass

Miracles in Aotearoa New Zealand

351

V

vagina pain 506
Valdez, Rafina 227
Van der Hulst, Wilma 597
Van der Koeff, Jo-Anne 240
Van der Mije, Anne 184
Vankuylenburg, Roger 215
Van Veen, Karen 491
vasectomy reversal 566
Vaughan, Christine 244
Verneer, Anita 340
vertigo 140
    balance problem 140
Vick, Shona 92
Victory Christian Centre 71, 185, 235, 502, 583
Vine Church 582
vision
    blurred 443
Vision Church 59, 77, 389
voice box
    nodules 139
    vocal cord damage 143
    vocal limitations/loss of voice 139, 143, 157
vomiting 151, 154, 156, 316, 324, 350, 492
Vosper, Andrew 150
Vossen, Nadia 117

W

Waddell, Angela 565
Waiheke 263
Waiheke Island 100, 153
Waihi Beach Christian Centre 109
Waikanae 106, 148, 199, 364, 380, 454
Waimotu, Hector 160
Wainuiomata 185
Waipa Cove 246
Wairoa 161
Wairoa Apostolic Church 273
Waitara 54
Wakelin, Prue 130
Walker, John 280
Walker, Leslie 90
Walker, Penny 135
Wallace, Noeline 64
Wallis, Louise 487
Wanaka 46, 91, 295, 361, 579
Wanganui 61, 89, 234, 305, 326, 419, 439, 520
Wanganui Central Baptist Church 305
Warboys, Karen 77
Ward, Kerry 556
Ward, Maureen 325
Warren, Maria 384
warts 579
Watkins, Justine 553
Watkins, Pauline 388

Index

Watson, Judith 508
Watson, Lucy 342
Watson-Paul, Catherine 594
Watson, Thelma 315
Wawatai, Ann 230
Weatherall, Mary 245
Weggery, Trish 560
Weidknecht, Erick, Katrina & Zach 572
Wellington 64
Wellington, Valerie 54
Well of Life Church 189, 201, 433
Wells, Lyn 283
Wells, Naomi 59, 389
West Auckland 120, 139, 467
West City Christian Centre 356
West City Christian Centre Church 227, 246, 325, 360, 386, 434
West City Church 349
Westside Apostolic 134
Whaanga, Dawn 300
Whaanga, Peter 280
Whakatane 81, 129, 147, 157, 177, 213
Whakatane Apostolic 595
Whangamata 64
Whanganui 141, 301
Whangaparaoa 260
Whangarei 58, 68, 70, 78, 101, 105, 106, 134, 150, 152, 204, 205, 207, 233, 241, 248, 262, 309, 312, 325, 351, 361, 367, 372, 388, 482, 492, 572
Whitby 243
White, Verna 38
Whiting, Lynne 539
Whitmore, Heather 366
Wightman, Julie 250, 489
Wijohn, Leona 192
Wilkie, J. 179
Williams, Lorraine 160, 420
Williams, Nicole 73, 353
Williams, Tania 486
Willis, Monica 88
Wilson, David 174
Wilson, Gary 507
Wilson, Harriet 133
Wilson, Leeanne 423
Wilson, Rebekah 405
Wilson, Ruth 370
Wimuta, Roger 258
windpipe abnormality 598
Windsor 365
Winton 308, 402, 519
Witene, Alena 597
Witstyn, William 424
Witt, Debbie 123
W., J.A. (Sonny) 128
Wolff-Parkinson-White syndrome 365
Women's Aglow 366
Women's Aglow, Gisborne 258

Women's Aglow, Mt. Maunganui 214
Wonglyn, Angela 401
Wonglyn, Bernice 316
Woods, Diana 382
Woodward, Melody 567
Word of Life Church 410, 461
Worsfold, Jonathan 109
Wosthuizen, Carol 367
Wright, Eva 312
Wright., F. 256
Wright, Lynette 136
Wright, Phil 266
wrist(s) 306, 308
    avascular necrosis 306
    broken 308
    infection 477
    limited movement 308
Wynyard, Roger 510

Y

Yeatman, Annette 203
Yeatman, Ruth 139
Young, Elizabeth 279
Young, Percy 261

Z

zero-negative polyarthritis 533
Zongeren, Jan Van 48
Zwies, Ellen 128

About the Authors

Nick Klinkenberg

Nick Klinkenberg has been a senior pastor in New Zealand for over 25 years. During this time, he enjoyed having Weston minister in his churches. Nick now operates in an overseeing role to a number of churches and travels extensively in NZ, Australia, USA, and Europe—speaking, coaching and mentoring leaders. He is passionate about seeing God's power move in people's lives and new churches being started.

Nick has authored several books: *Multiplication, Daily Medicine*, and *How to Start a Church For Dummies*. He is actively involved in Western Europe where his passion is to ignite church-planting movements.

Nick and his wife Karen have been married since 1978. Karen's life Scripture is 2 Peter 1:3 and Nick's life Scripture is Ephesians 3:20-21. Nick and Karen have three adult sons and five grandchildren.

Josh Klinkenberg

Josh and his wife Amberley are the directors of InFlame Ministries. They live in Tauranga, New Zealand with their three children, Elijah, Rain, and Indie. InFlame began as a worship school on a small island off the coast of New Zealand and has quickly become a national training ground for creatives across all streams in the body of Christ. Now known as InFlame Academy, they have a heart to see the body of Christ living in intimacy and power. Josh travels working with numerous churches, training and activating them into the supernatural. As a worship leader, speaker, producer, author, and musician, Josh travels throughout New Zealand and further afield. Josh and Amberley have a heart to see the indigenous cultures redeemed, restored and released into their full expression within the kingdom. Josh's life and ministry is marked by signs, wonders and miracles, especially in the area of physical healing. As well as being Sounds of the Nations NZ directors, Josh and Amberley are Jesus Culture Music artists and have released their EP "Our Love" through Jesus Culture Music.

www.inflameworshipschool.com

www.joshandamberleyklinkenberg.com

A Note from Zoe Ministries Trust

Weston Carryer founded Zoe Evangelistic Ministry in 1993 to spread the gospel of Jesus Christ and extend the Kingdom of God on earth in accordance with Mark 16:16-20 and Matthew 28:19-22, equipping saints for the purpose of ministry according to Ephesians 4:11-12, and supporting the needs of the poor according to Matthew 25:35-40.

While God has called Weston home, his legacy endures through Zoe Evangelistic Ministry. The Ministry continues to fulfill his vision by supporting a range of charities and missionaries. These faithful men and women of God are sharing the gospel in a practical manner by supporting the poor, working with widows and orphans, teaching new believers the essentials of the Christian faith, and training leaders in Africa and Asia to minister and lead others to Christ.

If you would like to support Zoe Evangelistic Ministry financially or in prayer, or would like more information about the ongoing work of the ministry, please contact the secretary at:

zoeministrynz@gmail.com

Resources

Multiplication: Inspiration and Tools For Church Planting (book)

Nick Klinkenberg

Mission leaders around the world all agree that the best way to fulfill the Great Commission that Jesus gave to us in Matthew 28:19-20 is to plant new churches. If this is true, we need to put all our resources including finances, energy, and focus into church planting.

Multiplication answers the 'why', the reasons for, and the how of church planting. It also has many practical tools that existing churches and groups are able to use.

Available at: www.visionschurches.com

Daily Medicine: Thoughts From His Word (book)

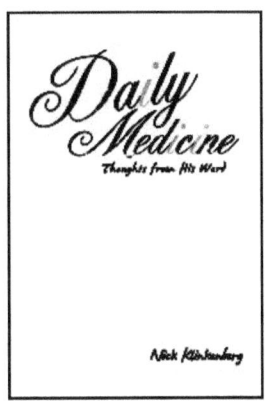

Nick Klinkenberg

This easy-to-read devotional book will empower you to believe God for your miracle of healing. Thirty-one short chapters (1-2 pages), with a Scripture and a comment, will encourage you to contend for your miracle. It also answers very difficult questions on the subject of healing, plus it contains a daily prayer guide (The Lord's Prayer). This book is a very practical yet supernatural tool.

Available at www.visionschurches.com

MIRACLES IN AOTEAROA NEW ZEALAND

The Art of Healing- A Journey Into the Miraculous (book)

Josh Klinkenberg

The *Art of Healing* is the self-told story of a life journey into the miraculous. Josh Klinkenberg shares the keys of the Kingdom, and insights he has gained through walking a road that few have had the opportunity to travel.

Josh shares profound revelations to activate you into a life of healing and the miraculous. He also addresses many of the commonly held "hard questions" in regards to healing like, "What about Job?, "What about God's sovereignty?", Is it God's will for everyone to be healed?", and "Can everyone heal the sick?"

Follow the journey of Josh and Amberley Klinkenberg as they take you on a ride of a lifetime into the very heart of God where you will discover an adventure that has been waiting for you since the bringing of time!

Available at www.inflameministries.com

Resources

For more information about R. Weston Carryer and other resources contact:

Zoe Evangelistic Ministry

Tauranga, New Zealand
www.zoeministry.co.nz
zoeministrynz@gmail.com

InFlame Ministries

Tauranga, New Zealand
www.inflameministries.com
info@inflameministries.com

Vision Churches International

Hamilton, New Zealand
www.VisionChurches.com
nick@visionchurches.com

www.ingramcontent.com/pod-product-compliance
Lightning Source LLC
Chambersburg PA
CBHW060354250426
43670CB00051B/2382